Language in Society 20

Principles of Linguistic Change

Language in Society

GENERAL EDITOR
Peter Trudgill, Professor in the Department of Language and Linguistics,
University of Essex

ADVISORY EDITORS
Ralph Fasold, Professor of Linguistics, Georgetown University
William Labov, Professor of Linguistics, University of Pennsylvania

Principles of Linguistic Change

Volume 1: Internal Factors

WILLIAM LABOV

BLACKWELL
Oxford UK & Cambridge USA

Copyright © William Labov 1994

The right of William Labov to be identified as author of this work has been asserted in accordance with the Copyright, Designs and Patents Act 1988.

First published 1994

Blackwell Publishers
238 Main Street
Cambridge, MA 02142
USA

108 Cowley Road
Oxford OX4 1JF
UK

Library of Congress Cataloging-in-Publication Data

A CIP catalog record for this book is available from the Library of Congress.

ISBN 0-631-17913-5
      0-631-17914-3

British Library Cataloguing in Publication Data

A CIP catalogue record for this book is available from the British Library.

Typeset in 10 on 12 pt Plantin
by Photo·graphics, Honiton, Devon
Printed at T.J. Press Ltd, Padstow, Cornwall.

This book is printed on acid-free paper

For Uriel Weinreich

Contents

Contents

Editor's Preface

The *Language in Society* series has produced a number of volumes over the years which we immodestly feel have represented very important milestones in the development of linguistic knowledge, theory, and practice. It is certain, however, that most of the authors who have already contributed to the series, recalling their own personal scholarly debts to William Labov, would gladly acknowledge that the current eagerly awaited volume is the most important of them all. The truth of the matter is that without William Labov there would be no *Language and Society* series. Nor would the (other) editors of the series – or any other practitioners of secular linguistics – be doing what they are doing today. William Labov has not only had an enormous influence on the development of secular linguistics; he actually started it. Without him, there would have been no tradition of empirical linguistic research in the speech community which, even if many linguists insist on referring to it as "sociolinguistics," has been one of the most important of all developments in 20th century descriptive and theoretical linguistics. Having been the originator of this way of doing linguistics, moreover, Labov has for thirty years remained at its very forefront and has continued to be not only its senior and most influential practitioner but also its best. The series is therefore enormously pleased to be able to publish this book, especially since by bringing Labov's latest research and thinking before an even wider audience, future generations of linguists will be inspired and encouraged to realize that, while studying the language of real people as they speak it in the course of their everyday lives may not be the only and is certainly not the easiest way of doing linguistics, it is the most essential and the most rewarding.

Peter Trudgill
University of Lausanne

Notational Conventions

The following notational conventions will be used throughout the three volumes of this work.

Phonetics and phonology

Italics indicate words in their orthographic form.

Bold type indicates the abstract phonological elements that define historical word classes: short **a**, long **ē**, **ai**. A word class is the complete set of words that contain the phonological unit that the class is named for, and that share a common historical development. Word classes as intact unities are relevant to a particular period of time, as chapters 15–18 of volume 1 will show. For these words, length is indicated by a macron: **ī**, **ē**, etc.

Brackets [ ] indicate IPA phonetic notation. The superscript notation for glides [aⁱ] is generally not used. Almost all the diphthongs discussed are falling diphthongs, so that the first element is the nucleus and the second element the glide: [aɪ], [ɛə], etc. The English upgliding diphthongs are usually shown as [aɪ], [aʊ], [eɪ], [ou], [ɪi], [ʊu], as these are the conventional forms most easily recognized. Where sources have used [ɩ] and [ɷ] I have retained those forms for the lower high vowels.

Slashes / / are used to indicate phonemes.

Parentheses ( ) indicate linguistic variables, which frequently cover the range of several phonemes: for example, (æh), (oh). The parenthesis notation indicates that attention will be given to the systematic dimensions of variation and the constraints upon it.

Angled brackets < > are used for the output of a variable rule, and within the environment of that rule, to indicate constraints that favor the output. In categorical rules, angled brackets indicate strict cooccurrence.

Acoustic plots used in this work show F2 on the horizontal dimension, with high values on the left and low values on the right, and F1 on the vertical dimension, with high values at the top and low values at the bottom. Both scales are linear. Though diagrams with logarithmic second formant displays correspond more closely to even perceptual spacing, the more expanded view of the second formant is helpful in exploring the dimension of peripherality, which plays an important role in many chapters of volume 1.

Research projects

Throughout this work, references are frequently made to the results of research projects conducted at the Linguistic Laboratory of the University of Pennsylvania under grants from the National Science Foundation. In many cases, the references are to publications in which those results were reported. In other cases, however, unpublished data and analyses are cited, and here it is often more appropriate to refer directly to the research projects themselves. The following abbreviations are used:

LES   The study of the Lower East Side of New York City, the major component of the study of social stratification and change in the New York City dialect, as reported in Labov 1966.

LYS   A Quantitative Study of Sound Change in Progress, 1968–1972. The spectrographic study of patterns of chain shifting in a range of British and American dialects, together with a review of the historical record for such patterns, as reported in Labov, Yaeger, and Steiner 1972.

LCV   Project on Linguistic Change and Variation, 1973–1977. The investigation of sound changes in progress in Philadelphia, based on the long-term study of 11 neighborhoods and a random survey of telephone users, as reported in Labov 1980, 1989a, 1990, Hindle 1980, Payne 1976, 1980, Guy 1980.

CDC   A Study of Cross-Dialectal Comprehension, 1987–1991. An experimental study of the cognitive consequences of the patterns of linguistic change and diversity described in LYS and LCV, as reported in Labov 1989c, Labov and Ash, to appear, Karan and Labov 1990.

Data from dialect geography

In general, the various projects of American dialect geography will be referred to as the *Linguistic Atlas records*. More specifically, the publications arising from these projects include *Kurath 1939* (a report on the methods of LANE, the Linguistic Atlas of New England), *Kurath et al. 1941* (detailed maps of LANE results, with full phonetic transcription of each item), *Kurath 1949* (establishing the basic divisions of the dialects of the Eastern United States, on the basis of regional lexical items from LANE and LAMSAS, the Linguistic Atlas of the Middle and Southern Atlantic

States), and *Kurath and McDavid 1961* (the phonetic and phonemic patterns of the same area based on LANE and LAMSAS records).

Several chapters utilize data from Orton and Dieth's *Survey of English Dialects* (1962–67), cited as *SED*.

Acknowledgments

This work is dedicated to Uriel Weinreich. He was, in the eyes of all who knew him, the perfect academic figure, and as my teacher and advisor, he protected me from all the evils of academic life. During the years that he supervised my dissertation, he was the chair of the Department of Linguistics at Columbia, the editor of *Word*, head of a major research project on semantics, creator and director of the *Language and Culture Atlas of Ashkenazic Jewry*, a major contributor to general linguistic theory, and a teacher supremely devoted to the education of his students. He died at the age of 41, in 1967. I thought that I already knew what I intended to do on entering graduate school, and Uriel never directly imposed his ideas upon me. Yet I found afterwards, in reading his unpublished papers, that he had anticipated many of the plans and ideas that I thought were my own. To appreciate his impact on the work published here, one should read the first part of Weinreich, Labov, and Herzog 1968, which is almost entirely his handwork. The last six months that he knew remained to him were devoted to the work that he thought was most important: the statement of a program for building linguistics upon empirical foundations.

The work reported in these pages rests largely on a series of research projects funded by the National Science Foundation from 1965 to 1992, and it could not have been done without that support. I am particularly grateful for the patient advice and oversight of Paul Chapin, the director of the Linguistics Program, as well as the many colleagues unknown to me who refereed the proposals and reviewed their merits and shortcomings.

In those research projects, I have had the pleasure of working with a remarkable series of associates and colleagues, and it is to them that I am most heavily indebted. They were as a rule graduate students in linguistics. Some have gone into other fields, but most have emerged as major contributors to linguistics, and I have drawn from the research and writing that they have done in the years that followed as much as from the work that we did together. The many citations and extracts from their work that appear in this volume will bear witness to the fruitfulness of their research and the independence of their insights. At more than one point in the exposition, it will be evident that my own thinking has been turned in new directions as a result of their contributions.

One of my earliest associates in the study of sound change at Columbia University was Benji Wald, who took time out from his work on Swahili to do interviews in Chicago and Boston that played a major part in the first formulation of the principles of chain shifting, which Wald and I presented to the LSA in 1968. At the same time, Paul Cohen did the first detailed study of the distribution of short **a** in New York City and northern New Jersey (Cohen 1970), which has been a major reference point for work on lexical diffusion in that complex area of English phonology.

The first half of this volume is largely a development of the quantitative study of sound change in progress by Malcah Yaeger, Richard Steiner, and myself at the University of Pennsylvania, reported in Labov, Yaeger, and Steiner 1972 and referred to here as LYS. Most of the spectrographic analysees displayed in chapter 6 are Yaeger's work, and if the general principles of chain shifting derived from them have value, it is the direct result of her energy and insight. Her fieldwork in Buffalo, Detroit, and Rochester is still an important part of our view of the Northern Cities Shift. Richard Steiner, who has gone on to be a leading figure in Semitic studies, explored the literature on sound change in Indo–European for LYS. More than anyone else, he introduced me to the tradition of careful and accurate scholarship in historical studies, though he did not relieve me of my personal tendency toward error.

The work of the Project on Linguistic Change and Variation (LCV) in Philadelphia and Eastern Pennsylvania, carried out from 1973 to 1979, is reported throughout volume 1 and will be the central data source for volume 2. The research group consisted of Anne Bower, Elizabeth Dayton, Gregory Guy, Don Hindle, Matt Lennig, Arvilla Payne, Shana Poplack, Deborah Schiffrin, and myself. Lennig set up the first computational and mathematical configuration for our vowel analyses, and Hindle maintained and developed it. Hindle's dissertation (1980) was based on the analysis of the extraordinary recording made by Payne of Carol Meyers in the course of an entire day, combined with his telephone survey of Philadelphia. The insights gained from his treatment of the social and stylistic variation in vowel systems play a crucial role at many points in this volume. Payne, Bower, and Schiffrin developed the art of sociolinguistic fieldwork to the highest point that I have had the opportunity to observe, and jointly analyzed the demographic and social patterns of the data. They also carried out the analysis of sociolinguistic variables and short **a** in Philadelphia that forms the basis of a number of chapters in this volume. Dayton did the instrumental analyses of the vast bulk of the Philadelphia vowel systems; the fact that this is now the best-known vowel system in the world is largely due to her energy, persistence, and skill. Payne combined her fieldwork in King of Prussia with middle-class speakers with her study of the acquisition of the Philadelphia dialect by out-of-state children (Payne 1976, 1980), which plays a major role in many chapters of this volume.

Other work on the acquisition of Philadelphia phonology has been important in the arguments. Gregory Guy and Sally Boyd contributed studies on the acquisition of *-t,d* deletion, which has become increasingly significant for our understanding of variation (Guy and Boyd 1990). Most recently, Julia Roberts has pursued this question with studies of children 3 to 5 years old; the results of her dissertation are an important resource at several points here and in volume 2.

LCV research on sound change and merger in Eastern Pennsylvania provided a background for the work of Ruth Herold on the merger of /o/ and /oh/ in that area (Herold 1990). Her intrepid and exciting work developed new concepts of the mechanism of merger that I have drawn upon extensively in part C of this volume.

Poplack's research in the Puerto Rican community of Philadelphia began in the LCV context (Poplack 1979, 1980, 1981). This research grew into the major study of variation in Spanish inflections that has been the basis of many further studies over the past years, and appears as the centerpiece of the study of the functionalist hypothesis in chapter 19. Poplack was the first to apply quantitative methods to the intricate problem of simultaneously measuring structural, semantic, and cultural influences on linguistic behavior. Guy plunged into the study of consonant cluster simplification with results that are now located at the solid center of variation theory (Guy 1980), and has continued to develop new theoretical insights that have advanced the field immeasurably. His work on variation in Portuguese inflections provides the crucial arguments on which our understanding of the functional hypothesis is finally based.

In the early 1980s, the Linguistics Laboratory at Penn turned to the study of the interface between the black, Hispanic, and white communities in Philadelphia. Results of the Project on the Influence of Urban Minorities on Linguistic Change [UMLC] will appear in volume 2, and there the contributions of John Myhill, Wendell Harris, Sherry Ash, and Dave Graff will play a prominent role.

The Linguistics Laboratory then turned to the Study of Cross-Dialectal Comprehension [CDC], an examination of the cognitive consequences of the linguistic changes in progress during the 1970s. As codirector of the laboratory, Sherry Ash has been the central figure in the organization of this and other research projects. Her own study of the vocalization of /l/ in Pennsylvania (1982) is an important complement to our studies of vowel systems, since it interacts with them at many points. The work of the CDC project is cited at many points in this volume, but will be an even more important element in volume 3. Ash carried out fieldwork in Chicago and Birmingham that provideds an accurate view of the most advanced stages of the Northern Cities Shift in the late 1980s.

The CDC research group included Sherry Ash, Gayla Iwata, Mark Karan, Ken Matsuda, Corey Miller, Julie Roberts, Robin Sabino, and myself. Iwata and Matsuda contributed vowel analyses of Chicago and Birmingham speakers of a much more detailed character than any that had been done before. Roberts and Sabino carried out more naturalistic studies of decoding that will be reported in volume 3. Karan and Miller worked with me on the experimental analysis of categorization and discrimination of near-mergers in Philadelphia, the main material of chapter 14. I am particularly indebted to them for the ingenuity and energy with which they carried out these crucial experiments.

At an early stage of this investigation of near-mergers, we were struck by the apparent paradox that people were able to produce distinctions that they could not hear. Leigh Lisker reminded us of the important distinction between *perception* and *labeling*, which motivated us to develop experiments that distinguished both types of behavior as reported in chapter 14.

Among my colleagues at Penn, I am especially indebted to Donald Ringe, who has given new significance to the concept of an alliance between historical linguistics and dialectology. He has guarded me against the most egregious errors that an outsider to historical and comparative linguistics can make, and in my efforts to appreciate the many grand theories of sound change to be found in the archives of Indo–European studies, instructed me in the difference between sound argument and idle exposition. I am indebted in particular for his directing my attention to the intricate developments in the vowel systems of North Frisian that are cited in chapter 5.

The general theme sounded in these pages is that the intelligence of linguists is to be respected; the resolution of the puzzles and paradoxes that are attempted here is also based on the principle that one should pay attention to the evidence that has led our predecessors to take the positions they did. This point of view applies equally well to the present. Many of the inquiries, investigations, and assessments in this volume are in response to the innovative and insightful work of William S.-Y. Wang on competing sound change, lexical diffusion, and dialect mixture. I have tried to follow his lead in developing more adequate computational means to deal with the massive data of dialect geography, in search of more adequate empirical grounds for the linguistic principles that we are testing. The contributions of Wang's students C.-C. Cheng, Matthew Chen, Chinfa Lien, Zhongwei Shen, and Mieko Ogura are prominent throughout the second half of this volume. Though my own alignment on all issues is not identical with theirs, I have never failed to be impressed by the force of their arguments and the relevance of their data.

At several points in the chapters to follow, I have reviewed the history of extended controversies that were never resolved. Many of these represented an opposition between the philological and the linguistic point of view, and unfortunately, the failure to agree often corresponded to the gap between those who had the clearest command of the facts and those who had the best grasp of the principles that those facts could illustrate. I find that I am increasingly indebted to an array of linguists who have consciously devoted their energies to closing that gap. I would like to acknowledge my indebtedness to Robert Stockwell, whose penetrating investigations of the history of English both anticipated and illuminated my own at many points. His most recent work, in collaboration with Donka Minkova, has opened up avenues for the connection between the past and the present that I have only begun to follow, and unfortunately only briefly touched on in these pages. In a somewhat different fashion, I have tried to absorb into my own work the original and creative contributions of David Stampe and Patricia Donegan, who bring a broad typological perspective to bear on the same set of problems, centering about that most remarkable of phenomena, the English Great Vowel Shift. In my treatment of that topic, I have tried to signal the overlap between my work and that of Stockwell, Stampe, and Donegan, and I find that it has become increasingly difficult to separate my own conclusions from what I have learned from them.

One would expect any sociolinguistic work to recognize the contributions of Charles Ferguson. For this volume, I have had occasion to return again and again to a short paper that he gave in 1945 on short *a* in Philadelphia. It was not published until 30 years later, in a volume in honor of another great contributor to the short **a** matter, George Trager. At each rereading, I found that I had failed to appreciate the full weight of Ferguson's observations, though I hope that in the final outcome (chapter 18), the circle has been closed.

As the narrative of this volume develops, it will be increasingly obvious (and perhaps irritating to some) that the protagonists are Osthoff, Brugmann, Leskien, and Delbrück. It would be redundant for me to express any further appreciation of their contribution, especially since I have only an imperfect grasp of it. But curiously enough, the current linguist I am most indebted to is one whose published opinion is that the same Neogrammarians are simply and empirically wrong. Paul Kiparsky's (1989) review of phonological change is the most recent of several papers that aim to integrate sociolinguistic studies of variation into current phonological theory. It is not a new experience for me to modify my own views in the light of Kiparsky's assessments. Yet I had no expectation of doing so as I read his letter reviewing my final statement of the Middle Atlantic short **a** situation in chapter 18 of this volume. To my surprise, a few calculations showed me that he was right in arguing that Payne's data were consistent with the formulation of a lexical rule rather than a split of underlying forms. Chapter 18 has therefore been restated within the framework of Kiparsky's lexical phonology, with grateful appreciation of his interest.

Throughout my sociolinguistic career, I have had many occasions to recognize the contributions that Anthony Kroch has made to my thinking about the fundamental issues of change and variation. Volume 1 ends with a statement of the evolutionary perspective on functional effects that is based on his formulation, and the succeeding volumes will respond in many ways to the questions that he has raised on the social motivation of sound change as well as his own findings on the patterns of syntactic change.

To another colleague, Gillian Sankoff, it is a great pleasure to express my thanks for an unending flow of support, insight, and inspiration. Though her work will appear more explicitly in volume 2 than volume 1, her less visible contributions are found throughout.

Finally, and without benefit of any further editing, I would like to express my appreciation of and admiration for the work of the copy editor of this book, Anne Mark. It is now a very different text than the one that she first took in hand. From her red pencil there has come a steady stream of corrections, emendations, and reorganizations that restored clarity to a muddied text and grace to a tortured style. Only in the deepest confidence would I reveal to an intimate associate how many mistakes, contradictions, and reversals of meaning have been detected by her vigilant eye. You the reader are even more in her debt than I, for you have been saved from the thankless task of unraveling riddles that I had never intended to set.

The author and publishers wish to thank the following: Academic Press Ltd for permission to publish Figure 8.3, adapted from Hashimoto, K. and K. Sasaki, 1982, On the relationship between the shape and position of the tongue for vowels, *Journal of Phonetics* 10: 291–299. Cambridge University Press for: Figure 8.1 from Ladefoged, Peter, 1964, A phonetic study of West African languages, *West African Language Monographs* 1; Figures 14.1, 14.2, 14.3 and Tables 14.1, 14.2, from Janson, Tore and Richard Schulman, 1983, Non-distinctive features and their use, *Journal of Linguistics* 19: 321–336. Indiana University Press for: the extract on p. 18 from Osthoff ansd Brugmann 1876, trans. Lehmann, Winfred P., ed., 1967, *A Reader in Nineteenth-century Historical Indo-European Linguistics*. Kenkyusha Ltd, Tokyo, for: Figure 17.1 and Table 17.1, from Appendix E and Figure 3.2 in Oguro, Mieko, *Historical English Phonology: A Lexical Perspective*. Paul Jen-Kuei Li for: Linguistic variations of different age groups in the Atayalic dialects, 1982, *Tsing Hua Journal of Chinese Studies*, new series, 14: 167–191. Monica Lindau for: Figures 8.4 a, b, c, from Vowel Features, 1978, *Language* 54: 541–563. Terence Nearey for: Figure 8.2 from Nearey, Phonetic feature system for vowels, 1977, University of Connecticut Dissertation. David Sankoff for: Figure 20.6 from Terrell, Tracy, Diachronic reconstruction by dialect comparison of variable constraints: s-aspiration and deletions in Spanish, 1981, in Sankoff, D. and H. Cedergren, eds., *Variation Omnibus*, Alberta: Lingustic Research, pp. 115–124. William S. Y. Wang for: Table 15.1 from Cheng, Chin-chuan and William S. Y.

Wang, 1972, Tone change in Chaozhou Chinese: a study of lexical diffusion. *Papers in Linguistics in Honor of Henry and Renee Kahane*, pp. 99–113, also in Wang, William S. Y., 1977, *The Lexicon in Phonological Change*, The Hague, Mouton, pp. 86–100; Table 16.4 from Wang, William S. Y., 1989, Theoretical issues in studying Chinese dialects, *Journal of the Chinese Language Teachers' Association* 25: 1–34. Every effort has been made to identify materials requiring permissions and to clear these with the parties concerned. Information regarding any possible omissions will be gratefully received by the publisher for acknowledgement in subsequent reprintings.

Introduction:
The Plan of the Work as a Whole

Organization

This investigation into the principles of language change will be presented in three volumes,
which will cover the following general areas of inquiry:

Volume 1
Internal factors: the study of apparent time and real time; principles governing chain shifts; mergers, splits, and near-mergers; the regularity of sound change; functional effects on linguistic change.

Volume 2
Social factors: the actuation problem; the social location of the innovators of change; change and the curvilinear pattern; the role of sex in linguistic change; the effect of ethnicity and race on change; the gravity model of diffusion; the social motivation of change.

Volume 3
Cognitive factors: the effect of change on comprehension across and within dialects; the acquisition and transmission of variable rules; principles of syntactic change and grammaticalization; the forms of variable rules and their place in the grammar.

The separation of "internal" from "external," "linguistic factors" from "social factors" may not seem practical to those who view language as a unified whole where *tout se tient*, or to those who believe that every feature of language has a social aspect. My own approach to the problems of language change has most often been associated with the use of sociolinguistic data to establish the social motivation of change. In light of the foundations laid in such works as "The Mechanism of Linguistic Change" (Labov 1965), "Empirical Foundations for a Theory of Language Change" (Weinreich, Labov, and Herzog 1968), and "The Social Setting of Linguistic Change" (Labov 1972), it is reasonable to ask whether internal factors can be successfully separated from social factors.

No complete separation is intended. Volume 1 will necessarily include considerable information on the social distribution of linguistic variables. In addition to the historical processes reviewed, the main sources of data will be studies of the spontaneous production of members of the speech community. Since these data are identified with particular persons, times, and places, they do not lose their identification with the community from which they are drawn. These investigations are intended to represent the real process of linguistic change in the community, and in that sense, they are "sociolinguistic". In the same sense, all systematic studies of variation are sociolinguistic, and the variationist perspective cannot be applied without regard to particular speech communities. But the questions raised in volume 1 do not differentiate among community members by their social characteristics. Most of the problems considered in this volume concern relations within phonetic, phonemic, and morphological systems and the effects of sound change on the capacity of sounds to distinguish meanings. They fall within the *constraints* and *transition* problems defined by Weinreich, Labov, and Herzog (1968). The last part of volume 1, dealing with how meaning is preserved in the course of linguistic change, involves the *evaluation* problem. The mode of analysis remains internal to the system: relying on the distribution of tokens of variants to see how any listener would be able to deduce the meanings they were intended to signal.

Volume 2 falls more properly within the domain of sociolinguistics, since the independent variables are social factors. It begins the investigation of the causes of change by searching for the location of the innovators within the social system. This inquiry involves all six of the major independent variables of sociolinguistics: sex, age, social class, ethnicity, race, and community size. Here the members of the speech community are differentiated by their social status within the community as well as their relations to other communities. The exploration of social factors leads to the study of patterns of communication, the homogenizing and intensifying effects of social networks, and the transmission of variable elements across generations and across historical periods. One of the central problems to be raised is one that was not clearly identified in previous research: how change that continues in the same direction over long periods of time is transmitted from one generation to the next. This volume is therefore concerned with both the *embedding* problem and the *evaluation* problem as defined by Weinreich, Labov, and Herzog (1968). It also attempts a contribution to the *actuation* problem, and considers why, in the major cities of the United States, sound change appears to be accelerating.

In any division into internal and external or social factors, the bipartite aspect of the embedding problem will become evident. On the one hand, any given change is embedded in the structural matrix of linguistic forms that are most closely related to it, and the change will be restrained, redirected, or accelerated by its relation to other forms. In this sense, the embedding problem is an implicit aspect of the constraints problem. On the other hand, a change is embedded in the structure of the speech community. To understand the causes of change, it is necessary to know where in the social structure the change originated, how it spread to other social groups, and which groups showed most resistance to it. Since embedding in a larger structure inevitably involves multiple causation, the solution to any embedding problem requires multivariate analysis. The multivariate analyses that are reported in these volumes almost always include both internal and external factors. When the analyses are carried out, it appears that the two sets of factors – internal and external – are effectively independent of each other. If an internal factor is dropped or changed, changes appear in other internal factors, but the external factors remain unchanged; if an external factor is dropped or changed, other external factors change, but the internal factors remain as they were (Sankoff and Labov 1979; Weiner and Labov 1983). Moreover, the internal factors are normally independent of each other, while the external factors are heavily interactive. These basic sociolinguistic findings provide the methodological rationale for the way the material in volumes 1 and 2 is divided and for the separate discussion of internal and external factors.

This work lays no claim to complete coverage of the principles of historical linguistics; it is devoted to those issues that can be illuminated through the study of change in progress. The attack on these problems does not benefit from the analysis of many kinds of linguistic change that are of increasing importance in the study of language variation. None of the studies of the speech communities to be introduced in volumes 1 and 2 will show examples of syntactic change currently in progress.[1] The main research results on syntactic variation have emerged from the diachronic studies of texts by Kroch and his students (Kroch 1989b; Santorini 1989). These studies have produced powerful and important principles of change that intersect with the concerns of volume 1 in chapter 20 only. However, as the work progressed, it became increasingly apparent that there are further questions to be answered concerning the cognitive consequences of linguistic change, how variation is perceived and evaluated by individuals, and the status of variable rules in synchronic grammar. These matters are dealt with in volume 3, which draws from recent experimental results on cross-dialectal comprehension, from observations of the acquisition of variation by young children, from longitudinal studies of the same speakers

---

[1] The best vantage point for studying current syntactic change is found in developing creoles, as in the study of relative clauses in Tok Pisin (Sankoff 1980). The general principles that emerge from that work revolve about changes in the grammatical roles of morphemes, the motivation of syntactic change in discourse, and processes of grammaticalization, and these will be important elements in the discussions of volume 2 and 3.

over several decades, and from the analysis of syntactic change over long periods of time.

Theory, principle, description, explanation . . .

The conception of "linguistic theory" that is used in this work is not necessarily the same as that presented in most work on synchronic linguistics, nor that advocated by students of sociolinguistics who argue for the construction of a "sociolinguistic theory". The dominant approach to theory construction in our field is to build a model that corresponds point for point to each element of language structure, and to state the rules for relating parts of the model to each other and to the empirical facts. Though this is a useful proceeding, and we will benefit from it at many points, it is not the only way to go about the business of increasing our knowledge of language and language change. Though some readers might look forward to finding "a theory of language change" in these volumes, it would seem to me a bizarre and fruitless undertaking to model all possible relations between past and present states of a language.

The approach to theory taken in this work is more akin to the one used in the evolutionary sciences of geology and biology than to the formal modeling of logic or computer science. We begin with general questions about the routes, mechanisms, and causes of change, questions that are most often derived from the work of earlier investigators. To answer them, we select communities that show changes in progress of a sort that promise to be most illuminating, and make observations of a representative sample of speakers from community. From these observations, we make inferences about what is happening in the community as a whole. In the best cases, we then select other communities that are best suited to test the generality of the inferences we have made, and combine all the data we have to confirm, correct, or reject those inferences. The result of this expansion of our knowledge is a small number of generalizations of wide scope, or *principles*, which we have good reason to think are true. The principles must of course be logically related. Principles governing chain shifts, for example, must be related to principles governing mergers, since mergers are the converse of chain shifts. A set of logically related general principles might certainly deserve to be called a theory, if it is useful to do so. Theories as a form of general knowledge are to be highly valued, though ultimately, as we will see, the chief value of a theory is in establishing the most important matters of fact.

As our principles grow stronger, it is increasingly possible to make deductions about what we can expect to find in new communities undergoing change. Deductions are strategies that locate the sites for renewed testing and refinement of the principles. But the overall goal is to proceed steadily from the known to the unknown, enlarging the sphere of our knowledge on the foundation of observation and experiment in a cumulative manner.[2]

We hope that the linguistic generalizations or principles will interlock in such a way that they may be combined into simpler and more general statements, and this will be a major goal of our undertaking. Such simplification is often called *explanation* in synchronic or even diachronic linguistics. I will be using the term in a different sense. As chapter 1 of this volume will argue, it is not likely that the explanation of language change can be drawn from linguistic structure alone, since the fact of language change itself is not consistent with our fundamental conception of what language is. We might try to explain change by pointing to certain weaknesses of linguistic structure, but such limitations can only provide an opening for the effect of forces that operate upon language from some other source. To explain a finding about linguistic change will mean to find its causes in a domain outside of linguistics: in physiology, acoustic phonetics, social relations, perceptual or cognitive capacities. Many of the experimental and observational procedures to be reported here are aimed in that direction. A set of propositions that relate general findings about language change to general properties of human beings or of human societies will certainly deserve to be called a theory of language change.

[2] The converse procedure, which is often used in synchronic linguistics, is to construct a model that forces us to provide an answer to the most general questions, on the basis of whatever information we have, and, from this model, to make deductions about empirical facts that will confirm or disconfirm the model. This procedure of moving from the unknown to the known is rapid and productive, though it does not necessarily have cumulative results, and it is not clear that it can be applied to the general study of linguistic change.

Part A

Introduction and Methodology

1

The Use of the Present to Explain the Past

In historical linguistics, we pursue the facts of language change: the primary goal is to determine what happened in the history of a language or language family. The *fact* of language change is a given; it is too obvious to be recorded or even listed among the assumptions of our research. Yet this fact alone – the existence of language change – is among the most stubborn and difficult to assimilate when we try to come to grips with the nature of language in general as it is reflected in the history of a language.

Language is conceived here as the instrument of communication used by a speech community, a commonly accepted system of associations between arbitrary forms and their meanings. There are many other conceptions of language, each with its own value, but they all involve the association of a sign and its meaning, which in turn depends on the Saussurean concept of opposition and distinctive differences. Language change involves a disturbance of the form/meaning relationship so that people affected by the change no longer signal meaning in the same way as others not affected – older people in the same community, or people of the same age in neighboring communities. The result is a loss of comprehension across dialects and ultimately, mutual unintelligibility.

If language had evolved in the course of human history as an instrument of communication and been well adapted to that need, one of its most important properties would be stability. No matter how difficult a language was to learn, it would be easier to learn if it were stable than if it continued to change, and no matter how useful a system of communication was, it would be more useful if it could be used to communicate with a neighboring group without learning a new system. The fact of language change is difficult to reconcile with the notion of a system adapted to communication, unless we identify other pathological features inherent in language that limit this adaptation.

The argument does not apply to linguistic communities isolated from each other over long periods of time, where there is no pressing need to communicate. Geographic separation naturally and inevitably leads to linguistic separation. But the studies of linguistic change in progress that provide the basic data for the work in hand have demonstrated that geographic separation is not a necessary condition for language divergence.

People living in the same cities, attending the same schools, and exposed to the same mass media may be differentially affected by linguistic change so that over time their linguistic forms become increasingly differentiated.[1]

If the fact of language change were a constant, and closely correlated with language use, it could be studied by any of the other means used for the analysis of erosion, wear, and breakage. But it is not in any way constant, except in the fact of its existence. Change is sporadic in a deep sense, moving rapidly over some regions of structure until they are distorted beyond recognition in a century or two, then arresting so suddenly that rules once normal and inevitable become inconceivable and unnatural in a decade, disappearing for millenia to provide the illusion of stability. The English system of long vowels has undergone a repeated series of chain shifts from the earliest records of the language, while the short vowels have been almost unaffected by change. Yet as we will see, a sudden and unexpected rotation of the short vowels of English has erupted in the Northern Cities of the United States, a massive change that bears no resemblance to any chain shift previously recorded in the history of the language.

The phenomenon we are studying is irrational, violent, and unpredictable. To develop *principles of language change* might therefore seem a quixotic undertaking, as many students of change have concluded.[2] What seemed to be unshakeable principles to one generation of scholars appear to be circular or contradictory formulations to another. Historical linguistics is marked by the prevalence of contradictions and paradoxes that offer a rich array of challenges to the scholar who would resolve them. To consider how this might be done, it may be helpful to review some of the problems of interpreting historical data, and the methods used to deal with them.

1.1 Problems in the interpretation of historical data

The principal strength of historical linguistics lies in its ability to trace many linguistic changes over long periods of time. This broad temporal perspective serves to insulate historians from the academic uncertainties of the present. With ten to twenty centuries of language development in view, historians can feel more secure than formal linguists, who are guided

---

[1] The most striking examples stem from studies of the divergence of the Black English Vernacular from white dialects (Bailey and Maynor 1987; Labov and Harris 1986). But the same effect can also be observed in small rural areas within the same ethnic groups. The centralization of /ay/ and /aw/ on Martha's Vineyard differentiated members of the Yankee population as a result of their orientation toward future careers rather than their present situation (Labov 1963), and the same phenomenon has been observed in many other areas (Holmquist 1985, 1988; Eckert 1988; Habick 1980).

[2] See, for example, Bach and Harms 1972 ("How Do Languages Get Crazy Rules?") and Postal 1965.

chiefly by their personal intuitions about the present state of the language. Historical linguistics rests firmly on the objective and wide-ranging character of its data.

But the data that are rich in so many ways are impoverished in others. Historical documents survive by chance, not by design, and the selection that is available is the product of an unpredictable series of historical accidents. The linguistic forms in such documents are often distinct from the vernacular of the writers, and instead reflect efforts to capture a normative dialect that never was any speaker's native language. As a result, many documents are riddled with the effects of hypercorrection, dialect mixture, and scribal error.[3] Furthermore, historical documents can only provide positive evidence. Negative evidence about what is ungrammatical can only be inferred from obvious gaps in distribution, and when the surviving materials are fragmentary, these gaps are most likely the result of chance.

Historical linguistics can then be thought of as the art of making the best use of bad data. The art is a highly developed one, but there are some limitations of the data that cannot be compensated for. Except for very recent times, no phonetic records are available for instrumental measurements.[4] We usually know very little about the social position of the writers, and not much more about the social structure of the community. Though we know what was written, we know nothing about what was understood, and we are in no position to perform controlled experiments on cross-dialectal comprehension. Our knowledge of what was distinctive and what was not is severely limited, since we cannot use the knowledge of native speakers to differentiate nondistinctive from distinctive variants.

A typology of evidence

New developments in linguistics sometimes take the form of broadening the field of inquiry, where the accepted methods of the discipline are

---

[3] Problems of scribal error and scribal practice are discussed in Stockwell and Barritt 1951, 1961. For methods of distinguishing political and geographic dialects from temporal sequences, see Toon 1983. Many historical linguists have developed ingenious methods to isolate these effects and locate texts or subtexts that have the highest probability of approximating the spoken language. Arnaud (1980) selects the letters of women novelists as the most likely to reflect the development of the English progressive in speech. Dees (1971) focuses on the feminine oblique case of demonstrative pronouns in tracing their evolution from the 12th century onward, avoiding the special epic conventions associated with the masculine protagonists of medieval epics. Like others he finds that dramatic texts such as the Miracle Plays, no matter how conventionalized, reflect the spoken language more closely than prose. In the history of Chinese, it has been particularly important to isolate the archaizing effects of the literary tradition from the development of the current language; for one ingenious means of doing this for the oldest stratum, see Shi 1989, and for a detailed investigation of the results in more recent dialects, see Wang and Lien, to appear.

[4] The problem of inferring phonetic forms from written records is most severe for ideographic scripts. Evidence from the history of Chinese plays a major role in recent discussions of the regularity of sound change (Chapters 15–16), and here the problems of dialect mixture and phonetic opacity are magnified.

applied to new topics that had not been considered before. This is the path followed in discourse analysis, the typology of word order, and the ethnography of speaking. The route followed here is the converse; it applies new methods to the resolution of older unresolved questions, which have frequently generated inconsistent or even contradictory evidence. The contradictions may concern matters of fact or general principles; it will be helpful to use a terminology that makes this distinction consistently.

FACTS, GENERALIZATIONS, AND PRINCIPLES

At the most concrete level, the facts that a historical inquiry is based on are observations of the incomplete records of the past, as described above. The term *fact*, as I will use it, designates a true synthetic predication about a particular singular object.[5] The object in question need not be concrete. A fact may concern an object as concrete as a letter (whether it is scratched, inked, or typed) or a manuscript (its length, its date). But a fact may concern a more abstract entity like a text (its author, its rhyme scheme) or a dialect (its prevalence in a given territory, its membership in a language). And as the opening of this chapter argued, there is the fact of language itself (its existence, its use by people or any given person). A fact may be so difficult to determine that we can only have theories about what it is (the origin of language), yet in this use, it remains a fact even when we do not know what it is: that is, an unknown fact.

Predications made about a plurality of objects are then *generalizations* ("Dialects are difficult to distinguish from languages"). Unlike a fact, a generalization may be disproved. If it is a statement about all members of a class ("No OE text predates the 8th century"), it will be disproved by a single fact that is inconsistent with it; if it is an existential statement ("In OE manuscripts, letters are sometimes scratched in"), it can be disproved only when every fact is inconsistent with it.

Since facts form the data of a field of inquiry, this terminology throws into relief the process by which theory creates data. Abstractions are not discovered like concrete objects, but invented. The abstractions invented by a given theory may generate new facts. The concept of "vowel shift" does not seem to have been used in the 19th century, and the recognition of the English Great Vowel Shift is usually attributed to Jespersen (1949:chap. 8; 1st ed. 1909). Before this term was available, one could

---

[5] This is consistent with the conventional expressions "determine the facts of the matter" and "that is a fact." In this sense, there is no such thing as a false or mistaken fact. Every piece of data then represents a fact, though we may be mistaken about what the fact is. We may report that word W has vowel V on the basis of a given text, but if we recognize the possibility of scribal error, we may report more accurately that the scribe wrote V in word W in that manuscript. There is of course another use of *fact* to mean "any predication" as in "The facts in his paper are wrong." It must of course be specified that a fact is a synthetic statement. Analytic statements like this definition are not facts but conventions of discourse.

make generalizations about English vowel changes in Early Modern English, and indeed the concept of the Great Vowel Shift is based on several such generalizations (the changes involve long stressed vowels, preserve distinctions, are symmetrical in front and back). Once the Great Vowel Shift was accepted as a singular entity, one could state facts about it (the dates of its beginning and end).

It follows that many predications are in limbo, struggling for the status of facts. They may be predications about subjects that are not generally recognized as singular entities (a new language grouping) or as entities at all (a new semantic primitive, the language of dolphins). In this sense, all facts are social facts, since they must draw on a generally accepted linguistic convention if they are to be recognized in a field of discourse.

The term *principle* will be reserved for maximal projections of generalizations. A principle is a generalization that is unrestricted in its application in time or space. Thus I will not be speaking about "principles of English vowel shifting" or "principles of Indo-European sound change," but about "principles of vowel shifting" and "principles of sound change." The distinction between *generalization* and *principle* provides a simple way of distinguishing between inductive and deductive approaches to building linguistic theory. An inductive approach creates generalizations slowly as the data base grows, moving step by step to statements of increasing generality. A deductive approach may move from one or two examples to the statement of an unrestricted (or "universal") principle, and then attempt to predict other facts or data from the logical implications of this and other principles.

As the title of this work indicates, it will be concerned chiefly with the principles of language change: the confirmation or revision of older principles and the introduction of new ones. The new principles to be reported here are basically the results of an inductive process of increasing generalization. The initial data were drawn from the detailed investigation of a few American English speech communities, and gradually broadened to include past and present data drawn from language change in a fairly wide variety of language families. On the other hand, many of the original principles were first formulated at an early stage in the inquiry (1966–68), under the influence of the linguistic tendency to maximize the generality of statements as quickly as possible, and were modified only gradually in the years that followed. In discussing these new principles, I will try to follow a middle path between inductive prudence and deductive presumption, bearing in mind the limitations of the data base in the range of phenomena and languages considered, as well as the exceptions and problematic cases that challenge the validity of the argument as a whole.

PARADOXES OF EVIDENCE

Much of historical linguistics deals with questions of fact, and only indirectly with matters of principle. For many important questions, the general theory of language change might equally well have predicted one outcome or the other. The factual nature of the issues does not imply that there are no difficult problems to be resolved; on the contrary, most of the long-standing disputes of historical linguistics are disagreements about matters of fact. These disputed questions vary in scope over a wide range: arguments about a single lexeme (the origins of *O.K.* (Read 1964)), about a class of segments (whether the OE short diphthongs were phonemic (Stockwell and Barritt 1951; Kuhn and Quirk 1953)),[6] about the history of entire languages (whether Yiddish originated in a Romance or Germanic territory (King 1988)), or about the relation of whole language families (whether Thai is a sister branch of Austronesian). In some cases, the resolution of such a long-standing dispute is swift and decisive, as in the determination that the language of Linear B was Greek (Chadwick and Ventris 1958). In other cases, the disagreement seems to resist resolution for a very long time, as the evidence for each point of view seems to be massive and irrefutable. In their sharpest form, these internal disagreements may be called *paradoxes of evidence.*

The discipline has many ways of resolving these issues. Internal evidence is reexamined for its validity. External evidence is brought to bear from neighboring fields of expertise (settlement history, literature, and demography), which may show that the contradictions were really the result of a lack of homogeneity in the object being studied. But despite all efforts toward resolution, the positions of the disputants may remain fixed over their scholarly lifetimes.

One dispute that I have been involved in myself concerns the origins of Black English and its recent directions of change. There is ample evidence to support contradictory views on both questions. Volume 2 will report on this controversy and attempt to contribute to a resolution, though the main focus will be on the more general principles of the relation of racial segregation to language change.

UNEXPECTED FACTS

Other questions of fact are not so much the subject of dispute as a source of surprise and even irritation. When a completely unexpected regularity appears, we are faced with two embarrassing questions: why it should be so, and why we did not expect it to be so. The more regular the phenom-

---

[6] A matter of principle was involved here originally, in the matter of scribal practice: whether native speakers would transcribe subphonemic variants. But the bulk of the dispute as it developed concerned factual questions about the lexicon.

enon, the more puzzling the question. In studies of chain shifting, it has been found that long or tense nuclei consistently become less open and never more open (LYS:chap. 4; chap. 5 of this volume). But no clear answer has yet been given for why this should be so. A number of other such facts are reported in LYS and in part B of this volume.

Each of these unexpected discoveries is a continuing challenge to the theory of linguistic change. They are facts in search of a principle, and in this sense they are intermediate between questions of fact and questions of principle. It is possible that explanations for some of these effects will open new fields of research that will overshadow the problems that are the focus of the chapters to follow. However, the topic of these volumes is not so much the explication of new findings as the effect of these new findings on well-known issues of linguistic change, and their contribution to the resolution of long-standing contradictions in the data and the theories of historical linguistics.

PARADOXES OF PRINCIPLE

There are many well-accepted facts of historical linguistics that violate well-accepted principles. One such case is the merger of English /ay/ and /oy/. In the 18th century, it was consistently and reliably reported that *line* and *loin*, *vice* and *voice*, *pint* and *point* were pronounced the same (chapter 10). Yet in the 19th and 20th centuries, these two word classes separated cleanly, with only an occasional crossover in local dialects. This will appear to be a clear violation of Garde's Principle (1961): that mergers are irreversible by linguistic means. In the literature of historical linguistics, the only solution put forward was that of Jespersen (1949:330), that spelling was responsible for the unmerger. But this suggestion has found little support among those who have examined the effects of spelling on mergers. Even where the spelling clearly differentiates the two classes, speakers of the merged dialect cannot reliably differentiate them.[7]

It has often been attested that when facts contradict a well-accepted principle, they are likely to be rejected. This was the case with observations that in minimal pair and commutation tests, speakers sometimes fail to label distinctions that they make consistently in production (chapter 12). This finding violates the principle stated by Bloomfield (1926) that "such a thing as a 'small difference in sound' does not exist in language": in other words, no matter how small a phonetic distinction may seem to outsiders, native speakers will have no difficulty in identifying it if it consis-

---

[7] The ongoing merger of long open **o** and short open **o** in the United States offers many opportunities to test this issue. Herold (1990) investigated this problem in Ontario, and found a fairly high degree of success among local speakers in separating long and short open **o** words as spoken by New Yorkers. However, 25% of the subjects who succeeded in separating the classes did so wrongly; that is, the labels were reversed.

tently distinguishes two groups of words. Chapter 12 will conclude with a dramatic account by David de Camp that shows in detail how data that contradicted this principle were rejected and excluded from his dissertation by a committee of linguists.

In addition to disagreements between facts and principles, there are disagreements over principles that have remained unresolved for a very long time. In such cases, there is a large body of data that support one principle, and a sizeable number of facts that support the other. It is only natural that these disputes should draw more attention than arguments over facts, since they may affect outcome of many particular analyses.

THE NEOGRAMMARIAN CONTROVERSY
The most famous argument over principles is certainly the controversy over the Neogrammarian principles of sound change, which motivates much of the research reported here and provides the framework for parts D and E of this volume. Many linguists still maintain that the Neogrammarian formulation of the principles of sound change gives historical and comparative linguistics the firm foundation on which cumulative work can proceed (Bloomfield 1933:364; Hockett 1965). Yet while the practice of historical linguists assumes the regularity of change, it is generally agreed that the massive data of dialect geography supports the contrary view, that "each word has its own history" (Gilliéron 1918; Malkiel 1967). Over several decades, the contradictions between these two bodies of evidence have aroused a wide range of responses (chapter 16); yet there seems to be general agreement that the lexical isoglosses of dialect geography fail to coincide in the way that the regularity hypothesis would predict. When the questions raised by the Neogrammarians are recast within a structuralist perspective, the issue is plainly a substantive one: what is the fundamental unit of sound change? In Bloomfield's formulation, it is *phonemes* that change (1933:364). The opposing view has been recast as a theory of lexical diffusion (Wang 1977), in which it is argued that the basic unit of change is the *word*. Close-grained studies of intermediate stages should be able to distinguish between the two possibilities.

Chapters 15 and 16 will demonstrate that there is good evidence to support both sides of this argument. We are faced with a paradox of principle: language behaves as if the significant unit affected by sound change is the phoneme, and also as if the unit of change is the word.

The turn to synchronic principles

In the effort to resolve such contradictions and long-standing disputes, diachronic linguists have often turned to the principles of synchronic linguistics. The use of synchronic principles is particularly appropriate when the methods of comparative linguistics lead to abstract reconstructions that are linked only indirectly to the evidence of attested languages.

It is a reasonable requirement that a reconstructed language should conform to the definition of possible language structure provided by present-day theory and typology. One would have to be suspicious, for example, of a reconstruction with more nasal vowels than oral vowels.

A second application of synchronic theory is derived from the general theory of markedness. "Natural" linguistic changes are similar to unmarked features of the grammar, in that they are more common than marked forms and simpler (that is, they lead to simpler forms, rules, or grammars). The reconstruction of former languages cannot be governed directly by markedness theory, since highly marked forms do occur; but it is possible to argue that the changes implied by the reconstruction should be "natural" changes (Greenberg 1969). The same logic can be applied to accounting for the mechanism of change between any two attested states of a language, as in the explication of the English Great Vowel Shift. Kiparsky (1989) reviews a wide variety of proposals to distinguish between natural and less natural phonological processes and their implication for phonological change.

The typological tradition initiated by Greenberg classifies linguistic structures and changes on the basis of their surface characteristics, while the search for natural changes within the generative tradition deals with much more abstract arguments. It is evident that more abstract modes of analysis have the capacity to unify a larger range of phenomena. But the connection with the work of historical linguists becomes more difficult as the theory becomes more abstract. To apply the principles of an abstract and formal linguistic theory to a language that has been described with the traditional tools of historical linguistics, it is necessary to recast the description in the terminology of that particular synchronic theory. Few abstract models have shown the stability needed to justify such an effort.[8]

There is no doubt that language structure is abstract and hierarchically organized, and efforts to unify and explicate linguistic changes must use principles considerably removed from the surface data. At many points in this work, the application of current synchronic formalisms to the data on hand will be examined, particularly in response to the important contributions of Kiparsky (1989). However, I do not believe that cumulative advances can be based on the reanalysis of facts already known and long considered by linguists working in other frameworks. The contradictions and paradoxes of historical linguistics will be approached here by the introduction of new data, of a type not available before. Studies of linguistic change in progress, which complement the strengths and weaknesses of

---

[8] King (1969) represents an effort to apply the generative notion of simplicity to the principles of historical change; for a critique of that effort, see King 1975. Stockwell and Macaulay (1967) assemble a number of such efforts to connect the current state of generative grammar with historical linguistics.

traditional diachronic data, should illuminate features of the past that were hidden from view, and so contribute toward the resolution of long-standing questions of historical linguistics.

1.2 The study of change in progress

In the 19th century, historical linguists made strong and explicit statements about the importance of studying the living language.

Only that comparative linguist who for once emerges from the hypotheses-beclouded atmosphere of the workshop in which the original Indo-European forms are forced, and steps into the clear air of tangible reality and of the present in order to get information about those things which gray theory can never reveal to him, and only he who renounces forever that formerly widespread but still used method of investigation according to which people observe language only on paper and resolve everything into terminology, systems of rules, and grammatical formalism and believe they have then fathomed the essence of the phenomena when they have devised a name for the thing – only he can arrive at a correct idea of the way in which linguistic forms live and change, and only he can acquire those methodological principles without which no credible results can be obtained at all in investigations in historical linguistics and without which any penetration into the periods of the past which lie behind the historical tradition of a language is like a sea voyage without a compass. (Osthoff and Brugmann 1876; translation from Lehmann 1967:202)

Broadly, this statement was designed to reinforce the importance of data drawn from German and other living languages as opposed to the documentary evidence of classical languages, which had been weighed more heavily in the earlier tradition. When the authors spoke of studying living languages, they do not seem to have been thinking in terms of their own introspections about German, but in terms of objective descriptions of local dialects.

In all living dialects the shapes of sounds peculiar to the dialect always appear much more consistently carried out throughout the entire linguistic material and maintained by the members of the linguistic community than one would expect from the study of the older languages accessible merely through the medium of writing: this consistency often extends into the finest shades of a sound. (Osthoff and Brugmann 1878; translation from Lehmann 1969:201–202)

Osthoff and Brugmann may have been aware that their own speech patterns were heavily influenced by the written language, and therefore not free from the weight of the classical traditions that they hoped to escape from. In any case, the only objective studies available to them were dialect monographs, and among these they were particularly struck by the regular patterns found in Winteler's (1876) description of the Swiss German dialect.

Though Osthoff and Brugmann prized dialectological evidence of the spatial reflexes of diachronic change, they did not call for studies of change in progress in the living languages. The first such study was carried out by Gauchat from 1899 to 1904 in the small Swiss village of Charmey. As a Romance dialectologist and staunch opponent of the Neogrammarian doctrine of the regularity of sound change, Gauchat was convinced that the Neogrammarians had overestimated the homogeneity of rural dialects. His report showed many variables that fluctuated with age: for example, the oldest generation used palatalized /l'/, the youngest generation used /y/, and the middle generation alternated between /l'/ and /y/ (1905). Gauchat believed that he had succeeded in refuting the Neogrammarian belief in the regularity of sound change, and reported that the "unity" of the community so essential to Neogrammarian doctrine was "null." In response, the Neogrammarian Goidanich (1926) argued that Gauchat's results did not reflect sound change, but instead resulted from dialect borrowing: the middle generation borrowed some forms from their parents, and some from their children, but abandoned their own pronunciation entirely. This bizarre argument rested on the Neogrammarian belief that sound change must proceed gradually and uniformly, so that all members of a given community (or generation?) use the same form: either /l'/, a phonetic form intermediate between /l'/ and /y/, or /y/.

It is generally believed that the Neogrammarians were misled by the exceptional simplicity of Winteler's data on the Kerenzen dialect, and that other explorations of rural and urban dialects showed variation that was inconsistent with their doctrine (Bloomfield 1933:322; Kiparsky 1989:369). Sociolinguistic studies of modern speech communities are cited as evidence of the heterogeneous character of the speech community in general (Kiparsky 1989). Yet the heterogeneity that is so fundamental to the sociolinguistic view of the community (Weinreich, Labov, and Herzog 1968) is an *ordered* heterogeneity that is not obviously inconsistent with the Neogrammarian concept. The central question is whether the process of sound change affects every word in which the given sound appears in the same way. To assess the regularity of dialectal variation, it will be necessary to introduce new methods for gathering and analyzing data that were not available to the originators of the Neogrammarian principles. Though they found most dialectologists arrayed against them, chapter 17 will show that their original confidence in the testimony of dialect geography was not misplaced.

Introduction of new principles

New data are not automatically applicable to an old problem; frequently the relevance of new data depends upon a new principle that was not evident to earlier investigators. The continuity or similarity between the present and the past then gives us the license to apply this new principle. The reported unmerger of /ay/ and /oy/ in Essex will not prove to be a violation of the principle that sound changes cannot be reversed, but a violation of a different principle: that "there is no such thing as a small difference in sound." The many modern examples of such violations lead to the introduction of a new principle of "near-merger": if a stable distinction between two word classes is minimal and depends upon a linguistic feature that normally does not function alone to distinguish word classes in that language, native speakers may not be able to use it to distinguish words. The principle modifies the traditional notion of contrast by establishing that the contrastive function of a phonemic distinction may be suspended without losing the historical integrity of the word classes involved. Chapter 12 develops the current evidence for this principle, and chapter 13 applies it to several historical cases of falsely reported merger, including the case of /ay/ and /oy/.

The fundamental paradox of historical linguistics

Even when we have the correct principle at hand, there is no immediate and obvious recipe for adding new data from the present to resolve the classical debates of the past. One cannot simply add 20th-century data to 16th-century data as if they were drawn from the same speech community, since the earlier community no longer exists. The use of the present to explain the past then depends not only on new methods and new data, but also on locating points of contact and similarity between the present and the past that would justify the application of the new data.

This is not a trivial problem. In fact, it involves more profound difficulties than any we have seen before. If the past were identical to the present in every way, the use of the present to explain the past would be simple and straightforward. But it would also be unnecessary, for there would be nothing to explain. The interest of historical linguistics rests on the fact that the past was different from the present – witness the fact of linguistic change. If it were not so, there would be no need for historical linguistics. The historical approach to the understanding of any aspect of language – understanding how it came to *be* – would not exist.

Given that the past differed from the present, there is no way of saying in advance how different it was. The differences between past and present may apply not only to the forms and rules of the language, but also to how those forms and rules were applied and how they changed.

These considerations lead to an appreciation of a paradox of historical linguistics that is as fundamental and profound as the Observer's Paradox in synchronic linguistics. It begins with the fact noted earlier that the records of the past are inevitably incomplete and defective. The task of historical linguistics is to complete that record by inferring the missing forms:

reconstructing unattested stages, extrapolating to complete the missing forms for attested stages, and reconstructing the intervening states between them. All this activity implies that the nature of the differences between past and present is known in advance. The Historical Paradox can be stated more briefly.

The task of historical linguistics is to explain the differences between the past and the present; but to the extent that the past was different from the present, there is no way of knowing how different it was.

The uniformitarian principle

From the preceding, it should be evident that the application of data from changes in progress to the problems of the past is dependent upon the linguistic version of the *uniformitarian principle*. The principle is so central to the work reported here that it will be essential to give some space to its origins and history. Christy (1983) traces the uniformitarian principle in the historical sciences of the 19th century, particularly in geology and philology, and the following remarks are much indebted to his account. The principle was first formulated by the Scottish geologist James Hutton in 1785, but it was first made the foundation of modern geology by Charles Lyell in his *Principles of Geology* in 1833. It is briefly that

knowledge of processes that operated in the past can be inferred by observing ongoing processes in the present. (Christy 1983:ix)

Uniformitarianism was opposed to *catastrophism*, the dominant view in geology and biology. Catastrophists held that the origins of the earth and of living things were to be found in sudden and unique events in the past, and that all living species have been fixed in their characters since then. The Biblical accounts of the creation of the earth by God and the origin of languages at the Tower of Babel were the sudden events that linked geology and linguistics to religious authority. In the course of the long debate, illustrious scientists like the anatomist Cuvier supported catastrophism by hard evidence drawn from the fossil record.

The major proponent of the uniformitarian principle in linguistics was William Dwight Whitney, who made it a central point in his *Language and the Study of Language* (1867). Whitney's older brother Josiah Dwight Whitney was a prominent geologist, and the two brothers were intimately familiar with each other's work. Whitney himself made many references to the parallels between geology and linguistics. In his discussion of the origin of language, he argues,

So far back as we can trace the history of language, the forces which have been efficient in producing its changes, and the general outlines of their modes of operation, have been the same. .... There is no way of investigating the first hidden steps of any continuous historical process, except by carefully studying the later recorded steps, and cautiously applying the analogies thence deduced, [just as] ... the geologist studies the forces which are now altering by slow degrees the form and aspect of the earth's crust. (1867:253, quoted in Christy 1983:84)

The Neogrammarians were directly influenced by Whitney, as Brugmann testifies:

Among the many valuable contributions of William Dwight Whitney to linguistic science is one especially important and fundamental principle. It may be stated in these words. In explaining prehistoric phenomena of language we must assume no other factors than those which we are able to observe and estimate in the historical period of language development. The factors that produced changes in human speech five thousand or ten thousand years ago cannot have been essentially different from those which are now operating to transform living languages. (1897:1–2, quoted in Christy 1983:82)

Though Whitney endorsed this principle as a basis for reasoning in linguistics, he was little inclined to the study of everyday language that is the central data source for the work reported here. He considered dialectal variations from his own standards as speech errors to be condemned or even prosecuted. The Neogrammarians rejected the limitations of Whitney's approach and, as we have seen, developed vigorously the idea that the understanding of classical languages of the past is to be found in the living dialects of the present.[9]

  Today, it would seem that linguistics has accepted the uniformitarian principle and its consequences, as geology, biology, and other historical sciences have done. But the implementation of uniformitarian thinking requires intimate contact with the actual processes of change in the present, and that type of study is relatively recent. Dialectology in the United States and elsewhere has traditionally focused on rural dialects, because these seemed to reflect best the earlier patterns of settlement history that were the major target of the discipline. As in most rural areas of other industrial countries, these dialects are receding. New technology makes the rural vocabulary obsolete, and young people abandon traditional phonetic and grammatical forms in favor of urban standards, anticipating their own migration to urban centers. It is therefore commonly reported by dialectologists that local dialects are disappearing, and that we have entered a new

---

[9] Whitney's approach to the causes of linguistic change is not the topic here, but it illustrates the kind of thinking that the Neogrammarians reacted against: "Such phonetic changes ... are inevitable and creep in of themselves; but that is only another way of saying that we know not who in particular is to blame for them. Offenses must needs come, but there is always that man by whom they come, could we but trace him out" (1867:43).

period of linguistic convergence instead of divergence. But research in urban areas shows the opposite. Since 1972, I and others have been reporting evidence of continued sound change in the dialects of the major English-speaking cities. In every large speech community studied in the United States, Canada, and Australia, we observe the vigorous developments of the local vernacular to be described in these volumes.

The innovative role of cities is not new: there is good reason to think that cities have always been the center of linguistic innovation, and that most rural dialects are relics of developments that began in the cities and spread to progressively smaller speech communities until they reached the countryside. But these communities are as a rule suffering from the decline in agriculture and a shrinking local population, so that they do not characterize the major trends in American dialects.

The uniformitarian principle is the necessary working assumption for all the investigations to follow. To the extent that this principle depends on uniformities in the physiological basis of language, it must be correct, since there is no indication of differences between the linguistic past and the present in this respect. But the uniformitarian principle is more problematic where social differences are concerned, and we must be alert to its limitations here. Our overall results on sound change in progress show that the present development of mass media and electronic communication has no detectable effect in retarding sound change. Yet the belief that these new developments must affect language change cannot be entirely wrong: there are certainly some consequences of the more rapid diffusion of politically dominant forms of speech. We must also be wary of extrapolating backward in time to neolithic, pre-urban societies with an entirely different social organization. For many of the languages of Asia, Africa, and South America, the historical record is short, and it is possible that different principles may have applied in their early development.

Gradualism versus catastrophism

The most general and influential formulation of the uniformitarian principle, that of Lyell (1833), was strongly committed to gradualism: the concept that the current state of the earth, over long periods of time, is the result of the small and continuous effects of erosion, sedimentation, metamorphosis, and orogeny that can be observed everywhere around us. The opposing view that some present-day formations were produced by unique and violent events in the past was associated with the religiously motivated doctrine of catastrophism. This gradualist view became a rigid dogma that has only recently been relaxed in geology (Gould 1980).[10] In linguistics,

---

[10] Gould (1980) argues that the new catastrophism has been strongly motivated by the success of Bretz in explaining the *coulee* formations in the channeled scablands of eastern Washington

we must be careful not to confuse a commitment to uniformitarian thinking with a commitment to gradualism.

It is well known that catastrophic events have played a major role in the history of all languages, primarily in the form of population dislocations: migrations, invasions, conquests, and massive immigrations. Other abrupt political changes have led to alterations in the normative structure of the speech community, with radical substitutions of one prestige norm for another, and consequent long-term effects on the language. When we deal with the effect of external factors on language change in volume 2, we will encounter strong evidence for the view of Martinet (1955) that significant external effects are of this catastrophic type, while all gradual effects are internal, structural reactions set off by these rare disruptions of the speech community. It will appear that such catastrophic changes are more common than previously believed, and that the history of many urban speech communities would lead us to expect massive population changes several times in a century rather than once in a millenium.

In any case, linguists are in no position to endorse a gradualist version of the uniformitarian doctrine. The external history of most languages shows the uneven path of development that corresponds well to the sporadic character of sound change. Recent reemphasis on demographic history[11] may put us in a better position to correlate the two profiles – social and linguistic – and thus respond to Meillet's suggestion that

the only variable to which we can turn to account for linguistic change is social change, of which linguistic variations are only consequences. We must determine which social structure corresponds to a given linguistic structure, and how, in a general manner, changes in social structure are translated into changes in linguistic structure. (1921: 16–17; my translation)

It remains to be seen whether the two types of uneven development can be fitted together, or whether language change and social change are both erratic and independently motivated.

Limitations of the uniformitarian principle

We can sum up this discussion of the uniformitarian principle by repeating the Neogrammarian insight that this principle is a necessary precondition for historical reconstruction as well as for the use of the present to explain the past. But we have also seen that it is in fact a necessary *consequence* of the fundamental paradox of historical linguistics, not a solution to that

---

by a single flood of glacial meltwater and the violent effects of vast volumes of water suddenly released.

[11] Most strongly evidenced in recent explorations of the histories of pidgins and creoles (Baker and Corne 1982; Bickerton 1984; Singler 1987), but also well motivated by work in dialectology (Trudgill 1986; Herold 1990).

parodox. If the uniformitarian principle is applied as if it were such a solution, rather than a working assumption, it can actually conceal the extent of the errors that are the result of real differences between past and present.

Solutions to the Historical Paradox must be analogous to solutions to the Observer's Paradox. Particular problems must be approached from several different directions, by different methods with complementary sources of error. The solution to the problem can then be located somewhere between the answers given by the different methods. In this way, we can know the limits of the errors introduced by the Historical Paradox, even if we cannot eliminate them entirely.

1.3   Introduction of new methods

The chapters to follow will apply data from the synchronic study of linguistic change in progress to historical problems. By this means, I hope to reinforce the natural alliance of dialect geography, sociolinguistics, phonetics, and historical linguistics – fields that share a common interest in objective data. The connections that we can make today were not possible a hundred years ago, since they depend to a large extent on new technology.

- The development of high-quality battery-operated tape recorders makes it possible to capture the systematic character of spontaneous speech and so replaces the older technique of "asking the informant" (Voegelin and Harris 1951).
- Techniques for the representative study of the speech community allow us to trace the process of change across the social structure, and so locate the innovators as well as those who resist and oppose the change.
- With current computational methods for the instrumental analysis of the speech wave, it is possible to provide objective measurements of the process of change for large bodies of data.
- The application of probability theory to the data allows us to extract higher-order regularities that govern variation in the community.
- With new methods for the multivariate analysis of discrete linguistic variation, one can provide objective evidence for more abstract analyses of the changes that are taking place.
- Subjective impressions of 'same' and 'different' can be correlated with actual distributions of phones in the course of speech, as well as with experimental tests of speakers' ability to recognize the distinctions they make themselves.
- Subjective impressions of the social status of linguistic variants can be verified with maps of social distributions of use and experimental studies of subjective reactions to various forms.

These new methods will be applied to many long-standing problems throughout these volumes. The reported historical unmerger of /ay/ and /oy/ will be studied by applying instrumental analysis to the nearest related phenomenon available in the present: the speech of Essex County in southeastern England (chapter 13). The regularity of sound change will be pursued through a multiple regression analysis of data from the study of change and variation in Philadelphia (chapter 16). Multidimensional scaling will be applied to the data of dialect geography to explore the insights of Osthoff and Brugmann on the regular course of sound change in local dialects (chapter 17).

Variation and invariance

The character of the data generated by the new methods to be used requires further innovations in analytical methods and the mathematical treatment of the data. Evidence for the changes that we will be studying is to be found in variation across decades in real time and in variation across age levels in apparent time. But these are not the only sources of variation in the data. To extract evidence for change in progress, we must separate the variation due to change from the variation due to social factors like sex, social class, social networks, and ethnicity, and from the variation due to internal factors like sentence stress, segmental environment, word order, and phrase structure.

The problem can be approached by a number of methods, of varying degrees of sophistication. If the data base is large enough, it can be subdivided along many dimensions, and a comparison of the cross-tabulations of subgroups can reveal much of the internal structure of the data. But in most cases, we will want to rely on the forms of multivariate analysis cited above, which examine the contribution of many constraints on the data simultaneously. For studies of sound change in progress, where the dependent variable is continuous, stepwise multiple regression will be used. The treatment of discrete binary or trinary variables will draw on the variable rule program (Cedergren and Sankoff 1974), which is designed to take into account the specific properties of linguistic data. We will also use principal components and multidimensional scaling, which are more independent of the linguistic theory involved, and accordingly more difficult to interpret. Yet the theory-free character of these methods can yield exceptionally strong conclusions when the results coincide with the categories predicted by a particular theory.

All these methods focus our attention on the precise distributions of variation in the linguistic structure and the social matrix. Given the nature of the proceeding – the extraction of general principles from the spontaneous use of language – we will not normally be pursuing exceptionless universals that uniquely determine the linguistic output without regard to any concomitant constraints. Whatever the proportion may be of invariant to variable linguistic rules, the study of change intersects only tangentially with the pursuit of invariance. True enough, the end result of many linguistic changes is reported as an invariant outcome, where the original form or rule is said to be entirely extinct. However, this study will turn up more than a few cases where the variation continues over enormous stretches of time, and others where the same process is renewed as if it had never ended. The close examination of the present shows that much of the past is still with us. The study of history benefits from the continuity of the past as well as from analogies with the present.

2

An Overview of the Issues

This chapter summarizes the argument of volume 1. It outlines the questions to be raised about linguistic change, the opposing answers given in the past, the types of evidence found on each side of the issues, the new types of data introduced to resolve these oppositions, and the new principles that will be introduced to resolve the problems and paradoxes of linguistic change.

Part A: Introduction and methodology

Chapter 1 has already introduced the general methodological principles for this enterprise, and in particular how the present can be used to explain the past. Chapter 2 is this summary of the issues. Chapters 3 and 4 provide the methodological foundation for the study of change in progress. They describe the techniques for this type of study, discuss some unresolved problems, and consider how to interpret the results of some recent studies of change in apparent time and real time.

Chapter 3 focuses on the study of apparent time: the distribution of linguistic forms across age groups in the speech community. It begins with a review of the methods that have been used to study change in progress. In response to the paradox that sound change is both too fast and too slow to be observed, it considers the types of inferences that can be drawn from mathematical and graphic displays of changes in apparent time, exemplified by studies of changes in progress in the New York City and Philadelphia vowel systems. It includes an account of the instrumental and analytic methods used to derive the age coefficients that are used throughout this work as measures of change in apparent time.

Often no real-time information is available concerning a sound change. Chapter 3 considers this common situation and asks, "What can we learn about change in real time from distributions in apparent time?" Some answers are provided by internal distributions in the Philadelphia vowel system, in particular the relative positions of "fast" and "slow" allophones that correlate with various stages in the history of a change. In the early stages of a sound change, some allophones move more rapidly than others and reach a more advanced position. At a later stage, the pattern in apparent time will show an odd situation: the age coefficients associated with the more advanced allophones are smaller than those associated with the less advanced allophones. These data are used to refine our understanding of the characteristic trajectory of linguistic change from initiation to completion. Finally, chapter 3 consolidates the evidence for the stability of phonological systems that is the basis for interpreting data drawn from apparent time.

Chapter 4 is devoted to real-time studies, of two kinds. In the first type, comparative data are drawn from earlier studies with entirely different aims, methods, and theoretical perspectives. These include the systematic records of dialect geography, as well as the fragmentary observations, occasional transcriptions, and more detailed descriptions typical of the historical record. The uses and limitations of such records are reviewed. The interpretation of these records necessarily involves the search for qualitative comparisons rather than quantitative ones.

The second source of real-time comparisons is the result of more deliberate procedures: the return to a speech community to replicate as closely as possible an earlier study of linguistic variation. Until recently, only one such restudy had been carried out: Hermann's 1929 replication of Gauchat's 1899 investigation of Charmey. Now, however, data are available from restudies of five major sociolinguistic investigations:

1 Fowler's 1986 replication of Labov's 1963 New York City Department Store Study (Fowler 1986; Labov 1963)
2 Cedergren's 1982 restudy of her 1972 investigation in Panama City (Cedergren 1973, 1984)
3 Trudgill's 1983 restudy of his 1968 survey of Norwich (Trudgill 1974a, 1988)
4 Thibault and Vincent's 1984 restudy of the 1971 Montreal survey (Sankoff and Sankoff 1973; Thibault and Vincent 1990)
5 Restudies of the Philadelphia speakers from the 1973–76 LCV project, interviewed in 1990 for research on language change in normal aging.

The methodology of real-time restudies is at an early stage of development, and there are many open questions. The most reliable results are derived from replicating the same methods, without necessarily obtaining data from the same speakers, but important conclusions can also be drawn from rerecording the same individuals. The results of the restudies will allow us to assess more precisely the reliability and validity of research on linguistic change in progress. As in the earlier work of Hermann (1929), the question is not easily resolved. The earlier data usually appear to have been a mixture of age-grading and real-time change, and the task of distinguishing these proves to be a formidable one.

Chapter 4 finally returns to the problem of modeling linguistic change according to the various possibilities revealed by the comparison of apparent-time and real-time data. It raises the question of what models are recaptured by what methods, and how studies can be designed that will not obscure as much as they reveal.

Part B: Chain shifting

The first problem to be faced in describing sound change is whether all types of change are possible, or whether there are limitations on what types of change can take place. The search for possible constraints on linguistic change is almost as broad an area as linguistics itself. An overview of recent work would include the study of semantic change, syntactic development, changes in word order, and the grammaticalization of morphological elements as well as phonological and phonetic change. A broad view of the issues can be derived from reviews of directions and constraints on phonological change (Kiparsky 1989), morphological change (Joseph and Janda 1988), and syntactic change (Kroch 1989b).

The attack on the constraints problem that is presented in part B is confined to a small part of this field: it is limited to phonetic and phonological change, and within that area, it focuses on stressed vowels. This is partly because the most detailed data on change in progress derive from instrumental studies of English vowel shifts. Among the languages of the world, English is one of the few that have developed or maintained complex systems of more than 10 vowels. This is not the most promising base for developing general principles of linguistic change. Nevertheless, the rotations, shifts, and mergers of vowels are among the major forces that lead to linguistic diversity throughout the world, and the changes that characterize the history of English appear to follow principles that can be traced across many language families.

The simplest kinds of vowel shifts involve movement of a vowel to an empty position in the vowel system, in turn leaving behind an empty position. There are very few constraints on such simple movements: it is not difficult to find examples of vowels becoming higher or lower, backer or fronter, rounded or unrounded, nasalized or unnasalized. But when these simple movements are combined in interlocking sets – chain shifts – the situation is quite different. The systematic character of sound change appears most clearly in chain shifts, and a number of unidirectional patterns appear.

The study of chain shifts cannot be isolated from the study of parallel movements, which have been widely discussed in the search for principles of linguistic change. Parallel shifts, or shifts that restore parallelism, formed much of the evidence for the principle that all linguistic change can be explained as a process of simplification (King 1969). Many of the chain shifts to be considered in part B exhibit both parallel and chained movements; we will have ample opportunity to consider the relations between these two types, and to see if their development can be described in terms of increasing generality of phonological rules.

Chapter 5 begins with three general principles of chain shifting that have been derived from the joint study of changes in progress and the record of completed changes. In chain shifts,

Principle I: Long vowels rise.
Principle II: Short nuclei fall.
Principle III: Back vowels move to the front.

To determine whether these are indeed valid constraints on change, it is first necessary to show where they have empirical content – in what configurations they can be seen to operate. The cover terms *tense* and *lax* must also be related to the terms *long* and *short* that are generally found in the historical record. Chapter 5 undertakes these tasks, reviewing the evidence that supports these principles and distinguishing some true counterexamples from some apparent ones.

The chain shift principles do not apply in isolation: that is, in any given historical development, two or more of the general principles are combined. These combinations are restricted to a relatively small number of chain shift patterns that recur throughout the languages of the world.

Chapter 5 also confronts some serious contradictions of principle in the historical record. These concern vowel movements that should have led to permanent mergers according to Garde's principle of the irreversibility of mergers (chapter 1), but did not. Typical is the case of Yiddish diphthongization. Like other Germanic languages, Yiddish diphthongized MHG **ī** and **ū** to [ai] and [au]. But in Yiddish, **ī** became diphthongized to [ɪi] and descended to [ai] without merging with MHG **ei** on the way. How did this happen? Traditional accounts provide no answer. A similar problem is the much-discussed case of *day* and *die* in the Great Vowel Shift, which also fails to show the merger that phonological theory would predict as [æi] rises to [ei] while [ɪi] descends to [ai]. A new problem is exposed in Early Modern English concerning four front vowels before /r/ – the supposedly irregular development of words spelled *ea* before /r/ (*rear, fear, tear [N], tear [V], bear, wear,* etc.). Closer examination shows that all of the exceptions to the regular development toward /ihr/ are from a particular etymological subclass: words with OE short **ĕ** in open syllables, such as **bĕran** 'to bear'. This class remained in mid position throughout the history of English. But how could it not have merged with the **ær** class of *rear, fear,* etc., as this class rose from [æ:r] to [e:r] to [i:r]? In all of these cases, the historical record violates the expectations that arise from current understandings of how vowel systems work: problems for later chapters to resolve.

Chapter 6 takes up the constraints problem with data from chain shifts in progress, based on instrumental measurements of vowel systems in a variety of American and British dialects. It introduces a new conception of English phonological space, and a new conception of the feature *peripherality* shared by other Germanic and Baltic languages that show the diphthongization of [iː] and [uː] to [ɪi] and [ʊu]. Both front and back vowel spaces are divided into two regions of phonological space: a peripheral region, near the outside of the vowel space, and a nonperipheral one, closer to the center. It is then proposed to modify the basic principles of chain shifting to assert that tense vowels rise along the peripheral path, and lax vowels fall along the nonperipheral path. Evidence for this principle comes from instrumental studies of a variety of English vowel systems that display chain shifts in progress.

Chapter 7 applies the proposed modifications of chapter 6 to the problems and contradictions that were exposed in the review of the historical record in chapter 5. The solutions depend upon the possibility that the earlier phonological systems also showed the peripheral and nonperipheral tracks that are found in modern phonological systems. The existence of such a model of phonological space can only be inferred, since early phonetic accounts have no way of indicating more than two or three categories along the front–back dimension, and more are required to support this model of phonological space. The theories of chapter 7 demand a more detailed look at the uniformitarian principle as it might apply to such large-scale phonological structures.

To support the proposals made in chapter 6, it is necessary to show what kinds of rule formulations would serve to describe the path of sound change predicted by the principles. Chapter 7 proposes phonological rules for the vowel shifts and discusses what modifications would be required in the inventory of features and rule operations.

Chapter 8 is a further exercise in simplifying and reducing the rules and principles for chain shifting. It begins by acknowledging the heterogeneity of the rules found thus far and asks whether a single, unrestricted vowel shift rule can simultaneously raise the tense nuclei along a peripheral track and lower the lax nuclei along a nonperipheral track. Much of the discussion involves the crucial transformation of [iː] to [ɪi] and [uː] to [ʊu], where a high tense vowel changes into a diphthong with a lax centralized nucleus and a tense offglide. The same question arises with other types of diphthongizations, such as the development of tense vowels to ingliding diphthongs in proto-Romance and modern English dialects.

Chapter 8 also explores the possibility of reducing the three chain shift principles to a single principle relating the degree of openness of a vowel to its peripherality. This in turn would make it possible to describe complex chain shifts by a single rule that makes use of an alpha convention.

As a further simplification, chapter 8 considers the possibility of expansion conventions, to predict that the nucleus of a diphthong will become progressively more open if the same subsystem contains no other diphthongs, in a process governed by the step-by-step rules that operate on monophthongs. Thus it would be helpful to show that the nucleus of /iy/ moves to a low position by the same process that governs the shift of /ey/ to /iy/.

Chapter 9 investigates constraints on shifting across subsystems of vowels: shortening, lengthening, diphthongization, and monophthongization. Such shifts across subsystems have been much less thoroughly explored than shifts within subsystems, but they form an essential part of the general theory. For if the principles that govern chain shifting were entirely unidirectional, the result would be highly asymmetrical vowel systems, with tense vowels concentrated among the high vowels, and lax vowels concentrated among the low vowels. Since this is not so, there must be mechanisms for redistributing the vowels, with low vowels entering the tense subsystem, and high vowels entering the lax subsystem. Chapter 9 sketches some contributions in this area, where certain problems of historical linguistics are beginning to be clarified. It introduces five additional principles that govern chain shifting across systems and raises some questions concerning the relations of nasal and glottalized subsystems to the unmarked set of vowels.

Part C: Mergers and splits

By definition, chain shifts preserve the capacity of the phonemic system to make distinctions. If all sound changes shared this property, then the understanding of linguistic change would be much more straightforward; we could not avoid the inference that change was dominated and controlled by the communicative function of language, and the losses in mutual intelligibility caused by chain shifting might seem a minor problem. But merger – the converse process that eliminates functional distinction – is as common as or more common than chain shifting, and it represents an immediate subtraction from the functional capacity of the vowel system. If we were to accept an information-preserving principle as binding on language, then the very existence of mergers would be as remarkable a paradox as any encountered so far. A more realistic view acknowledges that information-preserving tendencies are at best only tendencies, and searches for a way to assess the strength of competing tendencies in a way that will account for mergers. Chapters 10 through 14 pursue the principles that govern both vowel mergers and the opposing phenomenon: the split of one phonemic element into two.

The discussion begins with two paradoxical situations. Chapter 10 presents cases in the history of English where two word classes were reported to have merged, yet afterward separated with very little disturbance in the composition of each class. These are the converse of the paradoxes of chapter 5, where expected mergers did not take place. Perhaps the best-known instance is the development of ME long open ɛː in early modern English: the word class that is now generally spelled with *ea*. According to the traditional sound law, ɛː → eː → iː. A number of reports by orthoepists indicated that in the 16th century this vowel was merged with the reflexes of ME **aː** and **ai**, so that *meat* and *mate*, *sea* and *say* sounded alike, a situation also reported for Hiberno-English today. Though some writers of the time did not report such a merger, the evidence of spelling errors and rhymes shows that many Londoners of the period could not reliably distinguish the two word classes. It is thus surprising that a century later, most words of the *meat* class were merged with the /eː/ class, so that *meat* is now homonymous with *meet* and *sea* with *see*. Schematically:

$$16\text{th century} \quad \rightarrow \quad 17\text{th century}$$

$$\text{meet} \qquad \qquad \begin{Bmatrix} \text{meet} \\ \text{meat} \end{Bmatrix}$$

$$\begin{Bmatrix} \text{meat} \\ \text{mate} \end{Bmatrix} \qquad \qquad \text{mate}$$

Under the well-accepted principle that mergers are irreversible, this would seem to be impossible. The behavior of the *meat* class is indeed contradictory: it appears to be the same as the *mate* class and yet it appears to be different. If we were to try to resolve this contradiction by rejecting either the subjective judgments of the orthoepists or the objective evidence for the merger, we would be rejecting the major sources of data used to trace the history of English.

The second case addressed by chapter 10 is the reported merger of /ay/ and /oy/ in the 18th and 19th centuries. There is general agreement that in the standard London English of this period, and in many other dialects, the word class containing *vice, isle, pint, tie*, etc., fell together with the class containing *voice, oil, point, toy*, etc. Yet in the late 19th and early 20th centuries, these two classes separated and are now distinct. This case is clearer than that of *meat* and *mate*, since there is much less disagreement in contemporaneous reports. It should have been impossible for the two classes to separate, and yet they did. The only explanation that has been advanced is that of Jespersen: that the influence of spelling was responsible. But as noted in chapter 1, this suggestion has been recognized as a desperate expedient at best, and has received little credence among those familiar with the behavior of actual speakers.

Chapter 11 addresses the problem of locating the general principles that govern mergers and splits. It begins by reviewing some of the evidence for Garde's Principle that mergers are irreversible by linguistic means, and it further defines the cases of chapter 10 as paradoxes of principle. The spatial correlate of Garde's Principle is Herzog's Principle: that mergers expand at the expense of distinctions. Evidence from Yiddish and American dialectology is introduced to support this principle. Various proposals for the mechanism of merger are then examined, and a new perspective introduced by Herold (1990) is presented: that merger represents the acquisition rather than the loss of information. Finally, the various causes of merger are considered, and Garde's Principle is restated as a scale of relative difficulty of reversal depending on the causes and mechanism of merger.

Next chapter 11 takes up the converse of merger: the phonemic split, which has received considerably less attention in the literature. Three types of splits are presented: those due to the loss of a conditioning factor, those due to borrowing from external sources, and those involving the redistribution of members of one word class into two (known as lexical splits). Two lexical splits are examined in detail: the split of Old English short diphthongs and the split of short *a* in closed syllables in the Middle Atlantic states. Properties of lexical splits are then related to the more general problem of dealing with marginal phonemic distinctions. Marginality is in turn related to the central problem of the learnability of distinctions, which is another way of looking at the reversibility of mergers. Payne's (1976) study of the acquisition of the Philadelphia dialect in King of Prussia is reexamined in relation to this problem, since it concerns the learning both of new phonetic rules and of new phonemic categories.

Chapter 11 then considers the sociolinguistic status of mergers, contrasting these with other phonological changes by an absence of social affect and a very low degree of social awareness. The discussion involves other evidence that has been presented for the reversal of mergers, and considers whether there exist social conditions that might suffice to overcome the force of Garde's Principle. Finally, the paradoxical character of all the evidence presented so far is reviewed.

Chapter 12 introduces the puzzling phenomenon of "near-mergers" that have appeared in many studies of modern speech communities. Until these cases were discovered, it was assumed that the presence of any physical distinction between the realization of word classes automatically implied the ability of native speakers to recognize, label, and use the distinction to signal semantic differences. The chapter first reviews the general notion of contrast that underlies this assumption of the symmetry of production and perception, and the empirical means available for testing it. It introduces early empirical evidence for asymmetry, and notes the difficulty that linguists had in accepting data that contradicted their fundamental assumptions.

Chapter 12 then considers four cases from LYS that show this asymmetry of production and perception, with the additional illumination provided by later research: the merger of *source* and *sauce* in New York City; the merger of *fool* and *full* in Albuquerque (and in Salt Lake City); the merger of *cot* and *caught* in central Pennsylvania; and the merger of *too* and *toe* in Norwich. The chapter then reviews the extraordinary resistance that linguists have shown to accepting the evidence for this asymmetry of production and perception, ending with a graphic picture provided by David de Camp of how evidence for a near-merger of /o/ and /oh/ in San Francisco was rejected at his dissertation defense in the 1950s.

Chapter 13 applies the findings of chapter 12 to the paradoxes introduced in chapters 10 and 11. The reported mergers of the 16th and 18th centuries are reexamined in light of near-mergers and the new conception of the asymmetry of production and perception. Data are introduced from studies specifically designed to examine the possibility that the anomalous situations reported for earlier periods were actually the result of such near-mergers. The 18th-century developments of /ay/ and /oy/ are examined more closely in the historical record. From a review of the mechanism developed by Nunberg (1980), it appears that the most frequent reports of merger were given for allophones that would be expected to be physically closest to each other. Further data are introduced from an instrumental study of the dialect of Essex County, England, where according to all dialectological reports the 18th-century merger has continued to the present day. For three older speakers, the word classes of /ay/ and /oy/ were found to be in close approximation but acoustically separate on nonperipheral and peripheral tracks. In commutation tests based on their own and others' speech, these speakers showed considerable confusion in their attempts to label their own /ay/ and /oy/ productions. We may infer that this 20th-century near-merger reflects a situation that prevailed more generally in the English of the 18th century.

The reported merger of *meat* and *mate* in 16th-century England is then reconsidered in light of the proposal that this too was a case of near-merger (Labov 1975a). More recent evidence is provided by the recent work of Milroy and Harris in Belfast. Older speakers in Belfast continue to pronounce *meat* with the lower mid vowel [meːt] that was characteristic of 16th-century London. They are not generally capable of distinguishing words in this class from words in the long **a** class (*mate*, etc.). But Milroy and Harris show that the two classes are distinct, with a great tendency for the *mate* class to rise to high position and develop diphthongs. This reinforces the view that the earlier reported merger of *meat* and *mate* was in fact a case of near-merger, and provides a case parallel to that of the lengthened short **e** words discussed in chapter 5.

Chapter 14 addresses the cognitive question, "How is it possible for speakers to acquire and maintain a distinction they cannot recognize?"

Thus it might properly belong to the domain of volume 3; but since the answer is essential for understanding the phenomenon of near-mergers and the resolution of the paradoxes of chapter 10, the discussion is located here. The chapter reports experimental data on the contrast between *merry* and *Murray*, *ferry* and *furry* in Philadelphia, where some speakers have a clear distinction, others a full merger, and still others a near-merger. One series of experiments involves commutation tests and minimal pair tests on this distinction for both Philadelphians and non-Philadelphians. Another experimental device, the "Coach Test," allows us to address the question whether speakers who fail to label the distinction in formal tests may still use it accurately in unreflecting semantic interpretation. The results show that all Philadelphians are impaired in their ability to recognize and label the contrast of /e/ and /ʌ/ before intervocalic /r/, while non-Philadelphians have no difficulty at all. It is concluded that the semantic contrast between these two categories is suspended in Philadelphia. The further question of how the physical distinction is maintained, and how linguistic categorization is related to psychoacoustic discrimination, is assigned to volume 3.

Part D: The regularity controversy

Part D aims at a resolution of the paradoxes of principle that resulted from the long controversy between supporters and opponents of the Neogrammarian position on the regularity of sound change. These issues involve the mechanism of change: lexical regularity, the role of grammatical conditioning, the relation of analogy to sound change, the role of dialect borrowing, and the effect of meaning on sound change. The resolution of disagreement on these issues bears on our view of the nature of language as a whole, which will be pursued in part E. If grammatical and semantic information is irrelevant to the basic mechanism of language change, then the forces of change that have molded language to its present shape must be considered essentially dysfunctional. Many linguists have found it hard to accept this position, since they see around them intact linguistic systems that appear to have survived these changes with their communicative functions unimpaired. Furthermore, the characterization of sound change as completely mechanical calls into question the rational character of language itself, or at least the strength of its rational component. This part of the investigation must inevitably play a role in the discussion of the causes of change in volume 2, and will lead us toward a better understanding of the balance between the rational and nonrational components of the linguistic system.

Chapter 15 begins the discussion by introducing the nature of the controversy and reviewing its status as a true paradox of principle. The general approach applied here is that paradoxes of principle cannot be resolved without recognizing the evidence for the positions on both sides. The chapter then presents recent evidence for lexical diffusion that has reinvigorated opposition to the doctrine of the regularity of sound change. It reviews studies of Chinese dialectology, showing the lexically gradual transitions of abrupt phonetic changes. Cheng and Wang's (1972) study of the split of Middle Chinese tones in modern Chaozhou provides the classic case of the splitting of homonyms over time. Li's (1982) report on the Atayalic dialects of Formosa shows the word-by-word diffusion of labial to velar stops. Shen's (1990) study of speech perception in the Shanghai dialect displays a word-by-word collapse of the distinction between ã and ũ. The focus then moves to the Philadelphia speech community, where lexical diffusion has already been demonstrated in the split of short **a** into tense /æh/ and lax /æ/. Data from the spontaneous speech of 100 Philadelphians show that the membership of the tensed short **a** category is expanding in a word-by-word fashion in two marginal areas: before intervocalic /n/ and /l/. The selection of words is roughly correlated with frequency, but the most frequent words are unaffected. The chapter then introduces a further report on the progress of lexical diffusion of short **a** from Roberts' (1993) work with children 3 to 5 years old in South Philadelphia.

Chapter 16 considers the same topics from the Neogrammarian viewpoint. The recent work of Lien shows that the Chaozhou split is not a change within the system, but the result of intimate mixture of the literary and colloquial dialects. On the other hand, the Atayalic shift of labials to velars reflects the character of internal sound change, but without any evidence of lexical conditioning: a quantitative examination of the data shows a fine phonetic determination of change. The regularity of sound change is further supported by close examination of large bodies of data from the Philadelphia vowel system, centered around the instrumental analysis of 5,000 vowels produced by a single speaker who was recorded throughout a single day (Hindle 1980). Homonyms in these data are not split, but show identical development. The same data base is used to examine the progress of sound change within the tensed /æh/ class that is the result of the lexical split of short **a** presented in chapter 15: fine-grained phonetic conditioning is found with no trace of lexical irregularity.

Chapter 17 pursues the regularity principle further through evidence from dialect geography. It is no accident that the major opponents of Neogrammarian regularity have been found among the ranks of dialectologists, particularly Romance specialists like Gilliéron. Proponents of lexical diffusion have turned to the evidence of English dialect geography to demonstrate that the basic mechanism of the Great Vowel Shift was a word-by-word shift, consistent with the slogan that "every word has its own history." Chapter 17 examines the development of ME ī and ū in Orton and Dieth's *Survey of English Dialects* (1962–67). Chi-square tests, regression analysis, and multidimensional scaling are used to discover how much phonetic conditioning is to be found in the data and how much lexical irregularity. The results show a fine-grained phonetic distribution of the classic Neogrammarian type for all members of the OE ī and ū word classes. Lexical diffusion is found, but only for items that shifted their word class membership from Old English to Middle English in processes that involved deletion and compensatory lengthening.

As a whole, chapter 17 shows that the most common interpretation of the evidence of dialect geography, which has dominated linguistic thinking for the last century and a half, may have to be revised. Osthoff and Brugmann seem to have been more correct than they knew in arguing that the development of dialects would show regular sound change in accordance with Neogrammarian principles.

While chapter 15 developed evidence for lexical diffusion, chapters 16 and 17 gave strong support to the view that regular sound change is the basic mechanism of change. Chapter 18 attempts to resolve the controversy by identifying the types of changes where each mechanism is most likely to be found. It begins with a closer study of the clearest available example of lexical diffusion in process: the tensing of short **a** in Philadelphia. The main evidence for the nature of the rule involved is drawn from Payne's comparison of the acquisition of the Philadelphia dialect by New Yorkers and by speakers of Northern Cities dialects. These data, combined with other arguments advanced by Kiparsky, lead to the conclusion that the short **a** split is best represented as a rule with lexical specifications in the framework of lexical phonology. The New Yorkers appear to assign the [+tense] feature with a lexical rule similar to their own and find it relatively easy to discriminate *mad, bad, glad* from other words with short **a** before /d/, while the Northern Cities speakers, who have a single tense phoneme /æh/, appear to be using an overgeneralized phonetic output rule and find such lexical specification relatively difficult.

These findings then contribute to the further development of the proposal put forward by Labov (1981) for the resolution of the controversy. Phonetic changes governed by low-level output rules are typically regular, in the Neogrammarian tradition, while higher-level processes that change membership in abstract categories tend to show lexical diffusion. The *abstractness* of a category is developed as a general criterion, defined by the number of measurable properties that must change independently when an element changes its category membership. The general proposal is tested with the help of Fónagy's (1956) survey of sound changes reported over the past several centuries.

Finally, chapter 18 raises the question why the short **a** class is split in the Middle Atlantic states, but is tensed as a whole in the Northern Cities. This issue is pursued with the help of the view developed by Ferguson, Wyld, and Jespersen that the Middle Atlantic short **a** tensing is not a new phenomenon, but a direct descendant of the southern British broad **a** tensing, in front position in the 16th and 17th centuries. The chapter then develops the implications of Jespersen's theory that the broad **a** split was in turn the descendant of lengthening in open syllables, with all the lexically irregular consequences of involvement with the inflectional paradigm of Middle English.

Part E: The functional character of change

Part E confronts the second aspect of the Neogrammarian controversy, which deals with the relation of sound change to meaning, and examines the effect of linguistic change on the primary communicative function of language. The Romance dialectologists who opposed the regularity hypothesis most fiercely also argued against the independence of sound change from meaning: they produced case studies to show that sound change was modified directly to avoid homonymic clashes. Dialectologists in the tradition of Gilliéron thus adopted the functionalist view that language is controlled by rational processes that optimize its performance as a means of communicating referential information. The issue has continued in 20th-century discussions of the functionalist hypothesis, which argues that there is a general tendency in language change to avoid the loss of information. Chapter 19 explores these issues with the help of quantitative studies of linguistic variation at the intersection of phonology and morphology. Much of the evidence involves synchronic variation, where studies of linguistic variation have put functional arguments to the test.

Chapter 19 begins with functional explanations of the chain shifts that were the topic of chapter 5. It raises the question whether it is possible to distinguish between chain shifts and parallel movements that are simple generalizations of phonetic rules. The types of functional explanation that would apply in one case or the other are quite different, and it appears possible that all chain shifts can be treated as a type of generalization similar to parallel movements.

The main focus of the chapter is on the variable deletion of final segments that are sometimes complete morphemes themselves: final /t,d/ in English and Dutch, final /s/ and /n/ in Spanish and Portuguese, and final /s/ in Ladakhi. In most of these cases, there is no evidence for change in progress, though it is usually assumed that the present stable situation must be the product of a transitional period when the realization of intact final consonants and inflections first began to vary.

One extreme functional position, adopted by many traditional linguists, is that no information is ever completely lost, since redundant information always exists. It would follow that the variable deletion of a meaningful segment would be tightly constrained by the amount of information present elsewhere in the utterance. Investigators in the variationist tradition have tried to take this position into account by entering into their multivariate analyses all possible sources of information in the text that might compensate for the loss of the inflection. The chapter addresses the question of whether speakers take the overall information state into account in choosing a zero or a full form of an inflection. It appears that most of the findings developed so far are *counterfunctional* in nature. They show that when speakers produce morphological information, they tend to follow with more information, and when they delete information, they continue to delete it. The chapter presents the argument of Guy (1981) that most of the functional effects that are reported are the products of a systematic bias in coding. It concludes that speakers do not take information states into account in choosing a grammatical inflection or a zero, but rather are influenced by mechanical and structural factors.

Chapter 20 accepts this conclusion but returns to the fact that in the long run, meaning is usually maintained when the variable forms that convey that meaning are finally eliminated. If speakers do not take meaning into account in their choice of variants, how do we explain this fact? Several synchronic studies clearly show the presence of functional compensation in a grammatical paradigm. Hochberg (1986) demonstrates a close correlation between the deletion of verbal /s/ in Puerto Rican Spanish and the use of subject pronouns. Yet Cameron (1992) shows that any increase in the use of pronouns in the Caribbean cannot be due to functional compensation for the loss of inflections, since underlying probabilities that determine pronominal use in Puerto Rico are identical to those that operate in the Spanish of Madrid, where inflections are intact.

The functional hypothesis that motivates the investigations of part E reflects the *means-ends model* of Jakobson: that the forms of language are best viewed as the effects of speakers' intentions to be understood and not misunderstood. Chapter 20 develops an explanation based on the opposite view: that functional effects are the consequences of understanding and misunderstanding. The first question to be answered is how stable variation is transmitted across generations. This is the process of *probability matching*, which has been investigated in some detail in experiments on animal learning and ethological studies of foraging. Chapter 20 reviews this material and applies it to the linguistic situation, where the pool of data used by the language learner to form probabilities is controlled by the consequences of understanding and misunderstanding. A mathematical model is developed that examines the consequences of two different underlying theories that may be adopted by the language learner: that zeroes represent singulars (a privative theory), or that zeroes may represent either singulars or plurals (a facultative theory). The first leads to conservative behavior, which would increasingly limit deletion across generations; the second leads to innovative behavior, which would rapidly eliminate inflections. The question is then asked how such competing options may be related to the observed situation with long periods of stability, punctuated by the rapid differentiation of individual dialects.

Finally, the chapter raises the possibility that the process of probability matching may actually facilitate the compensating readjustments of the grammatical system that were introduced at the outset.

Chapter 21 reviews the principles developed in chapters 5–20.

This volume is concerned primarily with the internal structure of linguistic changes: the constraints on change, the mechanism of change, and the ways in which change is embedded in the linguistic system. In the course of exploring these issues, it will appear that the absence of change may be even more difficult to account for than its presence. The long-term stability of many components of the linguistic system is even more striking than the rapid transformation of others. At a more abstract level, stability is implied by the fact that the uniformitarian principle, an inevitable response to the Historical Paradox, has actually been applied with considerable success in these studies. Volume 2 will be concerned with embedding in the social system, with the evaluation and with the actuation of change. It is in the social matrix of language behavior that we will hope to locate the causes of change and to account for the even more puzzling phenomenon of long-term stability.

3

The Study of Change in Progress: Observations in Apparent Time

3.1 Can sound change be observed?

The central topic of this work is the study of sound change in progress and its application to the historical record. The discussion of the uniformitarian principle in chapter 1 argued that the second step is practical. But we must ask the same question about the first step: Can sound change in progress be observed?

Plainly, the observation of a change in a language does not amount to a simple report: it requires observations of two states of a language and a guarantee of some continuity between the two – an assurance that in some sense, these are two states of the *same* language. If it is a qualitative observation, nothing further is required. The observer may report that some element is present in the language that was missing before, or that something has disappeared that was present.[1] For example, on Martha's Vineyard in 1961 a back centralized diphthong [ʌu] was frequently observed in *out*, *loud*, etc., alternating with [au] (Labov 1963). But the Linguistic Atlas records of the 1940s report only [æu] alternating with [au] (Kurath and McDavid 1961). More often we are dealing with quantitative changes: increasing raising of a vowel, more frequent vocalization of a liquid, or increasing duration of a segment. In this case we need more extended observations at each time period to ascertain the mean values at each time, and their range of variation, in order to determine that any differences in these means are indeed significant, and that the change over time is not simply the result of chance fluctuations in behavior.

This simple view of the matter has overlooked a crucial question: What does it mean to observe the state of a *language*? If we assume an ideally homogeneous language, then it suffices to observe any individual speaker, but this is immediately belied by the inquiry itself: by inquiring into change, we are questioning the homogeneity of the object. Satisfactory observations of qualitative differences are usually confirmed by a scattering

[1] As we will see, such qualitative observations are not the most common in the study of change in progress, but they play a crucial part in relating changes in apparent time to changes in real time.

of reports of a given feature from various sectors of the speech community at one time, and the complete absence of such reports at a later time. If the people we observed were all borne and raised by native parents, we can say that the community now contains people who speak in a different way, and if the difference is not the result of some obvious borrowing from neighboring or prestige dialects, we feel justified in reporting a significant change in the state of the language. In the case of quantitative studies, things are not so simple. We must begin with a representative sample of the community, and the observers must be tested for the reliability of their observing skills. Then we must either locate the same speakers at a later time (a panel study), or we must construct a second representative sample (a trend study). Since no such sample is ever without its limitations, we must show that the two samples do not suffer from different limitations. If the same observer is not available to make the second set of observations, it is not enough to compare two reliability studies: we must find a way of relating the two sets of observations to some absolute standard.

The conditions for a satisfactory quantitative study over time are rarely met. Panel studies are expensive; losses are heavy; and few funding agencies will support a project over the required 5 or 10 years. It is more economical to base a trend study upon a previous quantitative study, but it is rare to find that scholars 5, 10, or 20 years ago were interested in the same problems that occupy us now, or that they went about solving them in the same way.

At the time that the current series of sociolinguistic studies in the speech community began, there was therefore no straightforward way of tracing change in progress in a way that would satisfy all criticisms, and more indirect means were needed.

Traditional negative arguments

In my first approach to this problem, I cited a well-known statement of Bloomfield.

The process of linguistic change has never been directly observed; we shall see that such observation, with our present facilities, is inconceivable. (1933:347)

The problems that troubled Bloomfield were twofold: the gradual and almost imperceptible character of the changes, and the mixture of true sound change with deviations from other causes (dialect mixture, speech errors, analogical combination, and the like). Essentially, however, his view was that sound change is too slow to be observed. The studies of change in progress in English-speaking cities show that this is hardly the case (Labov 1966). The movement of nuclei from the most open position to the most closed position – from low to high – can be traced within three or four generations. The quantitative study of new and vigorous changes in Philadelphia shows a rate of movement that would cover the available distance within phonological space within four generations, if it were to continue at the maximum rate. In fact, changes move much more slowly at the beginning and the end of their trajectories (Kroch 1989a; Shen 1990), and the speed of movement across generations in midcourse is underestimated by any measure that extends from the very beginning to the very end.

On the other side of the matter, Weinreich, Labov, and Herzog (1968) have cited Hockett's (1958) argument that phonemic change is altogether too fast to be observed.

Sound change itself is constant and slow. A phonemic restructuring, on the other hand, must in a sense be absolutely sudden. . . . [T]here is no reason to believe that we would ever be able to detect this kind of sudden event by direct observation. (Hockett 1958:456–7)

The sudden event referred to here is conceived as a change in the phonemic status of a distinction.[2] Our current studies of dialect divergence are evenly divided between rotations and chain shifts, which Hockett would identify as sound change, and phonemic restructuring by splits and mergers. Chapter 12 will show that the presence or absence of a distinction is not a simple binary matter. Instead, the process of sound change may narrow a distinction to the point that its semantic role is suspended. This intermediate state of affairs, distributed irregularly among individual speakers and listeners, may apparently last for several centuries. In other cases, growing familiarity with merged dialects will lead to a gradual abandonment of the contrastive function of an opposition by speakers who still maintain it themselves (Herold 1990; chapter 17).

The result of the two traditional positions was to remove the study of sound change in progress from the realm of empirical possibilities. Both arguments misrepresent the difficulties: a result typical of the mode of discourse that draws on thought experiments rather than real observation. Yet as the opening section pointed out, there are many difficulties to be overcome in any such enterprise. Unless they are satisfactorily resolved, Bloomfield and Hockett may turn out to be right in the long run.

3.2   Distributions in apparent time

The first and most straightforward approach to studying linguistic change in progress is to trace change in apparent time: that is, the distribution of

---

[2] Hockett conceives of this change as taking place in one speaker or "a tiny group of speakers." In line with the general approach to language as a property of the speech community, I would prefer to avoid a focus on the individual, since the language has not in effect changed unless the change is accepted as part of the language by other speakers.

linguistic variables across age levels. If we discover a monotonic relationship between age and the linguistic variable, or a significant correlation between the two, then the issue is to decide whether we are dealing with a true change in progress or with age-grading (Hockett 1950), a regular change of linguistic behavior with age that repeats in each generation. This issue has been the major focus of almost all earlier studies of change in progress, and it will be the focus of much of this chapter and the next. The most decisive way to interpret the data of older speakers is to study changes in the same individuals in real time, the topic of the next chapter. Much that is said here about apparent time will be illuminated by the findings of the next chapter. But first it will be necessary to look at some of the problems involved in obtaining a clear and accurate view of the apparent-time dimension.

The oldest age group

It seems obvious that any student of the speech community will record the speech of its oldest members. Yet there are quite a few difficulties in obtaining good samples of spontaneous speech from people in their 70s, 80s, and 90s. Some show physical deterioration that interferes with their speech: loss of teeth, hoarseness of voice, and lax articulation. Others show deterioration of mental abilities: loss of memory, interest, and attention. When speech is seriously affected by senile decay, we can hardly take it as evidence for the language structure that the speakers used when they were young. On the other hand, many older speakers do retain the clarity and precision of their speech. I myself have been fortunate enough to interview many people in their 80s and 90s who were almost the "perfect" subjects. They would speak vigorously for many hours, with very little guidance, about the very subjects I was most interested in, and gave a wealth of personal narratives and insightful observations about the community. In the sections to follow, we will look more closely at whether their use of linguistic variables can be accepted as characteristic of the state of the language some 40 or 50 years ago. The point to bear in mind is that a random sample of the community is not likely to give us the intact samples of the speech of the oldest generation that we need. Instead, we usually have to supplement our sample by searching out older speakers with an intact and flourishing linguistic competence. There is no obvious risk of bias in such a search, since it is not likely that the survival of their mental linguistic skills is correlated with their use of the linguistic variables that were socially significant in their youth.[3]

---

[3] We would be running a risk if we were to seek out the older speakers who have a great reputation in the community as storytellers and "characters." They are usually people who have a great gift for elaborating linguistic structures on the basis of the smallest events in real

The next chapter will review evidence from real-time studies that will be particularly pertinent to evaluating the evidence from the oldest age group.

The youngest age group

It also seems natural to extend the age range of our speakers downward to include the youngest members of the community. But how young can we go and still say that we are studying the language of the speech community? It is evident that 2-year-olds lack a great deal of the linguistic knowledge that would qualify them in this way. Their deviations from the adult pattern are most likely developmental differences (that is, true age-grading).[4]

The question that remains is this: How young is the youngest stratum of speakers that will give us evidence on the state and direction of a linguistic change in progress? In New York City, Labov (1966) found that the raising of (eh) in *man* and (oh) in *lost* was most advanced in the youngest group of speakers, from 8 to 19. In Norwich, Trudgill (1974a) found that the backing of (el) in *belt* was most extreme in his youngest age stratum, from 10 to 19 years. Cedergren (1973) found that the lenition of (ch) in Panama City was most extreme in Spanish speakers from 14 to 20. All of these results would seem to indicate that adolescents, and preadolescents, are the leading edge in the progress of sound change, and that any study must be sure to include extended recordings of their speech.

None of the studies cited above give values for the very youngest speakers, the preadolescents from 8 to 11, since they are included with the adolescents. Usually, a sample of the speech community includes only a scattering of such speakers. It is rare to find a community sample that allows us to compare the speech of the youngest speakers with a full age range of speakers of comparable social background. However, figure 3.1 provides

---

life: tall tales, yarns, and outright "lies" designed to amuse their listeners. The language that they use is likely to show stereotyped and archaic forms that fit in with the special nature of the speech event itself. The people we look for as representative of the oldest stratum of the speech community are quite the opposite. They have the ability to talk in a serious and straightforward way about the most serious events of their lives. In most cases, they are not known as gifted speakers, and the stories that they tell may not have been heard before by members of their own families.

[4] A number of linguists have urged us to look at the speech errors of young children as the source of incoming linguistic changes (Halle 1962); see Saussure 1949 for a general assessment. But even if these variations include forms that are later adopted by adults, they are simply one of the sources of variability in language from which linguistic change is selected. The point of view developed here, echoing Weinreich, Labov, and Herzog (1968), is that linguistic change is not a change in individual habits, but rather the diffusion of new individual forms into the wider community, and the adoption of these forms as new and binding conventions. The speech errors of children have no privileged relation to the specific language changes that affect a given community.

some useful information on this question. It is an analysis of the progress of a well-advanced sound change: the New York City variable (oh) through different age levels for Jews and Italians in careful speech (Labov 1966:chap. 8). The (oh) variable is the height of the nucleus of the ingliding vowel in *coffee, lost, awful, law,* etc. It progresses through four stages:

1	[ɔ°]	low
2	[Ω°]	lower mid
3	[o°]	upper mid
4	[ʊ°]	high

The (oh) index is formed by multiplying the mean value of the (oh) tokens by 10. A value of 30 is conservative, similar to the realization of the vowel in *nor, or* in most parts of the Eastern United States. A level of 20 reflects the general New York City norm, and values from 10 to 19 show the presence of the high, overrounded variant that is most characteristic of the latest stages of the change.

Figure 3.1 shows a sudden advance in the variable in the second oldest

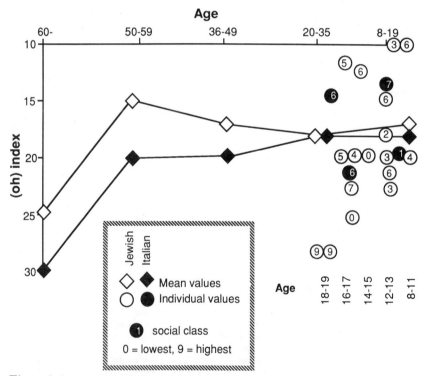

Figure 3.1.   The distribution of young speakers in the development of New York City (oh)

group, for both Jews and Italians, and then a general leveling out toward a norm of 17–18. Superimposed on this view are the values of 21 children of the New York City subjects: this expands the two mean values at the extreme right of the diagram. To interpret these data, one must bear in mind that (oh) in the speech of New York City adults fits the general principle of the "curvilinear pattern": that change from below is led by the interior social groups, rather than the highest or lowest group (Labov 1972:294). Thus, we find the highest nuclei (and lowest values of the index) for the central social groups 3–7, and conservative values for the lower classes 0–2 and the upper middle class 9. The children of the adults reflect the same pattern. Above the mean are a cluster of 7 individuals, in classes 3–7, mostly class 6. At the bottom of the distribution are two upper middle class youth and one lower-class youth. Table 3.1 shows the results of a multiple regression analysis of the youth, taking the (oh) index as the independent variable, and age and membership in the interior social classes 3–7 as the dependent variables. There is a sizeable effect of social class: the (oh) index is almost 5 points lower for the interior social groups. This is matched by an effect of about the same size for age. The difference between a 20-year-old and an 8-year-old is 12 * .326, or 3.912. But this effect is not significant, since there is a second cluster of younger speakers around the (oh)-20 level.

On the whole, the evidence indicates that we must take into account data from speakers as young as 8 years old in tracing a variable through apparent time.

Clarifying trajectories in apparent time

It might seem at first that there is no difficulty in describing the relations of a particular variable to the dimension of apparent time. One can set up appropriate age groups and chart the mean values of the variable for each group; or one can examine the relation between the age of each individual and that person's value for the variable and correlate the values of the variable for each individual with their ages. Yet there are many situations where only a vague distribution in apparent time appears at first, and it is the analyst's task to disengage the stronger relationship that may lie within

Table 3.1 Effect of age and membership in an interior social class on the (oh) index in New York City [N = 36]

	Coefficient	t	p
Interior social class 3–7	−4.538	−2.77	<.01
Age	.326	1.24	n.s.

the data. This situation arises when the distribution is not uniform throughout the community, but is strongly concentrated in speakers of a particular ethnic group, social class, or sex.

Such a case is well illustrated by two parallel variables in New York City: the backing of (ay) from [ay] to [ɒy] and the obverse fronting of (aw) from [aʊ] to [æʊ]. These two variables lie well below the level of social awareness among New Yorkers and, unlike (oh), show little stylistic variation. The Lower East Side study did not focus on (ay) and (aw), but recorded only a single characteristic value of the variable for each speaker, the modal value for the first five occurrences. The phonetic scales used to code the variable were as follows:

(ay)		(aw)	
5	a	5	a
6	ɑ	4	a>
7	ɑ>	3	æ<
8	ɒ<	2	æ
9	ɒ	1	æ
10	ɒ⊥	0	ɛ⊤
11	ɔ	−1	ɛ

The individual values for (ay) and (aw) are displayed in the scattergram of figure 3.2. The scale on the left-hand side combines the (ay) and (aw) index, centered about their joint conservative value of 5.

Figure 3.2 shows the entire age range of 158 New York City subjects, from 8 to 73 years old. The circles represent the (ay) values and the crosses represent the (aw) values. At the central value of 5, a large number of crosses are superimposed on circles: these are the most conservative speakers. It is evident that the two series diverge for the youngest speakers, with extreme values of (ay) as high as 11, and extreme values of (aw) as low as 0. Even a visual inspection shows clear evidence of change in apparent time.

However, the two regression lines diverge only slightly. The line for (ay) is almost flat, with a slope of −.004, and explains only a very small percentage of the variance, as shown by an r^2 of .002. The line for (aw) has a steeper slope of .013 but still accounts for only 5% of the variance. We can understand this difference between the overall impression and the regression lines by noting that a number of (ay) symbols cross over into the (aw) territory, and that this holds for the younger speakers as well as the older ones. Such fronted nuclei are hardly characteristic of the New York City dialect. On reflection, it is apparent that the low (ay) values must represent monophthongal pronunciations of (ay) with [æ:]. These are obviously Southern forms, suggesting that we examine separately the black speakers in the New York City sample. Figure 3.3 shows the age

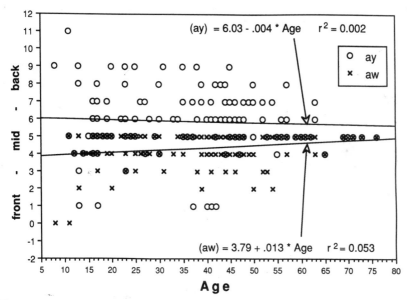

Figure 3.2. Distribution of (ay) and (aw) in apparent time for all New York City speakers [N = 158]

distributions of (ay) and (aw) for the 31 black speakers. No strong monotonic tendencies are evident, but the regression lines run in the opposite direction from those of the community as a whole. The (aw) line has a negative slope, meaning that values become greater as age becomes smaller, and the (ay) line has a positive slope. Though neither is significant, they indicate that the black subsample has a different distribution in apparent time from the rest of the community.

The next step is to examine the patterns of (ay) and (aw) in the white community alone. In figure 3.4, the black group has been removed from the main sample, and we see the distribution of (ay) and (aw) for all white New York City subjects. Now the (ay) and (aw) symbols overlap only along their central common front, the value 5. Only one person shows a fronted value of (ay): a 55-year-old Jewish woman. Otherwise, moving from right to left, we see a steady shift of the circles upward and crosses downward. For the very youngest speakers, the concentration of symbols at the central value comes to an end. The speakers below 16 show widely divergent forms of both (ay) and (aw). Since each speaker is represented by only a single value, this representation may exaggerate the uniformity of the shift, but it underlines firmly the point raised in the last section: a study of apparent time must extend downward in the age range to include preadolescent as well as adolescent speakers. The regression lines fitted to the data show the symmetric divergence that is truly characteristic of the

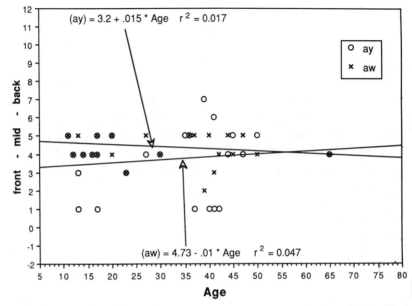

Figure 3.3.   Distribution of (ay) and (aw) in apparent time for black New York City speakers [N = 31]

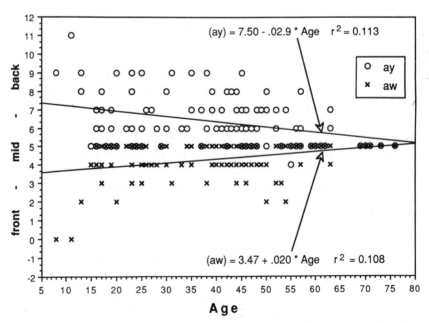

Figure 3.4.   Distribution of (ay) and (aw) in apparent time for all white New York City subjects [N = 127]

speech community, with an origin at 5 on the right, spreading toward values of (ay)-8 and (aw)-3 on the left. The relations indicated by these lines are now significant, and each accounts for 11% of the variance.

As illustrated in figure 3.5, our view of the sound change in apparent time can be sharpened even further by focusing on the central social classes: the upper working class and the lower working class (3–5 and 6–8 in the socioeconomic scale used in New York City). As with (oh), the New York City data for (ay) and (aw) display the curvilinear pattern that change from below is led by these interior classes. Figure 3.5 isolates the pattern for these 70 speakers: the regression lines diverge even more sharply, and the percentage of variance accounted for has risen to 14% for (ay) and 16% for (aw).

The statistics on these regression analyses can be compared directly in table 3.2, which shows the successive age coefficients for the three analyses, and the level of significance for each.

Figure 3.3 showed that the black community in New York City treats the variables (ay) and (aw) in a very different manner from the white community. If only these two variables were concerned, the removal of the black speakers would be a suspiciously ad hoc procedure. But the study reported in Labov (1966) found that blacks did not participate in any of the sound shifts characteristic of the New York City vernacular, and since then the same pattern has been demonstrated in Philadelphia (Labov 1980;

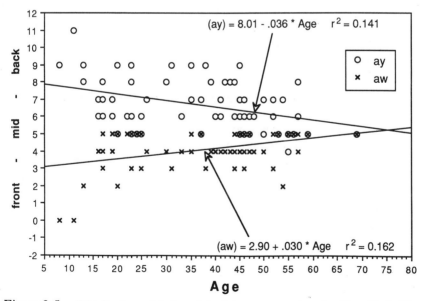

Figure 3.5. Distribution of (ay) and (aw) in apparent time for New York City upper working class and lower working class subjects only [N = 70]

Table 3.2   Age coefficients of (ay) and (aw) for three sets of New
York City speakers

	(ay)	*(aw)*
All NYC speakers [N = 149]	−.005	.014*
White NYC speakers [N = 115]	−.029**	.021**
White social classes 3–8 only [N = 65]	−.034*	.030**

*$p < .01$ **$p < .001$

Labov and Harris 1986; Ash and Myhill 1986) and observed in most other
areas of the North and the South (Bailey and Maynor 1987).

These studies show that the speech communities in most northern cities
are in fact two distinct communities: one white, the other nonwhite. Within
the white urban community we typically find a geographically uniform,
socially differentiated dialect built upon a homogeneous structural base
(Labov 1989a). But not all variables behave in the same way for all social
groups. Figure 3.5 confirms the general finding of an association between
change from below and a curvilinear pattern in the social class hierarchy.
Since changes from below proceed first and at a faster rate among the
interior social groups, a clear view of the change in apparent time then
requires that we examine these innovating groups separately to get a clear
view of the main direction and rate of progress of the apparent change. At
the same time, we lose information on the behavior of the variable among
the less advanced social groups. In the progressive refinements of Figures
3.2–3.5 information is lost as well as gained.

3.3   Refining the measurement of sound change

In the early studies we have been examining, the view of change in apparent time was limited by several methodological inadequacies. The first is
the method of measuring the dependent variable. In the New York City
study, the vowel shifts were estimated by impressionistic means. The phonetic alphabet was properly treated as a series of signposts along continuous phonetic dimensions, but distances along these continuous dimensions
were measured by a crude series of qualitative phonetic values and then
reconverted into a single pseudoquantitative dimension. It is "pseudoquantitative" because we have no guarantee that the series of impressionistic
ratings of "front–mid–back" are indeed aligned along a single dimension
of tongue position or sound wave property.

In 1968, I initiated a series of quantitative studies of sound change in
progress, with the idea that the tools of acoustic analysis could be used to

study the spontaneous speech of field recordings. These research projects have used a succession of instrumental methods, following the development of the most stable laboratory methods available through the 1970s and 1980s. Measurements have been based on the general finding that vowels can be discriminated by the central tendencies of the first two or three formants.[5] With all the limitations that one can put on this relationship, the two-formant plots have correlated well with impressionistic phonetics and increased the coders' confidence in their phonetic transcription. Furthermore, instrumental analyses have called to attention new relations that have subsequently been confirmed by listening. The first instrument to be used, the Kay Sonograph, was a slow and finicky electromechanical device, but estimates of the central tendencies of formants from narrow-band spectrograms achieved an error of less than 1/4 of a pitch period.[6] These provided the data for the diagrams and general principles derived from the Quantitative Study of Sound Change in Progress, 1968–1972 (LYS), including a detailed analysis of 10 New York City speakers. A second device was used in the Project on Linguistic Change and Variation, 1973–1977 (LCV), carried out in Philadelphia. This is the largest instrumental study of sound change that has been carried out so far; it includes acoustic analyses of the vowel systems of 120 speakers. The data are based on analysis of the spectrum with a real-time hardware device, the Spectral Dynamics 301C; the spectral information was then fed into a version of the linear predictive coding algorithm that operated on the frequency domain. This gave much greater speed and accuracy than the spectrogram, with an internal consistency within 5–10 Hz.

More recently, greater increases in accuracy and reliability have been achieved with software methods that apply linear predictive coding to the

[5] This was first clearly demonstrated by Cooper et al. (1952). The first two formants provide only a first approximation to the characterization of vowel timbre, but one that has proven useful in studies of dozens of sound changes. The greatest difficulties lie in the treatment of the high vowels. For [i] at least, it is generally considered necessary to combine information on F2 and F3 in some appropriate way, though there is no general agreement on the best method. Since none of the studies carried out so far has depended crucially on the position of [i], F2 position has usually been the only information given. Some overlaps in the F1/F2 plots of mid and high vowels have been observed in spite of the distinct acoustic impressions yielded by the vowels in question. This is the case for checked /ey/ and /iy/ in Philadelphia. Lennig (1978) was unable to resolve the overlap for Parisian /u/ and /o/.

[6] That is, ±25 Hz for most men, ±50 Hz for most women. The spectrograms departed from linearity in many irritating ways, especially in the large amount of noise in the first few harmonics, which made it difficult to isolate the first formant for high vowels. Furthermore, they were extremely sensitive to background noise, present in many field recordings. On the other hand, the combination of broad-band spectrographs for tracking formant movements and narrow-band spectrographs to measure position yielded fairly few gross errors compared to some current software methods.

digitized speech wave directly.[7] But as accuracy has increased, the difficulties in using these data to track sound change across the community have become more serious. Since speakers have very different vowel tract lengths and shapes, the absolute values of these measurements cannot be directly compared. Vowels that sound the same as spoken by men, women, and children will appear to have much higher F1 and F2 values for women than for men, and higher yet for young children. To use these data for a study of change across the community, it is necessary to solve the normalization problem: we must select a mathematical transformation of the data that will yield the same result as the normalizing operation of the human ear and brain, which compensates for these physical differences rapidly and automatically. LCV compared a number of normalization methods to find one that would eliminate differences due to vocal tract length, but preserve sociolinguistic differences in age and social class that were known by other measures to be characteristic of the community (Hindle 1978). The log mean normalization of Nearey (1977) proved to be satisfactory, and the vowel measurements to be discussed below have all been normalized by this method.

Multivariate analysis of continuous data

So far our view of change in apparent time has also been limited by the fact that we have been relating the dependent variable – the sound change in question – to only one independent variable at a time – in this case, the age of the speakers. But as we move along the age range of the sample, other social variables shift as well. The degree of upward social mobility in the Lower East Side was very great, so that on the average older speakers in the sample had lower educational achievement and occupational status than younger speakers.[8] The random sample of the Lower East Side obtained good representation of all social classes, but could not reasonably represent all age groups for all social classes. In general, no sample can represent in equal proportions all the factors that influence the dependent variable. As a result, a particular distribution in apparent time may actually reflect the distribution of other variables in the population.

Methods for multivariate analysis are designed to deal with this problem by measuring the effect of many factors simultaneously. LCV used multiple regression as the final step in the analysis of sound change in Philadelphia.

---

[7] Current configurations at the Linguistics Laboratory at the University of Pennsylvania use the WAVES+ package on a Sun workstation, and the CSL program of Kay Elemetric on a 386 Packard-Bell operating at 33 MHz.

[8] This is especially true of the Jewish group. It also applies to the Italians and other white ethnic groups, but to a lesser extent. It does not apply to the blacks, who were the only group to show downward social mobility as a whole (Labov 1966).

The following sequence of methods was designed to measure and locate the progress of linguistic change in the social structure:

1   (a) A series of long-term studies in Philadelphia neighborhoods selected to represent the socioeconomic, ethnic, and geographic patterns of the city. (b) A more rapid series of interviews with a random sample of telephone listings.
2   The measurement of stressed vowels for 120 speakers from the neighborhood sample and 60 speakers from the telephone sample by linear predictive coding as noted above.
3   The normalization of the mean values of these systems using the geometric mean.[9]
4   The application of stepwise multiple regression to these data. The independent variables for the stepwise regression are the mean formant values for each vowel for each speaker.

These Philadelphia vowels will play a major role in many discussions to follow. The synchronic reflection of the changes is a range of variability that will be referred to by vowel symbols in parentheses, as follows:

(ahr)   The raising and backing of the nucleus of /ahr/ in *bar, barred*, etc.
(ohr)   The raising and backing of the nucleus of /ohr/ in *bore, bored*, etc.
(æh)   The raising and fronting of the nucleus of tense /æh/ in the following subcategories:
    (æhN)   /æh/ before nasals in *can [N], can't*, etc.;
    (æhS)   /æh/ before voiceless fricatives in *calf, bath, cast*, etc.;
    (æh$)   /æh/ before /d/ in three words: *mad, bad, glad*.
(uw)   The fronting of the nucleus of /uw/ in *too, mood*, etc., but not before liquids.
(ow)   The fronting of the nucleus of /ow/ in *bow, road*, etc., but not before liquids.
    Both of these variables are subcategorized as
    (uwF, owF)   vowels in free syllables;
    (uwC, owC)   vowels in checked syllables.
(eyC)   The raising and fronting of the nucleus of /ey/ in checked syllables, as in *made, raise*, etc.
(aw)   The raising and fronting of the nucleus of /aw/ in *bow, about*, etc.
(ay0)   The raising and backing of the nucleus of /ay/ before voiceless

---

[9] In accordance with the principles discussed above, using the geometrical mean normalization of Nearey (1977).

consonants, as in *bite, fight,* etc.

(iyC)   The raising and fronting of /iy/ in checked syllables, as in *seat, seed,* etc.

(ʌ)   The raising and backing of /ʌ/ in *but, bud,* etc.

(i)   The lowering of /i/ in *bit, bid,* etc.

(e)   The lowering of /e/ in *bet, bed,* etc.

(æ)   The lowering of /æ/ in *bat, sad,* etc.

The dependent variable for the stepwise regression is the central tendency in hertz of a particular formant of a particular vowel. The independent variables available to the analysis are as follows:

1 Age
2 Education (in years)
3 Occupation
4 Residence value
5 Socioeconomic class (based on indicators 2–4)
6 A five-point measure of house upkeep
7 The neighborhood
8 A classification of social mobility
9 Four indices of participation in communication networks
10 Foreign language background
11 Generational status in the United States
12 Whether or not the person's telephone is listed

The algorithm produces a coefficient for each independent variable, indicating the strength of the correlation between that variable and the dependent variable, and, among other statistics, a *t*-value showing the significance of that figure. These coefficients $a_1, a_2, \ldots$ fit into a single linear equation of the form that estimates the value of a particular formant:

(1)   Formant x = Constant + a_1 * Factor$_1$ + a_2 * Factor$_2$
           $\ldots a_n$ * Factor$_n$

For the study of apparent time, we will be concerned with only the first two terms: a constant, and the age of the speaker. Thus, the second formant of the variable (aw), which registers the degree of fronting of the vowel, appears as follows:

(2)   F2(aw) = 2000 − 5.6 * Age

The value of the coefficient is negative, since younger age groups show higher values of F2. The estimate for a 40-year-old speaker would be 2000

− 5.6 * 40 = 1760.[10] We can use these coefficients to display the rate of change in apparent time for an entire vowel system (figure 3.6). The circles show the mean normalized value for the 14 vowels in a linear two-dimensional formant space.[11] The heads of the arrows show the estimated formant positions for speakers 25 years younger than the mean, and the tails of the arrows show the corresponding positions for speakers 25 years older than the mean, all other things being equal. The thickness of the arrows or vectors corresponds to the significance of the coefficients, as shown by the *t*-values. If the mean age for Philadelphia speakers is 40, we can fill out the model of (2) as follows:

(3) $F2(aw)_{65} = 2000 - 5.6 * 65 = 1636$
$F2(aw)_{40} = 2000 - 5.6 * 40 = 1760$
$F2(aw)_{15} = 2000 - 5.6 * 15 = 1916$

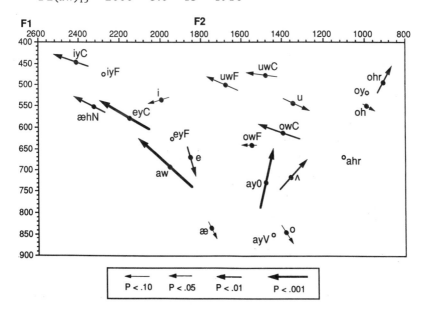

Figure 3.6. Movement of Philadelphia vowels in apparent time. O = mean values for 116 speakers in the neighborhood study. Vectors connect values for groups 25 years older and younger than the mean. ___F = free vowel; ___C = checked vowel; ___0 = before voiceless finals

[10] Of course, many other social factors are also involved in determining the mean value of a variable; these will be discussed below.
[11] This quantitative representation preserves the qualitative vowel relations of an IPA transcription, since acoustic relations are the basis of impressionistic notation. The relation to psychological representations would be sharpened by using a Mel scale for the second formant, and averaging F3 with F2 for high front vowels. But for the internal comparison of changes in progress, this simpler linear representation serves quite well.

Figure 3.6 then shows the motions of all Philadelphia vowels in apparent time. The three largest vectors are associated with three new and vigorous changes in progress: (aw), the fronting and raising of the nucleus of /aw/;[12] (eyC), the fronting and raising of the nucleus of checked /ey/; and (ay0), the raising and backing of the nucleus of /ay/ before voiceless consonants.

Age as a discrete variable

The treatment of age as a continuous quantitative variable simplifies and facilitates the analysis, but it is important to note that this treatment – like all elements of the multiple regression – is simply a linear approximation to a more complex relation. This approximation is a reasonable one as long as the relation between age and the linguistic variable is monotonic – for example, as long as each decrease in the mean age of a group of speakers is associated with an increase in the estimated mean of F2 of (aw).[13] Although this linear view is useful in comparing the relative movements of different variables, it tells us nothing about how the change proceeds through the various age levels of apparent time, which will be an important factor when we attempt to project this information into real time.

We can refine our view of the movements in apparent time by resolving the continuous dimension of age into a set of qualitative categories: ages 8–14, 15–19, 20–29, 30–39, 40–49, 50–59, 60–69, and 70 and over. These can be entered into multiple regression algorithms as "dummy" variables. If a given speaker falls into a given age range, he or she will be rated as "1" for that category, otherwise, as "0." One group is set aside as the residual group, and all others are compared with this one. The degree of significance of the coefficients then represents the significance of the difference between the given group and the residual group. In this multiple regression analysis, we will also retain the most significant social relations: occupation of the speaker (unskilled, skilled, clerical, managerial, professional) and social mobility derived from comparing the speaker's occupation with his or her parents' (upward, none, downward). We then obtain the results shown in table 3.3 for the age coefficients. The differences between the various older groups and the reference group 8–14 do not increase steadily, but rather appear to move by generations, for the adults at least: a younger generation 20–49 and an older generation 50 and above.

---

[12] Associated with this upward movement of the nucleus on the front diagonal is a reversal of direction of the glide, downward toward open [ɔ]. The most conservative forms of Philadelphia (aw) are [æʊ], while the most advanced are [eɔ].

[13] Treating socioeconomic class in this way has the destructive result of wiping out the existing relationship altogether. There is a curvilinear relation between socioeconomic class and the movement of (aw), so that the highest values are found in the intermediate social classes, and the lowest values are found in the highest and lowest social classes.

Table 3.3 Philadelphia F2(aw) coefficients for grouped age categories

Age group	8–14	15–19	20–29	30–39	40–49	50–59	60–69	70–
	0	–253	–362	–349	–325	–535	–552	–538

Multiple regression versus simple regression

We can use this more precise view to reevaluate multiple regression versus simple regression. Figure 3.7 compares the values for age groups for F2 of (aw), derived from multiple regression, with a simple regression using age groups alone, and the group means averaged arithmetically. All three curves begin with the same group mean for the youngest age group: 2345. The regression coefficients are then subtracted from this original mean value.

In this figure, the points derived by multiple regression preserve the monotonic relationship between age and the linguistic variable, with only insignificant fluctuations within each stage. In contrast, the simple regression (and the group means) show several reversals of the basic relationship. The 30–39 age group appears to be considerably more

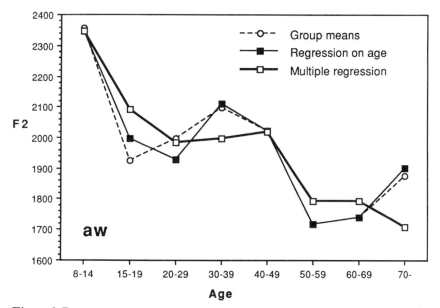

Figure 3.7. Distribution of F2 (aw) in apparent time by group means, simple regression and multiple regression

advanced than the 15–29 age groups, and the 70-year-old speakers also show a sudden upsurge by comparison with the two next younger groups.

It is not difficult to explain the difference between these sets of curves. We must infer that the 30–39 age group and the 70– age group both contain a relative excess of those occupational groups that favor the change,[14] so that the view of change in apparent time is confused. Figure 3.8 is the parallel display for a second new and vigorous change, the fronting of checked /ey/. Here too, the values derived from multiple regression show a smoother path of descent than those derived from simple regression and group means. It is only natural that Figures 3.7 and 3.8 show the same configuration, since the fluctuations in the simple regression are produced by the skewed characteristics of the same sample. If all the minor social factors were taken into account, we would expect an even smoother curve from multiple regression analysis.

We conclude, then, that (1) these data indicate that changes move by generations, rather than continuously through the population, and (2) a clear view of change in apparent time requires a multivariate analysis to take into account the effect of other social factors.

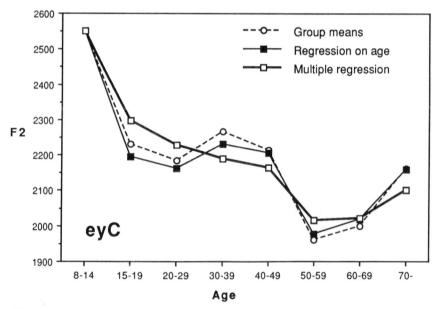

Figure 3.8.   Distribution of F2 (ey0) in apparent time by group means, simple regression and multiple regression

[14] These are primarily the skilled working-class groups. Occupation shows the same curvilinear distribution that we find in a combined socioeconomic index, in that the occupational groups with highest and lowest social status disfavor the changes in progress.

3.4 Inferences from patterns in apparent time

The next chapter will add real-time observations of the Philadelphia vowel system that will allow us to establish the stages of its evolution with considerable certainty. This combination of observations in apparent time and real time is the basic method for the study of change in progress. However, in many speech communities this method can't be realized: there simply are no observations in real time that we can use to calibrate and confirm the possibilities that are raised in apparent time. In such cases, we are strongly motivated to study the present in greater depth, and see what can be deduced about change in progress from the actual distributions in apparent time.

Rotations of the phonological system

The progress of sound changes in a speech community can be traced along two dimensions. The first is the age coefficient that was used in Figures 3.6–3.8, which shows the degree of differentiation across speakers by age. The second is the phonetic distance that the sound has moved from its point of origin. This point must be estimated in a way that is more general than a simple reference to the speech of the oldest members of a particular community. The notation that we use to describe English phonology in general is actually based on such a generalized starting point for current sound changes (table 3.4).[15] This notation projects /i/ as a high front vowel, /ey/ as mid front, /aw/ as low back, etc. Chapter 6 will present and justify this notation in greater detail; here we can note that it provides a point of

Table 3.4   The general phonological pattern of current English dialects

	Short		Upgliding				Ingliding	
			Front Glide		*Back Glide*			
	Front	*Back*	*Front*	*Back*	*Front*	*Back*	*Front*	*Back*
High	i	u	iy		iw	uw	ih	uh
Mid	e	ʌ	ey	oy		ow	eh	oh
Low	æ	o		ay		aw	æh	ah

[15] A description of such a conservative phonology is found in Kenyon and Knott 1953 and in Trager and Smith 1957. Another approach to estimating the relative extent of a sound change is to compare an urban dialect like that of Philadelphia with descriptions of the dialects just outside its influence (Kurath and McDavid 1961).

reference from which we can estimate the extent of sound change in a particular dialect. Thus, we can see that the lowering of (i) to [ɪ⊤], has progressed only a short distance from the starting point [ɪ], whereas the fronting and raising of (aw) to [e:ɔ] has shifted quite far from the point of origin [aʊ]. There is no age coeficient associated with (ahr), but the Philadelphia pronunciation [ɔɚ] is well removed from the original [ɑɚ].

Figure 3.9 displays 11 Philadelphia sound changes along these two dimensions.[16] All allophones participating in the shift are combined, so only one variable is shown for (æh), (ow), and (uw). The horizontal axis arranges the variables according to the phonetic distance they have moved, from complete movements across phonemic boundaries on the left to almost imperceptible shifts on the right. The vertical axis is the age coefficient, in the form of its effect on one generation of 20 years. The age coefficient derived from multiple regression is multiplied by 20 in the case of F2 variables and by 40 in the case of F1 variables. To be able to compare changes that affect F1 with those that affect F2, we must take into account that a typical sound change moves 200 Hz on the F2 dimension as it moves 100 Hz on the F1 dimension. Thus, distance along the front diagonal, in the direction of the vectors shown in Figure 3.6, is calculated as follows:

(4)   Height = F2 − 2 * F1 + constant

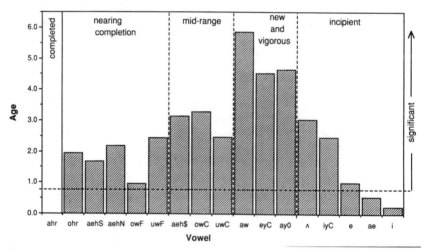

Figure 3.9.   Age coefficients of 11 Philadelphia sound changes by degree of phonetic shift. Age coefficient: 20× for (eyC), (aw), (ow), (uw), (æh), (ahr); 40× for others

---

[16] This includes all the vowels involved in past, present, and potential Philadelphia sound changes, including the completed and incipient shifts displayed in figure 3.6, along with the allophones of (æh) not shown there.

This adjustment is of course only an approximation, but it gives the right order of magnitude, as the consistency of the results will show.

Figure 3.9 gives us a purely synchronic basis for stratifying the sound changes into five classes:

Incipient	(i), (e), (æ), (iyC), (ʌ)
New and vigorous	(ay0), (eyC), (aw)
Midrange	(æh$), (owC), (uwC)
Nearing completion	(ohr), (æh$), (æhN), (owF), (uwF)
Completed	(ahr)

The S-shaped curve

The rise and fall of the age coefficients in figure 3.9 reflects the general observation that sound changes begin at a slow rate, progress rapidly in midcourse, and slow down in their last stages (Bailey 1973:77; Weinreich, Labov, and Herzog 1968; Kroch 1989a). The rate of sound change thus follows an S-shaped curve, or ogive. Figure 3.10 shows the abstract shape of such a curve, in this case generated from the cumulative frequencies of the binomial distribution.[17] There are many other functions, such as the cumulative normal distribution or the logistic function, which produce

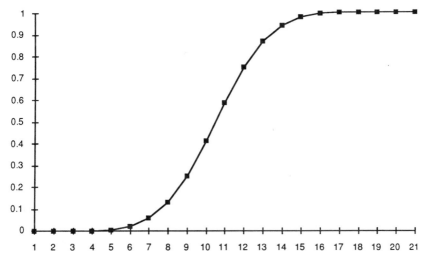

Figure 3.10.   S-shaped curve produced by cumulative frequencies of binomial distribution

[17] These are cumulative values of the successive coefficients of a binomial expression, in this case beginning with x^{20}, attached to $x^{19}y^{1}$, $x^{18}y^{2}$, etc. They represent the relative frequencies of combinations of x's and y's in a large number of sets of 20 equiprobable binary choices between x and y.

curves of this general shape. Such distributions describe the unstable competition between two forms, and can be generated by a model in which the probability of contact between the two governs the rate of change. If we follow Bloomfield (1933: 46) in constructing a map of all the speech exchanges that take place in a community, then the overall probability of an exchange involving the two forms is low at the beginning of the change, maximal at midpoint, and minimal at the end.

In the case of two competing linguistic forms, the sociolinguistic model proposed by Sturtevant (1947) is quite consistent with the scenario for the first half of the change. Two competing sounds are associated with the social values characteristic of the speakers who use them, and the progress of the change is associated with the adoption of the values of one group by members of the other. Thus, at the beginning of the change, speakers of the older form are rarely exposed to the newer form, so that little change or transfer can take place. The rate of change will be greatest when contact between speakers is greatest, that is, at midpoint.

This model might seem to predict a rapid movement to completion in the second half of the change, since speakers of the conservative form would be surrounded by speakers of the newer form, and it is their conversion that governs the rate of change. The fact that speakers of the newer form rarely hear the older form might seem irrelevant, since they are not undergoing change. This would be true if we were dealing with a binary change, like a life-or-death struggle where each contact ends with the triumph of one form or the other. But if we posit that the pressure to change is very slight, and that the shift at each speech contact is also very slight, then the rate of change will fall, since the number of speech events where the shift occurs is diminishing.

If we proposed other mechanisms of change, which depended on the newer form being easier to produce or easier to understand, a similar pattern would result, as long as the amount of change depended on the frequency of contact. We will return to these issues when we consider the mechanism of linguistic change in part D.

Figure 3.11 shows the concrete relationship between the S-shaped curve of development and the rate of Philadelphia sound changes. Each of the 11 sound changes is placed along the curve by matching the slope of the line (divided by 100) to the age coefficient determined in figure 3.9. The incipient sound changes are at the lower left, and the nearly completed and completed changes at the upper right. The new and vigorous changes begin with (ay0) and (eyC) just past the point of inflection of the curve, and (aw), with a slope of 1, is exactly at midpoint.

These results fit in with our understanding of how sound changes are generalized throughout the structure. We can see that the fronting of the three back upgliding vowels begins with (uw), and is generalized first to

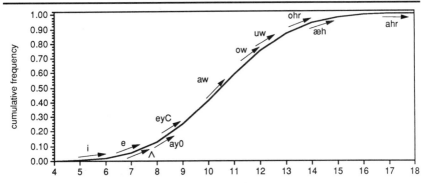

Figure 3.11. Placement of Philadelphia sound changes on S-shaped curve.
Slope of arrow (y/x) = (age coefficient of figure 3.9)/100

(ow) and then to (aw). The centralization of the nucleus (ay0) is generalized to (ʌ).

The results displayed in figure 3.11 will be compared with data from several other sources in the chapters to follow, which will allow us to confirm or reject the inferences drawn from the study of apparent time alone.

The internal relations of allophones and subgroups

The last section produced a global view of the 11 Philadelphia sound changes, with a regular relationship between the rate of change and the degree of advancement of the change. We can use apparent-time data to probe much more deeply into the behavior of the changes we are dealing with, by calculating the age coefficients separately for different allophones and for different subgroups. In this section, we will pursue this approach by examining the difference between the age coefficients for men and women.[18]

To begin with the basic facts: for all but two of the Philadelphia sound changes, women show much more advanced forms than men. Table 3.5 shows the normalized mean formant values by sex for the 116 speakers of the Philadelphia Neighborhood Studies.[19] It is evident that women have substantially higher F2 values for (eyC), (æhS), (æhN), (æh$), (aw), (owC), (owF), and (uwC).[20] One new and vigorous change is dominated

---

[18] We will not be dealing with the substantive question of how the sexual differentiation of language interacts with linguistic change, which has been explored elsewhere (Labov 1990) and which will become a major focus of attention in volume 2.

[19] It is assumed here that the normalization methods have eliminated the major part of the difference between men and women that is the result of differences in vocal tract length (Hindle 1978). Volume 2 will examine this issue more closely.

[20] The most fronted allophone, (uwF), shows an advantage for men, but measurements in this area are subject to considerable error.

Table 3.5 Normalized mean formant values of
Philadelphia sound changes by sex

	Women		Men	
Vowel	F1	F2	F1	F2
eyC	580	2202	575	2112
æhS	568	2207	595	2125
æhN	544	2375	561	2285
æh$	544	2240	589	2102
aw	687	2021	695	1902
ay0	750	1489	712	1475
owC	618	1428	610	1362
owF	649	1636	630	1519
uwC	490	1530	469	1440
uwF	502	1682	502	1721

by men: (ay0). Here men show much lower F1 values, the main index of
the change.

When we are dealing with an advanced, nearly completed change, we
can expect to find that the rate of change for the most advanced allophones
and the most advanced speakers is greatly reduced. Conversely, those allophones and groups that were slower to arrive at this point will now be seen
as moving faster. Figure 3.12 shows this relationship for the two more
advanced allophones of /æh/, the nearly completed changes (æhN) and

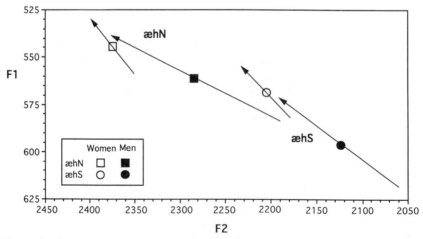

Figure 3.12.   Age coefficients for (æhN) and (æhS) by sex for the Philadelphia
neighborhood study

(æhS). In this diagram, the rate of change in apparent time is shown in a two-formant space, registering changes in F1 as well as F2. As in figure 3.6, the age coefficients are shown as vectors passing through the mean values: the head of the arrow represents the expected values for speakers 25 years younger than the mean, and the tail the values for speakers 25 years older than the mean. We see a steady upward movement along the front diagonal, which defines the phonological dimension of height, rather than a shift of F2 or F1 alone.[21] Note that here it is not the slope of the vector that registers the size of the age affect, but the length of the arrow. As we expect, the change is most advanced before nasal consonants. For both allophones, women are more advanced than men. But it is also quite clear that the rate of change, as measured by age coefficients, is greater for men than for women.

To elaborate on this point: It is to be expected that all the sound changes on the upper half of the S-shaped curve will show the relationship that the allophone that had been moving slower is now moving faster. As figure 3.12 illustrates, this pattern is stronger for men than for women.[22] The rate of change among women has slowed to the point that there is actually no significant age effect, and the differentiation between men and women is maximal, as we would expect when social awareness reaches a maximum.

Figure 3.13 shows the comparable view of two new and vigorous changes, (eyC) and (aw). Here it is also true that the mean values for men are behind the mean values for women. But there is no significant differ-ence in the age coefficients, which follow the same path at the same angle.

The vectors of Figures 3.12–3.13 are of course only approximations of the actual path of the change through apparent time. Figures 3.7 and 3.8 showed a more accurate view of the changes in grouping age by decade, using dummy variables to show the effect of each decade rather than a single quantitative regression. We can look more narrowly at the apparent-time data by doing the same for the two allophones of (æh). Figure 3.14 contrasts the development of (æhN) and (æhS) by decade, showing F2 values only. For (æhN), there is considerable fluctuation from one decade to the next, but men and women show almost exactly the same up and down movement. As Figures 3.7–3.8 suggested, this may be due to the effect of alternate generations. For (æhS), the two sexes show somewhat less coordination.

Each diagram in figure 3.14 shows the regression equations for both

---

[21] The F1 coefficients are usually smaller and at a lower level of significance than the F2 coefficients, and they show more random fluctuation. In chapters to follow, we will define phonological height as distance along the diagonal defined as $\sqrt{F2^2 - (2*F1)^2}$.

[22] In the case of (æhN), we must bear in mind that this is the one element of the Philadelphia sound changes that is closest to the type of stereotype that dominates the New York City speech community (Labov 1966).

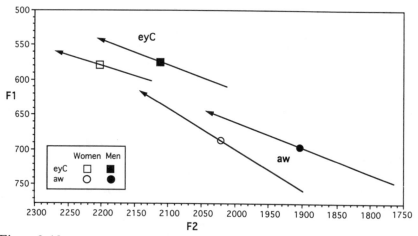

Figure 3.13. Age coefficients for (eyC) and (aw) by sex for the Philadelphia neighborhood study

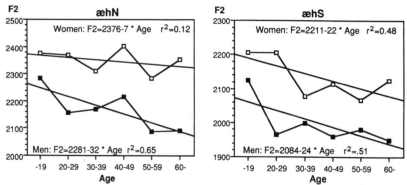

Figure 3.14. Fronting of (æh) allophones by decade for men and women

men and women. The slopes of the lines clearly illustrate the difference between the sexes. For (æhN), men show a slope of −32, whereas women show a slope of only −7; for (æhS), the two are identical. The same relationship is shown by the amount of variation explained by each line. For (æhN), r^2 shows that 65% of the variance for men is explained by the regression, but only 12% for the women; for (æhS), there is no difference. This indicates that for (æhN), there is very little effect of age among women, and a considerable effect among men.

In the same way, figure 3.15 displays the behavior in apparent time for the new and vigorous sound changes, (eyC) and (aw). Here there is no great difference between men and women, though there is a slight tendency for the youngest speakers to close the gap between the two sexes, and men

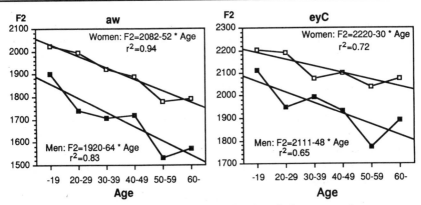

Figure 3.15. Fronting of (eyC) and (aw) by decade for men and women

do show a greater slope for (eyC) than women. In the case of (aw), the two lines are almost parallel. The regression line fits the points quite well, as indicated by the amount of the variance that is explained by age. Sexual differentiation is a constant throughout these sound changes, and it is not until the change is almost completed that it levels out among women and accelerates among men.

The youngest sound change that we can examine accurately with these tools is the centralization of /ayO/, shown in Figure 3.16. In this case, we are well down into the lower part of the S-shaped curve. Here the greater

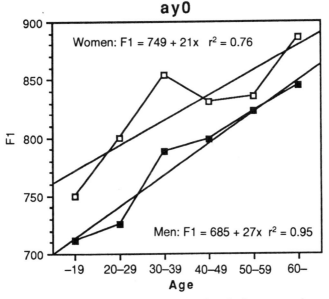

Figure 3.16. Centralization of (ay0) by decade for men and women

slope is shown by the more advanced group, the males. Among older speakers, the difference between men and women is quite small. There is some indication that the youngest group of female speakers is beginning to catch up.

It appears that the inferences to be drawn about change in progress from apparent time are not negligible, and that this type of analysis can be pursued profitably when no real-time data are available. We can conclude that much is to be learned by exploring age distributions, especially when the finer structure of the speech community is taken into account. It will be interesting to see to what degree the apparent-time inferences of this chapter can be confirmed by juxtaposing them with real-time data, both for the general principles and for the particular findings concerning sound changes in Philadelphia.

4

The Study of Change in Progress: Observations in Real Time

To the best of my knowledge, no one who has studied linguistic change in progress has ever made the error of confusing change in apparent time with change in real time.[1] It is obvious that distributions across age levels might not represent change in the community at all, but instead might represent a characteric pattern of "age-grading" that is repeated in every generation (Hockett 1950). Many well-established sociolinguistic variables exhibit such age-grading, where adolescents and young adults use stigmatized variants more freely than middle-aged speakers, especially when they are being observed.[2] Given a clear age distribution in apparent time, we have the problem of interpreting this result: Does it represent change in progress or not?

The obvious answer to the problems involved in the interpretation of apparent time would be to rely upon observations in real time, that is, to observe a speech community at two discrete points in time. Any differences between the two observations might be taken as a definitive answer to the question, What kinds of changes have taken place? Indeed, such real-time differences are what we mean by linguistic change, in the simplest and most straightforward definition of the term. Yet it turns out that there are many serious and unexpected difficulties in carrying out real-time studies and in making valid inferences from them.

4.1 Ways of making real-time observations

There are two basic approaches to the problem of accumulating real-time data. The simplest and most efficient is to search the literature dealing with the community in question and to compare earlier findings with current ones. The second approach is much more difficult and elaborate:

[1] Though it is not uncommon for those who are reading such reports for the first time to call this problem to the attention of the investigator, in person or in print.
[2] This is particularly true of such stereotyped variables as (dh) in *these*, *them*, *those*, etc., which shows strong age-grading in Philadelphia and New York City (Labov 1966).

to return to the community after a lapse of time and repeat the same study.

Reviewing the past

The first step for a well-trained investigator is to search for any previous study that bears on the subject under investigation. One should automatically make use of the past to interpret the present – this is the normal procedure of historical linguistics. The results of such a search will show both the advantages and disadvantages of historical investigations in general. As noted in chapter 1, historical linguistics must come to grips with data that are inherently bad, in the sense that they are fragmentary – the result of a series of historical accidents that determined first what was set down in writing, and then what part of that written record was preserved. On the other hand, the same accidents give the record its primary advantage as objective evidence – it was not created to prove any point that we might have in mind, or to serve the purposes of some research program that we have set in motion.

In the study of linguistic change in progress, we will therefore be fortunate to find in the literature any evidence bearing on the variables that we are actually dealing with. What we do find is not always easy to relate to our own interests, since the authors of previous studies had different concerns and used different methods. Points of exact comparison are few and far between.

This raises the issue of quantitative versus qualitative comparisons. Quantitative comparisons are not apt to be very useful. Earlier observations of what "sometimes" or "often" occurred cannot easily be compared with the frequencies of recent studies. Phonetic transcriptions of vowels cannot easily be compared for degrees of backing, fronting, raising, or lowering, nor can those of obstruents be compared for degrees of frication or voice onset time. Dialectologists in the field are often quite conservative in their notation, and they tend to limit their entries to variants of the forms they have encountered before, even when sound changes have advanced across several levels of the sound system. The Linguistic Atlas transcriptions of New York City speech in the 1940s showed the notation [æ⊥] for tensed /æ/ in *half, pass, last, bad,* etc., indicating a slightly raised variety of [æ] (Kurath and McDavid 1961). This would imply a sizeable retreat from the level recorded by Babbitt (1896), who indicated [ɛːᵊ] for this class. But fortunately, Hubbell (1962) was able to monitor tape recordings made by Linguistic Atlas informants, and he observed the homonymy of *bad* and *bared.* This is a particularly useful observation since it avoids the uncertainties of phonetic notation and rests solidly upon qualitative observations of 'same' and 'different'. We can then eliminate the possibility that the age distributions of the 1966 study represent age-grading, and we can reconstruct three phonetic levels for the most advanced phonetic form of tensed /æh/ in New York City:[3]

1895 [ɛːᵊ] → 1940 [eːᵊ] → 1960 [iːᵊ]

A similar use of data from the *Linguistic Atlas of New England* (Kurath et al. 1941), gathered in the 1930s, made it possible to interpret the apparent-time gradient from Martha's Vineyard (Labov 1963). The variables being studied here were (ay) and (aw), the centralization of the nuclei of /ay/ and /aw/. These retrograde movements appeared to reverse the effects of the Great Vowel Shift, though they might have also represented the continuation of an earlier stage of an incomplete opening of the nucleus of ME **ū**. Linguistic Atlas records showed occasional slight centralization of /ay/, with an [a⊥ɪ] notation. There is no guarantee that the notation does not represent vowel nuclei considerably more centralized than this, even approaching the extreme [əɪ] of the 1960s. But fortunately, the differences in the treatment of /aw/ were qualitative, not quantitative. No trace of the centralization of /aw/ appears in the Linguistic Atlas records. The only alternations found there opposed the inland rural [æω] to the urban and coastal [aω]. The /aw/ evidence was therefore decisive in demonstrating that the changes in apparent time recorded on Martha's Vineyard in 1961 were evidence of change in progress in real time.

As we will see, phonetic notations and general observations are less easy to interpret than qualitative statements based on the fundamental linguistic notion of 'same' and 'different'.

Repeating the past

The converse of the strategy just outlined is to make use of the present to interpret the past: to return to the scene of an earlier study and repeat it as closely as possible. If we are willing to devote the same amount of time and effort as the original investigator, we will be able to say decisively whether the change has continued to advance in real time or whether the same distribution in apparent time repeats itself. Before we invest so heavily, it is important to consider whether the outcome will be so decisive that the game is worth the candle.

There are two radically different types of longitudinal studies, which involve radically different problems of interpretation. In the terms used in sociology, they are *trend* and *panel* studies.

---

[3] The changes in the system also involve changes in the subclasses of short **a** words affected. Babbitt refers only to the "broad *a*" class that includes short **a** before voiceless fricatives and nasals. The present New York City system is a much larger set that includes all words with short **a** before voiced stops.

TREND STUDIES

The simplest type of replication is a trend study. We enumerate the general population in the same way, draw the sample population in the same way, obtain the data and analyze them in the same way – but *x* number of years later. If we are dealing with a large urban population, it is highly unlikely that the new sample will include any of the same individuals. But if we follow the same controlled procedures, the sample will be representative, and it will produce the most reliable type of replication.

For such a study to yield a meaningful portrait of linguistic development, it is essential that the community have remained in a more or less stable state in the intervening period. If drastic changes in its demographic makeup have taken place, the changes we observe in language may have little to do with the logic of linguistic change in progress. What we observe is external change in the language – the kind of change that took place in English speech communities in the course of the Norman invasion. In the long run, such externally motivated changes may be more important for the history of the language than internal developments, but they depend upon a chain of causes and effects that lie well outside linguistic relations. For this reason, it has been very difficult to trace changes in progress in the Black English Vernacular in the decades following the Great Migration of southern rural blacks to the northern cities – the largest single population shift in the history of the United States (Bailey and Maynor 1987). From 1940 to 1980, successive generations in the black community had entirely different linguistic environments.

PANEL STUDIES

The second approach to observations in real time sidesteps the problem of replicating the sampling method of the previous study by using the original sample. A panel study attempts to locate the same individuals that were the subjects of the first study, and monitors any changes in their behavior by submitting them to the same questionnaire, interview, or experiment. This is an expensive and time-consuming procedure, if it is planned as a panel study from the beginning, for the initial sample must be large enough to take the inevitable losses into account. An unplanned panel study will be left with a reduced sample, perhaps too small for statistical significance, but nonetheless extremely valuable for the interpretation of the original observations.

Several linguists have returned to the community they originally studied and have replicated their work, but the pursuit of the same individuals was usually not a part of the basic design.[4] A complete panel study was constructed in Montreal in 1984, based on the original sample of 120 speakers

---

[4] See the discussion of Cedergren's real-time restudy of Panama City in section 4.4.

in the Sankoff–Cedergren study (Sankoff and Sankoff 1973). Under the direction of Thibault and Vincent, field workers located and interviewed 50% of the original sample, a remarkably high proportion. It is expected that the results of this restudy will add a great deal to the further interpretation of the many studies already completed in Montreal.

Another way of following the same speaker across time is by the use of recordings. In their study of the Copenhagen dialect, Brink and Lund (1975) gained considerable time depth by collecting phonograph records of earlier speakers; the oldest recorded speaker was born in 1816. Moreover, they were able to obtain recordings of the same speakers at different periods in their lives – in one case, after an interval of 50 years. These are invaluable data for the study of changes in the community, and for studies of change or the absence of change in individual systems.

The richest body of recorded data on a single speaker is certainly that collected for Sarah Gorby, the Yiddish folk singer. Prince (1987) examines this large corpus, covering many decades and over 80 recordings, for changes in the frequency of features of Gorby's Bessarabian dialect, as opposed to standard Yiddish. This investigation used techniques of multivariate analysis to reveal systematic changes in the singer's strategic use of local dialect over her lifetime. One important finding for the general study of historical processes is the distinction between open and closed word classes. In Gorby's style shifting, open class words were far more malleable than closed class words. In the discussion to follow, it will appear that the mechanism of vowel shifting is particularly sensitive to this dimension.

4.2 Stages in the mechanism of linguistic change

Among the most intricate sets of linguistic changes are those that involve complex vowel systems, with intimate interdependence among the movements of individual vowels, and the mechanism of change in such systems remains a central problem. A classic problem of this type is the reconstruction of the mechanism of the English Great Vowel Shift – to identify the initiating changes, and to show the sequence of steps as a causal chain (Jespersen 1949; Wyld 1936; Martinet 1955; Dobson 1957; Stockwell 1964, 1978). In part B, the study of chain shifts now in progress will greatly enhance our ability to reconstruct this mechanism, extrapolating from the principles that govern current changes to reinterpret the changes of the past.

The procedures outlined in the previous sections provide the data needed to determine the time dimension for current changes. Once the data from apparent time have been correlated with real-time data, it is possible to reconstruct a chronology of the various steps, and to correlate this chronology with the sociolinguistic characteristics of each stage. We will necessarily be concerned with the level of social awareness of each stage. Some variables are the overt topics of social comment and show both correction and hypercorrection (*stereotypes*); others are not at the same high level of social awareness, but show consistent stylistic and social stratification (*markers*); still others are never commented on or even recognized by native speakers, but are differentiated only in their relative degrees of advancement among the initiating social groups (*indicators*). In earlier treatments of the mechanism of linguistic change, these types were correlated with chronological stages, stereotypes being the oldest and indicators the youngest (Labov 1965). In this volume, we will be able to carry the discussion considerably further on the basis of several decades of quantitative research.

Change from above and change from below

Any general consideration of linguistic change must first distinguish between change from above and change from below, a distinction first established in these terms in the New York City study (Labov 1966). "Above" and "below" refer here simultaneously to levels of social awareness and positions in the socioeconomic hierarchy. *Changes from above* are introduced by the dominant social class, often with full public awareness. Normally, they represent borrowings from other speech communities that have higher prestige in the view of the dominant class. Such borrowings do not immediately affect the vernacular patterns of the dominant class or other social classes, but appear primarily in careful speech, reflecting a superposed dialect learned after the vernacular is acquired. Frequently the newly borrowed linguistic features are inconsistent with the vernacular system, and their use involves correlated changes in other features. For example, the introduction of constricted [r] into an *r*-less dialect involves shifts in the realization of all the vowel nuclei before /r/, sometimes with accompanying mergers. This inconsistency may prevent the change from above from being integrated with the rest of the system, and the borrowed element with its associated changes may form a separate subsystem for many generations (Fries and Pike 1949).

Changes from below are systematic changes that appear first in the vernacular, and represent the operation of internal, linguistic factors. At the outset, and through most of their development, they are completely below the level of social awareness. No one notices them or talks about them, and even phonetically trained observers may be quite unconscious of them for many years. It is only when the changes are nearing completion that members of the community become aware of them. Changes from below may be introduced by any social class, although no cases have been recorded in which the highest-status social group acts as the innovating group.

Real-time data on Philadelphia sound changes

The following discussion of stages in the mechanism of sound change will focus on change from below and will use the Philadelphia vowel system as the paradigmatic example. This vowel system was selected for the most detailed sociolinguistic and instrumental examination because it is currently affected by a more extensive series of sound changes than any other dialect yet studied. Fourteen of the 20 vowel phonemes are involved in change.[5] Figure 3.6 showed the size of movements in apparent time as vectors of varying length and thickness. We can combine this evidence from apparent time with four sources of real-time evidence on the development of the Philadelphia dialect:

1 A brief phonetic transcription of "The North Wind and the Sun," published by L. Sprague de Camp in *Le maître phonétique* in 1933.
2 The Linguistic Atlas records, based on fieldwork by Guy Lowman in the 1940s (Kurath and McDavid 1961).
3 An article on the Philadelphia dialect by R. Whitney Tucker published in *American Speech* in 1944.
4 Ferguson's (1975) description of short **a** in Philadelphia (first presented in 1945, and based on observations made from 1940 to 1969).

The combination of real- and apparent-time data can be used to reconstruct five stages of change in the Philadelphia vowel system, proceeding from the earliest to the latest, or in present-day terms, from the oldest to the youngest.

1 *Completed changes.* The backing of /ahr/ from [aɔ˞] to [ɒɔ˞] characterizes all Philadelphia speakers, from the upper class to the lower working class. There is no age vector associated with the mean value, which is located in lower mid back position. This vowel is never discussed and never shifts: it is completely below any level of social awareness. According to Tucker (1944:40),

[t]he developments just mentioned [backing and rounding] are to be noted especially before *r: a* is distinctly rounded, i.e., pronounced as open *o* [ɔ]. But *-ar-* is never confused with *-or-*, for in the latter pronunciation the *o* is rather long and very close [o]. Contrast therefore *far* [fɔːr]: *four* [foːr].

2 *Changes nearing completion.* The raising of /ohr/ toward /uhr/ forms

---

[5] Of the seven upgliding diphthongs, /uw, ow, aw, ey, ay, oy/ are involved in change; only /iy/ is relatively stable. Of the six short vowels, /i, e, æ, ʌ/ show incipient movement. Of the seven ingliding vowels, /æh, ah, oh, uh/ are involved in change; /u, o, ih, eh/ are stable. See figure 3.6.

the second part of a chain shift with the previous change, as noted in the quotation from Tucker. Figure 3.6 shows a small upward age vector continuing. When the change is completed, /ohr/ and /uhr/ are entirely merged, forming homonyms of *moor/more, lure/lore, boor/bore*, etc. For most Philadelphians, these are indeed homonyms, but not for all. In reading word lists and pronouncing minimal pairs, many Philadelphians correct their native [uɚ] to [oɚ].

The tensing and raising of (æh) is the most marked stereotype of the Philadelphia system. Figure 3.6 shows a moderate level of movement in apparent time, which varies widely among the three major allophones of tense /æh/: (æhN) is clearly the most advanced. Figures 3.9–3.14 illustrate this further, showing that the apparent-time configuration of (æhN) is closest to the configuration associated with a change nearing completion. The real-time evidence offers little information on the degree of raising in Philadelphia in earlier times. Ferguson (1975) generally identifies the tensed (æh) with the vowel of *care* – that is, a lower mid vowel – but many of the oldest speakers recorded in the 1970s show much higher vowels. The main tensing occurs in closed syllables before front nasals and front voiceless fricatives (Payne 1980; Labov 1989a).

A second aspect of change associated with /æh/ is the set of items included in this category. The split of /æ/ and /æh/ involves a complex set of phonetic, grammatical, and lexical conditions, which will be presented in detail in chapter 15. In addition to the three basic phonetic categories indicated by the allophones before front nasals (æhN), voiceless fricatives (æhS), and the words *mad, bad, glad* (æh$), there are many other grammatical and phonetic conditions that govern membership in this category. Ferguson (1975) provides a good baseline for the period 1940–1970, and the apparent-time changes in the data from the 1970s can be calibrated against this description. The most significant fact is that Ferguson does not note any tensing before a morpheme-internal /n/ or /l/, environments that show considerable tensing in the 1970s and 1980s.

As the oldest of the socially marked changes in Philadelphia, (æh) has become a social stereotype and is now aligned with the socioeconomic hierarchy. This stratification is so dominant, and so easily recorded in impressionistic transcription, that it served as the test for the normalization algorithm referred to in sections 3.3 and 3.4. Any reasonable normalization algorithm should preserve the social stratification of this variable.

3 *Midrange changes.* The fronting of (uw) and (ow) is one of the best-known markers of Philadelphia speech, and differentiates Philadelphia from New York City (which shares (æh) as a sociolinguistic variable). This fronting is not new; Tucker (1944:41) already describes it as quite advanced.

'Long *o*', for instance, as in *old*, *go*, is pronounced [ɛːʊ] or [œːʊ] – the first element open, either rounded or unrounded, and with a very lax enunciation . . .. In *oo* the first element appears to be an open *i*, prolonged [ɪːʊ].

However, Tucker states several times that this fronting occurs before /l/. In the current Philadelphia dialect, it clearly does not: /uw/ and /ow/ are in extreme back position before /l/ (see figure 4.13a). Since Tucker notes that there is no fronting before /r/, and this situation prevails today, we must accept the idea that this is a phonological change that took place between 1940 and 1970. It is consistent with other changes that show a gradual movement away from the characteristic Southern States form of the Southern Shift.

The age vectors in figure 3.6 are of moderate length. Two separate allophones are shown: free and checked.

Though (uw) and (ow) are not as prominent to Philadelphians as (aeh), they are the most easily identified feature of Philadelphia speech for outsiders. As Tucker says, "It is this sound, more than any other, that makes Philadelphia speech seem affected or 'sissified' to other Americans" (1944:41). (uw) and (ow) show only moderate correction in formal speech and reading.

4 *New and vigorous changes.* Three variables show long and heavy vectors on figure 3.6, representing the largest and most significant age coefficients in the system. The first is closely integrated with the fronting of the back upgliding vowels just discussed: the fronting and raising of the nucleus of (aw) from a conservative position of [æʊ] to an advanced position of [e⊥ɔ]. No previous study reports a nucleus more advanced than [æ]. Tucker (1944:41) notes that

[t]he diphthong written *ou* or *ow* has [æ] instead of [ɑ] as its first element, as is regularly the case in Southern dialects; so here again we seem to find a kinship with the South. In the North this sound is chiefly rustic.[6] Examples: *house* [hæːʊs], *down* (dæːʊn).

The second is (eyC), the retrograde movement of checked /ey/,which moves up to a position that considerably overlaps /iy/. There is no trace of this shift in any previous record. On the other hand, there is ample evidence for the movement of the free allophone in the opposite direction (see the discussion of the Southern Shift in chapter 6). Tucker (1944:41) gives an extreme description – "In 'long *a*' as in *day*, the first element ranges from [æ] to [a]" – with no hint of a contrary movement in checked position.

---

[6] See the case of Martha's Vineyard cited earlier in the chapter.

The third is (ay0), the centralization and backing of the nucleus of /ay/ from [ay] to [ʌy] before voiceless consonants. Here Tucker's evidence provides the kind of qualitative contrast that is decisive (1944:40).

Both the [aɪ]-type diphthong and the [ɑʊ]-type diphthong exist in only one quality, whereas, in most American dialects the first element is shortened and modified in quality before a voiceless consonant – the precise sounds vary according to locality. (In my own speech, for example, the short sound, as in *night* or *out*, seems to be identical with the vowel of *but*; contrast with [ɑ] in *ride*, *loud*.) No such distinction is made in the Philadelphia dialect.

Figure 3.6 displays apparent-time evidence that the centralization of (ay0) was a new and vigorous change in Philadelphia in the 1970s, and figure 3.16 shows that it hardly existed for the oldest generation.[7] Here Tucker's evidence is again decisive in the interpretation of the situation as a change in real time.

None of these new and vigorous changes have risen to any prominent level of social awareness. They are never referred to in discussions of language with community members, in newspaper articles on the Philadelphia dialect, or even by phoneticians. They show no evidence of correction in careful speech, though their realizations are responsive to social situations (Hindle 1980) and they do show consistent patterns of social evaluation in subjective reaction tests.

5 *Incipient changes*. Figure 3.6 shows a number of small and nonsignificant vectors that represent incipient changes in the Philadelphia system. No trace of these shifts is found in any previous real-time record. They are detectable only instrumentally, and though some may represent chance fluctuations, they form patterns that match significant changes and reflect the overall dynamic of the system in a coherent manner. These include the falling and backing of the short vowels /i/ and /e/, and the raising of /ʌ/ in a direction parallel to the centralization of (ay0). They show no social correlations or subjective responses.

Figure 4.1 superimposes this classification on the curvilinear array of Philadelphia sound changes that was first displayed in figure 3.9. The rate of change in apparent time is slowest for almost completed changes, and fastest for new and vigorous changes. Conversely, the level of social awareness is maximal for almost completed changes, and minimal for new and vigorous changes. Figure 4.1 can be read as a synchronic view of layers in apparent time, from left to right.

---

[7] But see some tendency in a recent study of a very old speaker in figure 4.12.

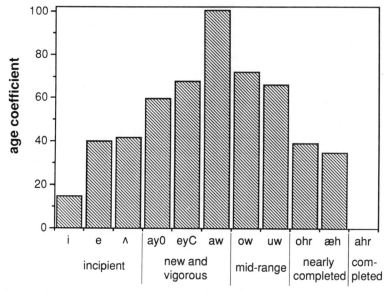

Figure 4.1. Five stages of Philadelphia sound changes by age coefficient

4.3 Relations between apparent time and real time

The interpretation of real-time data, drawn from panel studies or trend studies, requires an underlying model of how individuals change or do not change during their lives, how communities change or do not change over time, and what may result from combinations of these possibilities. The simplest combinations produce four distinct patterns (table 4.1).

There should be no difficulty in interpreting the first two patterns. (1) If the behavior of individuals is stable throughout their lifetimes, and the community remains at the same level, there is no variation to analyze, and we have *stability*: the stable, invariant, homogeneous situation that was once considered optimal, the ideal pattern that Gauchat set out to test and

Table 4.1 Patterns of change in the individual and the community

		Individual	*Community*
1	Stability	Stable	Stable
2	Age-grading	Unstable	Stable
3	Generational change	Stable	Unstable
4	Communal change	Unstable	Unstable

disprove. (2) If individuals change their linguistic behavior throughout their lifetimes, but the community as a whole does not change, the pattern can be characterized as one of *age-grading*.

The third and fourth combinations are not quite so transparent. (3) *Generational change* is the normal type of linguistic change that we have been considering so far – most typical of sound change and morphological change. Individual speakers enter the community with a characteristic frequency for a particular variable, maintained throughout their lifetimes; but regular increases in the values adopted by individuals, often incremented by generations, lead to linguistic change for the community. (4) The converse of this pattern is *communal change*, where all members of the community alter their frequencies together, or acquire new forms simultaneously. This is a common pattern of lexical change, as Payne (1976) found in her study of speakers entering the Philadelphia community. It appears to be a basic pattern for syntactic change as well, as Sankoff and Brown (1976) found in the development of Tok Pisin relatives and as Arnaud (1980) found in the development of the English progressive.

What methods find what models

How do these patterns of change relate to different methods of studying the community? If we confine our observations to distributions in apparent time, we will detect those conditions that lead to a differentiation of generations: that is, age-grading and generational change. We will not be able to distinguish between these two. Nor will we be able to detect the existence of communal change, since it will be indistinguishable from stability.

A panel study, on the other hand, will detect conditions where the individual either changes or is stable: age-grading and communal change. But a panel study by itself will not differentiate between these two, or between stability and generational change, since it provides no view of the community except through the behavior of the same individuals. Let us suppose that a community study was completed at time t_0 with no evidence of change in apparent time for a given variable (v). A panel study at time t_1 located 50% of the old subjects, and showed that their use of (v) had advanced by 20% on the average. Since no age-grading was present at time t_0 it might be assumed that this must represent a communal change in (v). But it might also represent age-grading that did not exist at t_0 but arose in response to a new superposed norm introduced into the community after that time.[8]

Since a trend study includes two studies of apparent time, it will both detect unstable behavior of individuals and distinguish stable from unstable

---

[8] For just such a case, see the discussion of the Department Store Study replication in section 4.4.

communities, differentiating all four of these patterns. In that sense, the trend study would be the best possible approach to gathering data on linguistic change. It has only one limitation: it produces no information on the behavior of individuals over time. That information, provided by panel studies, is essential for interpreting the many studies where little or no real-time data are available.

4.4 Four real-time replications

In order to assess the complexities of replicating previous studies, and the difficulties of interpretation, we will consider four such real-time investigations in detail. In each case, it will appear that the results do not point to any one of the models of change and stability outlined above, but instead to a combination of these patterns.

Hermann's restudy of Charmey

The earliest and best-known trend study was carried out not in a city but in the small village of Charmey in the Suisse Romande. E. Hermann (1929) returned to the village to replicate the work that Gauchat had carried out from 1899 to 1904 (Gauchat 1905). Gauchat had been motivated by the desire to test (and to challenge) the Neogrammarians' concept of a homogeneous, unified local dialect. He found changes in apparent time for five linguistic variables: three elements of the vowel system, and two consonantal changes.

$$a^\circ \rightarrow \alpha\colon \qquad l' \rightarrow y$$
$$o \rightarrow a^\circ \qquad \theta \rightarrow h$$
$$e \rightarrow e^i$$

Gauchat reported his observations in a qualitative form, richly endowed with ethnographic reports of the speech of particular individuals. Hermann did not claim the same intimate knowledge of village ways and speech patterns, but he interviewed 40 speakers with particular attention to the variables of interest, and he listed all of these individuals with their characteristic patterns. He found that the monophthongization of /a°/ was obviously complete, that the diphthongization of /o/ had advanced considerably, and that the diphthongization of /e/ was not quite finished. In Hermann's time, the main variation in the diphthongization of /o/ was in the environment before /r/, which had not been affected in 1904. On the other hand, the aspiration of /θ/ had not advanced, but showed the same type of variation that Gauchat had found in 1904. Hermann's replication demonstrated dramatically that Gauchat had indeed succeeded in locating linguistic change in progress; but it also showed that real-time information was needed to resolve the ambiguity of data drawn from apparent time.

The interest of Hermann's data grows considerably when we tabulate the differences between men and women across generations. For the change in progress represented by the diphthongization of /o/ before /r/, women were considerably ahead of men; in the middle generation (30–60), they showed 67% diphthongization versus 50% for men; in the youngest generation (below 30), they showed 90% diphthongization versus 80% for men. On the other hand, men showed a slightly greater tendency than women to aspirate /θ/. This reversal of the behavior of the sexes is consistent with the difference between an active change in progress, where women are most often in the lead, and a stable sociolinguistic variable, where men tend to use the reduced forms more often (Labov 1972:chap. 9).

Studies of large urban communities require a variety of different methods of gathering data to obtain a clear view of the range of styles characteristic of the community, and their social distribution. Any one method is limited by its characteristic errors, but a combination of methods with complementary sources of error allows us to make strong inferences about the structure of variation both in the vernacular and in superposed varieties. One of many such methods is the rapid and anonymous survey, which is particularly well suited to replication by trend studies.

Fowler's Department Store Study replication

The New York City Department Store Study (Labov 1966) was the first such rapid and anonymous survey. Its focus was the variable (r): the frequency of constricted [r] in final and preconsonantal position, which had been introduced into New York City as a superposed prestige variable in the years following World War II.[9] The change that this study traced was not a change in the vernacular use of (r), but rather a change in the positive evaluation of (r) as a norm for careful speech, which affected all speakers born after 1922 (Labov 1966:chap. 12). Figure 4.2 shows the social and stylistic stratification of (r) found in the sociolinguistic interviews conducted in 1962–63 with 81 adult speakers from the Lower East Side study. Despite two decades under the new prestige norm, the New York City vernacular remained r-less. In casual speech, all social classes except the upper middle class showed percentages of constricted [r] close to zero, and significant percentages of [r] appeared only in more formal styles. The upper middle class, on the other hand, used [r] 20% of the time in casual speech; as the dotted line indicates, the younger members of that group show a mean value twice as high.

---

[9] The introduction of (r) reversed the prestige relations of r-ful and r-less dialects that dominated speech classes and the mass media in New York City in prior years. Since the New York City study of 1966, it has become evident that a similar reversal has taken place in all of the r-less areas of the Eastern United States: in Eastern New England, and in the Upper and Lower South.

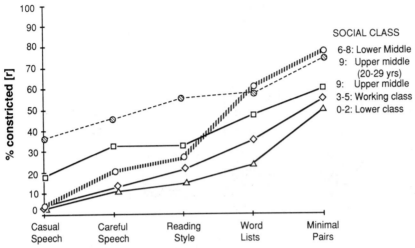

Figure 4.2. Social stratification of (r) in New York City

The Department Store survey reported in Labov 1966 examined this variable by an entirely different method. In two afternoons in 1962, I gathered information on the use of (r) from 264 individuals in three department stores: Saks, Macy's, and S. Klein, which were socially stratified by location, prices, advertising, and many other objective indices. The results confirmed the patterns of distribution of (r) found on the Lower East Side: social stratification, stylistic stratification by social class (the store), by occupation (floorwalkers, sales clerks, sweepers), and by age. The most complex pattern shared by the two studies was the reversal of distributions in apparent time for different social classes. For the lower middle class (represented by Macy's in the Department Store Study), the highest (r) values were found among speakers 45–60 years old, who were the most sensitive to the new prestige pattern, whereas other social classes showed steadily increasing (r) values for lower age groups.

In 1986, Joy Fowler replicated the Department Store Study in minute detail. Since S. Klein was no longer in business, she substituted May's, a similar lower-status store of the same size in the same area. The stratification of these stores remains identical to the original comparison of 1962.[10] She approached the same number of people in each store, asking

---

[10] Figures showing the stratification of the three stores were provided in a similar restudy in 1984 by Jeff MacDonald. The stores were differentiated by their advertising in the middle-class *New York Times* and working-class tabloid *Daily News*. On November 11–13, 1984, the *Times* had 5 2/3 pages from Saks, 12 1/2 from Macy's, and 0 from May's; the *News* had 0 from Saks, 7 from Macy's, and 11 2/5 from *May's*. Women's dresses were advertised at $265 for Saks, $118 for Macy's, and $13.99–$29.99 for May's. Indirect incandescent lighting is used in Macy's and Saks, with no guards visible; May's uses bright fluorescent lights and conspicuous uniformed guards on each floor. Saks employees wore conservative fashions and

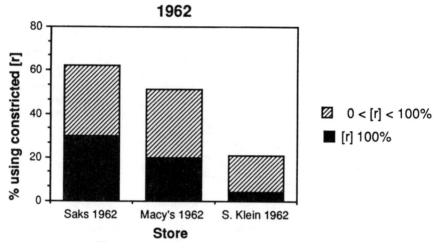

Figure 4.3a.   Overall stratification of (r), 1962

for a department that was located on the fourth floor. On receiving the answer, she then said, "Excuse me?" and obtained a second, more careful repetition of "Fourth floor."

Fowler's restudy shows that the structure of (r) in New York City is remarkably stable. Each of the relations reported in the 1962 study reappears in her data in detail. Figures 4.3a and 4.3b show the overall stratification of (r) for the three stores in 1962 and 1986. In each case,

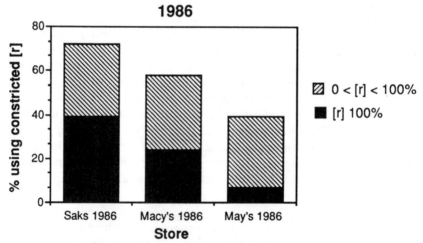

Figure 4.3b.   Overall stratification of (r), 1986

hairstyles; Macy's employees tended to show sporty, punk hairstyles and trendy fashions; May's employees did not use marked fashions or hairstyles.

the three stores are stratified in the same way, by the percentage of speakers who used 100% constricted [r] in their responses, and by the percentage who used [r] variably. Figure 4.4 shows a detailed replication of the stylistic behavior of the department store speakers. The stratification of the three stores is preserved for each of the four basic utterances: *fourth* and *floor* uttered the first time, and *fourth* and *floor* repeated with emphasis. Each /r/ in *floor* gets more constricted [r] than the preconsonantal /r/ in *fourth*, and the emphatic utterances get more [r] than the unemphatic ones.

In the same way, the 1986 study replicated the 1962 results for occupational stratification within the stores, for the differentiation of ground floor and higher floors in Saks, and for the ethnic differentiation of subjects.

Fowler's exact replication allows us to approach a fundamental question concerning the mechanism of linguistic change. We have seen that the effect of the new prestige norm was not to modify the vernacular of most

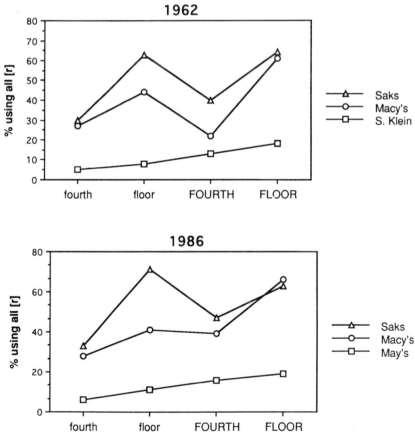

Figure 4.4. Differentiation of (r) by style in 1962 and 1986

New Yorkers, but rather to produce variable behavior in formal situations. Yet the *r*-less vernacular norm was also once a prestige pattern, introduced under the influence of London in the early 19th century.[11] How do such variable prestige patterns become consistent vernacular patterns? Most speakers acquire the use of constricted [r] as a superposed form, long after their vernacular patterns are set. One suggestion that was advanced in 1966 looked to the hypercorrect behavior of the lower middle class for this mechanism. Since lower middle class speakers use even more [r] in their most formal style than the upper middle class, they may impress this form upon their children in instructional styles, and so give them the early practice that leads to consistent motor patterns.

Our present concern with distributions in apparent time is illuminated by the intricate parallels of figure 4.5. For both 1962 and 1986, younger speakers use constricted [r] in Saks, but the reverse pattern is seen in Macy's: more frequently the older the speaker, the more [r].

In all the diagrams given so far, the 1986 figures are somewhat higher than the 1962 figures. Change in real time has taken place. Figure 4.6 shows that the percentage of speakers who used [r] 100% of the time increased in all three stores in the 24-year period, but the difference is much greater for the highest-status store, Saks.[12] The same figure shows a rather different picture for the percentage of variable [r] or "some [r]." Saks and Macy's show only a small upward movement, but the lowest-status store shows a dramatic increase, to the same level as the others. The use of (r) as a stylistic variable has increased strikingly among the lowest-status employees but they exhibit nowhere near the same control over this variable as the Saks employees.

Figure 4.7 shows a consistent age pattern in the behavior of each social class. It compares the rate of increase for all [r] for the three age groups of Saks employees and the three age groups of Macy's employees. (As figure 4.5 indicated, the order of the three age levels is reversed for the two stores). The slopes of increase are similar for the three age groups in Saks – from 11% to 13%. On the other hand, the *rate* of increase has accelerated for the younger speakers in Macy's, indicating the increasing influence of the (r) pattern of the upper middle class.

Fowler's study provides clear evidence of generational change in progress in real time, but it is quite slow compared with the evolution of the

---

[11] Walker (1791) was the first to note the general *r*-less pattern in London, with such transcriptions as *caad*, though Wyld (1936) notes early spellings that indicate loss of /r/ before /s/ in *person*, etc. This means that the original settlers of New York City could not have had a consistently *r*-less vernacular, but acquired this norm under the influence of the new London prestige form, just as citizens of Boston, Richmond, Savannah, and Charleston did.
[12] As Figure 4.2 shows, the only group of speakers on the Lower East Side who used constricted (r) to any extent in their casual speech was the younger upper middle class, who reached an overall mean of 40%.

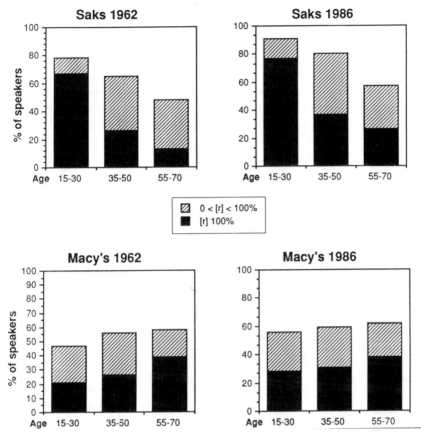

Figure 4.5. Age stratification of (r) in Saks and Macy's in 1962 and 1986

New York City vowel system or the palatalization of /l/ that Gauchat observed in Charmey. There is also evidence for repeated age-grading, in both the highest and second highest status groups. The age-grading effect is much larger than the generational change: in Saks, the shift of all [r] from the youngest group to the group 20 years older remains at the high rate of 40%, whereas the upward movement after 24 years is only 10%.

The precise replication of the Department Store Study shows that the sociolinguistic structure of the speech community is perhaps even more stable than anticipated. Under the pressure of the new *r*-pronouncing norm, New York City speech is changing slowly. Contrary to what I originally expected, the hypercorrect behavior of the lower middle class, reflected in the pattern of Macy's employees, has not resulted in any sudden advance of *r*-pronunciation as a whole.

Here it should be pointed out that such an acceleration was reported by MacDonald in a 1984 replication of the Department Store Study, which

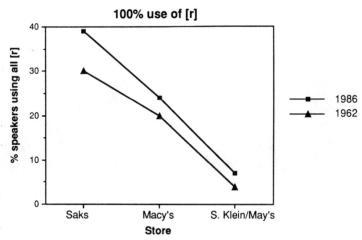

Figure 4.6a.   Increase in 100% (r) use in three New York City department
stores, 1962–1986

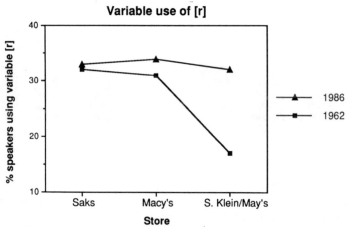

Figure 4.6b.   Increase in use of variable (r) in three New York City department
stores, 1962–1986

also used Saks, Macy's, and May's.[13] MacDonald found that 60% of
speakers interviewed at Saks, 73% at Macy's, and 54% at May's used all
[r], and that 10% of speakers interviewed at Saks, 18% at Macy's, and
9% at May's used some [r]. Thus, MacDonald found much higher rates
than Fowler for all [r], with a proportionately higher increase for Macy's.
Within this overall framework, all other comparisons show the expected

---

[13] See footnote 10 for MacDonald's data on the stratification of the three stores.

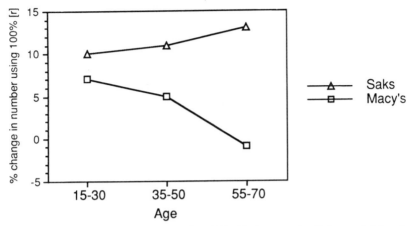

Figure 4.7. Increase in the use of 100% (r) by age in Saks and Macy's, 1962–1986

stratification – by sex, by floor, and by occupation. It may be that the expected acceleration of this prestige pattern, led by the lower middle class, has occurred in New York, but there are several reasons to believe that Fowler's replication is more accurate than MacDonald's. First, Fowler exactly replicated the number of subjects in the original study, whereas MacDonald interviewed only about half as many.[14] Second, MacDonald had particular difficulty in obtaining subjects in Macy's, where he could not formulate a question to which the unambiguous answer was "Fourth floor." The Macy's and May's samples were heavily biased toward younger speakers, with only 4 subjects in the oldest third for each store, which explains part of the high values for these two stores. Third, the paradigm of four responses was largely incomplete. For the 37 subjects who gave complete responses, the leading position of Macy's disappears, and the usual stratification is found for "all [r]": Saks 77%, Macy's 54%, and May's 26%. Finally, the transcription seemed to be biased toward "all [r]," which may be due to shorter exchanges, or a tendency to hear a shwa as [r].

Clearly, it is not easy to achieve reliability for trend studies that involve repetitions of the same procedures by different investigators. Fowler's

[14] Labov and Fowler each interviewed 68 speakers at Saks, 125 at Macy's, and 71 at S. Klein/May's; MacDonald interviewed 68, 68, and 35 speakers at the respective stores. MacDonald reports a strong internal constraint on the fieldwork as the reason for the lower numbers in his study: "It seemed important not to reveal the nature of my endeavor. All three stores have numerous security guards whom I deemed it important to avoid. I also suspected that each of the stores also employs television surveillance. Thus it seemed better to linger as short a time as possible in any one area of each store in order to arouse the least suspicion." He also reports that the fieldwork took 10 hours as opposed to the 6.5 hours of the original study.

execution was the most careful, and her results the most conservative. My own observations of the New York City (r) in recent years agree with Fowler's in showing little change. We can conclude, then, that the effect of the hypercorrect pattern of the second highest status group has not led to an overall revolution in the stratification of (r) in New York City. In Fowler's data, it is reflected only in the emphatic repetition of *floor*, where Macy's employees surpass the level of the Saks employees. The repetition of *fourth floor* corresponds to the careful speech of the sociolinguistic interviews in 1962; figure 4.4 shows that the chief increase for Macy's employees is in this careful speech. The upper middle class continues to lead in the use of [r] in less monitored styles, whereas the lower middle class leads in more careful styles. It follows that any overall increase in the use of this prestige form in the vernacular depends upon the gradual increase in use among the highest-prestige speakers. This may have been the mechanism in the early stages of the formation of the 19th-century *r*-less vernacular, but at some point in the process we must expect a sudden acceleration.[15]

Cedergren's restudy of Panama City

In 1969–71, Henrietta Cedergren carried out a sociolinguistic study of the Spanish of Panama City (Cedergren 1973). One of the five main variables that she studied was the lenition of (ch) in *muchacha, che, muchos*, etc., which involved a shift from the affricate [č] to the fricative [š]. This was the only variable that showed a clear pattern of change in apparent time. No real-time evidence was available to interpret these data, but there were other indications that the apparent-time pattern represented change in progress.[16] In 1983, Cedergren returned to Panama City and repeated her sampling procedure to create a trend study.[17] One of her chief goals was to provide the real-time evidence that would decide whether the lenition of (ch) was in fact a change in progress. The following analysis is based on data that she presented to the 1984 NWAVE meeting.

Figure 4.8a shows the data on the (ch) index for the two studies.[18]

The age groupings that Cedergren set up for the two studies differ slightly in figure 4.8a. I have aligned the two sets of categories as closely

---

[15] As chapter 3 showed, we would expect the importation of [r] to follow an S-shaped curve; but in the case of this prestige pattern, we are still at the lower tail with a shallow slope.
[16] In the case of (ch), the monotonic relationship with age was coupled with a curvilinear relationship with social class. The other four variables showed the opposite pattern: a monotonic relationship with the class hierarchy and a more or less flat relationship with age. This was one of the main pieces of evidence that led to the curvilinear hypothesis (Labov 1980).
[17] Cedergren did locate some of the same subjects, but interviewing the original sample of speakers was not the primary design of her restudy.
[18] The (ch) index was based on a 3-point scale: 0 for the affricate, 1 for the intermediate palatalized form, and 2 for the clear fricative. The average value multiplied by 100 formed the index.

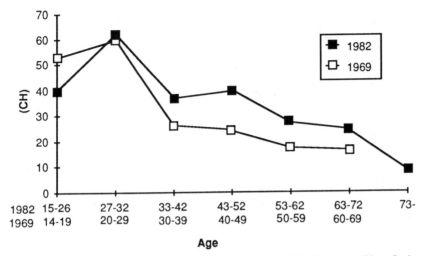

Figure 4.8a. Real time changes in the lenition of (ch) in Panama City: Cedergren's trend study, 1969–1982

as possible.[19] The 1969 study showed a steady rise in lenition as age decreased, a peak in the second youngest age group, and then a slight decline in the youngest group. The same pattern is found in the 1982 study, which suggests – from a qualitative point of view – the existence of age-grading. On the other hand, there is clear evidence of an increase of 10%–15% for all but the two youngest age groups, which indicates the presence of linguistic change in progress.

How can we decide whether the model of age-grading fits these data better than the model of generational change? Figures 4.8b–c project both of these abstract models against the actual observations. In Figure 4.8b, the model of generational change is applied to the 1969 data. Speakers who were 15 years old in 1969 would be 28 in 1982. Assuming that individual use of (ch) is stable, we plot the 1969 values from figure 4.8a, and then we project each value for 1969 one unit to the right, which is the nearest approximation we can make, given Cedergren's age groupings. We then compare these projected values with the observed values for 1982. On the whole, the two sets of values do not match very well. Only one age group (50–59) shows a coincidence. Otherwise, the observed values are closer to the 1969 values than to the projected values.

---

[19] In her original NWAVE presentation, Cedergren showed groups of the same chronological age in each column. This is a natural strategy, but would be more suitable if the restudy were indeed a panel study. The present mode of display, which groups together subjects of the same relative age in apparent time, appears to be more revealing of the processes at work here.

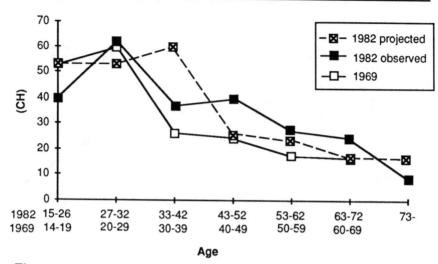

Figure 4.8b. Model of generational change of (ch) in Panama City: Projected and observed values for Cedergren's restudy

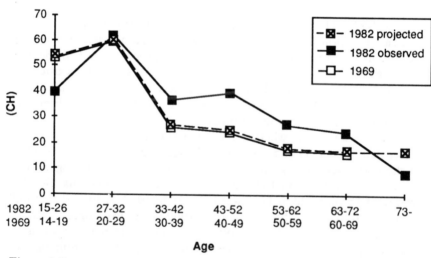

Figure 4.8c. Model of age-grading of (ch) in Panama City: Projected and observed values for Cedergren's restudy

Figure 4.8c is the corresponding diagram for the age-grading model. Here the model is very simple. Since each age grouping represents the same relative position in apparent time, the model predicts the same value for the 1982 group as the 1969 group. The results are quite clear. For all but the two lowest age groups, the actual observations run parallel to the projections of the age-grading model, but at a level 10%–15% higher.

Thus, the majority of the population continues to advance in the lenition of (ch). But for the second highest group this process appears to have reached its limit, and the youngest group displays the opposite effect – a retreat from the ongoing process.

These data show a remarkable parallel to the importation of constricted [r] into New York City. In each case, age-grading is the dominant configuration. In succeeding generations, speakers follow the same pattern across apparent time. But there is also a steady increment of the process at a lower level, showing that a real-time change is taking place. This suggests that in trying to decide which model is correct for a given process, we may have been setting up a misleading opposition between age-grading and generational change. It is possible that age-grading is involved in the mechanism of real-time change for certain types of linguistic change. The two changes we are considering here are not obviously of the same type. The adoption of constricted [r] is a change from above, and the lenition of (ch) is a change from below: no exterior model is involved. In terms of the process of change, we find both similarities and differences. On the one hand, in each case the middle-aged and older speakers appear to be gradually acquiring the norm of the younger speakers. On the other hand, the lenition of (ch) seems to have reached its peak and is retreating, whereas the importation of constricted [r] is continuing steadily.

Trudgill's revisitation of Norwich

Trudgill's study of the English city of Norwich was carried out in 1968 (Trudgill 1974a). The original sample was a random selection of 60 speakers who were born between 1875 and 1958; at the time of the study, they were between the ages of 10 and 93. In 1983, Trudgill returned to Norwich and carried out a restudy of a somewhat different form from those summarized above (Trudgill 1988). To get a real-time perspective on the apparent-time view of stable variables and changes in progress, he added 17 speakers between the ages of 10 and 25 – a group comparable to the teenage group of his original sample, who were from 10 to 20 years old at the time. Trudgill's method gives us only one point of comparison, but it is an efficient one.

The restudy uncovered a number of changes in progress that had not been evident in 1968. For some, like the shift of /θ/ to /f/, there was no trace at all in the earlier study; 15 years later, 70% of the speakers showed this feature. For others, like the labialization of /r/, there was only a scattering of cases in 1968, which Trudgill ascribed to individual variation; by 1983, it was apparent that this process was a general trend. The fronting of the nucleus of /u:/ in *moan, soap, toe*, etc., did not appear in the 1968 sample, though it did show up in some of the adolescents I interviewed a few years later (LYS:chap. 6). In 1983, the process was well under way. There is no doubt, therefore, that adding a new sample of younger speakers – a truncated trend study – was effective in updating our view of what is happening in Norwich.

The most important restudy for present purposes concerns the clearest example of change in progress in the Norwich study: the backing of (el) in *help, belt, hell*, etc. Here the biggest increases for the youngest age group in 1968 had been in spontaneous speech, with a smaller rate of change in reading style and word lists. In the restudy, the relative rates of change were reversed. There was only a slight upward movement in the backing of (el) in spontaneous speech for the new adolescents, but a sizeable increase in reading style and word lists. Trudgill's account for this phenomenon is that the change had practically reached completion, with the merger with wedge, so that *hell* and *hull* were homonyms. But in 1968, the change was stigmatized; in 1983, it was becoming accepted as the norm for the community. We will have occasion to review this logic in volume 2, when we deal with the progress of recent sound changes in American English.

4.5 The stability of individual phonological systems over time

None of the cases examined so far has supplied evidence of stable individual systems. Nevertheless, there is evidence to show that in some circumstances phonological structures are remarkably stable throughout an individual's life. This is a crucial matter for the study of linguistic change in progress. Despite the clear value of real-time data, many studies of speech communities will have only apparent-time data to deal with. For most areas of the world, we have no previous studies of linguistic variation to interpret, and in very few cases will we be able to return to restudy a community. If we can define the situations where stability of individual systems is the rule, we will be freer to associate distributions in apparent time with changes in real time, or at least to infer the existence of real-time changes with a high degree of probability.

Types of change

In approaching this topic, it is important to distinguish different stages of sound change and their relation to social and stylistic stratification. Almost by definition, changes from above involve instability in the phonology of the individual, who acquires the superposed features late in life and gradually improves in his or her ability to produce this feature. The issue of stability is of interest only for changes from below, which reflect more directly the history of the language and the linguistic factors that we want to reconstruct. Among changes from above, we must also distinguish various types, since as the study of New York City demonstrates (r), the late stages in this process are often accompanied by conscious correction and alterations of vernacular performance.

Instrumental measurements of parents and children

The many vowel systems analyzed in LYS include both communities for which real-time data are available and communities for which they are not. The most convincing evidence for the stability of individual systems lies in the analysis of 10 speakers from New York City, who replicate in detail the attested and reconstructed history of the New York City vowel system. If individual systems were not stable, and communal change was characteristic of vowel systems, they would all reflect slight variations on the most advanced linguistic system. But in fact, the realizations of tensed (æh) range from low front [æ:] for the oldest speakers to high front [i:ᵊ] for the youngest.

LYS shows parallel patterns for many different speech communities for which real-time data are not available. Most relevant here are analyses within families. Figures 4.9a and 4.9b show the typical progress of an active chain shift across generations, in this case the Northern Cities Shift in Detroit. In this dialect, the entire short **a** word class is tensed to /æh/ and undergoes fronting and raising. The advancement of a particular token

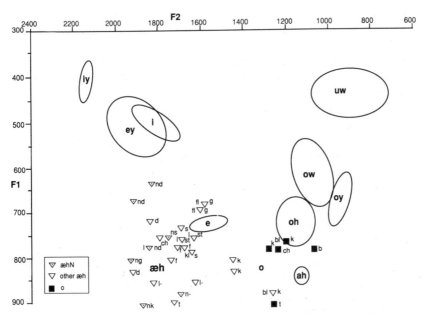

Figure 4.9a. Vowel system of James Adamo, 55, Detroit

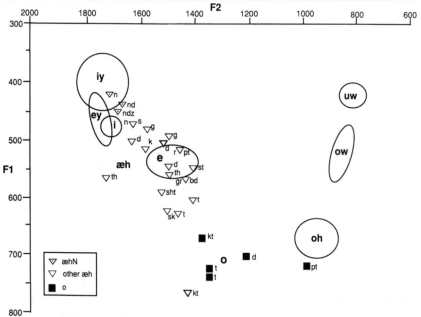

Figure 4.9b.   Vowel system of Chris Adamo, 13, Detroit

depends primarily on its phonetic environment, the following segment exerting the most powerful influence.[20]

Figure 4.9a shows the pattern of the Northern Cities Shift for the father of the family, James Adamo, 55. The /æh/ word class shows a globular distribution in low front position. Clear indications of raising are found only for the most favorable environments – before word-final apical nasals, as in *hand* and *stand*. Even these remain at the [æ⊥] or [ε] level, no higher than lower mid position. The short *o* words in the /a/ class are all in low back position, phonetically [ɑ].[21] This is an extremely conservative exemplification of the Northern Cities dialect.

Figure 4.9b shows the vowel system of the son, Chris Adamo, 13. The entire /æh/ class is shifted upward in an elliptical distribution. Again, the most advanced tokens occur before word-final /n/ and /nd/, and they reach lower high position, overlapping the nucleus of /iy/. The least advanced

---

[20] The relative degree of advancement is influenced by the manner of articulation of the following segment, in the order nasals > voiceless fricatives > voiced stops > voiced fricatives > voiceless stops. Point of articulation follows the ordering palatal > apical > labial, velar.

[21] As in the Middle Atlantic states, the short **a** token that is the lowest and farthest back – namely, *black* – has a following voiceless velar stop and a preceding obstruent-liquid cluster. This is located in the [ɑ] position, in the midst of the short **o** distribution. Both Figures 4.9a and 4.9b exemplify the fine-grained phonetic conditioning that is typical of regular sound change in progress, an issue that will be brought to the fore when we consider the controversies concerning the mechanism of sound change in chapter 16.

tokens, for words like *tapped* and *grabbed*, are in lower mid position. The rest of the tokens are spread out in a pattern that allows every phonetic influence to be registered, patterns that will become important in part C in considering the mechanism of change. The least advanced tokens are those with following voiceless stops, with following velars lagging behind following apicals. Again, the most conservative token of short **a** is found in the midst of the advancing short **o** distribution. The short **o** words are now in low central position, not far from the region of phonetic space that the short **a** words departed from. The most advanced tokens of short **o** are those preceding /t/ (as in *not*, *got*), and the most conservative are those preceding labials.

This radical shift across generations is characteristic of new and vigorous changes. In this most active stage, the trajectory of the change covers half of the available phonological space in one generation, and three-quarters in two. It is of course possible that age-grading is present, and that 40 years ago, James Adamo's speech pattern was closer to the one that Chris shows now. We have no real-time data that would resolve this question. It is possible that both /æh/ and /o/ are age-graded, and that in the course of time both vowels regress toward a previous norm. However, it is extremely improbable that the same systemic relations would then be found in both vowel systems. Age-grading is most typical of the more conscious types of style shifting and correction, whereas change from below proceeds in the highly organized, phonetically controlled patterns that we see here.[22]

Longitudinal studies of older speakers

Among the real-time studies of recent years, the one that bears most directly on the issues raised in this chapter is the longitudinal research on the effects of normal aging on language in Philadelphia.[23] In these studies, the same interviewer prepared for the reinterview by carefully studying the original tape recording, and discussed the same topics and obtained many of the same narratives as in the first interview. Though the data are still under analysis, this highly controlled study has already provided evidence indicating what kinds of changes can be expected to take place in the later years of life.

Evidence on phonetic changes in the 70s and 80s is crucial to the interpretation of many sound changes in progress. Apparent-time data frequently show a curve in which the sharpest drop-off in a variable is found for the oldest speakers. This appears in the case of New York City (oh)

---

[22] New Yorkers have a strong tendency to correct the variable (oh) in *lost, coffee, awful*, etc., from upper mid to low back position in their careful speech. The raising of (oh) is parallel to the raising of the nucleus of /oy/. But there are no attested examples of correction of /oy/, which remains as [ʊⁱ] or [uⁱ] even in word lists.

[23] Research sponsored by the National Institutes of Health.

in figure 3.1 and for New York City (aw) in figures 3.2–3.4. In the case of Philadelphia (aw) in figure 3.7, the greatest lag is found for the generation over 50. Some part of this effect might be due to changes in the vocal tract or manner of articulation of older speakers, and not to generational change in real time. Note that all three of these changes involve increases in peripherality and raising of tense nuclei.

Let us suppose that speakers undergo a relaxation of the articulatory muscles in their later years that leads to a laxer pronunciation. Their (oh) variable might decline from [oˑ] to [Ωˑ] as a result of such laxing, yielding the illusion of change in apparent time. If of course the change involved laxing or centralization, such a general tendency would yield the opposite effect: it would minimize the appearance of a real-time change in apparent time. However, a laxing of articulation might not be general to all points in the system; it might represent a contraction of phonological space, which modifies the extreme points without altering the central areas. In that case, the standard deviation of the system as a whole would be smaller.

One of the first subjects reinterviewed in the Philadelphia longitudinal studies was Jenny Rosetti. She was a central figure in one of the South Philadelphia neighborhoods studied by Anne Bower in 1973–76, and is a representative speaker of the older Italian working-class groups. At the time of her first interview in 1973, she was 68. In 1990, when she was 85, Bower reinterviewed her on the same topics, and obtained most of the same narratives.[24] Table 4.2 shows the overall parameters of the stressed vowels in these two interviews.[25] It is immediately apparent that there are no overall changes in the base of articulation. The mean difference in F1 is only 12 Hz, and the difference in F2 of 73 Hz is within the range of

Table 4.2   Means and standard deviations of the overall vowel system of Jenny Rosetti at ages 68 and 85

Age	Mean		N	Standard deviation	
	F1	F2		F1	F2
68	699	1951	220	217.5	595.5
85	711	1878	207	239.4	613.4

[24] The interview done in 1973 used a Nagra IV-S tape recorder at $3\frac{3}{4}$ in/sec, with a Sennheiser 140 lavaliere microphone. The 1980 interview was done with a Panasonic DAT recorder and a Sony ECM55, at $7\frac{1}{2}$ in/sec. Analyses were carried out by Laura Koenig using the LPC routine of the WAVES+ package.

[25] All vowels with primary lexical stress are included, except those with initial glides or initial obstruent + liquid clusters, and those with liquid finals.

chance fluctuation, about one-eighth of the standard deviation. Moreover, there is no shrinkage of the periphery: there is a slight increase in the standard deviation rather than a reduction.

Table 4.3 examines the individual vowels of Jenny Rosetti's system. If the changes in apparent time shown in figure 3.6 are actually the product of age-grading, we should see a retreat in the older pattern. If the contrary

Table 4.3 Comparison of vowel nuclei for Jenny Rosetti at ages 68 and 85

Vowel measurement	*Mean difference*	*t*	*N (1973/1990)*
Advancing with age?			
/æhS/-front diagonal	331	1.57	6/9
/æhN/-front diagonal	324	1.38	9/10
/æh$/-front diagonal	100	0.40	6/2
/æh/-front diagonal	300	**2.38	21/21
/ayO/-back diagonal	−296	−1.30	5/7
/ayV/-F2	−310	**−2.38	9/16
Retreating with age?			
/owC/-F2	−134	−0.82	15/6
/owF/-F2	−139	−0.54	5/8
/uwC/-F2	−241	−0.90	9/9
/uwF/-F2	−156	−0.60	6/6
No change evident			
/i/-F1	118	0.69	15/9
/e/-F1	−5	−0.12	9/13
/æ/-F1	−117	−2.00	17/16
/o/-F1	39	0.64	10/9
/o/-F2	57	0.49	10/9
/ʌ/-F1	−31	0.37	7/10
/ʌ/-F2	−132	1.14	7/10
/u/-F1	−41	−0.06	6/7
/u/-F2	−143	−0.96	6/7
/iyC/-F1	−41	−1.22	21/10
/iyC/-F2	−45	0.3	21/10
/iyF/-F1	35	0.37	7/6
/iyF/-F2	−235	−1.12	7/6
/eyC/-front diagonal	81	0.54	23/11
/eyF/-front diagonal	378	0.97	5/6
/aw/-front diagonal	−348	−1.30	8/19
/ayV/-F1	21	0.17	9/16
/oh/-F1	−4	0.48	10/10
/oy/-F1	−77	−1.00	6/3

**p < 0.01; all other differences, p > .05.

phenomenon appears – if the sound change advances, indicating that the speaker is participating in the changes that take place around her – this would indicate that the rate of change is actually greater than figure 3.6 indicates. The table shows differences in F1 values for those vowels that were found to be moving primarily on that dimension, F2 for those changes that involved only F2, and distance moved along the front or back diagonal for the changes that followed those routes.

The first section of table 4.3 shows those vowels that give any indication of advancement in the later period. The two major allophones of /æh/ – /æhN/ (before nasals) and /æhS/ (before voiceless fricatives) – both show an advance of over 300 units along the front diagonal that is the path of increasing height for tense front vowels.

$$\text{Height}_{\text{FRONT}} = \sqrt{F2^2 - (2 * F1)^2}$$

The differences fall short of the .05 level of significance as the *t*-values indicate. The third allophone, /æh$/ (before /d/ in *mad, bad, glad*), shows a smaller and less significant effect in the same direction. Combining the three allophones does produce a significant result at the .01 level, with 40 degrees of freedom.

Of the other changes in progress, only (ay0), the centralization of /ay/ before voiceless finals, shows a sizeable advance along the back diagonal.

$$\text{Height}_{\text{BACK}} = \sqrt{F2^2 - F1^2}$$

Since this centralization involves a lowering of F1, the negative sign in the mean difference column indicates the advancement of the change; however, it falls well short of significance. There is a significant backward shift of the other allophones of /ay/, shown as /ayV/-F2. We know from individual observations that this tendency exists in Philadelphia, but it does not show up as a change in apparent time, so we cannot relate this fact to the current problem. Figure 4.10 shows the distribution of the /ay/ means involved with bars indicating one standard deviation.

The second section of table 4.3 shows the vowels that display any suggestion of a retreat in the later period. The middle range changes that involve the fronting of back upgliding vowels /uw/ and /ow/ all show a moderate decline of about 150 Hz in the F2 dimension. However, the scatter of tokens is such that they all fall well short of significance. When the four allophones are combined in a single index, the effect is not augmented.[26] Although the consistency of this effect is striking, it is not enough in itself to argue for an age-grading effect.

---

[26] Because of the skewing of the distribution of tokens of /owC/ and /owF/, the age difference disappears when they are combined.

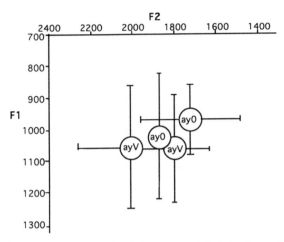

Figure 4.10. Means and standard deviations of (ay) for Jenny Rosetti at age 68 and 85

The third section of the table is by far the largest: it shows the vowels that give no significant indication of change, and it confirms the general stability of the system. Most of the mean differences are small; those that do show sizeable differences are well within the range of chance fluctuation.

We will want to pay particular attention to the three new and vigorous changes: the raising and fronting of /aw/ and checked /ey/, and the raising and backing of /ay/ before voiceless consonants. The (aw) variable shows no significant change in either direction. As noted above the (ay0) variable means do not differ significantly, but in the 1990 recording, several tokens appeared in a truly centralized and backed position. Figure 4.11 shows this distribution: though it is suggestive, Fischer's exact test shows that it may arise through chance in 1 case out of 6.

The same pattern appears in the case of (eyC). Here there is no suggestion of a shift in the overall mean, but once again advanced tokens appeared in the 1990 interview, as shown in figure 4.12. In this case, the distribution is not so likely to be the result of chance. Three of the 11 tokens of (eyC) were in this advanced position in 1990, but none of the 21 tokens were in 1973. In only 1 case out of 33 would such a pattern arise by chance.

This development of the Philadelphia vowel system for one speaker in real time is characteristic of the relatively small number that have been investigated so far. There is no overall change that would justify a reinterpretation of the apparent-time data as the result of age grading. The most significant shifts are in the reverse direction: they show older speakers influenced slightly by the changes taking place around them. Although the

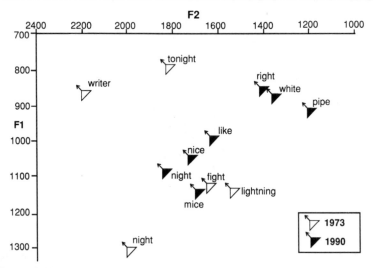

Figure 4.11. Distribution of (ay0) tokens of Jenny Rosetti at age 68 and 85

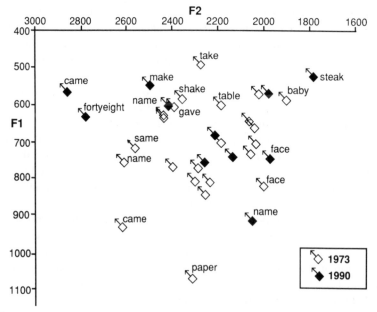

Figure 4.12. Distribution of (eyC) tokens of Jenny Rosetti at age 68 and 85

advanced position of (æh) is the most striking effect, this is most likely to be a stylistic shift. Since (æh) is the oldest and most socially marked of the Philadelphia changes, we can expect that speakers will show less and less social correction as they get older. The marginal effects seen in the newer sound changes can more likely be viewed as borrowing than as over-all shifts.[27] The statistical stability of the system can be contrasted sharply with the significant differences across speakers of different ages reflected in figure 3.6.

The acquisition of the Philadelphia dialect

Further inferences concerning the stability of individual systems can be found in Payne's (1976, 1980) work on the acquisition of the Philadelphia dialect. The longitudinal studies of the Philadelphia speakers focus on older speakers in a constant environment, where we have the least reason to expect change. Payne's research instead focuses on adults in their 30s and 40s who were raised in other areas using well-documented phonologi-cal patterns, and indicates what changes in their system were brought about by 10 or 20 years of exposure to the very different environment of the Philadelphia dialect area.

Payne's study used the same neighborhood that was selected by LCV to represent upper middle class speech in Philadelphia. This was King of Prussia, a new community that had grown up since World War II as indus-trial parks in the area attracted the automotive, electronic, and computer industries. Approximately half of the residents came from Philadelphia, and half came from neighboring dialect areas: New York City, New England, and the Midwest. Payne's investigation focused on the success of the children of in-migrant families in learning the Philadelphia dialect. We will be looking at her results at several points in this volume, particu-larly in relation to the complex split of Philadelphia short **a** into tense and lax forms. Here we are interested in comparing out-of-state children and adults in their acquisition of the lower-level Philadelphia sound changes of figure 3.6.

Children who came to the Philadelphia area when they were less than 10 years old showed a very high rate of acquisition. For example, 25 of the 34 children came from dialect areas with back /uw/ and /ow/; 13 showed only fronted tokens of /uw/ and 17 only fronted tokens of /ow/, and no children failed to show some fronting.

Figure 4.13a displays the principal long and upgliding vowels in the sys-tem of Joyce Cameron, 11, who came to Philadelphia from Cleveland when she was 4 years old. The characteristic Philadelphia pattern shows at every point.

[27] The idea that parents borrow some of their phonetic forms from their children is obvious when it comes to vocabulary, and can be seen in other forms of behavior as well, such as music and fashions (see Katz and Lazarsfeld 1955). Chapter 16 will review Goidanich's (1926) response to Gauchat's study of Charmey, which argued that instead of sound change, he had found only patterns of borrowings between generations.

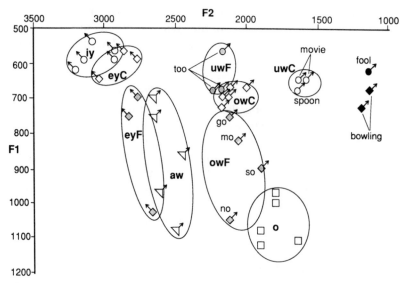

Figure 4.13a. Vowel system of Joyce Cameron, 11, Cleveland/King of Prussia
Shaded symbols = free vowels

- The front upgliding vowel /ey/ is split into two parts: the checked vowels in *ate, name,* and *date* are in high position, overlapping /iy/,
  reflecting the retrograde movement of this allophone in the Philadelphia system.
- The monosyllabic free vowels in *days, say,* and *bay* follow a radically
  different pattern, extending to fully open position.
- The Philadelphia /aw/ is faithfully reproduced, with an [e] nucleus that
  glides back and down. Only one /aw/ token is in low position.
- The back vowels show the regular fronting of /uw/ and /ow/ except
  before /l/, where *fooling* and *bowling* are in extreme back position, sharply differentiated from the other vowels.
- There is a split between checked and free /ow/, parallel to the conditioning of /ey/: checked *most, road,* etc., are high, whereas free *no,
  go, so* extend to low position.[28] The free *too* is the most fronted of the
  /uw/ words, reflecting the Philadelphia pattern.

In King of Prussia, the parents of out-of-state children showed minimal

---

[28] This is not the most characteristic Philadelphia pattern, as figure 3.6 shows. Normally, the
free /ow/ class is more fronted than checked /ow/, rather than more open. This part of the
system represents a Cameronian reinterpretation of the Philadelphia system.

tendencies to acquire the Philadelphia dialect. Figure 4.13b displays the corresponding system of Anna Cameron, 35, Joyce's mother, who had also spent 7 years in Philadelphia. Her upgliding vowels show the intact Cleveland pattern at each point.

- The long vowels /iy/ and /ey/ are compact in high front position, and free and checked allophones are undifferentiated: the /ey/ class includes *ate, stable, date,* and *play.*
- The /aw/ nucleus is in low back position, with no reflection of the special Philadelphia phonetics.
- /uw/ and /ow/ are in high and mid position. One token of *too* shows some fronting. But most importantly, there is no differentiation of vowels before /l/. As the figure shows, *school* is no backer than *movies,* and *bowling* is distributed with all other /ow/ words.

This difference between children and adults can be ascribed to biological changes in the parents' language-learning abilities, to differences in the social environment of parents and children, or to differences in social motivation. For our studies in apparent time, the important fact is that the phonological patterns of the adults remained stable.

The stability of category structure

Although the aging process or a new environment causes some variation in the realization of phonetic tokens and in the output of low-level phonetic

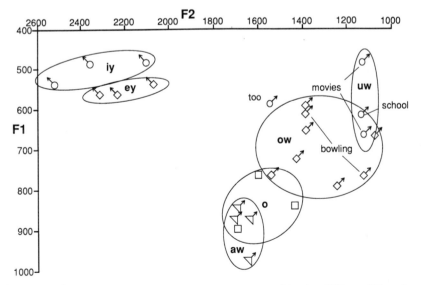

Figure 4.13b. Vowel system of Anna Cameron, 35, Cleveland/King of Prussia

rules, there is considerable stability in the underlying structure – the distribution of lexical entries in the categories of the system. Many people who travel through different dialect areas are convinced that they change their speech radically with their environment: that they are in effect "chameleons." But close examination of their speech shows that the changes are less extensive and more limited than they thought. The distribution of lexical tokens in phonemic categories is the most stable feature of the dialect and serves to define the dialect origin of a speaker with considerable precision.

This stability of category structure is obvious in the longitudinal studies of Philadelphia speakers exemplified by Jenny Rosetti. It also appears clearly in the behavior of the in-migrant adults in King of Prussia. More dramatic demonstration has come from several judicial cases where the principle of category stability has had important legal consequences. One involved a cargo handler in Los Angeles, Paul Prinzivalli, who was accused of making a series of threatening telephone calls to the Pan American ticket office (Labov 1988). Prinzivalli was a New Yorker, and the Los Angeles police, prosecutors, and judges thought that the recorded telephone threats were made by a New Yorker. In fact, the recordings showed the vowel system of Eastern New England, with a single low back vowel in which *bomb*, *on* and *off* are merged as /ɒ/ (figure 4.14a). Prinzivalli was recorded repeating the same messages; the analysis of his vowel system showed the New York City pattern in exact detail, with three phonemes in place of one: the low central vowel /a/ in *on*; the midback /ah/ in *bomb*; and the high back ingliding /oh/ in *off* (figure 4.14b).

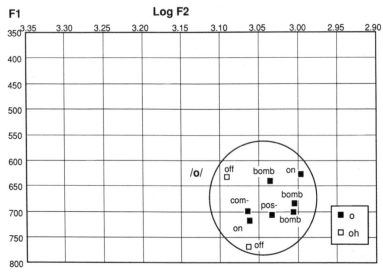

Figure 4.14a. Low back vowel phoneme of the bomb threat caller

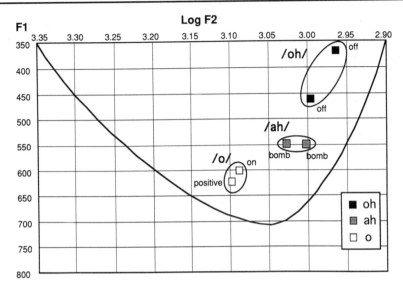

Figure 4.14b.   Back vowel phonemes of the bomb threat caller

After this testimony, the judge asked the defendant to rise and repeat the oath of allegiance to the United States. He then asked me if I could indicate any defining features of New York City speech in this passage. Among other things, I was able to point out the tense vowel in *flag*. The New York City dialect has tense /æh/ before all voiced stops, but in communities in near-by northern New Jersey, the first environment that shows a lax vowel is that before /g/. It was evident to the court as a matter of objective fact that the two speech patterns were uttered by different individuals, and Prinzivalli was acquitted on the basis of this evidence.[29]

Conclusion

We thus have two firm bodies of evidence on the stability of phonological systems. One set, consisting of trend studies, shows that variables operating at high levels of social awareness are modified throughout a speaker's lifetime, with consistent age-grading in the community. The other set, including community, family, and individual studies, shows that the phonological

[29] Sharon Ash acted as expert witness in a parallel case the following year, involving a Philadelphian who was accused of making threats to burn down a warehouse. The recorded telephone threats showed none of the defining features of the Philadelphia dialect, but the defendant, who had lived in New Jersey for many years, had preserved all these characteristics, and in particular the tensed and fronted nucleus of /aw/ in the name of the warehouse, *Mr. Howe*. Ash, who organized the dialect information for the defense, did a test survey of individuals who were asked to disguise their voices over the telephone. The subjects modified tempo, voice quality, and intonation, but none modified the segmental features specific to their geographical dialect.

categories that underlie the surface variation remain stable. Between these two is a vast array of data concerning the phonetic realizations of vowel systems, which show quantitative and qualitative differences across generations. These indicate that generational change rather than communal change is the basic model for sound change. As the panel studies based on reinterviews of the same subjects proceed, we will be able to state with more certainty how much age-grading is present in these records. From present indications, apparent-time studies may understate the actual rate of sound change, since older speakers show a limited tendency toward communal change, participating to a small extent in the changes taking place around them.

Part B

Chain Shifting

5

General Principles of Vowel Shifting

5.1 The constraints problem and the search for universals

In 1968, Weinreich, Labov, and Herzog outlined five problems to be solved in establishing the empirical foundations of a theory of language change. The first of these, the *constraints* problem, is to discover whatever constraints may exist on the form, direction, or structural character of linguistic changes. This definition of the constraints problem is not inconsistent with the search for a "universal grammar" that is the central thrust of formal linguistics today. The extension of this program to the study of language change would seek to establish a set of principles that define the concept "possible linguistic change" and that distinguish possible from impossible changes. At the heart of this universalistic approach is the idea that there are abstract principles of language present in all human beings, which define or permit certain types of language change and prohibit others: in other words, that there are some possible linguistic actions that human beings never perform, since they are incapable of doing so, and that changes that depend on such actions will never be found.

There is no contradiction between the goals of the universalistic approach and the empirical program that is projected here. The aims are the same: to find the most general principles that govern language structure and language change. The two approaches differ in that the historical and evolutionary approach does not assume that there are any principles of linguistic behavior that are so isolated from all other factors that their operation will determine the outcome in every case. Studies of linguistic variation and change indicate that any such principle or rule, no matter how powerful, may be overridden in situations where many factors are unfavorable to its application.

Nevertheless, the initial results in this chapter will seem at first to contradict this statement. Section 5.2 begins with reports of chain shifts extracted from the historical record, inspecting and comparing their similarities in structure and direction. When a number of English dialects are charted, and when these results are compared with the array of chain shifts reported in the historical record, constraints emerge with a compelling, exceptionless character that would satisfy the most stringent demands of a universalistic approach. I will present these general principles of chain shifting in the spirit in which they were discovered – as unidirectional principles of linguistic change.

The field of view will then be enlarged to consider a number of apparent exceptions to the general principles, including retrograde movements that reverse the unidirectional principles. Some of these will be resolved within the view of phonological space that is developed in the chapters to follow. But the success or failure of this enterprise will not rest upon the defense of exceptionless principles. From the variationist perspective, we will ultimately accept the finding that there are no directions of vowel shifting that are forbidden to speakers of human language, but we will establish that some directions are taken far more often than others. Beyond the achievements of this chapter, we will begin to see the outlines of a broader study that will replace our qualitative principles with quantitative statements of a more sophisticated kind.

The systematic view of chain shifting that is developed here will then lead to the study of unresolved problems involving the relations of two fundamental kinds of phonological change: merger and chain shifting.

5.2 Three principles of vowel shifting

This section will present three general principles that govern the chain shifting of vowels.[1] They will first be stated in a form that applies to the completed chain shifts of the historical record; later they will be revised to take into account more precise information on chain shifts in progress.

(1) PRINCIPLE I
In chain shifts, long vowels rise.
PRINCIPLE II
In chain shifts, short vowels fall.
PRINCIPLE IIA
In chain shifts, the nuclei of upgliding diphthongs fall.
PRINCIPLE III
In chain shifts, back vowels move to the front.

Principle I has no clear exceptions in the data to be reviewed. Principle II applies generally to most of the available examples, but the historical record does contain exceptions (see section 5.4). Principle IIa applies to an

---

[1] This and most of the following sections are based on the original presentation of this topic in chapter 4 of LYS. A preliminary version of these principles was presented in Labov and Wald 1969 and further developed in Labov 1991.

even larger number of cases. It is properly seen as a part of Principle II, since the nuclei of upgliding diphthongs are normally single morae.[2] Principle III also applies quite generally, but a small number of exceptions have come to light in both past and current sound changes.

All of these principles were foreshadowed in observations made by Sweet (1888:19–21). But Sweet wrote before the concept of chain shifting had become general in linguistics, and his observations referred to individual sound changes. Although these principles may hold statistically for isolated changes, they do not apply with enough force to capture the general interest of linguists, and Sweet's principles were effectively lost. Principle III was reintroduced into the study of chain shifts by Martinet (1955) and Haudricourt and Juilland (1949). The three principles of chain shifting have reemerged in current studies of linguistic change in progress, where they apply with sweeping regularity to a very large number of vowel shifts.

Though these principles are stated in terms of chain shifts, I will not hesitate to use them to describe and classify individual movements where they apply.

The functional explanation of chain shifting

It is theoretically interesting in itself that these principles appear as powerful constraints on language change only in chain shifts. If the movement of vowels were entirely independent of each other, we would expect the force of any such principle to be diluted as we considered more than one movement at a time. If, for example, the tendency of /ɔ:/ and /o:/ to rise rather than fall each had a probability of .8, and the movements of these vowels were independent of each other, then the probability of /ɔ:/ and /o:/ both rising would be .64. Instead, the available evidence places it close to 1.00. This appears to confirm the basic notion that chain shifts reflect the functional economy of the vowel system: vowels move together to avoid merger and preserve their capacity to distinguish words (Martinet 1955).[3]

The term *functional* might well be taken to refer to a wide variety of ends-means relations. It originally indicated the linguistic function of communicating referential information, but there are many other functions that might be introduced, bearing in mind Bühler's (1934) trilogy of representational, affective, and directive uses and the further elaborations by Jakobson (1960) and Hymes (1961) to include aesthetic, ludic, metalinguistic, and phatic functions. Such wider excursions into functional theory are not immediately relevant to the major problems of this work. Many investigations show that phonological variables like chain shifts and mergers are

---

[2] This statement will be modified in the next few chapters, and ultimately Principle IIa will be restated to specify "*short* nuclei of upgliding diphthongs."

[3] This functional interpretation is not the only way to view chain shifts. For an opposing view, see chapter 17.

typically free of any emphatic, affective, or accommodative functions, and that they lie well below the level of social awareness (Herold 1990; Labov 1989a). Functional analysis of phonological changes must involve the capacity of features and phonemes to distinguish words and thereby convey representational information. If this capacity is diminished, and mergers occur, it is not to serve some other hidden function of the linguistic system. We may indeed call upon some latent functions of language in dealing with the motivation of sound change and its continued renewal, but that profound problem, important as it is, is not the central topic of this section. Therefore *the functional explanation of sound change* will refer here to the effort to account for the rotations, collapse, or expansion of the sound system through correlations with the amount of referential information conveyed by the system.

Martinet's concern with chain shifting springs from this relation of chain shifts to functional explanation. Principle III is an important element in Martinet's (1952, 1955) interrelation of structure, function, and economy, and his explanation of this principle is the only current explanation available for any of the three principles. In Martinet's view, Principle III is the result of two opposing tendencies: the asymmetry of the articulatory space of the supraglottal tract, and the phonological drive for symmetry. According to Martinet, more articulatory space is available for front vowels than for back vowels. Although this space easily accommodates four degrees of height for front vowels, the same array of four vowels produces overcrowding in the back, with a consequent threat to the margins of security of the back vowels. The pressure to relieve this overcrowding results in the movement of back vowels to the front. Haudricourt and Juilland (1949) reviewed all available examples of the movement of back vowels to the front in chain shifts, in French, Swedish, Greek, and other languages. They found strong confirmation of Martinet's views: in each case, the fronting was accompanied by a prior development of four levels of height in the back vowels.

We will return to this particular explanation and to the evaluation of functional explanations of chain shifting in general later in this section and at the end of chapter 6.

THE DEFINITION OF CHAIN SHIFTING

In order to demonstrate, defend, or explicate the principles of chain shifting, it is necessary first to define a chain shift. Chain shifts in general consist of minimal or extended chain shifts. A *minimal chain shift* is a change in the position of two phonemes in which one moves away from an original position that is then occupied by the other.[4] (Thus a chain shift is dis-

---

[4] The term *occupied* might seem to imply that the second phoneme takes up exactly the same position in phonetic space. It will ultimately appear that this is too strict, and that in many

tinguished from its opposite – a *merger* – in that a merger is a change in the relations of two vowels in which one assumes or approximates the position held by the other.) The two phonemes of a minimal chain shift may be referred to more briefly as the *entering* and *leaving* elements. An *extended chain shift*, then, is any combination of minimal chain shifts in which the entering element of one minimal chain shift replaces the leaving element of a second.

These definitions are neutral with respect to which is the *initiating* and which is the *responding* element in a temporal or causative sense, or indeed whether the two elements move together.[5] The schematic representations of chain shifts to follow will show the entering element as A, and the leaving elements as B, C, etc. A linear representation of a minimal chain shift will then look like (2).

(2) /A/ → /B/ →

The simple movement of A to position B will be represented as /A → B/, and the merger of two phonemes A and B will be represented as /A/ → /B/. In more complex cases, this notation will be useful in distinguishing a series of shifts from a series of movements, both obeying the general principles of chain shifting. Thus a single vowel may move /A → B → C → D/, as in the case of /ī → iy → ey → ay/, a movement that forms part of the Great Vowel Shift and follows Principle II. A similar phonetic pattern appears in modern sound changes but involves the chain shifting of four distinct phonemes:

/iy/ → /ey/ → /ay/ → /oy/ →

CAUSAL LINKS

Though the definition of chain shifting does not establish a direction of causation, the linguistic context in which these events occur establishes a clear causal relation. The shift /A/ → /B/ → indicates a combination of events that have led to a situation in which the phonemic inventory /A/, /B/ is preserved. If only A had moved, or if A had moved before /B/, then there would now be only one phoneme /A = B/. Therefore, given the existence of sound changes affecting A and B, the chain shift in this form can be considered the immediate cause of the current capacity of the system to make distinctions. If the vowel system had shown parallel changes such

chain shifts, the second phoneme takes up a position that approximates that of the older one but is not exactly the same. (See chapter 9 on changes of subsystem and chapter 12 on near-mergers.)
[5] The question of push chains versus drag or pull chains will be discussed below.

as (3i) or unconnected changes such as (3ii), then no such causal relation would exist.

(3)

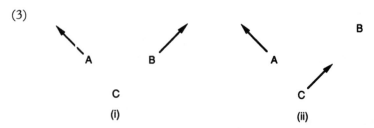

(i)　　　　　　　　　　　　　　　　(ii)

In (3i), if B had not been raised, the system would have been phonetically skewed, but this would not affect the amount of information it conveyed. In (3ii), if A had not been raised, the system would have been somewhat more symmetrical, but the functional utility of the system in the sense defined would have remained the same. But in (2), if B had not moved out of the position that A occupied, the system would have been radically altered in a functional sense.

Principles I and II make clear predictions about the basic cases where the entering and leaving elements differ in height:

(4)

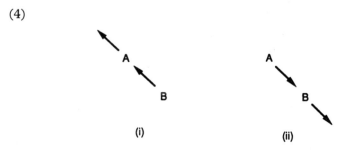

(i)　　　　　　　　　　　　　　　(ii)

In these simple cases, Principles I and II assert that (4i) is predicted for long vowels and (4ii) is strongly favored for short vowels, but that (4ii) will never occur with long vowels and (4i) rarely with short vowels.

In many cases, the leaving element is high or low and cannot move any farther in this direction. The leaving element may then undergo a nonlinear differentiation, as suggested by (5). Such nonlinear movements usually involve shifts to other subsystems – monophthongization, diphthongization, shortening, or lengthening – which will be considered in Chapter 9.

The chain-shifting principles do not apply in any obvious way to symmetrical systems that have as many front vowels as back ones, as in (6). If A, B, C are long vowels, what do Principles I–III predict about a chain shift that involves them? They do not predict whether A and B will rise, or whether B and C will rise. They do say that if A and B rise, C will not fall unless it is shortened.

(5)

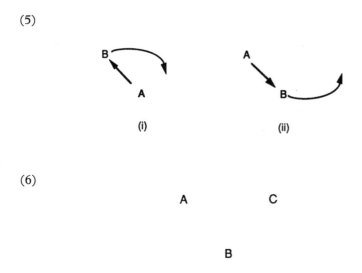

(i)   (ii)

(6)

     A   C

          B

How do these principles relate to vowel systems that do not have length distinctions, like Romance? In this case, the single vowel series behaves like the long vowels, and follows Principle I. To put it another way, the only simple vowels that follow Principle II are those that are marked as short in contrast to a series of long vowels.

Supporting evidence in the historical record

In searching the historical record for chain shifts, LYS cited instances of the three principles in a number of other languages – primarily from Indo-European, but also from other language families (see table 5.1). Certain languages are listed in several different columns in the table. That is because several principles regularly cooccur in characteristic patterns. Since it would be painfully redundant to study each application of each principle to each language, we will instead examine the major patterns of chain shifting and then how they are exemplified in particular languages.

5.3   The major patterns of chain shifting

As they are stated, the three principles of chain shifting are independent; but they are not free to combine in every possible way. A vowel can move front and down at the same time, or front and up, but it cannot move both up and down, and the principles do not mention movements to the back. It should not be surprising that the principles combine to produce only a small number of repeated patterns. The patterns originally recognized in LYS were based on the instrumental study of current dialects, but all but the fourth are well established in the historical record.

Table 5.1   Attested instances of the general principles of chain shifting in completed changes

Principle I raising of long vowels	Principle II lowering of short vowels	Principle IIa lowering of diphthongal nuclei	Principle III fronting of back vowels
English	North Frisian	English	Yiddish
German	Vegliote	Yiddish [Central]	Swedish
Yiddish		Yiddish [Western]	North Frisian
Swedish		Swedish	Romansh
Frisian		North Frisian	French
Portuguese		Romansh	Lettish
Swiss French		Vegliote	Greek
Romansh		Czech	Albanian
Greek		Lettish	Akha
Lithuanian		Korean	
Old Prussian			
Albanian			
Lappish			
Syriac			
Akha			

Conventions of the diagrams

The diagrams of this chapter are drawn in the simplest possible geometric form, reflecting the systems of features that are most widely used in historical phonology: high, mid, and low; front and back. The central position of /a/ is recognized only when the symmetry of the system demands it; otherwise, /a/ is shown as a back vowel, aligned with /o/ and /u/. The diagrams thus interpret the principles of chain shifting in terms of changes in distinctive features. Phonetic changes in redundant features are not necessarily relevant to the generalizations we are searching for. For example, lowering of front vowels within the phonetic vowel triangle usually involves some degree of backing, since the front-back distance between low vowels is much less than that between high vowels. This phonetic backing is not considered a violation of Principle III, and the phonological diagrams reflect this fact.

Historically attested graphic forms are shown in bold: **ie, uo**, etc. In historical descriptions, the phonemic status of a given vowel is not always made explicit, but unless evidence is given to the contrary, vowels are entered into the diagrams as phonemes. Phonemes are shown with the usual / / notation. When a vowel moves to a new phonetic position without either occupying the space formerly occupied by another phoneme or merging with it, its new phonetic form is shown in brackets [ ], even when this new phonetic notation is the letter conventionally used for the other phoneme in descriptions of the language. Brackets [ ] are also used for phonetic intermediate stages that must be assumed, when no corresponding graphic representation appears in the record.

To achieve consistency across diagrams, the segmental notation shows [w], [y], and [ə] for the targets of all glides. Thus the **ie** and **uo** of Germanic and Baltic are used in the discussion in the text, but they appear in the diagrams as [iə] and [uɔ]. Vowels interpreted as long in historical texts are usually indicated with a macron [v̄], and modern phonetic length is marked with a colon [v:].

In the diagrams that illustrate Pattern 1, the horizontal lines mark changes of subsystem (e.g., monophthong to diphthong) and the vertical lines mark changes of height within subsystems. (The principles that govern changes of subsystem fall outside the scope of this chapter, but are considered in chapter 9).

Pattern 1 chain shifts

The first pattern to be considered, shown in (7), is exemplified by the classic symmetry of the English Great Vowel Shift.

(7)   PATTERN 1

In (7), Principle I applies in the raising of the long vowels in both back and front, with the high vowels leaving the system of long monophthongs to become upgliding diphthongs. In the Great Vowel Shift itself, these patterns were realized as:

/ǣ/ → /ē/ → /ī → iy/
/ɔ̄/ → /ō/ → /ū → uw/

Principle II applies to the consequent lowering of the diphthongal nuclei, which from the descriptions of contemporary orthographers and grammarians would be represented as:

/iy → ey → ay/
/uw → ow → aw/

The actual mechanism of the Great Vowel Shift will be examined more closely in section 5.5; here we are simply concerned with the way in which Pattern 1 embodies the general principles of vowel shifting.

No other historical chain shift shows as elaborate a development of Pattern 1 as the English Great Vowel Shift, but the symmetrical raising and diphthongization characteristic of this pattern also appear in several other languages of northern Europe. As shown in (8), Common Czech (Kučera 1961) has undergone an upward movement of the mid tense vowels with diphthongization and lowering of the high tense vowels:

(8) THE CZECH VOWEL SHIFT

Common Czech contrasts with the standard literary form, where the shift did not take place. Urban speakers appear to move freely between the two forms, indicating that alternations of this sort can be grasped and applied by native speakers.[6]

A third example occurs in the Baltic language, Old Prussian (Schmalsteig 1964, 1968). The data are limited; but evidence of a Pattern 1 shift appears in Catechism texts. In Catechism II, old ē moved to ī while ī moved to ei, but in Catechism I, only the latter change is found. In all texts, a conditioned sound change moved ā to ū while ū shifted to ou or even au. Thus, there is some evidence that the lowering of diphthongal nuclei was operating in Old Prussian, maximizing the distance between nucleus and glide. Again, we can isolate in Old Prussian the coexistence of two distinct vowel systems, one more conservative and one more innovative, indicating the presence of an ongoing change and of social differentiation in the more advanced stages.

As shown in (9), Middle High German provides a somewhat more complex version of Pattern 1 that involves chain shifts across subsystems (Priebsch and Collinson 1958).

(9) THE MIDDLE HIGH GERMAN VOWEL SHIFT

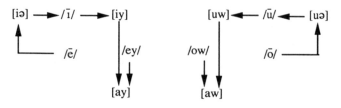

---

[6] The synchronic alternation does not actually correspond to a simultaneous historical process. The steps that led to the present contrast of Common Czech and standard Czech were separated by a considerable period.

The long mid vowels first rose in Old High German to ingliding vowels **ie** and **ou** (LYS:chap. 3). They were then monophthongized in Middle High German, but did not merge with the original long high vowels, which were in turn diphthongized to upgliding Vy and Vw. The nuclei of these new diphthongs were lowered to mid and then to low position, yielding modern [ay] and [aw]. The pair of original diphthongs **ei** /ey/ and **ou** /ow/ were lowered along with them, and there is a complete merger of /ey/ with /ay/ and /ow/ with /aw/ in the modern standard dialect.[7]

In Western Yiddish this process was continued further. As shown in (10), the original diphthongs **ei** and **ou** are now merged as monophthongal ā, and we infer that [ay] and [aw] were monophthongized and merged.

(10)   THE WESTERN YIDDISH VOWEL SHIFT

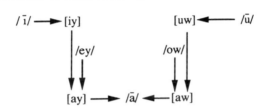

In the usual development from Middle High German a third series also participated in these changes: the front rounded vowels followed a development parallel to that of the front unrounded vowels at each stage.

Pattern 2 chain shifts

Pattern 2 involves all three principles, as shown in (11).

(11)   PATTERN 2

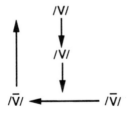

In this series of diagrams, horizontal arrows indicate distinctive fronting and backing, as well as changes of subsystem. In Pattern 2, a long back low vowel shifts to the front, following Principle III; the low front long vowel moves to high front position, following Principle I. In some cases,

---

[7] It is not clear when the merger took place: at mid position or at low position after a downward chain shift of *ei* and *ou*.

the new high front vowel develops an inglide; in others, it merges with /i/. The front short vowels fall, following Principle II.

Pattern 2 depends crucially on the existence of a low front /æ:/ and a relatively back /ɑ:/ or /ɔ:/, and as any taxonomy of vowel systems will show, this type of "square" system is much less common than the "triangular" systems with /e/ and /o/ flanking /a/. The chief instances of Pattern 2 are in modern English dialects that will be examined in chapter 6; examples in the historical record are not common. It is not accidental that the closest historical development parallel to modern Pattern 2 shifts is in North Frisian. Frisian shared with Anglo-Saxon the "Anglo-Frisian brightening" of Proto-West Germanic ā to ǣ. The ǣ phoneme, which also included the reflexes of monophthongized PWG **ai**, was then fronted and raised, developing an inglide in the *breaking* process that is widespread in Frisian.[8] Thus IE **ai** appears in the North Frisian dialects of Föhr and Amrum as *siap* 'soap', *sial* 'soul', *hial* 'whole', and IE ā as *bian* 'bone' (Wilts, Braren, and Hinrichsen 1986). Short /i/ falls to mid and low position, yielding *sat* 'sit', *batter* 'bitter', *madel* 'middle', and so on.

(12)   THE NORTH FRISIAN PATTERN 2 SHIFT

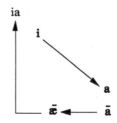

This is only part of a much more complex pattern, with considerable front-back symmetry, which we will consider below. The asymmetrical fronting of ā is the essential feature that brings it into the Pattern 2 framework. In other versions of Pattern 2, we will see that the creation of ingliding vowels is also highly characteristic of this pattern.[9]

Pattern 2 movement is also found in the history of Korean (Hong

---

[8] Breaking is often associated with the conditioned development of an inglide before /h, l, r, x/, etc., but unconditioned breaking of this type is a much more general process that will play a major role in the discussions to follow. It occurs quite frequently as long or tense vowels move from low to mid and high position, and is probably more common than the simple shift of monophthongs as in the Great Vowel Shift.

[9] Breaking is considerably more general in West Frisian, where /i:/ and /e:/ merge to /i:ə/, while /ɛ:/ and /a:/ follow a similar path that leads eventually to the short ingliding form /iə/ (Markey 1973).

1991:29; Lee 1961).[10] As shown in (13), in the transition from Old Korean to 13th-century Early Middle Korean, back **a** shifted to a central or front position, and the vowel that was occupying that slot was raised and fronted to fill a mid front hole in the pattern.

(13)   THE OLD KOREAN PATTERN 2 SHIFT

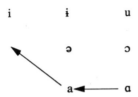

Perhaps the best-known example of fronting and raising along these dimensions is provided by the history of Greek, shown in (14). Rather than a Pattern 2 chain shift, this is an example of a Pattern 2 merger. The numbers on each path indicate the ordering of the events. Long ā and ɛ̄ moved along the same path, as in Frisian, but no inglide developed and no length distinction was maintained. The result in the modern language is a sweeping merger in /i/.[11]

(14)   THE GREEK PATTERN 2 MERGER

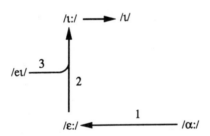

A Pattern 2 chain shift appears in the vowel shifts of the extinct Romance language Vegliote, spoken until 1899 on the island of Veglia in the Adriatic Sea off the coast of Yugoslavia (Hadlich 1965). As illustrated in (15), in an early period ɛ and ɔ moved upward to become ingliding vowels. Later

---

[10] The Korean data are cited in Hong 1991, with other references. I am particularly indebted to Yunsook Hong for drawing my attention to the complex Korean shifts. I have used a phonemic notation that reflects the features of the sounds in Old Korean; the traditional notation used by Lee and Hong reflects the sounds of modern Korean. Though this stage of the development of Korean fits in with the general principles of chain shifting, the later changes to be discussed below form a set of striking counterexamples.
[11] In addition to the mergers shown here, /oy/, /u/, and /u:/ eventually merged with /i:/.

(in Hadlich's Period IV), the short vowels moved downward in a chain shift that terminated in a merger in /a/.

(15)   THE VEGLIOTE VOWEL SHIFTS

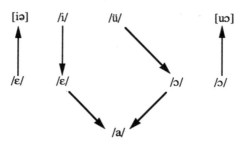

Do these movements follow the general principles of chain shifting in (1)? In the traditional notation, we see /ɛ/ and /ɔ/ rising at one stage and falling at another. If they are short vowels, they should not rise to high position in the first place. Like other Romance languages, Vegliote had lost the distinction between long and short well before these developments took place. In most other Romance languages, the single series of vowels follows the pattern of the tense or long vowels, which we may consider the unmarked case. To have a series of "short" vowels, it is necessary that they be opposed to some other series of "long" vowels as shorter or less peripheral. In this case, we do have the basis for such an opposition /i, ü/ stand in opposition to /iɛ/ and /uɔ/. These ingliding diphthongs developed from an /ɛ/ and /ɔ/ at an early stage. We can infer from the patterns of many other languages that these were tensed or lengthened vowels that developed inglides as they rose from lower mid to upper mid position. They then shifted to falling diphthongs /iɛ/ and /uɔ/, which were subsequently smoothed to /i/ and /u/. This lengthening, raising, and breaking of low vowels has already been exemplified by the development of (æh) in American English in chapters 3 and 4, and in North Frisian in (12) above. Before the monophthongization of /iɛ/ and /uɔ/ in Vegliote, these vowels undoubtedly formed a long subsystem, in opposition to the short vowels, which fell in accordance with Principle II.

There is more to the Vegliote story than this. Close ẹ and ọ ultimately developed into diphthongs with open nuclei (*fajd* 'faith', *sawl* 'sun'). This implies that they rose to high position, were diphthongized, and fell in the fashion of Pattern 1, and were therefore part of the long or tense series as opposed to the short vowels, /i, ɛ, u, ɔ/.[12]

---

[12] The only other Romance language to show such a pattern is Romansh, which is in close contact with Germanic languages. Though Vegliote was also an isolated language at the periphery of the Romance world, its contacts with Venetian and Serbo-Croatian could not be responsible for this development. Instead, I would suggest that it instantiates the independent

Pattern 3 chain shifts

Pattern 3 chain shifts, illustrated in (16), combine the raising of vowels under Principle I and fronting under Principle III. This pattern is frequently found in Romance languages, where there is only a single unmarked vowel series, and also in Germanic languages, where it affects the long vowels. As shown in (16i) and (16ii), it has two forms: the first operates on monophthongs; the second involves diphthongization of back vowels before the nucleus is fronted.[13]

(16) PATTERN 3

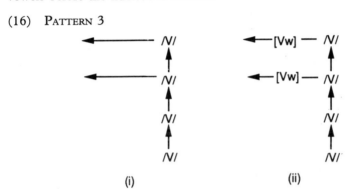

(i)   (ii)

The historical examples that we will consider here are all of type (i); in the discussion of contemporary changes in progress in chapter 6, examples of type (ii) will play a major role.

Germanic scholars have been conscious of the Pattern 3 shift from the earliest period. Prokosch (1930) presents the changes illustrated in (17) as the "Germanic Vowel Shift," representing changes that took place from Indo-European to Proto-Germanic.

(17)

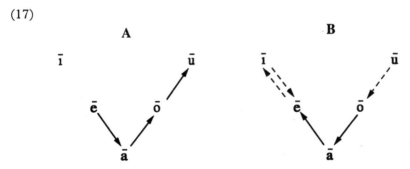

development of a more complex phonological space than that of other Romance languages. In the terms to be introduced in chapter 6, this would imply the existence of peripheral and nonperipheral tracks in both front and back.

[13] In some Pattern 3 chain shifts, the mid back vowel is fronted as well as the high back vowel. But as later discussions will show, this is not a proper part of the chain shift, as it is defined in this chapter.

The left-hand part, A, resembles the Pattern 3 shift that affected the long vowels, with the fronting components added in modern Germanic. The right-hand part, B, shows Prokosch's initial suggestion for an opposed lowering movement of the short vowels, following what we have called Principle II. The dashed lines indicate conditioned changes: the lowering of short ĭ and ŭ took place only before **h** and **r**, and in West Germanic when the next syllable contained **a**, whereas contrary raisings took place under other conditions. To maintain a general downshift of short vowels in Germanic, we will have to assume a series of general lowering, conditioned raising, and conditioned lowering. Even Prokosch, who believed in a general Germanic vowel shift, was forced to reject B as a particular statement about Germanic. It simply illustrates the principle emphasized by Sievers, that Germanic short and long vowels tend to move in opposite directions. We will return to this point at the end of chapter 6, in discussing possible explanations of the chain shift principles.

Pattern 3 shifts have been at the center of the functionally oriented discussions of Martinet and his students. Four European examples were treated by Haudricourt and Juilland (1949): French, the Portuguese of San Miguel, Swedish, and Greek. LYS presents a range of other instances of Pattern 3: from Western Europe, the Swiss French dialects of the Valais and Romansch; from Eastern Europe, Yiddish, Lithuanian, and Albanian; and outside of Indo-European, West Syriac and Akha, a Lolo-Burmese language.

The classic Pattern 3 chain shift is exemplified in Swedish and East Norwegian, one of the earliest chain shifts recognized (Haugen 1970; Benediktsson 1970).[14] It was initiated by the early lengthening of short /a/, and thus qualifies as a push chain (Benediktsson 1970). The next step was the backing of the original long ā to ɔ, yielding the Old Scandinavian system shown in (18). The Pattern 3 chain shift then applied to produce the raising and fronting shown by the arrows.

Because there was already a front rounded long vowel [ȳ] in the system, a contrast of rounding developed, with the older [ȳ] showing out-rounding, and the new [ü] distinguished by in-rounding. The distinction between out-rounding and in-rounding then adds another dimension to the structural constraints on chain shifting, though limited to this one position (Hammerberg 1970).

This is one of the examples cited by Haudricourt and Juilland to support their thesis that the fronting of back vowels occurs in response to overcrowding in the back: to reduce the four levels of height shown in (18). This is not the only way to reduce the number of height contrasts: other descendants of Old Scandinavian have diphthongized ɔ to /aw/.

---

[14] Benediktsson notes that it was described as a chain shift by the Norwegian dialectologist Amund B. Larsen.

(18) THE SWEDISH PATTERN 3 SHIFT

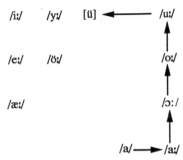

The many other Western European examples of Pattern 3 are too well known to need reviewing here. At one point, it seemed that Pattern 3 was an areal phenomenon, dependent on the regional dispersion of phonemic /ü/. There is indeed a heavy concentration of this chain shift pattern in Western Europe. But it is also found in Eastern and Southern Europe. The chain shift of Proto-Southern Yiddish shows /o:/ → /u: → ü/, with a subsequent unrounding of [ü] to [i]. The /o:/ that was raised to /u:/ had earlier been raised from /ā/. Thus, Central Yiddish /ši:l/ 'school' corresponds to NHG *Schule*, but CY /šu:l/ 'bowl' corresponds to NHG *Schale* (Herzog 1965).

In a more distant branch of Indo-European, we find evidence of a Pattern 3 shift in Albanian, illustrated in (19). PIE **ā**, **ō**, and **ū** are represented in Albanian by /o/, /e/, and /i/, respectively (Brugmann 1922). Since PIE **au** is represented by Albanian /a/, it seems clear that a chain shift is involved.

(19) THE ALBANIAN VOWEL SHIFT

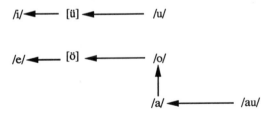

This is the variety of Pattern 3 (ii) where the fronting affects both high and mid back vowels, the most common variety in current English dialects. The intermediate stage [ö] is no longer attested, since PIE **ō** is fronted and unrounded to **ē** in Albanian; but some evidence of the [ü] remains.

There are also truncated cases of Pattern 3 that do not show fronting.

The Lithuanian development illustrated in (20) (Senn 1966) is limited to the raising portion of Pattern 3.

(20)　LITHUANIAN RAISING

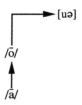

The development of inglides as long mid vowels rise, yielding **uo** from ō, is quite general in Eastern Balto-Slavic as well as in Gallo-Romance and Frisian. But whereas Lettish has only this movement, Lithuanian also has the raising of **ā** that identifies this as a chain shift.

Outside of Indo-European, a similar shift appears in West Syriac (Nöldeke 1880): /ā/ → /ō/ → /ū/, with a merger of /ō/ and /ū/ in high position. No other examples have been found in Semitic languages so far; this is only natural since most Semitic vowel systems have not developed far beyond the three-member system.

The Pattern 3 chain shift most remote from the Indo-European examples appears in Akha, a Lolo-Burmese language spoken by hill tribesmen living in an area overlapping China, Burma, Thailand, and Laos. Data on nine dialects have been examined by Bradley (1969) from reports by Lewis, Nisida, Roux, and others. Dialect 6, spoken in the central area between Burma and China, is of particular interest here because of the extensive fronting of the high back vowels. Akha has a series of glottal vowels in checked, glottal-tone syllables, as opposed to plain vowels in open-tone syllables. There was first of all a classic Pattern 3 shift of back vowels in glottal-tone syllables (underlined), as shown in (21).

(21)　THE AKHA CHAIN SHIFT I

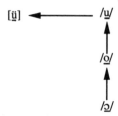

The older /u̠/, which then appeared as a new glottal phoneme /ṵ̈/, already had a counterpart in open-tone syllables. This vowel developed further to open /y/, followed by a fronting of open /u/. This left a considerable gap in the back: there was no /u/, /o/, or /ɔ/. Two of the three were supplied by another complex shift: /a/ rose to /ɔ/, while glottal-tone /o̯/ moved to nonglottal /o/. In parallel, the place of open-tone /a/ was filled by /ɔ̯/, which also lost its glottalization. These developments are shown in (22).

(22)   THE AKHA CHAIN SHIFT II

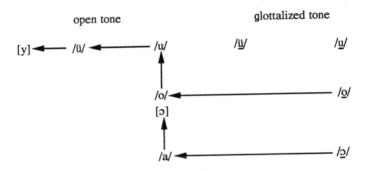

The second shift in open-tone syllables may also be considered an instance of Pattern 3, with the additional complication that the full raising of /a/ was forestalled by the entrance of glottal /o̯/ into the open-tone system. The final result is an unbalanced system with /ü/ but no /u/.[15] If the principles of chain shifting continue to apply in Akha, we would expect a further raising of /ɔ/ → /o → u/ in the open-tone subsystem.

Combined patterns

The examples given so far have focused primarily on the patterns individually. It is not uncommon to find assemblies of chain shifts that show the combined effects of all three patterns, which in turn exemplify several principles of chain shifting. Two such examples from Indo-European will indicate the ways in which chain shifting can affect entire vowel systems.

CHAIN SHIFTS IN EAST LETTISH DIALECTS
The East Lettish dialects reported in Endzelin's (1922) monumental study provide a richer inventory of vowel shifts than any other language, including the symmetrical pattern of raising and diphthongization that makes up Pattern 1, the raising in back vowels characteristic of Pattern 2, and the parallel development of ingliding vowels that feed into the chain shifts of monophthongs.

---

[15] This is one of the many counterexamples to the proposed universal that /ü/ always implies /u/ (Sedlak 1969).

Lettish and Lithuanian show a general raising of the tense mid vowels to high ingliding **iɛ** and **uɔ**, as we saw in (20); and a new long /e:/ and /o:/ are supplied from other sources. The phonemes that enter this complex series of shifts are shown in boldface in (23); these include the long mid vowels /e:, o:/, the high ingliding vowels /iə, uə/, and the long high vowels /i:, u:/.

(23)   EAST LETTISH CHAIN SHIFTS

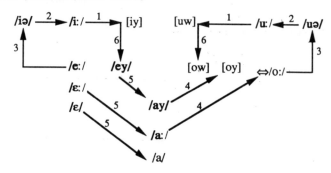

The numbers in (23) do not reflect the actual historical stages so much as a set of logical relations, including (under a pull chain model) what orderings would be necessary to arrive at the set of mergers and distinctions shown in the final configuration.

- Steps 1, 2, and 3 insert the ingliding vowels into the familiar symmetry of Pattern 1. The high monophthongs develop upglides; the ingliding diphthongs become monophthongs; and the mid long monophthongs rise and develop inglides, as we have witnessed in many other languages.
- Step 4 is an asymmetrical addition that adjoins Pattern 3 to the back portion of Pattern 1. The raising of the nucleus of /ay/ is motivated not by a chain shift relation but by the identification of the nucleus of /ay/ and /a:/.[16]
- Step 5 is a downward shift of the three mid front nuclei in /ɛ:/, /ɛ/, and /ey/.
- Step 6 is really the completion of Step 1, and might be included in it, but it could not logically be completed until /ey/ had been lowered in Step 5. Since there was no original /ow/, there is no problem in the back. At this point, however, the discrete pull chain model creates problems, since it presupposes a stage where monophthongal /i:/ and

---

[16] Chapter 6 will present a number of English dialects where a similar generalization unites the movements of /ay/ and /oy/ with those of /ahr/ and /ohr/.

/u:/ contrast with diphthongal /iy/ and /uw/. This is not a stable configuration, as far as I know. Apparently the phonetic differences are
not great enough to maintain the distinction, and we must assume
some degree of further lowering of the nucleus along with Step 2.

Two chain shifts of considerable complexity can be traced in this development:

/ɛ̄/ → /ā/ → /ō/ → /uə/ → /ū → ow/
/ē/ → /iə/ → /ī/ → /ey/ → /ay → oy/

The pattern of (23) contains many movements that exemplify the principles of chain shifting, but involved with them are several movements in
directions contrary to those principles. The movements of the front diphthongs are coupled with the raising of the lax nucleus of /ay/. This may
not be a genuine countermovement, since the tenseness of the nucleus of
/ay/ cannot be determined from the data; like the /ay/ of modern dialects
to be discussed in chapter 6, it may very well be tensed, backed, and
lengthened. The chain shift of the long vowels in the back involves the
lowering of front /ɛ̄/. It is clear that long /ɛ:/ did not shorten, since it did
not merge with /ɛ/. The lowering of /ɛ:/ is therefore a genuine violation of
Principle I. The fact that it is coupled with the upward movement of two
other long vowels may provide a motivation. The discussion of the pattern
in (6) indicated that Principles I and II would jointly predict a shortening
of the single vowel involved in downward movement. However, the principle could be modified to permit countermovement of an individual vowel
in association with movement in the predicted direction of two or more
other vowels.

So far we have been looking at a compilation of changes that take place
in many dialects. When we examine individual dialects, the raising of /ay/
is even less integrated into the pattern. The dialect of Aahof shows all the
changes together except one – the raising of /ay/ to [oy]. The dialect of
Setzen does exhibit the raising of /ay/, but here original **ei** does not fall all
the way to [ay] and remains at an intermediate level. Other dialects around
Setzen show [oy], but the link between the raising of **ai** and the lowering
of **ei** is not firmly established enough to motivate a clear violation of Principle IIa. We will see ample evidence on this point in the study of current
dialects in chapter 6.

CHAIN SHIFTS IN NORTH FRISIAN

The North Frisian instance of Pattern 2 was cited in (12). This is actually
an extract from the more complete configuration shown in (24) (Wilts,
Braren, and Hinrichsen 1986).[17]

---

[17] I am indebted to Don Ringe for calling my attention to the North Frisian case and for
providing the analysis given here.

(24)   THE NORTH FRISIAN CHAIN SHIFT

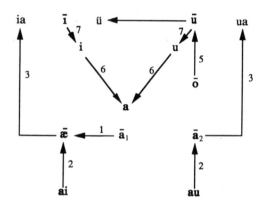

- Step 1 in this development was the separation of PWG ā into two vowels. The main body of ā words, designated ā₁, followed the path of Anglo-Frisian brightening, fronting to ǣ. The subset marked ā₂ remained central or back. This subset consisted of (1) words containing ā before nasals and (2) words containing short **a** that lengthened in the same environments that operated to produce lengthening of ǎ in English – before -*nd*, -*ld* and similar homorganic voiced clusters. We must assume that the allophone before nasals was originally considerably backer,[18] and that after the fronting of ā₁ it was joined by the lengthened ǎ reflexes.
- In Step 2, the ǣ category was joined by the monophthongization of **ai** and the ā₂ category by the monophthongization of **au**.
- Step 3 was the symmetrical raising and breaking of the long vowels, with ǣ proceeding to *ia* and ā₂ to *ua* (notations that both represent ingliding vowels).
- Step 4 was the fronting of ū to [ü] (an earlier umlauting of ū had already been unrounded).
- Step 5 raised ō to the high position that ū had vacated in Step 4.
- Step 6 was a symmetrical lowering of short **i** and **u** to /a/.
- Step 7 was a general – though not complete – shortening of the long high vowels to the positions vacated in Step 6.

On the whole, we can see that North Frisian adjoins Pattern 3 (Steps 4 and 5) to Pattern 2, though it is a more symmetrical version of Pattern 2 than is found elsewhere. The most interesting point in the process is the

---

[18] Again as in the case of OE short **a**, which shifted to **o** before nasals in a widespread change that was later reversed (Toon 1976).

relationship between the shortening of /iː/ and /uː/ and the development of the inglides. The logical numbering system allows this shortening to follow the development of the inglides, implying that there can be a stable contrast between inglides and monophthongs in high position. In the discussion of East Lettish in (23) above, it was suggested that there is no stable contrast between long monophthongs and upglides in high position. The same instability may hold for high monophthongs and inglides. If this is true, the development of high inglides will encourage the movement of high monophthongs to other phonetic forms.

5.4 Exceptions to the general principles

The historical and evolutionary approach outlined in section 5.1 leads us to expect exceptions to the general principles of chain shifting. We can expect that sooner or later factors that disfavor the principles will combine in concentrations powerful enough to reverse the direction of chain shifting. If we had enough data, we would expect to find that Principles I–III govern the outcome with frequencies varying from moderately high to close to 1.00, and we would be able to isolate those features of the contextual situation that are responsible for the principle's applying with a given probability.

Plainly there are not enough cases of completed chain shifts to set such a program in motion. What we can do is to estimate the relative force of the three principles by reviewing all of the exceptions that have come to light so far.

The evidence supporting Principle I is quite uniform, and the only violation is found in East Lettish: the lowering of ɛ̄ to [aː]. Both long monophthongs and long ingliding vowels rise in the course of chain shifts.

The evidence supporting Principle IIa shows a parallel uniformity. Again, it is the East Lettish dialects that provide a counterexample, the raising of /ay/ to [oy]. But this one case is not fully established as a part of the basic chain shift patterns.

The more general formulation of Principle II deals with short vowels and their tendency to fall in chain shifts. This follows Sweet's original formulation for sound changes in general, which was made without regard to chain shifting. It is easy enough to find many examples of short vowels falling in the historical record. For example, one of the earliest changes in Indo-European was the shift of short ŏ to ă, alongside the raising of ā to ō. But there are still not many cases of completed chain shifts that show the falling of short vowels. The best historical case is the falling of short vowels in North Frisian, linked by a chain shift mechanism to the shortening of long vowels.

One well-known movement of short vowels can be interpreted as an upward chain shift. London working-class speech shows [i], [e⊥], [ɛ] for the front short vowels /i/, /e/, /æ/ (Sivertsen 1960). In this case, there are no entering and leaving phonemes that would define a vowel shift. One might say instead that it represents an upward compression of the phonological space used by the short vowels. But if /i/ had not moved to an upper mid position, its margin of security with /e/ would have been seriously endangered. The same upward shift appears in Australian English (Mitchell and Delbridge 1965; Bradley and Bradley 1979). The New Zealand version of this short vowel perturbation illustrated in (25), is much more clearly a chain shift. Instead of moving farther up, the high front short vowel /i/ moves to the back, becoming a lower high central vowel, while /e/ moves to replace it, and /æ/ moves up behind /e/.

(25)   THE NEW ZEALAND FRONT SHORT VOWEL SHIFT

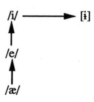

This clearly violates both Principle III (since a front vowel is moving to the back in a chain shift) and Principle II (since short vowels are rising together). It is possible that there are no general constraints on the movements of short vowels: we must end the survey of completed changes by concluding that this is a possibility.

The development of Korean vowels from the 13th century onward shows an even more extensive set of counterexamples, which make it seem as though an entirely different organizing principle were at work. Korean does not have a contrast between long and short vowels, so the single series of vowels would be expected to follow Principles I and III, moving up and to the front. But in the development of Early Middle Korean (13th century) to Late Middle Korean (15th century), we see extended chain shifts to the back and downward (Hong 1991; Lee 1961). The notation in (26) begins with the phonetic forms that were the result of the earlier shifts noted in (13), and the numbering again follows the logical sequence that must be assumed under a discrete pull chain model.

Here a downward movement in the back vowels (Steps 1 and 2) leaves a hole at high back position, which is filled by a backward shifting of the high mid central unrounded vowel (Step 3). This position is in turn filled by an upward movement of the mid central vowel (Step 4), followed by a backing of the mid front vowel (Step 5). If we consider the Korean vowels as the equivalent of a tense series, all but Step 4 run counter to Principles I–III. If we consider them to behave like short vowels, then Steps 3 and

(26) THE MIDDLE KOREAN VOWEL SHIFT

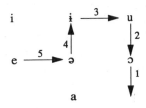

5 are counterexamples to Principle III. There is no doubt that the history of Korean vowels is different from that of all other languages considered so far. The one other feature that marks Korean as different is the coexistence with these monophthongs of two sets of rising diphthongs, /wi, we, wæ, wa, wɔ/ and /ye, yæ, yɔ, yo, yu/. It is hard to say how these rising diphthongs might interact with the monophthongs and affect their movements, since all other studies of chain shifts relate falling diphthongs to monophthongs.

On the whole, there are not many counterexamples to Principle III, and as we have seen, it commands a great deal of support. One extensive counterexample might well be considered here, though it is a change in progress rather than a completed one. Lennig (1978) studied the vowel system of modern-day Paris through sociolinguistic interviews with 90 Parisians. As shown in (27), the Parisian vernacular (*Parigot*) had undergone a Pattern 3 chain shift, where back /ɑ/ had moved up to [ɔ] or even [o], while /ɔ/, found only in checked syllables (*Paul, sotte*), had moved forward almost to the position of /œ/ in *peur* (Martinet 1958). Parallel frontings of allophones of /o/ and /u/ had also taken place, with a split of the allophones of /u/. Lennig found uniformly fronted [ʉ] following dental consonants (*tout, sous*) as opposed to labials and velars (*pour, coup*).

(27) THE PARISIAN CHAIN SHIFT

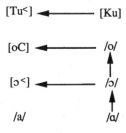

Lennig's work maps change in apparent time through a number of social dimensions, distinguishing the rate of change by sex and socioeconomic class. His results document a thoroughgoing reversal of (27). The change is led by the most conservative group in Parisian society: upper middle class females. At one end of the chain, the shift is triggered by the merger of /a/ and /ɑ/. This is accompanied by a back movement of the fronted elements and a downward movement of the raised elements. (28) reproduces the reverse shifts recorded in Lennig's instrumental measurements. Instead of the discrete numbered replacements shown in the previous diagrams, this diagram reproduces the partial shift in a continuous space characteristic of change in progress.

(28) THE REVERSE PARISIAN CHAIN SHIFT (after Lennig 1978)

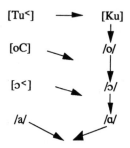

The Paris reversal runs counter to the two strongest principles of chain shifting: Principles I and III. It demonstrates that none of the principles of chain shifting is either absolute or isolated from social factors. If social pressures are strong enough, phonetic processes that are deeply rooted in the history of the language and the functional economy of the system can be reversed. Conservative pressures of this type can be traced in New York and Philadelphia (Labov 1966, 1989a). Here they operate to "correct" and reverse the oldest stages of change, which are completed or almost complete, but they do not affect the innovative forces and the new and vigorous changes that operate below the level of social consciousness. In Paris, the internal factors that lead to change from below are weaker, and the changes that led to the local vernacular all showed the properties of completed changes, at high levels of social awareness. It is under these conditions that the conservative factors in the speech community can operate in a systematic manner to reverse chain shifts as a whole.

5.5 Paradoxes

The exceptional cases considered in section 5.4 add depth and texture to our understanding of the principles outlined in section 5.3. Effective knowledge of a principle means knowing the scope of its application and its degree of generality, even to the extent of identifying it as a minor rather than a major tendency. In this section we will consider cases of a much more difficult kind that cannot be classified as exceptions. We will look at a number of historical developments that follow the paths of chain shifting outlined in (1), but lead to unacceptable consequences in that they violate principles at a much higher level of generality. It will appear that the beginning and ending stages are not compatible with the principles of chain shifting, since all known routes predict mergers that did not in fact take place.

As defined at the outset, a chain shift is basically the opposite of a merger. The general condition for a valid description of a chain shift is quite straightforward. Whatever path we describe for the chain-shifting vowels, they cannot at any time occupy the same position in phonological space: if they do so, they will by definition merge, and we will have described a merger rather than a chain shift. Scholars have not always been careful to observe this condition, or to draw the obvious consequences when it fails to hold. In a number of cases, we are presented with paradoxical descriptions, which state that merger was avoided, yet describe changes that must have led to merger. We will consider four such paradoxical descriptions. To clarify the logic of the situation, I will translate the traditional description into the formal notation of a discrete phonology based on an abstract binary feature system.

The Valais raising of back vowels

Gauchat, Jeanjaquet, and Tappolet (1925) collected data on the Romance dialects in the province of the Valais. In these data we can trace a shift in the western region where /ɔ/ rose directly to [u] without merging with /o/. The /ɔ/ involved here had two sources: in checked position, it descended from the /ɔ/ of Vulgar Latin, inheriting its openness; in free position, it was the result of the monophthongization of /au/. It is the checked allophone that is the immediate focus of our attention. For although /ɔ/, checked and free, rose to [u], checked /o/, the phoneme representing the reflexes of Vulgar Latin checked /o/, fell to [ɔ]. Thus, in the course of the chain shift, the leaving element and the entering element passed one another, as shown in (29).

(29)   VALAIS RAISING

To translate this diagram into rules, we would begin with the array of four features in (30), to distinguish four phonetic positions.

(30)

	high	low	ant	round
u	+	−	−	+
o	−	−	−	+
ɔ	−	+	−	+
a	−	+	−	−

The changes would then be represented by the following rewriting of [low] and [high]:

{V1}   OPEN-O RAISING 1

$$[\ \ ] \rightarrow [-\text{low}]/\begin{bmatrix} \rule{2em}{0.4pt} \\ +\text{round} \\ +\text{back} \end{bmatrix}$$

{V2}   OPEN-O RAISING 2

$$[\ \ ] \rightarrow [+\text{high}]/\begin{bmatrix} \rule{2em}{0.4pt} \\ +\text{back} \end{bmatrix}$$

{V3}   LOWERING OF CHECKED CLOSED-O

$$[\ \ ] \rightarrow [+\text{low}]/\begin{bmatrix} \rule{2em}{0.4pt} \\ -\text{high} \\ +\text{back} \end{bmatrix}\begin{bmatrix} +\text{seg} \\ -\text{syl} \end{bmatrix}$$

Rules {V1} – {V3} translate the traditional notation into binary features. {V1} differentiates the rounded /ɔ/, checked and free, from /a/, and raises it to mid position; {V2} continues the raising to high position. {V3} then lowers the non-high /o/ to low position.

How could this have happened? The traditional diagram (29) simply shows /ɔ/ and /o/ passing each other without merging. But rule {V1} makes it explicit that /ɔ/ and /o/ merge: the only feature that distinguishes them is [low], and after {V1} they are indistinguishable. There is no way that {V2} can apply only to the output of {V1} and not to /o/; it applies jointly to the merged class and predicts that both /ɔ/ and /o/, checked and free, should raise to [u]. {V3} would then apply vacuously only to /a/.

What solutions could be imagined in terms of such a distinctive feature matrix? First, one might introduce a fifth feature to distinguish /o/ from the raised /ɔ/ – say, [+ tense] for [o] as opposed to [− tense] for /ɔ/. The feature [tense] has been used to distinguish these two vowels in situations where four levels of vowel height would otherwise have to be recognized. But there is no basis for introducing this feature into Romance languages, and there would be no basis for maintaining the [− tense] feature once /ɔ/ had raised to [o].

Second, one might insist that the two word classes remained distinct even though the vowels had the same features.[19] One could defend such an approach if there were alternations that allowed the native speakers to maintain the identity of the word classes. Such alternations would have to be found for every word that remained distinct, however, and there is no basis for this in the Romance vocabulary.

Third, one might eliminate the two-step raising process and accomplish the entire raising with a single rule:

{V4}   OPEN-O SUPERRAISING

$$[\text{+low}] \rightarrow [\text{+high}]/\left[\begin{array}{c} \rule{1cm}{0.4pt} \\ \text{+back} \end{array}\right]$$

This would be equivalent to saying that /ɔ/ simply "leaped over" /o/. It would not be necessary to specify that [+ low] becomes [– low], since [+ high] is redundantly [– low]. It is true that all the past and present chain shifts that we have studied show that [ɔ] moves to [u] through the intermediate position of [o]. But an abstract enough phonology could dispense with this historical realism, if one were willing to introduce rewrite rules that effectively change two features at a time.

Fourth, one might write a flip-flop rule, which raises /ɔ/ and lowers /o/ at the same time:

{V5}   LOWNESS REVERSAL

$$[\alpha\text{low}] \rightarrow [-\alpha\text{low}]/\rule{1cm}{0.4pt}\left[\begin{array}{c} \rule{1cm}{0.4pt} \\ \text{+back} \end{array}\right]$$

This is the familiar flip-flop rule that Chomsky and Halle (1968) applied to the English Great Vowel Shift. Its merits and demerits have been much debated in the literature. As a description of what happened after the fact, this solution or the previous one might well be defended. But a flip-flop rule offers an account of the process as it happened only if it is accompanied by two firm theoretical positions:

1   There is no distinction between the change itself and the rules that describe the change: change in the language is nothing but the mental process of introducing new rules or altering old ones. This is of course the familiar position taken by Halle (1962).

2   Rule systems are isolated from the effects of the use of language. The fact that two generations used opposite phonetic values for /o/ and /ɔ/ in speaking to each other would then have no communicative consequences, and it would not lead to any confusion in the membership of the

---

[19] This was in fact the approach taken by Halle (1962) to the continued distinctiveness of the class of *mate* and *meat* in 16th-century English, to be discussed in chapter 6.

two word classes.[20] This might be particularly difficult to maintain in the light of Payne's work in King of Prussia, described in chapter 4. Her findings confirm the commonsense inference that children learn their word classes from their parents, and show further that it is very difficult if not impossible for a generation of speakers to relearn word class memberships in a uniform way later in life. This fact lies behind two of the most general constraints on language change:

(31) **Two segments that share the same set of distinctive features are indistinguishable in the language, and the word classes containing these segments are merged.**

(32) **Once two word classes have merged, they cannot be distinguished by any linguistic process.**[21]

The case of Valais raising therefore cannot be considered an exception to a rule, but must instead be considered a paradox of principle.

Yiddish diphthongization

Proto-Yiddish underwent the same Pattern 1 diphthongization of ī and ū to **ai** and **au** that was illustrated in (9) for Middle High German (Herzog 1965). This involved the merger of ī with **ei** as it descended to **ai**. But in Proto-Yiddish, the old **ei** remained at mid position and did not merge with the new diphthongs whose nuclei fell to low position. The same movement took place in the back, where ū fell to /aw/ (in Herzog's reconstruction) while **ou** shifted to **oy** and did not merge with the reflexes of OHG long ū. These developments are illustrated in (33). We have already seen that in Western Yiddish, the mid upgliding diphthongs /ey/ and /ow/ merged with MHG ī and ū, and then ultimately merged into a single /a/ phoneme.

(33) Proto-Yiddish diphthongization

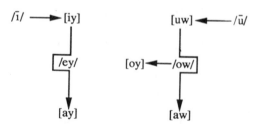

---

[20] See Chomsky and Halle's (1968: 256) reply to Stockwell (1964b).
[21] This is Garde's Principle (Garde 1961), which will play a central role in the discussion of mergers and their irreversibility in chapter 11.

But in Northeastern Yiddish /mejn/ 'mean' contrasts with /majn/ 'my'. The first comes from OHG **ei** /ey/, the second from OHG ī. The fact that the back vowels did not merge can be accounted for by the ordering of the shift of **ou** to **oy**. But the failure of Proto-Yiddish ī to merge with the older **ei** in its path to **ai** is not easy to explain. It presents the same kind of paradox as in the previous case. Rather than explore possible explanations at this point, I will proceed with a more complex problem, the lowering of the English diphthong /iy/ in the Great Vowel Shift, which involves some of the same issues as the formal description of the Yiddish diphthongization. The possible resolutions of the English example may in turn help to illuminate the Yiddish case.

The Great Vowel Shift I

The English Great Vowel Shift is the site of a parallel problem, which has been the focus of much discussion and disagreement. The earliest view of the vowel shift was provided by Jespersen in 1909. In Chapter 7 of volume 1 of his *Modern English Grammar* (1949), he introduced the term "Great Vowel Shift" and gave the chart shown in (34).

(34)   THE GREAT VOWEL SHIFT (Jespersen)

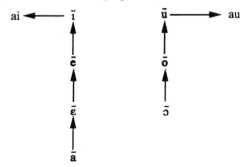

It is now usual to show the shift in Early Modern English as beginning with the reflex of ME ā as a low front vowel [æ:] in *name, grave*, etc. A second vowel shares the same nucleus: the reflex of ME **ai** in *day, maid*, etc., appears as [æy].[22] There is some disagreement on exactly when this was monophthongized and merged with **æ**, but it is generally thought to have undergone these changes in the 17th century, after the Great Vowel Shift had done its work.

The many discussions and explanations of the Great Vowel Shift after Jespersen's are reviewed by Wolfe (1972), who outlines some of the contro-

---

[22] In this discussion of the history of English diphthongization, I will use the broad phonetic notation of [y] and [w] for the English upglide, though in synchronic discussions /y/ and /w/ will be reserved for the phonemic notation of glides.

versies that I will deal with here; I rely heavily upon her careful review of the issues. The main focus will be on the front vowels, and in particular the mechanism by which ME ī descended to its present-day realization in most American and English dialects, [ay]. Some scholars (Orton 1933; Ellis 1874) take the straightforward view that the diphthong descended as a front vowel until it reached [æy], and then backed to [ay]:

(35)   Route 1
       ME ī → iy → ey → ɛy → æy → ay

But as Dobson (1968: 660) points out,

This view is altogether impossible. If the development had been that suggested, ME ī would have crossed the path of ME **ai** developing to [æi] and [ɛi]; most of the orthoepists who say that ME ī was [ei] still pronounced ME **ai** as a diphthong.

Thus, *die* would have merged with *day*, and *my* with *may*, which did not happen: there was never any tendency for these two vowels to be confused. A second approach, taken by Luick (1903), Jespersen (1949), and Zachrisson (1913) (and by Chomsky and Halle), is that the diphthong descended as a front vowel only midway, and was then centralized before falling further:

(36)   Route 2
       ME ī → iy → ey → əy → ay

But this would not have eliminated the merger at the midpoint /ey/. The solution implicit in Dobson's discussion is that the diphthongization of ME ī followed a centralized path from the outset:[23]

(37)   Route 3
       ME ī → iy → iy → əy → ay

Stockwell has defended this centralized path as both more realistic historically and more consistent with long-term developments in English dialectology (1964a, 1972, 1978; Stockwell and Minkova 1990). Stockwell (1972) introduced the feature [±peripheral] to account for the natural class of [+peripheral] vowels that are front-unrounded and back-rounded; such a feature also allows this centralizing [−peripheral] path to be described in a more formal framework. Lindau (1978) inserts this feature

---

[23] Dobson is unique among philologists in relating the solution to this problem to the path taken by modern-day dialects; we will return to his insights in chapter 6, which applies data from change in progress to this problem.

into a general framework for the phonetic basis for phonological features of vowels.

The options suggested for the Great Vowel Shift are diagrammed in (38). Each route is labeled with a number, so that it can easily be traced. The dashed line shows the route that ME **ai** must have followed in the opposite direction, and indicates where a merger with **ī** would be predicted.

(38)   GREAT VOWEL SHIFT OPTIONS

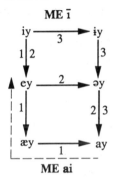

Routes 1 and 2 show the problem of the encounter with the path of the rising reflex of ME **ai**. Route 3 avoids this problem. But unfortunately, Route 3 does not fit in with the available evidence from orthoepists and grammarians. Wolfe undertook the task of investigating Stockwell's hypothesis from a sympathetic point of view. But after a careful review of four 16th-century sources (Hart, Bellot, Bullokar, Mulcaster) and thirteen 17th-century writers, she concluded that "the orthoepists offer no support whatsoever for the claim that centralization preceded lowering" (1972:171). She found that none of the orthoepists before Hodges (1643) identified the nucleus of *die, my,* etc., as anything but a front vowel, even though many carefully distinguished the nucleus from the glide; and that all the ones after Hodges tended to hear the nucleus as the central vowel of *nut,* etc.

The issues are therefore clear-cut, but the controversy is unresolved. How then do the proponents of Routes 1 and 2 explain that ME **ī** and **ai** did not merge? Of the various possibilities outlined in the discussion of the Romance back vowels, there is no more relevant ground in this case than in that one for introducing a new distinctive feature, such as [tense]; nor is there any more basis for claiming that alternations maintained the two word classes as distinct. A jump directly from /iy/ to /ay/ would be as easy to write as the superjump from /ɔ/ to /u/, but it is even less attractive because there is so much evidence for the intermediate stages. The flip-flop mechanism is the preferred type of description and is of course the one that has been advanced for the Great Vowel Shift:

{GVS1}   LOWNESS REVERSAL

$$[\alpha low] \rightarrow [-\alpha low]/\underline{\quad} \begin{bmatrix} +back \\ +long \\ +str \end{bmatrix}$$

This rule has all the advantages of efficiency, since it simultaneously handles the problem of the diphthongs that we are concerned with here, and also raises ME **ǣy** to **ē**. To endorse it, we must of course accept the theoretical positions given at the end of the discussion of the Valais back vowels. If we are not willing to accept these, we are left with the paradox that ME **ī** descended to [aɪ] without merging with ME **ai**, which ascended to [eɪ]. The same problem applies to the Yiddish development outlined earlier.

Vowels before /r/ in the Great Vowel Shift II

English shows a great deal of irregularity in the phonetic realization of words spelled **ea**, where it seems impossible to predict whether a nucleus will have [e], as in *great, break, wear, bear, tear* [V], etc., or [i], as in *meat, seat, fear, tear* [N], etc. The general case of *meat* and *break* will be taken up in chapter 6. This section will consider only the particular environment of words ending in /r/, which show much greater regularity than previous treatments would suggest.

The spellings are not a reliable guide to the word classes involved here. To follow the pattern of evolution, it will be necessary to embed the history of the **ea** words ending in /r/ in the history of all current English words with long front vowels before /r/ – that is, ingliding /ihr/ or /ehr/. The overall development is given in (39), which shows the various processes that operated on OE long front vowels before /r/ to produce the modern system. The many processes shown in (39) can be understood best as the composite result of a series of historically ordered rules {E5.1}–{E5.8}. This will involve the rest of the rules that are usually included in the Great Vowel Shift which was examined only in its first stage in the preceding section. We will need to look at all of these rules, though our focus is only on their application to words ending in /r/.

Before the Middle English period began, the OE ingliding diphthongs **ēo, ēa,** and **ĕa** lost their inglides, a process generally known as *Smoothing:*[24] The smoothing process amplified some of the other word classes before /r/ that are the participants in the scenario of (39). The diphthong **ēa** (phonetically [æːə] or [ɛːə] lost its glide and merged with **ǣ**, so that *téar*

---

[24] The phonetic realization of the short diphthongs is much disputed, but the subsequent history of all these diphthongs is quite straightforward if we assume that they merged with the reflexes of **ǣ**, as indicated here.

(39) RAISING OF FRONT VOWELS BEFORE /R/

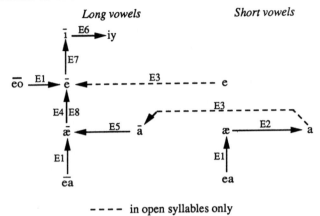

---- in open syllables only

{E5.1} SMOOTHING

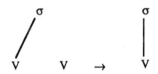

'tear [V]' fell together with *fær*, 'fear'. The diphthong ēo (phonetically [e:ə] merged with long ē, so that *déor* 'deer' fell together with *hér* 'here'.

At the start of the Middle English period, the short front vowels were shifted to center or back, so that in the development traced here, there is no difference between **æ**, **ea**, and **a** – they were all written as **a**:

{E5.2} BACKING OF æ

$$[+\text{low}] \rightarrow [-\text{ant}]/\left[\begin{array}{c}\overline{}\\-\text{long}\end{array}\right]$$

In the 11th and 12th centuries, English underwent a general lengthening in open syllables, the central process involved in the problem outlined here.[25] A large number of short ă vowels were affected by this process. Verbs like *faran* 'travel' and *sparian* 'spare' were lengthened, since they normally occurred with vowels following the stem /r/. Bisyllabic noun stems like *hara* 'hare' and *snara* 'snare' were also lengthened. In addition, many monosyl-

---

[25] For a close treatment of the many problems involved in characterizing "open syllable lengthening," see Minkova 1982 and Stockwell 1985. The major issues involved do not intersect with the treatment of low and mid vowels before /r/ that is the focus here, but they will be relevant in chapter 15.

{E5.3} LENGTHENING IN OPEN SYLLABLES

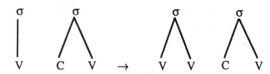

labic nouns and adjectives were lengthened where the oblique inflectional forms were taken as basic. Some additional compensatory lengthenings took place with the loss of intervocalic velars, as in *fæger* 'fair' and *stœger* 'stair'. At this point, there was no original long ā for these lengthened forms to combine with, since ā had been raised unconditionally to ɔ̄ in the Old English period. The lengthened forms therefore created a new long ǣ class.[26]

At the same time, lengthening in open syllables affected the short ĕ class. Thus, ĕ in the four verbs *beran* 'bear', *teran* 'tear', *swerian* 'swear', and *werian* 'wear', as well as in the nouns *bera* 'bear' and *pere* 'pear', was lengthened to ē̞.

The word classes involved were then amplified by large-scale borrowings in the 12th through 14th centuries, first from Norman French, and later from French, Norse, Dutch, and other sources. Borrowed **ar** uniformly joined the OE **ār** class, as in *pare* 'pare' and *scars* 'scarce' from French, *snara* 'snare' and *skerre* 'scare' from Old Norse, and *tare* 'tare' from Arabic. Borrowed **er** uniformly merged with the reflexes of the OE **ǣr** and **ēr** classes, as in *appere* 'appear', *spere* 'sphere', and *cler* 'clear' from French, and *gere* 'gear' from Norse.

The Great Vowel Shift then operated to produce the sweeping changes in vowel height that we have already considered. The discrete steps outlined here are not intended to suggest that the shifts happened simply and automatically; rather, they represent the end result of the process as it would appear to a speaker in the 17th century who had witnessed its completion. The ordering of the steps is dictated by what vowels stayed distinct and what vowels fell together.

The first logical step is then the raising of **æ**:

{E5.4}   æ RAISING

$$[\ \ ] \rightarrow [-\text{low}]/\begin{bmatrix} \underline{\quad} \\ +\text{long} \\ -\text{back} \end{bmatrix}$$

---

[26] This recreation of ā will play a major role in chapter 15, where the discussion of lexical diffusion versus regular sound change leads to an investigation of the origins of the short **a** split in the Middle Atlantic states.

The emptying of the low front long vowel position was accompanied by the formation of a large word class including the **æ** and **ē** classes and the many borrowings that had already amplified those classes as described above.

The next step is the fronting of **ā** to fill the vacancy created by the raising of **æ**. This fronting was included in the vowel shift in Jespersen's schema (34), but as previously noted, it is now generally shown as a precondition of the symmetrical vowel shift itself.

{E5.5}   FRONTING OF **ā**

$$[+low] \rightarrow [-back] / \left[\frac{\quad\quad\quad}{+long} \right]$$

There are many conflicting views on the ordering of the steps in the Great Vowel Shift. Luick (1903) argued that the raising of the mid vowels was the first step – a push shift.[27] Here I will follow the majority view of Jespersen (1949), Martinet (1955), Stockwell (1964a), and Stampe (1972) that the diphthongization of the high vowels was the first step in the vowel shift proper.

{E5.6}   DIPHTHONGIZATION OF HIGH VOWELS

$$\emptyset \rightarrow \begin{bmatrix} -voc \\ -cons \\ \alpha ant \end{bmatrix} / \begin{bmatrix} +high \\ \alpha ant \\ +long \\ +str \end{bmatrix} \underline{\quad\quad}$$

We need not pursue this rule farther along the various possible paths discussed earlier. It is followed in this logical sequence by the general raising of long mid vowels, both front and back. The rule is shown here with the usual constraint to long vowels that agree in backness and rounding, thus excluding /oy/ from its operation. This rule should apply to the **ēr** class in (39), made up of six sources: original OE **ē** in *hér* 'here', *wérig* 'weary', etc.; smoothed OE **ēo** in *déor* 'deer', *dréorig* 'dreary', etc.; lengthened OE short **ĕ** in *bera* 'bear', *werian* 'wear', etc.; OE **æ** in *fœ:r* 'fear', *rœ:ran* 'rear', etc.; smoothed OE **ēa** in *téar* 'tear', *néar* 'near', etc.; and many loans from French as in ME *appere* 'appear', *spere* 'sphere', etc.

{E5.7}   RAISING OF MID VOWELS

$$[\quad] \rightarrow [+high] / \underline{\quad\quad} \begin{bmatrix} +long \\ +str \\ \alpha back \\ \alpha round \end{bmatrix}$$

---

[27] For some interesting arguments in support of Luick's position, see Ogura 1990:45.

The last rule in the series, {E5.8}, completes the shift by moving the low front **ær** class into the mid position that was vacated by {E5.7}. This class now contains the reflexes of OE lengthened short **ă** as in *faran* 'fare', *bear* 'bare', etc., and French loans as in ME *chaere* 'chair', *feire* 'fair', etc.

{E5.8}   RAISING OF LOW VOWELS

$$[\ \ ] \rightarrow [-\text{low}]/ \begin{bmatrix} \underline{} \\ +\text{long} \\ +\text{str} \end{bmatrix}$$

So far, the development of **ēar**, **ǣr**, and **ēr** under rules {E5.1}–{E5.8} has been shown as regular. There are two irregularities in words of known origin that I have been able to trace, and they both involve function words. *Their* is from a Scandinavian model with **ei** and should have been raised to /ihr/ by regular processes. *There* is from OE ð*ǣr*ð*ēr* and would normally have been raised to /ihr/ as well. The analogical influence of the lax forms of these words is most likely responsible for their exceptional behavior. With the exception of one subclass to be discussed below, all ME **ǣr** and **ēr** words become /ihr/ in Modern English, and all ME **ār** words become /ehr/.[28]

THE EXCEPTIONAL SUBCLASS

In the description of rule {E5.7}, there was an odd inconsistency in the make-up of the **ēr** class: the examples 'bear' and 'wear' are not pronounced today with /ihr/ like the other members of the class. Irregularities in the words spelled with *ea* are not unexpected; chapter 6 will discuss the well-known cases of *meat*, *leak*, and *pea* versus *great*, *steak*, and *yea*. Yet the situation we are dealing with here is quite different. The exceptional behavior in words before /r/ is entirely concentrated in one subclass with a particular history: the group of short **ěr** words that were lengthened by rule {E5.3}. By every known linguistic principle and the rules projected here, they should have been carried along with the rest of the ME **ē** class to high position. But this did not happen.

Nine short **ě** words are involved. The six most common still have /ehr/, and the three less common have /ihr/:

---

[28] This statement carries no empirical weight for the vowels that were lengthened in open syllables, since the chief evidence for their lengthening is their ultimate development as /ihr/ or /ehr/.

/ehr/			/ihr/		
bear [V]	<	*beran*	smear {N,V}	<	*smerian, smeru*
bear [N]	<	*bera*	spear	<	*spere*
tear [V]	<	*teran*	weir	<	*wer, werian*
pear	<	*pere*			
wear	<	*werian*			
swear	<	*swerian*			

The development of lengthened ĕ shows more than a little irregularity: it is sharply differentiated from the uniform development of ǣr and ār. How then did lengthened ĕr fail to follow the path of other ēr? And how did the ǣr class pass this lengthened ĕr class without merging with it? These data, and this question, provide us with another paradox.

EXPLANATIONS

What kinds of explanations might be provided for these contradictory sets of data?

One approach might be to claim that the lengthening did not take place after all, or that it was only a partial lengthening, or that it took place much later. But the process of lengthening in open syllables was quite general in Early Middle English. It affected many word classes, and all during the same period. The low vowels showed no such irregularities: there are no examples of lengthened short ă words left behind. Furthermore, the lengthening process came to an end before the vowel shift applied, and (except for Scottish dialects) short /e/ in closed syllables went to the mid central vowel and merged with the reflexes of /ir, or, ur/, yielding the same vowel in *person, serve, fir, world,* and *fur.* Today, the only short /e/ words before /r/ are found in open syllable stems, like *merry* and *cherry.* In the closed syllables *tear, bear, pear,* etc., only long ingliding vowels or short mid central vowels are found. If lengthening had not applied to *bear, tear, pear,* etc., they would today be pronounced [bər, tər, pər], etc., to rhyme with *her* and *per.* Instead, they clearly maintained their membership in the long vowel class and eventually merged with raised ME ā to produce the modern /ehr/ class.

The notion of a superjump is not very useful here. The ME ǣ class might have jumped over the mid vowels and thus escaped merger with the class of lengthened ME ĕ words. But lengthened ME ĕ also failed to merge with original ME ēr and smoothed ME ēo, which were in mid position before they were raised to /ihr/.

Finally, a flip-flop rule would do nothing to solve this particular problem. True enough, rules {E5.7} and {E5.8} might be combined with other processes to produce rules for reversal of highness or reversal of lowness as in {GVS1}. But this would by no means explain why lengthened ME ĕ did not merge with the rest of the long mid vowels.

The fourth paradox therefore has no solution within the traditional articulatory framework or the mechanisms offered by a discrete, formal phonology.

6

Chain Shifts in Progress

Chapter 5 presented the unidirectional principles of chain shifting derived from the study of completed sound changes.[1] These principles were supported by a sizeable number of cases, with the exception of chain shifts of simple short vowels. The principles of chain shifting are not absolute. Even for the strongest ones, Principles I and III, exceptional changes were found operating in the opposite direction. However, the major problems in this exposition were not these exceptions, but the paradoxical cases of chain shifts that should have led to merger but did not. This chapter will examine chain shifts in progress in English dialects to see what additional information can be derived from instrumental measurements of the actual use of language in spontaneous speech. These studies will provide a much larger body of data in support of the three principles of chain shifting. This body of data will also be much richer than the historical record could provide; it will yield more information on the paths that vowels take through phonological space, the differentiation of allophones, the coherence of word classes, and the effects of environment. With the help of this additional information, I will try to illuminate and resolve the problems raised in chapter 4. To the extent that this effort succeeds, this chapter will have made progress toward the major program of this work, the use of the present to explain the past.

6.1 The general approach to change in progress

Social location of the speakers

Chapter 3 outlined general methods for the study of change in progress, as procedures for tracing trajectories in apparent time. The data for this chapter are drawn from studies that use these methods, ranging from the highly systematic sampling of urban populations in New York, Detroit, and Philadelphia to exploratory studies in London, Glasgow, Sydney, and

---

[1] In the actual course of development, the ordering was the other way around. The principles of chain shifting were derived from the study of ongoing changes, and then confirmed by the study of the historical record. (See LYS:chaps. 3–4.)

Atlanta.[2] All data are taken from spontaneous speech, recorded with the best available equipment under field conditions, using the techniques of the sociolinguistic interview to reduce the effects of observation (Labov 1984).[3] Representative surveys of entire speech communities provided the template of changes in progress for the broader range of communities that were explored less systematically. Of particular importance here is the location of the most advanced speakers in the social spectrum. The pattern now seems clear, at least for cities in the United States. In the course of change from below, the most advanced vowel systems are found among younger speakers: young adults and youth in late adolescence. Furthermore, these innovators are found among "interior groups" – that is, groups centrally located in the class hierarchy (see chapter 3 and Labov 1990). In terms of social class labels, this means the upper working class and lower middle class; in occupational terms, skilled workers, technicians, clerks, teachers, merchants, and leaders of local organizations and political parties. Among these social groups, the prototypical exponents of new and vigorous changes are apt to be speakers with the highest local prestige: upwardly mobile individuals from ethnic groups who have entered the community in the last three or four generations. In most of the vowel shifts that we will look at, women are considerably more advanced than men.

The findings of the systematic community studies then serve as a guide in selecting characteristic speakers in exploratory studies.[4] The view of sound changes in progress derived from the broad range of cities is based on sociolinguistic interviews with speakers selected to represent the most advanced stages of changes in progress, and other speakers from their families and neighbors who represent older stages of the changes, following the logic laid out in chapters 3 and 4. In most areas, we have the records of older working-class speakers in the 70–80 age range, who represent the oldest stratum available for instrumental measurement. The exploratory

---

[2] Most of the exploratory studies were done by myself. Contributions to this data base were also made by Benji Wald, Malcah Yaeger, and Sharon Ash.

[3] In almost all cases, the recordings were made with Nagra tape recorders, using lavaliere microphones that maximized signal-to-noise ratio. The recordings that were the basis of LYS and LCV used a speed of $3\frac{3}{4}$ in/sec and dynamic microphones such as the Sennheiser 214. Recent recordings made for research on cross-dialectal comprehension in Chicago, Birmingham, and elsewhere obtained a higher-quality signal, recording at $7\frac{1}{2}$ in/sec and using condenser microphones such as the Sennheiser 415 or a Panasonic DAT recorder with a Sony EC=55 microphone.

[4] In some cases, the exploratory studies cover a number of years and 10 to 20 families, which give enough basis for comparison to further confirm the general principles on social distribution outlined above. My series of exploratory studies in 20 British cities was extensive enough to serve as the basis for Houston's (1985) reconstruction of the history of (ing). Our view of Chicago now covers a period of 20 years and a wide range of social classes as a result of interviews carried out by Ash for CDC.

studies reported here do not as a rule include upper-middle-class or lower-class speakers, who display even more conservative patterns.[5]

The uniformitarian principle

Each section of this chapter applies the uniformitarian principle presented in section 1.2. The assumption throughout is that we can learn about the mechanism of past sound changes by studying changes taking place around us, always bearing in mind the Historical Paradox which tells us that we have no other choice but to do so. Nevertheless, using the present to explain the past is not a common strategy. One reason is the general reluctance of linguists to enter the community and study the language of everyday life. Another is the belief that sound change itself is a thing of the past. The data to follow will show that this is far from the case.

Speech styles

The sociolinguistic interviews that provide the data used here include a wide range of styles. The closest approach to the vernacular is found in *casual speech*, where attention to the forms of speech is minimal, and the most consistent representation of that style is to be found in excited, emotionally engaged speech. The major part of the interview, no matter how casual it may seem on first inspection, must be classed as *careful speech*.[6] Together, casual speech and careful speech are labeled *spontaneous speech*, as opposed to the *controlled styles* used in reading. The extreme formal end of the stylistic continuum is found in the reading of isolated words – lists or minimal pairs – where the speaker's attention is focused directly on pronunciation.[7] In every community, a small number of speak-

---

[5] In many American cities, the characteristic lower-class speakers are members of the black or Hispanic communities. As the New York City study first showed (Labov 1966:chap. 8; see chapter 2), they may appear at first to be conservative exponents of the local vowel system. Closer study shows that they are not oriented to the local vernacular development at all, but are instead oriented to a national pattern of koine formation within the nonwhite groups. In England, nonwhite groups are much more involved in the local vernacular sound system, as our exploratory studies show. However, all representatives of both British and American sound systems in this volume are drawn from the white community.

[6] One might wonder why sound changes in progress cannot be traced by obtaining samples of speakers interacting with each other, in group sessions. Only sociolinguistic interviews can provide the very large volume of speech needed for a complete analysis of the linguistic system, the complete identification of the speakers' personal histories needed for sampling the community, and the high-quality sound recordings needed for the accurate analysis of phonetic forms (Labov 1984).

[7] Bell (1984) argues that attention paid to speech is not the organizing principle of stylistic variation, but rather the audience that is being addressed. The main evidence for this position is the speech of the same radio announcers addressing different audiences. Though this demonstrates the importance of the audience, a much larger body of evidence shows great stylistic variation of speakers with a constant audience. Findings on the great stylistic difference between open and closed classes (Prince 1987) reinforce the importance of attention paid to speech as an organizing principle of style in speech outside of research settings. It seems clear that stylistic shifting responds to many independent variables and that no one of them can

ers can be found who show so little style shifting that this range is very narrow; for them, the phonetic realizations of words in deliberate reading are almost indistinguishable from the pattern of casual speech. Since the ordered heterogeneity of styles is a normal and functional aspect of socio-linguistic structure, such speakers have to be considered abnormal, even defective members of the speech community. The data presented here are drawn from the spontaneous speech of normal speakers.

The use of spontaneous speech as opposed to word lists means that in some cases the less common phonemes like /oy/ and /u/ are not well represented. But only in spontaneous speech will we find the most advanced tokens of linguistic change in progress, and we will need these to establish the direction and path of the change. If we filled in the pattern with tokens drawn from word lists, we would obscure rather than clarify the position of these phonemes with respect to the rest of the system. The type of shift found in such formal styles is often quite abrupt, and it is not clearly related to the distribution of variants found in spontaneous speech (LYS:fig. 3–3; Yaeger 1975; Labov 1989a).

For each speaker analyzed, the data of spontaneous speech will provide a wide dispersion of vowel tokens, ranging along the path of the change from more advanced to less advanced tokens. There is reason to believe that this range is correlated with the use of vowel variables in social interaction, even for the early stages of change from below. Hindle's (1980) study of a single Philadelphia speaker, recorded in a variety of social situations, showed that the more advanced tokens were used in intense social exchanges with peers. In the interview data we will use here, the most advanced tokens characteristically appear in emphatically stressed words in personal narratives. This is an important issue in the pursuit of the actuation problem and the social motivation of sound change that will be undertaken in volume 2. For our present study of the paths and mechanisms of change, it is sufficient to have a good representation of the range of variants used in spontaneous speech.

Instrumental measurements

The instrumental techniques used to derive the measurements also cover a wide range. The charts of LYS are based on the measurement of formant frequencies in narrow-band spectrograms. For the LCV studies of Philadelphia vowels, harmonic analysis was done by a hard-wired spectrum analyzer, and linear predictive analysis was then carried out on the data of the frequency domain. In more recent investigations of Philadelphia, Chicago, and Birmingham, linear predictive analysis is carried out directly on the

---

be considered an "essential" or "controlling factor." Yet attention paid to speech is a useful organizing principle for the study of change in progress, since it differentiates the various layers of change presented in chapter 2.

digitized speech wave. The measurements are all designed to yield estimates of the central tendencies of the vowel formants, at a given point in time selected to represent the characteristic value of the nucleus or glide.[8] The diagrams in this chapter, like those in chapters 3 and 4, will locate each nucleus on a doubly linear two-formant plot. The methods themselves are reported in detail in the various technical reports given in the references.

The outlines of phonological space

The principles of chain shifting were presented in chapter 5 in a discrete phonological space, defined by distinctive features. Since the data of this chapter are instrumental measurements of formant frequencies, the chain shifts shown here are necessarily portrayed in a very different manner: they are seen as taking place in a continuous phonetic space. The shape and internal structure of this space is one of the major concerns of this chapter.

The triangular acoustic diagrams displayed in figures 4.9 and 4.13 are based on the typical results of measurements that give us the outlines of phonological space. That space is a triangle, not the quadrilateral of impressionistic phonetics.[9] The dimensions of the triangle, shown in (1), are formed by the limits on acoustic productions. The top of the triangle is defined by the lowest F1 values for [i] and [u] – typically 300 Hz for men and 400 Hz for women. The bottom of the triangle is defined by the F1 values of the most open vowel of the system, about 900 Hz for men and 1100 Hz for women. Since we will be comparing qualitative relations within the triangle, the numerical differences in F1 between men and women will not be relevant.

(1)   THE VOWEL TRIANGLE

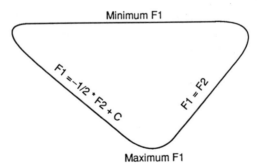

8 The formant may show a steady state, or more often a continuous trajectory with a relative maximum or minimum. See LYS (chap. 2) for the conventions used to select the points in time for measuring vowel nuclei.
9 Some speakers do show a quadrilateral acoustic space, but this is a relatively rare case that involves the absence of maximally open central vowels.

The two diagonals of the triangle are defined in quite different ways. In chapter 4, the dimension of height along the front diagonal was defined as $\sqrt{F2^2 - (2 * F1)^2}$. As an empirical fact, we find that the great majority of raisings are not simple alterations of F1, but rather combine changes in both F1 and F2 along this dimension. The outer limit of phonetic space is then defined as in (2).

(2) $F1 = -\frac{1}{2} * F2 + \text{Constant}$

The slope of this line, $-\frac{1}{2}$, is characteristic of the path that front vowels follow in the course of raising. In such a trajectory, each unit of increase in F1 is accompanied by twice the number of units of decrease in F2. The constant ranges from about 2800 for men to 3400 for women. The back diagonal is formed simply by the expression in (3),

(3) $F1 = F2$

for by definition, F1 is lower than F2, and it is not possible for a vowel to occupy the space to the right of this line, where F2 is lower than F1. Within the triangle, vowels may approach this line as F2 becomes lower and F1 higher, so that spectrograms may show only a single bundle of reinforced harmonics where theoretically we must expect two.

The Modern English vowel system

The various sound shifts in progress in English dialects operate upon a system that is basically the output of the Pattern 1 Great Vowel Shift, but only after one additional sound change of considerable importance that took place in the 17th and 18th centuries: the diphthongization of the long vowels /i:, e:, u:, o:/. This event reorganized English vowels into the system first presented in chapter 3 with three subsets: one set of six short vowels, and two sets of four upgliding vowels, as shown in (4).

(4)   SHORT   UPGLIDING

		FRONT		BACK	
i	u	iy		iw	uw
e	ʌ	ey	oy		ow
æ	o	ay	aw		

This notation provides an overall pattern that is a common starting place for the chain shifts we will be studying. It does not serve for all English dialects. For example, the diphthongization of high and mid vowels did not take place in all communities in the north of England, Scotland, and Ireland, so that the diphthongal system is more limited. The dynamics of the chain shifts in southern England, the United States, and elsewhere are a result of the structural relations shown in (4). The chain shifts that we will be studying take place largely within these three subsystems, and not across them.

The short vowels are shown here with the symbol /o/ in low back position. In the great majority of American dialects, this has been lowered and unrounded to [a], and merged with the allophone of ME short **a** after /w/ that was not fronted to [æ], in *want, watch, watt*, etc.[10] For our purposes, the notation /o/ is justified by two different sets of facts: (1) the productive morphophonemic alternation with /ow/ in *tone/tonic, telephone/telephonic, bio-/biology*, etc.; (2) the dialectal relations with the British dialects that preserve short rounded [ɔ] here, as well as the Canadian and New England dialects that use a rounded vowel for the result of merging long open **o** (see below). For the majority of American dialects and the minority of British dialects that use a variety of [ɑ] for this vowel, it will be understood that the low-level rule of unrounding, lowering, and centralization to [a] has applied.[11]

One might suggest the use of the less abstract /ɔ/ as a notation parallel to /æ/ in the front. But the general principle that controls our notation is to avoid using special characters until we are compelled to. Short open /o/ will be paired with long open /oh/ (see below), and /ɔ/ will be introduced only for the small number of dialects that preserve the distinction between /o/ and /ɔ/ before /r/.[12]

Until recently, the short vowels were quite stable in comparison with the long vowels, and had not moved far from their Middle English origins. The chief source of cross-dialectal variation was in tensing of the low vowels, with a lexical splitting of /æ/ and /o/. But as we will see, some of the most radical of the recent changes affect the short vowels, which are rotated systematically in the Northern Cities. The most important feature that establishes the unity of this subsystem is a structural one: these vowels occur only in checked position, never in free position:

(5) /i/ pit, sit   /u/ put, soot
    /e/ pet, set   /ʌ/ putt, but
    /æ/ pat, sat   /o/ pot, sot, watt, want

[10] And in many dialects that do not preserve distinctive length or inglide in the low central vowels, /a/ also includes the vowels of *father, calm, pajama, rajah, pa, ma*, etc.

[11] Historically, this unrounding occurred in the United States by the beginning of the 19th century. It was first noted by the spelling reformer Michael Barton in 1832, in comparing his own upper New York State dialect with that of Boston.

[12] One might ask whether the more abstract notion of /a/ could be used for the low front short vowel that I have labeled /æ/. The difficulty arises in relating the short vowels to the long and ingliding vowels, presented below. In many dialects, /æ/ splits into lax /æ/ and tense /æh/. Almost all dialects contrast this with the low central long and ingliding vowel /ah/ in *father, pajamas*, etc.

The front upgliding class is quite straightforward:

(6)   /iy/ be, beat
       /ey/ say, bait   /oy/ boy, Hoyt
                         /ay/ buy, bite

In addition to the northern British dialects mentioned above, there are a number of American dialects that retain monophthongal vowels where others have /iy/ and /ey/, even in free position. This has long been noted as a characteristic of dialects with a strong non-English substratum: in the Caribbean, in Ireland, in Pennsylvania-German areas (Reed and Seifert 1954; Kurath and McDavid 1961), and in Scandinavian-dominated regions of the North Central states (Allen 1973).[13] However, the chain shifts affecting the Vy class to be discussed in this chapter all have clearly diphthongized vowels even in checked position.

The back upgliding class contains three basic members and one marginal member, /iw/.

(7)   /iw/ fruit, dew   /uw/ boot, do
                          /ow/ boat, bow
                          /aw/ bout, bough

The diphthong /iw/ is found in a sizeable set of reflexes of French **u**, borrowed at a time when it was already somewhat fronted, as well as the Middle English diphthongs *few*, *dew*, etc. These were realized in many dialects as [jü] or [jɪu], which could be analyzed as containing /juw/. The phonemic distinctiveness of /iw/ was the result of the loss of the conditioning /j/ glide after apicals, creating a contrast between *dew* and *do*, *crude* and *croon*, *lute* and *loot*. The contrast disappeared in many dialects and remained marginal in others, so that it has not impeded the Pattern 3 movements to be presented here.

The diphthongization of the mid and high vowels left two long vowels in the system. Both were phonemes that had been formed from a variety of miscellaneous classes. In most dialects, long /ah/ is a limited class consisting of a few low central vowels in open syllables that were not fronted – *father*, *pa*, *llama*, *pajama*, *rajah*, *calm*, *salve*, etc. In various dialects of southern England and New England, the long /ah/ class is augmented by members of the broad **a** class. Long open **o** is the combined result of three different processes: the monophthongization of /aw/ in *hawk*, *caw*, etc.; the vocalization of /l/ in *talk*, *all*, etc.; and the tensing of short **o** in *lost*, *coffee*,

---

[13] In recent decades, these areas have undergone some remarkable new developments, which lie outside the range of data considered in this chapter. Long monophthongs have shown a tendency to develop inglides, especially in checked position.

dog, etc. (primarily in American dialects). The tensing processes that created the broad **a** class and augmented the long open **o** class share a basic phonetic conditioning (tensing before nasals and voiceless fricatives), and the same factors now appear in the tensing of short **a** in the Middle Atlantic states. (The formation of these three classes is examined in detail in the discussions of lexical splits in chapter 11 and regular sound change in chapter 15.)

In many dialects, the new tensed [æ:] and [ɔ:] are raised and develop salient inglides as they reach mid position, a process that was reflected in several of the historical changes reviewed in chapter 5. The length of these tense vowels is then prominently associated with inglides, and they become identified with the limited sets of ingliding diphthongs in *idea*, *yeah*, *boa*, and *skua*. These marginal classes then become augmented and develop important contrasts with the upgliding vowels. In New York City, for example, the trajectories of the diphthongs in *low* [lʌʊ] and *law* [lʊə] trace out the same areas of phonetic space, but in opposite directions. When tautosyllabic /r/ is vocalized to shwa in southern British and Eastern American dialects, the resulting ingliding vowels fall together with the others, producing a very large number of homonyms.[14] The subsystem of ingliding vowels will be designated Vh, using the semivowel /h/ to indicate the inglide.[15] A conservative system for an *r*-less Middle Atlantic dialect such as that of New York City then appears as in (8),

(8) /ih/ beard, theatre /uh/ moored, skua
     /eh/ bared, yeah   /oh/ baud, bored, boa
     /æh/ bad, salve, baa /ah/ bard, father

with the understanding that the processes of linguistic change often lead to the gradual merger of /æh/ and /eh/, and the merger of that class with /ih/, along with the merger of /oh/ and /uh/.

The inventory of vowels that will form the basis of our discussion of chain shifts is therefore as follows:

(9) SHORT   UPGLIDING   INGLIDING
                  FRONT   BACK
     i   u   iy   iw   uw   ih   uh
     e   ʌ   ey   oy   ow   eh   oh
     æ   o   ay   aw   æh   ah

---

[14] So that in New York City the combined effects of tensing and raising of short **a** and vocalization of /r/ produced homonyms of *bad* and *bared*, and ultimately of *bad*, *bared*, and *beard*, along with *law*, *lore*, and *lure*, and *laud*, *lord*, and *lured* (Labov 1966).

[15] This is a convenient and traditional notation, and it will ultimately assume considerable theoretical significance. This notation is possible because prevocalic /h/ is in complementary distribution with postvocalic [ə], though this argument does not carry the same decisive role in this discussion that it did for American structural linguists (Trager and Smith 1957).

This notation will be used throughout the discussions to follow.[16]

The concept of a word class

The expression *word class* has been used freely throughout the preceding chapters, primarily in the context of historically attested sound changes. A typical word class is the ME ū class: that is, all the words containing vowels that are reflexes or direct descendants of ME ū. This construct will play an even more important part in the chapters that deal with the regularity of sound change, since word classes and regularity imply each other. There is no problem in the concept of word class as far as diachronic description is concerned.

However, this chapter will also use word classes in synchronic descriptions of vowel systems. The presentation of chain shifts in progress is based upon synchronic views of individual vowel systems. As we saw in chapter 3, time depth is usually provided by contrasting speakers of different ages within communities, since the earlier real-time data are usually not comparable. The use of the standard set of word classes defined by (9) allows us to make comparisons across dialects, and to infer developments by the logical relationship between dialects. The vowel charts will show, not the phonemes of the dialects concerned, but the phonetic realization of the word classes defined by (9), which will be used for all the American and most of the British dialects to be described. They do not represent the most appropriate phonetic or phonemic notation for any one dialect; instead, they represent a framework that allows us to compare dialects. These word classes are relatively recent. They date back, not to Middle or Old English times, but to the late 18th or 19th century. At this point, the Great Vowel Shift and the subsequent diphthongization of mid and high tense vowels were generally accomplished. In most American dialects, short open **o** had unrounded to [a] and some short **a** words had become tensed to [ɛ:ə].

For any current dialect, the phonetic realization of a given word class may be quite far from the notation shown. What we have labeled as /i/ may fall to [ɛ] or [æ]; what we have labeled as /ey/ may rise to [i:ᴛ] or back to [ʌi]. By retaining the nomenclature of (9), we retain the ability to trace the development of sound changes from their recent starting point, and to demonstrate the opposing movements of the same elements in different regional dialects. When we consider mergers in chapters 10–13, the same technique will be useful in tracing ongoing changes.

In many cases, a given word class, which is a single phoneme in all

---

[16] Since we are dealing with stressed vowels, there is no shwa, and no central vowel, though this would be a serious omission if we were to aim at a complete analysis of some British or American dialects. The mid central vowel in *her* and *bird* will not enter into the economy of any of the vowel systems we are to consider and can be neglected for present purposes.

dialects, has divided into one or more allophones with radically different distributions. Thus, /ay/ is divided into (ay0), the centralized allophone before voiceless finals, and (ayV), the residual class before voiced consonants and final pause. The notation I have adopted throughout is an attempt to preserve the perceived identity of the word class, but also to reveal those radical differences in the phonetic histories of the allophones that can lead to split. In these cases, an additional consonant designates the allophones in question.

Conventions of instrumental vowel charts

In the sections to follow, the patterns of chain shifts in progress will be illustrated by two-formant diagrams based on instrumental measurements of vowel nuclei. The vertical dimension is F1 and the horizontal dimension F2. Both dimensions are linear, even though the mel or bark scales, which reflect perceptual distances more accurately, approximate a logarithmic scale about 500 Hz. Although a logarithmic contraction of the upper range of F2 is consistent with the perceptual data to be presented in the following chapters, the distinctions in production that are most important for our view of phonological space will be seen most clearly in a linear display.[17]

The timbre of a vowel will normally be shown by a single point, representing the central tendency of that vowel. In most cases, these are points of inflection of the vowel trajectories. The most common such point of inflection is the F1 maximum reached when the consonantal influence of the onset or coda is minimal. In the case of tense ingliding front vowels like [e:ə] in *man*, the central tendency is an F2 maximum that follows the F1 maximum. For the corresponding back vowels like [o:ə] in *lost* or [o:ɣ] in *Paul*, the measured point in time is an F2 minimum. Where no such point of inflection differentiates a long steady state, the earliest point is selected that shows no obvious consonantal influence. The selection of a single point should not imply that this represents all the perceptually important information about the vowel – obviously untrue in the case of a diphthong. The one point that represents a given token of a vowel can be compared with a point for another token of the same class, so that the overall distribution of the word class or phoneme can be registered. If the same rules for measurement are observed across speakers, we will be able to use these clusters of points to trace the progress of a sound change across apparent time, as in chapter 3.

The diagrams to be presented below are not complete representations of the vowel systems, but extracts intended to bring out particular relations

---

[17] A further reason for preferring the linear display is that it compensates for the absence of the F3 contribution in our displays. For high front vowels where F3 is within 500 Hz of F2, there is reason to believe that the perceptual effect is a combination of F2 and F3, though there is no agreed formula to represent that combination.

of importance to the principles of chain shifting. The word class on which we are focusing will be shown with individual tokens, usually surrounded by an ellipse, whereas other word classes that are included to show the contours of phonological space may be represented only by a circle registering the mean value. The symbols that will be used to represent vowels here and in following chapters are shown in (10).

(10) Vowel codes

V		Vy		Vw		Vh		Vhr	
ⵔ	i	ⵔ	iy	ⵔ	iw			⊕	ihr
◇	e	◇	ey	◤	aw	▽	æh	⬦	ehr
□	æ	▽	ay	◢	ow	▽	æhN	✚	ahr
■	o	◆	oy	◢	uw	✿	ah	⁚⁚	ɔhr
◆	ʌ					▼	oh	▼	ohr
●	u							⊕	uhr

The general conventions used to construct the symbols are listed in (11).

(11) Conventions for constructing symbols used to represent vowels

Height
  High vowels   Circles
  Mid vowels   Diamonds
  Low vowels   Squares
Backing
  Front vowels   Open symbols
  Back vowels   Solid symbols
Diphthongs
  Upgliding   Front and back upward arrows
  Ingliding   Triangles, crosses, etc.

6.2 Patterns of change in progress

Section 5.3 presented combinations of the elementary components of chain shifting that are most commonly found in the historical record. This section will investigate these patterns in greater detail as they occur in change in progress, using the instrumental measurements of spontaneous speech, and then will add a fourth pattern that is perhaps the most common in current English dialects, but not found in the historical record.

Pattern 1 and its extensions

The striking symmetry of Pattern 1 is not exemplified in any current English sound change. All the ongoing changes show the influence of Principle III on the back vowels, fronting them more than Pattern 1 allows. The symmetry of the Great Vowel Shift depends on the symmetrical fall of ME ī and ū to mid and low position. Many conservative English dialects now rest at the end point of this process, displaying a symmetrical pair of upgliding diphthongs /ay/ and /aw/ with the identical low central nucleus [a]. This is the case in the speech of northern New Jersey (my own dialect), and most of the speakers from the Northern Cities, including Albany, Rochester, Buffalo, Detroit, and Chicago. There are also many other dialects where /aw/ and /ay/ continue to move, in the pattern shown in (12).

(12)   EXTENSION OF PATTERN 1

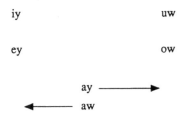

Several scholars have recognized the generality of Principle IIa and have proposed that it be understood as a form of nucleus-glide differentiation (Stockwell 1978; Stampe 1972; Donegan 1978).[18] The opening of diphthongal nuclei under Principle IIa certainly leads to an increase in the phonetic distance between nucleus and glide. This tendency is developed further by this extension of Pattern 1, and eventually reverses the opening movement. Figure 6.1 shows the vowel pattern of Chris Andersen, 73, the oldest of the 10 New Yorkers analyzed instrumentally by LYS. The conservative character of this system can be seen clearly in the parallel lower mid positions of (æh) and (oh). In Andersen's speech, the membership of the New York City /æh/ class is quite regular, in that words like *man, pass, half* are lengthened and more peripheral than other words; but the raising to mid and high position characteristic of younger speakers has not actually begun, and (oh) is equally conservative. The conservative orientation of (ay) and (aw) is equally clear. They are both squarely located in central position, with no tendency toward fronting or backing. In contrast, figure 6.2 shows the advanced New York City dialect of an upper

---

[18] The force of these contributions will be considered in more detail in chapters 7 and 8. The functional principles advanced by Donegan are more specific than nucleus-glide differentiation and involve the opposing need to maximize chromaticity and sonority.

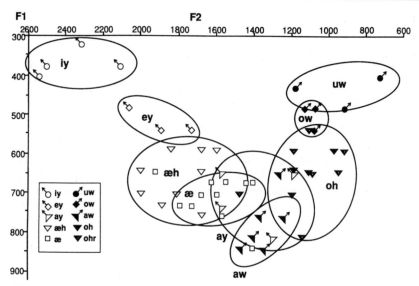

Figure 6.1.   Upgliding vowels of Chris Andersen, 73, New York City [1963]

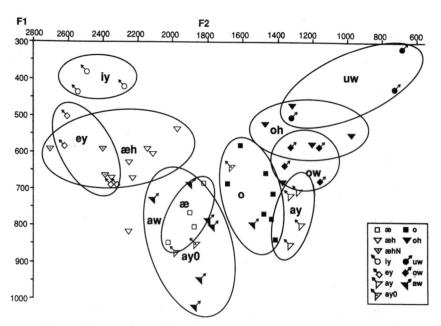

Figure 6.2.   Vowel system of Sue Palma, 37, New York City [1962]

working class speaker, Sue Palma, 37. Her long upgliding vowels /iy, uw, ey, ow/ show the same conservative, parallel position as those of Chris Andersen, while the tense ingliding /æ/ and /oh/ have now moved to upper mid position. The most recent New York City sound change has affected her /ay/ and /aw/ diphthongs. Except for the tokens before voiceless stops, /ay/ has shifted well to the back of /o/, and /aw/ has moved to the front and adopted a nucleus that is identified with lax /æ/.

A more extreme movement of /aw/ to the front is found in Philadelphia, where conservative speakers have [æu], at the same position as advanced New Yorkers, whereas younger speakers show [e:ɔ], with a fronted upper mid nucleus, and a reversal of the direction of the glide to lower back position.[19]

Many Southern U.S. and southern British dialects show /aw/ as [eü] with a fronted nucleus and /ay/ as a fully backed and raised [ɔɪ]. Figure 6.3 shows the upgliding vowel system of a London woman, Marie Colville, who was interviewed in 1968 in Hackney at the age of 39. She was born near Bethnal Green, identifies herself as a "regular Cockney, with none of your airs and graces," and shows the classic Cockney vowel system

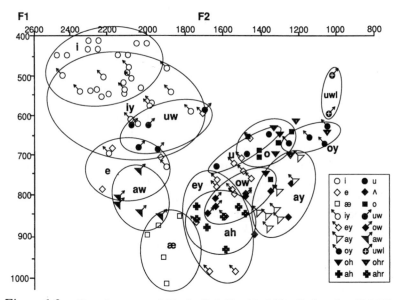

Figure 6.3. Vowel system of Marie Colville, 39, Milwall, London [1968]

---

[19] Though this is an unusual phonetic development, it may have been foreshadowed by the development of OE ēa, discussed in chapter 5. This was an ingliding vowel derived from an older Germanic **au**. Stockwell (1978) argues that this is a continuous tendency throughout the history of English.

(Sivertsen 1960). In this vowel system the nucleus of /aw/ has moved far-ther front and upward, so that it is clearly in mid front position and higher than the /ey/ diphthong. Symmetrically, /ay/ has moved to mid back pos-ition, higher than /ow/. Furthermore, it is involved in a chain shift with /oy/, which moves up to high position, [uɪ]. The abstract pattern for this extension of Pattern 1 is not simply (12) but (13).

(13)   EXTENSION OF PATTERN 1 CHAIN SHIFT

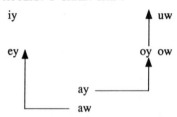

If this extension of the /aw/ shift is part of the chain-shifting pattern, it destroys the conformity of Pattern 1 to Principle II: the nuclei of upgliding diphthongs rise rather than fall. There can be no question that the move-ments of /ay/ and /oy/ form a chain shift, and that the nuclei are rising. It appears that our first effort to apply the general principles of chain shifting to change in progress has produced a striking counterexample.

PERIPHERALITY
This first reversal is the result not of weaknesses of principle but of an inadequate descriptive framework. The London vowel shift will ultimately appear as the closest replication of the Great Vowel Shift that can take place under present conditions (Pattern 4 below), and one that follows the same general principles. This result will not emerge, however, until we draw more information from the phonetic record and develop a framework that reflects more of the structure in the phonetic data.

The phonetic analysis of Marie Colville's system, figure 6.3, shows that the /aw/ tokens are considerably fronter than /ey/. Symmetrically, /ay/ is backer than other back vowels: in its lower range, backer than /ow/; and in its upper range, backer than short /u/ and short /o/. Higher up, /oy/ is also backer than other back vowels, along with /ohr/. But diagrams like (13) have no room for information of this sort: there is only one front and one back position.

This information may not seem to be immediately connected to the prin-ciples of chain shifting. However, the pattern of figure 6.3 is a recurrent one that must be taken into account in our view of phonological space. It occurs not only in the speech of Londoners, but also in many other dia-lects. A comparison with a Southern U.S. dialect will illustrate the general point. The principal difference between the London pattern and that of most Southern States dialects [SSE] is in the behavior of /ay/. In most SSE dialects /ay/ is monophthongized, and it either stays in central position or shifts to the front instead of shifting to the back as in London. However, the overall SSE pattern replicates those features of phonological space that are most crucial for our argument.

Figure 6.4 shows the vowel system of Jerry Thrasher, 20, of south central Texas. The pattern formed by the vowel nuclei is similar in many ways to that of Marie Colville, with the exception of the monophthongized /ay/, which remains in low central position. Among the back upgliding vowels, /uw/ is radically fronted, but the nucleus of /ow/ has moved downward, rather than to the front. As in London, /ow/ occupies a back position, but not as far back as other vowels. In central Texas, the far-back vowels do not include /ay/, but they do include the vowels before /r/, as in London.[20] Among the front vowels, /aw/ ranges from upper low to upper mid, in a long ellipse that is located in extreme front position. In contrast, the nuclei of the front upgliding diphthongs /iy/ and /ey/ occupy more central positions, just as in London.

These and other vowel charts to follow show that the phonological space occupied by English vowels is not adequately mapped by the four binary

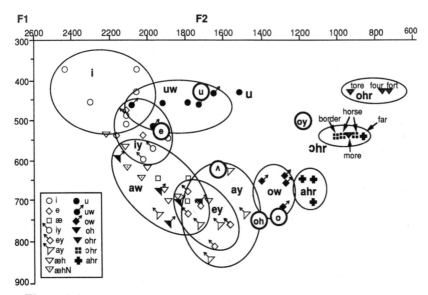

Figure 6.4.   Vowel system of Jerry Thrasher, 20, Leakey, Texas [1969]

[20] In London, /ohr/ has moved to high back position. In Texas, there is a chain shift in which /ahr/ moves up, overlapping and merging with /ɔhr/, while /ohr/ moves to the same high position as in London. These similarities are particularly striking because the London /r/ is vocalized, while south central Texas /r/ is consonantal. In general, vowels before vocalized /r/ retain this far-back phonetic location in spite of an apparent phonemic merger with other vowels (see chapter 12).

dimensions of distinctive features or the 3 × 2 charts of chapter 5 – at least not at the level at which sound changes take place. These representations lead to contradictory descriptions and fail to account for the mergers and chain shifts that have actually taken place. The triangular phonetic space in (1) is also unsatisfactory, since it gives no rules for relating the general principles of chain shifting to the observed chain shifts: in such an empty space, anything can happen. But this space does give us the footing on which a satisfactory account can be built.

In section 5.5, the term *peripherality* was introduced to describe the path of the high vowels in the Great Vowel Shift. As first conceived by Stockwell (1966), nonperipheral vowels are nonoptimal, in that they are not as clearly distinguished as peripheral vowels. Front rounded and back unrounded vowels are nonperipheral. In fact, such vowels do occupy roughly the same positions in two-formant space as the descending nuclei of /ey/ and /ow/ in figures 6.3 and 6.4. I will use the term *nonperipheral* and the feature [– peripheral] to describe any type of vowel nucleus that is plainly more distant from the periphery in its mean and distribution than another vowel of the same height. We can then elaborate our view of phonological space as shown in (14).

(14) Peripheral and nonperipheral paths in front and back

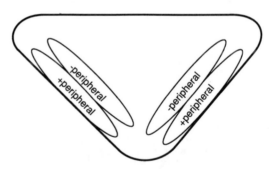

The vowel space (14) sums up the observations just presented about the extensions of Pattern 1 in London and Texas. In both front and back are two ellipses, one near the periphery of the vowel space, one closer to the center. The diphthongs /ay/ and /aw/ rise along the peripheral ellipse, while other upgliding vowels are located on the nonperipheral ellipse. Other chain shifts are spaced along the back ellipse, involving the raising of back vowels before /r/ (a part of Pattern 3, to be discussed below). These are also rising vowels. The arrows in (14) show that rising vowels follow a path along the peripheral ellipse.

How do these facts relate to the general principles of chain shifting? Since Principle I states that long vowels rise, some relation between length and peripherality is implied. This relation is not difficult to find: it is well known that in general longer vowels are located at the periphery of the vowel space, and shorter vowels are more centralized (Liljencrants and Lindblom 1972). The usual explanation is that short vowels do not reach their intended targets because before they have fully emerged from one consonantal transition, they are engaged in another. We might then say that long vowels rise along the peripheral track, because they are automatically located on that track. It is not dificult to look ahead and project a second adjustment of Principle II: that short vowels fall along the nonperipheral track.

This simple view is unfortunately not adequate. At the level at which sound change takes place, there is no direct relationship between length and peripherality in English vowels. It is true enough that /aw/ and /ay/ are phonetically long: in free position they range from 150 to 300 msec, as compared with 50–100 msec for short vowels. But there are other vowels in figures 6.3 and 6.4 that are equally long – /ey/ and /ow/ – and these are clearly located on the nonperipheral track.

So far we have considered only four of the six principal upgliding vowels: /ey, ay, ow, aw/. Of the other two, /uw/ is not relevant, since it is plainly in the grip of Principle III and follows another dynamic. But /iy/ is a crucial case. For both Marie Colville and Jerry Thrasher, /iy/ ranges from high front position to a centralized upper mid position. Is /iy/ located on the peripheral or nonperipheral ellipse? This question is answered by figure 6.5, which analyzes the /iy/ phoneme of Marie Colville in much greater detail. The segmental environment and stress pattern of each vowel are shown, in addition to its position in the two-formant space.

Figure 6.5 shows that the target of /iy/ is located not at the periphery of the vowel space, but at the centralized and lowest position of the distribution. This is where extrastressed vowels and free vowels are found. On the other hand, vowels with secondary or tertiary stress are found at the upper left, closer to the periphery. The most peripheral vowels are pronouns. It follows that the connection often made between peripheral position and length is reversed for Marie Colville's /iy/. The more time the speaker has to enunciate the vowel, the farther the nucleus extends toward the center of the vowel system.

Principle I states that long vowels rise, and these vowels are certainly long. Yet comparisons within and across dialects point to the conclusion that the nuclei of upgliding vowels /iy, ey, ow/ are not rising, but falling (see LYS:chap. 4). The general principles would then have to be restated in these terms: in chain shifts, some long vowels rise along the peripheral track, and other long vowels fall along the nonperipheral track. This is true enough, and in the long run will turn out to be extremely helpful; but at the moment it leaves us with no way of differentiating between those that rise and those that fall, so that the main contribution of Principles I and II is lost (Stockwell 1978:344).

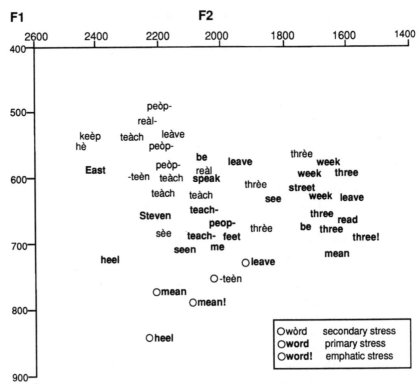

Figure 6.5. Detailed view of /iy/ of Marie Colville

The term *long* is necessarily used in two different senses throughout this chapter. On the one hand, it refers to vowels that were long in Middle English or Old English, and to their descendants by regular sound change. On the other hand, it refers to physical length, as measured by duration of the resonant portion in time. The term *long vowel* as used in Principle I refers to the abstract, historical category. An intervening category is needed if this abstract length is to be clearly related to the physical locations that I have called peripheral and nonperipheral. That category is [+ tense], which will be used here in the same way that it was implemented in Chomsky and Halle 1968: an abstract category that organizes English vowels into major sets. The name *tense* makes reference to a possible articulatory definition based on measurements of muscular tension, but my use of it is based on more indirect acoustic evidence. The feature [tense] will appear as an abstract assembly of several phonetic features; it will be applied not to vowels as a whole, but to nuclei or glides as distinct segments. In most Modern English dialects, tense nuclei are differentiated from lax nuclei in that they

- are located closer to the periphery of the two- or three-formant vowel space
- are relatively longer
- develop relatively greater amplitude
- are frequently separated from the following glide by transitions of much lower amplitude than the nucleus or the glide
- develop inglides if they are at mid or high position.

The classic tense nuclei of Modern English dialects are those of *man* and *law* in the Middle Atlantic states, and they are often heard and stigmatized as extreme sounds ("harsh," "nasal"). However, tense nuclei are also found in upgliding diphthongs, as suggested in the extreme developments of /ay/ and /aw/ to [ɒ:i] and [ɛ:o] in London, New York, and Philadelpha. Here the nuclei are peripheral, long, with considerable amplitude. They also develop low-amplitude midpoints between nucleus and glide, so that in extreme forms they can be heard as two syllables instead of one. Figure 6.6 shows the characteristic trajectory of a free /ay/ vowel spoken by Marie Colville: a fully stressed form of the word *I*. Each measurement shown corresponds to a 10-msec frame; the vowel is 180 msec long. It begins with a transition from low central position just front of center, and moves to a low back position, with a characteristic steady state of 60 msec. It then proceeds downward to a point of inflection in low central position before proceeding upward to the glide target, [ɪ]. This /ay/ might be transcribed

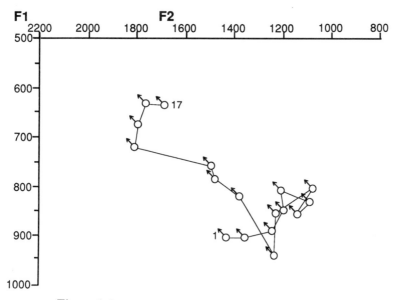

Figure 6.6. Trajectory of stressed *I* of Marie Colville

narrowly as [ᵃɒ:ɑ⊥ᶦ].[21] Similar complex trajectories are found for /ay/ in New York and Philadelphia.

This complex description of the tense/lax distinction should make it clear that it is not simply a terminological substitution for peripheral/ nonperipheral. The complex of features that makes up the [tense] category allows us to identify tense vowels independently of their position in two-formant space, and thereby gives empirical substance to the principles involved. If, for example, a pair of long vowels with distinct inglides were to be located on the nonperipheral track and were to move upward in a chain shift, their movement would constitute a marked exception to the general principles put forward here.

We can then restate the first two principles of chain shifting as follows:

(15) PRINCIPLE I
      In chain shifts, tense nuclei rise along a peripheral track.
      PRINCIPLE II
      In chain shifts, lax nuclei fall along a nonperipheral track.

These two principles describe the modern extensions of Pattern 1 and will apply to the various other patterns to be explored below.[22] But we have not yet answered the question of how diphthongs move from one category to the other. The nuclei of /iy/, /ey/, and /ow/ are lax by the definitions just given. How can we apply this definition of tense and lax to low central vowels? The model shown in (14) gives no clue. The concept of peripherality can easily and logically be extended to low central vowels. In the conservative dialects that show a symmetrical low central [ay] and [aw] for /ay/ and /aw/, the [a] nucleus is not usually the most open or nonperipheral vowel of the system. In figure 6.1, the /ay/ and /aw/ of the older New York City speaker are comparatively central, while the most extreme vowels of the system are the tense /ah/ in *father, God, bomb,* etc.[23] But as /ay/ moves to the back and /aw/ moves to the front, they regularly appear as the most open vowels of the system, as seen in figure 6.2. It follows that an intervening step between the falling of a diphthong to /ay/ and /aw/ and the raising of these nuclei along the peripheral track is the tensing of the nuclei. Such tensing is the automatic result of further lower-

---

[21] The combination of a steady state and a separate point of inflection is not confined to /ay/, but may be found in mid /ey/ vowels as well. Impressionistic transcriptions do not capture such complexity, and there is an unsolved problem: whether the steady state or the point of inflection corresponds most closely to the center of the nucleus as perceived.

[22] Stockwell (1978) formulates these two principles in a much simpler fashion as an upward drift of the V of Vh and a downward drift of the V of Vy/w. We will return to this approach, which has much to recommend it, when data from all of the patterns have been presented.

[23] In New York City, there is an additional tense/lax split in the low central vowel, contrasting /o/ in *not, body, hog* with /ah/ in *God, bomb* (Cohen 1970).

ing that moves the nucleus close to the periphery, that is, makes the low diphthongs the most open vowels of the system.[24]

This argument leads to the view of phonological space shown in (16).

(16) PERIPHERAL AND NONPERIPHERAL TRACKS

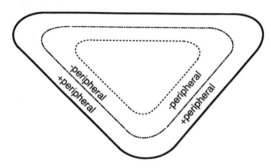

The ellipses of (14) were merely the reflection of the movements of individual phonemes. In (16), English phonological space is extended to two distinct tracks: a peripheral track that follows the outer limit of phonological space, and a nonperipheral track that follows this in parallel closer to the center of the system. The remaining space is central.

(16) extends the definition of the two tracks to the high central vowels [ɨ], [ɯ] and their lax counterparts. It is a logical extension of the definition of peripherality and will play a role in the application of the categories *tense* and *lax* to glides and their targets.[25] The general conception of peripherality made explicit here is that implied in Lindau's (1978:558) statement that "the lax vowels tend to be inside the tense vowels."

Pattern 2 and the Northern Cities Shift

The extension of the concept of peripherality to low central vowels permits us to approach the current realizations of Pattern 2 shifts and relate them to the basic principles of chain shifting. Although Pattern 2 is relatively rare in the historical records, it is a dominant force in American English dialects today, and it has been the focus of the most intensive investigation in recent years.

The clearest and most complete realization of Pattern 2 in current

---

[24] The situation here is parallel to the development of tensing and raising of /æ/ and /oh/ in New York City and elsewhere, which is not part of a chain shift. LYS showed that the first step in this process is the *lowering*, not the raising, of /æ/. That is, the tensing of /æ/ is essentially the movement of the lax nucleus from the nonperipheral track to the periphery of the vowel system, with additional length, so that [æ] becomes [æ^<:].

[25] The distinction between tense and lax high central vowels will play only a minor role in the discussions of the principles of chain shifting to follow, but it will reemerge as a crucial factor in a more radically revised view of phonological space in chapter 8.

English dialects is the *Northern Cities Shift*, one of the most vigorous sound changes now in progress in the United States. It combines the operation of Principles I and II, and illustrates fully the correlation of peripherality with the direction of sound change. It is the most complex chain shift yet recorded within one subsystem, involving six members of the English vowel system in one continuous and connected pattern. It is also a remarkable new development in English phonology: over the past millennium, most of the rotations have affected the long vowels; the short vowels have remained relatively stable.

Early evidence for the Northern Cities Shift can be traced throughout the Northern dialect area as mapped in Kurath and McDavid 1961, Marckwardt 1957, and Allen 1964. The shift was first explicitly recognized in an unpublished paper by Fasold (1969), who traced the raising of /æh/, the fronting of /o/, and the fronting of /oh/ among 24 speakers from the Detroit survey of Shuy, Wolfram, and Riley (1966). Fasold is, properly speaking, the discoverer of this extraordinary rotation of American English vowels.

As a first illustration of the Northern Cities Shift in progress in apparent time, we will look at the vowel system of a suburb of Buffalo, New York, examining data gathered in 1970. Our purpose will be to trace the path of the Northern Cities Shift through phonological space, following the changing relations between word class targets as a whole. But as sound changes proceed, phonetic conditioning exaggerates the differences between faster and slower elements so that allophonic differences become exaggerated. Since an understanding of phonetic conditioning is also essential, I will point out its major features.[26]

CHILI

The Northern Cities Shift is essentially an urban phenomenon. Callary (1975) demonstrates that the advancement of the shift (as measured by one of its major elements, the raising of tense /æh/) is tightly correlated with the size of the speech community. The larger the city, the more advanced the change. The most conservative system can therefore be viewed in the speech pattern of an older speaker from a small town. Figure 6.7 shows the vowel system of Frank Huber, who was 81 in 1970, and who lived in Chili, New York, a small town near Rochester. The stable vowels are indicated by their mean positions, while the distributions of the vowels involved in change – /æh/ and /oh/ – are shown as ellipses. In contrast to the situation in the London and Texas vowel systems examined above, the vowels /iy, ey, uw, ow/ show stable peripheral nuclei in high

---

[26] Chapter 15 will examine this phonetic conditioning in greater detail.

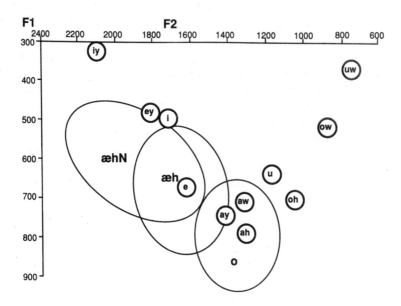

Figure 6.7. Vowel system of Frank Huber, 81, Chili, New York [1970]

and mid position.[27] This is one of the primary characteristics of the Northern Cities Shift. The corresponding short vowels /i, e, u, ʌ/ are relatively low and centralized. Whereas /oh/ is in lower mid back position, /o/ is in low center position, slightly to the back. Finally, the tensed short a, phonemically /æh/,[28] is in the process of raising. The vowel is distributed in a broad ellipse along the front periphery, with allophones ranging from upper mid to low central, where it is contiguous but nonoverlapping with

---

[27] In most cases, /iy/, /ey/, and /uw/ are monophthongal in checked position, and in some areas, they are monophthongal in free position. This is the basis for the report by Lehiste and Peterson (1961) that American English *bead* and *who'd* have simple long nuclei, and *hayed* and *node* have complex nuclei with single targets. Lehiste's subjects were educated speakers from an area north of Chicago.

[28] Throughout this chapter, the symbol /æh/ will be used to indicate the tensed short a in *hat, pack, last, bath, man*, etc. In the Middle Atlantic and Southern dialects, this is split between a lax /æ/ and a tense /æh/. In still other dialects, there is only one phoneme, /æ/, with a raised allophone before nasals. The symbol /æh/ is used in place of other signs of tensing (length, superior bar) to distinguish it from underlying tense vowels, and to emphasize that its raising is always accompanied by the development of an inglide as it reaches mid and high position. This inglide is an essential element in maintaining the distinction between /æh/ and /ey, iy/, since in the Northern Cities the nuclei overlap, and only the direction of the glide differentiates them. The notation /æh/ is therefore to be preferred to /æ/ for the Northern Cities.

/a/.[29] Most importantly for the present discussion, it is in peripheral position, clearly fronter than any of the other vowels in the system.

Figure 6.8 expands the data of figure 6.7 by showing the 136 measured tokens of /æh/ and the 23 tokens of /o/. The most advanced and least advanced /æh/ words are labeled, and the major contextual constraints are available for inspection. A following nasal consonant is clearly a powerful effect; words such as *hand, and, chance* are the most advanced, at upper left, and only a few such words with several following syllables appear at lower left: *example, animals*, etc. Among words with oral finals, words with initial obstruent clusters and several syllables are even lower and backer: *classify, flats, agriculture*. These tendencies are given a more precise expression in table 6.1, which shows the results of a multiple regression

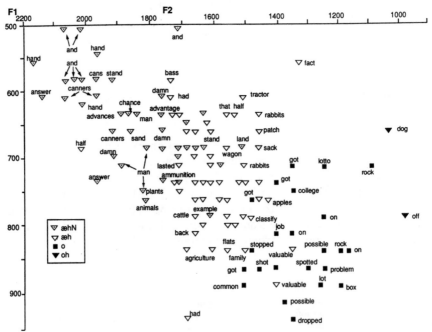

Figure 6.8.   Low vowels of Frank Huber

---

[29] LYS examines the phonetic conditioning of raising in some detail. Here as in all other dialects, the more advanced tokens are the vowels before nasal consonants, and the least advanced, neighboring /a/, are those with initial liquid clusters (*flat*) or following velars (*bag, back*).

analysis of the 136 /æh/ tokens. An initial liquid cluster has a powerful effect on both F1 and F2, raising the first by 106 Hz and lowering the second by 160 Hz. The individual word *and*, which is quite common in the data set, is marked by its higher position with a lower F1 coefficient, while the number of following syllables has an opposite effect, lowering the vowel considerably (the effect of two or three syllables is shown by multiplying the coefficient 24 by a factor of 2 or 3). On the other hand, F2 is significantly lowered by the general membership in the class of grammatical functors. Finally, the expected effect of a following nasal is shown: F2 is advanced by 144 Hz.

Figure 6.8 also shows marked contextual effects on the fronting of /o/, which is just beginning in this system. Words with initial velars and final apicals, like *got*, are always found in the frontest and highest position, while words with following velars, like *rock* and *box*, are farthest back.

Figure 6.9 shows the vowel system of Henry Ord from Chili, a generation younger than Frank Huber, who was 60 years old in 1970. The major difference between the two systems is the fronting and raising of /æh/, which now ranges from upper high – as high as /iy/ and fronter – to lower mid. The most advanced tokens of /æh/ are those with following nasals, like *can* and *hand*, except for those with initial liquid clusters, like *plant*. The least advanced tokens of /æh/ are those with initial liquid clusters and following syllables (*tractor*, *apple*); even these are raised some distance from [æ] and are well separated from advancing short /o/, the second element in the chain shift.

Table 6.1 Significant regression coefficients for phonetic and grammatical constraints on the raising and fronting of (æh) for Frank Huber, 81, Chili, New York [1970]

	Coefficient	t	P
F1			
Preceding obstruent + liquid clusters (*flat, graduate*, etc.)	106	3.11	.002
The word *and*	−136	−2.77	.006
Number of following syllables	24	2.17	.032
F2			
Preceding obstruent + liquid clusters (*flat, graduate*, etc.)	−160	−1.80	.074
Grammatical form (*that, had, am*, etc.)	182	2.88	.005
Following nasal consonant (*man, stand, family*, etc.)	144	2.93	.004

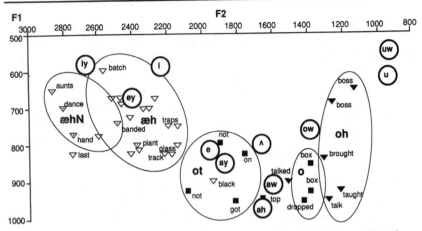

Figure 6.9.   Vowel system of Henry Ord, 60, Chili, New York [1970]

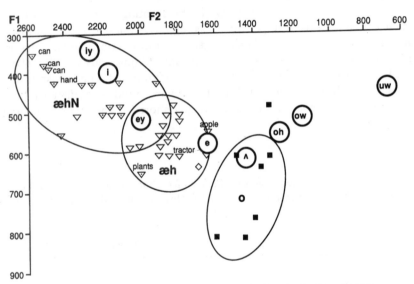

Figure 6.10.   Vowel system of Bea White, 54, Buffalo [1970]

BUFFALO
The LYS diagrams for the city of Buffalo include one for a 76-year-old woman with a system similar to that of Henry Ord. The next step forward in the Northern Cities Shift appears in figure 6.10, the vowel system of Bea White, a Buffalo resident who was 54 years old in 1970. Though /æh/ is not quite as high as in the speech of Henry Ord, it does not descend below upper mid position, even for words with initial liquid clusters like

plant, traps, track, and *glass.*[30] Short /o/ is split into two allophones: the more advanced, fronted tokens before apical consonants (*not, on, got*), with the emphatically stressed *not* the most in advance; and the set before velars and labials, which remains in low back position (*box, dropped*). At the same time, the third element of the shift appears: the downward drift of /oh/. Like /o/, this phoneme has begun to show a widening gap between the conservative and advanced tokens. In this case, the conservative tokens are those that disfavor lowering – words ending in apicals like *boss*. The more advanced tokens of /oh/ ending in velars (*talked*) have shifted forward, with one token overlapping /o/.

Figure 6.11 shows the next step in the Buffalo realization of the Northern Cities Shift: the speech pattern of Flo Danowski, who was 39 in 1971. At this point, /æh/ is almost entirely confined to high position (before nasals) and upper mid position (elsewhere).[31] The /o/ class has moved as a whole into low front position (along with the nucleus of /ahr/ and /ay/). The more advanced tokens of /o/ have now passed the low front target. The word *got* is the most characteristic of these: it is the leading element in the fronting of /o/, with initial velar and final /t/. The short /o/ in *got* has actually moved to mid front position. In listening experiments, it can be heard as [ɛ] in isolation; in context, it is heard as [æ] ([gæt]). At the same time, /oh/ has continued the drift toward a low central position, a tendency which becomes extreme among younger speakers.

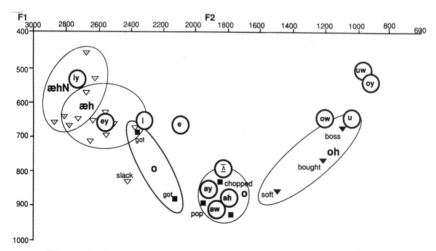

Figure 6.11. Vowel system of Flo Danowski, 39, Buffalo [1971]

[30] A more profound lowering effect is seen with *black*, which is located squarely in the [æ] region where /o/ is now found. *Black* is the most conservative, even eccentric word in other dialects and often overlaps with /a/, as in Philadelphia.
[31] Again, there is one exception, a word with an initial cluster and a following velar: *slack*.

This shift in phonological space exemplifies the problem of symmetrical structures discussed in chapter 5. Since one member of a subsystem must fall if the other rises, how can both be said to obey either Principle I or Principle II? In the Northern Cities Shift we see that the process begins with the tensing and raising of short **a** by Principle I, followed by the fronting of short **o**, which is motivated both by Principle III and by the chain-shifting tendency to fill the vacated short **a** space. The fall of long open **o** is a consequence of the basic chain-shifting principle itself, as developed by Martinet (1955). This principle may now be stated in the combined terminology of chapters 5 and 6:

(17)   THE CHAIN-SHIFTING PRINCIPLE
       When the phonetic space between two members of a subsystem is increased by the shifting of one member (the leaving element), the other member will shift its phonetic position to fill that space (the entering element).

The mechanism that underlies this principle will be explored in the discussion of functional explanations in chapters 19 and 20. At this point, the indeterminacy of the symmetrical structure can be resolved by saying that the direction of the leaving element follows Principles I–III, while the direction of the entering element may be governed by the basic chain-shifting principle. This asymmetry is a dynamic one, reflecting the temporal order of events; it will recede into the background in the two following chapters when we consider the rules that reflect the functional economy of the system as a whole.

(18) displays the first stage of the Northern Cities Shift on the peripheral/nonperipheral pattern of phonological space.

(18)   THE NORTHERN CITIES SHIFT I

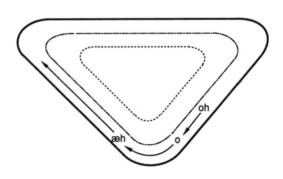

DETROIT

In chapter 4, the Northern Cities Shift in Detroit was introduced with diagrams of the vowel systems of a father and his son. Figures 4.9a,b show the progress of the shift for James and Chris Adamo, who were interviewed by Shuy, Wolfram, and Riley in 1965. These diagrams show a dramatic upward shift of (æh) in one generation, with a concurrent fronting of /o/. Three other Detroit speakers are analyzed in LYS, including Kathy, a 15-year-old girl who I interviewed in 1964. Though Fasold (1969) may have been the first linguist who noted the Northern Cities Shift, Kathy can claim priority through the observation she made at the end of the interview:

(19) It's so funny about New Yorkers. They say [bɑɾl] for [bæɾl], and they say [bæɾl] for [biᵀəɾl]!

Her /æh/ tokens are in high front position, and /æhN/ is at a level with and fronter than /iy/.

CHICAGO

The Northern Cities Shift has been observed in all the major cities in the Northern dialect area, from the White Mountains in Vermont westward: Rochester, Syracuse, Buffalo, Cleveland, Detroit, and Chicago. Chicago is the largest of these cities, and following the logic of Callary (1975), we would expect to find the Shift in its most advanced form there.[32] Fortunately, we have considerable time depth for Chicago, with interviews that range from 1968 to 1991 (including exploratory interviews carried out by Benji Wald and myself from 1968 onward and the more recent interviews by Ash conducted between 1989 and 1991 in connection with the CDC project). Over this period of 23 years, we can observe the development of the Northern Cities Shift in apparent time. Most of the speakers who will be examined here are from the upper working class or lower middle class, from 13 to 21 years old, and most are women.

I first became acquainted with the Northern Cities Shift in 1968, during

---

[32] Comparisons between cities are complicated by the fact that very different methods were used. Detroit is the most conservative of the recordings available, but they are based on the acoustic analyses of interviews carried out in 1965 by the research team headed by Shuy, Wolfram, and Riley (1966). The interviews were conducted by a number of field workers at a time when sociolinguistic methods were not well developed. Some of the most advanced features of the shift were first noted by Eckert in a suburb of Detroit in fieldwork as early as 1980 (1986, 1988). In Chicago, our first exploratory interviews were conducted in 1968, and our most recent in 1986. I will make use of this time depth to trace the development of the chain shift in comparable interviews and measurements. Again, the more advanced features that complete the shift are found in the recent interviews. Pederson (1965) shows none of the elements of the Northern Cities Shift, even among adolescents, but the absence of these features from the phonetic record may be a product of the methodology as well as the impressionistic notation used, both of the most conservative type.

interviews in Chicago with a group of boys, 16–18 years old. One of them, Tony, introduced me to his friend [ʒæn]. Thinking that he had said "Jan," I looked around for a girl. Then I realized that he was talking about his friend *John*. Later, Tony told me about his friend Marty, who went out on Lake Michigan in a small boat.

(20)   Tony: Well Marty, we went in the [læks] . . . and he got stuck
        in there, and they had to tow him out. [General laughter.]
        WL: What do you mean . . . in the where?
        Tony: In the [læ⁾ks]. [Laughs]
        WL: Whassat?
        Floyd: For a boat, you know.

The shift of /o/ to the low front position is so complete, and so startling, that this passage remains opaque for the great majority of listeners from other dialect regions.[33] The display of Tony's vowel system in figure 6.12 shows the pattern for word lists and reading style. We can see that the first two elements of the Northern Cities Shift are well established even in controlled speech. As with all Chicago speakers, we see the initial event that triggers the Northern Cities Shift – the raising of /æh/ to upper mid

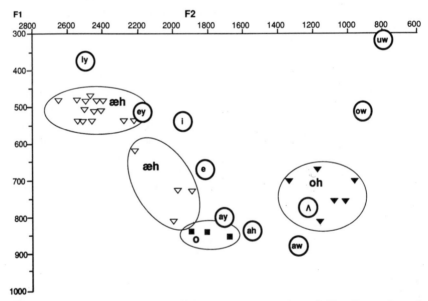

Figure 6.12.   Vowel system of Tony C., 17, Chicago [1968] (Reading and word
lists)

[33] We have used this passage in experiments on cross-dialectal comprehension to be described below, and the percentage of listeners who hear [læks] as *locks* is very low.

position. The Chicago raising is not quite as high as the Buffalo raising shown in figures 6.10 and 6.11. In Tony's speech, tense /æh/ is tightly concentrated in upper mid position, and short /o/ is established well front of center. In addition, short /e/ is relatively low, just above short /o/. A more systematic lowering of the short vowels along the nonperipheral track appears in the system of Carol Muehe, interviewed by Benji Wald in the Evergreen Park district of Chicago at the age of 16 in 1969. Carol Muehe showed many of the social characteristics of the leading exponents of sound change, which we will examine in more detail in volume 2. Like many of the speakers whose vowel systems will be considered here, she was a verbal leader of her peer group, centrally located in an upwardly mobile ethnic group that had arrived one or two generations before.[34]

Figure 6.13 shows the detailed distribution of /æh/ and /o/ in the vowel system of Carol Muehe. The range of /æh/ covers almost the entire front periphery, with a few tokens like *aunt* in upper high position, extremely fronted, and a few of the most conservative environments (*black, bang*) in low front position, contiguous with /o/. The most advanced /o/ words (again, tokens of *got*) are the most fronted and slightly centralized. /oh/ shows no pronounced lowering and centralization. The lowering of the short vowels /i/ and /e/ is clearly indicated. Short /i/ is not found in high

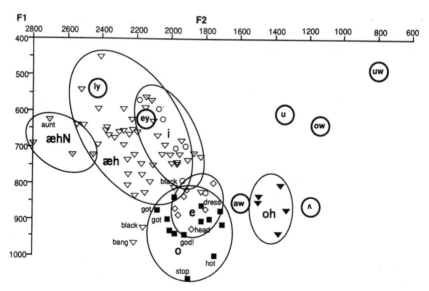

Figure 6.13. Vowel system of Carol Muehe, 16, Evergreen Park, Chicago [1969]

[34] Much of Carol Muehe's interview is taken up with a narrative about a fight in which she represented the interests of a friend who had been called a whore by a girl named Red [ræd].

position, but is lowered to mid (or even lower mid) position. Short /e/ in *dress* falls to low position, and overlaps the area of /o/. One emphatic token of short /e/, *head*, is the most open position along with the most open tokens of /o/. This extended Pattern 2 is shown in (21).

(21)   THE NORTHERN CITIES SHIFT II

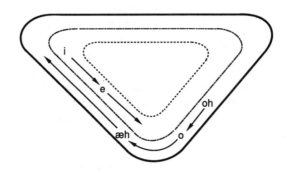

COMPLETION OF THE SHIFT: THE BACKING OF /E/ AND /ʌ/

In 1976, I interviewed a group of adolescent girls in a working-class area of Chicago with upwardly mobile, recently arrived ethnic groups of Slavic and Jewish background. This was a particularly lively session, which involved a large part of the dominant peer group of the block and featured excited accounts of a seance at a pajama party. This passage was used for an initial decoding experiment in the CDC study. Subjects were asked to decode lines a–n of the narrative (22) of Debbie S., who was 13 at the time of recording. Each line was played separately, together with that part of the preceding line following the / mark, so that the listener was always fully aware of the context.

(22)   WL: Did you ever do ouija boards?
       Debbie S.:
       a   No, we have seances.
       b   And so, at this one party, we had a seance an' –
       c   Well, my ma said we shouldn't be in 'em 'cause they're dangerous
       d   I just watched / what everybody did
       e   An' so when they were callin' [kɔˢn] this one person
       f   And they said, "If you're here, / knock on the wall."
       g   So all of a sudden / they hear a knock and they
       h   And they all come screamin', / run into the bedroom [bɛˀdrum],
       i   And turn all the lights on.
       j   / But then they did this other thing
       k   That [ðiˀt] they would ask the candle a question
       l   an' if it was yes, / they would tell the candles to move

m   and if it was no, they would have [heəv] it stand still.
n   And so, nobody really got scared of that [ði:ət].

Some of the striking results of these preliminary studies showed the following frequent errors in decoding:

1   The word *that* in line (22k) was frequently heard as *yet*, showing a shift of syllabicity not uncommon for advanced tokens of /æh/.
2   The word *have* in line (22m) was often heard as *hear*.
3   The word *that* in line (22n) was frequently heard as two words such as *the act* or *the fact*.
4   The phrase *they were callin'* in line (22e) was very often heard as *here comes*.
5   The word *bedroom* in line (22h) was heard as *budgeroom* or another nonsense word with a /ʌ/ nucleus.

The first, second, and third items are the result of the extreme raising of /æh/: the nucleus reaches high position and shows a tendency to break into two nuclei, with a low energy region at the position of most extreme fronting (F2 maximum). This anticipates the type of shift in syllabicity that was observed in chapter 5 in the Gallo-Romance raising of mid vowels.

The fourth item is not really a problem of the vowel system, but is a consequence of the vocalization of intervocalic /l/ in *callin'*. This occurs occasionally in Chicago but is far more frequent in Philadelphia and is a major factor in misunderstandings of Philadelphia speech.

The fifth item shows a new tendency: the backing, rather than lowering, of /e/. This is a common pattern among the speakers in this interview. *Debbie* was normally pronounced [dʌbi].

Figure 6.14 shows the vowel system of Debbie S. as a whole and locates the tokens in the seance narrative within that system. The *that* of line (22n) is indeed one of the most extreme examples of /æh/, but the *have* of line (22m) is only in lower high position, and the backing of /e/ in *bedroom* is not the most extreme. The range of /e/ extends backward to the /ʌ/ position, which is not the case in the other Chicago vowel systems illustrated in figures 6.12 and 6.13.

In the late 1970s, Eckert conducted studies of sound change in a suburban high school just outside Detroit. She documented in detail the social distribution of the first and second stages of the Northern Cities Shift. In an early report (1986), Eckert showed that the shift was most advanced among females of the upwardly mobile segment of the high school population: the social types known generally as "Jocks." Within the Jock group, the most advanced systems were characteristic of those who used language as a basis for negotiating social prestige: those engaged in student government and dramatics, and, prototypically, the "brokers" who transmitted

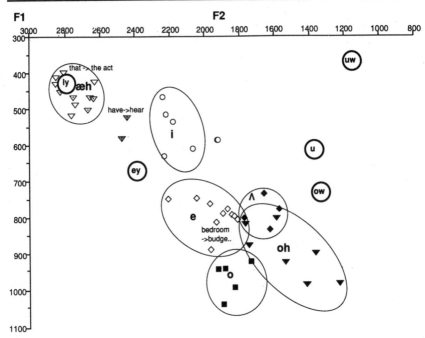

Figure 6.14.   Vowel system of Debbie S., 13, Chicago [1976], with location of extreme tokens in the seance narrative

information among the various high school groups. Eckert's ethnographically informed research gives further support to the view of the innovators of sound change found in the Philadelphia study, presented in section 6.1.

Eckert (1986, 1988, 1989, 1991) reports in detail on the latest stages of the Northern Cities Shift. Short /e/ shows two distinct patterns: a lowering to [æ], similar to that seen in the speech of Carol Muehe in figure 6.13, and a backing toward [ʌ]. These observations are confirmed by LYS and CDC studies in other Northern Cities: Rochester, Cleveland, and Chicago. Eckert's data show that the opposing high school group, the Burnouts, were leading significantly in backing of /e/ to [ʌ], while the Jocks strongly favored lowering of /e/ to [æ].[35]

Eckert was the first to observe a sixth element engaged in the Northern Cities Shift, which completed the circular character of this chain. She found that /ʌ/ was shifting backward toward the position formerly occupied

[35] Recall that backing of /e/ was also characteristic of the 1976 Chicago interviews. The name *Debbie, Deb* was regularly pronounced as [dʌbi, dʌb], and *bedroom* as [bʌdrum].

by long open /oh/. The result is the completion of the chain as shown in (23).

(23)   THE NORTHERN CITIES SHIFT III

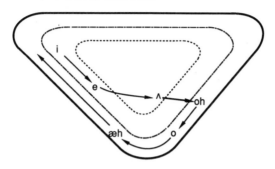

Recent interviews by the CDC project in Chicago have confirmed Eckert's observations, on the level of perception as well as production (Labov 1989c; Labov and Ash, to appear). No evidence of the backing of /ʌ/ has yet been found in the data from the 1960s or 1970s, and in the absence of other information we conclude that this is a new stage in the Northern Cities Shift, characteristic of the late 1970s and the 1980s.

From 1976 we can move 12 years ahead to 1988. Figure 6.15 shows the vowel system of Jackie H., 18, a freshman at the University of Illinois, Chicago Circle, recorded in 1988. This vowel system represents the fullest development of the Northern Cities Shift.[36] The means for both primary stress (bold type) and secondary stress (plain type) are shown for most vowels. The vowel triangle shown in the abstract schema of (23) is superimposed on the system: the first inner triangle is 66% of the size of the outer one, and the second inner triangle is reduced to 33%. Of the four long upgliding vowels, /iy/, /ey/, and /ow/ remain stable on the peripheral track. The fourth of these, /uw/, shows the tendency to shift forward that is now affecting most western and northern dialects. A tight group of nuclei are located in low central peripheral position: /aw/, /ay/, and /ah/ appear to share the same nucleus. The Northern Cities pattern is shown most

---

[36] Jackie H. was interviewed by Ash in the course of the CDC project, as part of a series of interviews to provide the test stimuli for the Gating Experiments. She is prototypical of the speakers involved: local, upwardly mobile young women from lower middle class backgrounds, verbal leaders of their immediate peer groups who use language as their primary instrument for negotiating social status. A wide range of sociolinguistic studies show that this group displays the most advanced forms of sound changes in progress (Eckert 1986; Labov 1980, 1991). The acoustic quality of these recordings was excellent (Nagra IVS recorder with a Sennheiser 415 microphone at $7\frac{1}{2}$ in/sec), the volume of speech was relatively high, and LPC analyses were closely correlated with auditory impressions. Figure 6.15 therefore gives us the most precise picture of the acoustic development of the Northern Cities Shift.

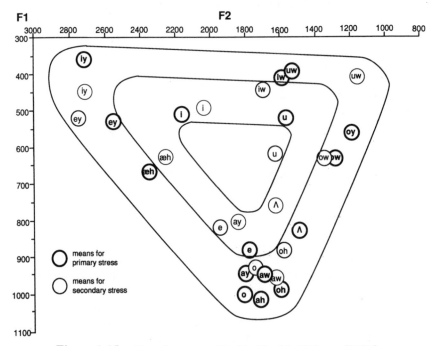

Figure 6.15.   Vowel system of Jackie H., 18, Chicago [1989]

clearly by the positions of the primary stressed means. (1) /æh/ is raised
to a mean mid position on the peripheral track; (2) the mean position of
/o/ is to the front of the other peripheral low central vowels; (3) /oh/ is in
peripheral low back position behind it; (4) /i/ has shifted back along the
nonperipheral track (and not down, as in other speakers' systems); (5) /e/
has moved both down and back, to the lowest position in the nonperipheral
track, adjacent to both /o/ and /ʌ/; (6) stressed /ʌ/ has shifted back to the
peripheral track, to the position formerly occupied by /oh/. Thus, figure
6.15 differs from the general model (23) in two respects: /i/ has moved
back rather than down, and /e/ has followed the downward track of (21)
more than the backing of (23). (As Eckert's work in the Detroit area shows
(1988), this is an option that is influenced by social position within the
group.)

The positions of the secondary stressed means are quite revealing. As a
rule, they are more centralized than the means for primary stressed vowels,
but for two of the newest and most active changes, one can see that the
secondary stressed vowels lag behind along the trajectory of the change.
This is the case for /e/ and /oh/ – with consequences for comprehension
to be examined shortly.

Figure 6.16 displays the distributions of individual vowels for the phonemes involved in change. /æh/ shows the expected long ellipse: in the most advanced position are vowels before nasals (*sandals*) and after an initial palatal (*Jackie*), and in the least advanced position are vowels with initial clusters and several following syllables (*grandmother*). Short /o/ forms a compact cluster in low front position: the actual degree of fronting is best shown by the perceptual experiments to be summarized below. Long open /o/ ranges more widely, with some tokens (*boss's*) in the original position. The most advanced tokens are *talk* and *talking*: one of the latter shows unusual fronting, but the distinction between /o/ and /oh/ is clearly maintained with a 200 Hz difference in F2 (/o/ mean 1802; /oh/ mean 1603; $t = 3.11$, d.f. 27, $p < .001$).

The most interesting distribution is that of /e/. It overlaps with /o/, but maintains a clear distinction in F1 (/e/ mean 874, /o/ mean 993; $t = 3.57$, d.f. 34, $p < .001$). It is closely juxtaposed to /ʌ/, but with a clear F2 difference (/e/ mean 1778, /ʌ/ mean 1485; $t = 3.81$, d.f. 25, $p < .001$). The approximation of the stressed /e/ tokens to the /ʌ/ distribution is a striking feature of all the Chicago speakers of this period.

The F2 distances traversed near the bottom of the vowel triangle are physically small, and the phonetic consequences of these acoustic shifts

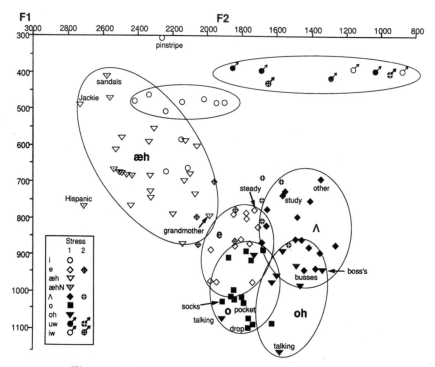

Figure 6.16. Short mid vowels /e/ and /ʌ/ of Jackie H.

can only be assessed by perceptual experiments. Figure 6.16 also locates the words spoken by Jackie H. that were used in the CDC Gating Experiments. Subjects were asked to transcribe words heard in isolation, then in a phrase, and finally in a full sentence. (24) is the full sentence for the item that focused on the word *socks*, shown on figure 6.16 as the frontest of the short **o** words.

(24)   Y'hadda wear [sæks], no sandals.

Of 157 subjects in the second series of CDC Gating Experiments carried out in 1990, only 7% heard the isolated item [s___ks] as *socks* (all but 1 from Chicago). Sixty-three percent transcribed it as *sax* or *sacks*, and an additional 26% as *sex* (all but 1 from Chicago and Philadelphia, where /e/ is lowered toward [æ]). Though the full context of the sentence clearly indicates the meaning of 'socks', this vowel was so strongly heard as a front vowel that 18% of the subjects could still not transcribe it as a token of /o/. (Twelve subjects, mostly from Philadelphia, wrote "wear slacks" as their solution to the problem.)

   The item given in (25) shows a sentence with three words involved in the Northern Cities Shift. The word *drop* is shown in figure 6.16 as the most open of the /o/ words. Since there is no word "drap," the tendency to write "drop" is reinforced. Yet 58% of the subjects used a short **a** in transcribing the isolated word. Item (25) also includes an example of backed /e/ in *steady*. Eighty-three percent of the subjects heard this as "study" in isolation, and in the phrase "[stʌ<di] for a minute," 74% retained this interpretation.

(25)   And I didn't know there was such a thing as an [ɛr pa<kɪt]. And
       we kept going up and down in the air and uh you get to a point
       where you're [stʌ<di fər mɪnɪt]. All of a sudden you just take this
       [mɛsɪv dra<p].

The Gating Experiment item given in (26) contains the word *busses*, shown on figure 6.16 as the lowest of the /ʌ/ tokens, and not far from Jackie H.'s realization of *boss*. Six-sevenths of the 157 subjects heard the isolated word as "bosses" – 83% – and surprisingly enough, this value did not change when they transcribed the phrase "[ðəbɔsɪz] with the uh–like the antennas on the top." The percentage of subjects who maintained "bosses" for the full sentence dropped only moderately, to 57%, and in this respect, Chicagoans were not significantly different from others.

(26)   I can remember vaguely when we had [ðəbɔsɪz] with the uh – like
       the antennas on the top that were attached to um – like, some

kind of like a wire. From, like, street pole to like, you know, like from street lamp to street lamp.

The Gating Experiments show that in both physical and perceptual reality, the Northern Cities Shift creates a full rotation of vowels from one phonemic category to another.

TEMPORAL ORDERING

The relative chronology of the Northern Cities Shift cannot be as precise as the chronology for the Philadelphia sound changes documented in chapter 4, but the raising of /æh/ is certainly the oldest change. Apparent-time data and the limited evidence from real-time differences in the data point to the following schema:

Changes nearing completion
1   raising of /æh/
Midrange changes
2   fronting of /a/
3   centralization and fronting of /oh/
New and vigorous changes
4   lowering of /i/ and /e/
5   backing of /e/
6   backing of /ʌ/

The first three changes clearly form a drag chain.

1   /æ → ih/
2   /o/ → /æ/
3   /oh/ → /o/

The ordering of the lowering of /i/ and /e/ is not clear, but this change most likely forms another drag chain:

4   /e/ → /æ/
4'   /i/ → /e/

The backing of /e/ and the backing of /ʌ/ form another link, and from all available evidence it is a push chain:

5   /e/ → /ʌ/
6   /ʌ/ → /oh/

Some evidence for the priority of Step 5 over Step 6 is found in the distribution of primary and secondary stressed vowels in figure 6.16. As already noted in figure 6.5, and in many other diagrams, the most highly stressed vowels tend to move farther in the direction of the change in progress.

CHAIN SHIFT CONNECTIONS OF /æh/ AND /i/, /e/ AND /o/

This outline of the Northern Cities Shift presents three separate sets of entering and leaving elements. But does the Northern Cities Shift as a whole constitute a chain shift as originally defined? The central question concerns a link between Steps 1 and 4', that is, the /æh/ → /i/ → relationship. The nucleus of the tense ingliding /æh/ does not move into the space formerly occupied by /i/, since they are on two distinct tracks. Furthermore, /æh/ is differentiated from /i/ by its prominent inglide. Whether /i/ moves down or to the back, it appears to be increasing its distance from /æh/. Without prejudging the question of functional explanation (chapter 19), it seems necessary to examine this linkage to see how it is related to the structural definition of a chain shift.

Whereas all the other stages of the Northern Cities Shift are related as entering and leaving pairs in accordance with the definition, there would seem to be no direct connection to unite the raising of /æh/ and the lowering of /i/, since /æh/ does not impinge directly on the margin of security of /i/.[37]

There is a parallel connection between the tense/lax pairs of /o/ and /e/: they are both attracted to the hole in the pattern resulting from the tensing and raising of /æh/. In figure 6.13, /o/ and /e/ overlap in this position. The major cluster of short /e/ words are located just back and center of the major cluster of /o/ words, so that /e/ lies in the nonperipheral track and /o/ in the peripheral track. But there are outliers of each group on all sides in the two-formant space, and one would expect that other phonetic features differentiate these two groups. The end result is a reorientation of /e/. Instead of lowering to a position that overlaps with /o/, it shifts back toward /ʌ/.

The links between the various stages of the Northern Cities Shift may be considered from a structural as well as a functional point of view. The shift involves the operation of all three principles: the raising of tense /æh/ along the front peripheral track by Principle I, the falling of lax /i/, /e/, and /oh/ along the nonperipheral tracks according to Principle II, and the fronting of /o/ by Principle III. The combined operation of these principles links the various steps in a structure that occurs repeatedly throughout the Northern Cities, a linkage that is not demonstrably due to direct communication or diffusion. If these are independent parallel developments, they are more likely to call for the "natural phonetic" explanations that will be

---

[37] This may not be entirely so. McKenzie (1918) reviews the history of ingliding diphthongization in seven languages (Romance, Old Irish, Finnish, Lappish, Livonian, Icelandic, Old High German) to show that upgliding **ei** could not have become ingliding **ie** directly, but must have passed through a monophthongization stage. We do not, however, find languages with a contrast between /ie/ [iə] and /i:/ [i:] or between /iy/ [ɪi] and /i:/ [i:].

reviewed at the end of this chapter, rather than the type of paradigmatic functional explanation advanced by Martinet (1955).

The discussion of this chapter has assumed so far that neighboring vowels on peripheral and nonperipheral tracks exert structural pressures upon each other that motivate, or at least partially motivate, the ensuing steps in a sound change. If this is true, it follows that vowels distinguished as [± peripheral] are not completely distinct in the sense that vowels distinguished as [± high] are. Chapter 12 will show that neighboring vowels on peripheral and nonperipheral tracks are in fact heard as "the same" by many members of the community, even though they are produced as physically distinct elements and remain distinct until they are separated by further sound changes.

The study of natural misunderstandings conducted in connection with the CDC project will help to illuminate this situation. The possible chain shift relations between raised /æh/ and other vowels can be demonstrated by the types of misunderstandings that occur. Of the 697 collected to date, 188 or 27% are traceable to dialect differences. Fifteen of these concern (æh) in one way or another. The speakers and listeners involved represent many parts of the country, since the raising of /æh/ reaches the highest position before nasals, and in almost every dialect, short **a** is raised in this position. Table 6.2 summarizes the misunderstandings that occurred.

The most surprising fact about table 6.2 is that the most common misunderstanding involving /æh/ arises not from confusion with other vowels

Table 6.2 Naturally occurring misunderstandings involving /æh/

Intended as	Heard as	N	
/ih/	/æh/	3	Gillian ⇒ Joanne
			cinnamon ⇒ salmon
			Ian ⇒ Ann
/æh/	/ih/	1	Ann ⇒ Ian
/ih/	/i/	1	Ian ⇒ in
/i/	/æh/	2	singles ⇒ sandals
			Linda ⇒ Landis
/æh/	/i/	5	sample ⇒ simple
			and ⇒ in
			Kodak ⇒ coding
			Ann ⇒ incoming
			Levan ⇒ Levin
/æh/	/e/	1	pans ⇒ pens
/eh/	/æh/	1	ANC ⇒ Nancy
/æh/	/iy/	1	Levan ⇒ Le Van

on the peripheral track, but from confusion with short vowels on the non-peripheral track. To understand this result, we will have to examine the instances more closely.

For linguists who reflect on the problems of misunderstanding, the most prominent kind of misunderstanding involves minimal pairs like *Ian* and *Ann*. Indeed, this is a very likely misunderstanding; those who name their children *Ian* or live in Ann Arbor are sure to collect examples, and two instances are found in the data. However, there are not many such minimal pairs, and when /æh/ is misunderstood for another ingliding form, it is usually the result of a combination with other phonetic misinterpretations. (27) shows how the vocalization of /n/ can lead to this result.

(27)   Charlotte T. [Virginia]: Cinnamon carrot cake—that sounds good.
       Robin S. [Long Island]: misunderstood as ⇒ Salmon carrot cake.

Those whose names contain ingliding vowels are subject to such misunderstanding. My colleague Gillian Sankoff notes that the incident recorded in (28) is not rare.

(28)   Hairdresser: What's your name?
       Gillian: Gillian.
       Hairdresser: OK, Joanne, we'll see you at 11:00.

Inglides are often created across word boundaries, as in (29), which confuses /eh/ and /æh/.

(29)   Bill: The ANC promised to use their influence . . .
       Gillian: Nancy? Nancy promised them?

In the sections to follow, we will see that the distance between /æh/ and /i/ in the Southern States is much less than in the Northern Cities area, since the nucleus of /i/ becomes tense and it develops an inglide. Though we do not have a phonetic record of what was spoken, the following cases probably represent a confusion of /æh/ and the ingliding /ih/:

(30)   A non-Texan told a Texan that the name of her son was *Ian*. The Texan couldn't understand why anybody would name a child something so strange as the preposition *in*. (observation reported by C. Feagin from J. Baugh)

(31)   Charlotte T. [Virginia]: Is Ann coming?
       Marybeth [Bucks Co., Pa.]: Incoming? Incoming from where?

In these cases, the ingliding /ih/ may actually have had a nucleus located on the peripheral track, and the confusion was among members of the same subsystem. But for eight cases of table 6.2, the misunderstanding appears to be between a peripheral and a nonperipheral vowel.

The most extensive example of confusion through the raising of the Northern Cities (æh) came to my attention during a visit to Cornell University. The organizer of a colloquium taught by visiting scholars was a young woman named Linda Le Van, born in a small town in New York State. Her name was first reported to me on a telephone message slip as *Linda Levine*. A number of graduate students in the Cornell psychology department, including 4 of 12 who attended the colloquium, also thought her last name was Levine. Linda herself said that her name had been misinterpreted Levin or Levine in high school, but she really only noticed it when she went to school in Athens, Ohio, and the error became very common in Ithaca.

All the examples so far involve /æh/ before nasals. The most extreme exponent of the Northern Cities Shift whom I met in New York State was at Syracuse University. Her use of *Kodak* was misheard as *coding* by a transcriber from Long Island.

The relationship here is a subtle one. No one would say that /æh/ will merge with /e/ and /i/ as it rises to [i:ə]. The instrumental diagrams show that the path followed by the nucleus is quite distinct from the lax vowels. On the other hand, the many phonetic features that separate the lax vowels from the tense vowels are not all to be relied on as distinctive in themselves. In the stream of speech, the inglide is often absorbed, neutralized, or neglected. Differences in height are obviously neutralized as /æh/ rises. This leaves as a permanent residue only the difference between the [+ peripheral] and [− peripheral] tracks. We will encounter ample evidence that this distinction is sufficient to maintain a productive difference but not necessarily a perceptual difference − hence the number of confusions between /æh/ and /i/ that we have witnessed, and the possibility that the lowering of /i/ and /e/ is linked to the raising of /æh/ as a way of maximizing the difference between them.

PHONETIC EVIDENCE FOR PUSH CHAINS

In discussions of chain shifting, many abstract arguments have been put forward concerning the relations between the entering and leaving elements in a chain. This issue is not relevant to the question of functional explanations (see chapter 19), since they will apply either to push chains (those in which the entering element moves first) or to pull or drag chains (those in which the leaving element moves first). The theoretical issue that motivates the discussion has to do with the nature of sound change itself. Those who believe that language change can only arise through changes in discrete (perhaps binary) rules can accept only pull chains (King 1969).

In this framework it is not conceivable that one phoneme can encroach on the phonetic space of another (or in Martinet's terms, reduce its margin of security). In the case of the backing of /e/, [−back] will either become [+back] or not become [+back]. But those who view sound change as taking place in a continuous phonetic and phonological space, as I do here, will see the issue of pull chains versus push chains as an empirical one. Two distinct kinds of data will be relevant. Naturally, we will consider any information on the temporal ordering of the elements concerned, in apparent or real time. For example, the historical evidence on the Swedish chain shift (chapter 5, (18)) indicates that the lengthening of short /a/ was the first step involved (Benediktsson 1970). In addition, the phonetic distribution of the tokens at any given time will reveal what is happening. In the first stages of a push chain, the distribution of entering element will be in close approximation to the leaving element, which may not in fact have moved at all. Of particular importance is the distribution of primary and secondary stressed vowels. As noted in our examination of figure 6.15, the primary stressed vowels of the entering element will be the most advanced for the entering element, but not the leaving element if the latter has not yet begun to shift.

Real-time evidence confirms these indications of a push chain status for the backing of /e/. The vowel systems of Tony in figure 6.12 and Carol Muehe in figure 6.13, recorded 20 years earlier, show a great distance between /e/ and /ʌ/. Figure 6.17 displays the vowel system of Mike Spencer, 18, recorded by Benji Wald in 1970. Spencer's system, like all those from the 1970s, shows no particular lowering or backing of /e/, and the gap between /e/ and /ʌ/ is as wide as in any dialect. Men are more conservative than women in all these shifts (as Fasold (1969) showed for the early stages of the Northern Cities Shift in Detroit). We can conclude that the approximation of /e/ to /ʌ/ is a product of the past 20 years, and that the backing of /ʌ/, which results in tokens such as those in (25), is even more recent and by no means as general.

PRINCIPLE III REVIEWED

The latest developments in the Northern Cities Shift introduce a counter-example to Principle III. Two vowels, /e/ and /ʌ/, move to the back instead of to the front as Principle III predicts. This is considerably stronger counterevidence than the exceptions noted in chapter 5. The Northern Cities Shift actually encompasses two contrary motions on the front/back dimension: /æh/, /o/, and /oh/ move forward, while /e/ and /ʌ/ move back. This suggests that a more adequate formulation would be as follows:

(32) PRINCIPLE III′

In chain shifts, tense vowels move to the front along peripheral paths, and lax vowels move to the back along nonperipheral paths.[38]

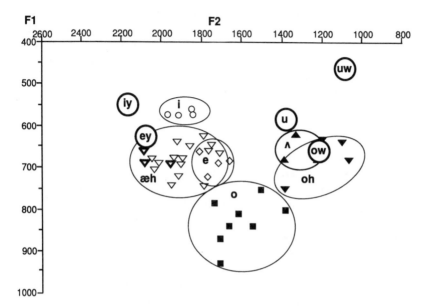

Figure 6.17. Short mid vowels /e/ and /ʌ/ of Mike Spencer, 16, Evergreen Park, Chicago [1969]

This formulation accounts for a number of exceptional movements in chain shifting. The Korean chain shift (26) in chapter 5 apparently represents the backward movement of lax vowels along nonperipheral paths, including the high vowels. The same can be said for the backing of /i/ in New Zealand English ((25) in chapter 5). However, the new formulation does not account for the fronting of tense vowels through the center, such as the fronting of /ow/ in Philadelphia, discussed in chapters 3 and 4. The following section will examine such fronting movements in detail and will offer ample opportunity to consider whether (32) survives as a satisfactory reformulation of Principle III.

Pattern 3 and the Southern Shift

The most common chain shift in the historical record of chapter 5 followed Pattern 3. This pattern combines the operation of Principle I and Principle III, as low vowels move up and back, while the high and mid vowels move to the front (see (16) in chapter 5). Pattern 3 does not appear in the Northern Cities dialects, where /ow/ is stable,[39] /oh/ moves down rather than up,

---

[38] In the discussion so far, *nonperipheral* has been used in two senses. In one sense, it has referred to the [–peripheral] track of (14). In the other, it has referred to any position that is not [+peripheral]. In the discussions to follow I will try to use it in the former sense.
[39] Though /uw/ was originally quite stable, this has changed in recent years, as we will see.

and /ah/ moves front rather than back. Pattern 3 does operate in a series
of English sound changes that are even more general than the Northern
Cities Shift, and quite opposed to it. This is the *Southern Shift*, which
governs the vowel systems of southern England, Australia, New Zealand,
South Africa, the southern Middle Atlantic states, the Upper and Lower
South, the South Midland, the Gulf states, and Texas.

LONDON

The London dialect illustrated by the speech of Marie Colville in figure
6.3 and John Gale in figure 6.21 shows only two elements of Pattern 3.
The word class of *nor, or, four, fort, cord*, etc., appears as /ohr/ in high back
position. This is of course an *r*-less dialect, but /r/ is not replaced here by
an inglide. Instead, /ohr/ develops an upglide, joining the word classes of
/oh/ in *law, cawed*, etc., so that all these words have [o⊥ᴜ]. The vowel that
formerly occupied this area, /uw/, is now a front rounded vowel, with a
front rounded upglide, [üᵘ]. As we have seen, the nucleus of /ow/ does not
follow the shift in parallel with /uw/, but instead falls along the
[±peripheral] track to a lower mid position. London then represents a
mixed pattern, with the symmetry of Pattern 1 and the asymmetry of Pattern 3. There is no doubt that a chain shift is involved, since /ohr/ and
/oh/ are now in the upgliding subsystem and would therefore be confounded with /uw/ if it had not shifted forward.

PHILADELPHIA

A more complete version of Pattern 3 can be seen in Philadelphia. The
mean values and vectors of figure 3.6 illustrate the movements of the back
vowels that respond to this type of chain shifting. The first part of the shift
concerns vowels before /r/, which move upward along the peripheral track,
terminating in a merger of /ohr/ and /uhr/: /ahr/ → /ohr/ → /uhr/. There is
a parallel raising of /oh/, but not of /ah/. At the same time, /uw/ shifts
forward. For the most advanced speakers, the unrounded nucleus of /uw/
is in the same front position as that of London /uw/, but the glide moves
back toward [u] rather than up to [ü]. In mid position, /ow/ moves forward
in parallel with /uw/. As chapter 3 showed, /ow/ is considerably behind
/uw/.

CENTRAL TEXAS

A similar pattern of chain shifting appears in many other dialects that participate in the Southern Shift. The central Texas pattern of Jerry Thrasher
(figure 6.4) shows /ahr/ in a similar lower mid back position and /ohr/ in
upper high back position, both following the [+peripheral] track. Here
there is a third back vowel in intermediate position, /ɔhr/ (exemplified here
in *Ord* and *horse*), as opposed to /ohr/ in *tore, four*, and *fort*). Since this
part of Texas lies between the areas where /ahr/ is merged with /ɔhr/ and

/ɔhr/ is merged with /ohr/, there is some migration among the three classes: *more* and *far* appear with the /ɔhr/ class. /uw/ is again in high front position; but /ow/ has followed the same track as in London, descending to a lower mid back, [–peripheral] position.

LYS also gives data for four west Texas speakers who show the same pattern of /ahr/ → /ohr/ → /uhr/, with /ow/ remaining in back position, and with different arrangements of /ɔhr/ and /ohr/.

Figure 6.18 shows four stages in the development of the New York City shift, /ah/ → /oh → uh/. The two vowels involved are /ah/ in *father, calm, pajama,* etc., and /oh/ in *law, salt, coffee,* etc. They are flanked by two vowels that do not participate in the shift but mark the end points in phonological space. In low central position is /o/, realized as [ɑ] in New York City. In high back position is /uw/; as /oh/ moves up to high position,

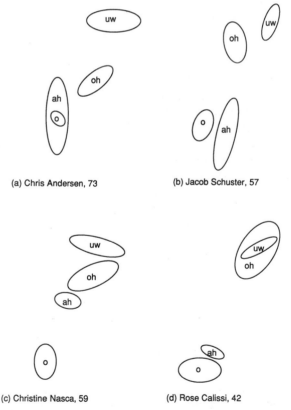

(a) Chris Andersen, 73

(b) Jacob Schuster, 57

(c) Christine Nasca, 59

(d) Rose Calissi, 42

Figure 6.18.   Four stages in the New York City shift of back ingliding vowels

/uw/ does not respond by moving to the front.[40] In the last stage, the nucleus of /oh/ overlaps the nucleus of /uw/ completely, but of course no merger takes place, given the opposing directions of the glides. There is therefore no necessary connection between the raising of ingliding vowels and the fronting of upgliding vowels. LYS presents a similar series of diagrams for the chain shift before /r/, /ahr/ → /ohr/ → /uhr/. This pattern is even more regular, and /uw/ overlaps /uhr/ at the end of the line.

If there is no necessary connection between the two parts of Pattern 3 – the raising and backing on the one hand, and the fronting on the other – then we must question whether the pattern reported by Haudricourt and Juilland (1949) in Europe should be identified with the extensively diphthongized English and German patterns. If we abandon the connection, we still have to ask why the fronting of /uw/ should be associated so regularly with the raising of back vowels.

NORWICH
Norwich, the principal city of the county of Norfolk in eastern England, is of particular interest for the study of chain shifting as well as for sociolinguistic research. Trudgill's (1974a, 1988) study of the social stratification of English in Norwich has contributed considerably to our knowledge both of the social location of change in progress and of the phonological mechanism of change. LYS presents an instrumental analysis of the vowel systems of five Norwich speakers I interviewed in 1973: the patterns fit closely the view of Norwich phonology and changes in progress given by Trudgill.

The word class inventory of (9) will not do for Norwich, which has retained several distinctions not found in any American dialects. One is a distinction between two mid back word classes that have fallen together elsewhere. The reflexes of ME **ow** in *snow, row, know, grow, show* appear in Norwich English as /ɔw/, upgliding diphthongs with a low back nonperipheral nucleus. They are opposed to the main class of Modern English descendants of ME ɔ words, which surface as /ow/ or /o:/ in most modern dialects: *soap, go, toe, boat,* etc. In conservative Norwich English, these show the effect of continued raising to [u:]. Concurrently, the reflexes of ME ō, which appear as /uw/ or /u:/ in most other dialects, shift to high front rounded position [ü], with a glide moving toward the front rounded semivowel [ɥ].

Figure 6.19 shows the vowel system in the spontaneous speech of Les Branson, 42 years old when interviewed in 1971. Here we will focus only on the Pattern 3 aspect of the Southern Shift in the back and high vowels, where Branson is quite conservative for a Norwich speaker. On the

---

[40] The chain shift is not perfectly regular in its operation, since as we can see here, /ah/ remains in low position for the fourth speaker in the series, even though it is in upper mid position behind /oh/ for the third speaker. This irregularity is not found for /ahr/.

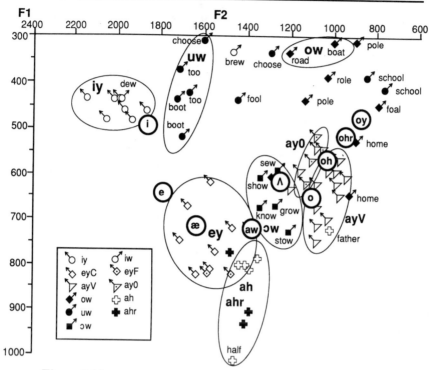

Figure 6.19. Vowel system of Les Branson, 42, Norwich [1971]

[–peripheral] track are located the nuclei of /ɔw/, /o/, /ʌ/, and /ay/ before voiceless consonants. On the [+peripheral] track are /ay/ final and before voiced consonants, /oy/ and /ow/ and /uw/ before /l/. The fronting of /uw/ is complete, except for one checked form of *choose* and the allophones before /l/.

Figure 6.20 shows the vowel system of Les Branson's son, David, age 14. The phonological system of the back vowels is the same. The special Norwich low upgliding phoneme /ɔw/ is represented by *throw* and *blow* in lower back mid position, close to the mean of short /o/ (though for David *know* is included in the /ow/ distribution). The /ɔw/ class appears to have shifted to the peripheral track. The mean of /ay/ is in upper mid position, again with a wide front-back range, with the allophones before voiceless consonants occupying a nonperipheral position. The largest difference between David's system and that of his parents' generation is found with /ow/. The main group of /ow/ words – *coast, know, note, go* – is clearly in the high peripheral position of [u]. But one word at least represents a second norm – *soak*, which is fronted more than halfway toward /uw/. This tendency in spontaneous speech led me to explore the contrast between /uw/ and /ow/ more carefully with minimal pairs and a commutation test:

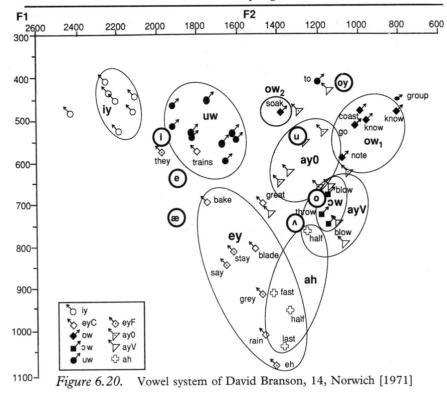

Figure 6.20. Vowel system of David Branson, 14, Norwich [1971]

here the nucleus of *toe* was fronted almost as far as the nucleus of *too* (for a detailed discussion, see figure 12.4). The main body of /uw/ words is tightly clustered in front nonperipheral position as [ü].[41] Norwich thus shows a double application of Pattern 3 fronting, like Swedish with its pair of high front vowels [y] and [ü]. In this fronting, /ow/ is fully diphthongized, like /ɔw/ and /uw/; the fronting is entirely confined to the nucleus, and all glides move back to [u].

Pattern 3 is represented schematically in phonological space in (33), where all the vowels involved move on the peripheral track. The Norwich data of figures 6.19–6.20 fit into this pattern. A clear chain shift link of entering and leaving elements connects the fronting of the high back vowel to the raising of the mid vowel. The first two stages plainly represent a drag chain:

$$1 \qquad /uw \rightarrow ü^u/$$
$$2 \quad /ow/ \rightarrow /uw/$$
$$3 \qquad /uw \rightarrow üw/$$

[41] One fully stressed word, *group*, is found in high back position, again registering the influence of initial liquid clusters.

(33)   PATTERN 3 CHAIN SHIFT

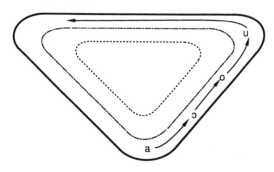

The neatness of the original Norwich pattern is all the more puzzling in
light of the development of Step 3 by the youngest speakers (to be presented in detail in figure 12.4), which threatens the margin of security of
the original /uw/. This step is another example of a push, rather than a
drag, effect. In Swedish, the original /uw/ has responded to this second
fronting by developing out-rounding, or by lowering and laxing of the
nucleus (Nordberg 1975). If the tendency for /ow/ to rise was created by
the vacancy in high back position, what force is responsible for the continued fronting of this phoneme? This is a recurrent type of problem that
functional approaches must resolve.

THE LINK BETWEEN /OH/ AND /UW/
There is no doubt that correlated movements of /ahr/ and /ohr/ represent
a chain shift. But is the fronting of /uw/ connected with these in a chain
shift relationship? A chain shift as originally defined would identify /uhr/
as a leaving element that would have moved to the center and so avoided
merger with /ohr/. The shift of /uw/ cannot have any relationship with a
tendency to avoid merger, since /uw/ differs from /ohr/ in the direction of
the glide, and of course in the presence of final /r/. Therefore, we might say
that the resemblance between the Philadelphia pattern and the European
examples (French, Portuguese, Swedish, Greek, etc.) is accidental. Before
we come to this conclusion, though, it will be helpful to examine a few
other cases.

FRONTING OF THE MID VOWELS AS A PARALLEL MOTION
At the end of the discussion of Pattern 2, it was suggested that the early
discussions of Principle III may have failed to distinguish between the
movements of tense and lax vowels. There is some evidence that periph-

erality plays the same role in the operation of Principle III that it plays in the operation of Principles I and II: namely, vowels move to the front along peripheral tracks and to the back along nonperipheral tracks. The fronting of the peripheral /ow/ was cited as an immediate and obvious counterexample to this generalization: Pattern 3 movements offer a rich variety of such frontings.

The first descriptions of Pattern 3 in LYS included the fronting of the mid back nucleus (/o:/ or /ow/), since it was commonly associated with the fronting of /u/. Yet further reflection indicates that the fronting of /o/ has no connection with either chain shifting or the principles of chain shifting. It is never linked directly with the raising of a back vowel that would otherwise merge with the mid vowel, but instead represents a generalization of the fronting of the high back vowel. In the English dialects examined so far, /ow/ is the result of the 17th-century diphthongization of /i:, e:, u:, o:/ to produce /iy, ey, uw, ow/ with lax nuclei.[42] When /ow/ is fronted, it is always in parallel with /uw/ and considerably behind it (see figure 3.6 for Philadelphia). In other dialects, like those of London or Texas, the nucleus of /ow/ falls to a low back [–peripheral] position. Though this resembles the movement of ME ū in the Great Vowel Shift, it is not associated with any chain shift. Instead, it appears to represent a generalization of the lowering of the nucleus of /ey/, part of the chain shift to be discussed as Pattern 4. Front/back parallelism is of course even more common than the generalization of movements of high vowels to mid vowels – for example, the parallel movements of /æh/ and /oh/, /ay/, and /aw/ in New York City (Labov 1966).

We then have no cases of a lax nucleus of /ow/ involved in a chain shift comparable to the backward movement of Lettish /ey/ cited in chapter 4 or the backing of lax /e/ in Pattern 2. The fronting of back vowels that is associated with chain shifting takes place either on the upper peripheral track, like /u/, or on the lower peripheral track, like /o/ in Pattern 2. There is no doubt that Northern Cities /o/ is a peripheral vowel. Whether the /u/ nucleus of /uw/ is lax or tense, peripheral or nonperipheral, remains to be seen.[43]

Pattern 4 in the Southern Shift

The final pattern to be considered in this chapter, Pattern 4, was not discussed in the resume of the historical record on chain shifting in chapter 5, though historical evidence can be found for it. It was foreshadowed in the chain shifts of East Lettish dialects in (23) of chapter 5, where for

---

[42] Though it should be emphasized that there are many English dialects where only some of these vowels are diphthongs, even in free position.
[43] The most extensive examples of fronting in chain shifts are to be found in the phonology of Norwich, where closer phonetic studies may resolve the question.

some dialects, /ay/ rose to [oy]. The more extended shift /ay/ → /oy → uy/ was found earlier in this chapter in the discussion of Pattern 1 extensions in (12). In New York and Philadelphia, this appears as an isolated chain shift, but in many other dialects, it is integrated with the overall movement of the front upgliding diphthongs, and it is the dominant mode of chain shifting of upgliding vowels that is found in present-day English dialects in the Southern Shift.

Pattern 4 begins with a laxing of the nuclei of /iy/ and /ey/, so that they are clearly located on the [–peripheral] track. The basic movement is a downward chain shift of these two nuclei. The nucleus of /ey/ falls, usually to the most open position, and the nucleus of /iy/ follows. There are two alternate forms of this pattern, which depend on the behavior of /ay/ when it reaches the bottom of the vowel system.

In the Gulf states, Texas, and many areas of the Upper and Lower South, /ay/ is monophthongized and shifts to the front as long [a:]. In southern England, Australia, New Zealand, and the coastal areas of the Eastern United States, /ay/ and /oy/ move up along the back [+peripheral] track. (34) shows the general pattern of movements in phonological space for these dialects.

(34)   PATTERN 4 CHAIN SHIFT

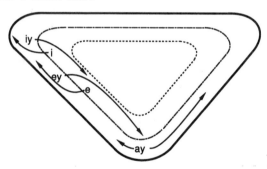

PATTERN 4 IN SOUTHERN ENGLAND
The concept of peripherality was introduced in this chapter through a study of the extension of Pattern 1 in London and Texas. In the vowel system of Marie Colville in figure 6.3, it was observed that /aw/ is fronter than /ey/. As the figure also shows, /ey/ has descended until it overlaps with the low vowel /ah/, and its present distribution indicates that it has descended along the nonperipheral track. In all the other southern English vowel systems presented in LYS (Norwich and London), /ey/ falls in the same way. For many younger speakers, /ey/ occupies the lowest position in the system. Figure 6.21 shows the upgliding vowels of another Londoner, John Gale, who was 23 when he was interviewed in Chelsea in

1968. Though the upward movement of /ay/ and /oy/ is not as advanced as that of Marie Colville, the downward movement of /iy/ and /ey/ is even more extreme.[44] The more emphatic, longer tokens of /iy/ and /ey/ are the more central and lower, indicating that their targets are at the advancing edge of the Pattern 4 movement (as figure 6.5 indicated in detail for Marie Colville's /iy/ distribution). In the front vowels, again we see that it is the raised and fronted /aw/ that defines the peripheral track most clearly. It is also evident that the short vowels /i/ and /e/ are peripheral, a tendency of the greatest importance in the dynamics of the Southern Shift.

Norwich speakers do not differ from Londoners in their implementation of Pattern 4. The two Bransons exemplify several stages of Pattern 4. For the more conservative speaker, Les Branson (figure 6.19), /ey/ extends to lower mid position, clearly less peripheral than the short vowels /i/ and /e/, though /iy/ does not show any clear movement away from the high front area. As noted in the discussion above, /ay/ is located in the upper mid peripheral area in the back. David Branson (figure 6.20) shows a front vowel area where the short vowels /i/, /e/, and /æ/ are plainly the most peripheral. As in his father's system, we see that /iy/ remains stationary in the high front area. But on the nonperipheral track, /ey/ displays an

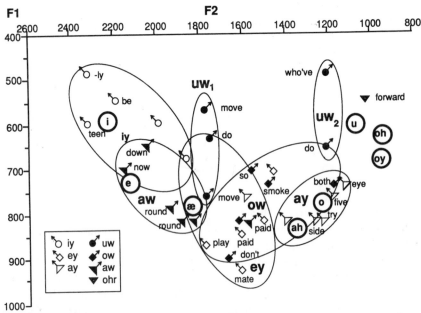

Figure 6.21.   Vowel system of John Gale, 23, Chelsea, London [1968]

[44] This must not be taken automatically as an indication of change in progress. In fact, the London version of the Pattern 4 shift appears to have been well established for over 100 years.

extraordinary range. The pronoun *they* and the word *trains* are in mid position; the rest of the /ey/ words are distributed in a long ellipse that begins in low position and extends downward – *bake, say, stay, blade, gray, rain, eh*. The most open vowel is the affective particle *eh*, which is even more open than the most open broad **a** word, *last*. This illustrates the general fact that most sensitive sociolinguistic variable in the southern British vowel system is /ey/, whose distribution in apparent time is most likely due to age-grading of a well-recognized and long-established social stereotype.[45]

PATTERN 4 IN THE UNITED STATES

Pattern 4 is also a part of the Southern Shift as implemented in American dialects. Philadelphia, as the northernmost of the Southern cities, was once a full participant in the process. Tucker reported in 1944 that Philadelphia /ey/ was the most open vowel in the system; the Philadelphia pattern is similar to Cockney in this respect (chapter 4). Philadelphia /oy/ has indeed risen to high position, and beyond: the nucleus of /oy/ is so close that it is often heard as a semivowel, with a shift of syllabicity, so that *choice* and *twice* can be confused. The backing and raising of /ay/ is not as general as in other areas (but see figure 4.10 and table 4.3 for the speech of Jenny Rosetti). Philadelphia thus shows in three out of four /Vy/ vowels a history of affiliation with the Southern Shift and Pattern 4. Recent developments show a retreat from this alignment, however, with the retrograde raising of /ey/ in checked position (figure 3.6).

In some dialects of the Southeastern United States, /ay/ moves to the back and the chain shift of Pattern 4 is activated. The Outer Banks of North Carolina is a relic area that shows an early and extended development of these processes. Figure 6.22 shows the front upgliding vowels of Monty O'Neill, a shrimp-boat captain from Wanchese, North Carolina, who was interviewed in 1973 at the age of 31. His system clearly shows the centralization of /iy/ and /ey/ on the [–peripheral] track, and the chain shift of /ay/ and /oy/ on the [+peripheral] track in the back. The backing and raising of /ay/ is the salient feature here: people from the Outer Banks are known as "Hoi Toiders" in the rest of the state, and the pronunciation of raised /ay/ as [ɔɪ] is a self-conscious stereotype that local speakers often correct.

THE TENSING OF SHORT VOWELS IN PATTERN 4

The discussion of the front vowels in Pattern 4 has focused so far on the centralization of the nuclei of the upgliding diphthongs that are the reflexes

---

[45] Most Americans become familiar with this variable through Shaw's *Pygmalion* and the musical version, *My Fair Lady*. (ey) becomes the symbol of a major breakthrough in the retraining of the London vernacular, when Eliza masters *The rain in Spain lies mainly in the plain.*

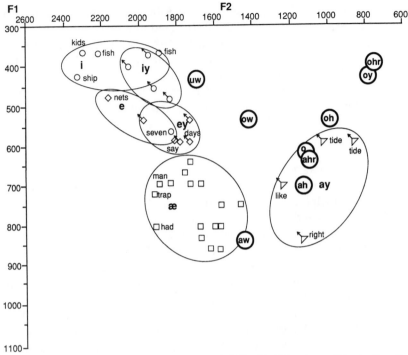

Figure 6.22.   Vowel system of Monty O'Neill, 31, Wanchese, North Carolina
[1969]

of the original Middle English front long vowels. The vowel systems presented have not been normalized to an absolute frame of reference, however: the location of the [−peripheral] track is relative to some other vowels
that occupy the [+peripheral] track. In the dialects undergoing the Northern Cities Shift, tensed /æh/, /iy/, and /ey/ occupied this position, and the
short vowels were centralized on the [−peripheral] track relative to these.
In the full development of Pattern 4, the highest F2 values are those of
the original short vowels, /i, e, æ/. These must lie on the [+peripheral]
track, since it is defined as the outer envelope of the vowels that the speaker
uses; and in reality, we have yet to find a dialect where there are not some
nuclei with a tense quality that impressionistically fall into the range of
cardinal [i, e, ε, æ].

In the clearest exemplars of Pattern 4, in London, Norwich, the Outer
Banks, and other areas of the Southern United States, the originally short,
lax vowels become [+peripheral]. In London, Australia, and New Zealand,
they remain phonetically short, so that they are clearly short, tense
[+peripheral] vowels. In the Southern United States, these originally short
vowels become long and ingliding. There are some Southern dialects where
the short vowels appear as lax and ingliding, and this is a possible articu-

lation for all dialects.[46] But for the majority of the vernacular speakers in the Southern States, the nuclei of these vowels are tense – as shown by exploratory interviews in the Outer Banks, Atlanta, Birmingham, Jackson, eastern and central Texas, and the South Midland areas of Knoxville, Bluefields. In the vowel system of Monty O'Neill (figure 6.22) the reversal of the originally tense and lax nuclei is evident, and similar patterns appear throughout the vowel analyses used earlier to illustrate Pattern 3 and Pattern 4 as they combine in the Southern Shift. Figure 6.23 shows the physical trajectories that correspond to the impressionistic transcriptions of inglides. There is a wide range in the degree of fronting of short /i/, with the most emphatic forms in the highest and frontest position. The word *skiff* begins with a fronted velar, so that the word follows a smooth trajectory from peripheral [i] to [ə]. The word *best* begins with a labial transition in a more centralized position, shifts to a peripheral mid position, and then moves to a centralized glide. In general, the glides of the new tense ingliding vowels follow a clockwise trajectory toward the target [ə], and the glides of lax /iy, ey, ay/ follow a counterclockwise trajectory.

The tense character of the new short vowels leads to widespread mergers before /l/. The word class of ME long ī before /l/ is realized as /ih/, which is a diphthong with a tense [+peripheral] nucleus and a lax [–peripheral]

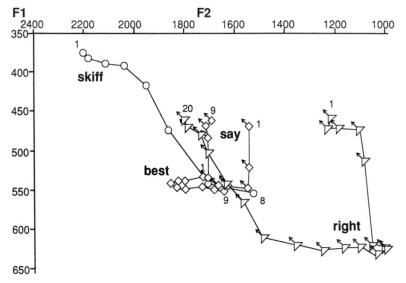

Figure 6.23. Trajectories for short ingliding and long upgliding vowels of Monty O'Neill

---

[46] The records of the American Linguistic Atlas are extremely conservative in this respect. All notations of front ingliding vowels in Kurath and McDavid (1961) show lax nuclei like [ɪə], never the [iə] that the acoustic analyses of this volume show.

glide. This is phonetically identical to the development of the originally short /i/ in general, and leads to a merger of originally short and long i before /l/: *hill* and *heel*, *still* and *steel* are homonymous throughout the area where the short vowels have become [+peripheral].

PATTERN 4′ IN SOUTHERN STATES ENGLISH
One of the most widespread features of Southern States English is the monophthongization of /ay/ to the long low center nucleus [a:]. This occurs generally in free position and before voiced consonants. The same process affects vowels before voiceless consonants, as in *nice*, *night*, *like*, etc., but it is usually restricted socially. In Southern cities, it is not uncommon to find highly educated, upper middle class speakers using [aᵉ] before voiceless finals, and [a:] elsewhere, while /ay/ is consistently monophthongal for working-class speakers.

The effect of this monophthongization is to truncate the second half of Pattern 4, so that the chain shift is confined to /iy/ → /ey/ → /ay/ → /a:/ →. This alternate route, which we may call Pattern 4′, is indicated in (34) by the short branch fronting from /ay/. Figure 6.4 shows the implementation of Pattern 4′ in the vowel system of Jerry Thrasher, of central Texas. It is evident that /iy/ and /ey/ are descending along the [–peripheral] track. The relative positions of /iy/ and /i/ are reversed. The descent of /ey/ has carried it very far away from short /e/: it extends from lower mid to the most open position of the system, fully overlapping monophthongal /ay/ (free and before voiced consonants). There is of course no merger, since /ey/ is fully diphthongized and /ay/ is monophthongized.

CROSS-DIALECTAL CONSEQUENCES OF PATTERN 4 IN BIRMINGHAM
The CDC project is concerned with the cognitive consequences of the chain shifts that are outlined in this chapter. We have already seen some of the effects of the Northern Cities Shift in the CDC Gating Experiments, which expose listeners to advanced tokens of sound changes as isolated words, as phrases, and as sentences. CDC chose Birmingham, Alabama, as one of the original target cities, and a number of younger Birmingham speakers were interviewed in the course of this work. Figure 6.24 shows the mean values of the primary stressed vowels in the system of Wendy P., 18, who was interviewed by Ash in 1989. This interview was carried out with the same equipment and analyzed with the same techniques as the interview with Jackie H. in Chicago, and figure 6.24 therefore gives us the prototypical view of the Southern Shift that is comparable to the advanced view of the Northern Cities Shift in figure 6.15.[47]

---

[47] No study of a Southern States city has yet established which if any of the various chain shifts that comprise the Southern Shift may actually be involved in change in progress. The analyses of the Southern Shift that are presented in this chapter show the consequences of

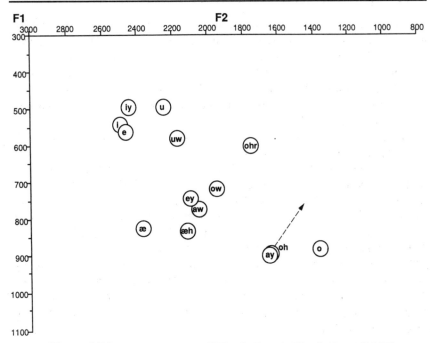

Figure 6.24. Vowel means of Wendy P., 18, Birmingham [1989]

The most striking characteristic of this vowel system is the extreme skewing to the front as a result of Pattern 3 chain shifts. The fronting of /uw/, /u/, and /ow/ presents an elliptical distribution with no representation in the high back area at all. Even /ohr/ is advanced to a position front of center. Figure 6.24 also shows clearly the effects of Pattern 4 shifts.

The front peripheral track is occupied by the original short vowels, /i, e, æ/, which are ingliding vowels with tense nuclei. A second feature of the short vowel distribution is that the /e/ mean is very close to the /i/ mean; it would be even closer, if we had maintained the same definition of word classes as in the Northern Cities. But the word *get* is realized with /i/ in most Southern dialects (i.e., the colloquial form is *git*), and the merger of /i/ and /e/ before nasals is too well established to allow *center* and *member* to be included in the calculation of the mean, which shows /e/ before oral consonants only.

The mean for the /ey/ nucleus is far below the /e/ mean, and it is clear that /ey/ has been centralized and lowered on a nonperipheral track.

There are several other features of figure 6.24 that make us realize we are dealing with a radically different organization of the vowel system from

the general principles of chain shifting for vowel systems, but they do not as yet apply directly to questions of the mechanism of change.

the Northern and Middle Atlantic pattern. A separate means is shown for /æh/ – representing environments that are tensed in the Middle Atlantic states – *ask, after, half, aunt*. But these vowels are not fronter and higher than the rest of the /æ/ distribution: they are backer and lower. The nucleus of /oh/ is not located along the back periphery, but is in low central position along with /ay/: it has in fact not an ingliding vowel, but a back upgliding vowel of the form [ɑu].

Figure 6.25 shows the actual distributions of the short vowels and front upgliding diphthongs. This figure reveals some of the dynamic tendencies of the Southern Shift that are hidden when only mean values are shown. Short /i/ has a very wide range, as in the case of Monty O'Neill, and includes many vowels with a nucleus far higher and fronter than the mean. We see *hit* [hiət] at the extreme high front position, and *sittin'* in a high central position – the kind of environmental effects analyzed by Sledd (1966) when he demonstrated that the "barred-i" of Trager and Smith (1957) was merely one extreme of a continuous series of umlaut effects. /iy/ has a similar mean, and also shows a wide F2 range for the locations of its nuclei, but the lexical distribution of /iy/ does not show the environmental effects of /i/: both free and checked forms are found in front and centralized positions.

Despite the extreme tensing of the /i/ nucleus in the most favored pos-

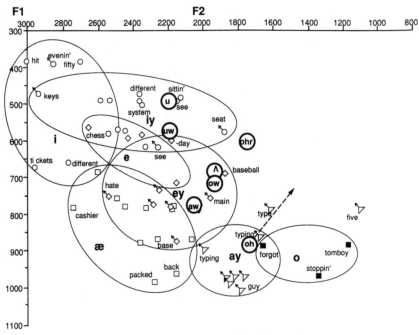

Figure 6.25.   Pattern 4′ chain shift of Wendy P.

itions, there is no tendency for merger between /i/ and /iy/. /i/ has moved into the class of ingliding vowels, /ih/, and it contrasts with the upgliding /iy/, which in turn has developed a highly differentiated nucleus. The trajectories of /i/ and /iy/ move in opposite directions: /i/ is ingliding, while /iy/ is upgliding. This is demonstrated quite clearly in the CDC Gating Experiments. One of the Birmingham items contained the word *kids* in the phrase *a bunch of kids*. Of the 67 Birmingham subjects, including those of college and high school age, not one failed to identify the vowel as /i/ (or in our terms, /ih/). But of 133 subjects from Chicago and Philadelphia, only 91 identified the vowel as it was intended, and 42, or 32%, heard it as a form of /iy/ mostly before an inglide: *keys, Kiev, peer, P.S.*, and so on.

Some tokens of /æ/ are quite fronted and clearly occupy the peripheral track. The distribution makes phonetic sense in the same terms as the Northern Cities Shift. The highest and frontest words are before voiced apical stops and voiceless back fricatives; the lowest and backest vowels are before voiceless velar stops.

The mean values for the low nuclei were not as informative as they might be. The actual distribution of /ay/ shows two major contextual effects. Words ending in voiceless stops like *type* may be centralized, and not monophthongized. The word *five* shows exceptional backing, as it often does in a wide range of English dialects.

As noted above, the most striking fact about this system is that short /e/ not before nasal consonants has risen along the peripheral track to overlap with /i/. This is not simply a characteristic of extreme pronunciations in excited speech, but is also found in the careful pronunciation used in the reading of word lists. For the CDC experiment on Controlled Vowel Identification, Wendy P. read a series of vowels in the /k___d/ framework. Her pronunciation of /e/ in *ked* as [kiⁱəd] was slightly lower than that of /i/ in *kid* as [kiəd]. The percentages of listeners who understood this vowel as /e/ were: Philadelphia 5%, Chicago 12%, and Birmingham 25%. The great majority of others heard Wendy's /e/ as /i/.

CHAIN SHIFT CONNECTIONS IN PATTERN 4

Pattern 4 shows more clearly than any other chain shift the clear separation of [+peripheral] and [−peripheral] tracks. Furthermore, each step seems to show the type of homogeneous juxtaposition that is most consistent with the functional interpretation of chain shifts. In the form of Pattern 4 that shows the backing of /ay/, the following steps can be recognized:

1		/oy/ → uy/
2		/ay/ → /oy/
3	/ey/ → /ay/	
4	/iy/ → /ey/	

And for the monophthongization of /ay/:

1   /ay → a:/
2   /ey/ → /ay/
3   /iy/ → /ey/

From Figures 6.4 and 6.24–6.25 it is evident that the new [a:] from monophthongized /ay/ remains a distinct phoneme, backer than /æ/ and fronter than /o/, which is realized as [ɑ]. Sledd argued in 1962 (Texas Conference 1962) that this /a:/ was a distinct new nucleus that must be added to the array of nine nuclei used in Trager and Smith (1957) – in other words, that the effort to set out an overall pattern of nine vowels had failed. From the point of view of an autonomous contrastive phonemics, this seems to be a valid argument. However, the CDC work on the perception of Southern vowel systems in Birmingham points in another direction, and before this symmetrical paradigm is revised, the evidence on cross-dialectal comprehension to be presented in volume 3 will have to be taken into account.

6.3   Some possible explanations of the principles of chain shifting

In the discussion of chain link connections, I have tried to focus on the structural relations between the entering and leaving elements, and their relation to the fundamental concept of chain shifting. This section will consider explanations that have been advanced for the general principles of chain shifting. Most of the recent efforts in this direction have emphasized functional explanations – tendencies to maximize the flow of information from speaker to addressee – and I will consider these first.

One of the earliest functional approaches to the explanation of chain shifting is that of Martinet (1952, 1955). His fundamental concepts of *field of dispersion* and *margin of security* must play a role in any discussion of the mechanism of sound change. Martinet proposed that the functional economy of the system should be understood as the result of the dialectic opposition between the cognitive demand for symmetry and the asymmetrical physiology of the supraglottal tract. As we saw in chapter 5, Haudricourt and Juilland (1949) applied this concept to Pattern 3 shifts and established a clear correlation between Pattern 3 and the existence of more than three degrees of height among the back vowels. Thus, Pattern 3 was seen as a functional reaction that relieved the crowding of vowels in the back – establishing an asymmetrical system in the process. Indeed, there is no doubt that the result of Pattern 3 chain shifting in Southern States English is extremely asymmetrical phonetically as well as phonologically, as shown in figure 6.24. The same logic that predicts a Pattern 3 shift in a language with more than three degrees of height among back vowels would predict the absence of Pattern 3 in cases where the number of distinctions in the back is reduced, as in the many American dialects with a merger of /o/ and /oh/ in *cot, caught*, etc. Furthermore, the shift would be equally unlikely in the Northern Cities area where /oh/ is laxed, shortened, and fronted.

Until recently, this prediction seemed valid. The vowel systems documented from Northern Cities speakers of the 1960s and early 1970s showed the nuclei of /iy, ey, uw, ow/ in stable peripheral positions with no trace of fronting of the back vowels. But starting in the late 1970s, dialects with the low back merger began to show fronting of /uw/ and /ow/. This fronting first came to public attention in the recordings of Valley Girls speech by Moon Zappa, but it soon became evident that the phenomenon was much more general. In the late 1980s, studies of San Francisco Bay area dialects reported fronting of /ow/ (Luthin 1987), and at the University of Pennsylvania Linguistics Laboratory, investigations of Los Angeles dialects showed fronting of /uw/ to high front nonperipheral position.[48] Furthermore, the Northern Cities speakers began to show marked fronting of /uw/ to at least mid central position. This appears clearly in all of the Chicago speakers recorded in the 1980s (contrast figures 6.15 and 6.16 with figures 6.12–6.14, which show no fronting at all). The fronting of /uw/ is not a part of a chain shift in any of the Western or Northern Cities dialects. Nevertheless, its occurrence throws some doubt on the logic of Martinet's explanation, since it suggests an independent cause that might well apply to the Pattern 3 chain shifts as well.

Pattern 4 introduces other aspects of chain shift relations that extend considerably beyond the question of movement and replacement. The tensing of the short vowels and the laxing of the nuclei of the originally long vowels leads to a dramatic reversal of phonetic realization and an increasing differentiation of the two series. These phonetic movements set the stage for the chain shift patterns that we have observed. It is attractive to try to relate the phonetic movements themselves to some more general pattern.

Stockwell (1978) introduces general arguments that would interpret and explain the patterns identified in LYS. In light of the repeated tendencies toward chain shifting of a particular type in English, he reduces Principles I and IIa to two statements of admirable simplicity (p. 344):

(35) The V of Vh and nonhomorganic Vy/w drifts upward.
The V of homorganic Vy/w drifts downward.

---

[48] A study by Tom Veatch of his younger sister's vowel system gave the clearest evidence on this point.

He accounts for these principles under a single tendency to maximize nucleus-glide distances (p. 343):

(36)   The single perceptual principle that optimal glides tend to maximize the distance of the glide predicts that [LYS's] principles I and II will be characteristic of a language with a vowel system of the English type.

Since Stockwell treats the peripheral/nonperipheral distinction as a formal device rather than a substantive description, the formulation of (35) seems clearly to be preferred. He relates these principles to *natural* perceptual tendencies without becoming engaged with the specific structure of phonological space exemplified here.

The analysis of vowel shifting by Stampe (1972) utilizes the more complex framework of Donegan (1978), which makes a principled use of the peripheral/nonperipheral distinction, in terms of a tendency to maximize vowel color and sonority. Donegan views tense vowels as *chromatic*, and lax vowels as *achromatic*. Thus, as the most sonorous vowel, /a/ has the optimal syllabicity and tone-bearing capacity, whereas /i/ and /u/ have optimum chromaticity and maximize distinctiveness. Stampe's and Donegan's treatment of vowel shifting depends on the basic principle that "if contextual factors do not interfere, vowels tend to polarize the three cardinal properties [labiality, palatality, sonority]" (Stampe 1972). Thus, in the course of linguistic change tense vowels tend to increase their chromaticity (Donegan 1978:118). At the same time, they lose sonority. Lax or achromatic vowels, on the other hand, are primarily characterized by their sonority, which they tend to increase through lowering (p. 136). Since achromatic vowels have no color to increase or decrease, they do not suffer any loss through this process. Donegan (1978) does not consider chain shifting specifically but rather stresses the implicational character of these relations in sound change as a whole: if tense vowels fall, then lax vowels fall also; if lax vowels rise, then tense vowels rise also. The most natural combination of these processes, of course, is for tense vowels to rise and lax vowels to fall.

These observations shed considerable light on the processes involved here. They are stated in terms that seem at first reading to be teleological: that speakers shift their vowels *in order to* be heard more clearly, or *in order to* distinguish the vowels one from another. Both Stockwell and Donegan assert that these changes are *natural*. However, the concept of naturalness and the concept of functional motivation appear to me to carry more ideological weight than the data presented so far can sustain. Chapter 19 will return to the topic of functional arguments concerning sound change as well as morphological change. Before concluding this chapter, I would like to consider mechanical explanations of the principles of chain shifting that are more consistent with the general findings of this volume.

Sievers's principle

Sievers (1850:279) offers a general explanation of the contrary tendencies of long and short vowels that were exemplified in Prokosch's diagram (17) in chapter 5.

> It is well known that short and long vowels are frequently differentiated by opposite directions of movement . . . .. The basis for this lies in the frequent operation of the law that the articulation of a sound will be the more energetic and complete, the more strongly it is present in consciousness, that is, the greater its amplitude and length. This accounts for, in the case of the long vowels, not only the raising of particular articulations of the tongue (in placement and degree of tension), but the increase in rounding, when it is present. The short vowels, on the other hand, which involve only a brief movement of the tongue, will not reach their specific amount of displacement from the rest position of the tongue, or tension, that is, there will be initiated a shift of the vowels with stronger articulations to sound with more neutral articulations, as far as tongue and lip position, as well as tension, is concerned.

Prokosch (1930) finds this persuasive for the Germanic case, but argues that it does not explain the fact that it is a specifically Germanic tendency, and not characteristic of other languages. We have seen that the principles involved are in fact more general. One reason that they are displayed more prominently in Germanic than in other languages is that Germanic uses a version of phonological space with peripheral and nonperipheral tracks both in front and in back, whereas other languages do not. The other important fact about Germanic is underlined by Prokosch (pp. 77–8):

> Sievers' definition of the underlying cause is abstractly true, but the effect followed only where the contrast between long and short vowels, as subsequent linguistic history shows, was sharply outlined in speech consciousness, that is, principally in the Germanic Languages.

Prokosch leans back toward the functional side, relating the principles of vowel shifting to a tendency to increase contrast. But it seems to me that the essence of Sievers's position is a mechanical one: that in pronouncing a long vowel, speakers tend to overshoot the target, whereas in pronouncing a short vowel, they tend to undershoot. This of course will not account for the lowering of lax vowels to low *peripheral* position. Part E will return to these issues in a more general evaluation of functional arguments.

7

Resolution of the Paradoxes

7.1 Introduction: scope of this chapter

This chapter will apply the findings of chapter 6 on changes in progress to the problems and paradoxes that were developed in the review of the historical record in chapter 5. Many of the solutions will already be evident, since the concept of peripherality has a clear application to the interpretation of completed chain shifts. But the mechanism for presenting those solutions is not so evident, particularly in dealing with changes in a continuous phonetic space. The fundamental drive behind formal notation is the search for simplicity – a way of presenting many diverse phenomena through the same rules. It has often been observed that the process of formalization and simplification tends to continue indefinitely, especially if the only limit is the ingenuity of the formalizers. This chapter will follow that path only as far as the particular cases will carry us. The search for further simplification and reduction of the chain shift rules will be the concern of the following chapter.

Formalization of the rules for chain shifting

Resolving the paradoxes of chapter 5 will require restating the rules given there. This chapter will have the auxiliary goal of restating vowel shift rules in a form that describes the process of chain shifting itself. To do so will require adjusting the rules to the findings of chapter 6, which reviewed changes in progress through the evidence of measurements in a continuous phonetic space and developed a revised view of the nature of the space used by English dialects. Because that phonetic space differs from the phonetic substratum that was assumed for earlier representations of English phonology, changes are required in the form of the rules that relate phonological structures to phonetic facts. The rules presented here originally grew out of modifications to the framework of Chomsky and Halle (1968) (*SPE*) and have themselves been modified by the insights resulting from the research summarized in earlier chapters. Rewrite rules of the *SPE* type originally had severe limitations, which have been overcome by recent developments in phonological theory. In particular, syllable structure was not recognized directly, being indicated instead by elaborate formulas in the CV notation. Here, rules involving syllable structure, including lengthening and shortening rules, will be stated in the framework of autosegmental phonology. However, the rules that describe the chain shifts themselves, including movements of raising, lowering, backing, and fronting, seem best stated as rewrite rules. The *n*-ary notation that will be used, and the conventions introduced to treat chain shifting as a single process, are presented as modifications of phonological rewrite rules.

To the best of my knowledge, there have been no attempts to write rules to represent the process of chain shifting. The many representations of the Great Vowel Shift, for example, are all assemblies of rules of different kinds. The general treatments of the subject cited in chapter 6 (Stockwell 1978; Stampe 1972; Donegan 1978) are not highly formalized from the point of view of rule statement.[1] The modifications of rewrite rules described here therefore represent an effort to state as exactly as possible what has been derived from the empirical investigations of chapter 6.

Although the space in which changes have been measured is continuous, the changes themselves need not be described in continuous terms. Indeed, they can be formalized at a number of different levels: at the phonetic level of continuous linguistic change; at an *n*-ary level where height, fronting, and even rounding may be represented as a linear dimension with anywhere from two to seven values; or at the binary level where every category is presented as a dimension with only two values.

The first approach might seem most appropriate for changes currently in progress. However, continuous data are not easily incorporated into the representation of chain shifts. A review of the figures in chapters 3, 4, and 6 will show that at any one point in time the various units of the shift are usually moving at different rates. For example, figure 3.6 shows that /ahr/ is not moving at all in apparent time, whereas /ohr/ is still moving slowly upward. Ultimately, a continuous model using quantitative data will illuminate the sequencing and causal links within the change. The regression coefficients given for the Northern Cities Shift in table 6.1 are typical of the data that will be needed to register the internal conditioning of change in progress and write phonetic implementation rules that are sensitive to the differentiation of the speech community (Liberman and

---

[1] The rules given in Stampe 1972 and Donegan 1978 are similar in structure to variable rules – for example,

$$\left[\begin{array}{cc} \text{chr} & \text{!lo} \\ \text{V} & \text{!tns} \end{array} \right] \rightarrow \text{higher}$$

which states that chromatic vowels become higher; the lower and tenser they are, the more susceptible they are to this process. But whereas variable rules are confirmed or disconfirmed by quantitative studies of production in a given speech community, there are many difficulties in applying a principle of accountability across languages, dialects, and time periods that would lead to a reliable enumeration of chain shifts (see below). The rules to follow are designed to describe what actually happened in a given speech community over time.

Pierrehumbert 1984). But the chain shift aspect itself, in which vowels move simultaneously while remaining distinct, requires a certain degree of discreteness. The level that captures the chain shift phenomenon in a simple and straightforward way is the discrete *n*-ary level, rather than the binary level.

One could represent the chain shift phenomenon by a set of observations about a set of binary rules. The history of intervocalic consonants in British Celtic provides one of the most symmetrical and systematic examples of consonantal chain shifting (Martinet 1955:266–7).

(1)   -pp-   -tt-   -kk-
                 ↓   ↓   ↓
                 -p-   -t-   -g-
                 ↓   ↓   ↓
                 -b-   -d-   -g-
                 ↓   ↓   ↓
                 -β-   -ɣ-   -ð-

These shifts could be described as a series of three binary changes:

(2) a. [–tense] → [–cons] /V___V (lax stops become fricatives)
     b. [–long] → [–tense] /V___V (single stops are voiced)
     c. [ ] → [–long] /V___V (geminates are simplified)

One would also have to specify an extrinsic order: 2(a) → 2(b) → 2(c). But even these rules and this ordering are not sufficient to formally recognize this process as a chain shift. One would also have to add the observation that if the rules had not occurred in the extrinsic order given, the result would have been one or more mergers of the series concerned.

A simpler way to show the chain shift as a single process would be to write a single rule. To do so, we would have to recognize that the three subrules (2a–c) are parts of one process, moving in one direction along one dimension such as a sonority hierarchy, or its converse, an obstruence hierarchy. Let us consider what the formalism would look like if we converted [±sonorant] to [*n*-sonority] with steadily decreasing values that would be consistent with the ordering:

(3) geminate or long stop > voiceless stop > voiced stop > voiced fricative

We could then formulate a rewrite rule with the feature [sonorant] on both left and right sides of the arrow, and an increment on the right. It would also have a variable repeated on both left and right, with an increment or decrement on the right:

(4)   [z son] → [$z+\alpha x$ son] / . . .

In such a format, the variable z can take on any value, discrete or continuous, that is established for a hierarchy of consonantal marking. In this case, we might establish a discrete 7-point series with values for obstruence of 0 voiceless geminate, 1 voiceless stop, 2 voiced stop, 3 voiced fricative, 4 liquid, 5 semivowel, 6 vowel. It is understood that the usual binary notation [±feature] is a shorthand for [±1 feature], where the ± value indicates a choice between +1 and −1. Greek letter variables like α and β take one of the values +1 or −1. In the case of a symmetrical rule, α will be assigned its value by some feature of the environment. To describe the historical changes listed in (1), the value of α will be set at − since this is a lenition process:

(5)   [z son] → [$z - x$ son] / . . .

Since z appears on both sides of the arrow in (4), the rule will not eliminate any distinctions. Whatever value of z separates two segments before the rule applies will separate them after it applies, since the increment or decrement x applies equally to both. If two consonants are separated by one degree of sonority before the rule applies, they will be separated by one degree after it applies. No metaconditions or extraneous discussion are needed to represent the chain shift phenomenon.

A vowel chain shift can be presented in a similar fashion, using an n-ary dimension of fronting, backing, or rounding. LYS used the following notation to describe both the Great Vowel Shift and its modern successors:

(6)   [z high] → [$z+\alpha x$ high] / . . .

To describe changes in progress by functions in a formant space, z and x will be real numbers, and the feature of height will take continuous values. In the representations to be used here, z and x will take values in an n-ary dimension, designating three to five discrete levels of height.[2] As in (4), the variable α takes only two values, +1 or −1, in agreement with some other feature that determines whether the chain shift is rising or falling. A further simplification can be imposed on this chain shift schema: namely, that $x = 1$ (i.e., that no unit of the feature dimension can be skipped by such an instruction). This will be the basic rule form for vowel shifting in the discussion to follow, always bearing in mind the possibility that a less

---

[2] LYS used five degrees of height to describe the Great Vowel Shift and phonological rules associated with it. This included 0 for the low central [a], 1–3 for low, mid, and high vowels, and 4 for the glides.

restrictive interpretation of *x* may be required at a later point. Thus the rules will appear in the following form:

(7)   [*z* high] → [*z*+α high] / . . .

The paradoxes of Chapter 5 reviewed

Section 5.5 presented four problems in interpreting the historical record of chain shifts. In each case, the changes that appear to have taken place should have led to mergers that did not in fact take place. Given the assumptions about phonological space and rule formats in these descriptions, the distinctions that were maintained were *impossible distinctions*. The Proto-Romance distinction between open and closed **o** should have been eliminated in the Valais; the Proto-Yiddish distinction between **ei** and **ai** should have disappeared in modern Yiddish; and the Middle English distinctions between **æy** and **iy**, **ǣr** and **ēr** should have been merged in Modern English. We did not consider these cases to be exceptions to a rule, since they appeared to violate principles that were more solidly established than the chain shift rules we were investigating: the principle that two segments with the same set of features are indistinguishable, and the principle that mergers are irreversible. The operation of these principles should have produced mergers, but it did not. We might of course consider the principles disproved, and abandon them. However, these four cases are not sufficient to dismiss or even question the principles involved, since they rest on a vast body of evidence in the history of many language families. The paradox has to do with the nature of linguistic principles: How can linguistic principles apply in general and yet not apply in particular? In other words, how can they apply and not apply at the same time?

The nature of the evidence in Chapter 5

The four cases of unexpected failure to merge are similar in one important respect. In each case, the problem lies not in the evidence or the principles, but in the concept of phonological space that was available to the original description. Once the view of phonological space is enlarged by adding the concept of *peripherality*, and that view is projected back into the past, it appears that the two segments that did not merge may not have shared the same set of features. In the geometry of this phonological space, there is room for segments involved in linguistic change to pass each other in front or in back, if one is on the [+peripheral] track and the other is on the [−peripheral] track. The figures of chapter 6 display such an acoustic space specialized for rising and falling segments, and a number of distinctions maintained by the [±peripheral] feature in the course of changes now in progress:

- Rising /æ/ and falling /e/ did not merge in the Northern Cities Shift.
- Falling /e/ and fronting /o/ did not merge in the Northern Cities Shift.
- Rising /aw/ and fronting /ow/ did not merge in Philadelphia.

This enlarged view of phonological space makes concrete use of the [±tense] distinction, applied to the differential paths followed by tense rising /æh/ and lax falling /e/. We are used to this distinction of fronting and backing in the differential positions of tense [i,e] and lax English [ɪ,ɛ],[3] and we assume that in Middle English the long vowels were more fronted than the short vowels. No one is surprised that long ē did not merge with short ĭ as it rose past it in the course of the Great Vowel Shift.[4] The evidence of chapter 6 went considerably beyond these commonplace observations. We observed /oy/ and /ay/ rising along a [+peripheral] track, and /iy/ and /ey/ falling along a [–peripheral] track, in accordance with the general principles of chain shifting; yet there is nothing in the conventional phonetic transcriptions of these vowels that would have predicted these measurements. In fact, it is rare to distinguish tense and lax nuclei of upgliding diphthongs; but when this is done, it usually refers to length rather than fronting or backing. Occasional observations of slight fronting and backing can be found in the literature, but the systematic placement of all English front and back nuclei on one of these two tracks is the product of instrumental observations.

Once the measurements are made, a trained ear can become sensitive to many distinctions of fronting and backing of vowel nuclei, and can predict the instrumental distinctions displayed in chapter 6. But this is not the common practice of dialectology. The notational arsenal of dialectologists contains as many as 16 distinctions of height, but only 3 degrees of fronting and backing.[5] The insensitivity of the ear to F2 distinctions as compared with F1 distinctions is the major fact – physical or psychological – lying behind the paradoxes of chapter 5 and their resolution.

Varieties of phonological space

The more abstract types of phonological space are completely defined by the features that the rules operate upon. But the type of feature represented

---

[3] Though many English dialects have lax nuclei for /iy/ and /ey/, many others use monophthongal varieties with peripheral [i:, e:], even in free position. More commonly we find diphthongized forms with nuclei fronter and higher than the corresponding lax short vowels, but still not as front or high as cardinal [i, e].

[4] Although short ĭ and long ē did fall together in Romance when the length distinction was lost. This may mean that at one time Latin had a phonological space similar to that of the Germanic, Slavic, and Baltic languages, but that it collapsed into a simpler form at this time.

[5] For example, the notation of the *Atlas Linguistique de France* includes alphabetic symbols for four degrees of height in the front [i, é, è, á]. Each of these can be modified by being made more close with a subscript period, or more open with a subscript comma.

by [±peripheral] and [*z* high] is located within a more concrete phonetic space; as the discussion proceeds, I will exploit the implications of these phonetic lcoations. The rules themselves, operating on these features, are abstractions from this space. As rules become more abstract, they are also simpler and more general, and in this process of abstraction lies the primary motivation of rule-writing. We are therefore impelled to use the most abstract features that will describe the linguistic changes in question.

[±TENSE] VERSUS [±PERIPHERAL]
Given this direction of analysis, one might prefer to use the traditional [±tense] notation to register these distinctions and avoid introducing the more concrete feature notation of [±peripheral]. It would not be unreasonable to do so, and the rules to follow could well be written with [±tense] in place of [±peripheral]. In English dialects, [+tense] is realized as [+peripheral], and [−tense] as [−peripheral]. But the matching is not one-to-one. A tense vowel can be located in the central, nonperipheral space. The long central monophthong in the British Received Pronunciation version of *girl* and *fur* certainly qualifies as tense through its length and its steady-state quality, and its phonological distribution (free as well as checked) shares the same alternations with /r/ as other members of the tense /Vhr/ set in *fear*, *fair*, *four*, etc.

The intimate relationship of tenseness and peripherality in modern English dialects is also found in other branches of Germanic and in other Indo-European families, Baltic and Slavic in particular. But it is not shared by all: Romance, Greek, and Celtic show no signs of the Pattern 1 or Pattern 4 movements that suggest a peripheral and a nonperipheral track. The analysis of French vowel systems shows three rather than four areas for phonemic targets in phonological space: an area for front vowels, an area for back vowels, and an area of mixed (front rounded) vowels:

(8)   PARISIAN VOWEL SPACE (after Lennig 1978)

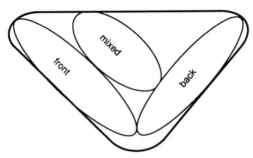

Consistent with this type of phonological space in Romance languages is the absence of any diphthongization of /iy/ with a [−peripheral] nucleus. There is one remarkable exception to this generalization, which appears in the discussion of extensions of Pattern 1 in Romansh in chapter 5 (Grisch 1939; Camenish 1962). Romansh shows strong indications of peripheral and nonperipheral tracks. But the fact that the one Romance language to show such developments is surrounded by German speakers, and intimately engaged in bilingual contact with German (Weinreich 1968), reinforces the notion that peripherality is not a feature of Romance structure. Rather, it enters only as a result of strong external contact.

When vowels in Romance languages rise toward /i/, they often merge with it. This is true of many other branches of Indo-European. Greek provides the most spectacular example. The merger of the front vowels in Greek was reviewed in (14) of chapter 5 in a set of orthogonal features; after the loss of length, eight vowels ultimately fell together in a single /i/ phoneme. In our current view of phonological space, this appears as (9).

(9) THE COLLAPSE OF GREEK VOWELS INTO /i/

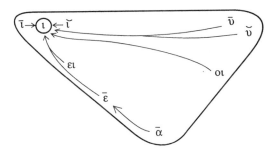

[±PERIPHERAL], [±TENSE], [±LONG]

The term *tense* is not common in the historical record; the intimate union of peripherality and tenseness that we see in current dialects would normally appear as reference to a series of *long* vowels. Greek had a stable system of long and short vowels for a considerable period. Was length correlated with peripherality, and did a peripherality distinction collapse along with length? There is no evidence pointing in that direction – no diphthongization of ī or ū. Moreover, the classic Greek long mid vowels were *lower than* the short vowels (Sturtevant 1940). On the other hand, Latin long vowels had the same relationship to the short vowels that we find in northern European languages today. There is some evidence of a shift in progress in late Latin: the important fact, referred to above, is that when length was lost, short ĭ fell together with long ě, and short ŭ with ō (Pope 1934:89). Either the long mid vowels were rising or the short vowels were falling. The loss of length might have been promoted by the lack of supporting (redundant) features like peripherality. Yet it seems unlikely that Latin, alone among southern European branches of Indo-European, had the type of phonological space we have been examining in Germanic.

There is no reason to think that length distinctions are in general correlated with peripherality. Hungarian, for example, has no qualitative distinction between long and short high vowels.[6] There are great qualitative distinctions between long and short /e/ and long and short /o/, but these are
distinctions of height, arranged along the periphery. Hungarian seems to
have a three-track system, like French, and in addition shows no vowel
reduction to shwa.

TYPES OF TENSENESS

The peripheral/nonperipheral opposition is one of the most prominent
means of differentiating subsystems of vowels in many languages, but it is
by no means a universal exponent of the cover feature [tense]. In languages
that oppose sets of vowels in ways that resemble the Indo-European
tense/lax distinction, peripherality may not be involved at all. Stewart
(1967) shows that Akan has a strict vowel harmony system that opposes
the two sets of vowels displayed in (10).

(10)   WEST AFRICAN VOWEL SPACE

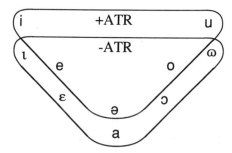

When the opposition tense/lax is applied to this system, the upper set is
labeled [+tense]: it is clearly not [+peripheral], since it includes the mid
central vowel /ə/ but not /a/. The term *raised* has been used for the upper
set /i, e, u, o, ə/. However, a number of studies show that the variation
between the two systems is due to changes in the size of the pharynx,
controlled by the position of the tongue root and the larynx. Stewart shows
that this set is characterized by the advancing of the tongue root and lowering of the larynx, while the set /ɪ, ɛ, ɷ, ɔ, a/ is characterized by retraction
of the tongue root and raising of the larynx. Since Stewart's paper
appeared, the feature [advanced tongue root] or [ATR], has been applied
as a substitute for [tense] in a number of languages (Perkell 1971), but
without benefit of the cineradiographic data that Stewart provides for

---

[6] Though to be sure, this is an unstable distinction with a marginal status for many Hungari-
ans, and one that Hungarian typewriters dispense with.

Akan. [ATR] is an attractive way of describing the tense set of English vowels; it recalls Sweet's terminology of *narrow* versus *wide* for the long and short vowels. However, Lindau (1978:558) shows that tongue root position in German and English is correlated with tongue height, and therefore cannot function as an independent feature to distinguish long and short vowels in those languages. She concludes that although there is no single phonetic feature that will define the tense/lax opposition, the peripheral/central axis is the most general, and supports the use of [±peripheral] as the chief phonetic realization of [±tense]. For the West African vowel harmony sets, Lindau proposes the opposition *expanded/constricted* rather than *tense/lax*.

As far as the principles of chain shifting are concerned, the value of the term *tense* would be lessened if it were tied to a specific physical measure. It follows that the particular relationship between tenseness and peripherality that we have been concerned with is specific to a large group of languages, where [±tense] is a useful cover term for a variety of oppositions that generally have to do with whether more energy is expended in articulation, or less. Peripherality is one particular specification of this expenditure of energy, but as noted above, it cannot be rigidly related to tenseness, given the possibility of long central vowels. Peripherality is more abstract than the physical measurements, since it is a relative term – referring as it does to a phonetic target relatively closer to the vowel periphery than another target. And we have not set the bounds for the [+peripheral] and [−peripheral] tracks in terms of percent or proportion of the vowel space involved. Nevertheless, peripherality can be demonstrated by objective measurements of sets of vowels, and it is tied to the properties of phonological space in the languages under investigation. In the Germanic and Baltic language families, and those Romance languages influenced by Germanic, peripherality is the principal feature determining the direction of movement within the tense and lax subsystems. In most Romance languages, the vowels that agree in backness and rounding behave in accordance with Principle I, while the others, the "mixed vowels," do not.[7]

If the rules that we are writing are ultimately to be understood in terms of physical and psychological behavior, it would be best to keep them close to the physical evidence, and if they are to be connected to the variable and erratic course of sound change, it is best to keep them close to the properties of particular languages. For both of these reasons, I will retain the feature [±peripheral] in the rules for chain shifting within subsystems. Chapter 9 will take up chain shifting across subsystems.

---

[7] There is some evidence that in chain shifting, such mixed vowels fall, as in the Eskilstuna dialect of Swedish (Nordberg 1975) and as in the Belfast dialect of Anglo-Irish, where diphthongs with front rounded nuclei fall.

7.2   Resolution of the paradoxes

Valais raising

The view of the back vowels in the Valais provided in chapter 5 can be recast in the phonological space of chapter 6:

(11)   RAISING OF THE BACK VOWELS

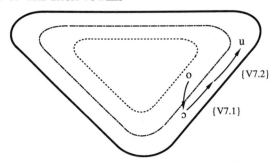

As one solution to the problem of how /o/ and /ɔ/ remained distinct, chapter 5 proposed that they were distinguished by a feature like [±tense]. There was no evidence to support such a notion in French phonology. However, the data reviewed in chapter 6 led to the inference that the phonetic space of the Valais did include the feature [±peripheral]. Such an inference is represented geometrically in (11). The basic chain shift would then be described by the following rule:

$$\{V7.1\}[z\ \text{high}] \rightarrow [z + \alpha\ \text{high}] / \left[\begin{array}{c} \overline{} \\ +\text{back} \\ \alpha\text{peri} \end{array} \right]$$

If we recognize (conservatively) three degrees of height, then /ɔ/ will be [1 high], [o] will be [2 high], and [u] will be [3 high]. The [+peripheral] vowel, /ɔ/, will rise from [1 high] to [2 high], and the [−peripheral] vowel will fall from [2 high] to [1 high]. At no point in this process do the two segments share the same set of features, no matter how the two parts of the rule are ordered.

In this particular chain shift, there is only one segment moving up and one segment moving down, so that the binary feature [±low] can be used. The rule form conventionally used for flip-flops could then be substituted:

$$\{V7.1'\}\quad [\alpha\text{low}] \rightarrow [-\alpha\text{low}] / \left[\begin{array}{c} \overline{} \\ +\text{back} \\ \alpha\text{peri} \end{array} \right]$$

That is, we need not regard the Valais movement as a chain shift; instead, we can view it as an exchange of positions. This result leads us back to the status of flip-flop rules and their relation to the process of linguistic change. Introducing the concept of peripherality allows us to eliminate the puzzling or paradoxical character of flip-flops as instantaneous reversals that children would have to learn from parents who had no such rule. Instead, they now appear as special subtypes of chain shifts where the movements in opposing directions are limited to one step. Rules for flip-flops, like rules for any other chain shift, may be taken as a summary statement of a completed change, or a simplified account of the trajectories actually followed by the changes as they happened.

For the purposes of this discussion, I will use the more general format of {V7.1}, since it shows the relation of the Valais back vowel movements to other chain shifts.

It remains to ask whether it makes sense to attribute a feature derived from Germanic phonological space to a Romance language. The earlier discussion of phonological spaces has already built a strong case against this notion. But the special position of Romansh, which shows signs of the four-track system, was an integral part of that discussion. The Valais is also a French-speaking area backed up against the German-speaking border. Though there is no record of the intimate kind of bilingualism that was recorded among the Romansh, it is not illogical for the Valais to appear as one French dialect with a [±peripheral] distinction. No other French dialect has been reported to show the exchange of closed and open /o/.

There remains the further raising of the original /ɔ/ from [o] to [u]:

$$\{V7.2\} \quad [-low] \rightarrow [+high] \ / \ \left[\begin{array}{c} \rule{1.5em}{0.4pt} \\ +back \end{array} \right]$$

Can or should {V7.1} and {V7.2} be combined into a single rule? From one point of view, they should, since the complete process ends with a high [u] vowel. There may be some condition on chain shifts that insists that they continue their original movement as far as possible into any empty areas of phonological space. Such an Expansion Convention might be applied to ME ī and ensure its full descent to /ay/. That is an attractive possibility that will simplify and explain many of the movements in chain shifting, but there are difficulties that might prevent us from adopting it. Section 8.2 will consider the arguments for and against an Expansion Convention. For the moment, I will retain {V7.2} as a separate rule.

Diphthongization in the English Great Vowel Shift

The best-known and most widely disputed of the paradoxes under consideration is the path of diphthongization of ME ī in the Great Vowel Shift. Chapter 5 showed that if the nucleus of *my* and *ride* was a front vowel, as all the testimony of grammarians indicated, then there was no obvious way that this word class could have escaped merger with the diphthong that proceeded from ME **ai** in *may* and *maid* /æy/. The solution that we may project backward into the 16th century is that the phonological space of Early Modern English was similar to that of English dialects today. This is the pattern shown in (12).

(12)   THE GREAT VOWEL SHIFT IN [±PERIPHERAL] PHONOLOGICAL SPACE

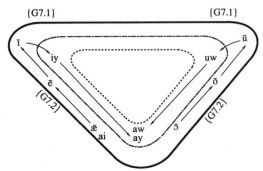

In this phonological space, it is evident that the reflexes of ME ī may be diphthongized to /iy/, with a lax, [–peripheral] nucleus, and descend to /ay/ as front vowels, without merging with the reflexes of ME **ai**.

Chapter 5 cited Dobson's observations on the fundamental problem of the Great Vowel Shift: that ME ī could not have been diphthongized and lowered as a front vowel without merging with ME **ai**. On the other hand, the consensus of the historical testimony was that ME ī was a front vowel throughout this period, and not the type of central vowel that would have been written with a **u**. Though Dobson did not have the phonetic basis for tracing this path explicitly, he made the relative connection in discussing why the orthoepists of the early period (Palsgrave, Smith, Lodwick, Bullokar) did not report a diphthongal character for ī:

> The failure was one of practical phonetic analysis . . . . An exact parallel is provided by Australians and Cockneys at the present time, who are quite unaware that they often pronounce [əi] for StE [i:] (or rather [ɪi]; theoretical training in phonetics does not always improve their acoustic perception). (1968:659)

Diagram (12) shows rules {G7.1} and {G7.2} applying to front and back vowels. Rule {G7.1} describes the diphthongization of the high vowels, which is generally recognized to be the initiating factor in the vowel shift (Martinet 1955:248–56).[8] It is a dual process that dissimilates the two

---

[8] As noted in chapter 5, Luick (1903) argued for the contrary view, that the Great Vowel Shift was initiated by the raising of the mid vowels; and there is evidence from the dialect geography of the north of England to support this. Where ME ō was fronted to ē, the diph-

identical morae of a high vowel: the first mora becomes [–peripheral], which automatically involves lowering and centralization, and the second becomes [–vocalic].[9]

{G7.1} DIPHTHONGIZATION OF HIGH VOWELS

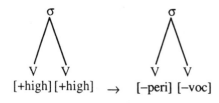

$$\text{[+high] [+high]} \rightarrow \text{[–peri] [–voc]}$$

Given this differentiation of high vowels, the vowel shift follows.

{G7.2} VOWEL SHIFT

$$[z \text{ high}] \rightarrow [z+\alpha \text{ high}] / \begin{bmatrix} \underline{\hspace{1cm}} \\ \alpha\text{peri} \\ \beta\text{round} \\ +\text{str} \\ +\text{long} \end{bmatrix} \quad [\beta\text{round}]$$

Rule {G7.2} uses roundness agreement to specify that the vowel shift rule does not apply to /oy/ or to /iw/ (the long high vowel of *fruit, rude,* etc.): here the nucleus does not agree with the glide in rounding.[10] (Stockwell (1978) converts this condition into a positive requirement for the vowel shift: it applies only to "homorganic" diphthongs. This makes sense in terms of nucleus-glide differentiation, since heterorganic diphthongs are already more differentiated.) The vowel shift rule is also specified to apply only to stressed vowels, so that it does not raise unstressed vowels such as the ō in *window* or *follow.* Otherwise, {G7.2} applies to all peripheral vow-

thongization of ū was inhibited. Nevertheless, Stockwell (1978) presents strong arguments that the diphthongization of the high vowels can be tracked back to Middle English. Stampe (1972) independently shows that the shortening of ME ī before palatals implies the absorption of front glides by palatals.

[9] It is not necessary to specify any further features to prevent the rule from applying to the long vowel in *fruit, tune,* etc. It seems reasonable to believe that the underlying form of that vowel was diphthongal /iw/ in Early Modern English as it is today.

[10] At the time that this rule applied, there probably was no /aw/ involved in the chain shift, so that it is not necessary to specify that the nucleus agrees with the glide in backness and rounding, but simply to continue the line of {G6.1} that it agree in rounding, as first indicated in {E5.7}. This constraint applies automatically to the other half of the rule, since the preceding rule ensures that the relevant [–peripheral] nuclei will be followed by glides that agree in rounding.

els, including the diphthong **ai** (/æːy/), just as its modern relatives apply to /ay/ and /oy/. The operation of {G7.2} can be followed in (13), which shows the values assumed for all the variables for the front vowels where $\beta = -$.

(13)	Input	z high	α	β	$z+\alpha$ high	Output
	ǣ	1 high	+1	−1	2 high	[eː]
	ē	2 high	+1	−1	3 high	[iː]
	ïi	3 high	−1	−1	2 high	[ɛ⁼ı]

For peripheral vowels, with $\alpha = +1$, the rule adds one unit of height, which in the front brings ǣ to [eː] and ē to [iː]. The output of the previous rule is [−peripheral] [ïi] where $\alpha = -1$; this is lowered to [ɛ⁼ı]. This leaves the vowels in their early 17th-century positions. The nucleus of *my*, *ride*, etc. is now in mid position, distinctly a front vowel as it appears in the descriptions of the orthoepists. Nevertheless, it is distinguished by its nonperipherality from the nucleus of *may*, *raid*, etc. A later rule moves the nucleus of [ɛ⁼ı] to low position.

THE USE OF [αPERIPHERAL]

The operation of vowel shift rule {G7.2} depends crucially on the use of [αperipheral] for its symmetrical operation. Everything that has been learned from this review of past and present chain shifts indicates an association of laxing and [−peripheral] with the lowering of the diphthongal nuclei. On this association rests the explanation of why *die* and *day*, *ride* and *raid* did not merge − as well as the whole connection between chain shifts past and present on which this investigation is based.

The crucial question for any such symmetrical rule is how to prevent it from applying to the originally short vowels /i, e, æ/. *SPE* specifies the feature [+tense], since the diphthongized reflexes of ME ī and ū are differentiated from the short vowels by that feature. Why, then, does the symmetrical vowel shift rule {G7.2} not lower the short lax vowels?

Since the rule affects all [+peripheral] nuclei followed by glides or obstruents, but only [−peripheral] nuclei followed by glides, there appears to be considerable asymmetry in its application, which might require an embarrassing and awkward condition (*if* [peri] = −, *and* [−cons] follows, *then* . . .). But there is a single feature of English phonology that identifies the set of originally long vowels and diphthongs (which now form the upgliding, long, and ingliding subsets; see chapter 6). Though there are many processes in current English that lengthen originally short vowels and shorten originally long vowels, the abstract category of [± long] remains intact. This category depends upon privileges of occurrence that are in turn linked to underlying prosodic structure, rather than surface phonetic form. The most general continuing characteristic that differentiates the originally short vowels from all others is that they do not occur in word-final or stem-final position in underlying representation.[11] Membership in this category influences the phonological structure of the vowel system at many structural levels. At the level of representation used in chapter 6, English has general constraints on underlying forms that exclude the sequences shown in (14),

(14)

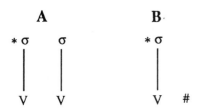

or conversely, a redundancy rule (15) such that a vocalic segment implies either [+consonantal] or [–vocalic] in the following segment.[12]

(15) $\qquad [\ ] \rightarrow \left\{ \begin{matrix} -\text{voc} \\ +\text{cons} \end{matrix} \right\} \Big/ \left[\begin{matrix} +\text{cons} \\ -\text{voc} \end{matrix} \right] \underline{\quad}$

Thus, the originally long vowels and diphthongs are free classes, while the originally short vowels are checked. I will continue the convention of using [±long] as the most abstract classifying feature of English vowels (Halle and Mohanan 1985).[13] Rule {G7.2} uses [+long] to exclude the originally short vowels from its scope. The feature [±len(gthened)] will be reserved for lower-level operations that are more closely connected to the physical realizations of duration.

THE CHAIN SHIFT CONNECTIONS OF THE GREAT VOWEL SHIFT

The symmetrical character of the Great Vowel Shift allows the rule {G7.2} to capitalize on two kinds of symmetry: front/back, and peripheral/nonpe-

---

[11] For those who wish to represent the final vowels of *pillow*, *window*, *city*, and *happy* with /o/ and /i/, this definition can be amended by stating that free vowels can occur in final stressed syllables, checked vowels cannot.

[12] The only exception to this strong constraint that I know of occurs in the phonetic output of the New York City vernacular, where stressed *her* is realized as [hʌ] and, more rarely, other words with rimes in /ǝhr/ are pronounced with final [ʌ].

[13] There is general agreement on the need for an abstract classifying feature other than [±tense], which operates at a lower level of abstraction. A vowel such as /æ/ can change from the lax to the tense category without losing its identity as a [–free] vowel, since there is no change in its privileges of occurrence.

ripheral. The first kind is an obvious type of generalization that simplifies the rule statement and is not involved with the chain shift mechanism itself. The second kind of symmetry does involve a link of the chain shift type. The leaving vowel is ī; the entering vowel is ē. If the rules were written without {G7.1}, with the high vowels in monophthongal condition, then the three steps in the front vowels would be linked by the same proposed causal mechanism. But since ME ī is first changed to /iy/ – narrowly [ɪi] – there might seem to be no immediate reason why it could not stay in that position while [e˞] moved to [i:]. The symmetry of [±peripheral] would not then proceed from any structural tendency to avoid merger.

The issue has already been raised in regard to the link between raising and fronting in Pattern 3 shifts. Like /u:/ and /uw/, /i:/ and /iy/ are not identical; but neither are they distinct. We do not have any example of stable distinctions between high monophthong and diphthong /i:/ vs. /iy/. Instead, we find inglide vs. upglide (/ih/ vs. /iy/), long vs. short (/i:/ vs. /i/), or monophthong vs. mid diphthong (/i:/ vs. /ey/). Peripherality does not appear to be as easily recognized as height by the perceptive apparatus, though the two are produced with equal consistency by the speech production mechanism. In functional terms, the output of {G7.1} is not a phonemic distinction strong enough to provide a margin of security against a new /i:/ arising from /e:/. It follows that in the sense of preserving distinctness, all the links of the chain shift sequence /æ:/ → /e:/ → /iy → ey/ have the same status. In each case, if the element to the left of the arrow had moved to the position of the element to the right of the arrow, and the element to the right had not itself moved, then the two elements would not have been distinct.

The formalism of {G7.1} and {G7.2} does not express this concept. The two rules are quite different in form and function, and do not exhibit any causal relationship. If they could be integrated into a single rule, that relationship would become explicit – a problem to be addressed in chapter 8.

Yiddish diphthongization

The diphthongization of Proto-Yiddish poses the same problem as the Great Vowel Shift. Less information is available on the phonetic forms involved, but the evolution of the language leads us to assume the development shown in (16). Projecting our knowledge of current dialect possibilities into the early history of Yiddish, then, we locate Proto-Yiddish **ei** on the peripheral path. To the extent that the past was governed by the same principles that operate in the present, this location accounts for two facts: (1) when the nucleus of Proto-Yiddish ī descended along the nonperipheral path, following Principle II, it did not merge with [+peripheral] **ei** (or more specifically, **ēi**); (2) the diphthong **ēi** did not join in the falling process.

(16) YIDDISH DIPHTHONGIZATION IN PHONOLOGICAL SPACE

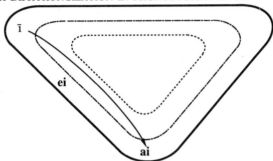

On the other hand, we must assume a [–peripheral] **ĕi** for the Middle High German that was the ancestor of German dialects that merge **ei** and **ī** in modern /ay/.

English raising of vowels before /r/

The fourth problem posed in chapter 5 was perhaps the most intractable. The traditional framework provided there offered no means of explaining why the Modern English reflexes of lengthened OE **ĕr** did not merge with the descendants of OE **ǣr** and **ēar** as they rose to mid and then high position. It was clear from the prior and later history of words like *bear*, *tear*, and *pear* that (1) they *had* been lengthened, and (2) this lengthening had taken place long before the Great Vowel Shift began.

The view of phonological space presented in chapter 6 opens up the one possibility that would account for the factual situation outlined in chapter 5. OE **ĕr** was lengthened in open syllables, but remained in nonperipheral position. In (17), all the sound changes that were originally mapped in (38) of chapter 5 are displayed in the new view of phonological space.

(17) SOUND CHANGES AFFECTING FRONT VOWELS BEFORE /r/

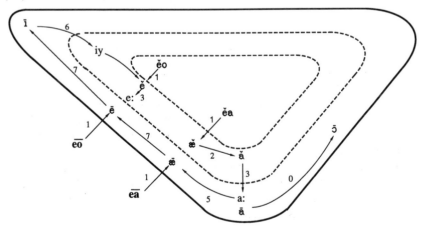

The numbered steps correspond to the series of rules that were ordered in real time to arrive at the present-day result. Most of the rules given in chapter 5 remain unchanged. The late Old English smoothing rule {E5.1} is shown as bringing ēo, ēa, ĕa, ĕo from a separate subsystem of ingliding vowels into the vowel triangle. The smoothing rule, which remains the same, is repeated here as {E7.1}.

{E7.1} SMOOTHING

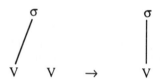

The Middle English backing of OE ǽ {E5.2} remains essentially the same, though we now replace [–long] with [–peri]:

{E7.2} BACKING OF ǽ

$$[+\text{low}] \rightarrow [-\text{ant}] \ / \ \left[\begin{array}{c} \underline{} \\ -\text{peri} \end{array} \right]$$

Rule {E7.3}, lengthening in open syllables, may be given the same expression as in chapter 5 ({E5.3}), the spreading of V to VV before CV. It is repeated here as {E7.3}.

{E7.3} LENGTHENING IN OPEN SYLLABLES

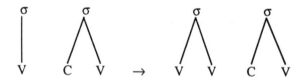

This does not violate the constraint against VV, as stated in (14) and (15), which forbid this sequence in two successive syllables, not in a single syllable. The feature [+long] is then spread across two elements in the CV skeleton, as shown in the equivalence of (18).

Rule {E7.3} is thus equivalent to the conversion of [–len] into [+len]. At the same time, it also describes the conversion of a [–free] vowel into a [+free] vowel, since it is a fact of English that all vowels of the structure shown in (19) are free vowels, and (18) implies (19).

(18)

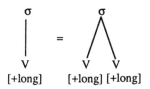

(19)

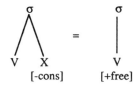

Lengthening in open syllables did not occur in final position, of course, but only in medial position, since no short vowels occurred in final position in Old English.[14] The checked vowels lengthened by {E7.3} acquired the feature [+free], but they would not actually occur in free position. Rather, they would be free vowels with defective distribution, without corresponding allophones in word-final position. If they had been immediately identified with some other phoneme that had such allophones, that situation would have been resolved.

The graphic representation in (17) indicates that no such resolution occurred for lengthened ĕr. As the events that followed clearly demonstrate, the new /e:/ remained distinct from the reflexes of OE ēr. Rule {E5.4} as stated would not produce this result. On the contrary, it would

---

[14] If one were to accept the argument of Minkova 1982 that "lengthening in open syllables" was actually compensatory lengthening in closed syllables after the loss of final shwa, this statement still holds, though the rules will take on a different form.

merge the new /e:/ with the old ē along with ǣ. When it is restated as {E7.4}, it merges only ē with ǣ.

{E7.4} ǣ Raising

$$[\ ] \rightarrow [-\text{low}] / \begin{bmatrix} \overline{} \\ +\text{peri} \\ -\text{back} \end{bmatrix}$$

The lengthening of open syllables by {E7.3} also affected the low central vowel **a**, as we have seen. The new /a:/ is raised by {E7.5}, again substituting peripherality for length.

{E7.5} Fronting of **a**:

$$[+\text{low}] \rightarrow [-\text{back}] / \begin{bmatrix} \overline{} \\ +\text{peri} \end{bmatrix}$$

The Great Vowel Shift now takes place. The three rules given as {E5.6–8} are now replaced by {G7.1–2}. In (17), their effects are indicated by 6 and 7.

WHY DID LENGTHENED ĔR NOT MERGE WITH ĒR?
The lengthened short vowels [e:] and [a:] in (17) are shown, not in boldface type with macrons associated with the original historical record, but rather with the phonemic notation /e:/, since the nature of the alteration of the original forms and their phonemic status is the focus here. The main purpose of the analysis is to find a reasonable phonological framework that will allow us to describe the facts in a coherent manner – one that will not violate the basic assumptions and principles of phonology and historical linguistics. The introduction of the feature [peripheral], and the distinction between peripherality and length, achieves this end. But as always, a new solution raises new questions. It remains to ask whether we can explain why /e:/ behaved in such an odd manner. In the past several chapters, we have seen three shifts of [–peripheral] vowels to the [+peripheral] track: the tensing of /æ/ and /o/ in modern American dialects; the tensing of short /a/ in the Northern Cities Shift; and of course the most immediate parallel within the Great Vowel Shift, namely, the movement of lengthened ǎ into peripheral position and its subsequent upward movement. If the lengthened low vowel before /r/ moved into the peripheral track, why did the corresponding mid vowel not do so?

The answer seems reasonably clear from the fact that there was no ā in peripheral position when lengthening in open syllables took place. The original ā had shifted to back ɔ some time earlier in Old English (the vowel of *bát, stán* moving to /ɔ:/). Whether or not the lengthened /a:/ immediately became peripheral, there was no structural impediment to its doing so, and its participation in the raising rule {E7.4} indicates that it was peripheral at that point. On the other hand, the same movement of lengthened **ĕr** would produce immediate mergers: *bear* with *beer*, *tear* [V] with *tear* [N], *pear* with *peer*, and *wear* with *we're*.

Chapter 5 pointed out that these lengthened **ĕr** words nevertheless did eventually merge with other words: *bare* and *bear* with *bare*, *tear* with *tare*, *pear* with *pare*, *wear* with *ware*. If a functional argument explains the failure to merge in one case, how can it explain the occurrence of merger in the next?

One might well look to the effect of the following segment for an account. We know that the intervocalic /r/ of late Old English was not an interlude but a syllable-initial /r/, since "open syllable" implies exactly that. Whether this /r/ was a flap or some other form of articulation, it was not likely the humped or retroflex [ɚ] that developed in Modern English. Considerable evidence indicates that the phonological space available for vowels before /r/ has been steadily contracting, and the number of distinctions has shrunk accordingly. Before tautosyllabic /r/, the original high and mid short vowels have all merged in checked syllables: *bird, herd, word*, and *worm* all show the same vowel. In open syllables before /r/, many dialects have merged /ey/, /e/, /æ/, and even /ʌ/, as in *Mary, merry, marry*, and *Murray*. The originally long vowels have developed inglides before /r/, and show an equally wide range of mergers.

In modern Scots English, where a strongly consonantal, even trilled [r] is maintained, the distinction between short /e/ and other short vowels before /r/ is also maintained. Thus, *kernel* is quite distinct from *colonel*, and *person* from *purse in*.

The effect of syllable-final /r/ is not symmetrical, however. Most modern /r/ articulations show a marked lowering of both F3 and F2, and the shift of vowels before tautosyllabic /r/ to [−peripheral] position is a product of the general tendency of these vocalic allophones to show lower F2 before /r/. Applied to the back vowels, this leads to a [+peripheral] position, and a greater tendency for the vowels before /r/ to participate in upward chain shifts, as we saw in the discussion of Pattern 3.

It is hardly fanciful, then, to infer that when the original lengthening took place in open syllables, the phonological space available to vowels before /r/ was equivalent to that before other obstruents; that at the time of the Great Vowel Shift, it was not greatly contracted; but that by the 17th and 18th centuries, tautosyllabic /r/ had become heavily involved with the preceding nucleus and sharply restricted the number of distinctions possible. Furthermore, this contraction of phonological space led to a shift of front vowels before /r/ to the [−peripheral] track. Thus, it is not unreasonable that lengthened ĕr did not merge with neighboring ē for several centuries, but that it eventually did so as the distinction between [+peripheral] and [–peripheral] front vowels became smaller and smaller.[15]

---

[15] This contraction of phonological space before /r/ was not a simple one-way movement. When final /r/ was vocalized at the end of the 18th century, it was once again possible for the vowels of *beer*, *bare*, etc., to become fully [+peripheral]. The upward shift of /ihr/ and /ehr/ along with /æh/ in New York City (Labov 1966) testifies to this.

8

Reduction of the Rules and Principles

8.1 Reduction of the rule system

Chapter 7 carried out the substantive task of explaining and resolving the four paradoxes of chain shifting that were first presented in chapter 5, using the concepts of phonological space that were developed in chapter 6. These three chapters followed the central model of this investigation, using the present to explain the past. We came to the conclusion that in the Valais, /ɔ/ rose as an ingliding vowel along the back peripheral track, while /o/ fell along the nonperipheral track. In early Modern English, the diphthong /iy/ fell with a lax nucleus along the nonperipheral track, while the diphthong /æy/ rose with a tense nucleus along the front peripheral track. In the history of Yiddish, the diphthong **ei** maintained its independence by the same mechanism. Finally, it was concluded that in Middle English, **ĕr** was lengthened in open syllables, but not fronted to the peripheral track until after the operation of the Great Vowel Shift. This means that length and peripherality, though closely associated in English phonology, remained as distinct features and could be realized separately.

Though these resolutions are satisfactory in terms of the particular events that occurred, the rules and principles as stated leave something to be desired. The description of the Great Vowel Shift requires two discrete rules of radically different types. The three principles of chain shifting show considerable redundancy and overlap. This chapter will pursue a simpler statement of these rules and principles.

The heterogeneity of the Great Vowel Shift rules

Three of the four problems in chapter 7 concerned the Great Vowel Shift or processes allied to it. Though the rules needed to capture this process are greatly reduced from previous accounts, the fact remains that {G7.1} is a prosodic rule of diphthongization, quite different in form and character from the basic chain shift rule {G7.2}. For those who would consider the diphthongization of high vowels the initiating condition for the vowel shift, this makes sense, and it is conventionally understood that the "removal" of ī made room for the raising of ē. Yet as chapter 7 argued, the diphthongization to [iy] does not actually create a segment distinct from [i:].

It follows that for ē to rise to [i:], an additional process must apply to further differentiate [iy], and that is accomplished by the symmetry of the vowel shift rule {G7.2}, governed by [αperipheral]. Though this resolution is neat enough, it leaves us with two distinct events, the diphthongization and the vowel shift. If diphthongization was the *cause* of the vowel shift, in the sense that it was the initiating condition, then what was the cause of diphthongization?

Stockwell (1978) presents the two opposing tendencies of raising of long vowels and opening of diphthongal nuclei as essentially the same phenomenon. The two statements given in (38) of chapter 5 are so similar that they are easily seen as aspects of a single process of nucleus-glide dissimilation. This symmetry is partly a product of Stockwell's long-standing position that English has had ingliding vowels from the beginning, and that the long monophthongs that were subject to the Great Vowel Shift can be treated structurally as Vh inglides. Under this account, diphthongization is seen as a distinct process – a long-term tendency in English phonology that precedes and follows the period usually assigned to the Great Vowel Shift. Stockwell's view of English structure as homogeneous over time is persuasive, given the repeated fronting of low vowels; tensing, raising, and ingliding; laxing, lowering, and upgliding.[1] Whether or not we accept the Vh hypothesis for Early Modern English depends on our view of the nature of the second mora in the high and mid long vowels. But the symmetry of the tensing and laxing processes can be accepted by focusing on the first mora as either tense or lax. The following discussion will follow the spirit of Stockwell's simplification, within the view of phonological space that was developed in chapters 6 and 7.

If we can reduce these two processes to one, it will be possible to see the Great Vowel Shift and many others as a single event, repeated over time with variations according to the initial inventory of vowels. The tendency of long vowels to rise is not an isolated phenomenon in the history of English, confined to the 16th and 17th centuries. It was seen first in Old English with the raising of original ā to ō. Jespersen suggested that

---

[1] If Early Modern English had a free alternation of V: with Vh, a radical structural reorganization must have occurred in English sometime in the 17th or 18th century. Certainly today, the situation is quite different. In many modern American, British, and Caribbean dialects, upglides alternate with or substitute for long monophthongs, not only in checked position, but also in free position, and American English speakers quickly identify long monophthongs as variants of the upgliding vowels. On the other hand, short vowels frequently alternate with inglides. Most American listeners are familiar with the ingliding short vowels shown in figure 6.23, and have no difficulty in identifying them as variants of the short vowels. Thus, today, Vh alternates with V, and V: with Vy. In the 1970s, among younger speakers in Fond du Lac, Wisconsin, and a number of rural areas nearby, I encountered a tendency for monophthongal V: to develop inglides. Monophthongal long vowels in *pole, motor, boat* developed inglides as [poːəl, morɚ, boət]. Such pronunciations were almost impossible for speakers from other areas to understand or accept. Recent research has not shown this tendency to be generalized or spreading rapidly.

the first step in the Great Vowel Shift was the raising of the new **ā** from lengthening in open syllables (see (34) in chapter 5). Though we set this notion aside in chapter 5, developments to follow in this chapter will reintroduce and justify it. Other raising processes before and after the Great Vowel Shift show that the application of Principle I to long vowels is a continually renewed aspect of English phonology.

Unrestricted vowel shifts

We will first look at the formulation of the vowel shift rule {G7.2}, with the goal of generalizing it further to cover the diphthongization process described by {G7.1} as well. Rule {G7.2} altered degrees of height, based on an *n*-ary set of values ranging from 1 to 3. In this chapter, we will develop the same *n*-ary set, with the additional possibility of viewing the most open vowel, **a**, as [0 high] (see table 8.1).

The vowel shift rule is repeated here as {G8.1}.

{G8.1}   Vowel Shift

$$[z \text{ high}] \rightarrow [z + \alpha \text{ high}] \ / \ \begin{bmatrix} \underline{\quad\quad} \\ \alpha \text{peri} \\ \beta \text{round} \\ +\text{str} \\ +\text{long} \end{bmatrix} \quad [\beta \text{round}]$$

What range of values can such a rule apply to? Chapter 7 applied it to [1 high] and [2 high] among the peripheral vowels, and [3 high] among the nonperipheral vowels. The simplest way to treat the rule, however, is not to restrict it at all. If we take this idea seriously, the vowel shift rule should apply to [3 high] among the peripheral nuclei as well as the lax nuclei, that is, to [i:] as well as to [æ, ɛ, ɪ].

If the rule applies to a [3 high, +peripheral] vowel, the output will have

Table 8.1   Feature assignments for vowel shifting

	Binary		N-ary
	high	low	high
[i, u]	+	−	3
[e, o]	−	−	2
[æ, ɔ]	−	+	1
[a]	−	+	0

to be [4 high]. What is the phonetic interpretation of such an output? It is not at all difficult to locate, since by every principle of sonority and articulatory phonetics, the next step after [i] is [j], and the next step after [u] is [w]. The feature [4 high] clearly indicates a semivowel.

The application of the vowel shift rule to [i:] and [u:] will therefore reduce the syllabic nucleus to a marginal element and produce a result with less than the minimum sonority required for a syllabic nucleus.[2] In the actual development of these sound changes, a sonorous nucleus is supplied. Thus, in the front vowels we would have the derivation [i:] → [j] → [ij].

This convention needs no special statement, since it merely extends the application of the vowel shift rule to its full possible scope and interprets the result in light of accepted principles of sonority. It eliminates the special diphthongization rule {G7.1}. However, it leaves us with the same output as the diphthongization rule did originally. To obtain the differentiation of [i:] → [e⁺y] that was proposed as the minimally distinct one for further vowel shifting, we would have to reapply the vowel shift rule on the [−peripheral] side of the ledger.

The solution to this problem will bring us closer to a formal rule that captures the notion of diphthongization.

THE DIFFERENTIATION OF MORAE

The general vowel shift rule {G8.1} preserves the defining feature [+long], identifying the original set of Middle English phonetically long and structurally free vowels. It must not be forgotten that long vowels contain two morae, and long monophthongs two identical morae. This is the phonetic character of the input to the vowel shift rule. In all cases other than the one we are dealing with, application of the rule to both morae is effectively simultaneous. Though one might formally apply the rule to each mora in turn, the result would be the same as applying it to both morae simultaneously. But in the case of a [3 high] input, the situation is different. If one mora becomes [4 high], the other cannot do so without reducing the syllabic nucleus to the sonority of a glide. The immediate consequence of raising is a qualitative change in the relations of the two morae. As one mora is raised to [4 high], it loses its [+vocalic] character; the other retains

---

[2] This argument can easily be overstated. Many languages of the world have whispered vowels, and high central vowels with buzzing, fricative-like qualities (Mandarin). Kotsinas (to appear) reports that the modern Stockholm urban vernacular has shifted the long high vowels /i:, y:/ to extremely high positions with considerable fricativization. Recorded examples show backing in some environments, but devoicing and nonsonorous nuclei in others. In a review of spreading of the feature [+ consonant], Kaisse (1992) cites the Uyghur development of forms like /ʔit/ and /ʔuka/ to [ʔšt] and [ʔɸwka] with fricative nuclei (Hahn 1991). We cannot then argue that the development of more sonorous nuclei is an automatic consequence of raising to a level higher than high vowels, but it is the dominant reaction of those languages that have a nonperipheral track in their version of phonological space.

it. The raised mora is also more peripheral than the unraised one; like all phonological features, peripherality is contrastive, and the unraised mora automatically becomes [–peripheral]. The Dissimilation Effect 1 {DE1} registers these two changes.

{DE1}   Dissimilation Effect 1
The development of a [4 high] mora is accompanied by the laxing of an adjoining mora.

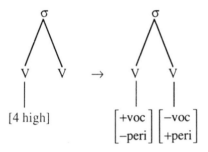

The [4 high] mora is rewritten as the corresponding upglide, so that [+vocalic] is converted to [–vocalic]. Its [+peripheral] status is preserved. The preceding mora retains its [+vocalic] status but becomes [–peripheral]. I have written out both values of [vocalic] and [peripheral] for the two segments, though only one is changed for each, in order to throw into relief the dissimilating character of this effect.

Diphthongization is usually thought of as the addition of a glide to a nucleus. There are many sound changes of this type – most often conditioned changes (like the development of palatal glides before velars, or inglides before liquids) but also unconditioned ones (like the general diphthongization that followed the Great Vowel Shift). The diphthongization of high vowels that formed part of the Great Vowel Shift is not of this type. Rather, it is the result of a dissimilation of the two morae, as the raising tendency behind the Great Vowel Shift applies to high vowels. The Dissimilation Effect 1 on ME ī and ū would follow from their response to the pressure of the vowel shift rule to raise peripheral vowels. The result is the splitting of the monophthong into two parts: one maximally peripheral and the other maximally nonperipheral. This is in fact the historical route by which audibility has been preserved, as the system effects the minimal changes that make a [4 high] element audible and pronounceable.

If a rule is to apply to two morae, our first intuitive notion is to apply it to the first mora. This is in fact what happened with the Old English breaking of **ea, eo, io** to produce ingliding vowels, and more recently with the tensing and raising of short **a** and short **o** in *man, bad, law,* and *lost.* In the Great Vowel Shift development of long high monophthongs, it is obvious that the second mora was affected first. If the first mora had been raised, the output would have been identical to the ingliding vowels. At the moment, we must register the historical fact that it was the second mora that was raised.[3]

The vowel shift rule then applies to the mora that was not affected before. Since this is now [−peripheral], it is lowered to [2 open]. Thus the application of raising to long high vowels in the analytical perspective of an *n*-ary feature framework involves the three steps shown in table 8.2. (In table 8.2, the dissimilating features are shown in boldface/italics.) The usual output of a diphthongization rule like {G7.1} is a diphthong often written as [iy] or [ɨy], where [y] is a general symbol for a front upglide that is actually more phonemic than phonetic. Certainly there are many such diphthongs and many such diphthongization rules. But it has been noted at several points that there is no evidence for a vowel system with a distinctive contrast between [i:] and [iy] or between [i:] and [i:ə]. Since the overall effect of the vowel shift rule is to raise ME ē to [i:], a true chain shift rule that preserves minimal distinctions cannot reasonably produce a high diphthong [ɪy] as the result of shifting ME ī. The overall result is a minimally distinct set of monophthongs and diphthongs:

(1)   OUTPUT OF THE VOWEL SHIFT RULE {G8.1}

[i:, u:]   →   {G8.1, DE1}   →   [e$^>$y, o$^<$w]

[e:, o:]   →   {G8.1}   →   [i:, u:]

[æ, ɔ:]   →   {G8.1}   →   [e:, o:]

In this formulation, a single application of the vowel shift rule produces

Table 8.2   Application of {G8.1} to long high vowels

	Mora		${G8.1} \atop \{→\}$	Mora		${DE1} \atop \{→\}$	Mora		${G8.1} \atop \{→\}$	Mora	
	1	2		1	2		1	2		1	2
[long]	+	+		+	+		+	+		+	+
[high]	3	3		3	4		3	4		2	4
[peri]	+	+		+	+		−	+		−	+
[voc]	+	+		+	+		+	−		+	−

[3] One way of approaching the matter is to note that the distinctive contour of long monophthongs extends the [+peripheral] character of the vowel to the second mora, which is just what does not happen with ingliding vowels. The development of the ingliding vowels in current sound changes is a conditioned tensing (see chapter 11), while the Great Vowel Shift was syntagmatically unconditioned.

its output – subject to the additional lowering of the diphthongs in later centuries. *Single application* here does not mean that the rule immediately transforms Middle English into Early Modern English, or that it grinds out Early Modern English by continuous processing. Rather, the rule sums up in a single statement processes that affected the speech community over several centuries. By describing the whole process in a single statement, it links the separate elements to the general principles of vowel shifting, and consequently to a single causal connection. What that cause is, we do not yet know, but the simpler and more unified our account of the change is, the greater the likelihood that we can explain how it came about.

How does this account of the change fit in with the view that diphthongization of high vowels was the initial step in the Great Vowel Shift? The basic notion of a chain shift rule governed by the $z+\alpha x$ operator is that it applies to all segments simultaneously, that is, to all values of z in the defined range. As we have seen, a realistic definition that fits in with the sweeping character of vowel shifts is that z is essentially undefined – that the rule affects all of the vowels in the designated n-ary dimension.

If the rule did not affect all of these z values at the same time, it would be nothing more than an abbreviation for a collection of rules that could apply in any order, whose order needs to be specified to avoid merger. Yet we know from every empirical study of change in progress that vowels move at different rates, and that there are initial and final movements. In the Philadelphia back chain shift, /ahr/ no longer shows any change in apparent time, whereas /ohr/ continues to move upward toward /uhr/ (figure 3.6). The chain shift rule does not describe the *process* of chain shifting but rather its end result; it should be viewed not as a lever that moves segments but as the mold into which they fit. It is therefore consistent with either a gradual and simultaneous movement of all vowels or a discrete series of successive movements, bearing in mind that those successive movements must be ordered in such a way as to arrive at the final result described by the vowel shift rule. Such an ordering would begin with diphthongization and proceed from high to low, with the raising of ǣ and ɔ̄ as the last step.

The diphthongization rules do create a special status for the movements of ī and ū. We have established $x = 1$ in $z+\alpha x$, though it might be set at any real value. But the Dissimilation Effect establishes a discrete change of features, so that the shift from [i:] to [ɪy] happens as soon as the second mora is produced as contrastively more peripheral than the first. Even if the movement of the first mora from [i] to [y] and the second from [ɪ] to [e>] were gradual, this convention reflects a discreteness in perception: there is a minimal difference between nucleus and glide that can be heard as diphthongal.

The way in which the vowel shift rule controls the movements of individual vowels will be explored further in the discussion of the Expansion Convention in section 8.2. But first it will be helpful to examine the differentiation of the two morae more closely.

ALTERNATIVE MODES OF DIPHTHONGIZATION

At first glance, the application of the vowel shift rule to successive morae seems like nothing more than a formal device to achieve the desired unification. Its relation to linguistic structure becomes more evident when we consider (1) that it represents the basic operation of syllabification, that is, the selection of the syllabic nucleus; (2) that it is equally capable of representing the important linguistic process of resyllabification; and (3) that there are two alternative modes of treating two successive morae which are actually realized in linguistic history.

Long monophthongs are converted into diphthongs in two different ways. First, in the Great Vowel Shift and other Pattern 1 configurations, the first mora becomes the nucleus (a "falling" diphthong) and is quickly differentiated from the glide target. In the version just given, this was represented as the raising of the second mora – that is, the continued upward movement of the tense vowels reaches its maximum first in the second mora. Second, in some cases the second mora falls behind the first even before high position, or [3 high], is reached. In Romance, Germanic, Lithuanian, and other languages, it is common for this to happen as long vowels rise from mid to high position (LYS:chap. 3). The **ie, ia** and **uo, ua** graphic conventions reflect this fact directly (LYS:sec. 3.8.1; Rauch 1967).[4] Our best modern interpretation of this notation is an ingliding diphthong, where the second mora moves to a central position.

Many English sound changes in progress show the development of an inglide, which seems to be more characteristic of English now than in earlier periods.[5] When /æ/ is first lengthened and tensed to /æh/, the tendency to ingliding is fundamental to the articulation, even though it is not immediately apparent. As the vowel rises to [ɛ:ə] and [e:ə], the differentiation of the lengthened vowel into peripheral and nonperipheral morae is increasingly obvious. Furthermore, the vowel develops a radically different acoustic trajectory. (2) shows the characteristic trajectories for *bad* with tense and lax vowels. In the lax case on the right, there is a simple F1 maximum, showing the central tendency of the nucleus. The upper mid tense vowel on the left shows both F1 and F2 maxima. Furthermore, the F2 maximum, which seems to be associated with the acoustic impression of maximum height, is also a point of lowest amplitude. As the vowel rises

---

[4] There are several alternative ways of interpreting these spellings, for example, as the addition of a palatal onglide. Older spellings in German like *heer, hear, hiar* preceding *hier* argue strongly against this interpretation.

[5] The current direction of diphthongization in the raising of tensed /æh/ and /oh/ would appear to have a structural motivation: the presence of upgliding diphthongs /ey/ and /ow/ already in the language.

to high position, there is an increasing tendency to hear it as two distinct nuclei. (See the discussion of the seance narrative in (22) of chapter 6, where *that* [ðiːət] is heard by speakers of other dialects as *the act* or *the fact* or *yet* with a shift of syllabicity.)

(2)   CHARACTERISTIC TRAJECTORIES OF TENSE AND LAX VOWELS IN *BAD*

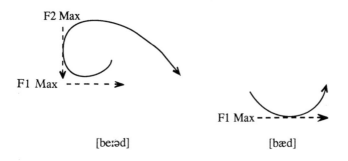

[beːəd]   [bæd]

As ingliding diphthongs reach maximum height, the next step in the advancement of sound change is a shift of syllabicity to produce a rising diphthong, and the subsequent lowering of the diphthongal nucleus. This is the history of an early Proto-Romance development that has produced the following paradigm from tonic free open **e** and **o** (Pope 1934; Brunot and Bruneau 1949):

(3)

Latin	French	Italian	Spanish
pĕtram	pierre	pietra	piedra
pĕdem	pied	piede	pie
ŏvum	oeuf	uovo	huevo
fŏcum	feu	fuoco	fuego

Although there are differing views on the origin of these rising diphthongs, the standard view is that they were originally falling and were produced by a gradual raising of the first element. This view is supported by Algerian inscriptions that contain the earliest examples of Latin diphthongization, with *ee* as well as *ie* (*meeritis* for *meritis*), just as in the German examples.

Evidence from the Valais is again important. Standard French and most northern French dialects show the pattern of (3), where the inglide develops in front, but the back vowels are fronted monophthongs. In the eastern Valais, no fronting took place, and there, as we have seen, tonic free open /ɔ/ is found as monophthongal [u]. Earlier, we argued from the internal logic of the situation that /ɔ/ must have risen along a peripheral path, while checked /o/ fell on a nonperipheral path. The Valais must have participated in the Proto-Romance development of this tonic free open vowel, and it must have shown the same inglides. That inglide does not appear today, but the loss of inglides is one of the most common of the changes that affect [uᵊ]. It therefore appears most likely that free /ɔ/ rose as a lengthened vowel with a peripheral nucleus and a centering inglide.

The Romance development of rising diphthongs represents the application of the mirror image of the Dissimilation Effect 1 {DE1} and this can be collapsed with {DE1} to produce a more inclusive version:

{DE1'} DISSIMILATION EFFECT 1 [revised]

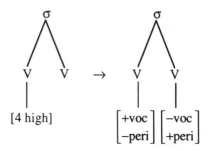

There is of course no need for two formulations. The rule differentiates a two-mora syllable with a [4 high] mora into a semivowel and a lax nucleus, irrespective of the placement of [4 high]. By applying the mirror image convention of an asterisk on the input, we can indicate that both orders apply.

When {DE1'} applies to ingliding vowels, with [4 high] first, the rule changes the [−vocalic] feature on the following segment to [+vocalic]; it remains [−peripheral]. Thus the dissimilation of the two segments now produces a change of syllabicity, from a falling to a rising diphthong.

In the diphthongization of high monophthongs, we had no clear motivation for selecting the second mora for raising as a historical fact. For the ingliding tense vowels, there is no choice. The first mora is considerably higher than the second, and it will be raised to [4 high] first. For long monophthongs, we will have to specify that the second mora is raised first. At present, we have no examples of a breaking of high vowels /iː/ → [iə] in a chain shift, though the reverse is built into the East Lettish shifts (chapter 5). It is also important to bear in mind that the raising of a high vowel to [4 high] and the Dissimilation Effect apply only to languages in which the [−peripheral] option is available. For other languages, a rule with the output operator $z+\alpha x$ cannot apply to [3 high] vowels.

DISSIMILATION EFFECTS ON LOW VOWELS

The problems analyzed so far have focused on integrating the diphthongization of the high vowels into the single vowel shift rule. If the proposed solutions are useful there, they should also be useful at the other end of phonological space, when rule {G8.1} applies to vowels that are minimally high. In this discussion, I will follow the indications in chapter 6 that show the range of [a] to be lowest in phonological space, lower than [æ] or [ɑ], along with other vowels that are no lower than these. Therefore, it is reasonable to assign [1 high] to [–peripheral] /a/, and [0 high] to [+peripheral] /a/. When the nucleus of /ay/ or /aw/ reaches [0 high], it automatically becomes [+peripheral] by the definition of that feature.

Chapter 6 has already indicated the logic of the obvious next step for chain shift rules. The nucleus of an upgliding diphthong that is [0 high], affected by a chain shift rule of the form [z high] → [$z+\alpha x$ high], will be raised to [1 high]. As we have seen, this moves /ay/ to [ɑy] and /aw/ to [æw]. The tendency to nucleus-glide differentiation is obviously at work here. It is expressed directly in Dissimilation Effect 2 {DE2}:

{DE2}   DISSIMILATION EFFECT 2

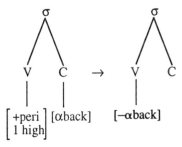

When a diphthong with a [+peripheral] nucleus begins to rise, {DE2} automatically moves /aw/ to the front and /ay/ to the back. But the [0 high] location represents a fork in the path of chain shifting, and this is only one possible route. The other route is not a part of the vowel shift rule. Instead of continuing the path of nucleus-glide differentiation, the glide is weakened and assimilated, along with its backness or frontness, to the nucleus. Monophthongization of /ay/ to [a:] is thus a termination of the vowel shift process as expressed by {G8.1}.

8.2   Reduction of the principles

The vowel shift rule {G8.1} is economical, as rules are supposed to be, and it expresses in a symbolic notation the connection between the rising and falling parts of the chain. But it also suggests that Principle I and Principle II are somehow the same principle. Certainly whatever explanation would be given for one would apply, inversely, to the other, for these are, after all, symmetrical principles from the beginning. Principle III was from the outset altogether asymmetrical. In chapter 6, (32) provided a symmetrical reformulation in which back vowels move to the front along peripheral paths, and front vowels move to the back along nonperipheral paths. In this section, I would like to explore the notion that the revised Principle III and the conjoined Principles I and II are versions of the same principle. It is possible that there is only one principle of chain shifting, and not three.

This section will begin with a proposal to reduce the three principles to a single principle, with an accompanying modification of the model of phonological space. This will lead to some further economies in formal statement, which will be used to express in a concise way the complex chain shifts that make up the four patterns and the two major tendencies of Modern English dialects: the Northern Cities Shift and the Southern Shift. Since the Northern Cities Shift is the most complex of the modern chain shifts, with many variables at an early stage of development, it will be important to examine the logical and causal relations of its elements in some detail.

The asymmetry of phonological space

Though Principles I and II are symmetrical in the front-back dimension, they are in essence asymmetrical principles. The opposing constraints for peripheral and nonperipheral nuclei are not reversible – if they were, the principles would have no meaning. The possibility of joining Principles I and II with Principle III rests on joining their two asymmetries. Why should peripheral vowels move *up* by Principle I and *front* by Principle III, instead of *up* by Principle I and *back* by Principle III? There must be some connection between fronting and raising, backing and falling. Our first task, then, is to explore any asymmetries in the underlying phonological space, which until now has been portrayed as almost symmetrical: the slope of the back periphery is steeper than that of the front periphery, but the horizontal boundaries are all level: high, mid, and low are shown as parallel in front and back.

THE ASYMMETRY OF [i] AND [u]
The articulatory triangle that we have been sketching here projects [i, a, u] as three equivalent terminal points of phonological space. But the types of sound changes reviewed in chapters 5 and 6 do not point to any equivalence of [i] and [u]. When a sound moving up the peripheral track reaches [i:], we have seen only one option available for further movement. If it does not diphthongize and develop a lax nucleus, it remains in place and merges with any new sound approaching [i]. Since this option depends on the existence of a phonological space with a [–peripheral] track and since most systems do not have such a space, [i] often functions as a dead end for sound changes, as in the case of Greek (see (9) in chapter 7). In the high back corner, the situation is quite different. If a sound moving up

reaches [u], it may diphthongize and develop a lax nucleus, but it may also front towards [ü]. This fronting movement does not depend on any special configuration of phonological space, since all systems have a high periphery by definition. Whether or not the fronting sound is direted toward [ʉ], [i], [ü], [iu], or [i] depends on many factors in the system; the basic fact is that the fronting of [u] opens a wide variety of possibilities.

In its relation to sound change, then, [u] may be regarded as a way station, while [i] is a terminus.

THE AMBIVALENCE OF [a]

The most open vowel [a] has a somewhat different status from the vowels at the upper limits of the vowel triangle. It is the main juncture where descending nonperipheral vowels enter the peripheral track. At this point, some vowels ascend along the front periphery, while others ascend along the back periphery. We have seen that in Old English, long ā moved back and up, while in Early Middle English, the new lengthened short ă in open syllables moved front and up. One could argue that the direction of movement depends on whether the vowel began the movement slightly to the front or to the back of center. But some phonemes will be located at [a] in dead center, and if others are shifted to the front or the back, this raises the question of how they got there. In the oldest varieties of New York City English, /aw/ and /ay/ had identical nuclei, but as the system evolved, /aw/ moved to the front along the peripheral track, and /ay/ to the back.

There are two clear principles that determine which direction a peripheral [a] will take, and both have functional interpretations.

1 The front/back balance of neighboring phonemes is a decisive factor in determining whether an /a/ phoneme will shift phonetically to the front or the back. Moulton (1962) demonstrates decisively that the phonetic position of /a/ in Swiss German dialects is linked to the existence of an /æ/ or /ɔ/ phoneme. Any skewing of the system of neighboring phonemes is reflected in the allophones of /a/: systems with /æ/ but no /ɔ/ show back varieties of /a/, those with /ɔ/ but no /æ/ show front varieties, and so on.

2 The tendency to nucleus-glide differentiation is a widespread phenomenon. Insofar as /aw/ and /ay/ retain their diphthongal status, their phonetic shifts show increasing distance between the nucleus and the glide. This is incorporated into the vowel shift rule {G8.1}, as discussed in section 8.1.

We then have only two major types of movement along the peripheral track, both extending from [a] to [i]: one along the front path from [a] to [æ] to [i], the other along the back path from [a] to [ɔ] to [u] to [i]. In items of the number of discrete phonetic targets usually recognized, the second path is considerably longer than the first. These distances can be expressed as degrees of opening:

(4) 5   4   3   2   1
    a → æ → ε → e → i

    8   7   6   5   4   3   2   1
    a → ɑ → ɔ → o → u → ʉ → ü → i

This assignment of n-ary values is radically different from any displayed so far, in that there are five steps of openness along the front periphery, but eight along the back. This is another aspect of the asymmetry of phonological space that is the main topic of this section.

THE FEATURE [OPEN]

The asymmetries of sound change can be summed up by describing vowel shifts as governed by a single feature of *openness*, as shown in (4). It is not an acoustically based feature, for on the whole, the asymmetry of [i] and [u] is not reflected in a two-formant space.[6] On the other hand, all studies of the articulatory apparatus converge on representations that show [u] in an intermediate position between [a] and [i]. In no articulatory view can [u] be considered to occupy a high back corner. If we use the location of the narrowest constriction of the vocal tract to determine the relative backness of a vowel, the vowel that is most back is clearly not [u], but [ɔ]. Figure 8.1 is a typical result of X-ray tracing of tongue positions of vowels close to cardinal position – in this case, the vowels of Ngwe (Ladefoged 1964). The insert tracing of the highest position of the tongue shows [u] as just the type of way station that our discussion of sound changes indicated. Figure 8.2 is Nearey's range-normalized plot of tongue body positions in American English vowels (Nearey 1977). Figure 8.3 shows Hashimoto and Sakawi's (1982) plot of tongue positions, based on cineradiographic data of Perkell (1971) for American English. All of these show an elliptical distribution where the vowels follow two paths from [ɑ] to [i], one in the back and one in the front. There seems to be no question

---

[6] The unnormalized acoustic envelopes that have been presented in the figures of chapters 3, 4 and 6 are not perfectly regular and uniform. Some are regular triangles with distributions of /iy/ and /uw/ nuclei at the same F1 level; others show skewing in one direction or another. The 54 systems analyzed in LYS were compared to see whether the highest front vowel (/iy/, /ihr/, or /æh/) was higher than, equal to, or lower than the highest back vowel (/uw/, /oy/, or /ohr/). High front was higher than high back in 25 cases, there was no difference in 3 cases, and high front was lower than high back in 26 cases. There are some interesting biases from dialect to dialect, but they do not correspond to the actual direction of sound change. In the Northern Cities, Detroit, Rochester, and Buffalo show a preponderance of /iy/ higher than /uw/ (11/1/2), while Chicago shows the reverse (1/0/5). London and Norwich show a predominance of /iy/ lower than /uw/ (2/0/8), while Texas shows /iy/ higher than /uw/ (4/0/1). There are no obvious correspondences with age or sex.

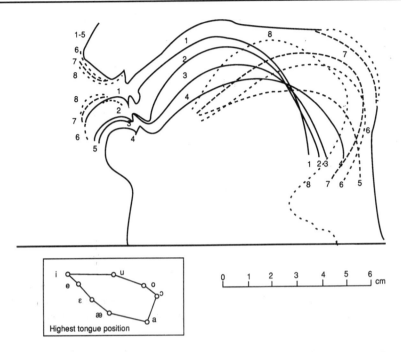

Figure 8.1. Tongue positions for eight near-cardinal vowels of Ngwe [1 = i, 2 = e, 3 = ɛ, 4 = æ, 5 = a, 6 = ɔ, 7 = o, 8 = u] (from Ladefoged 1964)

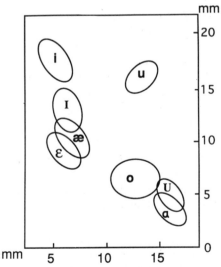

Figure 8.2. Tongue body positions in American English vowels
(from Nearey 1977)

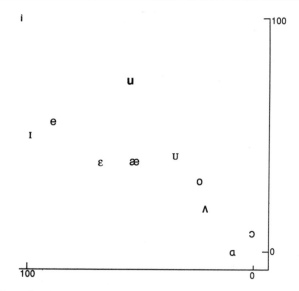

Figure 8.3.   Hashimoto and Sasaki's (1982) plot of tongue center position for the cineradiographic data on American English vowels provided by Perkell (1969)

that mappings of tongue positions will show elliptical distributions, radically different from the triangular or trapezoidal distributions of acoustic data. It is not entirely clear how this articulatory asymmetry relates to the asymmetry of the chain shifts we have been studying, since our generalizations have been based almost entirely on acoustic or impressionistic data (which are essentially acoustic). We can get some further insight into this problem by using data provided by Lindau (1978) in her survey of vowel features. They are based on studies of five male speakers of American English, pronouncing the 10 vowels of the Peterson-Barney (1952) series in the /h__d/ context.[7] Figure 8.4a shows the mean values for these speakers in the linear F2 × F1 plot of chapter 6. Figure 8.4b returns these data to the original form used by Lindau, where the abscissa is F2 – F1. This view of the acoustic data shifts [u] toward the front and begins to eliminate the high back corner. Figure 8.4c is the result of measurements that Lindau carried out on cineradiographic data. The horizontal axis locates the highest point of the tongue on a line parallel to the hard palate; the vertical axis is the perpendicular distance of this line from the edge of the upper teeth. The shape of phonological space is again seen to be the elliptical

---

[7] It is not easy to relate these speakers to the patterns developed in chapter 6, since they are described simply as "from the Midwest," with the additional note that a panel of three linguists agreed that they spoke the same variety of American English. Given the data of figure 8.4a, we can assume that this dialect was not strongly influenced by the Midland tendency to participate in a Pattern 3 shift, and that there was minimal fronting of /uw/.

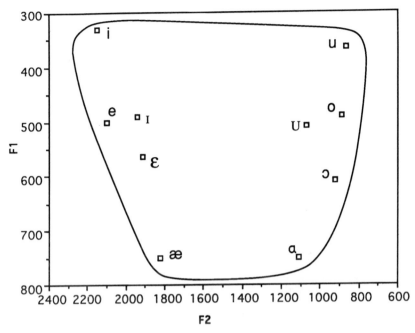

Figure 8.4a.   Mean values of American English vowels in the /h___d/ context (adapted from Lindau 1978). Mean normalized values of F1 and F2

pattern of figures 8.1–8.3, with no evidence that [u] occupies a high back position.

The most promising basis for an explanation of the principles of chain shifting within subsystems was presented briefly at the end of chapter 6: Sievers's (1850) early conception that vowels pronounced with greater length and energy will show a tendency to move toward more exaggerated, or more extreme, positions farther from the position of rest. Donegan's (1978) conception of a tendency to maximize chromaticity depends upon a trapezoidal or triangular conception of phonological space, while the simple mechanical conception involved in Sievers's view is quite compatible with the elliptical phonological space of figure 8.4c. Furthermore, Sievers's view of the mechanism is essentially physiological, while Donegan's is acoustic. We can therefore move with greater confidence toward a reformulation of the principles of chain shifting in terms of a dimension of openness that has its firmest basis in physiology, restating in a more compact form the relationship between raising, fronting, backing, and lowering. We can sum up the principles of chain shifting as a single principle that establishes an inverse relationship between peripherality and changes in openness:

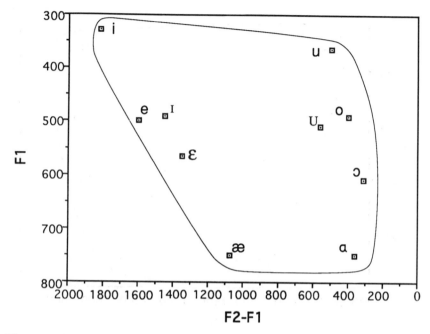

Figure 8.4b. Mean values of American English vowels in the /h___d/ context (adapted from Lindau 1978). Mean normalized values of F1 and F2 – F1

(5) In chain shifts, peripheral vowels become less open and nonperipheral vowels becomes more open.

A Pattern 3 shift like that operating in Norwich can then be described by the rule shown in (6), which now combines the raising of back vowels and the fronting of high vowels.

(6) $[z \text{ open}] \rightarrow [z - x \text{ open}] / \left[\dfrac{\overline{}}{+\text{peri}} \right]$

A Pattern 2 shift like the Northern Cities Shift can be described by the rule shown in (7).

(7) $[z \text{ open}] \rightarrow [z - \alpha x \text{ open}] / \begin{bmatrix} \overline{} \\ \alpha\text{peri} \\ +\text{ant} \\ -\text{free} \end{bmatrix}$

This rules applies only to front, originally short vowels – that is, to [−free] vowels, not to the peripheral /iy/, /ey/, etc. It will front tense /o/ to [æ:ˁ],

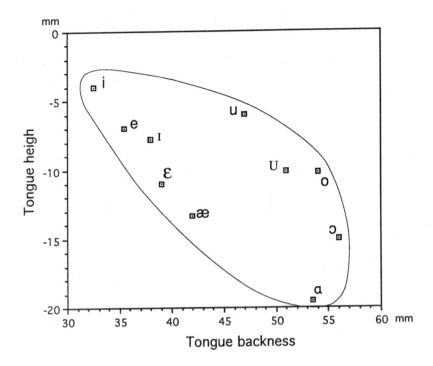

Figure 8.4c. Mean normalized positions of the highest point of the tongue in American English vowels in the /h_____d/ context (adapted from Lindau 1978)

raise tense /æ/ to [ɛ:], lower lax [ɪ] to [ɛ], and lower lax /ɛ/ to [æ>]. At present, we still have no general convention for continuing the raising of /æ/ to [iə], and no way of predicting when lax /ɛ/ will back to /ʌ/ instead of falling to [æ>].

Pattern 1 and Pattern 4 chain shifts will not be affected by this convention. The symmetry of Pattern 1 does not require a feature of openness to capture the full generalization. In fact, substituting [open] for [high] in {G8.1} would produce the wrong result: after diphthongization of ME ū: the nucleus of [ʊu] would front to [ü] instead of falling to [a]. It would follow that this concept of a phonological space dominated by the global feature of openness was not operating in Early Middle English.

The front/back symmetry of Pattern 4', which follows the tensing of /ay/, does not require the feature [open]. However, it is not inconsistent with it. A Pattern 4' rule, such as that operating in Norwich, will have the following form:[8]

_____

[8] A certain amount of redundancy still remains to be extracted from such rules. The notation —α . . . α is redundant since according to the principle in (5), openness will always be inversely related to peripherality.

(8) $[z \text{ open}] \rightarrow [z - \alpha x \text{ open}] / \left[\dfrac{\quad}{\alpha \text{peri}} \right] \begin{bmatrix} -\text{cons} \\ -\text{back} \end{bmatrix}$

This rule will lower the nuclei of /iy/ and /ey/, and raise the nuclei of /ay/ and /oy/. When the least open peripheral vowel in the shift reaches [uy], this version of the rule predicts that it will be fronted.[9]

The Expansion Convention

The rules written so far show movement in single units, where $x = 1$ in the original schema (7) of chapter 7. Section 7.2 raised the question whether chain shifts might be governed by an Expansion Convention to extend movements as far as they can go without creating mergers. Though this is an attractive proposal in many ways, it runs into several serious difficulties.

The impulse to write such a condition would seem to have two aspects: *compulsion* ("Go as far as you can!") and *avoidance* ("Stop when you see a merger coming!"). Both suggest that sound change is endowed with foresight and purpose, congenial enough to those who have inherited Jakobson's teleological orientation (chapter 1). At a later point (chapters 19–20) we will ask whether language does in fact react to language change in a way that preserves meaning and if so, how this might be accomplished. For the moment, however, we will postpone this issue and formulate the Expansion Convention in an objective manner.

(9)   THE EXPANSION CONVENTION
       Given a process of sound change described by a rule
            $[z \text{ fea}_i] \rightarrow [z + \alpha x \text{ fea}_i] / \ldots$
       apply the rule to any one segment by increasing x until a segment
       bearing $[z + \alpha(x+1) \text{ fea}_i]$ would be nondistinct from another
       segment, or until $z - \alpha x = 0$.

It is important to bear in mind that the chain shift rule that (9) focuses on is not a rule governing the behavior of individuals. An individual does not carry out a chain shift, or maximize a distribution. The rule is a generalization describing the behavior of a speech community over time, and

---

[9] This has not happened in Norwich. But the history of Romance languages shows that when Latin **ē** was diphthongized to [e$^>$i] backed to [ɔi], and raised to [ui], a shift of syllabicity took place, and the resulting rising diphthong showed the fronting of its nucleus to [wə]. This older process raises the question as to whether this revision of the vowel shift rules has any application to Romance languages that do not have the [±peripheral] feature in front and back. It was noted above that in languages without a tense/lax or long/short distinction, the unmarked series is to be taken as [+tense], and Romance vowels accordingly rise along the periphery. This is inevitable in terms of the feature [peripheral], since if there is only one series, it must be peripheral by definition.

it seeks to unify a number of distinct stages or phenomena that may take as long as three generations. Without asking how such a convention is effected by the speakers of the community, let us review the current evidence for such a generalization.

COMPULSION

We have seen many examples of vowel shifts that have extended beyond the single unit of movement predicted by the rules written in this chapter. They can be grouped under three headings: lowering, raising, and fronting:

1 The further lowering of ME ī and ū from [ey] to [ay] and [o˂w] to [aw] in the English Great Vowel Shift, in Middle High German, and in Yiddish.
2 The further raising of tense /æh/ from [ɛ:] to [i:ə] in the Northern Cities Shift in Buffalo, Rochester, Chicago, and elsewhere; the raising of Valais /ɔ/ to [u].[10]
3 The further fronting of /uw/ from [ʉw] to [üw] in the Southern Shift in Philadelphia and elsewhere.

On the other hand, all phonemes do not immediately expand to fill intervening space. In the historical record, Common Czech shows the diphthongization of Ɪ to **ei**, ū to **ou**, with no further lowering of the nucleus, and the same limitation can be observed in Old Prussian. But we do not have enough information on the other developments in these systems to comment intelligibly on them. The diagrams of chapter 6 show that /iy/ has remained in high position for many dialects involved in Pattern 4, even though /ey/ has fallen to low position (see for example, Norwich, figures 6.19–6.20). Though we are of course looking at an intermediate stage, and /iy/ may eventually fall to mid position and fill the gap, these dialects do not seem to exhibit an overpowering compulsion for this to happen immediately. It is interesting to note that the examples in 1–3 above all concern nucleus-glide differentiation. We cannot argue that all diphthongs show maximum nucleus-glide differentation, but it does appear that in the course of chain shifts, there is a strong tendency for this condition to be realized.

The discussion of the Expansion Convention so far has implicitly assumed a single target or norm that moves from low to mid to high. But this is misleading. The most important evidence for the Expansion Convention is found in the distribution of phonemes involved in change in progress. In the majority of the sound changes we have studied, the allophones of a given phoneme expand across the available space, differen-

---

[10] As noted above, it is most likely that the raising of Valais /ɔ/ took place as a peripheral ingliding vowel, so that it is parallel to the raising of /æh/ in the Northern Cities Shift.

tiated according to the effect of the environment. Most of the diagrams of the Northern Cities Shift show /æh/ as a long ellipse ranging from high to lower mid position. At one extreme is /æh/ before nasals in high position, and at the other is /æh/ after liquid clusters in lower mid position (see figure 6.8, ranging from *hand* to *flats*; figure 6.9, from *aunts* to *glass*, *track*; figure 6.10, from *can* to *tractor*; figure 6.16, from *sandals* to *grandmother*). The same allophonic expansion undoubtedly occurred in the diphthongizationof high vowels in the Great Vowel Shift. As the sound change reaches completion, such extended allophones assemble into a tightly constrained cluster at the most advanced end of the distribution (for the example of /æh/, see figures 6.2, 6.11). The mechanism by which the sound crosses an unoccupied phonological space is therefore not a steady progression from point A to point B, but rather the expansion of fast and slow allophones to the limits of unoccupied territory.

AVOIDANCE

The second half of the Expansion Convention is formulated as a distinctness requirement. Because we are dealing with an *n*-ary notation, the convention can look ahead at the *n* + 1 case. Thus in Pattern 4, /ay/ initially expands over [ɑi, ɒi, ɔi]. While /ay/ is at [oi] and /oy/ is at [ui], this is the full range of available space. To be sure, when phonemes expand to the limits of phonological space, they are constrained by the physical parameters of the articulatory apparatus and its acoustic reflections. When /æh/ expands to [i:ə], it cannot become any higher and still be a vowel. But even here there are routes that the vowel might follow into occupied territory. The ingliding [i:ə] could conceivably be monophthongized to [i:] and so encroach on /iy/; or be shortened and so shift further into the territory occupied by /i/; or show a shift of syllabicity to /ja/. To show which of these routes are preferred, possible, or unlikely, the principles for changes across subsets of vowels must be investigated. But in general it can be said that the phonological space of any phoneme is limited by the space occupied by other phonemes, and that any expansion beyond that point will lead to merger.

How can we estimate the strength of the tendency to avoid merger? It is well known that one of the weaknesses of the functional interpretation of chain shifts (Martinet 1955) is that it considers and explains chain shifts but ignores the many mergers that do take place, such as the large set of mergers into Greek /i/ shown in (9) of chapter 7. An accountable study that balances chain shifts against mergers is not easy to accomplish. The enumeration of chain shifts depends on the number of different languages and dialects we set up. Is the Northern Cities Shift a single phenomenon? Or do we count separately the avoidance of merger in Chicago, Rochester, and Buffalo? The Great Vowel Shift is usually described as a single set of changes. But the *Survey of English Dialects* (Orton and Dieth 1962–67) shows that it occurs in many different stages across the landscape and with different possibilities of merger in many communities (chapter 17). Pattern 3 chain shifts occur in many Romance dialects: are these the same event or parallel events? There are no simple answers to such questions, so that a quantitative survey of mergers vs. chain shifts seems to be a remote possibility.

A different strategy is to search for those events that run counter to general tendencies, and see how they might be explained. These fall into two categories: (1) chain shifts that deviate from the paths predicted by the general principles; (2) mergers that occur where continued chain shifting might have been expected.

The rest of this chapter will review all the exceptional cases that can be located in the chain shifts considered in chapters 5–7.

Deviant chain shifts   In the normal course of Pattern 1 and Pattern 4 shifts, the diphthong with the most open nucleus – /iy/ or /ey/ – descends to [ay] and to [+peripheral] position. Three deviations from this pattern can be identified.

Romansh is one of the exceptional Romance languages that show a diphthongization of /i/ to [ɪi]. As we follow the Romansh developments in various communities, the reflexes of Vulgar Latin ī and ō appear as [i] and [u] in some dialects (e.g. Surselva, Sutselva; Grisch 1939). But in the Sotsés region diphthongs develop. The front diphthong does not follow the usual course of opening to [ay]. Instead, it shifts to the back, to [oy].[11] On the other hand, the parallel back vowel does descend to [aw] and then proceeds to [ɛw] and [ew], following the full route of the Pattern 1 extension. We can account for this lack of parallelism by the fact that VL e is also diphthongized, and occupies the [ay] position. In (10), I have assumed that these diphthongizing dialects of Romansh have acquired the Germanic phonological space, and I have displayed the sound shifts as if the diphthongal nuclei were lax, an assumption that remains to be verified by measurement. The developments of (10) are not actually chain shifts but parallel movements comparable to the extensions of Pattern 1. Nevertheless, they show the mechanism of avoidance that prevents the reflexes of VL i from merging with the reflexes of VL e, deviating from the expected parallelism with the back vowel.

A similar shift occurs in southern Sweden (Swenning 1909; Hedström 1932), where the Germanic diphthongization along a [–peripheral] track is expected. In the province of Småland and neighboring regions, the monophthong /e:/ is diphthongized; in some areas it is lowered to [ay] and in others it appears as [oy]. In those areas where /e:/ appears as [oy], a second

---

[11] In the original version of Principle III, this would have been an exception, but in the revised version, the shifting of lax nuclei to the back is the rule rather than the exception.

(10)   DIPHTHONGIZATION IN THE SOTSÉS REGION OF ROMANSH

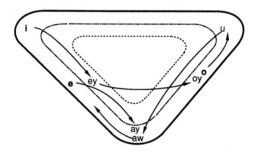

diphthongization of both long and short /a/ has taken place, as shown in (11).

(11)   DIPHTHONGAL MOVEMENTS IN SOUTHERN SWEDISH

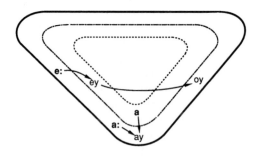

Again, this is a case of parallel movement rather than chain shifting, but it illustrates the same deviation from the typical route /ey/ → /ay/ → /oy/.

The third case of avoidance is the failure of the lengthened **ĕr** in Middle English to assume the expected peripheral position. The overall view afforded by (17) in chapter 7 showed that **ăr** words were lengthened and rose along the peripheral track to yield *bare, fare,* etc., since no OE **a:** remained as a result of original backing and raising. But in the interpretation given here, **ĕr** words remained in the [−peripheral] position.[12]

Mergers in chain shifts   Also relevant to this examination of the functional interpretation of chain shifts is the occurrence of mergers in the midst of the shift. Mergers are never easy to explain, since they obviously interfere with the main business of phonemes: to distinguish one word from

---

[12] In this case, the following /r/ environment must have contributed to the avoidance effect, since it did not occur with **ĕ** in other environments.

another.[13] But mergers that occur in the course of chain shifting are even more striking, since they are surrounded by events that have the opposite effect – the maintenance of distinctions.

The chain shifts considered here include very few cases of merger. The most prominent examples occur in the course of Pattern 3 shifts, especially before /r/. In London, New York, and Philadelphia we find the shift in (12), with a merger of the last two word classes.

(12)   /ahr/ → /ohr/ → /uhr/

One could attempt to explain this by citing the small number of minimal pairs involved, but there are in fact more than a few for such a limited environment, as shown in (13); and of course there is a much larger set of near-minimal pairs or rhymes. The actual number depends on the presence or absence of palatal onglides in words like *lure* and the lowering to [o] in words like *poor* in various dialects.

(13)	dour	door	boor	bore
	lure	lore	spoor	spore
	sure	shore	tour	tore
	moor	more	poor	pour

For an account of this merger, we must instead look to more general principles of chain shifting. Surprisingly enough, there are no examples of the fronting of /uhr/ in the dialects considered so far. The combination of a peripheral high back nucleus and a centering glide is apparently not consistent with the conditions that lead to fronting. In the London, New York, and Philadelphia dialects, this constraint holds for following liquids /r/ and /l/. It appears to hold for dialects where final /l/ is dark and often vocalized. It does not hold for Southern U.S. dialects where final /l/ is relatively clear. In this case, words like *school* show a fronted [ü] and participate in the full development of the Pattern 3 chain shift. But words ending in /r/ do not: in this case, both /uhr/ and /ohr/ can be lowered and the inglide is frequently truncated (yielding [foə] or [fo] for *four*, [pʊə] (unmerged), [poə], or [po] for *poor*).

The generalization then holds that a peripheral high back vowel followed by a centering glide does not participate in Principle III or become less open under the revised General Principle given in (5).

---

[13] One would normally look to the functional load of distinctions in order to explain which mergers take place and which do not. But such loads are not easy to measure; the current CDC studies of misunderstandings in everyday life show that it would be a serious underestimation to examine only the preceding and following consonants in isolated words (King 1969). The examples of misunderstandings given in chapter 6 show how difficult it is to imagine the contexts in which confusion takes place.

Another example of merger in the midst of chain shifting can be found in the Great Vowel Shift, where the three-way distinction of ME long vowels ā ~ ɛ̄ ~ ē in *mate* ~ *meat* ~ *meet* was reduced to two. How this happened and the mechanism involved will be considered in the following chapters.

The study of chain shifting does not then provide many examples of unexpected mergers; examples of unexpected avoidance are easier to locate. This situation reinforces the case for a functional interpretation of chain shifting. But it does not resolve the question of how such functional effects take place, which will be the major topic of chapter 20.

9

Chain Shifts across Subsystems

The principles of chain shifting considered so far have focused on movements within a simple F1/F2 space: fronting, backing, raising, and lowering. But many of the diagrams have shown other types of changes integrated with these chain shifts: monophthongization, diphthongization, development of inglides, smoothing, lengthening, and shortening. The general principles that govern such shifts across subsystems have not been investigated as thoroughly as those discussed so far. However, they are essential to understanding the overall operation of chain shifting. For if Principles I–III or the revised General Principle (5) of chapter 8 predicts unidirectional movements, what prevents the development of highly skewed systems? What, for example, prevents Principle I from collapsing all long vowels into /i:/ and /u:/? If chain shifts are rotations that preserve the functional economy of the system, then exits and entrances from a given chain become essential to preserve the economy of the system as a whole. Where such exits are closed, as in Greek, we observe wholesale merger.

Chapter 8 extended the vowel shift rule to include the transformation of monophthongs into upgliding diphthongs, and looked briefly at the transformation of diphthongs into monophthongs. But these are only two of the ways that sound change moves across subsystems. A complete review of the data and the problems is beyond the scope of this work, but this chapter will examine some of the issues involved, with a few examples of unidirectional movements, and will present some additional general principles that govern chain shifting across subsystems.

9.1 The concept of subsystem

The notion of "subsystem" is indissolubly connected to the notion of hierarchy in linguistic structure. If all features were at the same level of abstractness, there would be no subsystems. But there is reason to think that changes in place of articulation, the main topic of the preceding discussion, are the most concrete types of sound changes, tightly tied to particular acoustic dimensions and articulatory gestures. The diagram of

English vowel structure first presented in chapter 3 and developed in chapter 6 is repeated here as (1). This is a relatively abstract portrait of phonological space, with bilateral symmetry and three degrees of height for each subsystem.

(1)   THE ORGANIZATION OF ENGLISH VOWELS

SHORT		UPGLIDING			INGLIDING	
		FRONT		BACK		
i	u	iy		iw	uw	ih	uh
e	ʌ	ey	oy		ow	eh	oh
æ	o	ay		aw		æh	ah

Many languages have a wider range of well-developed vowel subsystems: subsystems of rising diphthongs (Korean), nasal vowels (French, Portuguese), glottalized vowels (Akha), and so on.

The organization shown in (1) is motivated by a wide range of structural arguments. For the study of sound change, the most important consideration is the distribution of confusions and mergers. The subsystems can be defined as sets of vowels that are maximally subject to pairwise confusion, whereas confusions across subsystems are less common. This follows both logically and empirically from the fact that vowels differ from neighbors in their own subsystem by only one phonological feature. While corresponding elements of different subsystems, like /i/, /iy/, and /ih/, differ by only one phonological feature at this level of abstraction, they are in most cases distinguished from each other by multiple phonetic features. For example /i/ and /iy/ differ by length, the presence of a glide, the peripherality of the nucleus (which in turn involves distinctions of both F1 and F2), voice quality (Di Paolo and Faber 1990), and energy contour. As a result, variation in the realization of any one phonetic feature rarely leads to overlap across subsystems. This is what is meant by the *abstractness* of certain features. If the distinction between long-and-ingliding and front upgliding vowels depends upon many phonetic differences between them, then the label "long-and-ingliding" does not correspond to any one phonetic feature. Rather, it is an abstract label for a category.

This high degree of differentiation across subsystems does not hold for all the corresponding members. At some locations within a subsystem, phonetic differences from a neighboring system will be reduced. These are the entrance and exit locations where changes in subsystem membership are most common. The recognition of such entrance and exit locations is essential for the understanding of the phonological economy that governs the course of sound change.

9.2 Evidence from naturally occurring misunderstandings

Before we begin the search for such exit and entrance locations, it may be illuminating to review evidence for the organization in (1) that is drawn from the CDC collection of natural misunderstandings. This material, first used in chapter 6 to investigate possible functional links between elements of chain shifts, is a collection of 697 observations made from 1984 to 1990. The purpose of the collection is to compare misunderstandings in everyday life with the results of the controlled experiments on cross-dialectal comprehension to be presented in full in volume 3.

We can use these data to study the nature of English subsystems. First, we can examine the validity of the organization in (1) by comparing the frequency of misunderstandings within and across subsystems, in line with the logic presented above. Furthermore, we can determine entrance and exit locations by finding where elements in a given subsystem are most likely to be confused with elements of another subsystem, and where they are not. This will give us some measure of the relative phonetic distances that separate corresponding elements of two subsystems. Finally, we can locate the phonetic environments that condition such confusions by reducing the phonetic distance between segments in different subsystems.

These data from natural misunderstandings are not used here to argue that such misunderstandings are the causes of change. Actually, the evidence is ambiguous in this respect. The data include misunderstandings that are the result of change in progress, like the raising of tensed /æh/ to [i:ə] and the lowering of /e/ to /æ/ in Chicago. The proportion of items motivated by dialect differences has been fairly constant over time: it is a little more than one-quarter, or 27%. The majority result from overlaps of relatively stable vowels, like /i/, /e/, and /æ/ in Philadelphia.

Several dozen observers, most of them linguists, were recruited to collect these data. They were equipped with a standard printed protocol for recording the misunderstandings as soon as possible after they occurred. The observers noted the date, the dialect backgrounds of speakers and listeners, and the misunderstanding itself in as full a context as possible. They then estimated the time that elapsed between the misunderstood utterance and the correction of the misunderstanding. They also noted how the correction took place: during the utterance, by a query or gesture from the listener, by subsequent turns of talk, or through later nonverbal events. Inevitably, some observers were biased toward particular kinds of events that they were interested in, like the results of merger. It therefore seems likely that the proportion of dialect-motivated understandings was inflated by the interests of the CDC research project. However, observers were instructed to make every effort to note all misunderstandings, including those that depended not on any difference in sounds, but on structural factors or referential ambiguity. The greatest difficulty was found not in a bias toward one kind of misunderstanding, but in the observers' tendency to forget an event if it was not written down shortly after it occurred.

Misunderstandings that arose when people were speaking in very noisy environments, using poor telephone connections, or shouting across distances were not included. Nevertheless, it is not difficult to distinguish those utterances that were relatively noisy from those that were heard more clearly. When the phonetic conditions are truly degenerate, the report shows massive misunderstandings where only a few stressed syllables of the original utterance are preserved. The rest is reanalyzed with considerable ingenuity. These *global misunderstandings* are exemplified in (2)–(4).

(2)   A   [says]: The mayor found an answer for the Eagles.
      B   [hears]: Ralph Nader found an anwer for the needles.
(3)   A   [says, over a cordless phone]: This is A from the Linguistics Laboratory.
      B   [hears over the phone]: This is A from cystic fibrosis.
(4)   A   [says]: You could have acetate sheets that flop over each of them.
      B   [hears]: You could ask the cheese to flop over each of them.

The opposite type of event, *local misunderstanding*, depends upon a misinterpretation of a specific segment, while the rest of the utterance is faithfully reproduced. Though this may be due to faulty hearing conditions, it is much more likely to be due to the phonetic realization of the particular segment. The following two local misunderstandings focus on the relation of /æ/ and /e/:

(5)   A   [says]: I'd go to the Acme and bag.
      B   [hears]: I'd go to the Acme and beg.
(6)   A   [says]: The house has a yellow door and lattice windows.
      B   [hears]: The house has a yellow door and lettuce windows.

For the study of subsystems of English vowels, it will be most efficient to examine local misunderstandings that depend upon the differential interpretation of vowels. This will exclude a large number of global misunderstandings like (2)–(4), as well as 45 misunderstandings that depend upon structural and not phonetic factors. In addition, we will exclude cases that depend upon differences in phonemic inventory: for example, 20 cases that depend upon the merger of short **o** and long open **o**. This leaves 154 local misunderstandings of the relevant type.

Global differences within and across subsystems

Given the greater separation of vowels across subsystems, one might have predicted the total number of misunderstandings within subsystems to be much greater than that across subsystems. However, this is not true. The totals for the two types are almost the same: there were 78 cases of misunderstandings within subsystems, and 74 across subsystems. One might therefore conclude that the concept of subsystem is not significant in natural misunderstandings. However, a closer examination of the distributions shows that there are radical differences between the two types.

In the study of changes in progress in English vowel systems, we find that certain consonantal environments have a particularly strong effect on the realization of vowel nuclei and glides:

- Tautosyllabic following /r/ contracts the periphery of phonological space, so that fewer distinctions are possible in the vowel system: only one short vowel (*fir, her, fur, world*) and three to six long vowels (*fear, fair, far, for, four, boor*), with considerable variability in the organization and number of distinctions from one dialect to another.
- Following nasal consonants enlarge the periphery of phonological space, but acoustic effects of nasality reduce phonological distinctiveness in both nuclei and glides (not only in *pin, pen*, etc., but also in *think, thank, song, gong, time, Tom*, etc.).
- Following consonantal laterals can lower F2 drastically if they are dark. The ongoing vocalization of /l/ in American dialects leads to a number of other effects that can drastically affect understanding. Syllable-final /l/ becomes a glide that is sometimes heard as a back rounded [o] or [u], in *goal, people*, etc., sometimes heard as [ə] in *call, sale*, etc., and sometimes confused with nasality. When intervocalic /l/ is vocalized, the glide combines with the preceding and following nuclei to produce a radically different vowel, often confused with /aw/, so that *bounce* and *balance* are homonyms.
- Preceding clusters of obstruent plus liquid have a strong effect on formants of the following nuclei, for front vowels in particular. F2 is lowered considerably, yielding vowels that are physically much backer than the normal distribution of the phoneme. Thus the phonological space available to front vowels is reduced; *green* and *grain* become less distinct, and *black* enters the field of dispersion of *block*.

If we examine the distribution of the naturally occurring misunderstandings across these four environments, a radical difference between those within subsystems and those across subsystems appears, as shown in figure 9.1. More than three-quarters of the misunderstandings across subsystems are found in these special environments, and almost half are due to the

Within sub-systems [N=78]   Across sub-systems

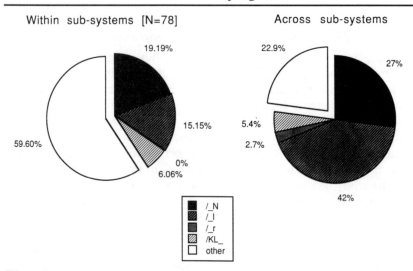

Figure 9.1.   Distribution of local vowel misunderstandings within and across
subsystems

effect of following /l/. But only two-fifths of the misunderstandings within
subsystems are in special environments. Most of the other three-fifths are
confusions in simple monosyllables checked by obstruents (*jag → jock,
bad → bed,   bugs → box,   hicks → hex*, etc.)   or   in   polysyllables
(*lattice → lettuce, loaner → lunar, mother → model*, etc.).

What is the significance of this particular distribution of misunderstandings across subsystems? The four special environments have the effect of
reducing the phonetic distances between neighboring phonemes. For
example, before final /l/, glides tend to be reduced or absorbed (or fused
with the glide that results from fully vocalized [l]). As a result, the monophthongization of /ay/ or /oy/ before /l/ precedes monophthongization in other
environments (and is implied by them). The same can be said for /aw/. As
noted above, the effect of a following nasal consonant is to reduce the
number of distinctions between vowels, resulting in the widespread merger
of /i/ and /e/ before front nasals. Though the effects of this merger were
not included in the 154 cases studied above, the general tendency of following nasals is to reduce the phonetic distance between neighboring vowels.

The pattern of misunderstandings within subsystems is remarkably regular, as reflected in figure 9.2 for the short vowels. Misunderstandings
between vowels are indicated by four integers separated by slashes. The
first represents the general, unmarked case (= "other" in figure 9.1); the
second, vowels before nasals; the third, vowels before liquids; and the
fourth, vowels preceded by liquid clusters. The numbers located along
straight lines between the vowels represent misunderstandings between

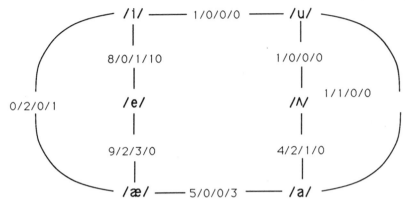

Figure 9.2. Naturally occurring misunderstandings between short vowels. /w/x/y/z/ = unmarked/before nasals/before liquids/after liquid clusters

adjacent vowels. The two curved paths represent misunderstandings between vowels separated by two features: /i/ and /æ/, and /u/ and /a/.

The number of misunderstandings among the short vowels is roughly the same for all adjacent pairs of vowels except those adjacent to /u/, and this is obviously due to the low frequency of this phoneme. Otherwise, it is clear that for each of the neighboring pairs of phonemes, the majority of the misunderstandings involve the unmarked environments: 28 out of 40, or 70%. But only 1 of the 5 cases of confusion between vowels separated by two units is in the unmarked environment, and 4 are in the special environments. Since /i/ and /æ/ are separated by two phonetic features within this subsystem, it is only when some special condition reduces the phonetic distance radically that confusion is likely.

Crossover locations

The regular distribution of confusion among the short vowels contrasts sharply with the asymmetrical distributions involving misunderstandings across subsystems. This asymmetry will yield some additional evidence on the principles governing transitions between subsystems. As we will see in the study of historical changes, transitions between subsystems do not occur randomly, nor do they occur at all points equally. The relation between /i/ and /iy/ is not the same as the relation between /a/ and /ay/.

Table 9.1 focuses on the upgliding diphthongs and shows all the naturally occurring misunderstandings in which these phonemes were confused with phonemes in other subsystems. Some of these misunderstandings reflect the loss of the glide (or of tenseness or of length), either in production or in perception, where the upgliding diphthong was perceived as a monophthong.

Table 9.1 Monophthongization and diphthongization in naturally occurring misunderstandings

	Monophthongization				Diphthongization			
	General	/__N	/__l	/KL__	General	/__N	/__l	/KL__
iy					1		1	
uw			2				2	
ey	5	3			2		1	
ow			10	1			1	
ay	5		3			2		2
aw	3	1	4		1	2	4	
Total	13	4	19	1	4	4	9	2

(6) A [says]: Why do you have a frown on your face?
     B [hears]: Why do you have a fan on your face?
(7) A [says]: . . . because of the pine trees.
     B [says]: There are no palm trees in Canada!

Others reflect the perception of a glide where none was intended:

(9) A [says]: Is that ladder still downstairs?
     B [hears]: Is that liner still downstairs?

The first and most obvious fact about Table 9.1 is that there is very little shifting of subsystems among the high vowels /iy/ and /uw/ in these samples of present-day English. In the case of /uw/, all the alternations are the result of the effects of a following /l/, reflecting the ongoing merger of high vowels before /l/ in many dialects of American English (Bailey and Ross 1992).

Mid and low vowels are more often involved in confusions. In 8 cases, /ey/ was heard as /e/. In 5 of them, no major conditioning factor was present:

(10)   A [says]: The DSM loudspeaker doesn't have spatial effects.
       B [hears]: The DSM loudspeaker doesn't have special effects.

However, 3 of the 8 cases show the effect of a following nasal. In the case of /ow/, 10 of 11 confusions with monophthongs are associated with a following /l/.

In the case of the low upgliding vowels /ay/ and /aw/, there is a substantial amount of monophthongization under general conditions, but almost all of the diphthongization is due to special phonetic environments. This is most evident in the confusion between a following /l/ and a /w/ glide. Three examples of this reported in Philadelphia involve a confusion between *balance* and *bounce*:

(11) A [says]: You meet two kinds of people in life, some can balance their checkbooks and some can't.
      B [hears]: You meet two kinds of people in life, some can bounce their checkbooks and some can't.

It is possible that such special conditioning can have a catalyzing effect in promoting a more general sound change. But the study of chain shifts that we are engaged in here largely focuses on unconditioned changes. We can sum up the situation reflected in naturally occurring misunderstandings by saying that production and perception of vowels show a general tendency toward monophthongization of low upgliding diphthongs (and the front mid vowel), but no general tendency toward the perception of spontaneous diphthongization where none was intended by the speaker.

9.3 Changes of peripherality

The special conditioning environments of section 9.2 usually operate by affecting the degree of peripherality of the nucleus. Thus strongly constricted following /r/ contracts the volume of phonological space, leading to a nonperipheral subsystem with fewer distinctions. Following nasals have the reverse effect, leading to more extreme positions of the nucleus. In the studies of the lexical regularity or irregularity of changes in part D, we will see that these special environments play an important role in the mechanism of change across subsystems, either as leading or as conservative elements. One of the most important such changes for the history of English involved lengthening in open syllables, the complex process affecting the development of vowels before /r/ that was studied in chapters 7 and 8. The main concern of this chapter will be unconditioned changes that result in the expansion or contraction of phonological space. This in turn will often involve the relations of peripheral and nonperipheral tracks, and the shift of a vowel from one to the other. The operation of the asymmetrical Principles I–III would lead to the concentration of all peripheral vowels at the top of the vowel space, and all nonperipheral vowels at the bottom, if there were no mechanism for changing from one unidirectional tendency to the other. Changes of subsystem are relevant to this problem only because most subsystems are either peripheral or nonperipheral (see table 9.2). Thus a change from short to ingliding vowels is bound to involve increases in peripherality, which may be gradual or discrete, while

Table 9.2   Distribution of peripherality by subsystem

	Peripheral nuclei	Nonperipheral nuclei
Short	no	yes
Long monophthongs	yes	yes[a]
Upgliding diphthongs	yes	yes
Ingliding diphthongs	yes	no

[a] Though long monophthongs are usually peripheral, there are many vowel systems that show nonperipheral long vowels, in the form of mid central or mixed vowels. None of the chain shifts that we have considered here involve such long nonperipheral vowels, and the principles that govern their movements are not well known.

a change from long monophthongs to upgliding diphthongs may or may not involve shifts of peripherality.[1] The changes in peripherality, which reflect higher-level laxing or tensing, occur at specific places within the subsystem, referred to above as exit and entrance locations. These exits and entrances involve a shift of phonetic category for a vowel involved in a change: after the change, it is a member of a different subsystem. I will refer more simply to this type of change as a *change of subsystem*, meaning a change that includes such a shift across the boundaries of subsystems. Since changes of subsystems are bound to involve changes in peripherality, the first task in developing principles for changing subsystems is to specify the principles that govern the location of these points.

Peripherality principles

The first peripherality principle concerns the result of lowering under Principle II.

(12)   PRINCIPLE IV:
       THE LOWER EXIT PRINCIPLE
       In chain shifting, low nonperipheral vowels become peripheral.

As noted above, this principle does not necessarily lead to a change of subsystem. It most often applies to the nonperipheral nuclei of upgliding vowels, as when [ɪi] from ME E ī falls under Principle II to [ɛ˃ɪ] and then to [ɐɪ] and [aɪ] (figure 6.1), or the [ɛ˃ɪ] representing Modern English /ey/ falls to [aɪ] (figures 6.3, 6.19, 6.20). The nonperipheral nucleus of the

---

[1] The investigations of part D will show that irregular sound changes or lexical diffusion are characteristic of such laxing and tensing at other points in the subsystem.

original [ᴇ˃ɪ] then typically becomes the most open vowel of the system as a whole, [a]. If the glide remains, the nucleus continues the shift under Principle I, moving up and back to peripheral [ɒ˃ɪ] and [ɔ˃ɪ], while original [ɔ˃ɪ] moves up to high position (figures 6.3, 6.19, 6.21). In other cases, the vowel leaves the subsystem of upgliding diphthongs and becomes a long monophthong, [a:] or [aˑ]. Both routes vacate the [aɪ] position and permit other vowels to occupy it as chain shifting continues (figures 6.4, 6.25–6.26).

A symmetrical pair of options is open to the reflex of ME **ū**, as it diphthongizes to [ʊu] and falls to [ʌu], [ɐu], and [au]. It then either advances toward [æu] or is monophthongized to [a:].[2]

When the upglide persists, the direction of further chain shifting of both /ay/ and /aw/ is controlled by Principle I, as the tense nucleus rises along a back or front peripheral track.

When the Lower Exit Principle applies to lower short monophthongs, there is only one option if a low vowel continues chain shifting without merger: to leave the nonperipheral subsystem, which normally means the lengthening of [a] to [a:].[3] The Swedish Pattern 3 shift displayed in (18) of chapter 5 can be summarized as follows:

(13) /a/ → /a:/ → /o:/ → /u: → ü/

This shift was apparently initiated by the lengthening of short /a/ (Benediktsson 1970).[4]

The Lower Exit Principle appears to be unidirectional. None of the chain shifts considered involve the shortening of a peripheral low vowel, though this is common enough as an individual change.

The existence of a Lower Exit Principle implies the existence of an Upper Exit Principle. This can be formulated as follows:

(14) PRINCIPLE V:
      THE UPPER EXIT PRINCIPLE
      In chain shifting, one of two high peripheral morae becomes nonperipheral.

---

[2] London, Philadelphia, New York, Texas, and Birmingham all show the fronting of /aw/ (figures 6.3, 3.6, 6.1, 6.4, 6.25), though there is considerable monophthongization in London. The Pittsburgh dialect, which has not been studied here, shows a consistent monophthongization of /aw/ to [a:].

[3] In Glasgow, /i/ falls to [ɪ] and /e/ to [æ⊥]. But only a small number of /e/ words are realized in this position. The majority are tensed and have risen to [ɛ:ə] or [e:ə].

[4] Most of the cases of lengthening of low vowels involve a great deal of lexical irregularity (chapter 18), and it therefore seems likely that this process operates at a higher level of abstraction than the other mechanisms discussed here.

This principle is a simpler and somewhat more general formulation than the Dissimilation Effect 1 used in the description of the Great Vowel Shift diphthongization in chapter 8. While the dissimilation effect was shown to be a categorical result of raising to [4 high], the Upper Exit Principle describes one of the unidirectional paths by which an element can leave the system of long monophthongs. As formalized in (15), it does not depend upon a concept such as [4 high], or mirror imaging. The left-hand side shows the typical configuration for long vowels, assuming a rule that will spread the [+high] feature to both morae. The right-hand side simply states that one of these two will become nonperipheral, and so remove the vowel from the subsystem of long monophthongs.

Such a rule has two cases:

    (a) V:→[−peri][+peri]
    (b) V:→[+peri][−peri]

(15)

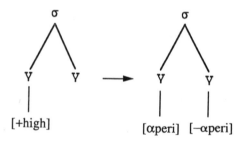

We saw case (a) operating in all the examples of Pattern 1 in chapter 5: it is in a sense the essential condition of that chapter. It sets up the conditions for the continued application of Principle I to the remaining long monophthongs, Principle III to the remaining back monophthongs, and Principle II to the diphthongs just produced.

If the Upper Exit Principle were confined to case (a), it would be of more limited application than the others, since it would apply only to a specific group of language families – those that permit the laxing of the nucleus of /i/. Case (a) operates freely in Baltic and Germanic languages.[5] But it does not apply to the Indic, Greek, Italic, Celtic, or Albanian branches of Indo-European. In these languages, /i/ shows a strong tendency

---

[5] Though the phonetic structures involved occur in Slavic languages, there is no record of chain shifts comparable to those in Baltic languages, and it is therefore not clear how the Slavic languages relate to this dichotomy.

to remain /i/, even under the heavy pressure of merger with other languages. As we have seen, it is found only in those Romance languages that
have had close contact with languages that have such laxing rules. Thus
it is the Baltic and Germanic languages that show the complex structure
of phonological space that the Upper Exit Principle demands: peripheral
and nonperipheral tracks in both the front and the back. The other languages either have a simple vowel system, with five to seven members or
fewer, or develop a tripartite phonological space with back, mixed, and
front vowels. In most of these other languages, case (b) operates freely to
produce ingliding vowels, as chapter 5 shows throughout.

Is the Upper Exit Principle unidirectional? For case (a), it appears to
be. There are no recorded cases of chain shifts involving the monophthongization of /iy/ or /uw/, though again this is common enough as an individual
phenomenon. Most of the dialects that show long high monophthongs are
the result of language contact (Anglo-Irish, Caribbean dialects, Hispanic
dialects in the Southwest, German-influenced dialects in Texas, Pennsylvania, and the North Central states, and Scandinavian-influenced dialects
in the North Central area). Some Scots and North England dialects retain
monophthongs as a result of the nonoccurrence of the Great Vowel Shift
or Early Modern English diphthongization. But there is no record of chain
shfits that reverse case (a). On the other hand, case (b) is plainly symmetrical. The smoothing of ingliding diphthongs to monophthongs is quite common (see English Smoothing {E5.1} and the East Lettish chain shifts in
(23) of chapter 5).

Given this difference in symmetry, we would have to restate the Upper
Exit Principle:

(14′) PRINCIPLE V:
THE UPPER EXIT PRINCIPLE (revised)
**In chain shifting, the first of two high morae may change
peripherality, and the second may become nonperipheral.**

Since unconditioned breaking is included in the Upper Exit Principle, we
might be tempted to modify the principle further to include the many cases
of breaking of long monophthongs as they rise from mid to high position.
This process is very general: it is found in Middle High German, in East
Lettish, in Vegliote, in other chain shifts reviewed in chapter 5, and in the
Pattern 3 chain shifts of American English reviewed in chapter 6. Like the
other changes of subsystem, it necessarily involves changes in peripherality.
One might want to modify the Upper Exit Principle to include this breaking of [e:] and [o:], but such a move would introduce a number of compli-
cations. It would vitiate the force of the Upper Exit Principle *as* an upper
exit principle. It would increase the asymmetry of breaking and laxing.
Most importantly, the breaking of mid vowels appears to be a dynamic

phenomenon, which occurs only in the course of the raising process, while the Upper and Lower Exit Principles can be the initiating elements of a sound change. It therefore seems best to formulate a separate principle:

(16)   PRINCIPLE VI:
       THE MID EXIT PRINCIPLE
       In chain shifts, peripheral vowels rising from mid to high position develop inglides.

The dynamic character of the process involved here is shown in (17), where [–high] is altered to [+high]. One might further accentuate this feature by writing a variant of an *n*-ary chain shift rule, indicating that the breaking occurs as [2 high] becomes greater than [2 high]; but this would impose an unjustified precision on our present limited knowledge.

(17)

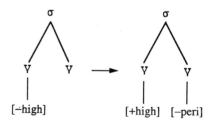

In American English, this principle reflects the well-known tendency for the tense vowels /æh/ and /oh/ to develop inglides as they rise past mid position. But this is not a change of subsystem in the sense that we have been using this term; rather, it is the development of an inglide within an ingliding subsystem. The /Vh/ series of American English is typically monophthongal in low position and ingliding in mid and high position (Trager and Smith 1957; Stockwell 1978). Even though the Mid Exit Principle applies to the phonetic realizations of American English, its use to describe changes of subsystem will apply primarily to vowels that are members of a distinct set of long monophthongs that shift to an ingliding form.

    Smoothing, the opposite of breaking, did apply to long Old English vowels, so that the distinction between the ingliding long vowels e͞o and i͞o, and their corresponding monophthongs e̅ and i̅, was lost. However, this process was not part of a chain shift. As an aspect of chain shifting, the Mid Exit Principle appears to be asymmetrical.

    A third peripherality principle that regulates shifts of subsystems is a simple consequence of the relative nature of linguistic units:

(18) PRINCIPLE VII:
      THE REDEFINITION PRINCIPLE
      Peripherality is defined relative to the vowel system as a whole.

Peripherality is not an absolute location in phonological space but, like height or frontness, a relationship determined by the elements of the system as a whole. A peripheral element is closer to the outer envelope of the vowel system than a nonperipheral element, as defined in (16) of chapter 6. It follows that a set of vowels may be assigned to another subsystem without any shift in their position, as a result of the shift of other vowels. The Redefinition Principle is so named because it governs change induced by the redefinition of one or more vowels as peripheral or nonperipheral. Its operation is evident in the Vegliote shifts, where the creation of peripheral ingliding vowels **ie** and **uo** led to the redefinition of the original set of unmarked vowels as lax, and their lowering in a chain shift (see (15) in chapter 5). It is even more apparent in the Southern Shift. The laxing of the nuclei of the upgliding diphthongs, and their subsequent centralization and lowering, leads to a redefinition of the originally short vowels as lax. In British, Australian, and New Zealand English, this leads to an upward movement of short tense vowels (figures 6.3, 6.19–21), and in Southern States English, it leads to the creation of tense ingliding vowels with nuclei that range from the position of the older short vowels to extremely front, that is, from [ɪə] to [iːə] (figures 6.4, 6.23–6.25).

9.4 Some complex changes across subsystems

The principles of section 9.3 that govern changes across subsystems all effect changes in the peripherality of nuclei or glides. These principles can be seen operating in many of the vowel systems and rules discussed in chapters 5–8. For example, as we saw in section 9.3, the Upper Exit Principle is a generalization of the Dissimilation Effect that described diphthongization in the Great Vowel Shift. However, most of the chain shifts discussed in chapters 5 and 6 were introduced to illustrate movements within subsystems. This section will review two complex chain shifts that chiefly involve changes across subsystems, to see how the principles apply in this case.

Central Yiddish

The chain shifts recorded for Central Yiddish (Herzog 1965) show systematic aspects of movements across subsystems.

This Pattern 3 back chain shift is joined by some elements that resemble Pattern 4, but the main structure consists of two sets of shifts across

(19)   CHAIN SHIFTING ACROSS SUBSYSTEMS IN CENTRAL YIDDISH

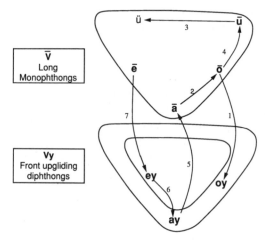

subsystems. The earliest part of the process is the diphthongization of ō
to /oy/ (Step 1). It is followed by the raising of ā to [o:] (Step 2). There
is no immediate necessity for a further raising to [u:]. In fact, there would
be reason for this not to take place, since the position is already occupied
by ū. The full Pattern 3 chain shift follows, however: the fronting of ū to
[ü] (Step 3), followed by raising of [o:] to [u:] (Step 4). The vacancy
created by the upward movement of ā is filled as the **ai** of *mayn* 'mine' is
monophthongized to [a:] (Step 5); the **ei** of *meyn* 'think' is lowered to [ay]
(Step 6); and the long close ē of *betn* 'ask' is diphthongized to [ey]
(Step 7).

This intricate series of changes can be thought of as a combination of
several distinct shifts. But in a further effort to grasp the unitary character
of chain shifting, we might search for a way to describe these movements
as inherently connected. Steps 2, 4, 5, 6, and 7 are all connected to a
preceding step by the general Chain-Shifting Principle given as (17) in
chapter 6. The only steps that are not so governed are Steps 1 and 3,
which are both leaving elements that initiate the chain shift. Step 3 is the
familiar fronting that initiates Pattern 3 chain shifts, and Step 6 is the
familiar lowering of /ey/ in the course of Pattern 4. Steps 1, 5, and 7 are
changes of subsystem, but only Step 5 is governed by a general principle
of chain shifting – in this case, the Lower Exit Principle. Steps 1 and 7
are parallel diphthongizations of mid long vowels that are motivated only
by their role in the general pattern of chain shifting.

East Lettish

The complexities of Central Yiddish pale beside the chain shifts that take
place in East Lettish (Endzelin 1922), first presented as (23) in chapter
5. The East Lettish sound shifts combine almost all the principles of vowel

shifting observed so far. The majority of these developments are actually shifts across subsystems rather than shifts within a subsystem. The subsystems are separated here in (20), where the relative peripherality of each subsystem is shown by an appropriate vowel triangle. Ingliding and long vowels show peripheral triangles, short vowels nonperipheral triangles, and upgliding diphthongs both. In this framework, we can see that the only shift of peripherality affecting a nucleus occurs when /ey/ falls to /ay/.

(20)   EAST LETTISH SHIFTS ACROSS SUBSYSTEMS

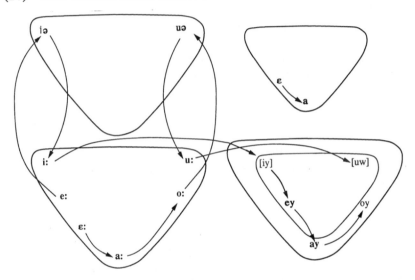

The development of **ie** and **uo**, representing ingliding phonemes /iə/ and /uə/, is a key element in this series of events, a process shared by Lithuanian and Latvian generally. In the East Lettish dialects, these ingliding vowels are monophthongized to [i:] and [u:]. In the front, the older /i:/ falls to /ey/ by way of /iy/; older /ey/ moves to [ay]; and in some dialects (e.g., Setzen), older /ay/ moves to [oy]. The position of old ingliding /iə/ is then taken up by /e:/, which rises to become a second tense ingliding vowel as /uə/ is replaced by /o:/. Among the front vowels, both long and short /ε/ fall. The lowering of the long vowel might be considered an exception to the general principles, if it were not connected to the expected raising of long vowels in the back.

The changes in subsystem are entirely symmetrical:

(21)

		Front	Back
a.	Diphthongization	i: → ey	u: → ow
b.	Monophthongization	iə → i:	uə → u:
c.	Breaking	e: → iə	o: → uə

These are highly patterned events. (21a) exemplifies case (a) of the Upper Exit Principle (15′) and (21b) is the converse of case (b) of that principle, which, as we have already seen, is symmetrical. 21(c) exemplifies the Mid Exit Principle in its most straightforward form.

9.5   Glottal and nasal subsystems

As long as the study of chain shifts is confined to Indo-European languages, we are apt to be more concerned with transitions between long and short vowels than with other oppositions between subsystems. Other language families will provide more instances of transitions that involve subsystems of glottalized, creaky-voice, and nasal vowels. Most often, we will observe transitions between these marked sets of vowels and the unmarked or plain vowels. One might then consider an eighth principle of chain shifting that specifies this as the normal route, since it follows almost automatically from the markedness relation.

(22)   PRINCIPLE VIII:
       THE UNMARKING PRINCIPLE
       In chain shifts, elements of the marked system are unmarked.

Chapter 5 presented two stages of chain shifting in Akha (see (21) and (22) of that chapter). The second stage, reproduced here as (23), shows the Unmarking Principle in operation. In Akha, the two sets of vowels are marked by the presence of open tone (the unmarked category) versus glottalized tone (the marked category). The upward shift of mid and low open tone vowels, in a Pattern 3 configuration, is followed by the unmarking of the mid and low glottalized tone vowels.

(23)   THE UNMARKING PRINCIPLE IN AKHA

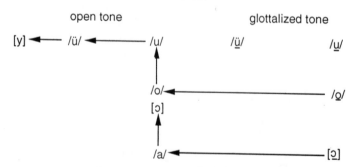

Where we apply this marking principle to the sets of long and short vowels in Indo-European, it should follow that long vowels (the unmarked category) are shortened more often than short vowels are lengthened. For the chain shifts that we have reviewed, this is true. But the lengthening of low vowels is a common theme in the review of sound change in English and other Germanic languages in chapters 5 and 6. The lengthening of Swedish short /a/ triggered the Swedish Pattern 3 chain shift (chapter 5, (18)). The tensing and raising of English short **a** in the Northern Cities Shift was followed by a tensing and fronting of short **o**.

The relations between oral and nasal vowels can be explored in the Tupi-Guarani languages, which are generally characterized by parallel sets of oral and nasal vowels. Soares and Leite (1991) set up six oral and nasal vowels as characteristic of the protolanguage, a 2×3 system with two degrees of phonological height, backing, and rounding:

(24)   Proto-Tupi-Guarani vowel system

i   ɨ   u   ĩ   ɨ̃   ũ
e   a   o   ẽ   ã   õ

Soares and Leite show that most of the languages in this family have been affected by a series of raising movements, which centralized the mid low vowels and in some cases continued this raising to merge the resulting mid vowels with high vowels. These movements did not involve shifting directly. Tapirapé typically shows the conditioned raising of /a/ to [ə] before nasals, and the unconditioned raising of /ã/ to [ə̃]. These two processes might be condensed into a single rule (25).

(25)
$$
\begin{bmatrix} -\text{round} \\ -\text{ant} \\ \langle -\text{nas} \rangle \end{bmatrix} \rightarrow [-\text{low}] \ / \ \underline{\hspace{1cm}} \ \begin{bmatrix} -\text{syl} \\ \langle +\text{nas} \rangle \end{bmatrix}
$$

But we can assume that this complex combination is the result of a prior assimilation rule – the nasalization of oral vowels, before nasal consonants. (25) then dissolves into two simple processes, both low-level phonetic operations with no phonological consequences for the inventory of phonemes, and can be written as (26) and (27).

(26) $[+\text{low}] \rightarrow [+\text{nas}] \ / \ \underline{\hspace{1cm}} \ [+\text{nas}]$

(27)
$$
\begin{bmatrix} -\text{round} \\ -\text{ant} \\ \langle +\text{nas} \rangle \end{bmatrix} \rightarrow [-\text{low}]
$$

The chain-shifting aspect of these Tupi-Guarani sound changes is triggered in Tapirapé by an extension of (26) that nasalizes all low vowels. It can be thought of as a parallel to the wholesale tensing of short **a** in the Northern Cities Shift, as compared with the conditioned tensing in New England or on the West Coast, where only short **a** before nasal consonants is affected. On the one hand, this extension represents a counterexample to the Unmarking Principle, since the nasal vowels are evidently the marked subsystem. On the other hand, the nasalization of low vowels recurs in many languages in many periods, favored by the general tendency for the velum to be lowered with low vowels (Chen and Wang 1975). LYS found that in Cardiff, /a/ before vocalized /r/ was not only lengthened and fronted but also nasalized to form a phonological opposition to oral vowels, so that [hæ:š] (*hash*) contrasted with [hæ̃:š] (*harsh*). A similar but less fully developed tendency is found in Boston. In the light of these considerations, it may be that the Unmarking Principle should be refined to define markedness and unmarkedness relative to the specific configurations of vowel features and the mark concerned.

The Tapirapé chain shift involves a movement of /o/ into the place vacated by /a/, and a downward movement of /u/ into the place vacated by /o/.

(28)   Tᴀᴘɪʀᴀᴘᴇ́ ᴄʜᴀɪɴ ꜱʜɪꜰᴛ

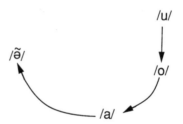

Chapter 5 introduced the general principles of chain shifting Principles I–III, with the proviso that a single series of vowels, as in Romance, would be considered the equivalent of the long series in a long-short opposition, and would follow the chain-shifting pattern with the long (or tense) vowels. In Romance languages, there are always more oral vowels than nasal vowels, which are the result of a relatively recent process of nasalizing oral vowels before nasal consonants with the subsequent loss of the conditioning factor. In the Tupi-Guarani languages, there is no evidence that the nasal vowels are so derived, and they are equal in number to the oral vowels.[6] It may very well be that in this context, the nasal vowels function as the equivalent of the tense or long vowels in Indo-European languages.

---

[6] Except for Asurini and Guajajara, where all nasal vowels have been denasalized.

Diagram (28) shows two vowels being lowered and one raised, but this may be an artifact of the phonemic notation. In a number of Tupi-Guarani languages, including Tapirapé, /o/ is represented by [ɔ] in many or most environments, and the major phonetic process is fronting. A phonetic approximation of the shift will therefore appear as shown in (29), which is remarkably similar to the Pattern 2 configuration of the Northern Cities Shift.

(29)   PHONETIC PATTERN OF THE TAPIRAPÉ CHAIN SHIFT

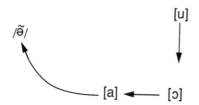

This chapter began with evidence from natural misunderstandings that strengthens the empirical base for our conception of phonological subsystems and a hierarchy of organization in phonology. Given the importance of subsystems, the problem remains of specifying the routes that change follows in moving elements from one subsystem to another. In preceding chapters, our view of the principles of chain shifting was limited to Principles I–III, along with the patterns that they form in combination. This chapter has added five peripherality principles, which describe how vowels in one subsystem typically make the transition to another. These principles make maximal use of the view of phonological space that was derived from the close study of changes in progress, and therefore rest on a reasonable body of empirical evidence. However, the study of changes across subsystems is by no means as advanced as the study of changes within systems. The principles presented here are designed to generate further interest in the problems involved. Numerous modifications and additions will most likely be required as more cases are investigated.

Part C

Mergers and Splits

10

Some Impossible Unmergings

The changes that affect the sound system of a language fall into three complementary categories: rotations, mergers, and splits. The first maintains distinctions, the second eliminates them, and the third creates them. The last three chapters have dealt with rotations or chain shifts and the general principles that control these shifts. Through the study of sound changes in progress, we were able to resolve paradoxical reports of distinctions that were maintained when mergers might have been expected. The next four chapters, which focus on mergers, reverse this view.

This chapter presents paradoxical reports of mergers that would not have been expected, given the events that followed. Chapter 11 examines the general properties of mergers and phonemic splits, and whether or not mergers can be reversed. Chapter 12 studies similar situations in modern dialects and introduces the concept of "near-merger." Finally, chapter 13 applies the evidence from existing dialects to resolve the paradoxes in the historical record, and introduces other evidence to reinforce the proposed solutions.

10.1 The unexpected maintenance of distinctions

In 1962, Halle published a paper that effectively created the field of generative phonology. He elevated phonemic analysis to the level of what had been called morphophonemics, and effectively argued against the existence of two systematic levels of representation with two sets of rules relating underlying forms to surface representations. This meant that the inventory of distinct segments that appeared in the base forms was considerably more abstract than those projected by structural linguists, and a much wider range of alternations was taken into account in recognizing these distinctions.

In one application of this reasoning to historical linguistics, Halle dealt with the well-known problem of the changing relations of three English word classes that are often exemplified by *mate*, *meat*, and *meet*. The general picture that he presented[1] can be summarized as follows:

---

[1] On the basis of information attributed to S. J. Keyser.

(1) | Type | ME class | ME value | 16th century | 17th century |
|------|----------|----------|--------------|--------------|
| meet | ē | [e:] | [e:] | [i:] |
| meat | ēā | [æ:, ɛ:] | [ɛ:] | [i:] |
| mate | ā | [a:] | [ɛ:] | [e:] |

Each of these word classes has a fairly complex history; in Middle English their various sources were merged by several processes – smoothing, raising, lengthening in open syllables – into the three categories shown.

The ME long ē class is inherited directly from OE ē (*meet, sweet, beet, deed, heed, he*) and ēō, īō (*she, be, flee, tree, weed, deep*).

The ME ēā class includes words derived from OE ēā (*flea, leaf, seam, steam, team, heal*), OE ǣ (*sea, read, lead, meal, steal*), and ON ǣ (*seat*), along with the results of the lengthening of short open ĕ in open syllables (*meat, eat*).

The ME long ā class represents the short ă words that were lengthened in open syllables: *hate, ate, late, lame, game, wade*. At some point in its development, the ā class merged with the ME **ay** class derived from OE ǣ (*day, maid, laid*, etc.), as discussed in chapter 4 in relation to the Great Vowel Shift. When and how this happened does not affect the present discussion of the relations between ā and ēā.

These classes were augmented in Middle English by large numbers of borrowings: chiefly from Anglo-French and Old French, but also from Dutch, German, Latin, and Scandinavian languages. The ā class was augmented by borrowings from numerous languages (*fade*, from French; *mate*, from Dutch; *fate*, from Latin). The ē and ēā classes took in many French words with various qualities of *e*: close, open, lengthened, long, and diphthongal (*treat, treason, reason, preach, cream, veal, seal*, etc.). How many of these were borrowed into the ēā class is an open question. The fact that many are spelled with *ea* does not decide it. Many words of diverse origins that were never associated with the ēā class were also spelled with *ea*: *dear, breast* from OE ēō; *beadle* from OE y. Conversely, many words of the ēā class are spelled otherwise: *greed, greet, leech* from OE ǣ. The original assignment of loanwords to a particular native class must be decided by their subsequent history: their participation in the changes that the native class undergoes. But this can only be investigated when the behavior of the original word classes inherited from Old English is determined. We will focus here on the original word classes as defined above and will bring in the Middle English borrowings only when they are introduced by arguments in the literature. Since the modern spellings are unreliable guides to membership in these classes, the evidentiary status of a particular word must be traced from its entrance into the language.

From (1) it appears that the three classes were distinct in Middle English, as ē, ā, and ēā; that in the course of the 16th century, ēā became identified with ā; and that somehow by the 17th century ēā was disengaged from ā and merged with ē. Halle explained this reversal as simply the reorganization of the rules for realizing the same set of underlying forms, ē, ā, eā. He assumed without discussion that the three underlying forms had remained distinct throughout the 16th century, during the time that ǣ and ā were apparently both realized as [ɛ:]. But it seems reasonable to ask *how* that could have happened.

The usual argument for the retention of underlying forms in the face of sound change is based on alternations. We can set up a similar table for *sane* and *sanity*,

(2)	Type	ME class	ME value	16th century	17th century
	sane	ǣ	[aː]	[ɛː]	[eː]
	sanity	ǣ	[æ]	[æ]	[æ]
	man	ă	[æ]	[æ]	[æ]

and argue that the underlying identity of *sane* and *sanity* is preserved by the regular alternations *sane/sanity*, *Spain/Spanish*, *stable/establish*, etc. Though *sanity*, *Spanish*, *establish*, and *man* all share the same vowel on the surface, the underlying form of the first three is quite different.

We might attempt to follow the same strategy by locating alternations of **ea** words. There is a small set that alternate with short ĕ: *break/breakfast*, *clean/cleanliness*, *mean/meant*. If the shortened **ea** words all alternated in this fashion, then it would be possible for 16th-century speakers to distinguish the underlying form of *break* from *brake* on the one hand and from *breek* on the other. But this strategy would serve only for the few words that showed such alternations. It would be of no value in distinguishing *beat* from *bate*, *meat* from *mate*, *feat* from *fate*.

Chomsky and Halle (1968) assign underlying forms to entire classes of long vowels on the basis of alternations shown by some members.[2] But no mergers are involved: it is simply a case of rotating the sets of long vowels by a phonetic rule to match the underlying forms of sets of short vowels. Thus alternations can help us undo the work of chain shifts. But grammatical alternations have no value in explaining the reversal of a merger. On the contrary, the very existence of *break/breakfast*, *clean/cleanliness*, *mean/meant* would motivate the splitting of the eā class, with *break*, *clean*, and *mean* joining long ē and the others remaining with ā. It is somewhat surprising to find that one of the few alternations in the verbal system – *break/broke*, *speak/spoke* – did not have enough influence to preserve the identity of the eā class. *Break* is one of the five well-known exceptions to the reversal of the ā ~ eā merger. From the late Old English period, *speak* and *break* shared membership in the same narrow class of short ĕ words that were

---

[2] However, there is considerable disagreement on whether this should be done. Others argue that it should be done only for those words that alternate.

lengthened in open syllables and joined the e̅a̅ class. Yet in spite of their close association in this alternation, *break* and *speak* now appear in different word classes.

The relevance of alternations to the restoration of a merger has not been discussed in the generative literature, to the best of my knowledge, and Halle's article remains as an unmotivated claim for the retention of under-lying forms.

The situation remains inexplicable. Before we assume that there really is something to explain, we must examine the historical situation more closely. Is there really good evidence for a merger of a̅ and e̅a̅? And was e̅a̅ extracted from a̅ as a whole to rejoin e̅ without losing its basic integrity as a class?

10.2   The reported merger of *meat* and *mate*

Philologists generally agree that the three word classes e̅, e̅a̅, a̅ were dis-tinguished by three different long front vowels in the early 1500s, and some believe that this distinction continued throughout the century. But there is also evidence for the existence of two other systems of front vowels:

(3)   I   II   III

    e̅   e̅   ⎧ e̅ ⎫
    e̅a̅   ⎧ e̅a̅ ⎫   ⎩ e̅a̅ ⎭
    a̅   ⎩ a̅ ⎭   a̅

For theories of language that depend upon the model of a homogeneous speech community, this is a particularly difficult and confused case to deal with. It involves many of the features that we are now familiar with from the study of normal, heterogeneous speech communities: inherent and sys-tematic variation, regional dialects within urban speech communities, and class stratification.

Evidence for and against the merger

The type of evidence that has proved most trustworthy in such situations is based on the study of speech production. In the historical record, this corresponds to the study of misspellings, puns, and rhymes, which are the type of evidence emphasized strongly by Wyld (1936) and Kökeritz (1953). For example, Wyld cites the following misspellings:

(4)   *to spake to her* (C. Stewkley in Verney Memoirs, iv, 464, 1695)
    maneing 'meaning' (Lady Brill Harley, 40, 1639)

St. Jeamsis Park (Later Verney Letters, 1:37, 1697)
to have her bed mead (Later Verney Letters, 1:75, 1700)[3]

The first two show the use of the ā spelling to indicate the ēa class, the second two the use of the ēa spelling to indicate the ā class. Such symmetrical misspelling patterns are typical of mergers. At the same time, this is not the type of accountable evidence that we are used to in the quantitative study of speech communities. To follow a principle of accountability, Wyld and Kökeritz would have to report the proportion of misspellings for distinct vowels versus the proportion of misspellings for vowels they consider nondistinct. Instead, they provide qualitative evidence that can only point in one direction.

The evidence of orthoepists and grammarians, the main focus of Jespersen, Luick, and Dobson, is better balanced, but it has the defects of most subjective reports: it is usually conservative in that it represents the systems that have been recognized and discussed in the past; the patterns of the most formal, reflective, and audio-monitored speech; and the behavior of the highest prestige, most visible social classes. Four authors from the late 16th century testify to the existence of System II in (3). Laneham in 1575, Bullokar in 1580, Bellot in 1580, and Delamothe in 1592 all state that ēa and ā words are homonyms or that they rhyme.

On the other hand, Hart (1569) reports System I, with all three word classes distinct. Mulcaster (1582) and Whythorne (Palmer 1969) agree.

There is also production evidence for System III. For example, Shakespeare rhymes *teach thee* with *beseech thee* (Venus and Adonis 404, 406); Spenser rhymes *seas* and *these*, *streeme* and *seeme*. Spellings such as *spyking* (Henry Machyn 1550) and *birive* (Harvey Letters 1573), also argue for the identification of ēa and ē.[4]

In the 17th century, grammarians no longer reported Systems I or II. The great bulk of ēa words were distinct from ā for Florio in 1611, Gill in 1621, Wallis in 1688 (Lehnert 1936), Price in 1665, Miège in 1688, and Cooper in 1687. By the end of the century, the ēa words not before /r/ had almost all been assigned to the ē class.

Faced with this evidence, historians of English construct radically different chronologies for the raising of these vowels. The traditional view is that the first merger could not have happened, and therefore it did not. Jespersen (1949), Luick (1921), and Dobson (1968) thus conclude that ā and ēa never merged, on the principle that if they had merged, they could not afterward have separated; and they arrange their chronologies accordingly. Zachrisson at first held the same opinion (1913) but later argues

---

[3] The first cited in Wyld 1936:211, the last three in Wyld 1936:401.
[4] Cited by Wyld (1936:209). Note that both the spelling *streeme* and the rhyme argue for the identity of the vowels here.

that there were some dialects in which the merger had taken place. Wyld (1936) and Kökeritz (1953) also accept the reports of the grammarians that at least for some dialects, ā and ēā had merged.

[I]n a list of words pronounced alike though written differently, 'Voces quae eandem habent pronunciationem', &c., Cooper includes *meat – mate*. Surely if this means anything it means what we have already tried to establish, that M.E. *ā* and M.E. *ē²* had both the same sound in the seventeenth century, if not much earlier, and further, if we can ever learn anything from the Orthoepists, we may learn that this sound was a *mid* and not a *high* vowel. (Wyld 1936:210–11)

Wyld and Kökeritz argue that the first merger was never actually reversed, and instead see a replacement of one dialect by another. System III is said to have been a southeastern importation, arriving with speakers from Kent and Essex, which gradually won out over the older London dialect. The Southeast was well advanced in the general raising of the long tense vowels; OE ī¹ and æ² were both raised to a tense mid [e:] in Kentish, often spelled **ie** as in *gier* and *cliene* (Wyld 1936:41).

Social factors

So far this volume has focused on the internal mechanism of sound change, and questions concerning the social motivation of change have been reserved for volume 2. But internal and external mechanisms cannot be entirely isolated, and at this point we must consider how the larger context interacts with the linguistic facts summarized above.

Wyld is a leading exponent of the view that social factors play an important role in linguistic change, and he has documented many cases of regional features becoming sociolinguistic variables in London. His views fit closely with Sturtevant's (1947) position that the progress of a sound change is closely tied to its role as a symbol of social conflict, articulated in greater detail in studies of sound change on Martha's Vineyard, in New York City, and in Philadelphia (Labov 1963, 1965, 1980). In this scheme, the trajectory of a sound change across the community may be outlined as follows:

1 A linguistic change begins as a local pattern characteristic of a particular social group, located at the interior of the social hierarchy.
2 The change may be accelerated by its use as a symbolic claim to local rights and privileges, defending the original group against claims by new groups entering the community.
3 As the change becomes generalized throughout the group, it becomes associated for others with the social values attributed to that group.
4 The change then gradually spreads to those neighboring populations that take the first group as a reference group for social values, and it

is often reinterpreted and accelerated further by groups first gaining entrance to the social structure.[5]

5 As the opposition of the two linguistic forms continues, it may symbolize an overt opposition of social values. This association of linguistic and social values may rise to the level of social consciousness and result in a stereotype, subject to irregular social correction, or it may remain below that level and result in an unconscious marker.

6 Finally, one of the two forms wins out. There follows a long period when the disappearing form is heard as archaic, a symbol of a vanished prestige or stigma, and is used as a source of stereotyped humor until it is extinguished entirely.

7 After the change is completed, the older pronunciation may be preserved in place names or fixed forms, and it is heard as a meaningless irregularity.

The changing status of e̅a̅ fits this model quite well. The change must be seen as an acceleration of processes that had already been operating in English, on and off, for more than a thousand years. The chief process is the raising of tense vowels, following Principle I. This raising was accelerated in London by the arrival of a large southeastern population whose speech showed a more advanced level of the basic chain shifts. There is strong evidence for the existence of socially marked dialects in 17th-century London, when the change had reached Stage 6. System III was then taken as a stereotype associated with a marked group of speakers. In a well-known quotation, Gill (1621) stigmatizes the affected or effeminate pronunciation of the Mopsae, who used an "Eastern Dialect," saying (in Gill's notation) "kēpn" instead of "kāpn" for *capon*. Later in the century, we can follow in the work of orthoepists like Cooper (1687) the progression of the shift by lexical diffusion in favor of the higher value for e̅a̅. The opposition was still alive in the 18th century. Tuite (1726) reports that the English differed in using high or low vowels for many e̅a̅ words, with Londoners leading in the use of high vowels. Today the issue is dead (Stage 7). The older pronunciation of the e̅a̅ class survives in a set of well-known irregularities (*great, break, steak,* etc.), to be discussed below, and in occasional place names like *Preakness*, New Jersey (pronounced [preɪknɪs]) and *Leakey*, Texas ([læɪki]).

The evidence for social oppositions is necessarily late, since it depends upon reactions formulated when the change is essentially over. Yet it seems

---

[5] Some groups reside in the community but are excluded from full participation in it, like the Portuguese or Indians on Martha's Vineyard and the 19th-century Irish or the present-day blacks and Hispanics in New York City and Philadelphia. When the third- or fourth-generation members of these groups gain access to the jobs, political positions, or social privileges that earlier generations were excluded from, they frequently adopt the linguistic symbols of local identity in a more extreme form (see Labov 1980; Poplack 1978).

to reinforce the evidence for the existence of competing systems in London.

Nevertheless, Wyld's explanation for the emergence of System III is not entirely persuasive. On one obvious point, it cannot stand as it is. Neither the older London System I nor the southeastern System III had a merger of ā and ēa. How then did London speakers acquire it?

To pursue this problem, we must continue to call upon the uniformitarian approach and apply principles derived from sociolinguistic studies of change in progress. In applying them, we can provide some plausible interpretations and so illuminate the past by the present as we do the present by the past. The basic principle that we will use springs from the initial observations of an association between a curvilinear pattern in the social hierarchy and a monotonic pattern in the age range. Change in apparent time is regularly associated with the advanced position of a social group located in the interior of the social hierarchy: not the highest, dominant class, or the lowest, underprivileged class, but rather the second highest status group (merchants, clerks, salespeople, teachers, local politicians) and the established skilled working class (artisans, mechanics, foremen).

In London, the raising of ēa and ā was most advanced among the merchant class, not the highest social class. Hart was one of the landed gentry and a court herald: he reports a low vowel for ā and a lower mid vowel for ēa. Those who testify to the merger of ēa and ā were tradesmen's sons, like Bullokar and Laneham. Here we can see the outlines of a middle-class pattern opposed to an upper-class pattern. If our present understanding of sociolinguistic patterns applies, we would not expect to find sharp divisions between the two that would establish them as separate dialects. The predominance of the merchant class in the raising process would be a quantitative pattern comparable to the dominance of the upper working class in Philadelphia sound changes (Labov 1980).

Within this framework of class differentiation, a second principle is required to motivate the reported merger:

(5) THE PRINCIPLE OF STRUCTURAL REINTERPRETATION
When a set of associated sound changes spreads from one group to another, the relative position of the associated elements changes.

Thus on Martha's Vineyard, the centralization of (ay) was accompanied by a secondary centralization of (aw) among the Yankees. When the change spread to the Portuguese and Indians, the relative positions of (ay) and (aw) were reversed, with (aw) now leading (Labov 1963). In 16th-century London, the raising of the ā class was apparently the primary sociolinguistic variable, as seen in Gill's late reflections on it in 1621. We have no record that raising of the e͞a class was stigmatized. The merger of a͞ and e͞a was characteristic of Londoners who were influenced by the southeastern model to accelerate their raising of a͞ without raising e͞a. Eventually, the e͞a class was raised, but this process was not completed until a century later.

A uniform chronology for sound change in 16th-century London is certain to encounter contradictions. These are as baffling as those found by linguists who tried to write a uniform description of New York City speech and ended by describing it as a massive case of "free variation" (Labov 1966:chap. 2). This preference for homogeneity also leads to rejecting most speakers' linguistic behavior as capricious, unreasonable, and harmful to the body politic. Thus Dobson, the most vociferous defender of the 16th-century spelling reformers of London, points out that they focused on a formal pronunciation of what was considered "good English," to the exclusion of newer forms that reflected ongoing changes in progress.

> The reformers did of course take as the basis of their phonetic spellings what they regarded as good English pronunciation – which was usually their own – and they did as a rule avoid recording vulgarisms unless to condemn them. (1957:193–4)

Though Dobson shows a certain degree of class prejudice, current research shows that his assessment is not completely off the mark. The processes that lead to such situations do appear to involve conflict between social groups, and conflict, to be sure, is considered destructive by most detached academic observers of the social scene. Yet these processes also involve assimilation, emulation, upward social mobility, and the acquisition of external standards for speaking behavior – phenomena that are not all negative in their effects on speakers' life chances. A balanced view must take into account the fact that language serves many ends for its users. If we are correct in assigning social motivations to sound changes, we can hardly expect them to be completely dominated by the need to preserve distinctions. It is indeed surprising that as many distinctions survive as they do, and a major problem of this work as a whole will be to account for that fact.

In this case, we must accept the possibility that a large population in 16th-century London could not distinguish between *meat* and *mate*, *heat* and *hate*, *feed* and *fade* in their spelling and their conscious observations, and easily accepted this equivalence in puns and rhymes. We must eventually confront an even deeper problem: if this merger did occur, how was it reversed? But first we must ask whether a successful reversal indeed took place, or whether, as some would suggest, only a rough approximation to the original word classes survives.

The regularity of irregular changes

Among the many irregularities of English spelling, some of the most prominent are associated with *ea*, and though spelling is not an infallible guide
to the word classes involved, it does reflect much of the problem of
accountability in tracing historical changes. In chapter 5, we found a certain amount of erratic behavior with respect to *ea* before /r/: while *wear*,
swear, *tear*, *bear* [N], *bear* [V], and *pear* stayed in mid position, *spear*, *smear*,
and *weir* did not. In this case the most frequent words behaved in a regular
fashion, and the three exceptional words were far less important to the
language. But when we examine the larger class derived from ME $\bar{ea}$, some
of the most frequent words turn out to be exceptional. This is the group
that Samuels (1965) refers to as "those *enfants terribles* of traditional *Lautlehre*":

(6)   great, break, yea, steak, drain

With or without a merger with $\bar{a}$, the very existence of these exceptions
has posed a difficult challenge for the traditional Neogrammarian view of
the regularity of sound change. We can understand how place names could
be left behind, along with rare and learned words, but these five are common, ordinary words and their irregularity is puzzling. If the shift of $\bar{ea}$ to
high position was the product of irregular dialect mixture, why did it work
so regularly for all words but these five? On the other hand, if sound change
is basically regular, why do so many sound changes show residua like these,
giving aid and comfort to the opponents of the Neogrammarian doctrine?
The five residual words are too many to fit the model of regular change,
and too few to be explained by random mixture. Samuels (1965:150–3)
reviews the many efforts to solve the difficult problem of accounting for
these words. He concludes that functional factors – the need to avoid homonymy – only partly account for the behavior of these words, and endorses
the view of Walker (1791) that a mid vowel in *great* and *break* is an effect
of sound symbolism, the more open sound being "deeper and more
expressive of the epithet *great*" and "more expressive of the action [of
breaking]" (as cited in Jespersen 1949:338).

We will return to the general problem of the regularity of sound change
in part D. But in this particular case it will appear that the problem of
irregularity has been overstated. A reexamination of the historical evidence,
along with data from current spectrographic studies of change in progress,
shows that the irregularity is largely illusory.

The form *yea* can first be set aside as an entirely different phenomenon.

It seems to have risen to [yi:] as part of the regular process in the 17th century, but afterward reformed to [ye:] along with *nay*.[6]

Three of the remaining words – *great*, *break*, and *drain* – begin with consonant plus /r/. Of course, historical linguists have noted this fact, but they have been quick to discount it because a great many **ea** words were raised after initial /r/:

(7) *r* is followed by [i:] in *read, treason, breach, grease, cream, preach,* etc. (Jespersen 1949:338)

To this list one might have added *ream, real, reap, rear, dream, bream, scream, treat*, etc. Jespersen did not let the matter rest there, and in a more strenuous effort to reduce these irregularities he developed analogical arguments for *great* and *break* as well as *yea*. But the argument against phonetic conditioning had been overstated, and the strength of the argument for it had not been exhausted.

Jespersen's argument has three limitations. First, his list of words with preceding /r/ is motivated only by spelling. Perhaps because he treated the matter in haste, perhaps because he had too much confidence in the spelling system, Jespersen (like many others) seemed to believe that the word class involved here, the "ea" class, was a group of words spelled with *ea*. On the other hand, these scholars surely knew that the vagaries of English spelling were the result of many historical accidents, as well as of the systematic confusions documented above. The word class we are discussing descended as a coherent set from OE **æ̆**, **e͞a**, and lengthened **ĕ**. But only one of the words in Jespersen's list is a member of this group. The ME word *breach* has no clear OE origin, and can only be traced to earlier forms with short **i,y**. The other words all of French origin, and entered English at different times, with different lengths and different vowel qualities.

(8) OE   **æ̆**   read
     ME   **e** (<? OE **y,i**)   breach
     OF   **e**   grease
     OF   **e:**   cream, preach
     OF   **ai**   treason

As noted earlier, one cannot describe the behavior of the **e͞a** class by loan-

---

[6] *Nay* is itself irregular. It is derived from OF *nei*, and should have risen to high position as well as *yea*. The fact that these vowels are both lowered indicates sociolinguistic processes affecting words of affirmation and disaffirmation, in which the vernacular favors more open forms. Compare the variant forms of *yes*, pronounced [jeə, jɛə, jiə], and of French *oui*, pronounced [wɛ, wæ].

words assigned to it, since the proper assignment of the loanwords depends upon their conformity to the development of the class they are assigned to.

Second, Jespersen did not distinguish between initial /r/ and consonant groups with /r/. In current studies of sound change in progress, this has proved to be a critical distinction. The instrumental studies of change in progress have provided ample evidence for the special behavior of obstruent/liquid clusters in regard to the parallel phenomenon of the raising of /æh/ – see figures 4.9, 6.8, 6.10, 6.13, 6.16 and table 6.1. At a later point, we will use these data to reexamine the Kr clusters in some detail. For the moment, it is enough to point out that the allophonic class we are dealing with here is not vowels after /r/, but vowels after initial clusters with /r/: /br, dr, gr/. In the list of five exceptions to the raising of e̅a, there is one representative of each cluster: *break, drain, great*. So far, I have not been able to locate a single example of the e̅a word class with such initial clusters that was raised. All current descendants of this word class that began with consonant plus /r/ are in mid position.

We have already seen that *yea* was not an exception to the main process, but was actually raised to [i:]. There remains one word, *steak*, which was borrowed in late Middle English from ON *steik*. It is not properly speaking a member of the e̅a class as defined here, though traditional discussions place it in this class. As Jespersen (1949:339) points out, [steɪk] is the regular continuation of ON **ei**; it is only the spelling that is irregular (cf. *they, their, bait, swain, raise,* all from ON **ei**).

There is of course another area where the irregular behavior of the **ea** class has been noted: shortening before /d/. I will not attempt to investigate this phenomenon here, but will return to it in chapter 18. As far as the *meat/mate* situation is concerned, we can simply sum it up under the following rule:

(9) In the 17th century, members of the e̅a class either were shortened to /e/ or rose to high position and merged with the e̅ class, except those beginning with initial clusters of consonant plus /r/, which merged with the a̅ class.

If e̅a did merge with a̅, the reversal was clean and complete.

10.3   The case of *loin* and *line*

So far, the /oy/ diphthong has not played a major role in our discussions of English sound change. It participates with /ay/ in the Pattern 4 chain shift, moving to high position along the peripheral track. But it was not a part of the Great Vowel Shift, which applied only to vowels with similar backing and rounding in nucleus and glide. In many ways, /oy/ remains an isolated element in English phonology. It shows odd alternations with /ʌ/, like *point/punctual*, and stands out from all the other Vy diphthongs in that its glide normally traces the full distance from the nucleus to the high front target.

This section will trace the history of the reported merger of ME **ī** and **oi** in the 17th and 18th centuries, and the reversal of that merger in the 19th.

There was no phoneme corresponding to modern /oy/ in Old English. ME **oi** comes from a number of disparate sources from the Middle English period onward:

1 From Latin **au** + **i**, as in *joy*.
2 From Latin short **ŏ** + **i**, as in *oil*.
3 From Late French **oi** derived from earlier **ei**, as in *loyal*.
4 From Latin **ō** or **ŭ** + **i**, as in *moist, point*.
5 From obscure (unknown) sources, as in *boy* and *toy*.

The traditional view, maintained by Sweet, is that group 3 was kept distinct from the rest as /uy/ until the mid-17th century, when the nucleus [u] unrounded and fell to [ʌ] along with short /u/, producing a merger with the descending ME **ī** at [ʌy].

However, the confusion of /ay/ and /oy/ seems to have begun earlier than this lowering of /u/. The first signs appear in 15th-century misspellings. Kökeritz (1953:216) cites a number of Shakespeare's rhymes that point in this direction, as well as inverted spellings: *smoil* for 'smile' and *imply* for 'employ'. Moreover, early merger of /ay/ and /oy/ was not confined to the /oy/ class. The assignment of an "open" or "closed" vowel to words in the /uy/ class shows that the /oy/ ~ /uy/ distinction was confused in the 16th century. Hart (1551), for example, shows *coin* and *voice* with an open /o/ nucleus, but *join* with /u/; all of these are /uy/ words. The /oy/ word *boy* appears with a /u/ nucleus in Hart's account.[7] The assignments to /uy/ and /oy/ by other orthoepists show many such examples in the 16th and early 17th centuries (Nunberg 1980).

The general recognition of the merger appears in the late 17th century when Coles (1674) identifies *line* and *loin*, *bile* and *boil*, *isle* and *oil*, including in these equivalences both /uy/ and /oy/ types. Cooper (1687), Aicken (1693), and Jones (1701) confirm these observations. Other phoneticians of the period list a wide variety of words as homonyms. Free variation between /ay/ and /oy/ appears in the rhymes of Dryden, Butler, and Pope, as in these lines from Pope's *Essay on Criticism*:

---

[7] As often noted, this raising may be due to the effect of the labial initial in *boy*.

And praise the easy vigour of a line
Where Denham's strength and Waller's sweetness join.

By the end of the 18th century, this merger had become a major social stereotype, stigmatized by Rudd (1755), Kenrick (1773), and Nares (1784). Kenrick concedes that some words had been so completely merged that a reversal would now be considered affected:

A vicious custom prevails, especially in common conversation, of sinking the first broad sound entirely, or rather of converting both into the sound of *i* or *y*; thus *oil, toil* are frequently pronounced exactly like *isle, tile*. This is a fault which the poets are inexcusable for promoting by making such words rhime to each other. And yet there are some words so written, which by long use, have almost lost their true sound. Such are *boil, join,* and many others, which it would now appear affectation to pronounce otherwise than *bile, jine.* (quoted in Ellis 1874:1057)

But at the same time, the merger was already in retreat, and fewer and fewer homonymous pairs were given by writers toward the end of the 18th century. In 1799, Adams cites only *bile* and *jine* as /ay/ pronunciations of /oy/ words.

In most Modern English dialects, /ay/ and /oy/ are distinct, with only a few crossovers remaining in local speech. Today, some American dialects use [baɪl] for *boil*.[8] But otherwise, words proceeding from ME **ī** are clearly separated from the word classes that make up ME **oi**. How could these two phonemes have merged and then unmerged? The general opinion is that spelling was responsible:

The disappearance of *ai* for *oi* in polite society is no doubt due to the influence of spelling. (Jespersen 1949:330)

In this opinion, Jespersen is joined by others: Luick (1903), Wyld (1936), and Kökeritz (1953). The argument is advanced because it is the only one conceivable. Indeed, orthography may have had more influence than in the case of **ēa** and **ā**, where the conventional modern spellings provide only an uncertain clue to the word classes involved. Spelling was more standardized during the main period of confusion of /ay/ and /oy/. Nevertheless, there are many reasons to doubt that it could have been the means by which such a clear separation was achieved.

The reports of the merger are quite general, and not attributed to polite London society only. In the modern London vernacular, however, /ay/ and /oy/ are quite distinct. The vowel system of Marie Colville in figure 6.3, one of many London systems analyzed in LYS, shows /ay/ backed and

---

[8] Especially with the meaning 'a small, turbulent stream'.

raised along the peripheral track to the original position of /oy/ [ɔɪ], with /oy/ shifted upward to high position. This dialect is the direct inheritor of the "common speech" stigmatized by Kenrick for its merger of /ay/ and /oy/. Most other southern British dialects show such a clear separation, as LYS found in such widely separated areas as Birmingham, Manchester, and Southampton. The Pattern 4 chain shift can be traced through other systems presented in chapter 6: Norwich (figures 6.19–6.21) and the Outer Banks of North Carolina (figure 6.22). There is only one area in England where a merger of /ay/ and /oy/ appears in current dialect records: the county of Essex in the southeast.

Before we come to any final conclusion on whether spelling might be responsible for the unmerging of /ay/ and /oy/, it will be helpful to review the general properties of mergers and splits, which will be the main topic of the next chapter.

11

The General Properties of Mergers and Splits

Chain shifting is essentially the avoidance of merger; yet mergers are much more common in the history of languages than chain shifts. We now turn to the general principles that govern this other aspect of sound change. While the general principles governing the diffusion of mergers have been prominently discussed in modern linguistics, the mechanism of merger itself is a relatively new topic in sociolinguistic research. This chapter will sum up what is generally known about mergers, and will add some recent findings of sociolinguistic studies. It will also deal with the converse of mergers: the emergence of new distinctions, and the occurrence of phonemic splits.

The state of our knowledge of splits is the converse of the state of our knowledge of mergers. Much attention has been paid to the mechanism of splits, but almost none to their consequences for the diffusion of change or to their cognitive consequences for language learners. This is understandable, since (at first glance) the mechanism of merger is quite simple, while the occurrence of a split demands explanation. In the case of merger, we tend to say simply that "Two vowels fell together," whereas something more complex certainly has to happen for a split to come about. On the other hand, the diffusion of mergers is a prominent and common event that has drawn a great deal of attention. For the very same reasons that mergers spread, splits do not. It might seem, therefore, that there is very little for the study of language change to focus on. But the reversal of mergers reported in the last chapter, if it occurred, would be a kind of split, which implies the acquisition of a distinction and its diffusion. To evaluate these reports seriously, we will have to pay attention to the learnability of distinctions and the spread of such learning.

Some linguists would like to distinguish between the origin of a language change and its diffusion. It may be useful to repeat here the position of Weinreich, Labov, and Herzog (1968) that there is no useful distinction to be made between the two. The discussion of naturally occurring misunderstandings in chapter 9 avoided the implication that individual mistakes in production or perception are directly related to the process of change. An individual may utter a deviant expression, and do it many times, without influencing the language. The change in the language comes about when other speakers adopt this new feature, and use it conventionally to communicate particular forms and meanings. Although innovation may start with the influence of a prominent individual, it is not the act of innovation that changes the language, but the act of influence. Thus the change and the first diffusion of the change occur at the same time.

With these provisos in mind, let us proceed first to the most prominent property of mergers for the student of language change: their unidirectional character.

11.1   The irreversibility of mergers

It is generally agreed that mergers are irreversible: once a merger, always a merger. This first and most important property of mergers throws into sharp focus the paradoxical character of the two reports of reversal that were reviewed in chapter 10. The principle was first stated clearly by Garde in his review of the history of Slavic inflections.

A merger realized in one language and unknown in another is always the result of an innovation in the language where it exists. Innovations can create mergers, but cannot reverse them. If two words have become identical through a phonetic change, they can never be differentiated by phonetic means. (1961:38–9 [my translation])

Since word classes are defined as phonological units, not morphological or syntactic, this means that they cannot be reversed by any operation dependent on linguistic structure. We may translate this into a more general form as the first of several principles governing mergers:

(1)   GARDE'S PRINCIPLE
Mergers are irreversible by linguistic means.

A word class is a historical accident. It is composed of a very large number of brute facts that have no explanation or connection with any other linguistic facts. The fact that /piyk/, meaning 'apex', contains the vowel phoneme /iy/ is a fact that must be learned when the word *peak* is first learned. The behavior of language learners shows that at first this arbitrary character applies to whole utterances. It is then gradually restricted to words and to morphemes as the regularities of the language become apparent. The choice of /t/, /d/, or /əd/ for the English past tense has nothing arbitrary about it. If an alternation is clearly recognized, then the brute facts to be learned take on a more abstract form. For example, if the alternation between /i/ in *sing* and /æ/ in *sang* were established as clearly as the *-ed* past tense alternation, then the morpheme {sing} would be represented as /sVng/ + /i-æ/ ablaut. Analogies of this sort have their limits, of course. As we saw in chapter 10, the relation *speak/spoken, break/broken* was not strong enough to keep *speak* and *break* in the same word class. But no matter how many such alternations we find, the vast majority of facts about the phonemic composition of the lexicon are arbitrary assignments inherited from the history of the language, which are not to be explained by any other fact.[1] This in effect is what is meant by the arbitrariness of the linguistic sign.

The irreversibility of mergers is then intimately connected with an even more general principle of linguistics. The fact that linguistic signs that make up historical word classes are arbitrary means that restoring a merger would involve relearning each of these facts. If /ay/ and /oy/ had merged into one phoneme /ay/, then the language learner would acquire *joint, point, pint, boy, by, bye, buy, spoil, oil, cloy* as /dʒaynt, paynt, bay, spayl, ayl, klay/. A restoration of the merger would mean learning that *joint* contains /oy/, *point* contains /oy/, *pint* contains /ay/, *boy* contains /oy/, *by* contains /ay/, *bye* contains /ay/, *buy* contains /ay/, *spoil* contains /oy/, *oil* contains /oy/, and *cloy* contains /oy/. I have written these facts out in full to emphasize that there is no way to speed the learning by grouping words into sets.

One might say that /oy/ is a relatively small class. But the learner trying to acquire the new distinction would only know that after mastering it. The new category assignments have to be learned for all members of the merged /ay/ class. Some frequency of hypercorrect forms is thus inevitable among those trying to learn a phonemic distinction not native to their own dialect.

It follows that it is much harder to unmerge a merged category than to learn the word classes of an altogether new language. Nonnative language learners have only to remember the list of facts; native language learners have to unlearn the old facts acquired from their parents, and learn a new set. It is not enough to learn that *joint* contains /oy/, *point* contains /oy/, *pint* contains /ay/, and so on. What native learners must learn is far more cumbersome: that *joint* does not contain /ay/ but does contain /oy/, *point* does not contain /ay/ but does contain /oy/, *pint* does not contain /oy/ but does contain /ay/, and so on.

The *difficulty* of reversing mergers is then deduced from more general principles of linguistics. The *impossibility* of reversal established by Garde's Principle is not a deduction, but rests on empirical observation. Garde's Principle does not say that it is theoretically impossible for a person to reverse a merger accurately. It is based on the empirical observation that at no known time in the history of languages has such a reversal been accomplished by enough individual speakers to restore two original word

---

[1] Evidence for the existence of sound symbolism marks the limitations of this statement and of the arbitrariness of the linguistic sign (Fónagy 1979).

classes for a given language as a whole. The following sections will present some of the evidence that supports the principle.

The expansion of mergers

The strongest evidence for the irreversibility of mergers comes from large-scale investigations of dialects where there were as many opportunities for the reversal of mergers as speech communities studied. Chapters 3 and 4 presented apparent-time and real-time studies as ways of tracing the progress of change. Dialect geography offers a third approach. The current spatial display of variation can be related to changes that originated at a particular time and radiated outward. For example, a pattern of expansion can be detected around an urban center where a change was first reported (Trudgill 1974b). Changes normally progress up along lines of communication, like river valleys, and lag behind in mountainous areas. Newer forms overlap the patterns displayed by older forms, leaving identical forms in widely isolated relic areas. These patterns facilitate the interpretation of spatial dispersion in terms of temporal change, with the result that dialect geography is one of the most powerful tools available for interpreting the past by means of data drawn from the present. Herzog (1965) uses this evidence to establish a principle that may be viewed as a corollary of Garde's Principle:

(2) HERZOG'S PRINCIPLE
     Mergers expand at the expense of distinctions.

Herzog illustrates his general principle with data drawn from his study of the Yiddish of northern Poland. In this geographic area, two sets of mergers affected the high vowels of Yiddish.

1   Length was lost in general in the Northeastern dialects of Yiddish, and those Polish dialects bordering on Lithuania show a merger of original /i:/ and /i/, /u:/ and /u/:

(3) THE NORTHEASTERN YIDDISH MERGER

```
        Proto-Yiddish        Northeastern Yiddish

        zin 'mind'
                        >       zin
        zi:n 'son's'

        zun 'sun'
                        >       zun
        zu:n 'son'
```

2   In central Poland, where length was maintained, the high back vowels /u:/ and /u/ are fronted to [ü:] and [ü] and unrounded, to merge with

/i:/ and /i/. This termination of the Central Yiddish chain shift in a merger was noted earlier in chapter 6.

(4) THE SOUTHERN YIDDISH MERGER

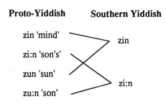

In one area of northern Poland, these two sets of sound changes overlap. Both real-time data and the dialect configurations leave no doubt that this overlapping area is the result of an eastward expansion of fronting and a westward expansion of the loss of length. Herzog poses the hypothetical question, How many distinctions will remain among /i:, i, u:, u/ when loss of length crosses the merger of front and back vowels? Linguists reply in various ways, depending on their views about which distinctions are most important in a language. But Herzog's Principle leads to a clear conclusion: none. Since mergers expand at the expense of distinctions, only /i/ will be left as a result of the intersection of these two processes in the region between Northeastern and Southern Yiddish. This is in fact what has happened. (See the map in Weinreich, Labov, and Herzog 1968:136).[2]

THE EXPANSION OF MERGERS IN AMERICAN DIALECT GEOGRAPHY

One of the major dialect boundaries in the Eastern United States is that dividing the North and the Midland: a line running across Pennsylvania, separating the northern tier of counties from the rest. This is a major geographic, agricultural, rainfall, and population boundary, and it is not surprising that disparate linguistic features bundle tightly along this line. The heavy dark line crossing Pennsylvania from west to east in figure 11.1 is a bundle of isoglosses established by lexical differences between the North and the Midland (Kurath 1949), coinciding with two major phonological isoglosses (Kurath and McDavid 1961).

First, the distinction between voiceless /ʍ/ and voiced /w/ is maintained in the North but lost in the Midland. It is an important distinction before front vowels and shows a good many minimal pairs:[3]

[2] This is one of the many dramatic instances of the mechanical character of sound change, as well as the force of Herzog's Principle. We will return to it in evaluating the functional principle in chapters 19–20.
[3] In English generally, /ʍ/ did not survive before back vowels, where it appears as /h/ in *who, whore*, etc., before rounded vowels. *What/watt* and *Juan/wan* provide the only contrast in the unrounded back vowels, and this distinction holds only for comparatively few speakers.

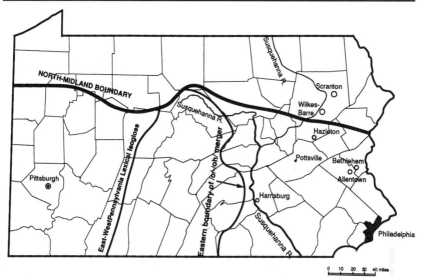

Figure 11.1. Isoglosses in Pennsylvania

(5) wheel/weal   which/witch
     whit/wit   whither/wither
     Whig/wig   whale/wail
     whey/way   where/wear
     while/wile   whine/wine
     when/wen

The merger has expanded rapidly at the expense of the distinction. The Northern Cities studies mentioned in chapter 6 have not found any speakers who maintain the distinction in New York State (Rochester, Syracuse, Buffalo).

Second, the distinction between historically closed [o] and open [ɔ] before /r/ is now preserved as a phonemic contrast in many r-pronouncing dialects in the north of England, but not in southern Britain. In the United States, it was maintained until recently in the Northern and Southern dialect areas but was merged in the Midland area in all Linguistic Atlas records. The general representation of English vowels in (1) of chapter 6 shows that the /ohr/ ~ /ɔhr/ opposition is the only point where a distinction between [o] and [ɔ] is required, and its rapid disappearance may be reinforced by its structural isolation. Though there are few minimal pairs, the distinction is scattered widely through the lexicon.[4]

---

[4] The lexical distribution of this distinction is shown in Kenyon and Knott 1953. The words that have the low vowel in some dialects but not in others are shown with both /or/ and /ɔr/, and those that have the closer vowel in those dialects show only /or/.

(6) *Minimal pairs*   *Unpredictable patterns*

/ohr/	/ɔhr/	/ohr/	/ɔhr/
four	for	pork	storm
mourning	morning	port	porpoise
oar, ore	or	porch	
borne	born	fort	fork
fourth	forth	store	stork

This distinction is now disappearing rapidly in the Northern dialect area. None of the speakers we studied in the Northern Cities have maintained it. It is still strong in Eastern New England (see LYS, figure 27, and Laferrière 1979 for Boston) and in the South. LYS shows a nonoverlapping distribution for /ohr/ and /ɔhr/ for seven speakers from the Outer Banks, and three speakers from Atlanta. But one of the younger Atlanta speakers shows the merger characteristic of the North, and there are other indications that the distinction is weakening in the South. (See figure 6.4 for central Texas, where two tokens of /ahr/ and one of /ohr/ appear in the /ɔhr/ area.)

Spelling clearly marks the /ʍ/ ~ /w/ distinction. American schools have taught that it should be maintained.[5] But that fact has not prevented its rapid disappearance. The /ohr/ ~/ɔhr/ distinction is not easily related to spelling. Although some /ohr/ words have long vowel spellings (*four, ore*), many do not.[6] This difference in relation to spelling is not reflected in the rate of disappearance of /ohr/ ~ /ɔhr/, which is no faster than /ʍ/ ~ /w/.

The low back merger in American English   The largest single phonological change taking place in American English is the unconditioned merger of the historical word classes containing long open o and short open o, phonemicized in the majority of Eastern dialects as /oh/ and /o/. This opposition of length has proved to be unstable in all English dialects. In many dialects, the two phonemes have been further differentiated phonetically. In the south of England, the long vowel /oh/ has tended to rise to a far back, overrounded position, while short /o/ has remained stable as a centralized, lower back rounded vowel. In most American dialects except Eastern New England and Charleston, short /o/ is lowered and unrounded to

[5] A working-class New York City speaker interviewed in 1962 reported that one of the things he appreciated most about English class in high school was being taught that there was a difference between *which* and *witch*. At the time of the interview, though, he was not sure what that difference was (Labov 1966:493).

[6] It is not to be expected that the average speaker would grasp the rule that /ohr/ is found after labials, especially /p/, in monosyllables like *port* or words derived from monosyllables (*portal*) but not after polysyllables like *porpoise*.

[a];[7] and in many of these, long /oh/ is raised and ingliding. A third possibility – merger of the two – is realized in four major areas of North America: Eastern New England, Eastern Pennsylvania, the Far West, and Canada.[8] A study based on the responses of long-distance telephone operators in 1966 showed that the merger was expanding in all of these areas, especially in the West. A transition zone surrounding the Far West was found to pass through Minnesota, Iowa, Kansas, the Panhandle of Texas, southern Arizona, and southern New Mexico (Labov 1991). Responses varied in the major cities of San Francisco and Los Angeles. More systematic investigations by Terrell (1975) in Los Angeles showed that this variability is confined to older people: all younger speakers showed the merger.

Figure 11.1 also shows the dialect boundary separating Eastern from Western Pennsylvania, determined by lexical boundaries (Kurath 1949). A second dialect boundary is located some distance to the east: this is the eastward limit of the expansion of the low back merger of /o/ and /oh/. Studies of the density of travel in Pennsylvania, as determined by average daily traffic flow on highways, indicate that the lexical boundary falls in a natural trough of communication. One way of relating the boundary between Eastern and Western Pennsylvania to lines of communication is to compare traffic flow across that boundary with the traffic flow for other possible locations of the boundary. Figure 11.2 plots 12 possible transits for north-south boundaries across the state of Pennsylvania against the minimum daily traffic flow per mile that would cross such a boundary. The lexical boundary found by Kurath is at a minimum location in this figure. This indicates that fewer people travel across that line than would travel across any parallel isogloss farther to the east or west (Labov 1974). However, the /o/ ~ /oh/ isogloss line is located farther to the east, up the slope of the communication pattern. We can conclude that the merger boundary has been pushed eastward under the pressure of mergers to expand, in this case against the natural tendency for boundaries to follow minima in networks of communication.

Herold's (1990) study of the low back merger focuses on developments in Eastern Pennsylvania. She first traced the progress of the merger by means of telephone interviews throughout the central part of the state, and then carried out intensive studies of particular communities in the

[7] See Trudgill 1974 for this development in Norwich. When /o/ is unrounded, it often merges with various small vowel classes that remained or developed after the lengthening in open syllables and fronting of /a/ to /æ/: words after /w/ (*watch, wash, walrus*), and shortened members of the broad *a* class (*father, pajamas, llama*, etc.).

[8] This merger must have taken place in the early 19th century. The American spelling reformer Michael Barton, from Duchess County, New York State, gives strong evidence of this throughout his work (1830–2). He differentiates his own pronunciation in this respect from that of New England orthographers, and criticizes Walker "in making the sound of *o* in *not*, and *a* in *far* to be different."

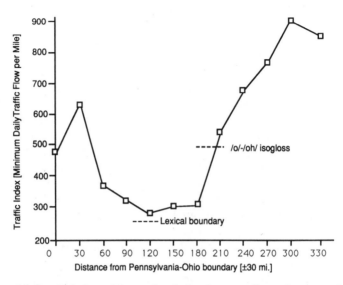

Figure 11.2.   Relation of Pennsylvania isoglosses to lines of communication

transitional zone. The first results showed a dramatic spread of the merger into the area around Scranton, Wilkes-Barre, and Hazleton, where no previous mergers had been reported. Initially, it appeared to be the result of an expansion of the Western Pennsylvania merger almost to the eastern margin of the state. However, closer study suggested a different interpretation. Figure 11.3 superimposes Herold's results on the low back merger as traced in the Linguistic Atlas records of 1940 (Wetmore 1959). The Atlas records show an outer limit for the merger that extends eastward to the Susquehanna River, but stops short of the northern and southern tier of counties. Surrounding this region is the outer limit of merger in Herold's telephone survey of 1988: it has expanded to include the southern and northern counties, crossing the influential North-Midland boundary, but it has not actually crossed the Susquehanna River eastward. From figure 11.3, it is apparent that the new eastern area of low back merger is isolated from the older western area. Herold demonstrated a close correlation between the degree of merger and coal mining, and traced the origin of the eastern merger to the rapid expansion of this region's population in the early 1900s through the in-migration of coal miners from Slavic-speaking areas. She concluded that this merger is an independent phenomenon, the creation of a new dialect through this massive change in the composition of the speech community.

   Within the eastern region, the merger is expanding rapidly from the original coal-mining towns to other communities. The most dramatic evidence

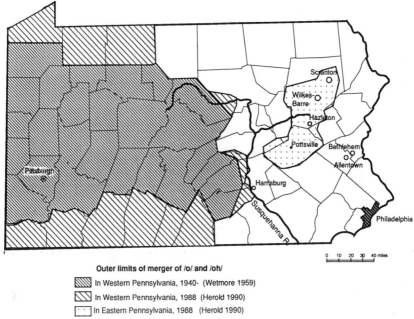

Outer limits of merger of /o/ and /oh/

In Western Pennsylvania, 1940- (Wetmore 1959)

In Western Pennsylvania, 1988 (Herold 1990)

In Eastern Pennsylvania, 1988 (Herold 1990)

Figure 11.3.   Outer limits of /o/ ~ /oh/ merger in Pennsylvania in 1940 and 1988

of this rapid expansion is found in Pottsville, a town of 18,000 in the north-central part of the region. In July 1977, members of the LCV project studied the progress of a number of sound changes in cities and towns of Eastern Pennsylvania, and they carried out minimal pair tests with 13 youth, aged 12–14. In July 1988, Herold returned to Pottsville and obtained minimal pair results from 16 youth in the same age range. Figure 11.4 shows the results for two minimal pairs: *cot ~ caught* and *Don ~ dawn*. Clearly, the merger had made spectacular progress in 11 years. Herold's data also show two features that are characteristic of the progress of mergers: that females are in advance of males, and that categorization or judgments are in advance of pronunciation.

The expansion of conditioned mergers   A number of conditioned mergers are also taking place in American English, and show evidence of expansion. Recent studies show that the merger of /i/ and /e/ before nasals is a 20th-century phenomenon, and that in many areas it is more complete for younger speakers than for older speakers (Brown 1990, Bailey and Ross 1992). In much of the Southern United States, including central Texas, there is a conditioned merger of /iy/ and /i/ before tautosyllabic /l/, so that

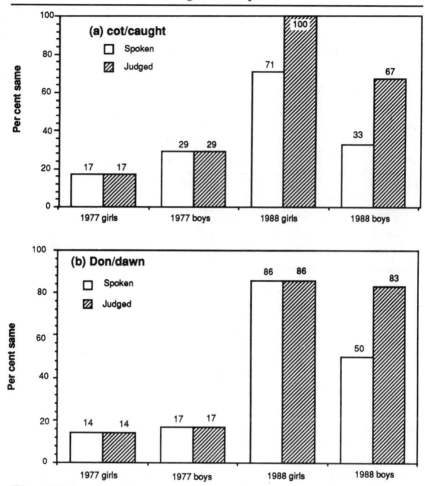

Figure 11.4.   Progress of o/oh merger in Pottsville as shown by minimal pair
results by sex in 1977 and 1988. (From Herold 1990.)

feel and *fill,* *steel* and *still* are both pronounced with a tense, ingliding [iə].[9]
In the Southwest, /uw/ and /u/ are commonly merged before /l/, so that
fool and *full,* *pool* and *pull* are pronounced alike. (This phenomenon, in the
form of a "near-merger," is one of the topics of chapter 12.) Since both
mergers before /l/ are expanding, there are many communities in Arizona
and Utah where they are found together (Di Paolo 1988).

The dialect geography of the United States is particularly active in terms
of the recent formation of new dialects, chain shifting, and ongoing merg-

---

[9] This is of course one of the consequences of the Pattern 4 shift. In figures 6.18 and 6.20–
6.23, it is evident that the position of the nuclei of /i/ and /iy/ overlap. Before /l/, the upglide
that distinguishes /iy/ disappears, and a merger follows.

ers. Yet in other areas with longer traditions, the steady expansion of mergers is found as well.

The mechanism of mergers

This section will address the internal aspect of the transition problem for mergers. The question is to determine by what route two phonemes become one: how the individual words and phoneme targets move in relation to each other. In recent years, considerable attention has been paid to this question:[10] Trudgill and Foxcroft (1978), Harris (1985), Herold (1990), and Shen (1990) have developed a number of models and provided empirical evidence to support them.

MERGER BY APPROXIMATION

The process that is closest in character to the chain shift movements is *merger by approximation*: the gradual approximation of the phonetic targets of two phonemes until they are nondistinct. The merger may result from the coalescence of two vowels, as happened with French /a/ and /ɑ/ (Lennig 1978). In this case, the resulting vowel may show a mean value intermediate between those of the original two. But the mergers that we have observed as the end stages of chain shifting, like the Greek mergers into /i/ (see (9) of chapter 7) or the merger of /ohr/ and /uhr/ in New York City (figure 6.17), do not show such intermediate forms. The merged phoneme has the same mean value as one of the members of the merger, but with an enlarged class membership.

MERGER BY TRANSFER

Merger by transfer is a unidirectional process in which words are transferred gradually from one phonemic category to another. As a rule, it is not consistent with a result that shows an intermediate phonetic form. Mergers by transfer are characteristic of stable sociolinguistic variables, where one form has acquired a social stigma or prestige – in other words, they are characteristic of change from above. The examples of this mechanism provided by Trudgill and Foxcroft (1978) illustrate the spread of mergers that have long been established in the dominant standard language. The merger of Belfast /a/ and /ɑ/ typifies a word-by-word mechanism of this kind (Milroy 1980). And in a study of the merger of /ã/ and /ɑ̃/ in Shanghai using native speakers' perceptions of sameness, Shen (1990) finds a pattern of word-by-word transfer.

MERGER BY EXPANSION

Herold (1990) investigated the mechanism of the /o/ ~ /oh/ merger by means of a detailed study of the town of Tamaqua in Eastern Pennsylvania.

---

[10] My discussion of this topic is heavily indebted to chapter 2 of Herold 1990.

She examined the spontaneous speech and minimal pairs of 28 residents from 9 to 91 years old, and carried out an acoustic analysis of 10 speakers. Because of the ways in which the word classes were formed, the phonetic environments of /o/ and /oh/ are highly skewed. In the 19th century, short **o** had undergone a split into a tense /oh/, which joined the word class of long open **o**, and a residual lax /o/. As in the current split of short **a**, the tensing showed a high degree of phonetic conditioning, affecting common words with following back nasals and voiceless fricatives, so that the /o/ phoneme has only the less common words of this type (*ping-pong* and *King Kong* with /o/ vs. *strong, song, wrong* and *long* with /oh/; *Goth, doff*, and *foss* with /o/ vs. *cloth, off*, and *loss* with /oh/). In order to determine conclusively that a given speaker has a distinction in spontaneous speech, multivariate analysis of the instrumental results is needed to take into account phonetic conditioning and word class membership. A multiple regression procedure was carried out, similar to that reported in chapter 6 for Frank Huber (table 6.1). In this case, a separate analysis was undertaken for each speaker, and the word class coefficients, showing the effect of membership in the /o/ or /oh/ class, were determined. When this was done, it was clear that the three oldest informants, aged 83, 81, and 74, have sizeable coefficients for word class membership for both F1 and F2, with a significance level in all cases of $p < .0005$. None of the younger speakers approach this level, though some effect of word class membership was found even for them.

With respect to the mechanism of merger, the most revealing data come from comparing the speech of J. Hogan, 81, with that of his son W. Hogan, 46. The father has highly significant word class coefficients of 124 for F1 and 209 for F2, which means that all other things being equal, membership in the /o/ class predicts an F1 124 Hz higher and 209 Hz fronter than membership in the /oh/ class. For the son, the corresponding figures are 22 Hz and 26 Hz, with no statistical significance at all. Figures 11.5a and 11.5b show the distribution of /oh/ and /o/ tokens in the spontaneous speech of the father and the son. For the father, the two vowel classes show very little overlap; for the son, they show complete overlap. What neither the merger-by-approximation model nor the merger-by-transfer model predicts is that the two vowel systems occupy the same phonetic space. The phonetic range of the new phoneme is roughly equivalent to the union of the range of the two phonemes that merged.

These results are typical of those obtained from all Tamaqua speakers who exhibit the merged system. Herold found no intermediate stages in the progress of this merger. All merged speakers produce tokens of the new phoneme that are [ɑ]-like, tokens that are [ɔ]-like, and tokens that are intermediate in quality. In this *merger by expansion*, the lexical constraints on the distribution of the two former phonemes are removed, and the range that was previously divided between the two phonemes is used

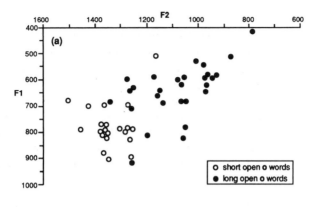

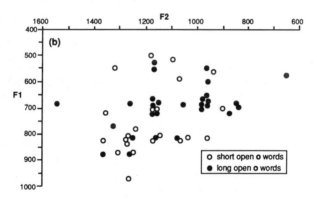

Figure 11.5. /o/ and /oh/ in spontaneous speech for two generations of speakers from Tamaqua, Pennsylvania. (a) J. Hogan, 81, (b) W. Hogan, 46

for the new phoneme, with allophonic distributions in appropriate areas of the new range.

It is clear that there is no single mechanism of merger, but several radically different ones. The task of future research is not to prove which is correct, but to determine where one or the other occurs. Our immediate problem is to see how these mechanisms are related to the steady expansion of merger, bearing in mind that they operate at different rates. Merger by transfer is the slowest; merger by approximation may take three or four generations; and merger by expansion appears to be complete in a single generation.

Misunderstanding and the suspension of phonemic contrast

In order to pursue this subject fruitfully, we must consider the immediate cause, beyond the internal mechanism of merger. What factors might lead members of a speech community to remove lexical restrictions in a sudden and categorical way?

Merger represents a loss of information, as far as the capacity of the linguistic system to distinguish meanings is concerned. The unidirectional expansion of the merger may therefore result in a loss of communicative capacity on the part of those who acquire it. Herold (1990) puts forward a view of the merger process that reverses this commonsense position. She proposes that the following series of events takes place:

1 Through changes in the population of the speech community, or through changes in nearby communities, speakers who make a phonemic distinction develop extensive contacts with speakers who do not.

2 The two-phoneme speakers often misunderstand what the one-phoneme speakers have said, since they interpret an allophonic variation as a phonemic distinction.

3 The one-phoneme speakers, on the other hand, do not misunderstand the two-phoneme speakers – not because they can use the phonemic difference, but because they do not attend to it in deciding what is being said. Given what is for them a complete homonymy between *Don* and *dawn*, they rely on the same types of syntactic, semantic, and pragmatic information that they use in their own speech.

4 After a certain period of time, the two-phoneme speakers cease to attend to this phonemic distinction themselves, since it is not reliable.

5 This decision may produce the sudden collapse of the distinction, as in Tamaqua. On the other hand, the two-phoneme speakers may continue for some time to produce the distinction without using it for semantic interpretation.

Herold's suggested mechanism for the expansion of mergers therefore represents a gain of information on the part of the two-phoneme speakers, not a loss. They learn that there are speakers who do not make the distinction, and they cease to misunderstand those speakers by adjusting their system accordingly. One might ask whether people are capable of adjusting their system only where necessary – in talking to one-phoneme speakers. This does not seem to be possible for two reasons. First, as the merger progresses, there is an intimate mixture of systems within the same community, and listeners cannot distinguish one type of speaker from another except by interpreting their utterances. Second, sociolinguistic studies show that mergers rarely rise to the level of overt social consciousness. Listeners attend to the realization of particular sounds by other speakers, but not to how many distinctions they make.

Herold draws support for her theory from results of the CDC project, which shows that speakers who rely on a given phonetic form will frequently and persistently misunderstand utterances when that form is altered by sound change (Labov 1989c). The CDC data that bear most directly on Herold's proposal are from the studies of natural misunderstanding, which were cited in chapter 6 to show the confusions produced by the raising of (æh), and in chapter 9 to show the hierarchical nature of subsystems. Of the 188 dialect-motivated misunderstandings in the collection, 35 involve mergers. They are all mergers that have been cited in previous pages: /o/ ~ /oh/, /in/ ~ /en/, /iyl/ ~ /il/, and /uwl/ ~ /ul/. There are four possible relations between speakers that are relevant to Herold's hypothesis, which generate the four cells in table 11.1. If Herold is correct, the largest number of misunderstandings should be found when two-phoneme speakers interpret what one-phoneme speakers have said.

To produce this table, I have used only the 27 local misunderstandings, where only 1 or 2 segments are involved; many of these are minimal pairs. In cell (a), there are only 2 events involving two-phoneme speakers and listeners; these are technically accidental and not dialect-motivated, but are included to show the low rate of such events. In cell (d), there is only 1 event involving a one-phoneme speaker and a one-phoneme listener. This might well understate the frequency of actual misunderstanding. The data were largely collected in Philadelphia, at the University of Pennsylvania, and although this academic community includes many speakers from the South, the West, and Canada, they are in the minority; we would expect a higher number if the data had been collected in Montreal or Denver. The crucial comparison is between the asymmetrical cells (b) and (c). There is no bias in the data collection that would lead to the great difference found here. Only 1 of the 24 cases involves a two-phoneme speaker, and 23 cases show the predicted relation of a one-phoneme speaker and a two-phoneme listener.

The great majority of the 28 mergers – 21 – involve /o/ ~ /oh/. Some

Table 11.1 Distribution of naturally occurring misunderstandings of /o/ and /oh/ by phonemic system of speaker and listener

	Listener			
	Two-phoneme		*One-phoneme*	
Speaker				
Two-phoneme	a	2	b	1
One-phoneme	c	23	d	1

involve minimal pairs that one might think of as unlikely, such as *awed* and *odd*, and *pa's* and *paws*. Yet the following misunderstandings actually occurred:

(7) Broadcaster 1, Hawaii [says]: . . . and how did the people react to the eclipse?
Broadcaster 2, Hawaii [says]: I'd say they were awed!
Patricia Donegan, Baltimore [hears]: I'd say they were odd!

(8) K. Parks, Wisconsin [says]: Well, I can call auto repair places.
Ruth Herold, Connecticut [hears]: I can call Otto . . . repair places.
[thinks that the speaker is proposing to call Otto Santa Ana, who would know about repair places]

It is also true that the most likely minimal pairs occur often. The records contain four cases of *Don* and *Dawn*.[11] The most spectacular concentration of misunderstandings involves a pair that is not minimal: *coffee* and *copy*. For one-phoneme speakers, the vowel is a rounded and backed allophone before labial /p/, an unexpected rounding that is identified as /oh/ by two-phoneme speakers. The intervocalic /p/ is not sufficiently distinct from intervocalic /f/ to prevent the confusion.[12]

(9) Carl Roberts, Boston: How did the coffee machine work out?
[referring to a coffee machine loaned to the Penn Colloquium]
Sherry Ash, Chicago: [starts to tell a long story about her problems with a copying machine until interrupted; a Philadelphian present hears *coffee*, but decides she has misheard it when Ash starts to reply]

(10) Gillian Sankoff, Montreal: [passing copy shop, 11/28/86]: This is too far; if we're in a hurry we won't save any time to come here for a copy shop.
William Labov, northern New Jersey [aware that they have passed a copy shop, looks around for a coffee shop]: Coffee shop?

(11) Gillian Sankoff, Montreal [passing copy shop, 6/21/90]: Oh! Copy shop! Here it is!
William Labov, northern New Jersey [looks for coffee shop, wondering why G. is looking for one since they just had coffee; knows that they are looking for a copy shop]

(12) Gillian Sankoff, Montreal: I wonder if there's a copy [kɔpi] place near the airport.

[11] Partly because for two years the Department of Linguistics at the University of Pennsylvania included a faculty member named Don Ringe and a graduate student named Dawn Suvino.
[12] The size of this collection is augmented by the convergence of the two items, *copy* and *coffee*, at scholarly meetings, and the recent emergence of copy shops along with coffee shops, but the range of items listed goes beyond this.

William Labov, northern New Jersey [thinks]: Why would she need coffee?

(13) David Sankoff, Montreal: It's time to make the copies.
      William Labov, northern New Jersey: But I've already had my coffee.

(14) David Sankoff, Montreal: I'll get your copy right away.
      William Labov, northern New Jersey [thinks]: Why is he getting us coffee?

(15) Ann Taylor, Vancouver: Do you have the copy key?
      Don Ringe, Kentucky: Is there a key to the coffee?

(16) Ruth Herold, Connecticut: These are copied from Maurice Sendak.
      Woman, background unknown: I thought you said you were getting coffee for Maurice Sendak.

The frequent repetition of this pattern may not lead most speakers to a conscious awareness of the effects of merger, but it may well lead them to rely less on the distinction and eventually to abandon it entirely. The effect on language that is at work here is not external in the sense of invoking extralinguistic factors. Neither social prestige nor the stigma of change from above is involved. But it is external motivation in the sense that contact between different speech communities is concerned. Herold distinguishes between these two dimensions to show when each of the three mechanisms might be most likely to occur (see table 11.2). We will return to this scheme after considering a larger range of changes in the linguistic inventory.

The relative likelihood of merger

The introduction to this chapter argued that there is no meaningful difference between "linguistic change" and "diffusion of linguistic change." In that sense, Herzog's Principle – that mergers must expand – would itself be the cause of mergers, and the mechanism presented above would merely be the means of implementation that determines the rate of merging. But this starts from the fact that a given phonemic distinction has merged in at least one speech community. There is another sense of "cause" that

Table 11.2 Mechanisms of merger by type of change and motivation

	Externally motivated	*Internally motivated*
Change from above	merger by transfer	
Change from below	merger by expansion	merger by approximation

bears on the critical opposition between chain shifts and mergers. Why in the course of sound change do some vowels fall together, and others maintain their differences? A number of discussions in chapters 5 through 9 have touched on this question. The various answers that have been given can be categorized in the following way.

(a) *The functional load of the opposition.* This is the number of different lexical items that are differentiated by a phonemic opposition, and conversely, the number of homonyms that would result from its loss. This line of argument has been explored by many investigators, notably King (1969); see also Wang 1967. For further evaluation of functional load arguments, see part E. For present purposes, it will be important to distinguish between two types of functional load:

(a₁) *The number of minimal pairs that depend on the distinction.* This determines the amount of lexical homonymy that would result if the merger took place. This measure in turn depends on both the size of the word classes and the accidents of history – how many of the possible frames happen to be filled. If there are few minimal pairs, very few words will become homonyms even if the classes are large. Thus the merger of /o/ and /oh/ makes homonyms of only a few frequent words: *cot/caught* and *Don/dawn* are the most notable. Yet as we have seen, the major source of misunderstanding is *copy/coffee*, an opposition that would not have entered into calculations that examined minimal pairs only. We may refer to this factor more specifically as a measure of *lexical opposition.*

(a₂) *The extent to which the distinction depends on minimal pairs.* This is equivalent to the predictability of the distributions. If one or both of the phonemes show a skewing in distribution, and those skewings are almost complementary, then the phonemic distinction will be maintained by only a small number of lexical items. Thus the distributions will be highly predictable. We may refer to this factor as a measure of *lexical predictability.* High lexical predictability implies low lexical opposition, but not vice versa.

(b) *The number of distinctions already made along that phonetic dimension.* This is a major factor in the explanations advanced by Martinet (1955) and Haudricourt and Juilland (1949) for chain shifting as well as merger. The number of stable oppositions that are possible along any one dimension varies according to the type of phonological analysis, but for height it is evidently three and rarely four, and for fronting and backing, or rounding, it is two and rarely three. It is argued, for example, that three levels of height are the most that can be maintained in the back, and four in the front.[13]

---

[13] Chapter 6 showed that the existence of only three degrees of height in the back did not prevent the fronting of /uw/ in the Western United States and the Northern Cities area.

(c) *The number of phonetic features on which the opposition depends.* It is generally agreed that an opposition maintained by several features is more stable than an opposition that depends on only one. Thus the distinction of length in Hungarian is unstable in the high vowels, where it is the only feature separating /i – i:/ and /u – u:/; but it is stable in the mid and low vowels, where vowel quality as well as length separates long and short.

(d) *The discriminability of the phonetic features on which the opposition depends.* Some features are said to be inherently more effective than others in maintaining phonemic oppositions. Chen and Wang (1975) argue that the feature of length itself is weak in maintaining phonemic oppositions, and that any distinction that depends on length alone is unstable, as opposed to place of articulation, nasality, etc. Chapter 6 introduced evidence from natural misunderstandings that peripherality is another such weak feature; chapters 12 and 14 will amplify this point.

(e) *Limitations in the range of movements that would avoid merger.* The view of phonological space outlined in chapter 6 motivates vowel merger whenever (1) a unidirectional process has reached the limits of the acoustic or articulatory space of any one subsystem, and (2) movements into other subsystems are not characteristic of the group of languages involved. Why the route /i/ → /iy/ is open for Germanic, Baltic, and Slavic branches of Indo-European, and not for others, remains an open question; however, this fact indicates that such arguments are not universal but are tied to the systemic features of particular language families. The widespread merger of /o/ and /u/ before tautosyllabic /r/ is a product of the fact that the back rounded vowels do not move frontward before the central inglide.

The multivariate nature of causation

The overall configuration that brings about mergers undoubtedly is a multivariate situation, involving a combination of these factors. Thus when the lengthened ME **ĕr** words eventually fell together with the lengthened ME **ǽr** words, so that *bear* became homonymous with *bare*, (c) only a single feature (peripherality) was involved, (d) that feature was a weak one, and (a₁) only a few oppositions were involved. In the case of the merger of /uhr/ and /ohr/, (a₁) only a few oppositions separate the /uhr/ and /ohr/ classes, (c) only a single feature – height – separates them, and (e) both routes /uhr/ → *[üɚ] and /uhr/ → *[uᵘɚ] appear to be unavailable. There is considerable dispute over the phonemic status of the OE short diphthongs **ea, eo, io** (Stockwell and Barritt 1951; Kuhn and Quirk 1953). If they were phonemically distinct from /æ, e, i/, the loss of that distinction by smoothing was associated with (a₁) low lexical opposition, (a₂) high lexical predictability, and (c) a single phonetic feature of ingliding, which rarely maintains a distinction alone.

Given the multiplicity of factors, various mergers can be differentiated according to the major factors or combination of factors involved. We are now in a position to return to the major question with which this chapter began: whether the type of cause underlying a merger might be related to the possibility of its being reversed.

The relative difficulty of reversal

If two phonemes are completely merged, by definition the functional load is zero. What difference would it make to the possibility of reversal if the original merger had been caused by a low functional load? Low lexical opposition (a_1) would make no difference, since reversal means not simply the reinstitution of the phonemic difference in the minimal pairs, but the restoration of the two original word classes as a whole. But high lexical predictability (a_2) *would* facilitate reversal as well as merger, since restoration of the original situation would depend only on the learning of a few minimal pairs.

If a merger was encouraged by (b) overcrowding along a particular dimension, the reversal would be more difficult than otherwise, since the restoration of that overcrowding would threaten the margins of security of all the neighboring phonemes. It is not immediately clear how (c) the size of the phonetic distinction would affect the reversal of a merger. From the point of view of production, it would be difficult to learn to produce several new features. For example, one might say that to learn the Eastern /o/ ~ /oh/ distinction, a speaker from California would have to learn to produce a high back tense overrounded ingliding vowel as opposed to a low central lax unrounded vowel. But the restoration of a distinction reestablishes, not the original phonetics, but the original distributions. The major source of difficulty is then the perceptual aspect. The factors that lead the one-phoneme speaker to perceive the whole range as "the same" might be eliminated. If the distinction that speakers of the merged dialect were trying to learn was a subtle one phonetically, it would be less salient and more difficult to learn. The same argument holds for (d) the discriminability or perceptual strength of the phonetic distinction.

If a merger was encouraged by (e), a blocked route for the end point of a chain shift, then a reversal would certainly be the most difficult of all, since it implies the reversal of the whole series of movements.

We then have the hierarchy shown in table 11.3, which ranks the difficulty of reversal according to the causal factors behind the original merger. Any merger that was associated with a cluster of factors like (d,b,e) would be the least likely to violate Herzog's Principle and Garde's Principle. On the other hand, a merger that followed high lexical predictability of a distinction but had none of the traits (c,d,b,e) would be the most likely to be reversed.

Table 11.3   Relation of factors causing merger to the possibility of reversal

Rank		Factor behind merger
Facilitating		High lexical predictability (a_1)
Neutral		Low lexical opposition (a_2)
Disfavoring	least	Single phonetic feature (c)
		Weak phonetic feature (d)
	↓	Crowded phonetic dimension (b)
	most	Blocked chain shift route (e)

Before we apply the logic of this result to the cases of reported unmerger, we must examine the obverse of mergers: the properties of phonemic splits and their origins in the history of languages.

11.2   Phonemic splits

Most reports of phonemic change involve mergers: the reduction in phonemic inventory. This simple fact would lead to the odd conclusion that most languages are steadily reducing their vowel inventory. Since any overview of language history shows that this is not so, it stands to reason that just as many phonemic splits must take place as mergers. For reasons that are not entirely clear, it is not easy for students of the speech community to locate the ongoing creation of phonemic distinctions. But there are enough cases in the historical record to provide a detailed taxonomy of splits. The properties of splits will be important in the investigation to follow: not only with regard to the reversal of mergers, but also in dealing with the regularity of sound change in part D. Without trying to replicate the extensive discussions on this topic (see Hock 1986), I will try to summarize the main properties of splits as they relate to the problems of this chapter and those to follow.

A *split* is the division of a preexisting phoneme to create a new phonemic distinction. It is not the only way in which new phonemic distinctions are created. New phonemes can be created by the integration of borrowings of phonemes, yielding segments with a new configuration of features that did not exist in the language before. An example is the incorporation of /oy/ into English, discussed in chapter 10.

Loss of the conditioning factor

The classic and most common form of split occurs when two allophones become distinctively different through the loss of the environmental factor that conditions their difference.[14] In non-Southern American dialects that show fronting of /uw/ and /ow/, this process is inhibited before /l/ as well as /r/. Typically the following pronunciations are heard:

(17)   too [tü^u]   tool [tu$^>$ɫ]
       go [gɛ$^{>u}$]   goal [go$^>$ɫ]

In many of these dialects, particularly that of Western Pennsylvania, the dark final /l/ that conditions this difference is undergoing vocalization in final position. After back rounded vowels, as in the words cited in (17), the /l/ may disappear entirely, producing the following surface opposition:

(18)   too [tü^u]   tool [tu$^>$:]
       go [gɛ$^{>u}$]   goal [go$^>$:]

In this case, there remain many alternations that allow a more abstract analysis to reconstruct the underlying /l/ (*tool/tooling, goal/goalie*), and there is no reason to recognize a new phonemic distinction in underlying forms.

More profound changes in the language were produced by the process of vowel lengthening in open syllables in late Old English discussed first in chapter 5. Long ā had been backed to ɔ̄, so there was no long ā at this point in the history of the language. Lengthening in open syllables could not create such a phoneme; it could only create long allophones in open syllables, short allophones in closed syllables. The phonemic split between long ā and short ă came about when the conditioning factors were worn away by continued sound change, which had first reduced final vowels to shwa, and then dropped the shwa. Thus the final *-e* in *name, same, made* was reduced and eventually disappeared, leading to a major phonemic contrast between /æ:/ and /æ/ in *made/mad, same/Sam*, and so on.

Borrowing

In many languages, new phonemes are introduced by a gradual process of borrowing from an exterior source, with a period of "coexistent phonemic systems" (Fries and Pike 1949), nativization of the marked morphemes, and final assimilation into a single phonemic system. The simplest case is that of a phoneme that simply does not exist in the borrowing language. As we have seen, Modern English /oy/ has no Old English origins, but

---

[14] This pattern is frequently referred to as the "Polivanov" factor after the Russian linguists who first described it.

derives from various Latin and Late French sources as well as from certain unknown and isolated roots. It is more common to find that borrowed words break an established allophonic pattern and so create a new contrast. Old English had no contrast between [f] and [v]: [f] never occurred medially and [v] never occurred initially. Almost all the contrasts that exist today are based on borrowed words with initial /v/, which first came into the language from French (*vagabond, very, village, voice, vulgar*, etc.). Once the massive French borrowings had established this pattern of initial /v/, borrowings from other languages resisted assimilation to the native pattern of initial /f/. There are only a very few words that are not Latinate. *Vixen* and *van* are from southern British dialects where only /v/, not /f/, occurred in initial position; *Viking* is a late Norse borrowing, replacing OE *wicing*.

Lexical splits

The preceding two sources of new phonemic contrasts preserve more or less intact the existing word classes, reorganizing or adding to them. The source of new phonemes that is of particular interest here actually divides a preexisting class along lines that cannot be predicted by any rule. Such lexical splits will play a major role in this chapter and in later ones that consider lexical diffusion versus regular sound change.

I know of no lexical split that consists simply of a random reapportionment of phonemes into two different classes. Such a historical change seems inconsistent with what we know about linguistic behavior. We do not find the unmotivated recreation of the brute facts of word class membership. Instead, such lexical splits display a high degree of conditioning, and what seems at first like a complex rule of distribution. Closer examination of the situation shows that a rule is not justified, and that mastery of the new distribution demands knowledge of each particular lexeme.

The properties of such lexical splits may be summed up in the following list. A typical lexical split of one word class into two shows:

1 A complex set of phonetic conditions that predicts the great majority of lexical assignments, but not all.
2 A number of phonetic conditions that specify particular words.
3 A variety of grammatical conditions involving inflectional and derivational suffixes, irregular verb paradigms, auxiliary status, and grammatical functors generally.
4 Variable behavior of derived words, particularly abbreviations and back-formations.
5 Irregular patterns of proper names and learned words depending on the age of acquisition.
6 A strong effect of word frequency.
7 Unmotivated lexical exceptions.

BRITISH BROAD **a**

The classic example of such a lexical split in English is the British broad **a** class. Broad **a** is found before nasals in borrowings from French words originally spelled with *au* like *dance* and *chance*, or words spelled with *a* like *lance, France,* and *plant* – in the majority of monosyllabic words ending in clusters of /n/ plus a voiceless obstruent. It also occurs before front voiceless fricatives in *half, laugh, bath, pass, past,* with a pattern of phonetic conditioning independent of etymology. Grammatical insights may help the second dialect learner formulate the rule that gives broad **a** in bimorphemic *chancy* but not in monomorphemic *fancy*, bimorphemic *can't* but not monomorphemic *cant* ('slang' or 'tilt'), monomorphemic *class* but not derived *classic*.[15] But no phonological, grammatical, or etymological rule will tell the second dialect learner that broad **a** is used in *class* but not *mass* 'substance, crowd'[16] both of French origin, though it is variable in the ecclesiastical *mass* of Old English origin; in *pastor* but not in *pastern*, both of French origin; in *plaster* from Old English but not *plastic* from Latin. A very adroit language learner may attack the situation before nasals by deducing that broad **a** occurs only before clusters, never before a single final nasal. If the cluster begins with /m/, it must further be specified as / __mpl/, which yields broad **a** in *sample, example*, but not *camp, lamp*, etc. Unfortunately, the learner must then learn to say *ample* as /æmpl/ and not /ahmpl/. The /n/ clusters are even more difficult, with broad **a** in *demand, command, slander*, but not in *land, grand, pander* (Jones 1964; Ferguson 1975). In each case, there is a tantalizing suggestion of an explanation – in some cases a hint of a high style for broad **a** versus a low style for short **a**, old patterns for broad **a** versus new ones for short **a** – but these tendencies are only tendencies, explanations after the fact. The one true path for learning the broad **a** class is to absorb it as a set of brute facts as a first language learner, or failing that, to be enrolled in a British public school in early childhood.

THE MIDDLE ATLANTIC SHORT **a** SPLIT

Much of the recent discussion of lexical splits has focused on the behavior of short **a** words in the Middle Atlantic states, in a range of urban dialects from New York, northern New Jersey, Philadelphia, Baltimore, and points farther south. We have already had many occasions to look at the sound change involved: the tensing of /æ/ to /æh/ and raising to [ɛː, eː, iː]. Though the entire short **a** class is affected in the Northern Cities, the Middle Atlantic states show a complex selection.[17] The northern New Jer-

---

[15] The *-ic* suffix shortens vowels consistently, of course, as in *tone/tonic, placate/placid.*
[16] Cf. *Iolanthe*: "Bow, bow, ye lower middle classes, bow ye tradesmen, bow ye masses." This is sung by British choruses with broad **a** in the first line, short **a** in the second.
[17] As also happens in the South, though this has not yet been investigated in detail.

sey pattern was first described in detail by George Trager, writing about his own speech. In a series of articles (Trager 1930, 1934, 1940), he developed more and more insight into this distribution, beginning with the idea of a complex allophonic distribution, and ending with the clear conclusion that this was a lexical split.[18]

The New York City pattern has been described in fine detail by Cohen (1970). It shows all of the properties listed above:

1   Tensing in closed syllables before voiced stops, voiceless fricatives, and front voiceless nasals.
2   Variable behavior before voiced fricatives in open syllables (*magic, imagine*).
3   Analogical tensing in open syllables before inflectional boundaries (tense *planning, passing,* lax *planet, passive*), and laxing in function words (*an, am, had, have, can*).
4   Variability before derivational boundaries (*classify, passable*) and abbreviations (*gas, math*).
5   Irregular laxing in learned words (*alas, adz,* lax *mad* 'insane' vs. tense *mad* 'angry').
6   Tensing in word-initial position in common polysyllables like *after* but not uncommon polysyllables like *Afghan*.
7   Absolute lexical exceptions like tense *avenue* (all other instances of short **a** before /v/ are lax, especially in open syllables and initial position).

Though we are now likely to regard the short **a** situation as a lexical rule rather than a phonemic split, it will appear that such lexically conditioned rules share many properties with phonemic redistributions.

THE DISPUTABILITY OF LEXICAL SPLITS AND THE **OE** SHORT DIPHTHONGS

It follows from the general properties of lexical splits that they are not easy to recognize analytically. Naive speakers of the language of course do not recognize the split until a very long time after it has occurred, since the phonemic oppositions are set up only gradually, and the traditions of the language identify the new phonemes as varieties of the old. As noted above, it took George Trager three studies and many years of analysis to recognize the phonemic status of the short **a** split in his dialect. Indeed, a hallmark of lexical splits is that linguists dispute the status of the two new phonemes – that is, they often disagree about whether a lexical split has taken

---

[18] Halle and Mohanan (1985) refer to the first of Trager's articles in their treatment of English segmental phonology, but unfortunately were not aware of the others. Their limited information about the short **a** split led them to propose that it is governed by a phonetic rule.

place. One of the longest such disputes in the history of American linguists concerned the status of the Old English short digraphs **ea, eo, io** (Stockwell and Barritt 1951, 1955, 1961; Kuhn and Quirk 1953). These graphic forms were all reflexes of front short vowels ă, ĕ, ĭ in Germanic, in contexts that generally lead to "breaking," or the development of inglides, particularly before tautosyllabic liquids as in *earm* 'poor', *bearn* 'child', *eall* 'all', *miolc* 'milk'. The distribution of these short diphthongs shows many of the properties of a lexical split. Yet their actual phonetic conditioning was quite idiosyncratic, with many fine details of distribution, and included vowels before and after velar /h/ as well. Stockwell and Barritt proposed that the short diphthongs were phonemically distinct from the corresponding short vowels, on two basic grounds: that the phonemic principle leads us to expect that scribes register only phonemic distinctions, and that the facts of distribution justify this view. Kuhn and Quirk disagreed, pointing out many factual limitations in the original argument, and the dispute continued over several decades and many articles.

Marginality and reversability

One of the most interesting facts about the Old English short diphthongs is that they were eliminated from the language in early Middle English, and the Old English graphic conventions gave way to simple ă, ĕ, ĭ. If **ea, eo, io** did signal a phonemic split, that split was reversed, and the integrity of the original word classes was restored. Since this reversal is a merger, and mergers expand at the expense of distinctions, this is not an unlikely event. The logic of the situation suggests, in fact, that the results of lexical splits are more likely to be reversed than other phonemic distinctions, since they depend on a smaller number of opposing elements.

The smoothing of the short diphthongs was only a part of the general smoothing processes operating at the end of the Old English period. In chapters 4 and 6, we saw that this smoothing merged $\overline{ea}$ and ā, $\overline{eo}$ and ō, so that the loss of the short diphthongs cannot be considered the result of an instability peculiar to them. Nevertheless, there is a sense in which the results of lexical splits fall short of the full phonemic oppositions characteristic of the major historical word classes. In the terminology we developed for mergers, they show high lexical predictability and low lexical opposition. As a result, they should be easier to reverse than other linguistic changes.

11.3 The unlearnability of distinctions

A second approach to the empirical basis of Garde's Principle is to examine the relative success of native speakers of a language in acquiring the systems of other dialects. All of the evidence given so far shows mergers spreading. It is apparently very easy to acquire a merger from another dialect, and we hardly need more proof of that fact. But the strength of Garde's Principle lies in the converse: the difficulty of acquiring a distinction for speakers who have a merger. This section will examine the available evidence on this point. The strongest kind of evidence comes from natural situations, when people move into new dialect areas where they and their children are surrounded by speakers who use a different system. Information can also be derived from field and laboratory experiments, where subjects are asked to imitate, recognize, or identify the patterns of another dialect.

Lexical splits offer a strategic research site for an inquiry into the learnability of distinctions – the obverse of the reversability of mergers. The advantage of studying a split is that speakers of all other communities who are in contact with it are in the position of the "merged dialect" faced with a distinction. Normally, they will not learn it, and we might expect that their influence would erode or slow the progress of the split. This might well occur on the frontier between two communities. But it would be another matter if we were to take a small number of speakers of the merged dialect and place them in the midst of the community with the split, far from any contact with their original communities.

The acquisition of the Philadelphia dialect

This contact situation was found in King of Prussia, the suburb that was the focus of Payne's (1976, 1980) study of the acquisition of the Philadelphia dialect introduced in chapter 3. The Philadelphia dialect exhibits a wide range of phonetic variables that must be acquired by a language learner, but also a lexical split of the type just outlined.

The land occupied by King of Prussia was devoted to farming up to 1945. In the next 25 years, industrial parks attracted chemical, automotive, electronic, and computing industries to the area. The technical and professional employees who were brought to these factories and laboratories settled down in the immediate suburban area, rather than in Philadelphia, which is a 40-minute drive away. About half of the new industries' personnel were Philadelphians who moved to the suburbs, and half were from out of state. In the area studied by Payne, most of the families were middle class and Catholic, and had from 3 to 7 children. This provided an appropriate setting for studying the capacity of children to learn the Philadelphia patterns. For the children, the social situation provided powerful motivation for learning, and the structure of the families yielded a wide range of possibilities for comparing the age of entrance into the community with the number of years spent in it.

One of the primary concerns of the King of Prussia study was the relative influence of family and peers on the acquisition of language. In earlier studies in New York City, it was found that second generation New Yorkers showed the same phonetic patterns as speakers from the third and fourth generations. The fact that parents spoke Yiddish, Polish, Italian, or German did not prevent their children from participating in the evolution of the New York City vernacular in the same way as children whose parents spoke that vernacular.[19] But this effect may have been due to the low social status of the parents' foreign accent; children may have picked up the social cues that this was not an appropriate model for language learning. The King of Prussia context gave parents a much greater advantage. The immigrant families in the study came from New York City (3), Massachusetts (3), upstate New York, Western Pennsylvania, Cleveland, and Kansas. At least in the adult world, their vernaculars had greater prestige than the local Philadelphia vernacular.

One might think that the sheer number of out-of-state families in some areas would strengthen their influence to the point that the Philadelphia pattern could not exert the normal effect it would have on isolated families. Payne's sample was therefore balanced to include two blocks that were predominantly Philadelphian, two that were about half out-of-state, and two that were predominantly out-of-state. No significant differences were found among the three types.

THE ACQUISITION OF PHONETIC VARIABLES

As noted in chapter 3, the out-of-state adults showed minimal tendencies to acquire the Philadelphia dialect, and preserved their basic phonetics and phonology intact. Their children, on the other hand, acquired the phonetics of the Philadelphia dialect rapidly and accurately. To measure this effect, Payne selected five Philadelphia sound changes that showed the maximum contrast with other dialects: (aw), (ay0), (oy), (ow), and (uw).[20] For all variables except (aw), a majority of the out-of-state children showed complete acquisition – that is, there was no discernible difference between their speech and that of local children. All children showed at least some fronting of (uw) and (ow), and even the most difficult variable for the children to acquire – (aw) – was acquired to some degree by 80% of them.

Figure 11.6 shows the percentage of children with complete acquisition

[19] In New York City, it was possible to carry out a statistically valid comparison between two groups of first and second native generation speakers: upper working class Italian men, and lower middle class Jewish women. There was no significant difference between the first and second native generation in each set, indicating no significant effect of having parents who were native speakers of Italian or Yiddish. Effects of ethnicity did appear in the preferential raising of (æh) by Italians and (oh) by Jews, but this was not related directly to the speech pattern of parents (Labov 1976).

[20] There would be no point in using (æh) as a phonetic index, for example, since all dialects show some raising of /æh/.

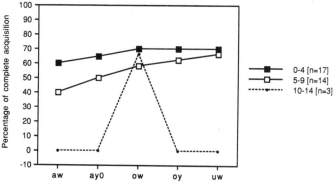

Figure 11.6. Percentage of complete acquisition of Philadelphia phonetic variables by out-of-state children in King of Prussia by age of arrival

according to their age of arrival in the King of Prussia area.[21] The legend shows the total number of children in each age range, but the actual number of out-of-state dialects that could be used for comparison was a subset of these.[22] In each case, the children who arrived before the age of 5 show the highest level of acquisition, and those who arrived between the ages of 5 and 9 approximate this result. The figures for the older children, who arrived between the ages of 10 and 14, are based on only 3 cases; we must expect that a larger number would show a higher level of acquisition, and that the high level for (ow), based on the speech of 2 out of 3 children, would fall. The discussion of the transmission of change in volume 2 will reexamine this situation through a multivariate analysis, and show that in fact membership in social networks is a more powerful influence than age of arrival on the acquisition of the Philadelphia phonetic pattern. Here we are concerned with the linguistic factors that bear on this process.

The ordering of the variables reflects the social and chronological trajectory of sound changes outlined in chapter 4. The new and vigorous changes (aw) and (ay0) are the lowest in social salience and show the lowest rate of acquisition. The middle-range changes (uw) and (ow) are

[21] The classification of acquisition or nonacquisition was based on qualitative differences, not quantitative. Children were rated only if their parents' dialect was qualitatively different from that spoken in Philadelphia (for example, if it showed no fronting of (uw) or no centralization of (ay0)). Payne's categories *complete* and *partial* therefore refer, not to the relative degree of advancement of the phonetic forms, but to the frequency with which any form within the Philadelphia range was used. In fact, the children's phonetic variables were relatively advanced. For the children acquiring these patterns, they function as markers of the Philadelphia community, not of sound changes in progress, and they are cited here in the parenthesized notation that indicates sociolinguistic variables.

[22] Not all variables could be used for children from all areas, since in some cases there was no contrast with the Philadelphia dialect. New York City, for example, shows the same raising of (oy) to [uy] as Philadelphia. The actual numbers available for each were: (aw) 20; (ay0) 34; (ow) 25; (uw) 25; (oy) 20.

the most salient. The fact that 2 of the 3 older children showed acquisition of (ow) suggests that it is more salient than (uw), and this fits in with other evidence: popular discussions of the Philadelphia accent refer often to (ow) but never to (uw). (Although (oy) is a well-advanced sound change, it is not salient in New York City or Philadelphia, and never shows correction even in the most formal speech.)

The full acquisition of the Philadelphia variables refers not only to the phonetic forms used but also to their distribution. The rules governing these distributions are all quite simple. For (aw) and (oy), there are no conditions: all instances of the variables are affected in the same way, and there are no allophonic differences that are relevant to the Philadelphia vernacular. The variable (ay0) occurs only before voiceless finals. An equally simple rule defines (uw) and (ow): front all nuclei in syllables not terminated with a liquid.[23] The phonetic variables are all defined by low-level surface rules, and there are no further rules that operate on their output.

THE ACQUISITION OF THE TENSE/LAX DISTINCTION

When we turn to the acquisition of the underlying set of categories to which the surface rules apply, a radically different situation prevails. The most sensitive indicator of the acquisition of Philadelphia phonological structure is a lexical split: the division of the historical short **a** word class into tense /æh/ and lax /æ/. The Philadelphia split has all of the complexities of the New York City split sketched earlier. This distribution was first introduced in the discussion of the raising of /æh/ as a phonetic variable, and it will be the topic of more intensive examination in several chapters to follow. It has been studied in some detail since the 1940s (see Ferguson 1975, LYS 1972, Payne 1976, and Labov 1989a).[24] This chapter will be concerned only with the invariant "core pattern," since the most straightforward way to study acquisition is to see whether learners have acquired an invariant pattern. Later chapters will focus on the variable areas of short **a** distributions in connection with the regularity of linguistic change.

Though the opposition of /æh/ and /æ/ appears as a phonemic split in a structuralist tradition, it is ultimately best treated as a complex rule in the perspective of lexical phonology, with lexical specifications which assign the features [+tense] or [−tense] to individual words where the rule

---

[23] One might have added the requirement that the mean value for free syllables be greater than that for checked syllables, which does not hold for all of the dialects that show this fronting. But Payne's study made no such restriction, since this distinction is far less salient than the main variable.

[24] The last study is a complete description of short **a** in the spontaneous speech of 100 Philadelphians from the LCV Neighborhood Study.

would produce a different result. Figure 11.7 is a chart of the consonants that normally condition a preceding tense /æh/ in the Philadelphia dialect. A solid line surrounds the front nasals and front voiceless fricatives, indicating that vowels in closed syllables are tensed before these consonants. This chart does not show the expected association of nasals with voiced stops and the close affinity of voiceless and voiced fricatives, but instead combines two series of consonants that appear to have no features in common. The dashed line indicates that three words before /d/ are also tensed (*mad, bad, glad*) but that all others (*sad, dad, brad, fad,* etc.) are lax. The odd distribution in this chart is now fairly familiar to those who have been studying American dialects, but it still poses hard questions for both language change and general phonology: how it came about, and how it is to be represented. These issues will be developed in greater detail in chapters 15 and 18.

The out-of-state children who arrived in King of Prussia had to learn three basic facts about the Philadelphia dialect in order to reproduce the core pattern:

1 Short **a** is lax before any back consonant (palatal or velar).
2 Short **a** is tensed in closed syllables before front nasals and front voiceless fricatives.
3 Short **a** is tense in three particular words ending in /d/.

Each of these distributions posed different problems for children who had different native short **a** distributions. But the overall results were comparable. Of 34 out-of-state children, none reproduced the full pattern, and only one reproduced the core pattern.[25]

The contrast with the acquisition of the phonetic rules is even more

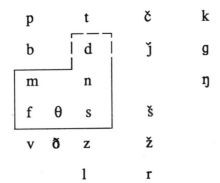

Figure 11.7.   Consonants following short **a** that condition tensing in Philadelphia

[25] A closer view of their partial success will be given in chapter 15.

extreme than this. The only children who showed the core pattern were those whose parents were born in the Philadelphia area. We conclude that the underlying categories, acquired as first dictionary forms in the child's vernacular, are not easily relearned. It follows that the traditional position of dialectologists is correct with regard to underlying forms: the structural homogeneity of a speech community depends upon those whose parents (and possibly grandparents) were raised in that community, and who remained in it themselves throughout their formative years. This position does not hold for phonetic output rules or the lexicon: here we find that the second generation speakers (and those who arrived before the age of 8) are equivalent to third and fourth generation speakers (see footnote 19).

The situation reflected in King of Prussia can be seen in many other speech communities. In the People's Republic of China, the standard language adopted by national policy is *pu tung hwa*, a dialect that is defined as having the phonology of Beijing and the grammar of Northern Mandarin. The phonology of the Beijing dialect includes a distinction between two series of apical consonants: dental and retroflex. But most other dialects and languages of China either do not make this distinction or do not preserve the lexical classes of Beijing. The great majority of those who must learn this standard as a second dialect do not acquire a consistent control of the dental and retroflex series (Lehmann 1975; Escure 1987). In France, a similar problem confronts speakers from the central and southern areas of the country, who do not have the standard phonemic distinction between upper and lower mid vowels that establishes /e/ and /ɛ/, /o/ and /ɔ/ as separate phonemes. These speakers have the same phonetic range as speakers of the standard language, but for them the two sets are in complementary distribution. An important part of the front distinction rests on the contrast heard in the imperfect *trouvait* [truvɛ] and conditional *trouverait* [truvərɛ] versus the participle *trouvé* [truve]. Despite strenuous efforts on the part of teachers, it proves to be an extremely difficult distinction to learn, and it is not clear how many speakers succeed in doing so.

Sociolinguistic forces

So far, it might seem as though Garde's Principle were absolute: that distinctions are unlearnable, and that mergers are irreversible in an absolute sense. This would be an error. I do not believe it is realistic or fruitful to declare that there are things human beings cannot learn because they are constitutionally incapable of doing so. We have seen that there is a logical hierarchy of difficulty in learning distinctions. Given the right social conditions, it is reasonable to think that a distinction can be reintroduced into a speech community in a consistent way.

What social conditions might make this possible? First, it must be noted that the changes in phonological inventory that we recognize as mergers and splits proceed well below the level of social consciousness. But unlike the phonetic movements of individual sounds and chain shifts, they remain at this level, without social prestige or stigma, long after they have gone to completion. For social pressures to be brought to bear on the reversal of mergers, there must be an overt campaign to bring the problem to social attention and bestow prestige on the distinction. Yet this is not a normal development. As a rule, mergers and splits have no social affect associated with them.

ABSENCE OF SOCIAL AFFECT

The evidence for the absence of social affect of splits and mergers is massive and overwhelming. Yet in another sense, it is almost entirely negative. Systematic study of social distributions and social affect has been directed to variables that in fact show social distributions and social affect, like the development of the new prestige marker (r) in New York City (Labov 1966), the use of short /o/ in Boston (Laferrière 1979), and the unrounding of short /o/ in Norwich (Trudgill 1974a). No one has as yet undertaken an experimental or observational study of social responses to a variable merger or split because there has been no preliminary report that would justify such an expenditure of time and effort. However, such studies have been carried out in communities as part of larger studies of ongoing sound changes, some of which are mergers, and we can use this fact to compare the social affect registered for the sound changes themselves and the mergers or splits of the phonemes involved.

We have had many occasions to refer to the raising of /æh/ and /oh/ in New York City and Philadelphia, and the development of the high ingliding vowels [i:ə] and [u:ə]. In New York City, these sounds carry a strong and consistent social stigma, as shown by vigorous correction in formal styles, subjective reaction tests, self-report tests, and overt discussion (Labov 1966:chaps. 7, 11, 12, 14). In Philadelphia, these reactions are less violent, directed almost entirely at the front vowel, and they are confined primarily to upper middle class and upper-class speakers. But in both cities, the raised /æh/ vowels are a major point of social comment. The offending sound is referred to as "harsh," "nasal," and "disgusting." In New York City, some speakers react with equal violence to the sound of raised /oh/.

Both of these sound changes begin and end with changes of phonemic inventory. As noted above, short open /o/ had been split into /o/ and /oh/, with unpredictable variation across dialects regarding which words stayed as /o/ and which were tensed to /oh/, joining the word class of *talk* and *law*. Short **a** was split into /æ/ and /æh/, again with unpredictable variation across the vocabulary. As the change progressed, the raised /æh/ in New York City merged with /ehr/ of the *r*-less dialect, and then with /ihr/, so that *bad, bared,* and *beard* were all potential homonyms. Among the most advanced speakers, /ohr/ merged with /uhr/, so that *shore* and *sure* were homonyms. In Philadelphia, the merger of /ohr/ and /uhr/ is the norm for most speakers, though there is considerable variation. Yet in the course of sociolinguistic studies, no speakers without linguistic training cited these splits or mergers as features of the New York City or Philadelphia dialect, complained about them, or stigmatized others for showing differences in inventory. Though many Philadelphians complained about the sounds used in *man, bad,* or *Camden,* no one noted that the vowels of *mad, bad,* and *glad* were tense, whereas the vowel of *sad* was lax. No one criticized Philadelphia speech because listeners could not distinguish *moor* from *more, lure* from *lore.*[26]

The most general unconditioned merger in the United States is of course the merger of short and long open **o** in *cot, caught,* etc. Many studies of this phenomenon have been carried out, but none have demonstrated any significant social awareness of it, nor are there any reports of speakers being stigmatized for failing to make the distinction or praised for making it. On the West Coast, New Yorkers are frequently stigmatized for using the high back ingliding /oh/ in *lost* and *coffee,* but not for making the distinction between *cot* and *caught.*

A similar lack of social affect is found in reactions to the ongoing merger of *pin* and *pen* in the Southern States. Comments always refer to the presence of [ɪ] in *friend, remember, pin,* etc., not to a merger between *since* and *sense, pin* and *pen, tin* and *ten,* etc.

All of these observations indicate that differences in phonological inventory – splits and mergers – are not normally the focus of social attention and that changes of this type do not carry social affect. This applies generally to abstract features of language. The interface between language and society is a narrow one. Members of the community perceive and react to surface structure: to words and to sounds. In each of the cases mentioned above, social attention is paid to sounds, not to their relations. Furthermore, it is paid not to sounds generally, but to sounds as exemplified in particular words. New York City (oh) is cited and perceived as the sound of the word *coffee.* Philadelphia (oh) is often cited as the sound of the word *water* – since that word has /o/ instead of /oh/ in many neighboring dialects.

One cannot say that there are no social reactions to structural facts. In New York City, the most strongly stigmatized sound of all is the upgliding

---

[26] Sensitive members of one community who have been exposed to a different arrangement of the short **a** inventory may report interesting and accurate observations, but these are not couched in terms of phonemic contrasts. The case of Murray A. is characteristic. Murray was born in New York City, moved to Philadelphia during his high school years, and then returned to New York after college. He said that Philadelphians made fun of his New York accent until he adjusted to the Philadelphia system. When I asked him how Philadelphians pronounced short **a** words, he was always right for those words where a contrast existed: for example, he was absolutely sure that Philadelphians used lax /æ/ in *sad, ran,* and *bag* – words where New Yorkers use /æh/. But he had no idea what vowel Philadelphians used in *bad, man,* or *past* – words where both Philadelphians and New Yorkers use /æh/.

centralized vowel in *third* and *first*, phonetically [əɛ] but usually spelled and stigmatized as *oi* in "Toity-Toid Street," etc. Among older, more traditional New Yorkers, /oy/ was pronounced the same way, and this merger was one of the few that has actually been referred to as a social stereotype. The normal way of referring to this structural fact is to say that people say *oil* for *earl* and *earl* for *oil*. Since there is no spelling that captures [əɛ], community members can only refer to the sound by reversing the lexical reference. On the other hand, some social stereotypes of this kind are accurate. In Utah, a standard stereotype of rural speech is "put the harse in the born," which indicates a reversal of /ahr/ and /ɔhr/. I first assumed that this was a social perception of a merger, but in fact, acoustic analyses of several speakers from Logan County have indicated that the two vowels were reversed.

THE INFLUENCE OF SPELLING AND CLASSICAL LEARNING

The school system would logically be the major instrument for a social program to reverse mergers. In the United States, most educational efforts to influence pronunciation are related to spelling, and given Jespersen's suggestion that spelling was instrumental in reversing the merger of *line* and *loin*, we should conclude by examining the relation between spelling and the educational programs that deal with mergers. What little concern the American educational system has shown for mergers has focused on consonantal issues that are most clearly reflected in spelling. The distinction between /w/ and /ʍ/ is consistently reflected in the spelling distinction between *w-* and *wh-*, and the intervocalic flap merger would be accurately reversed by following the *-t-* versus *-d-* spelling. Yet there is no evidence that teachers' efforts to reverse these mergers have been effective (see footnote 5).

Spelling is certainly brought to bear upon the lexical split of short **a**, since in most Eastern schools, teachers introduce short **a** words in reading lessons with a low front [æ]. The combined effort of school and parents to correct the stigmatized /æh/ has succeeded in completely reversing the tensing of short **a** for some upper middle class children in the Philadelphia and New York City area.[27]

The strongest influence of an educational system on language would probably be found in the effects of the tradition of classical learning in Arabic cultures. Several recent sociolinguistic studies of Arabic-speaking communities show that Islamic schooling has had a great impact upon the speech community. Abdel-Jawad (1981) examined the use of *qaf*, the uvular stop /q/, in a stratified sample of Amman in Jordan. In the history of Arabic, *qaf* is said to have merged with either /k/, /g/, or /ʔ/ many centuries

---

[27] In spite of my personal opposition to such correction, several of my own children raised in northern New Jersey consistently use [æː].

ago: /g/ in the Bedouin dialects, /k/ in the rural *fellahin* dialects, and /ʔ/ in urban dialects. But in modern Amman, *qaf* appears as a sociolinguistic variable, correlated with sex, social class, and urban/rural origins. It is not a case of the presence or absence of *qaf*, but of alternation with the other phonemes, /k/, /g/, and /ʔ/, each of which appears regularly in its own historical word class. *Qaf* itself is used by everyone in only a few words, like *Qur'an* 'Koran'.

Many of Abdel-Jawad's speakers showed very low percentages of *qaf* as a whole, and never used it in many words where they might have. But he found no occurrences of *qaf* in inappropriate vocabulary, that is, no hypercorrection, despite the total overlap with other phonemes. This means that all of the Amman Arabic speakers in the sample – no matter how much or what kind of education they had received – had preserved a knowledge of the *qaf* word class. Amman then seems to show a remarkable reversal of the mergers of *qaf* with these other phonemes.

One feature of the behavior of *qaf* in Abdel-Jawad's data points in another direction. The variable exhibits no phonological conditioning, but it does exhibit strong lexical conditioning. In a sociolinguistic study of the Arabic community of Cairo, Haeri (1991) looks closely at the distribution of *qaf* in that city. She concludes that the use of *qaf* is not controlled by a general sociolinguistic rule, but that it represents a series of lexical borrowings from the classical vocabulary. From this point of view, the *qaf* word class has not been restored in the Cairene Arabic system, but instead has been added as a parallel system that is not fully integrated into the language, comparable to the case discussed in Fries and Pike's (1949) original treatment of coexistent systems. Since each use of *qaf* occurs in an individual borrowed lexical item, there is no likelihood of the sound's being generalized to other parts of the vocabulary to replace /k/, /g/, or /ʔ/. Haeri contrasts the use of *qaf* with a new change in progress in Cairo, the palatalization of apical stops. She points out that this sociolinguistic variable shows a high degree of integration into the phonology of Cairene Arabic, and differs radically from *qaf* in its social and linguistic properties.

In any case, such consistent preservation of word class information may be attributed to a familiarity with Classical Arabic forms that is the product of the traditional Muslim educational system. We might therefore point to this example as one that shows the conditions under which the reversal of a merger is possible. This would require the intense social evaluation of a large number of lexical alternations of a type that is common enough in the honorific systems of such countries as Japan, Korea, and Tibet, but with the special provision that the alternants are distinguished by the use of a given phone that is no longer distinct in the common vocabulary.

THE ACQUISITION OF THE /ʌ/ ~ /ʊ/ DISTINCTION IN ENGLAND

The distinction between /ʌ/ and /u/ in British English is the result of a 17th-century lexical split. The primary process was the unrounding and lowering of /u/, which took place in the south of England but not the north. Trudgill (1986) notes that in northern areas there is an ongoing tendency for upwardly mobile speakers to acquire the standard distinction. It is not known how successful they are in this enterprise, since no accountable study of their performance has yet been undertaken. It may be instructive to look at the problems they face as a way of measuring the difficulty of acquiring a lexical split.

Like the lexical splits discussed earlier, this one showed strong phonetic conditioning, which may be useful to those who would acquire the pattern. The most important factor was the influence of a preceding labial consonant, which favored the retention of the rounding in *pull, put, puss, bull, bush, full, bush,* etc. There are many intricate subconditions to be learned: for example, /ʌ/ occurs before /g/ and /dʒ/, even after labial initials, as in *bug, mug, budge, fudge,* etc. – but not in *sugar* or the recent *boogie-woogie.*[28] Yet it is not clear that these rules will be useful, since the conditioning is far from complete, and the occurrence of the two phonemes is not predictable. /ʌ/ occurs in a number of words with labial onsets and apical codas: *mud, but, butt, bus,* with the minimal pairs *put/putt, puss/pus.* Note that spelling is no help in deciphering this distinction; the doubling of final consonants works in different directions for each pair.

The situation is further complicated by the results of the irregular shortening of /uː/ in *oo* words derived from ME ō, with its own intricate series of irregular phonetic conditionings. The northern speaker must learn to retain /u/ in many words before apicals (*foot, soot, good, wood, hood, stood, could,* etc.) and before /k/ (*cook, book, took,* etc.).[29] This creates a new series of oppositions, with minimal pairs like *stood/stud, could/cud, shook/shuck, look/luck, rook/ruck.* In this set, spelling does help those who would like to acquire the distinction, but only to a certain extent. The northern speaker must still learn by brute force that /ʌ/ is to be used in *flood, blood, glove, done, shove, hover, cover,* and many other words spelled with *oo* or *oCe.*

Given the importance of Received Pronunciation in England, large numbers of speakers from Yorkshire, Newcastle, Liverpool, and Leeds have made the effort to acquire the /ʌ/ ~ /u/ distinction. No doubt many have succeeded. But as Wyld (1936:3–4) points out, speakers do not acquire this class dialect through education – that is, through the study of books or any other form of individual effort – but through "opportunity and

---

[28] Actually derived by the shortening of long /uː/.
[29] The difference between *blood* and *good* is often attributed to the idea that the shortening of the first took place before the unrounding of short /u/, the latter after, but Jespersen (1949:334) points out that there is no basis for this ordering in the historical record.

experience." In fact, Wyld suggests that the Received Pronunciation would better be called the "Public School Dialect." The very creation of this standard depended on the fact that those who attended public schools (i.e., private boarding schools) acquired the distinction even if their families spoke a regional dialect without it. If such transformations were not possible, RP would not have become a unified form of expression free of geographic or ethnic influences. We thus have indirect evidence that the full acquisition of a lexical split is possible under the control of an educational system that places a strong emphasis on remaking behavior to eliminate all social variation. It is important to note that the children in these boarding schools subject to this retraining are a minority, live in the environment of the majority dialect nine-tenths of the year, and begin their training in preadolescent years.

It seems unlikely that such a transformation is possible in the community at large, or that the upwardly mobile individuals referred to by Trudgill could, by their own enterprise, listening to the various forms of the standard through whatever contacts they have, master this lexical split. A detailed study might show that some individuals succeed, and here the role of the mass media should not be dismissed in advance. Though the studies of sound change in progress show that mass media in the United States do not produce convergence in the community as a whole, it is possible that the media can serve as a template for individuals who are isolated from their peer groups and are strongly motivated to acquire an exterior standard.

12

Near-Mergers

So far, we have been considering merger, split, and the maintenance of contrast as a fixed set of possibilities, employing the fundamental conception of discrete classes that is shared by both the structuralist and the generative traditions. That linguistic categories are separated into mutually exclusive sets is perhaps the most fundamental concept of linguistics; without it, linguistic analysis as normally practiced would not be possible. I will refer to this position as the *categorical view*. It was not prominent in the study of chain shifting in part B. That enterprise was based on a concept of motion in a continuous phonetic space not subject to the categorical view, and the automatic application of the categorical view to the rotation of a fixed number of categories. Here in part C, mergers and splits have been considered within a categorical framework, and nothing presented so far would call the fundamental concept into question. However, this chapter will confront discoveries that make it difficult to maintain the categorical view without some modification. To proceed, we must first consider the assumptions and principles held in common by the various schools of phonology that share this discrete view of linguistic structure.

12.1 The conceptual basis of the categorical view

Though the categorical view favors discreteness, linguists have not ignored data that are difficult to categorize discretely. The history of phonology manifests a long series of struggles with marginal phenomena. But in each case, the struggle has been resolved by creating new discrete categories or new levels of organization, or by abandoning old restrictions, in order to preserve the notion of a discrete binary contrast between categories. Phonologists have wrestled with:

- the categorization of segments that are in complementary distribution except for a few lexical contrasts. The structuralist approach was to merge this situation with all other phonemic contrasts, under the slogan, "Once a phoneme, always a phoneme." The analysis of the Old English short diphthongs exemplified this approach (Stockwell and

Barritt 1951, 1955; Kuhn and Quirk 1953). The generative solution
is normally the converse: to derive the contrasting forms from a single
underlying form by a rule at the lexical level, and enter the contrasting
exceptions into the dictionary. Chapter 18 will consider such analyses
in various approaches to the Middle Atlantic short **a** split.

- the problem of segments that are in contrast only across grammatical
  boundaries. Moulton (1962) considers the case of German ich-laut
  and ach-laut, which can be recognized as two allophones of a single
  velar fricative if and only if the grammatical status of the suffix -*chen*
  is entered into the analysis. The structuralist solution is to ignore this
  boundary at the phonemic level, and recognize a single velar fricative
  only at a separate, more abstract level as a *morphophoneme*. The generative solution is to eliminate the distinction between phoneme and
  morphophoneme (Halle 1962).

- the status of phonetic elements that occur primarily in loanwords that
  are integrated to various degrees into the native vocabulary. The usual
  solution here is to recognize a distinct *coexistent system* (Fries and
  Pike 1949).

- the categorization of segments that are phonetically intermediate
  between two phonemes in environments where their contrast is neutralized, as in the much-discussed cases of English stops after /s/ or the
  intervocalic flap. One solution is to create a new type of segment, the
  archiphoneme, at a different level of organization, but it is more common to select one or the other phoneme as underlying on the basis of
  phonetic similarity or simplicity of the pattern.[1]

The marginal phenomenon to be considered here is somewhat different.
It arises when, as the result of sound change, two word classes that are
quite distinct in some dialects come into close approximation in a given
dialect. These cases have not been discussed in the traditional debates on
categorization and marginality. One reason is that the fine-grained phonetic observations or measurements that would show such approximation
have not been represented in the literature. As we will see, that fact is in
turn a result of the strength of the categorical view, which puts pressure
upon phoneticians to phonemicize their impressionistic transcriptions, but
also proceeds from a general theoretical bias against recording nondiscrete
phonetic information. By the end of this chapter, we will have encountered
dramatic testimony of a more powerful bias that leads to the suppression

---

[1] Hayes (1992) has called into question the existence of any such absolute neutralization on
the basis of work by Dinnsen (1985) on English flaps and Barry (1985) and Nolan (in press)
on nasal assimilation. In these cases, small differences in speech production persist that preserve the separate identity of the underlying forms. Hayes's use of such delicate phonetic
detail in phonological theory represents a striking departure from the categorical view.

of data not consistent with the categorical view. But first, we must explore more deeply the theoretical principles that mold the behavior of linguists so forcefully. With respect to phonology, the categorical view can be analyzed into six components:

1 *The concept of contrast.* The phonology of structural linguistics placed great emphasis on the concept of contrast, and much attention was given to deciding whether a particular phonetic difference was contrastive or not at a level of phonetic representation divorced from grammatical information. In a generative format, the goal is to identify underlying forms at the most abstract level of representation that can be justified. Apart from questions of level of representation, it is possible to identify general features of this concept that are held in common by all linguists. Contrast exists between types, which are exemplified by particular forms. Two types are in contrast when (a) there is at least one environment where the difference between them is the only difference between two utterances that differ in meaning; (b) the distribution of the two types is not predictable by any general rule; (c) native speakers are sensitive to the difference between the two types, at some level of behavior, but not to differences between tokens of the same types.[2]

2 *The concept of distinctiveness.* Membership in a contrastive category is determined by the presence or absence of one or more distinctive features. Any feature that is not distinctive is redundant, and is irrelevant to category membership.

3 *The discreteness of boundaries.* The boundaries between categories are infinitely sharp, in the sense that there are no intermediate forms. If the distinctive features that define membership in a category are all present in a given token, it is a member of that category, and if they are not all present, it is not.[3]

4 *The irrelevance of phonetics.* No matter how we approach phonology – as a distributional, behavioral, or mental pattern – it is the organization of phonetic material. All linguists would agree that one could not understand a phonology fully without some information on the phonetic material that had been organized. But once that organization is established, most of the phonetic information has to be set aside; phonological analysis is after all a data reduction procedure that is devoted to showing, from the perspective of the native speaker, that most differences don't make a difference. The amount of phonetic information provided in most phonological analyses is limited to the abstract set of features that are taken as distinctive.

[2] In the most precise sense, this is the phenomenon of *categorical perception*, as defined in the literature of experimental phonetics (Harnad 1987). The development of orthographies provides another reflection of this phenomenon (Stockwell and Barritt 1955).
[3] In theories of underspecification, distinctive features may not be present in underlying forms, but are derived by implicational relations.

Vowels are described as high, low, or mid, and finer differences in fronting, backing, raising, lowering, and rounding are ignored. It is even less common to find information on formant trajectories, amplitude contours, or energy distributions.[4]

There is a further motivation for the view that the relative phonetic distances between realizations of categories are not relevant to their categorical status. This position is the result of cross-linguistic experience that native speakers easily recognize and respond to phonetic differences that at first are almost imperceptible to the outside investigator. With familiarization and practice, the differences become much more apparent, and eventually the descriptive linguist cannot recapture the original impression that the categories are phonetically close. Such experiences led Bloomfield (1926) to formulate the following strong statement:

(1) Such a thing as a "small difference of sound" does not exist in language.

5 *The symmetry of production and perception.* It is generally assumed in linguistic analysis, and often formally acknowledged, that grammars and phonologies should be neutral with regard to the perspective of speaker and hearer. It is argued that we are all listeners as we speak, and speakers as we listen. From the phonological viewpoint, this means that a map of instrumental measurements of phoneme production should show the same structure as the output of a categorization or discrimination experiment.

6 *The reliability of intuitions.* The categorical view is strongly supported by the assumption that native speakers know what they can and cannot say and that they have free access to this knowledge. As a working principle, this has been an effective means of advancing analyses through the rapid accumulation of introspective judgments. It is of course only a working assumption: the more thoughtful theorists have recognized that there is no a priori guarantee that speakers have access to their intuitions (Chomsky 1964), but in practice, this principle governs almost everything that linguists do. It is not limited to the introspections of the theorist, but applies equally well to the elicitation of data from speakers of other languages. Voegelin and Harris (1951) criticize the procedures of mainstream field linguists, whose methodological principle (following Boas and Sapir) is simply "Ask the informant"; they argue that the reliability and validity of this method depend on the doubtful assumption that informants have free mental access to their language.

---

[4] Of course, one reason for the reduction of phonetic information is that much phonological analysis is based on secondary materials, where the analyst has available only a subset of the phonetic information provided in the original report.

There is ample evidence from experimental phonetics and sociolinguistic fieldwork that native speakers do think categorically about their language. Though the original evidence for categorical perception (Liberman et al. 1957; Pisoni 1971) has been criticized, extended beyond language, and reformulated (Harnad 1987), it remains a real phenomenon that can reinforce our confidence in the reliability of native speakers' intuitions. But a profound circularity underlies this confidence: for the tendency of the categorical structure to influence perception also makes it difficult for the native speaker to recognize any intermediate forms that are not governed by that structure.

12.2 Empirical procedures for establishing contrast

The empirical methods used for determining the contrastive status of phonemes in the speech community are designed to take into account the tendency of speakers to perceive and respond in categorical terms. Since these methods were used to obtain the data that will be the subject of this chapter, it is important to describe them in detail.

Minimal pair tests

A *minimal pair test* is a device for finding out whether two phonetic types are contrastive. The method is simple: a native speaker is asked whether two utterances that differ in meaning are 'the same' or 'different'. The utterances are phonetically identical except for one element, which is represented by a token of one type in one member of the pair, and a token of the other type in the other member. Thus a person may be asked to read the words *four* and *for*, and then say whether the two words are the same or different.

I have not found any detailed descriptions of minimal pair tests from the period of structural linguistics, when methods for describing languages were prominently discussed. In the study of the speech community, minimal pair tests have assumed increasing importance, and some specific methods have been developed that are important in obtaining replicable and reliable results.

1 The interviewer shows the speaker written versions of the two words, or pictures of two objects or situations.
2 The speaker is asked to pronounce the written words or name the objects or situations.
3 The interviewer makes an impressionistic transcription (at the moment, or later from a recording) of the two utterances.
4 *Without indicating in any way his or her own reaction on this point,* the

interviewer asks the speaker to say whether the two utterances sound the same or different.

5   If the speaker shows any confusion about the fact that the two utterances differ in meaning or spelling, the interviewer tries to clarify, for instance by saying, "If you only heard these two words spoken over the telephone, would you know which word was which?"

6   The interviewer records the speaker's full response.

7   If the 'same' and 'different' patterns of both speech and judgment are not clear and equivalent, further minimal pair tests are carried out with more tokens of the same type.

8   The analyst categorizes the production and judgment data as 'same' or 'different' (or as intermediate if appropriate).

Where no minimal pairs are available, near-minimal pairs can be used, such as *mirror* and *nearer*. The subject is then asked to say whether the two words rhyme or not. At present, there is no firm evidence that judgments on rhymes are less reliable than 'same' and 'different', though minimal pairs have the advantage of a closer relation to the communication test to be discussed shortly.

When minimal pair tests are done properly, two independent pieces of information result: one on how the speaker pronounces the words, and the other on how he or she evaluates any difference between them. These two observations then determine the entry in one of the cells of the four-cell table 12.1.

The six elements of the categorical view jointly lead us to expect that entries will occur in cells (a) and (d), where speech production and judgments of sameness are matched. This expectation is a correlate of the investment of the categorical view in the reliability of intuitions.

Since the purpose of the minimal pair test is to focus attention on speech, it is to be expected that sociolinguistic variables will shift radically toward formal styles in the test situation. When New Yorkers are asked to

Table 12.1   The four-cell table of the minimal pair test

		Spoken	
		same	different
Judged	same	a	b
	different	c	d

compare *god* and *guard*, they show the maximal tendency to pronounce a constricted [r] in *guard*, which is rare in spontaneous speech. The sociolinguistic variable is not whether *god* and *guard* are the same, but whether the /r/ is to be pronounced as a consonant or not. Chapter 11 argued that there is little social evaluation of the structural facts of merger or split. One might therefore think that minimal pairs alone would yield an accurate view of the phonemic inventory of a given dialect, without the need for detailed studies of the vernacular. However, there are other factors that lead to striking differences between the results of minimal pair tests and the pattern displayed in spontaneous speech. Speakers may be influenced by spelling; they may unconsciously adopt the norms of other dialects or of younger speakers in their own community. Studies of mergers in progress show that changes in speech perception precede changes in production. Within minimal pair tests, judgments of 'same' regularly exceed production as 'same' (figure 11.4; Di Paolo 1988), and by the same token, production in a minimal pair test will be shifted more toward the incoming norm than the system that the speaker actually uses. In addition to these factors, there are other differences between minimal pair tests and spontaneous speech that are more difficult to account for.

In discussing the problem of relating minimal pair data to spontaneous speech, Herold (1990) presents table 12.2, which shows the responses of 20 Canadians from London, Ontario, to minimal pair tests. From the spontaneous speech of these subjects and all other evidence about the region, we know that they had a total merger of /o/ and /oh/. But only 75% of the subjects gave the 'same'/'same' responses that correspond to cell (a) of table 12.1. Two of the cell (d) responses can be eliminated because the speaker made exaggerated distinctions that he admitted were not natural to him. One of the cell (b) responses to *Don/dawn* can be discounted because the speaker pronounced *Don* as [dɔn] and *dawn* as [dɑn]. Never-

Table 12.2 Treatment of /o/ ~ /oh/ minimal pairs by 20 subjects from London, Ontario (from Herold 1990, table 1.2)

Cell of table 12.1	Spoken	Judged	cot/caught	Don/dawn
a	same	same	15	15
b	different	same	1	2
c	same	different	2	2
d	different	different	2	1

theless, this leaves seven responses in cells (b), (c), and (d) that are difficult to interpret within the framework just given.[5]

Commutation tests

Despite all precautions, the information provided by a minimal pair test is both limited and uncertain. The judgments of 'same' and 'different' are influenced by a number of intervening variables that are not directly related to the physical relations of the speech pattern. A more reliable and more valid measure of the primary function of a phonemic contrast – its capacity to transmit information – is provided by *commutation tests*. Commutation tests were mentioned in the literature of the structural period (Harris 1951), but the first specific results of such tests were reported in LYS (chap. 6). These first efforts were relatively informal, with a certain amount of preliminary negotiation between interviewer and subjects; they have since been replaced by more carefully controlled procedures.

In commutation tests as first introduced, one native speaker is asked to read a randomized list of members of a minimal pair, and a second native speaker is asked to identify, in each case, which of the two possibilities has just been read. A secure phonemic distinction will produce 100% success, and a complete merger will produce a random result, with a mean value of 50% on repeated tests. One difficulty with this procedure is that if there is variation within the community, the experimenter does not know whether the rate of success is due to the ability of one speaker to produce the distinction or the ability of the other speaker to discriminate the tokens produced. The current method involves only one native speaker. The experimenter asks the subject to read a list of 14, 24, or 44 randomized words, including an equal number of each member of the opposing pair. This is recorded. The interviewer then dons earphones and turns the tape to a specified item on the list unknown to the subject (usually the fifth). The tape is then replayed starting with that item, and the subject is asked to identify each word. Since the purpose is to test the capacity of the distinction to convey meaningful information, the responses may be given as semantic labels rather than spelling labels. For example, in the contrast of *ferry* and *furry*, the speaker may be asked to identify *ferry* as 'boat' and *furry* as 'animal'. However, lower error rates can be achieved by giving

---

[5] It is of course important to relate the pronunciation in minimal pair tests to the larger pattern of speech production, since cell (b) might be filled by an accidental variation between the two pronunciations that had no significance and was not repeated regularly. This is to be checked by repeated application of the minimal pair test with the same and different items, as Step 7 in the minimal pair procedure indicates. The full interpretation of minimal pair results will require the background of a detailed study of contrast between the word classes involved in spontaneous speech. In the reports to follow, any difference in pronunciation that would fill cell (b) or cell (d) in table 12.1 will be related to evidence from spontaneous speech.

subjects a printed list with column entries for both words, and asking them to circle the correct one.

12.3 Near-mergers in the speech community

Until 1972, it was generally assumed that the four-cell table 12.1 had in principle one empty cell, (b). Although it was expected that spoken and judged responses would match, it was understood that not all responses would fall in the symmetrical cells (a) and (d). The influence of spelling sometimes leads to a response in cell (c); speakers often say that *ladder* is different from *latter*, even though they pronounce them alike.[6] However, it was always assumed that cell (b) was empty: if subjects pronounced the two sounds differently, they would judge them to be different. The basis for this assumption – which was more than an assumption, indeed a strong conviction – seems to have been the reasonable belief that speakers could not produce a distinction without having the ability to hear it. The existence of responses in cell (b) violates the implicit corollary of Bloomfield's principle (1), which may be expressed as follows:

(2) If a native speaker cannot discriminate between two sounds, then those sounds will be in free variation in his or her speech.

source *and* sauce *in New York City*

The first indication that (2) did not hold came from an instrumental study of the productions of /oh/ and /ohr/ obtained in New York City during the LYS project. In the preconsonantal position of words like *source*, /r/ is always vocalized to an ingliding shwa. Since the raised tense /oh/ in *sauce* is also ingliding, it was expected that *source* and *sauce* would be indistinguishable unless the /r/ was pronounced as a consonant. For many speakers, pairs like *god* and *guard* might be distinguished by vowel quality, since the nucleus of /ah/ is not as high or as back as the nucleus of /ahr/, opposed as [gɑd] to [gɒːd]. No subject and no investigator had ever suggested that *source* and *sauce* might be opposed by vowel color.[7] But when

---

[6] Such a case arose in my Lower East Side study (Labov 1966), where one speaker reported that he had learned in school not to merge /t/ and /d/ in intervocalic position. "I never paid attention to the rules of grammar until she started teaching to me, and I was so surprised at the way stuff is supposed to be pronounced . . . . She wrote the word *butter* on the board, and she asked me how to pronounce it, and I said [bʌɾɚ]. She told me that was wrong, and that's when I learned to pronounce *t*'s like a *t* – I used to pronounce them as *d*'s all the time." However, the only pronunciation the speaker actually used in these words was a flap (Labov 1966:348). Note that this is not unrelated to the issues raised by Dinnsen (1985) concerning whether the two flaps are neutralized.

[7] The merger is actually assumed rather than reported in Hubbell 1962, Wetmore 1959, and Kurath and McDavid 1961.

the New York City data were analyzed instrumentally in 1969, distinct patterns for the two word classes were repeatedly obtained.

Figure 12.1 shows the measured distributions of /ohr/ and /oh/ in three styles for a lower middle class Jewish speaker. The three diagrams show the positions of the nucleus of *source* and *sauce* in various controlled styles against the background of the pattern of spontaneous speech. The two overlapping ellipses show the distributions of /oh/ and /ohr/ in spontaneous speech: they are typical of the New York City measurements, which show (ohr) tokens extending farther back than (oh) tokens for 19 out of 20 speakers studied and higher for 16 out of 20 (LYS, figure 6.1). Figure 12.1a shows the nuclei of *source* and *sauce* as pronounced in a reading passage designed to juxtapose these two words:

(3) "And what's the source of your information, Joseph?" She used her sweet and sour tone of voice, like ketchup mixed with tomato sauce.

Here *source* is considerably higher than *sauce*. Figure 12.1b shows that in minimal pairs, the height difference disappears, but *source* is distinctly backer. Figure 12.1c displays the tokens of *source* and *sauce* from the following discussion:

(4) HL: [thoughtfully] ... *source* and *sauce* ... [vehemently] Well when you say the *source* of your information you don't mean the *sauce*, tomato *sauce* ... [excitedly] I would *know*, I would know when someone spoke!

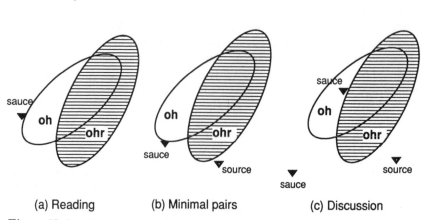

| (a) Reading | (b) Minimal pairs | (c) Discussion |

Figure 12.1.   Relation of /ohr/ to /oh/ in spontaneous speech (ellipses) and treatment of *source* and *sauce* in formal styles for Hazel Lappert, 42, New York City
[1962]

WL: But the *sound* is all I'm interested in . . .
HL: [thoughtfully] The sound is the same.

Again, the nucleus of *source* is well back of the nuclei of *sauce*. Although there is much individual variation and the two distributions overlap considerably, the New York City pattern is pervasive: whenever /r/ is vocalized, the nucleus of *source* is higher and/or farther back than the nucleus of *sauce*. What makes the data all the more surprising is that this distribution is the same one that is found in 100% r-pronouncing regions, even though the New York City vernacular has been consistently r-less for almost two centuries.

This type of response to the *source/sauce* minimal pair test falls in cell (b) of table 12.1. The speaker produces the two tokens with a marked phonetic difference, but judges the vowels to be the same. If this were the only case of its kind, it would certainly be judged a chance fluctuation. But five other cases came to light in rapid succession. Though these cases vary considerably in their consistency and phonetic character, they share the following features:

1 The opposing phonemes are differentiated by a smaller than normal phonetic distance.
2 This difference is most often an F2 difference, instead of a combination of F1 and F2.
3 There is considerable individual variation within the community: some individuals show a near-merger, others a complete merger, and still others a distinction.
4 Speakers who make a consistent difference in spontaneous speech often reduce this difference in more monitored styles.
5 Speakers judge the sounds to be the same in minimal pair tests, and fail commutation tests.
6 Phoneticians from other areas are better able to hear the difference than the native speakers.

LYS coined the term *near-merger* to describe this situation. Of the five other cases discussed in LYS, one concerns the merger of the tense and lax high back vowels before final /l/ in *fool* and *full*, *pool* and *pull*. I first found this merger among the Mexican-American youth in the western section of Salt Lake City, along with mergers of many other contrasts before /l/. It then appeared that the merger of /uw/ and /u/ before /l/ was the most general in the Southwest, overlapping with a merger of /iy/ and /i/ before /l/ that was expanding from a base farther to the east. The factors that govern these mergers in the Southwest are outlined in LYS (pp. 236–7); they have since been investigated in greater detail by Di Paolo in Salt Lake City (1988) and Bailey's research group in Texas (Bailey, Bernstein, and

Tillery, in press). The near-merger aspect first appeared in Albuquerque in 1969 in the speech of Dan Jones.

fool *and* full *in Albuquerque*

I first met Dan Jones in a session with a group of other high school students; their responses to the /uwl/ ~ /ul/ opposition varied considerably. Dan Jones read a list of minimal pairs with *fool* and *full*, *pool* and *pull*: he pronounced them the same and judged them to be the same. I met Dan later that day under more favorable conditions for recording casual speech, along with his girlfriend Didi, 16, and her brother Hal, 18. Figure 12.2a shows the distinction between /uw/ and /u/ that he maintained in his spontaneous speech (the F1/F2 scales are both twice the normal scale, as the distinctions to be studied are quite small). The tense vowel /uw/ is higher and farther back than /u/; *too* and *shoot* are differentiated from *hook* and *good* by both F1 and F2. There is also a distinction between /uwl/ and /ul/, but here only F2 distinguishes the vowels. This contrasts sharply with the results of the minimal pair tests carried out in the morning and the afternoon (figure 12.2b), where Dan judged *fool* and *full*, *pool* and *pull* to be the same; measurements of pronunciation show them to be quite close, with no consistent difference of either F1 or F2 between them. Both minimal pair tests indicate a merger, but speech suggests a distinction.

The commutation test was then introduced. Dan read a list of 20 randomly alternating instances of *fool* and *full*; Didi and Hal judged them as "double-O" or "double-L" words. To Dan these words all sounded the same, even though in reading them, he generally maintained the same difference that was found in his spontaneous speech. In the form of the commutation test used at that time, he was not the judge of his own speech. The judges did not show the same near-merger in their own speech: when Hal and Didi read the list, no one had any difficulty in distinguishing the words. However, they had a great deal of trouble deciding which of Dan's words were "double-O" and which were "double-L," although they were ultimately correct in 83% of their judgments.[8] Since 100% correct is normally the criterion for a passing grade on a commutation test, these results must be considered marginal.

Figure 12.2c shows the positions of the nuclei of the 20 words as Dan pronounced them in the commutation test. Except for one token of *fool*, the two distributions are closely approximated but distinct. Bearing in mind that the scales used here are twice the usual display, it is clear that the phonetic distance between these nuclei is much smaller than for the normal phonemic distinction, and this is reflected in the difficulty that

---

[8] When four Eastern judges (including three well-trained phoneticians) listened to the tape, they did not do as well: their average judgments conformed to the printed text in only 66% of the tokens.

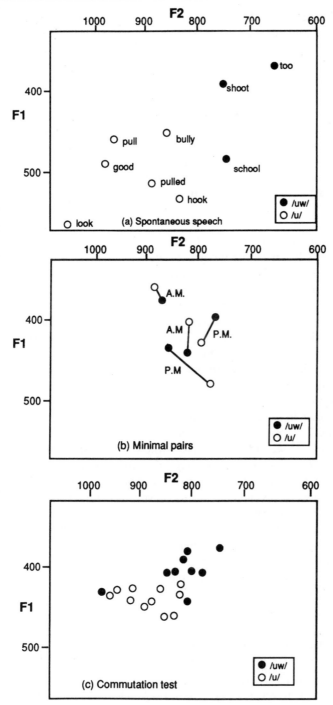

Figure 12.2. The /ul/ ~ /uwl/ contrast in spontaneous speech, minimal pairs and commutation test for Dan Jones, 16, Albuquerque [1971]

both phoneticians and local speakers have in distinguishing them. Though Dan Jones was not one of the judges, he repeatedly asserted that the two sets sounded the same to him. We therefore concluded that:

1 Dan Jones distinguished /uwl/ and /ul/ in everyday speech by differences in F2.
2 He categorized the two vowels as 'the same' in the ____ /l/ context, and on reflection, lost the phonetic differences that he habitually made.
3 He produced only a marginal distinction in a commutation test, which could be distinguished only marginally by others.
4 His close associates made a clearer distinction and could perceive the contrast better than he could.

THE MERGER IN SALT LAKE CITY

Dan Jones's behavior fits the general pattern of near-mergers as just outlined, though it is basically a report on one individual selected from the variety of responses obtained at the Albuquerque high school. As noted earlier, this merger was first observed in Salt Lake City, and was more extensively investigated as a part of the Intermountain Language Survey in Salt Lake City by Di Paolo (1988). High school students and their families were recruited as informants, so that Di Paolo's subjects can be categorized into three generations: the students [Generation 3], their parents [Generation 2], and their grandparents [Generation 1].[9]

In the Vowel Categorization Experiment, subjects first read a table with 10 categories in separate cells, each containing three exemplars of a vowel phoneme. The /uw/ cell contained *moot, hoot, and food*; the /u/ cell contained *could, book,* and *hook*. Subjects then read a list of 39 words, including *cool, full, pool,* and *pull*, and were asked to locate the cell with the vowel that matched that word and write the word in that cell. The subjects showed a general laxing tendency for all vowels before /l/. Table 12.3 shows results of this experiment that pertain to the /uw/ ~ /u/ distinction. The figures in this table show a relation between categorization and pronunciation that appears to be characteristic of near-mergers. In the youngest generation, merger in pronunciation has moved ahead rapidly, particularly among the females. This is a pattern that is also found in studies of the laxing of /uwl/ in Texas (Bailey, Bernstein, and Tillery, in press). But in

[9] Di Paolo and Faber (1990) investigated phonation differences in the /uwl/ and /u/ tokens of the Salt Lake City subjects. Their results may help to explain some of the anomalies in the F1/F2 plots, such as the fact that the isolated token of *fool* to the left of the *full* distribution in figure 12.2c is regularly heard as *fool*. Di Paolo and Faber's figures 9–18 show the F1/F2 positions of the vowel nuclei before /l/ for teenagers: the patterns in these figures are remarkably similar to Dan Jones's system in figure 12.2c, with the /uwl/ and /ul/ classes in close approximation.

the parents' and grandparents' generations, an earlier stage is visible where categorization is in advance of pronunciation. (Whether this reflects the actual temporal ordering of the process, or a later reaction of the older generations, will be illuminated in the more detailed studies of Philadelphia to follow.) But the relations between categorization and pronunciation shown here coincide with the general view of near-mergers. The filling of cell (b) in the minimal pair table 12.1 corresponds to the adult pattern in table 12.3.

cot *and* caught *in Pennsylvania: The Bill Peters effect*

Duncannon is a rural town in central Pennsylvania at the eastern edge of the /o/ ~ /oh/ merger as it expands from Western Pennsylvania. There, in 1970, I interviewed an 80-year-old man of German background named Bill Peters. In his spontaneous speech, Bill Peters showed a clear distinction between /o/ and /oh/; but in minimal pairs, he showed the near-merger of figure 12.3 in low back position, more typical of younger speakers. Apparently, he had unconsciously adopted the incoming merged norm as a guide in the minimal pair test, but not for speech. This is therefore a case of a consistent shift between formal and informal behavior. Herold (1990:182–6) identifies a number of older speakers in the transitional Eastern Pennsylvania towns of Pottsville and Tamaqua who display a similar shift toward the incoming norm in minimal pair tests. Of 5 speakers over 70 interviewed in Tamaqua, all of whom distinguished /o/ and /oh/ clearly and consistently in speech, only one 74-year-old man failed to show the influence of the merged norm in minimal pair tests. For example, 75-year-old Mrs. V. produced and perceived a substantial difference between /o/ and /oh/ in 5 out of 6 pairs, but hesitated in the case of cot and caught, first saying that they sounded the same, then changing her mind; in the case of Don and Dawn, she produced an almost indistinguishable pair that she evaluated as "slightly different." Thus the "Bill Peters effect" is quite

Table 12.3 Categorization and pronunciation of /uwl/ in Salt Lake City by age and sex (Di Paolo 1988, table 4). % responses other than /uw/ for *cool, school, pool*

	Generation 3		Generation 2		Generation 1	
	Male	*Female*	*Male*	*Female*	*Male*	*Female*
Categorization	20	27	17	17	8	27
Pronunciation	20	47	0	8	0	0
N	15	15	12	12	12	15

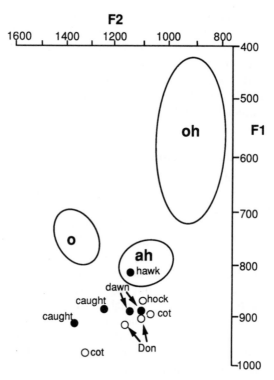

Figure 12.3.   /o/ and /oh/ in spontaneous speech and minimal pairs of Bill Peters, 80, Duncannon, Pennsylvania [1971]

general, and not dissimilar to the behavior of the adults in Salt Lake City in regard to *fool* and *full*.[10]

Near-mergers in Norwich

THE CASE OF *TOO* AND *TOE*

Since Trudgill's (1974a) comprehensive report on the speech community of Norwich, its vowel system and those of surrounding communities in Norfolk have yielded a number of important discoveries concerning sound change and dialect contact. In chapter 6, Norwich was used to exemplify a Pattern 3 shift that is quite distinct from the Pattern 1 shift of London (figures 6.19–6.21). The fronting of ME ō in *too*, *root*, etc., follows the path of many other southern English dialects: both the nucleus and glide

---

[10] It should be pointed out that Bill Peters is somewhat more consistent than these other speakers in two respects: he never hesitated in saying that the pairs were the same, and the two sets of tokens show a consistent but narrow differentiation. His speech therefore represents a clearer case of a near-merger than the more varied instances registered by Herold.

are front rounded vowels. In addition, the vowel of ME 5 in *so, stone, toe,* etc., is raised to [u:] in the conservative dialect. LYS reports that this nucleus is also fronted, though the glide keeps its high back target. Among the speakers I interviewed in Norwich in 1970 were two 14-year-old boys, David Branson, whose spontaneous speech pattern is shown in figure 6.21, and his close friend Keith. As David read a word list, the nuclei of the ME ō and 5 classes were in close approximation, although the glides went in opposite directions (figure 12.4a). The words *too* and *toe* were used in a commutation test with one boy as speaker, the other as listener. Keith

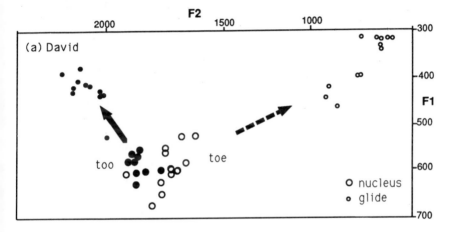

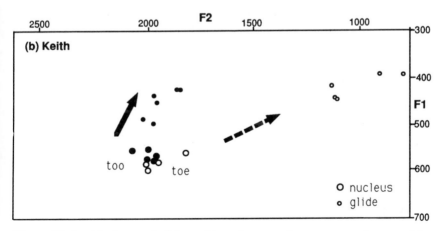

Figure 12.4. Nucleus and glide positions for *too* and *toe* commutation test, (a) as pronounced by David Branson, 14, Norwich, England [1971], (b) as pronounced by Keith, 14, Norwich, England [1971]

could not hear the distinction at all in David's speech, though it was pre-served in his own speech as well as in David's. David had no trouble in correctly naming each item produced by Keith as T-O-E or T-O-O, though the directions of the glides were not so sharply opposed in Keith's speech as in his own (figure 12.4b).

It is not merely the mistakes that Keith made that are important here: rather it is the total confusion that he showed in reacting to this test. His errors were concentrated on those items where the nuclei were closest; he was apparently trying to hear a difference in the position of the nucleus, and had not learned to listen to the direction and endpoint of the glides. This is all the more unexpected because his own productions are differen-tiated only by the glides. Keith thus demonstrates that a speaker can reliably produce a distinction without being able to hear it – or at least without being aware that he hears it. In some sense, Keith must have "heard" the distinction when he was learning the language, even if he could not turn his attention to it at the age of 14. At some level of unreflecting perception, he must have been monitoring his own production, but there is not the least doubt that he had come to the conclusion that the *toe* class and the *too* class were 'the same' in the linguistic sense. He was therefore unable to identify and label the two phonemes on the basis of the regular difference in the sound pattern, a difference that is found regularly in the speech of his best friend as well as his own.

The alternation between a focus on the nucleus and a focus on the glide is not unrelated to the stylistic shifts that take place as the speakers pay more and more attention to speech. As David focuses more and more sharply on the pronunciation of these vowels, the F1/F2 positions of the nuclei come closer and closer together. His *go* moves forward from an F2 of nearly 1400 Hz in speech to an F2 of 1750 Hz in the word lists. This is exactly the position of *toe* in the commutation test of figure 12.4a. Both David and Keith show the glide as the distinctive feature separating /uw/ and /ow/, and the position of the nucleus as the redundant feature. But since nucleus position is used to distinguish most other vowel pairs, it is possible that Keith was influenced to turn his attention to this feature to distinguish these vowels as well, with the resultant failure.

THE CASE OF *BEER* AND *BEAR*

In evaluating the evidence for the near-merger of *too* and *toe*, Trudgill notes that the word classes of *beer* and *bear* provide another example. All except the oldest Norwich informants regard these two word classes as identical (Trudgill 1974a), and dialect poetry rhymes the two:

Ah, more'n once I'a stopped there jus' to hear
Their lovely songs that fill the evenin' air.

However, actual productions of the /ihr/ and /ehr/ classes are quite different for all but the youngest generation of speakers. Older speakers show clear differences between the two phonemes. In this case, the distinction is characteristic of casual speech and tends to disappear in minimal pair tests, as Trudgill's figure 4.2 shows. The situation resembles that of Dan Jones in Albuquerque rather than that of Bill Peters in Duncannon, where a very narrow distinction is maintained in minimal pairs. If commutation tests were carried out for *beer* and *bear* in Norwich, we might indeed find the same near-merger as in Albuquerque or New York.

12.4 Resistance to the concept of near-merger

The cases of near-merger that have been considered so far are drawn from experiments carried out in the course of fieldwork in the speech community. The largest body of data cited stems from the New York City study, where 20 speakers were examined, but the most clear-cut instances are drawn from the behavior of single individuals in different communities (Dan Jones, Albuquerque; Bill Peters, Duncannon; David Branson, Norwich). Supporting evidence is contributed by the community studies of Di Paolo in Salt Lake City, Herold in Eastern Pennsylvania, and Trudgill in Norwich, but these do not provide for each speaker the clear disjunction between production and perception that defines the near-mergers for the three individuals just mentioned. Chapter 13 will take up the two cases of possible near-merger in the historical records that were first discussed in LYS, along with further evidence of near-mergers in the corresponding modern dialects and conclusive findings from the work of Harris and Milroy in modern-day Ireland that close the circle of the argument from present to past to present. Chapter 14 will pursue the issues more systematically by experimental methods, with the goal of resolving the paradoxical finding that speakers produce distinctions they do not seem to be able to perceive.

There is no doubt that the first observations on near-merger were considered paradoxical by those who heard them. At a number of oral presentations of the data, linguists and phoneticians rose to express their disbelief in the phenomenon, despite the wide range of data and the steady accumulation of evidence for it. Although it is true that every community that shows near-mergers also shows wide individual variation, the individuals who display the phenomenon are not difficult to find. In chapter 14, we will see that a community that has an opposition of this kind in the phonological system includes roughly equal numbers of speakers who preserve a distinction, speakers who have abandoned it, and speakers who display near-mergers.

How then can we account for the fact that near-mergers have not been reported before, and that linguists find it difficult to accept their existence? It is evident that the existence of a near-merger is inconsistent with four components of the categorical view outlined in section 12.1. In these cases of near-merger, it is not possible to maintain the binary opposition of membership described in point 3. In contravention of point 4, near-mergers demonstrate that there is such a thing as a small difference of sound. The existence of near-mergers also calls into question point 5, the symmetry of production and perception, and illustrates the great difficulties of evaluating introspections, despite the views outlined in point 6.

The most difficult problem raised by near-mergers is that from the productive viewpoint, there are two categories; from the perceptual viewpoint, only one. This is not merely a problem of description or nomenclature. How does a person learn to articulate each member of one category in one way, and each member of the other category in another way, if he or she cannot recognize the difference between the categories? This is a substantive issue of some weight.

There is a point of view commonly held in current linguistics that a theoretical framework is to be valued more highly than the facts that support it, based on the argument that a simple, clear theory that is contradicted by certain reported facts will ultimately prove to be right when such facts are investigated more carefully. It is also maintained that all facts are theoretical constructs and that observations can only be made within a theoretical framework. It is possible to find cases in the history of science that support this argument. But the opposite strategy seems to me more appropriate for the present state of linguistics, one that values above all the stubborn facts that resist explanation by any available theory. This study of linguistic change reports a number of such facts – repeated observations that were made in spite of all expectations to the contrary.[11] The development of the general principles in this volume is the result of a repeated series of inferences from resistant facts of this type. It seems to me that they provide the most powerful stimulus to the development of new methods and insights into the operation of the world around us.

The case of "near-merger" provides the most dramatic example of how a theoretical framework can prevent the recognition of facts. On June 23, 1977, I received a letter from David de Camp, two years before his death

---

[11] The framework in which these observations are embedded is the practice of reporting our impressions of objects and events with as little reliance on memory and intuition as possible. In the case of linguistics, the simplest observations can be fairly complex: speech sounds and the native speaker's interpretations of them. But when they are recorded immediately, by instruments or in writing, they are remarkably reliable and robust. The theoretical biases that interfere with such observations take effect primarily when time elapses between observation and recording, through a naive reliance on memory and introspection. These procedures for observation are a commonplace of the experimental method, as practiced in many fields, but they have only recently been applied to the study of spontaneous speech.

in 1979. It began with a reference to my 1975 article, "On the Use of the Present to Explain the Past," which was a first attempt to resolve the paradoxes presented in chapters 10 and 11 with data on modern near-mergers. De Camp said that he had wrestled with the problem of *meat* and *mate* as a graduate student and had met with no success, even though the key to the solution was "literally under my nose: right on top of my desk, as a matter of fact." He then explained what he meant by this:

This spring I had occasion to reread your paper, this time more thoroughly and really digested your pp. 840–849 (Current re-evaluation of speaker reports) which hold the key to your solution, and suddenly I was carried back to June of 1953 and my desperate attempts to defend a dissertation involving precisely this issue. In my study of San Francisco phonology, my sampling techniques (like those of everyone in 1951) were hardly sophisticated and no portable tape recorders were available, but at least I was confident of my phonetics. I had just spent two years doing a lot of raw transcription, checking it with that of other transcribers and against my subsequent retranscription of phonograph records. That is, I was sure until the whole linguistic establishment of Berkeley landed on me in the defense examination.

The trouble was that I followed up my interviews with a perception pair test, and all four mathematical possibilities showed up: people who could hear and produce a contrast, people who could neither hear nor produce, people who could hear but not produce, and even people who could produce but not hear. My examining committee, supplemented by several other linguists who came along for the fun, grudgingly allowed that the third possibility just might, though probably wouldn't occur, but insisted that the fourth was flat impossible. They insisted that I had just mistranscribed the data. For a fleeting moment I considered bringing one of my San Francisco speakers into the lab at Berkeley where Y.R. Chao had an early-model Kay Sonograph, but I abandoned the idea, thinking that the committee members wouldn't be convinced anyway – and I probably was right. Well, I got the dissertation accepted by hedging the point with lots of might's and it seems's, and perhaps's, and in the portion I published, I toned this point down and even marked it with a self-defensively apologetic exclamation point. I don't think I've ever given you a copy, but I now think you might be interested in it, just as a chapter in history, especially the treatment of this problem (pp. 62–63).

For all practical purposes, however, your claim still holds that it had "not been reported before . . . that . . . speakers can report two sounds as 'the same' even though they regularly make the distinction in their own natural language," for I was indeed intimidated by such adamant resistance from the entire linguistic establishment, began to doubt the accuracy of my own ears, and certainly did not see the relevance to the problem of *mate/meat* which was also worrying me at just that same time. And so years later, when tape recorders and Sonographs had become common and when rigid structuralist theories (both Tragerian and Hallean) had relaxed so that such theoretically unacceptable facts could at least be reported, the curious San Francisco data were deeply repressed and locked away until even the first quick reading of your paper a few years ago didn't recall them to memory. Obviously there is no moral for our profession in all this, for modern theorists, when confronted by a discrepancy between their theory and the data, would all unhesitatingly question the theory rather than the data, wouldn't they? Wouldn't they?

13

The Explanation of Unmergings

This chapter will apply the observations of chapter 12 on near-merger to resolve the paradoxical situations introduced in chapters 10 and 11. The phenomenon labeled *near-merger* is not yet fully understood; indeed, it is not at all clear how speakers can maintain a distinction without being able to perceive it. We are therefore in the odd position of resolving a reported historical paradox by means of a present-day behavior that is paradoxical in itself. Nevertheless, we will plunge into the reexamination of the past with the expectation that further study of the present will clarify what is happening – an expectation that chapter 14 will attempt to satisfy.

13.1   The apparent merger of *line* and *loin*

The problem of the unmerging of /ay/ and /oy/ in the 18th century was developed in chapter 10. Chapter 11 established the principle of the irreversibility of merger with enough certainty to make this unmerger difficult to accept as it was first presented in chapter 10. The term *falsely reported merger* was used to describe this phenomenon in LYS on the basis of the eventual outcome – the reseparation of /ay/ and /oy/. Yet the phenomenon of near-merger presented in chapter 12 shows that such reports of merger can be quite consistent and genuine, in that they reflect a true inability of native speakers to perceive the physical differences between the two word classes involved. There is much more to be said about the apparent merger and unmerger of *line* and *loin* in light of this richer view of phonological possibilities. We will first look at Nunberg's reexamination of the historical evidence in light of the richer view of phonological possibilities derived from the study of modern near-mergers – a paradigmatic case of using present information to explain the past.[1] We will then return to the present to find a direct continuation of that earlier situation in a current dialect, and so illuminate both the present and the past by their similarities.

---

[1] Nunberg's first analysis of the data was presented as an appendix to LYS. A more detailed presentation was published as Nunberg 1980, and the discussion to follow is based on that material.

Finally, we will reexamine the impossible unmerging of *meat* and *mate* in 16th-century London, applying new data from current continuations of that many-sided phenomenon.

Nunberg's reanalysis of the reported merger

Nunberg began the study of *line* and *loin* with the benefit of LYS data on near-mergers in modern dialects, and applied this information to interpret the results of his quantitative examination of all available evidence (1980). A summary of his analysis will be the first step in our effort to resolve the apparent contradictions in the historical record.

The word classes that make up the modern phonemes /ay/ and /oy/ have very different histories. /ay/ is almost entirely the reflex of ME ī. The origins of that class, and its consistent development over time, will be presented in some detail in chapter 17. As noted in chapter 10, /oy/ is largely the product of French borrowings, ultimately derived from (a) Latin au + i, as in *joy, cloister,* (b) Latin ŏ + i, as in *oil, oyster,* (c) Latin ō or ŭ + i, as in *moist, point,* (d) Late French oi, as in *royal, loyal,* and (e) various obscure sources, as in *boy, toy.* As a result of this history, /oy/ appears only before apical consonants, and never before labials or velars.

Throughout Middle English, words of this class appear with both high and mid nuclei, spelled with **o** or **u**. Nunberg argues convincingly that a phonetic realization of [oi] or [ui] depends more on the phonetic environment than on etymology, so that I will refer, not to two phonemes /oy/ and /uy/, but to a single /oy/ phoneme with high and mid allophones.

In the middle of the 17th century, the [ui] allophones fell to a mid non-peripheral position, in parallel with the movement of the nucleus of ME ū as it fell along the path outlined in chapter 6. It was at this point that the phonetic realizations of /oy/ came into close approximation with the phonetic realizations of ME ī on its way to becoming the phoneme /ay/. To trace this process over time, Nunberg (1980) tabulated the testimony of 19 sources from Hart in 1569 to Adams in 1799 for 24 /oy/ words. The result is an array of almost 200 citations, which are categorized as showing for /oy/ the nucleus **u, o, i** (identical with the ME ī reflexes) or ə (central, but not identical with ME ī).

Nunberg's first analysis of these data concerned the 6 sources of the precentralization period, from 1569 to 1653, where only **u** and **o** appear as the nuclei of the diphthong. Table 13.1 shows the phonetic factors that favor the appearance of [u]. The first effect is consistent with phonetic measurements of modern dialects. Following nasal consonants are regularly associated with lower F1, and historical developments show that following nasals favor raising (Eckert 1980:191). The effect of a preceding labial is also consistent with the later development of /u/: lowering and unrounding rarely occurred in this environment. The higher proportion of [ui] before /l/ is not typical of modern dialects, and suggests a clearer final

Table 13.1 Effects of phonetic environment on height of the /oy/ nucleus in the precentralization period

Environment	Number of citations	Proportion of [ui]
__n(t)	15	.76
p,b__	16	.53
__l	14	.50
Elsewhere	18	.14

allophone of /l/ than in the modern period. The "Elsewhere" class includes final position, which strongly disfavors the [u] nucleus.

Nunberg's next step was to include the data of the centralization period, from 1687 to 1799, when the reports of the merger predominated. A joint study of the centralized and noncentralized citations led Nunberg to refine the phonetic categories given in table 13.1, producing the comparison shown in table 13.2 between the proportions of [ui] in the precentralization period and the proportions of [əi] in the centralization period. The word *boy* was differentiated from other labials since free position strongly disfavors both height and centralization, and initial palatal affricate **j** was removed from the "Elsewhere" condition since it favors centralization more than the other environments. The result is a remarkable correlation of .99 between the two indices.

Nunberg's analysis thus shows that the centralization that led to the reported merger of the /ay/ and /oy/ class did not affect all allophones equally. Instead, it affected nuclei that were heard by the phoneticians,

Table 13.2 Effects of phonetic environment on height and centralization

Environment	Precentralization period, 1569–1653		Centralization period, 1687–1799	
	Proportion of [ui]	N	Proportion of [əi]	N
__nt	.88	13	.82	18
__n	.58	7	.58	17
__l	.50	14	.57	48
p,b__ *	.63	12	.64	35
Elsewhere**	.04	11	.06	18

$r = .99$
*Excluding *boy*
**Excluding j__

orthoepists, and grammarians of the day as a form of [u]. It is not immediately clear why these nuclei should have been identified with the [əi] stage of ME ī as it descended to mid position, since [ui] is farther away from [əi] than [oi]. But it appears that this identification was a matter of perception rather than production. Garde's Principle of the irreversibility of merger leads us to believe that if /oy/ and /ay/ were distinct in later development, they were never totally merged in their physical distributions. The reseparation or "unmerging" was remarkably complete. Three words switched from /ay/ to /oy/: *boil* 'tumor', from OE *byl*; *groin*, from OE *grunde*; and *joist*, from OF *giste*. It may be noted that these all show favorable environments for the raising and centralization noted in table 13.2, and *boil* contains two such environments. Furthermore, Nunberg points out that these are all 16th-century conversions, which preceded the centralization of /oy/. In the other direction, *eyelet* moved to /ay/ from /oy/; this is derived from OF *oilet* by the route of an obvious folk etymology.

The final step in Nunberg's analysis dealt only with the retreat of centralization, manifested in a subset of 7 sources from 1755 to 1799. During this period, the 24 /oy/ words split sharply into two groups:

A: *point, appoint, joint, join, boil, broil, spoil*
B: *coin, loin, foil, oil, toil, joist, poison, boy, joy, toy, oyster, noise, voice, void, loyal, voyage*

Group A includes the two most favoring environments of table 13.2. For this group, there are only 2 citations with [o], for *broil* and *spoil*, both from Rudd in 1755, the first source in the series. The next three sources yield 6 simple identifications with the ME ī class. The rest of the citations alternate between identification with ME ī and identification with /oy/. In addition, a new feature appears: the "long **i**" pronunciation is stigmatized as "vulgar." There are 10 such citations.

The situation with Group B is altogether different. There are 17 citations that indicate an [o] nucleus, and only 3 that indicate a stigmatized alternation with "long **i**." These are *oil*, *toil*, and *poison*, all items with favoring environments.

The history of the /ay/–/oy/ "unmerging," as unraveled by Nunberg, appears to have followed a complex path through social, phonetic, and etymological domains. The approximation of certain /ay/ and /oy/ allophones appears to have been the result of sound changes affecting all branches of society, and proceeded in its early stages without social evaluation. The reseparation began as "long **i**" pronunciations of /oy/ words rose in social awareness. They were then stigmatized as characteristic of the working class, and the upper and middle class retreated from these phonetic forms. Reviewing the noted statement by Kenrick quoted in chapter 10, we can see that the observer analyzed the problem from a structural viewpoint ("converting both into the sound of *i* or *y*"), yet it was perceived as a lexical migration rather than a general merger ("there are some words so written, which by long use, have almost lost their true sound"). Throughout this development, two distinct pronunciations of the /oy/ class were observed, and only one of them was identified with "long **i**." If all words had alternated, then the restitution of the class would not be hard to understand. But as a rule, it was the original high allophone that was identified with "long **i**." This was a variable rule, with many elements of the phonetic pattern favoring or disfavoring centralization. But it had the effect of separating the vocabulary into two groups of words, and if the centralized forms had actually been identified with the **ī** reflexes, one of these groups would have been permanently merged into the /ay/ class.

We then return to the central problem of chapter 10: how can we explain the fact that a permanent merger did not occur? It seems likely that the path traced by the nuclei of the higher allophones of /oy/ is the same path that we inferred for ME **ū** in the course of the Great Vowel Shift, by analogy with the modern developments of chapter 6 (figures 6.3, 6.21). It begins of course with a lax nucleus, not [u] but [ʊ], and follows the back nonperipheral path downward. Though modern philologists tend to interpret orthographical **u** as [ə], this is because their conception of phonological space has been limited to three degrees of fronting and backing: front, central, and back. Once we recognize the existence of the back nonperipheral track, the behavior of these allophones of /oy/ is quite predictable. That is not to say that the lowering of the nucleus here is a simple continuation of the Great Vowel Shift as a whole; it occurred at least a century after the diphthongization was essentially complete. However, the lowering of the [ʊ] nucleus continued steadily over a much longer period of time, and in many modern dialects it has not yet descended to [a]. It is therefore quite likely that speakers of southern English dialects identified the nucleus of the higher allophones of /oy/ with the nucleus diphthong that proceeded from ME **ū**. Such identification is not a conscious process, but it is common enough in modern dialects. It can be observed in Philadelphia, where /ʌ/ has begun to shift up and to the back, following the path of the centralized nucleus of /ay/ before voiceless consonants (see figure 3.6).

This inference about the trajectory of the [ui] allophones of /oy/ is more than a speculation. The overwhelming evidence of table 13.2 shows that these allophones moved from a high position to a mid position more centralized than the [oi] allophones. We can add to this conclusion the two facts of chapter 10: that /ay/ and /oy/ were widely reported as merged and that the merger did not actually take place. From these three observations, it seems clear that the reflexes of ME **ī** and the originally high allophones of /oy/ were in the same kind of close approximation that we have observed for /oh/ and /ohr/ in New York City.

Figure 13.1 reconstructs this history in a two-dimensional acoustic

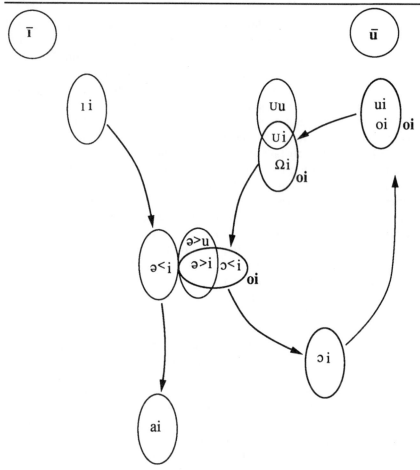

Figure 13.1.   Path of /oy/ allophones

space. It shows the high allophones of /oy/ following the path of the lax nucleus of ME ū in the Great Vowel Shift to a point where they closely approximated the descending ME ī. At this stage, they were still distinct in production from the /ay/ tokens, but so close that they were judged as 'the same' by most observers. In further developments, the nucleus of /ay/ continued to descend, and the nuclei of the centralized /oy/ allophones shifted back to merge with the other members of this class. Eventually, the nucleus of /oy/ became peripheral, and rose to upper mid and high position in many southern English and American dialects.

13.2   The near-merger of *line* and *loin* in Essex

The preceding argument follows the basic strategy of this volume in resolving paradoxes of the past by invoking further evidence from the present. Yet so far, the inferences are made from some distance. The evidence of near-mergers presented in chapter 12 comes from other variables in other dialect regions, far from the time and place where the merger of *line* and *loin* occurred. This evidence is persuasive because it deals with general principles of vowel movement and general principles of phonology. The most convincing data, however, would be actual recordings from the 18th century, which could be analyzed with current, instrumental techniques with their greater sensitivity to the front-back dimension. Such measurements might show that the physical realizations of /ay/ and /oy/ were indeed distinct, even while they were judged to be the same by Cooper, Jones, and Kenrick. Though these data are out of our reach, we can approximate them by examining the modern continuation of the merger in the dialects of present-day England. These can be found in the county of Essex, in southern England (figure 13.2), where Orton and Dieth's *Survey of English Dialects* (1962–67) (SED) shows a continuing merger of /ay/ and /oy/.[2]

To evaluate these data, we must first recognize the limits of the phonetic transcription used by the SED. The published records use a fairly narrow IPA transcription as far as the dimension of height is concerned. There are five alphabetic variants for vowel height, and each can be modified by diacritics for tongue raising [ə̝] or lowering [ə̞], which gives 15 possible levels of height. There are three alphabetic notations along the front-back dimension, with diacritics for advancement [ə̟] or retraction [ə̠]. But this second pair of diacritics is rarely used. For example, 16 out of 85 transcriptions for the word *core* in the East Midlands show vowel diacritics for raising or lowering, but none show diacritics for fronting or backing. The word *boil* shows 4 diacritics for raising or lowering, but none for fronting or backing. Occasionally, the backing symbol is used for the low central vowel [a̠], but it is not found with any vowels moving through the paths recognized here as nonperipheral. It is more common for the SED data to show a centralizing diacritic such as [ä] (the IPA notation that indicates coincidence with central position, aligned with [ə]), but not smaller degrees of fronting or backing. In short, the SED, like most dialect atlases, recognizes only three degrees of fronting and backing. It cannot reasonably be expected to register the close approximations and distinctions studied in chapter 12.

---

[2] In the discussion to follow, I will refer to the two word classes as /ay/ and /oy/, indicating the phonemes that are said to have merged in the 18th century and in Essex, but are now distinct in other dialects of England and America.

Figure 13.2. Eastern localities of the *Survey of English Dialects* (Orton and Dieth 1962–67)

This limitation is not arbitrary; it appears to represent real limitations on human ability to label degrees of fronting and backing. For intact linguistic signals, this limitation appears to be more severe than with the difference limen experimentally established with steady-state formants, where subjects can distinguish differences as small as 75 or 100 Hz for F2 (Flanagan 1955). The data of chapter 12 indicate that tokens that are separated by F2 differences of less than 200 Hz are most likely to be heard as 'the same'. Chapter 14 will provide more systematic information on this point.

In the SED records, we can examine the realizations of 30 words of the ME ī class, which are members of the /ay/ phoneme in most other dialects, and 8 words that fall into the /oy/ class (table 13.3). Thirteen of the /ay/ items are in morphemes ending in a voiceless consonant, 12 are before a voiced consonant, and 5 are in morphemes with free vowels or before

Table 13.3 SED words representing the /ay/ and /oy/ phonemes in most southern English dialects

/ay/			/oy/
_C^0	_C^v	_$C\#$	
knife	ivory	fly	poison
hayknife	hive	eyes	deadly poison
fight	died	bos-eyed	very poisonous
white	hide	eyebrows	oil
whitish	spider	dandelion	boil
height	blind		boiling
light	tire		boiled
lights	tires		groined
firelighting	fire		
righthanded	fireshovel		
scythe	iron		
slice	style		
dike			

hiatus. The 8 /oy/ words represent a more limited range of environments, and give us a reasonably close comparison only for words before /z/, /l/, and /n/.

Within the limitations of the SED notation, we find a complete merger of these two classes in Essex. Figure 13.2 shows the localities studied by the SED investigators in Essex and surrounding areas. The easternmost community in Essex and the most isolated is Tillingham (No. 13 on figure 13.2). In Tillingham, all words are recorded as [ɔɪ]. The same basic situation is reported for most of Essex. It is best illustrated by the contrast of *oil* (Orton and Dieth 1962–67:V.2.13) and *boil* (VI.11.6) with *stile* (IV.2.9), which includes combinations shown in table 13.4.

Localities 1 and 8 on the east show the standard distinction where the /oy/ class is differentiated by height, backing, and rounding, but Localities 6, 7, 12, and 15 on the north and west show a smaller distinction where

Table 13.4 SED transcriptions for ME ī before /l/ in Essex

	Distinction		Merger
stile	[aɪ]	[ɔ̆ɪ]	[ɔɪ]
oil, boil	[ɔɪ]	[ɔɪ]	[ɔɪ]

only backing is involved ([ɜ] indicates a fully centralized rounded mid nucleus). In the nine other communities /ay/ and /oy/ are fully merged.

For all the words listed in table 13.3, Locality 1 shows a stable distinction, but others show considerable variation.[3] For example, when we contrast *flies* and *eyes* with *poisonous*, we find that Localities 12 and 15 generally show a centralized [ɜɪ] for /ay/ and /oy/ while 6 and 7 continue to distinguish /ay/ as centralized and /oy/ as back. Locality 8 varies in this respect. A certain amount of fluctuation in impressionistic transcription is to be expected. But for Localities 2, 3, 4, 5 in the north, 14 in the south, and 13 in the east, we find consistent [ɔɪ] for both /ay/ and /oy/. In these areas, the 18th-century merger appears to have been continued with little variation.

I was able to listen to a tape recording of one of the SED subjects who showed this reported merger of /ay/ and /oy/.[4] Spectrograms for the few tokens of /ay/ on the tape did not appear to be in the same area of phonological space as /oy/. Instead, they were shifted slightly toward the center. Since /oy/ regularly appears as the most peripheral element in the back vowels, this situation suggested the possibility that /oy/ and /ay/ formed a peripheral/nonperipheral pair similar to *source* and *sauce* in New York City and *fool* and *full* in Albuquerque.

Spontaneous speech and minimal pairs

In the summer of 1971, I visited the village of Tillingham, among the most consistently merged of those reported. At that time, I interviewed three speakers: Jack Cant, 87, a retired farm laborer, and the brother of one of the SED informants; Leonard Raven, 70, a retired farm bailiff; and Mrs. Leonard Raven, 69, a housewife and former domestic worker. All three speakers came from Tillingham families. Though Mrs. Raven had worked in London for a number of years, Mr. Raven showed more effect of the standard language than his wife in shifting away from the vernacular forms. As in all sociolinguistic interviews, the major sections devoted to spontaneous speech were designed to approach vernacular style as closely as possible. In view of the rarity of /oy/ forms, I tried to elicit as many words in this class as possible. The interview with the Ravens was a family conversation, with considerable interaction; here I managed to elicit the pairs *voice/vice* and *loin/line*, before any discussion of language arose. I then asked

---

[3] Personal isoglosses between field-workers could not have been responsible for these differences, since the divisions just mentioned do not correspond to the allocation of communities to field-workers. The transcriptions for Localities 1 and 5 were done by Ellis, 7 and 15 by Barry, 11 and 12 by Wright, and the rest by Berntsen.

[4] I am indebted to Howard Berntsen for making this recording available, and for pointing out the nature of the problem.

directly whether these pairs were the same or different. They were 'the same' for Jack Cant and Mrs. Raven, and 'different' for Mr. Raven.

The left-hand portion of figure 13.3 outlines the vowel system of Jack Cant in spontaneous speech, with individual tokens of /oy/ and /ay/ displayed. It shows the Pattern 4 chain shift of /ey/, /ay/, and /oy/ in a form not dissimilar to that of London and Norwich. /uw/ has moved to high front position, and /ey/ has fallen to low central position. /ay/ has shifted to lower mid back position, as usual, and /oy/ is higher, as we would expect, ranging from mid to high back position. A few tokens of /oy/ are close to /ay/, but there is no more overlap than we would expect from any neighboring phonemes. One token of /ay/ is higher and more central, and overlaps the /oy/ range in height. This is the word *die*; it occupies the same position as the word *die* that was measured in the original SED recording.

The right-hand portion of figure 13.3 displays the /ay/ and /oy/ pronunciations of Jack Cant in minimal pair questions. These are closer together than in the spontaneous speech pattern, but again they are distinguished by height. The relationship here would have to be described as close approximation. Jack Cant appears to show the "Bill Peters effect," in that the norm of most conscious styles brings the two phonemes so close together that they sound the same. In these minimal pair tests, he declared all these words to be 'the same'.

Figure 13.4a shows the /ay/ and /oy/ tokens for Mrs. Raven, and figure 13.4b those for Mr. Raven. Though Mrs. Raven hears *line* and *loin* as 'the same' and Mr. Raven hears the two words as 'different', they show the

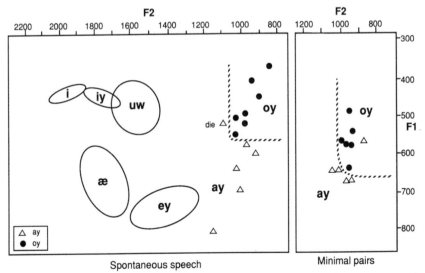

Figure 13.3. /ay/ and /oy/ vowels of Jack Cant in spontaneous speech and minimal pairs

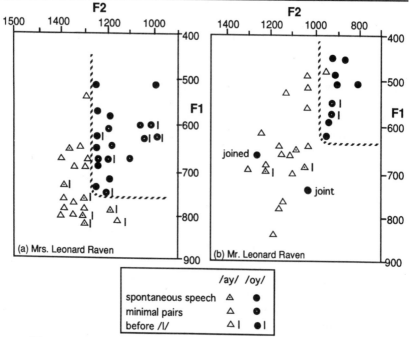

Figure 13.4.   /ay/ and /oy/ vowels of Mr. and Mrs. Leonard Raven

same distributions in spontaneous speech and minimal pairs. For both husband and wife, /ay/ is lower and/or less peripheral than /oy/. Words ending in /l/ are more peripheral for both speakers, but the same relations hold between /ayl/ and /oyl/ as with other allophones. Though some of Mrs. Raven's /ay/ tokens are as high as /oy/, these are clearly less peripheral; and though some /ay/ tokens are as peripheral as /oy/, these are clearly lower. There is no difficulty in drawing a boundary between the two sets.

In Mr. Raven's system, one /oy/ item has crossed over into the /ay/ class – the stem *join-*, mentioned by Kenrick (in the quotation of 1773 given in chapter 10) as one of the items that had to be accepted with /ay/ in the 18th century. Otherwise, we can draw a clear boundary between the two classes: basically a separation of [+peripheral] from [–peripheral]. Although the entire vowel systems of Mr. and Mrs. Raven are not shown here, they have the same overall organization as the system of Jack Cant in figure 13.3. This difference in peripherality is not a distinction between back and central vowels: the /ay/ words are in the back region, by no means equivalent to a central [ɜɪ]. In one IPA notation, they would be [ɒɪ]. Again, minimal pairs are closer together than the forms used in connected speech. It is understandable that these small differences may have escaped the dialectologist, who notes down the pronunciation of isolated words as delivered in relatively slow style. /ay/ and /oy/ are closely approximated, and differ along a dimension that is not usually registered by the impressionistic notation used.

Commutation tests

In the summer of 1972, I returned to Tillingham and met again with the three speakers I had interviewed the year before. I brought with me a commutation test prepared from the spontaneous speech of Jack Cant. Items 1–10 randomly alternated two of his pronunciations of *line* and *loin* in spontaneous, unreflecting speech, shown as the shaded tokens on the left-hand side of figure 13.3. Though they were selected as the most closely approximated tokens in spontaneous speech, they are clearly different in height. Items 11–20 alternated tokens of *loin* and *line* from speech where Jack Cant was consciously reflecting on whether these words were 'the same' or 'different'. These tokens display the usual small differences found in the minimal pair test.[5]

None of the three subjects passed the commutation test. Jack Cant, who originally rated *line* and *loin* as 'the same', gradually began to feel that there was a small difference between them. His comment demonstrates that native speakers naturally contradict Bloomfield's dictum that there are no small differences of sound in language: "There is a little difference but sometime they seem to be both the same." But Jack Cant was unable to identify his own productions of *loin* and *line*: his actual score was below chance, misidentifying the tokens 60% of the time. In further discussions, he reacted to *voice* and *vice* as 'the same', and insisted that there was no possible difference between *file* and *foil*. Mrs. Raven had the greatest degree of success in identifying Jack Cant's *line* and *loin*, though she had originally judged her own pronunciation as 'the same'. Her first 10 responses were all correct, though with some hesitations and revisions. The mistakes were concentrated in the second 10 items, where the tokens were spaced more closely. Mr. Raven, who originally thought that *line* and *loin* were different, had much less success in hearing the difference.[6]

During the discussion that followed, Mr. and Mrs. Raven both came to the conclusion that there was a difference between *line* and *loin* in the test tokens, and that it occurred in their own pronunciation as well. Mr. Raven, in particular, was able to exaggerate his natural pronunciation when reflecting on the difference.

---

[5] The tokens used for the commutation test differed along the F1 dimension only: In the first 10 items, the /ay/ items used had F1 values of 645 Hz and 605 Hz, while the /oy/ items had F1 values of 510 Hz and 575 Hz. For the second 10 items, the /ay/ token had an F1 of 685 Hz, and the /oy/ token an F1 of 575 Hz.

[6] The different results between Mr. and Mrs. Raven may be due to hearing problems. Mr. Raven is hard of hearing; his wife is not. Of course, hearing problems cannot be responsible for the general phenomenon of near-merger, since most of the cases cited earlier are from adolescent subjects.

(1) When you try to sound that L-O-I-N (lo̲:ɪn] I think people try to
     put that *o* in, more than they would if they just said [lʌɪn].

Mrs. Raven did not produce such a strong contrast in her own speech,
maintaining the slight differences shown in figure 13.4a, but she insisted
that the sound difference was useful in distinguishing the two words:

(2) "Loin of lamb," you do go like that, [lǫɪn], "loin o' lamb," 'n' if
     you want the [lɔ̜ɪn], the line, line or anything like that, you go like
     "Put the linen line [lǫɪn, lǫɪn]."

Nevertheless, she was not able to use the acoustic differences in the Jack
Cant tokens to identify words accurately, contrary to her expectation. As
noted above, the contrast from spontaneous speech was easier for her than
the series from the minimal pair test: her reactions to the former were
much faster and more accurate. This corresponds to Dan Jones's pattern
in Albuquerque: the difference made in natural speech tends to disappear
in the minimal pair test, as the subject reacts to his own judgment that
the two words are 'the same'. On further discussion, the difference may
be reestablished or exaggerated if the subject can consciously imitate other
dialects, as Dan Jones and Mr. Raven did.

The evidence from Essex thus reinforces the inference of section 13.1
that /ay/ and /oy/ were not completely merged in the 18th century, but
only closely approximated in a near-merger. Interviews with adolescent
speakers in Tillingham showed a much greater difference between these
vowels, with /ay/ becoming considerably more fronted. The retreat from
the near-merger was apparently under way, and there was no tendency for
the two word classes to be confused.

13.3 The near-merger of *meat* and *mate* in Belfast

The testimony of chapter 10 gave ample indication that a merger of *meat*
and *mate* was reported in the 16th century.[7] There is also no doubt that
the merger was reversed: chapter 10 also showed that the behavior of the
e̅a class was far more regular than most scholars have realized. Lengthened
ĕ words were shown to have remained in mid position while the originally
long word classes rose past mid position, without joining them. This provided strong evidence for the existence of a nonperipheral track in the front
vowels of 16th-century English.

---

[7] Harris (1985), relying largely on Wolfe 1972, seems to feel that the only evidence for the
merger of these two word classes is to be found in Wyld's arguments on rhymes and misspellings. However, chapter 10 cited four authors in the second half of the 16th century who
reported such a merger.

In LYS and in Labov 1975a, it was proposed that the *meat* and *mate* classes had not actually merged, but were reported as merged by many observers because they were in close approximation: that this situation was in fact another case of near-merger. This possibility came to the attention of Milroy and Harris, who were engaged in a sociolinguistic study of Belfast, and who had noted that among older speakers, the *meat* and *mate* classes were phonetically very close and were considered to be 'the same' by speakers of the Belfast vernacular. They began a close investigation of this case, and reported their results first in Milroy and Harris 1980. The following discussion recapitulates Milroy and Harris's data, briefly summarizes Harris's (1985) analysis, and presents my own interpretation of its implications for the overall argument of chapters 10–13. For a more extensive discussion of the *meat/mate* developments in the Belfast dialect and in other Irish, Scots, and English dialects, see Harris 1985.

The history of Belfast English is better known than that of many other English dialects. Patterson (1860) provides a list of 100 words that contain the reflexes of the $\overline{ea}$ or *meat* class, including many words spelled with *ea*, but also items such as *Jesus* and *decent*, often spelled "Jay-sus" and "day-cent" in Irish dialect literature. The vowel used in these words is apparently considered identical to the reflexes of the $\bar{a}$ or *mate* class. *Meat, please, weak* are often written as "mate, plays, wake." Other scholars who have treated Hiberno-English have generally considered the *meat* and *mate* classes to be 'the same'. Harris (1985:241) lists six such sources, and quotes the following song written in 1966:

> The Roost is next and for a rest
>   you can take a seat
> Before proceeding further to the
>   good oul' Golden Gate.

A number of other historical sources support the idea that the merger of the *meat* and *mate* classes must have taken place by 1700, and that it has been maintained to the present day by those who use the traditional pronunciation. However, the number of words in the *meat* class has been steadily shrinking, drained off into the $\bar{e}$ or *meet* class. Of 100 words noted by Patterson in the *meat* class in the 19th century, only 35 survive in the Belfast vernacular today.

The minimal pair and commutation tests used in other investigations are not suitable in the Belfast context, where the vernacular is highly stigmatized. All speakers have access to the more standard system where the *meat* class is merged with *meet*, and in such formal contexts as these tests provide, most speakers give the standard pronunciation.[8] The data used

---

[8] Harris (1985:294) notes that this seems to be true throughout Northern Ireland. An even greater degree of stigmatization prevails in New York City, and as a result the data on *source*

by Milroy and Harris were therefore drawn from only 8 of their 50 Belfast inner-city speakers: those who had made the greatest use of the vernacular *meat* alternants. These speakers were all men. A total of 60 tokens of the *meat* class were obtained, and 99 tokens of the *mate* class.

The information available on the speakers' perceptions of the contrast is therefore limited to observations made by the interviewers in discussions after the more spontaneous part of the interview was completed. Harris writes, "When [Belfast vernacular] speakers' attention is drawn to the non-standard variant, they generally agree that it is identical to the vowel in the *mate* class" (1985:241). Granting the general agreement on the part of phoneticians and native speakers that the vowels are 'the same', it remains to be seen whether they are the same in production. Four impressionistic levels of height were established for the nuclei:

    1 [ɪ]
    2 [e]
    3 [ęɪ]
    4 [ɛ]

The highest three nuclei were frequently accompanied by an inglide; the lower mid vowel [ɛ] was not, though it should be noted that the data included only two tokens of this variant. Differences between the two vowel classes were found in both the distributions by height and the frequencies of inglide. In table 13.5, more than one-third of the tokens of

Table 13.5 Distribution of *meat* and *mate* by vowel height and inglide in the Belfast vernacular (from Harris 1985, table 4.2)

		meat		*mate*	
	Word class	Glide	No glide	Glide	No glide
	Nucleus				
1	[ɪ]	0	0	33	0
2	[e]	18	2	54	6
3	[ę]	18	20	4	2
4	[ɛ]	0	2	0	0
	Total	36	24	91	8

and *sauce* were limited to those who did not insert an /r/ in the first word. However, unlike the speakers in Belfast, who consistently gave the standard pronunciation for *meat* and *mate*, the New York City speakers varied considerably from one another in their tendency to insert the /r/, even in minimal pair tests, so that enough data emerged to allow the analysis of chapter 12.

the *mate* class occur with a high nucleus, but none of the tokens of the *meat* class do. The modal height for *mate* is [e]; for *meat* it is [ę]. The situation here resembles that in New York City, rather than in Essex, since the amount of physical overlap appears to be considerable. The pronunciation [eə] is on the whole the most common; two-thirds of the *mate* class tokens and one-third of the *meat* class tokens occur with this vowel and are thus indistinguishable in this impressionistic transcription. On the other hand, the overall distributions are very different (chi-square yields *p* < .01). One-third of the *mate* class tokens occur with high vowels that were not heard with the *meat* class, and two-thirds of the *meat* class tokens occur with lower mid nuclei that are rarely associated with the *mate* class.

Another way of summing up the situation is to note that in roughly half of the utterances that include one of these words, listeners would be able to guess which word was which from the sound alone; in the other half, they would not be able to do so.

The overlap has not prevented the distinction between the two classes from being maintained for almost 300 years. The first report of merger in Hiberno-English was as early as 1700, and by Garde's well-established principle of the irreversibility of mergers, the distinction found in today's Belfast vernacular could not have been maintained if complete merger had occurred then or at any time thereafter. It follows that speakers are capable of tracing the frequency of occurrence of the two classes, as shown in table 13.5, and that this differential distribution is a part of their fundamental knowledge of the language, one that maintains the two sets of underlying forms.

The Belfast situation bears directly on the situation in 16th-century London.[9] It has been regularly reported that the *meat* and *mate* classes are merged in Belfast, but it is now evident that this is not so. If it is not so now, then it could never have been so in the past. The reports of merger dating from 1700 in Belfast then are actually reports of near-mergers, and imply that the London reports of the 16th century concerned near-mergers as well. These reports indicate an asymmetry of production and perception that is common to both communities, and they confirm the inferences we have made about the past on the basis of near-mergers in the present.

The role of peripherality

At many points in the preceding chapters, phonological problems have been clarified by taking into account the existence of peripheral and non-peripheral tracks in both the front and the back areas of English phonology.

---

[9] That is not to say to that the current Belfast vernacular mirrors the London vernacular of that time. In fact, Harris shows that throughout Ireland, Scotland, and England a great variety of relations between the *meat, mate,* and *meet* classes are found. Any one of these systems might be closer to the system of 16th-century London than the present-day Belfast system is.

This is a pattern of phonological space common to the Germanic and Baltic languages that show an upgliding diphthongization of long ī. In the spectrographic analysis of the Essex data on /ay/ and /oy/, it appeared that small differences in peripherality, difficult for native speakers to perceive, sustained a difference between these phonemes, just as they did in the several cases of chapter 12. In chapter 7, it was argued that several historical paradoxes can be resolved by accepting the possibility that vowels passed each other without merging, one rising on a peripheral track, the other falling on a nonperipheral track. It was proposed that this was the fundamental mechanism of the Great Vowel Shift. The inference receives further support when instrumental analysis is applied to languages that have been described before only by impressionistic means.[10]

This concluding section will consider whether such a peripheral/ nonperipheral distinction played a role in the reported merger and separation of *meat* and *mate*. Chapter 6 pointed out that in Modern English, tense vowels typically develop inglides as they rise to mid and high position, a development clearly demonstrated in table 13.5.

The preceding discussion of the SED records indicates that we cannot rely upon impressionistic transcriptions to register the small differences of fronting and backing that maintain certain distinctions. We can use the presence of inglides to infer small differences in the positions of the nuclei. The presence of marked inglides generally indicates a peripheral or tense position of the nuclei. For example, in the discussion of Vegliote in chapter 5, the breaking of the lower mid long vowels to forms written *ie* and *uo* was taken as an indication that these vowels now defined a peripheral track, and their rising on this track, along with the falling of other vowels along a nonperipheral track, was consistent with the general principles of chain shifting.

The Belfast *meat* and *mate* classes contrast not only in height, but also in the presence or absence of an inglide. However, the development of inglides is clearly related to height, and there are no significant differences between the word classes in this respect. This fact suggests that the distinction between the two classes is not accompanied by a difference in peripherality, since an equal tendency to develop inglides indicates an equal degree of peripherality.[11]

---

[10] Impressionistic descriptions of Dutch diphthongs, for example, usually do not show that the nuclei of upgliding diphthongs like **ei** are lax and nonperipheral, but this appears clearly in instrumental measures.

[11] It is true that Southern States dialects of American English exhibit a range of ingliding vowels from [iə] to [ɪə] (chapter 7), but this is a continuous range dependent on stress and syllabic environment. I do not know of any cases where two ingliding word classes are distinguished by the peripherality of their nuclei alone. It is quite common for two classes to be distinguished by the nature of the glides: either by the direction of the glide, as in the case of *toe* vs. *too* in Norwich, or the extent of the trajectory and the distance of its endpoint,

Harris (1985) discusses at length the range of features that distinguish the *meat* class from the *mate* class in various Scots and English dialects. In most of these dialects, the vowels exhibit differences in height, but that difference frequently reverses the historical relations of the two classes, with *mate* showing the higher vowels. The question is how the *mate* class became higher than the *meat* class without merging with it.

In only one of these dialects (the Scots of northeast Angus) does Harris find evidence of peripherality as the distinguishing feature (1985:269, table 4.6). It is more common for Scots vowels to be distinguished by length, since Aitken's Law, which redistributes length allophonically, applies to the *meat* class but not to the *mate* class. Wherever this redistribution applies, mid vowels are long before /r/ and voiced fricatives, and in morpheme-final position, but are short elsewhere. Therefore the reflexes of Scots *meat* are commonly short, whereas those of *mate* are long.

On the other hand, English dialects show various types of upgliding diphthongal developments of *meat* or *mate*, which serve to move them into different subsystems and effectively avoid merger.

We therefore have no reason to project differences in peripherality as the feature that distinguished the *meat* and *mate* classes in 16th-century London English. These two vowels were assuredly differentiated by height at one stage, reflecting the original distinction of [æ:] vs. [a:] or [ɛ:] vs. [æ:]. During the period when they were widely reported as the same (chapter 10), it is not likely that this difference in height was maintained. As we have seen, native speakers are quite sensitive to small differences in height, as opposed to fronting or backing. It is possible that the Early Modern English distinction was a difference in length. If it was a difference in diphthongization, it probably depended upon an inglide developed in the *mate* class, rather than an upglide. Harris points out that all but one of the dialects of English that distinguish three vowels – /e:/, /ɛ:/, /æ:/ – show ingliding rather than upgliding diphthongs.[12]

The most relevant facts concerning peripherality in Early Modern English have to do with the maintenance of the lengthened short **ĕr** words as a separate class. Chapter 5 showed that *wear, swear, tear, bear* [N], *bear* [V], and *pear* stayed in mid position as members of the **ær** class passed them in raising to high position. The only explanation available for this fact is that the vowels were lengthened but not fronted to peripheral position. Thus in Early Modern English there is evidence for a [±peripheral] distinction that was independent of length. If the **ær** class moved along a

---

as when in the most advanced Philadelphia dialect, /æh/ and /aw/ are distinguished as [e̝:ə] vs. [ɔ:ə].

[12] Harris notes that Cooper (1687) explicitly describes the *mate* class as consisting of "e lingual" followed by "u guttural." This has been considered a provincialism, derived from Cooper's Hertfordshire background, but it may describe the London feature that distinguishes the two classes.

[+peripheral] track, bypassing lengthened [−peripheral] **ĕr**, it is possible that the *meat* class, realized as [ɛ:], was also [−peripheral]. When the *meat* class rose to high position, it then became [+peripheral] and joined the /i:/ phoneme.

This is a possible account of the reversal of the differentiation of *meat* and *mate* in Belfast. But until we have instrumental measures of the Belfast vowel system to guide us, it will not be possible to decide this issue.

Determining the actual mechanism that operated upon the *meat* and *mate* classes is important for a full understanding of English phonological history. However, an explanation of the paradoxical unmerging of the two classes does not depend upon establishing this route. With the help of Milroy and Harris's work, we now infer with some confidence that the 17th-century relation between the e͞a and a̅ classes was that of a near-merger. The crucial point is that the Belfast data show an asymmetry of production and perception that confirms the original inference that the reports of merger summarized in chapter 10 were the products of a near-merger similar to those described in chapter 12.

14

The Suspension of Phonemic Contrast

Chapter 13 has added more evidence of the reality of near-mergers, and made it increasingly difficult to accept the categorical view without serious modification. If the testimony of David de Camp at the end of chapter 12 had not been enough to establish this point, the data from Essex and Belfast have made it even more necessary to recognize the asymmetry of production and perception that characterizes near-mergers. However, each case of near-merger introduced so far concerns the speech of a few individuals, who are admittedly not typical of all members of the community. The Essex data come from three persons, who varied among themselves in their perception of the *line/loin* contrast. Even the eight Belfast speakers who gave evidence on the *meat/mate* situation were selected as a special subset of older, conservative males. In every case we have studied, there is wide individual variation in reaction to the marginal phonemic contrast that assumes the form of a near-merger for a certain subset of the population. Does the existence of a near-merger for Speaker A affect Speaker B, who has a complete merger, or Speaker C, who makes a clear distinction? We do not yet have a clear view of how the phenomenon of near-merger affects an entire community, and where it is located in the speech economy of that community.

Even if every member of the speech community displayed a near-merger, it would still be difficult to understand what is happening here. The resistance of linguists to recognizing the existence of near-mergers is not entirely without motivation. The question remains, How can speakers produce a distinction without being able to recognize the sounds as different? As noted in chapter 13, unless we can answer this question, we are in the curious position of resolving one series of paradoxes by a behavior that is even more paradoxical: it would appear that some speakers have learned to produce a distinction that they cannot perceive.

This chapter will present the results of experiments that both illuminate this question and considerably enrich the data on near-mergers. A much larger number of subjects will be drawn into the arena, and we will get a much more complete view of the range of perceptual processes connected with this phenomenon. The subjects will not be selected by any criterion other than their membership in the speech community, so that each batch of subjects will span the range of contrastive relationships for the phonemic distinction in question. We will thus get a clearer view of the relation of near-merger to the speech of the community as a whole.

The first experiments to be reported here were designed by Tore Janson as a study of dialect differences in the categorization of Swedish vowels. Having encountered a series of surprising results that he realized were related to the near-merger phenomena reported in LYS, Janson characterized the underlying process as "the suspension of phonemic contrast," a formulation borrowed here as the title of this chapter. The main body of the chapter is then concerned with two series of recently concluded experiments undertaken in Philadelphia, which seem to provide clear answers to the questions raised above.

14.1 The categorization of Swedish vowels

Janson and Schulman (1983) report experiments concerning the categorization of 23 synthetic vowels by groups of Swedish subjects. Their paper begins with a direct attack on the discrete binary view of phonological structure that was discussed as the *categorical view* in chapter 13.

If a certain phonetic distinction is regularly used to convey distinctions in meaning, it is phonologically distinctive. Thus one of the presuppositions behind the concept of distinctiveness is that a phonetic difference is either distinctive or not distinctive. This can sound innocuous enough: cases in between do not regularly come to mind. However, there is at least one situation which may cause theoretical problems, and that is when phonetic differences are linked with differences in meaning in speech production, but the distinction is not utilized by the perceiver to distinguish meanings. (1983:321)

The initial condition that triggered this experiment is variation across Swedish dialects in the number of short front vowels. The Stockholm dialect has three long front vowels /iː, eː, ɛː/, but only two short front vowels, /i, e/. The present-day Stockholm /e/ is the result of a relatively recent merger between /e/ and /ɛ/. Though the Stockholm pronunciation has influenced many northern coastal areas, inland areas are generally unaffected, and maintain a system of three front short vowels, /i, e, ɛ/. Typical of such inland northern dialects is the municipality of Lycksele, which was used as a site for experiments on the perception of Swedish vowels.

A series of 23 synthetic vowel stimuli was prepared, starting with the natural pronunciation of [setː] by a Stockholm speaker. The OVE3 synthesizer was used to synthesize the vowels and adjust formant transitions for maximum naturalness. The F1 and F2 measurements of the 23 vowels are shown in figure 14.1. Subjects were first asked to read a list of 18 monosyllabic Swedish words, including two tokens of *sett* and two of *sätt*.

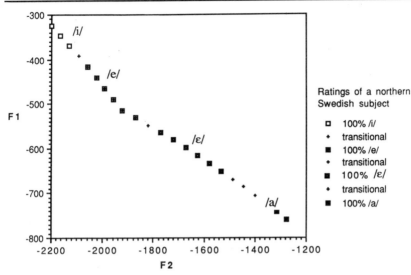

Figure 14.1.   Synthetic vowels for categorization experiment and areas of 100% categorization by a Swedish subject (from Janson and Schulman 1983)

The formant values of the recorded *sett* and *sätt* vowels were analyzed to obtain measures of production. Subjects were then asked to categorize a randomized series of 5 each of the 23 stimuli as one of the Swedish words *sitt, sett, sätt, satt*. On figure 14.1 the results are indicated for a northern Swedish speaker with a system of four vowels – not a subject of the main experimental series. Any point in the series where the subject scored less than 5 out of 5 correct is labeled "transitional" with a "+" symbol. This clear categorization into four vowels is the pattern that was expected from Lycksele subjects, if there were any correspondence between the production and perception of these vowel distinctions.

A first experiment was conducted with 15 Stockholm residents, born and raised in the city and suburbs, and 43 students at a Lycksele high school. As far as speech production was concerned, there were no surprises. The Stockholm speakers showed no significant difference between *sett* and *sätt*. A random sample of 10 of the 43 Lycksele students showed significant F1 and F2 differences for 9, and a significant F2 difference for the 10th. Thus the Stockholm subjects have a three-vowel system, and the Lycksele subjects a four-vowel system.

Results of the perception test

The results of the Janson and Schulman perception tests are given in terms of the width of the region of uncertainty at each boundary. The region of uncertainty is the number of contiguous stimulus vowels between regions where the subject exhibits complete certainty, or 100% identification. Thus

Table 14.1 Width of regions of uncertainty for perception
of Swedish vowels (from Janson and Schulman 1983:327)

	Boundary		
	/i–e/	/e–ɛ/	/ɛ–a/
Stockholm (N = 15)	2.9	7.1	1.5
Lycksele (N = 43)	3.7	6.9	2.5

in figure 14.1, the uncertainty of the /i-e/ boundary is 1, that of the /e-ɛ/
boundary is 2, and that of the /ɛ-a/ boundary is 3. Table 14.1 shows the
mean uncertainty for the two subject groups in the first experiment. There
is every reason to expect that table 14.1 would show sizeable differences
between the two groups of subjects for the /e-ɛ/ boundary, but instead they
are almost identical. For both, the region of uncertainty is so wide that it
occupies the entire space of the two intermediate vowels. Figure 14.2 is a
complete display of the categorization displayed by a speaker from another
northern Swedish dialect (not Lycksele), and figure 14.3 shows a typical
response from a Lycksele subject. It appears that for the Lycksele subject,
there is no perceptual distinction between the two mid vowels. In other
words, the perceptual reactions of the Lycksele students in these experiments are identical with those of the Stockholm subjects, even though
their productive systems are radically different.

  Though these synthetic stimuli were systematic and carefully controlled,
subjects may have missed cues from natural speech, or they may have been

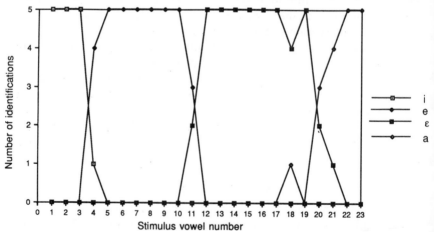

Figure 14.2.   Categorization of the /s____t/ continuum by a northern Swedish
subject, 47 (from Janson and Schulman 1983)

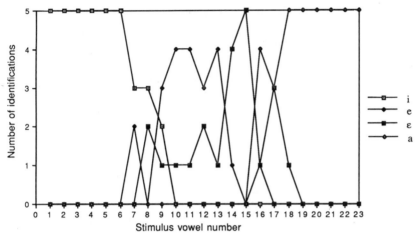

Figure 14.3.   Categorization of the /s___t/ continuum by a Lycksele subject
(from Janson and Schulman 1983)

unconsciously persuaded that the speaker was from Stockholm. A second
experiment addressed these problems by using as stimuli the natural pronunciations of *sitt, sett, sätt,* and *satt* from six Lycksele speakers and making
it explicit that the speaker was from Lycksele. The subjects were 34 Lycksele high school students and 34 Stockholm natives. The results reflected
the same general picture. For the identification of *sitt* and *satt*, the mean
error rate in Lycksele was 1.1%, in Stockholm 1.0%. For the identification
of *sett* and *sätt*, the error rate in Lycksele was 21%, in Stockholm 36%.
One of the most important parallels with our other studies of asymmetry
between production and perception is in the heterogeneous character of
the subjects' behavior. Table 14.2 shows the distribution of error rates for
the two mid vowels for both cities. Since there were two copies of two
pronunciations of each word by six speakers on the test tape, the total
number of possible errors was 48 for each subject. In Lycksele, 7 subjects
produced the error-free results that match their productive pattern, and 4

Table 14.2 Error distributions for perception of natural
Swedish front short vowels (from Janson and Schulman
1983:330–1)

	Lycksele	*Stockholm*
Group 1 (0–3 errors)	7	0
Group 2 (4–18 errors)	23	17
Group 3 (19–errors)	4	17

subjects showed the high rate of error, approaching chance. On the other hand, many Stockholm speakers were at the chance level, and none performed perfectly. Thus the Lycksele community is not equivalent to the Stockholm community in its perception of the mid vowels, but shows a variety of reactions to the task, as we have found in other communities.

Perhaps the most remarkable aspect of this work concerns a third experiment. Another group of Stockholm subjects was presented with the test tape of 23 synthesized vowels, and asked to identify the English words *sit, set, sat,* and *sot.*[1] The region of uncertainty for *set* and *sat* was only 3.8 vowels, almost 50% smaller than the 7.1 of the first experiment. Thus the difficulty in distinguishing between the mid vowels cannot be that the task is physiologically or acoustically difficult. The interfering factor appears to be the linguistic definition that [e] and [ɛ] are 'the same', adopted by both Stockholm and Lycksele subjects, and before they can respond to any categorization task, this linguistic definition intervenes. It is evident that the linguistic norms, which may be socially loaded or socially neutral, can affect tasks in ways that are independent of the productive system.

In evaluating this situation, Janson and Schulman make an immediate connection with the LYS data on near-mergers. They conclude that their subjects "maintain a distinction in their speech production which is not used for semantic differentiation between words in their own or their listeners' perception" (1983:333). They then proceed to inquire more generally into the function of nondistinctive features, and argue that the productive distinction between [e] and [ɛ] in Lycksele may function as a marker of local identity without serving to distinguish words. How then does it come about that these speakers do not distinguish [e] and [ɛ] in perception? Janson and Schulman characterize the situation in the following way:

Language users who employ an ordinary phonological distinction are exposed to speech in another dialect and/or another style in which this distinction is not upheld. Their response to this is to cease using the distinction for semantic differentiation in perception, which makes sense, since it has become inefficient for that purpose. (1983:335)

They thus anticipate the inference on the suspension of semantic contrast that Herold (1990) drew from her study of the merger of *cot* and *caught* in Eastern Pennsylvania, summarized in chapter 11.

Janson and Schulman's experiments have given us a much broader view

---

[1] The series does not in fact include the area of English [æ], since it follows a more centralized path in the lower mid region. When I listened to it, I was not sure that I would identify any word as prototypical *sat*, though some were closer to *sat* than to any other word. This problem may be not at all relevant to Stockholm speakers, whose knowledge of English phonetics, no matter how excellent, is mediated by their Stockholm system.

of the place of near-mergers in the speech community than we had before. Nevertheless, their inference about the suspension of semantic contrast is made on the basis of perceptual experiments that are not directly related to the process of semantic interpretation. There is some evidence that in the formal experimental situation, the social norms of the Stockholm dialect are interfering with the Lycksele speakers' use of their own dialect. Is it not possible that speakers use the "nondistinctive" feature to make distinctions in the unreflecting interpretation of speech in everyday life that they do not make in formal situations? A series of experiments undertaken in Philadelphia yields a much more direct answer to this question, and gives a more detailed picture of the range of behaviors that characterize "near-merger" in the speech community.

14.2 The suspension of contrast in Philadelphia

In pursuing the study of near-mergers, the LCV project was fortunate enough to find a relevant case within the Philadelphia speech community: a near-merger in the opposition of short /e/ and /ʌ/ before intervocalic /r/.

There are many well-known variations in the number of contrasting vowels in this position, illustrated in table 14.3. The geographic distribution of these systems has never been fully mapped. System I, with four different vowels, is found in New York City, the South, and areas of New England. System II, with a merger of *Mary* and *merry*, is characteristic of Maine and northern New Jersey. System III is quite widespread throughout the Midland and the West. System IV is found in a few areas of the West with strong /r/ constriction. System V is found in Philadelphia, where

Table 14.3 Contrasts of short front vowels before intervocalic /r/ in American English

I	II	III	IV	V
Mary	{ Mary / merry }			Mary
merry		{ Mary / merry / marry }	{ Mary / merry / marry / Murray }	{ merry / Murray }
marry	marry			marry
Murray	Murray	Murray		

the short /e/ in *merry* is centralized, quite distinct from the vowels in both *Mary* and *marry*, but merged with or in close approximation to the vowel in *Murray*.

In the LCV study of sound change in Philadelphia, we found subjects with complete merger of the /er/ – /ʌr/ contrast, with a clear distinction, and with a near-merger. No matter what their phonological pattern is, the majority of Philadelphians have only a small difference in F2 between vowels in the /er/ class and vowels in the /ʌr/ class. In spontaneous speech, this is heard most frequently as a mid central vowel in the common words *very* and *terrible*, and in the name of the suburb *Merion*. When minimal pair tests are conducted with *ferry*/*furry* and *merry*/*Murray*, three of the four cells are filled regularly. Minimal pair tests present only one or two items to judge 'the same' and 'different' from the point of view of speech production, and it is often hard to say whether these tokens are physically 'the same' or 'different'. To get a more exact measure of the proportions of merger, near-merger, and distinction, we can use the production information from commutation tests, which gives enough information to perform *t* tests on the significance of the difference between means. A recent experimental series of the CDC project produced the results shown in table 14.4, combining commutation test information with the judgments given in minimal pair tests. Within the city, 6 out of 21 speakers show the phenomenon of "near-merger." Suburban subjects show patterns much more similar to those of non-Philadelphians, though as we will see, they do display some influences of membership in the Philadelphia speech community. The one subject from outside Philadelphia who said that *ferry* and *furry* were 'the same' must have been temporarily confused, since in the commutation test itself, judging his own productions, he scored 100% like all others from outside the city.

Like many other near-mergers *ferry* and *furry* show a close approximation on the F2 dimension and no significant difference on the F1 dimension.

Table 14.4 Distribution of /er/ ~ /ʌr/ contrasts

		Speech production as shown in commutation tests					
		Philadelphia		Philadelphia suburbs		Non-Philadelphia	
		Same	Different	Same	Different	Same	Different
Minimal pair	Same	4	6	1	0	0	1
judgments	Different	0	11	0	3	0	13

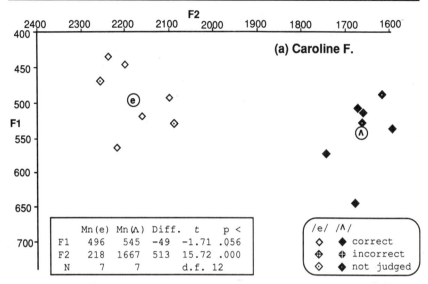

Figure 14.4a.   Clear distinction of Caroline F.

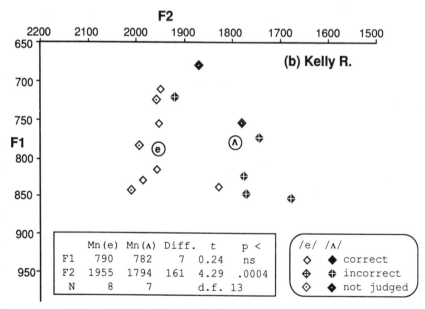

Figure 14.4b.   Nonoverlapping near-merger of Kelly R.

Figure 14.4.   Commutation test tokens produced by four Philadelphians

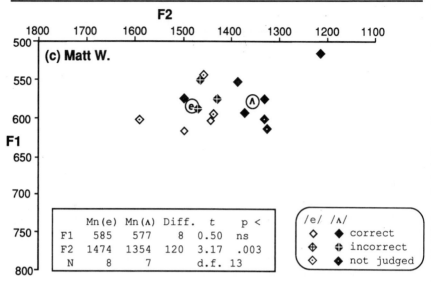

Figure 14.4c. Overlapping near-merger of Matt W.

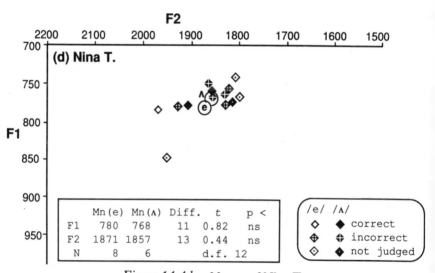

Figure 14.4d. Merger of Nina T.

Short /e/ before intervocalic /r/ shifts toward the center, where it rests next to /ʌ/, in a nonoverlapping or partially overlapping distribution. Figure 14.4 shows the *ferry/furry* tokens produced in commutation tests by four speakers. In each diagram, the positions of the individual /e/ and /ʌ/ tokens are shown as white and black diamonds respectively and the mean is shown as a circle containing the phonemic symbol. The scale is twice that of the diagrams shown so far, so that the distance between the tokens is twice as great as in the normal view. The tokens that were labeled correctly by the subject are solid figures; those that were labeled incorrectly are marked with crosses. The figures with dots in the center are tokens in the list that were read but were not used in the commutation test; they are used in calculating the mean. In the table at the bottom of each figure, the mean values for each word class are given for F1 and F2, with the differences, and a *t* test for the significance of difference in the means. It should be remembered that for non-Philadelphians, /e/ and /ʌ/ are not neighboring word classes like /i/ and /e/. Their means are quite widely separated, even before /r/, and there are no individual tokens in close approximation. Thus the non-Philadelphians' patterns resemble the patterns of /e/ and /ʌ/ found in Chicago in the early 1970s rather than the 1980s (Figures 6.12, 6.17 vs. Figures 6.14, 6.16).

Figure 14.4a shows a speaker with a clear distinction – Caroline F., with a mean F2 difference of 513 Hz between the two classes, and no /e/ token closer than 300 Hz to the nearest /ʌ/ token. There are no crossed diamonds, since she was one of the two Philadelphians who scored 100% in the commutation test.

Figure 14.4b shows a typical near-merger pattern in the commutation test tokens of Kelly R. There is a nonoverlapping distribution of /e/ and /ʌ/, and a significant difference between the F2 means of 161 Hz. Though this difference is greater than the just noticeable difference from a psychoacoustic point of view, it is considerably less than the difference needed for a reliable linguistic distinction.[2] Several tokens of opposing word classes are in close approximation, and obviously could not be distinguished one from the other. However, Kelly R.'s performance was considerably worse than this pattern would predict. She guessed *ferry* for all 10 words.

A second type of near-merger is shown in figure 14.4c, for Matt W. Again, there is a significant difference in the F2 means, at the .003 level, but it is reduced now to 120 Hz, and there are several overlapping tokens. This is similar to the New York City *source/sauce* pattern shown in figure 12.1. Though Matt W. scored only 7 out of 10, he labeled correctly the extreme tokens of /e/ and /ʌ/. In this respect, his ability to categorize his own productions was superior to that of Kelly R.

---

[2] This type of overlap is similar to that found for Keith in Norwich in figure 12.4b.

Finally, figure 14.4d shows a total merger in the commutation test pattern for Nina T. There are no significant differences between the means, and /e/ tokens are just as likely to be found to the back of /ʌ/ as to the front.

These diagrams show the physical correlate of the near-merger situation. It is the most common type of configuration in the Philadelphia community. Many of those who reported a distinction in the minimal pair test cannot pass a commutation test, as we will see, so that of the 11 subjects listed in table 14.4 as reporting and showing a distinction, only 5 made the type of clear and reliable distinction seen in figure 14.4a, whch was uniformly characteristic of non-Philadephians.

The labeling function vs. speech perception

The data just given provide additional confirmation of the finding that speakers are capable of maintaining a distinction in speech that is so narrow that it qualifies as "a small difference in sound." It remains to be seen what kind of role this difference plays in the linguistic system. While our investigation of chain shifts relied entirely on data from spontaneous speech, it is a common characteristic of near-mergers that the critical evidence is found not in spontaneous situations but in highly formal styles where maximum attention is focused on speech. Evidence from controlled styles is much less reliable, since many important allophonic differences are wiped out, and, depending on the particular sociolinguistic configuration, the mean values may shift backward toward an older, corrected value, or forward toward the apparent target of the change. Though a sociolinguistically sophisticated account of subjects' behavior in these formal situations can be given, a description based on such data does not have the inherent validity of a description based on spontaneous speech.

The question thus arises whether the asymmetry of production and perception in near-mergers is an artifact of commutation tests and minimal pairs. These formal situations ask speakers to perform a metalinguistic act, the *labeling* of linguistic categories: specifically, they are asked to associate a spoken form with a category by applying a label such as "animal," "double-L," "Merry Christmas," or "*sett*." This is quite distinct from the *perception* of features or contrasts, which is a largely unconscious act that enters into the *interpretation* of utterances.[3]

---

[3] The distinction between labeling and perception was first called to my attention by Leigh Lisker, in reviewing the problem discussed in this chapter. Herold (1990) makes the further distinction between labeling and correct identification. It is quite possible for a subject to develop a consistent and reliable labeling strategy that does not match the actual use of the distinction by those who maintain it. This was the case in Herold's investigation of the ability of Toronto speakers to deal with the New York City /a/ – /oh/ distinction. A number of them did show a consistent, 100% labeling function, but almost one-quarter of these reversed the labels on the words: what the speaker intended as *cot* was heard as *caught*, and vice versa. Thus we can identify three levels of behavior: perception, labeling, and correct identification.

The behavior that is studied in minimal pair and commutation tests cannot be considered irrelevant to linguistic structure. Throughout this chapter we will see that speakers who have physically distinct and well-separated phonemic categories have no difficulty in applying labels to them, and pass commutation tests with the expected 100% success. The impairment of the labeling function is therefore associated with the marginality of the phonemic distinction, in a combination of three factors: (1) the physical approximation of the targets, (2) widespread individual variation in the community, and (3) the loss of the labeling function itself. But as long as our data come only from methods that involve labeling, we cannot know whether or not the normal phonemic function – the use of a phonemic distinction to distinguish words in unreflecting interpretation – is also impaired.

The Coach Test

Since it is not likely that we will find the distinction between *ferry* and *furry*, *merry* and *Murray*, *Kerry* and *curry*, or any other minimal pair in spontaneous speech, it was necessary to devise an experiment that would test subjects' ability to use the /er/ – /ʌr/ distinction in an act of unreflecting semantic interpretation. To do this it was important that subjects not be in the least conscious of this distinction, and that they be reflecting only on the matters being presented by language, that is, the content, and not the form.

The general format adopted in this case was developed in previous experiments (Labov 1975b, 1988) in which subjects use their linguistic competence without reflection or introspection, applying the rules of grammar to the interpretation of sentences in a natural context. The experimental design for such *semantic disambiguation* has the following structure:

1 Subjects are asked to listen to a narrative in which one of the characters must make a choice, and to judge what was the right or wrong thing to do, or whether the character's decision was right or wrong.[4]
2 Near the end of the narrative, a sentence is constructed with alternate forms of a phonological, morphological, or syntactic variable. The narrative is designed so that the subject's interpretation of the events being described will be radically different depending on the variant that he or she hears. Subjects are randomly assigned to two groups. The first group hears one version; the second group hears the other.
3 The rest of the narrative consists of sentences that are all ambiguous with regard to the critical event, and are necessarily interpreted by sub-

---

[4] In this respect, the experiments are quite similar to the "moral dilemmas" posed by Kohlberg in the study of moral judgments (Kohlberg 1981).

jects in a manner consistent with their interpretation of the crucial sentence.

4   Subjects are asked for their opinions, and the investigator continues the discussion until it is clear how the subject has interpreted the critical event.

The semantic interpretations being studied in these experiments are often very subtle. When people are asked to listen to a single sentence, and immediately give an interpretation out of context, the results are frequently unreliable and unstable. But in the semantic disambiguation experiments, the interpretations are fixed in a context and serve as the basis for further interpretations, so that when the experimenter intervenes, there is usually no doubt about what meaning the subject has extracted from the test. The *Coach Test* was an experiment of this type, designed to test subjects' ability to use the /er/ – /ʌr/ distinction for unreflecting semantic interpretation. The design involved a minimal pair that would not appear to subjects as a minimal pair. Instead of using the usual minimal pair *merry – Murray*, I made use of a more subtle opposition: *Merion* (a Philadelphia suburb) and the combination *Murray in*. To do so, the narrative was designed to motivate the application of the nickname *Merion* to a girl and a moral choice between the selection of a boy or a girl. The story concerns the coach of a Philadelphia high school baseball team who were known as the "Also Rans" because they regularly finished second. One of the players was *Murray*, an earnest but hopeless fielder who dropped every ball that came to him. The coach made him happy by naming him his "First Utility Outfielder." The Board of Education then declared that girls could try out for the team, and a girl who had just come to the school tried out. She couldn't hit, but she could catch the ball fairly well. Her mother was a very aggressive type from Upper Merion, who kept needling the coach for not playing her daughter. The coach was exasperated and began calling the girl *Merion*; he finally placated her mother by naming her also the "First Utility Outfielder," sure that he would never need one. But during the crucial game, when the team might finally finish first, his center fielder tripped, fell, and was carried off. The coach was then faced with a difficult decision:

(1)   "I just don't know," he says, "If I put Murray in there and they hit one ball to the outfield, we come in second, again. The Council will nail my hide to the wall. But if I put a girl in there it will break the kid's heart. But if they hit something out there, that Merion might just catch it."
        So he thought about it a minute. "That's it.
        A   I gotta play Merion there."
        B   I gotta play Murray in there."
So that's what he does. So our pitcher gets hot, right. And none of

them hit the ball out of the infield. And we were really ahead. But Coach wasn't happy. He was sittin' there all worried. He says to me, "Do you think I did the right thing?"

Anyway, we won. And everybody was cheering away, but I didn't see Coach. He just disappeared. But I often used to wonder about that. You know: did he do the right thing?

Subjects hear a version either with sentence A, indicating that the coach chose the girl, or with sentence B, indicating that he chose the boy. Each subject is asked whether the coach did the right thing or not, and in the course of the discussion, the interviewer finds out whether the subject understood that the coach selected a boy or a girl.

The Coach Test is introduced with the instructions shown in (2).

(2)   I'd like to play a story for you that was told to us by a Philadelphian. It's about a problem that came up a few years ago that has to do with the right thing to do in a difficult situation, and we'd like to get your opinion about it.

The story is then played, and at the end, the interviewer asks, "What do you think? Was it the right thing to do?" After the subject gives his or her opinion, the interviewer says:

(3)   Let me play the coach's argument again, so you can get an idea of what his thinking was. Do you agree with him?

The interviewer then replays the section beginning with "I just don't know" to the end of the crucial sentences, "I gotta play Merion/Murray in there." In this replay, the stimulus word is switched, so that *Merion* is replaced by *Murray in* and vice versa. Non-Philadelphians who have a clear distinction between /er/ and /ʌr/ normally just change their interpretations, assuming that they did not hear right the first time. Occasionally, subjects detect an ambiguity, but they are never aware that the key terms have been switched. The reversal of the tokens of /er/ and /ʌr/ provides the strictest test of the phonemic functioning of the contrast: if /e/ and /ʌ/ are perceived as different phonemes in this context, then even in the most unfavorable situation where one interpretation has already been made, the presence of the other form will lead a listener to reverse the interpretation.

The Coach Test story was told by David De Pue, a graduate student at the University of Pennsylvania who is a native Philadelphian.[5] We prepared

---

[5] I am much indebted to Dave De Pue, not only for his realistic and convincing performance, but also for the addition of many colloquial forms, some specific to Philadelphia, which made the Coach Test more interesting and convincing.

one version with his natural pronunciation of *Merion,* and another with his pronunciation of *Murray in.* These were closely approximated, as in the speech of most Philadelphians. I also asked him to imitate my own much more distinct pronunciations, which he did in an accurate and natural manner. We prepared versions with these distinct forms, separated by an F2 distance of 250 Hz. We decided to attempt the experiment with the more distinct forms, and use the natural forms only if local subjects distinguished the first set accurately. Since this did not happen, all of the Coach Test data were gathered with the more distinct forms of the test stimuli.

When the Coach Test was first designed in 1976, it was presented to 15 Philadelphia subjects from the Neighborhood Study of the LCV project. In all of these tests, the stimulus was the sentence A form, where the coach selects the girl. Responses showed that close to 50% of the subjects thought the coach had selected the boy and 50% that he had selected the girl, and we came to the provisional conclusion that Philadelphians did not use the /er/–/ʌr/ distinction in their unreflecting semantic interpretations. In 1988, the CDC project began a controlled study of the /er/ – /ʌr/ distinction across dialectal boundaries, contrasting Philadelphians with non-Philadelphians. In this study, both the A and the B conditions were used, and the Coach Test was combined with minimal pair and commutation tests to give a full view of production and perception.

The contrast of /er/ and /ʌr/ in Philadelphia

EXPERIMENT 1
Experiment 1 included the following procedures:

1 A demographic inquiry into the subject's geographic and linguistic background.
2 The Coach Test.
3 Minimal pair tests including *ferry/furry.*
4 A commutation test. Each subject tape-recorded a randomized list of seven tokens of *ferry* and seven of *furry.* The investigator then played the tape from a point on the list unknown to the subject, and asked the subject to identify 10 words (5 *ferry* and 5 *furry*) by associating the word "animal" with *furry* and the word "boat" with *ferry.*

The formant positions of the nuclei of all *ferry* and *furry* productions were measured[6] and each subject was classified according to the degree of overlap of /er/ with /ʌr/.

---

[6] The GW 12-bit digitizer was used, and narrow-band spectrograms were prepared by the MacSpeech Lab I program on a Macintosh SE. The central tendency of the formants was

Thirty-six subjects, all students at the University of Pennsylvania or Drexel University, were exposed to this battery of tests; 21 were from the Philadelphia speech community and 15 from outside the region. In addition, 22 subjects were tested as a group at Drexel University with written responses; 12 were from the Philadelphia area.

The results illuminated the relationship between production, self-evaluation, performance in commutation tests, and perception of the distinction in discourse.

Results of the commutation tests   The commutation test revealed a dramatic difference between Philadelphians and non-Philadelphians. As table 14.5 shows, this difference is almost categorical. On this test, "Pass" means 10 out of 10 correct. This is a reasonable criterion, in view of the fact that non-Philadelphians achieve it with ease. When a commutation test involves a normal phonemic distinction, with normal margins of security, speakers have no difficulty in showing perfect performance. On the other hand, only 2 Philadelphians passed at this level. Their inability is not a product of the fact that they all show merger, however. As we saw in figures 14a–d, Philadelphians vary widely in both categorization (the minimal pair test) and production (distribution of tokens in the commutation test). Ten of the 21 Philadelphians said that *ferry* was different from *furry*, and this difference was reflected in percentage correct on the commutation test, as shown in table 14.6. Their mean scores are significantly better than those of Philadelphians who reported *ferry* and *furry* as 'the same', ($t = 2.38$, $p = .014$), even though they are considerably worse than scores of the non-Philadelphians ($t = 3.90$, $p < .001$).

This difference in performance on the commutation test can be related directly to the task that the subjects had to perform. Instrumental measurements of the tokens produced by subjects in the commutation test showed that half of them were like Matt W. or Nina T. in figures 14.4c and 14.4d: they showed overlap in /e/ and /ʌ/ before /r/ that made it impossible to

Table 14.5   Results of commutation test of *ferry/furry*

	Pass	*Fail*
Non-Philadelphians	15	0
Philadelphians	2	19

identified using the digital procedure outlined in LYS (chap. 2), which yields measurements with a maximal error range of one-quarter of a pitch period.

Table 14.6   Relation of minimal pair response to success on commutation test

	Mean % correct on commutation test
Non-Philadelphians [N = 15]	100
Philadelphians who respond 'different' in minimal pairs [N = 10]	78
Philadelphians who respond 'same' in minimal pairs [N = 11]	24
Philadelphians with nonoverlapping vowel patterns [N = 11]	79
Philadelphians with overlapping vowel patterns [N = 10]	51

obtain 100% correct scores.[7] The other half showed no overlap, and resembled either Caroline F. or Kelly R. in figures 14.4a and 14.4b. Without taking into account the more subtle point of the size of the margin of security – figure 14.4a vs. figure 14.4b – or the degree of overlap – figure 14.4c vs. figure 14.4d – we can ask whether the simple fact of overlap can predict success on the commutation test. The lower section of table 14.6 shows that it does. The 10 Philadelphians who produced nonoverlapping distributions were able to categorize the vowels more successfully than those who produced overlapping distributions ($t = 3.34$, $p = .0017$). But again, they were significantly worse than the non-Philadelphians ($t = 3.85$, $p < .001$). Indeed it is only natural that grouping subjects by minimal pair responses and by production patterns should yield the same results, since the two groups are the same except for one subject.[8]

The fact that the token distribution in production predicts success in identification suggests that we are not necessarily dealing with differences in the perceptual systems of Philadelphians and non-Philadelphians. It may be that given the Philadelphia tokens, the non-Philadelphians would do no better on a commutation test. Nor is there any evidence that Philadelphians would not be able to attend just as well to the difference between *ferry* and *furry* if they had produced tokens as distinct as those of the non-Philadelphians. So far, then, the results confirm the existence of wide-

---

[7] Always assuming that the F1 and F2 of the nucleus as plotted in figure 14.4 is an indicator of the central tendency of the vowel trajectory as perceived. There are of course other features that differentiate the words. We have not, as yet, detected any other acoustic feature that systematically differentiates /er/ and /ʌr/, but such features may exist.

[8] This subject had a clear distinction in production but heard *ferry* and *furry* as 'the same'. His two sets of vowels are opposed diagonally: /ʌ/ tokens have either lower F2 or lower F1. One token of *ferry* is within 50 Hz of the *furry* concentration on the F2 axis, but is much lower, over a 100 Hz away, on the F1 axis. This implies that at least for this subject, F2 is a more important dimension than F1.

spread variation in Philadelphia but do not indicate any fundamental alteration in the linguistic system. To pursue this question, we must examine responses to the Coach Test.

Results of the Coach Test   The Coach Test presents both Philadelphians and non-Philadelphians with the same stimuli. The results should answer two questions:

1   Does the impairment of Philadelphians' ability to distinguish /er/ and /ʌr/ hold for unreflecting semantic interpretation?
2   Is there any difference between Philadelphians and non-Philadelphians in this ability?

Table 14.7 gives positive answers to both questions. In the Coach Test, Philadelphians are worse than non-Philadelphians in their ability to interpret /er/ and /ʌr/ as indicating a girl and a boy respectively.[9] The non-Philadelphians did extraordinarily well on the Coach Test, with only 1 wrong out of 15. The Philadelphians were worse, but their performance is well above chance and the difference is not quite at the .05 level of significance.[10] In contrast with the commutation test, there was no observable correlation between results on the Coach Test and self-evaluation or

Table 14.7   Results of the Coach Test for Philadelphians and non-Philadelphians

	Correct	Incorrect
Non-Philadelphians	14	1
Philadelphians	14	7

$\chi^2 = 3.6$, $p = .06$

[9] "Correct" here means on the first response. We did not consider that a tendency to persist in the same interpretation when the tokens were switched in the second part of the test gave unambiguous information on the subject's linguistic system, since there are nonlinguistic factors that could lead a person to ignore a change in the input data. The second part of the test did show non-Philadelphians' greater sensitivity to the distinction through their ability to change judgments with change of input data, but the effect is a smaller one.
[10] Further applications of the Coach Test with groups produced a larger sample, and significant differences between Philadelphians and non-Philadelphians. It should be remembered that subjects were judging tokens of *Murray in* and *Merion* where the difference between /er/ and /ʌr/ was exaggerated by the Philadelphia speaker, in the direction of the non-Philadelphians' production. The F2 difference was 250 Hz.

vowel production. Table 14.8 shows the distribution of Coach Test answers when broken down by subjects' productions and self-evaluation on the minimal pair test.

EXPERIMENT 2: A STANDARDIZED COMMUTATION TEST
Although the results of Experiment 1 clearly show the suspension of phonemic contrast in Philadelphia, the strong results of the commutation tests do not allow us to detect differences in the perceptual systems of local speakers. Success in categorizing items on the commutation test was a direct product of the tokens that the individual produced. Results from another experiment, Experiment 2, confirm and extend these observations by allowing us to compare the ability of Philadelphians and non-Philadelphians to categorize the same series of vowel productions.[11] Experiment 2 used the same procedures as Experiment 1, but added two further commutation tests that would expose all subjects to the same stimuli.

The recorded tokens of two speakers were used for such standardized commutation tests: one whose productions of /er/ and /ʌr/ posed a very difficult problem for categorization, and one whose productions were relatively easy to categorize, within the characteristic Philadelphia range. Fig-

Table 14.8   Coach Test results for Philadelphians by self-report, production, and commutation score

	Correct	Incorrect
Minimal pairs		
Reporting merger	8	3
Reporting distinction	6	4
Vowel production		
With overlap	7	3
Without overlap	7	4
Commutation scores		
High	4	2
Medium	1	2
Low	9	3

[11] Experiment 2 was designed primarily to compare subjects' psychoacoustic abilities to discriminate sounds with their linguistic ability to categorize them. The full results will be presented in volume 3.

ure 14.5 shows the commutation test results for Laura M., who read an extended list of 42 tokens. There is a great deal of overlap of *ferry* and *furry*, yet we cannot call this system a merger. The difference in the F2 means is small but significant ($\chi^2 = 2.48\ p = .009$). Half of the /er/ tokens are more front than any /ʌr/ token, though the differences involved here are not much more than 100 Hz. A commutation test was prepared from a random alternation of five each of the two tokens indicated by surrounding squares on figure 14.5. These are near the two extremes of the F2 range of Laura M.'s articulation, but they proved quite difficult for subjects to label consistently.

Figure 14.6 shows the *ferry* and *furry* tokens produced by Jed F., a suburban Philadelphian with a clear distinction, a mean F2 difference of 281 Hz. Though this difference is not as great as that of most non-Philadelphians, it is representative of the type of clear distinction made in the city. No tokens are close to the neighboring word class, and the separation between the two distributions is sizeable. The commutation test was prepared from the two tokens marked with squares on figure 14.6. The /ʌr/ token was the only one that was wrongly labeled by Jed F. himself. However, he corrected himself after a short hesitation. This is the one that is closest to the /er/ distribution, but it is still 200 Hz from the /er/ mean, and not at all difficult for non-Philadelphians to recognize as *furry*.

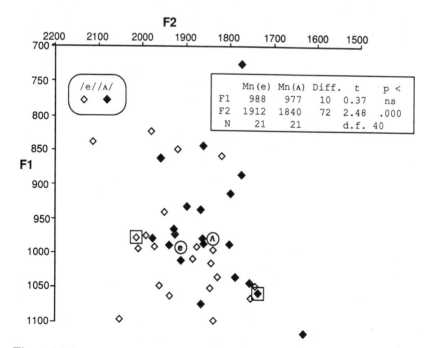

Figure 14.5. Commutation test tokens of Laura M. (overlapping near-merger)

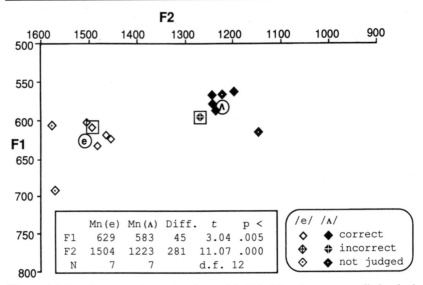

Figure 14.6.   Commutation test tokens of Jed F. (clear but narrow distinction)

The 53 subjects of Experiment 2 were a more varied group than the subjects of Experiment 1.[12] Seventeen subjects were from outside the Philadelphia area, 5 from the suburbs, and 31 from Philadelphia. Most of the subjects were recruited from the University of Pennsylvania community, but 8 were from working-class areas in North Philadelphia.[13] Fourteen black subjects were included, 11 from the Philadelphia area, and 3 from other areas. As in other studies, the black subjects proved to be members of a distinctly different speech community. None showed any tendency toward a merger of /er/ and /ʌr/.[14] Five subjects were drawn from the Phildelphia suburbs. Since all but one had a clear distinction between /er/ and /ʌr/, it seems likely that suburban speakers differ from the city population as a whole. We will therefore be comparing the performance of 20 white Philadelphians to that of 14 white subjects from outside of Philadelphia.[15]

---

[12] Subjects were recruited and tested by Corey Miller of the CDC project, who also did the instrumental analysis of the commutation and minimal pair test productions.

[13] These were members of the Guardian Angels, a volunteer anticrime group.

[14] Black Philadelphians performed better on commutation tests of their own productions than whites, but did worse than whites in the categorization of the speech of Laura M. and Jed F. in the commutation tests, as well as further discrimination tests based on the speech of Laura M. The categorization and discrimination patterns of the black subjects will be considered in volumes 2 and 3.

[15] Six from the Northern Cities, 2 from the Middle Atlantic states, 4 from the South Midland, 1 from eastern Texas, and 1 from the Far West.

Table 14.9 Commutation test of *ferry/furry* in Experiment 2

	Pass	Fail
Non-Philadelphians	14	0
Philadelphians	4	16

Table 14.10 Coach Test results in Experiment 2

	Correct	Incorrect
Non-Philadelphians	13	1
Philadelphians	14	5

$\chi^2 = 4.00, p = .05$

Table 14.9 shows results for the self-commutation test in Experiment 2. The responses are strikingly similar to those shown in table 14.5 for Experiment 1. The performance of non-Philadelphians is perfect, but only 20% of the Philadelphians completed the test without error.

Table 14.10 shows the results of the Coach Test, which are again very close to the results of Experiment 1. (One Philadelphian's responses were indeterminate.) Figure 14.7 shows graphically the similarity of results of Experiments 1 and 2 for both the commutation test and the Coach Test.

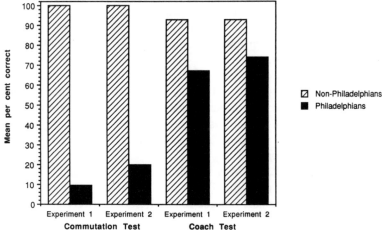

Figure 14.7. Comparison of Experiments 1 and 2 for commutation test and Coach Test

It seems clear from the evidence of the Coach Test that Philadelphians as a whole do not use the difference between /er/ and /ʌr/ to distinguish words. The results of the Coach Test are above chance, yet on the face of it, performance on the Coach Test is worse than performance on the commutation test. That is, if we assume that the Coach Test and the commutation test measure the same ability, then the commutation test is equivalent to 10 repetitions of the Coach Test. But applying the success rate for Philadelphians in Experiment 2 ten times gives $.737^{10}$ or .047. This would predict a success rate on the commutation test of less than 5%, instead of the 20% obtained (10% in Experiment 1).

This line of reasoning assumes that all Philadelphians use the distinction between /er/ and /ʌr/ to the same extent. But the commutation test scores indicate instead that *some* Philadelphians are capable of using this distinction to differentiate words. Let us assume that the small number of Philadelphia subjects who achieved 100% in the self-commutation test are also capable of matching the performance of non-Philadelphians on the Coach Test. This would mean that the 14 who gave correct answers on the Coach Test in Experiment 2 included the 4 who passed the commutation test. This turns out to be true. If we set these subjects aside, we can call the rest "normal Philadelphians." Then the proportion of normal Philadelphians who gave the correct answer on the Coach Test is not 14/19 but 10/15, or .67. (A chance performance would be 7.5/15, or .50). If we assume that the chance of success on any individual commutation trial is the same as that for the Coach Test, .67, then the chance of passing the commutation test for any of these 15 subjects is $.67^{10}$, or .018. Assuming that the .67 response on the Coach Test is the average success rate for a normal Philadelphian, we would not expect any of them to pass the commutation test, and this completes the argument. The majority of Philadelphia subjects cannot use the /er/ – /ʌr/ contrast to distinguish words. To put it in reverse, a success rate of 67% on the Coach Test is not inconsistent with a 0% success rate on the standardized commutation test. We are looking at the same form of behavior.

Let us now extend our view of the commutation tests to include the categorization of tokens produced by the speaker who exemplifies the near-merger, Laura M., and the speaker who exemplifies a Philadelphia distinction, Jed F. Table 14.11 displays success rates on the self-commutation test (as in table 14.9) and these two standardized commutation tests. In all cases, a passing score is 100%.[16]

The test involving Laura M.'s speech proved very difficult. No Philadelphian passed it, not even the 4 who passed the self-commutation test. Yet two non-Philadelphians did get 100%. If subjects were guessing ran-

---

[16] The numbers of subjects vary for the Jed F. and Laura M. tests, since they were added to the protocol of Experiment 2 after the series had begun.

Table 14.11   Results of commutation tests for self, Laura M. and Jed F.

	Self		Laura M.		Jed F.	
	Pass	Fail	Pass	Fail	Pass	Fail
Non-Philadelphians	14	0	2	7	7	2
Philadelphians	4	16	0	18	3	18

domly on these data, the proportion of success would be $.5^{10}$, or just about 1 out of 1000. This means that there is enough information in Laura M.'s tokens for a sensitive person to detect the pattern consistently.

The case of Jed F. is quite different. For the non-Philadelphias, judging these productions seems to be more difficult than judging their own, though the difference is not significant. It is not surprising to find that Philadelphians are significantly worse than non-Philadelphians. But it is surprising to find that Philadelphians have no more success in judging Jed F.'s tokens than their own. When we consider that over half the Philadelphia subjects have mergers or near-mergers, this means that they do not benefit from the clear (though narrow) distinction that Jed F. makes in production. The situation is somewhat clearer when we add the 4 suburban subjects to the city subjects, for a total of 25.[17] Of 7 subjects who have a clear distinction with no tokens of /er/ and /ʌr/ less than 200 Hz apart, 4 achieved 100% success on the self-commutation test. But of these, only 1 scored 100% in judging the speech of Jed F. It is evident that Philadelphians are not able to use the minimal separation of 200 Hz to consistently distinguish /er/ and /ʌr/.[18]

So far, we have been considering only the strict criterion of 100% success in Experiment 2. When we consider the actual rate of correct answers

[17] Jed F. is one of the 5 suburban subjects, so only 4 can be considered here.
[18] The striking difference in the difficulty of categorizing the Laura M. and Jed F. series can be illuminated if we look at the ranges of distribution of both sets of tokens. There was no difference in the crucial F2 dimension: the two tokens of Laura M. differed by 228 Hz and those of Jed F. differed by 221 Hz. As far as F1 is concerned, Laura M.'s *furry* was 81 Hz higher, and Jed F.'s only 13 Hz lower. However, if we examine the two distributions in figures 14.5 and 14.6, it is evident that there is a great difference in the pattern. Jed F.'s tokens are clustered into two sets that appear to cross a psychologically real boundary. Laura M.'s tokens form a continuous distribution, at a considerably higher F1 and F2 range. The higher F2 range for Laura M. is not merely a product of the female vocal tract: all of her tokens sound front to most listeners. In spite of the bias toward giving an equal number of answers for two alternatives, only 6 subjects did so. Twenty-seven heard more *ferry* than *furry* (with 5 subjects hearing only *ferry*); only 7 heard more *furry*. The mean responses for 40 subjects was 6.3 *ferry* and 3.7 *furry*. The major difficulty with forms produced by Laura M. is that the /ʌ/ tokens had moved well into the /e/ range.

in the commutation test, we obtain a more sensitive indicator of subjects' ability to use the /er/ – /ʌr/ distinction. Table 14.12 correlates the percentage correct in the categorization of *ferry* and *furry* in the three commutation tests with the type of distinction made by subjects in their self-commutation test. The first line shows the data for the non-Philadelphians, who all make a clear distinction. The second line displays the results for the 9 Philadelphians who also make a clear distinction (including the 4 suburban subjects). Despite the high performance of the Philadelphians, their mean scores are significantly lower than those of the non-Philadelphians ($p = .0147$). Results for the test based on the speech of Jed F. are very slightly lower for both groups: again Philadelphians are significantly worse ($p = .008$). Results for the Laura M. commutation test drop off sharply for both groups, and here there are no significant differences between them. This indicates that on the easier tasks, Philadelphians who make the distinction are impaired in their ability to categorize vowels, but on the more difficult tasks, their ability to categorize (and discriminate) is no worse than that of others.

Turning to the differences among Philadelphians, there is a significant effect on the self-categorization test between those who make a clear distinction and those with close approximation ($p = .056$). Though the other groups are graded in the way that we would expect, the differences are not

Table 14.12 Categorization of *ferry/furry* in Experiment 2 by type of production in self-categorization test

	% correct		
	Self	*Jed F.*	*Laura M.*
Non-Philadelphians			
Clear distinction	100(14)**	96.7(9)**	78.9(9)
Philadelphians			
Clear distinction	91.7(9)*	82.5(8)	73.8(8)
Nonoverlapping with			
close approximation	74(5)	76(5)	66(5)
Overlapping with			
significant difference			
in F2 means	68(5)	78(4)	56(4)
Merged	40(4)	77(3)	56(3)
All clear distinction			76.5(17)***
All merger and near-			
merger			57.5(12)

Significant differences with group immediately below: *$p < .05$, **$p < .01$, ***$p < .001$

significant. In the case of Jed F.'s speech, all Philadelphians are basically alike: the small difference between those with clear distinctions and others is not significant. With respect to the speech of Laura M., we find the converse. There are no significant differences among Philadelphians, but if we group the Philadelphians who show clear distinctions with the non-Philadelphians, the differences between them and all others is significant ($p = .009$).

We can sum up the results of this fine-grained examination of the commutation test by three findings that hold for the results of Experiments 1 and 2 generally. About one-third of the Philadelphia population shows a clear distinction; somewhat more than one third shows a near-merger; and a little less than one-third shows a full merger.

- Philadelphians with a full merger show the expected random response to self-commutation tests, and a severe reduction in the ability to categorize tokens that are clearly distinct.
- Philadelphians with a near-merger, either overlapping or nonoverlapping, do not show a significant improvement over speakers with a merger in their categorizations.
- Philadelphians with a clear distinction are significantly better than others in categorizing their own productions, but are not better than other Philadelphians in categorizing a clear Philadelphia distinction. They are better than others in categorizing a near-merger.
- All Philadelphians are worse than non-Philadelphians in judging either their own productions or a standard clear distinction.

These findings mean that, for Philadelphians in general, the semantic utility of the distinction is considerably less than for non-Philadelphians. Even the Philadelphians who would be expected to do better on the Coach Test and the commutation test, those who claim a distinction and keep their vowels distinct in production, scored significantly worse on these tests than non-Philadelphians.

Thus the near-merger of /er/ and /ʌr/ is accompanied by a reduction in the semantic contrast of this opposition. What is most remarkable about this development is that the entire community is affected by the decreased semantic use of the distinction. This gives partial confirmation to the proposal of Janson and Schulman (1983) and of Herold (1990) that speakers who make a distinction, but are in close contact with those who do not, find that the distinction is not useful and stop using it to differentiate words. The suspension of phonemic contrast in Philadelphia is not complete, but it is impaired to a degree that is correlated with the phonological system of the speaker. We are therefore looking at a dynamic process in Philadelphia, where the mechanism of merger is exposed for our inspection. The real-time status of the process is not yet evident: we do not know how fast the merger is proceeding, if at all. It is abundantly clear, however, that the phenomenon of near-merger is solidly entrenched in the process. Though previous reports of near-merger concerned a few individuals in each community, the near-merger affects a solid plurality of Philadelphia speakers, and appears to be an integral part of the linguistic economy.

The question remains, How can Philadelphians maintain nonoverlapping distributions, yet show such severe limitations in their ability to categorize their output? This is a question about discrimination rather than categorization. A further series of experiments, to be reported in volume 3, will investigate the ability of Philadelphians to discriminate the tokens along a physical continuum, and will analyze the ways in which the linguistic judgment that *ferry* and *furry* are 'the same', intersects with psychoacoustic detection, perception, and discrimination.

Part D

The Regularity Controversy

15

Evidence for Lexical Diffusion

The two remaining parts of this volume deal with the general principles that were the central concerns of the Neogrammarian linguists of the latter half of the 19th century: Leskien, Osthoff, Brugmann, Paul, and many others. The chief issues at stake are the traditional questions of whether sound change is or is not regular, and of how meaning is preserved, or is not, in the course of linguistic change. The quotations from Osthoff and Brugmann in section 1.2 make it clear that they were strongly oriented to the study of living languages and the program of using the present to interpret the past. They themselves did not control the techniques needed to deal directly with the speech community, and through an overemphasis on the role of the individual and of individual psychology, they removed themselves progressively farther from the possibility of doing so (Weinreich, Labov, and Herzog 1968). Their confidence in dialect geography could not then be supported by the mathematical methods needed to restore the underlying order to the apparent chaos of the surface data (chapter 17). Nevertheless, their fundamental insights into the nature of linguistic change have proved to be reliable guides for the study of the speech community, and the development of the evolutionary perspective of this volume. Many findings in the chapters to follow will provide strong confirmation of Neogrammarian principles. If the work presented here has a cumulative character, it is because it builds upon the firm foundation of Neogrammarian thought. Part D will deal with Neogrammarian position on the lexical regularity of sound change; part E with the Neogrammarian contention that sound change is modified only by the phonetic environment, and not by the need to convey information.

15.1 The regularity controversy

In chapter 1, the Neogrammarian controversy on the regularity of sound change was presented as a prototypical example of a long-standing, unresolved dispute over principles.[1] There is more than enough evidence to justify taking one position or the other – either that sound change is lexically regular or that it is not. But given this situation, one can take a firm position for one side only by dismissing or ignoring the evidence on the other side. We will see that some linguists acknowledge that there is evidence on both sides, while in practice they are committed to a single-minded program. Historical linguists assume that sound changes affect sounds, not words; exponents of lexical diffusion are intent on proving that sound changes affect words, not sounds.

The orientation toward linguistic research that is put forward in this volume approaches such controversies in a different spirit. It begins with respect for the intelligence of our predecessors, and for the evidence that led them to their conclusions. Careful consideration of the competing bodies of evidence leads to the conclusion that a higher-level theory is needed – one that will take into account, as well as account for, the findings on both sides of the controversy. Such a synthesis can be achieved only if we ascertain the conditions under which each of the opposing viewpoints is valid. This cannot be done by simply reshuffling the data already accumulated, or by manipulating and reorganizing what others have said – in a word, by trying to be more intelligent than our predecessors. The synthesis that is needed will make use of broader and richer data, drawn from a wider variety of sources and measured by more precise techniques.

Part D is devoted to the resolution, in this spirit, of the Neogrammarian controversy. It is now over a century old, and perhaps the most clearly stated issue in linguistic history. In the evolution of sound systems, is the basic unit of change the word or the sound? Our focus will be the question of the regularity of changes, as it was stated in categorical form by Osthoff and Brugmann (1878):

[E]very sound change, inasmuch as it occurs mechanically, takes place according to laws that admit no exception. (translated in Lehmann 1967:204)

The obverse of this "exceptionlessness" is lexical regularity: that when a sound changes, it affects every word in which that sound occurs in the same phonetic environment.

The most important elements of the Neogrammarian position as formulated by Osthoff and Brugmann are hidden in the phrase *inasmuch as it proceeds mechanically*. This phrase is designed to cover two types of exceptions to exceptionlessness. The first is *analogical change*, which involves conceptual relations that are not mechanical (or phonetic) in character. It

---

[1] This and the following chapter contain revisions and reformulations of the point of view first presented in Labov 1981. A considerable number of new facts have been incorporated, along with discussions of the issues that followed in the 10 years after the article appeared.

is widely recognized that one of the major virtues of the Neogrammarian position was the systematic role allotted to analogy (Kiparsky 1989:364). The second is *dialect borrowing*, which is generally considered to involve social relations of relative prestige that are not mechanical. Much of the argumentation concerning the Neogrammarian position concerns the identification of these two processes; the second will play a major part in the discussion to follow.

With respect to the issue of the regularity of sound change, it seemed clear that, until recently, the Neogrammarians had won the day.[2] Although dialectologists and philologists generally were still impressed with the facts that pointed to the slogan *Each word has its own history*, the mainstream of linguistic theory seems to have been Neogrammarian throughout the first century of the controversy. This holds not only for the American structuralists, and the absolute stance taken by Bloomfield (1933) and Hockett (1958), but for recent mainstream theorists as well. In the various efforts to apply generative phonology to historical linguistics, the dispute with the Neogrammarians has been mainly over the question of grammatical conditioning, not over the regularity of sound change (Postal 1968; King 1969; Kiparsky 1971, 1989).[3] Thus it was possible for Hockett (1965) to place the Neogrammarian hypothesis among the four great breakthroughs of linguistics, on a par perhaps with the theory of evolution in biology. The scholars engaged in comparative reconstruction in Indo-European, Austronesian, Sino-Tibetan, and other language families continue to recognize the regularity of sound change as the basic principle that unifies, rationalizes, and legitimates their activity.

However, the evidence in favor of the belief that sound change proceeds word by word has not disappeared. Interest has persisted in the work of classical opponents of the Neogrammarians, beginning with Schuchardt.[4] Moreover, the evidence for lexical diffusion has continued to accumulate

---

[2] Recent years have seen numerous republications, translations, and reassessments of the Neogrammarians' work. Most American linguists have been introduced to the Neogrammarians through the account in Pedersen 1962. Lehmann 1967 includes translations of a number of important Neogrammarian documents. The most important papers debating the Neogrammarian position are reproduced in Wilbur 1977; and the introduction to that volume gives a detailed account of the academic setting of the controversy. For recent scholarly reviews of the controversy, I draw on Hoenigswald 1978, Malkiel 1967, and Fónagy 1956.

[3] Kiparsky 1989 presents the most comprehensive statement of these issues to appear in recent years. It begins with the "exceptionless hypothesis" of the Neogrammarians, and argues (1) that it is an emprical claim, (2) that it is not imcompatible with the fact that each word has its own history, and (3) that it is contradicted by much evidence of grammatical conditioning and lexical diffusion. Kiparsky's views were formulated after the position developed in this chapter was first presented in 1981, and are in part a response to them. This and the following chapters will attempt to take into account, and respond to, Kiparsky's positions on dialect borrowing, lexical diffusion, and grammatical conditioning.

[4] Schuchardt's statement "Gegen di Junggrammatiker" is reproduced in Wilbur 1977. A more complete presentation of his point of view is available in Schuchardt 1980.

in the research efforts headed by students of Chinese. The traditional calm acceptance of the regularity of sound change can be maintained only by ignoring these linguists, together with their results. This chapter will review the original research on lexical diffusion by Wang, Cheng, Chen, Hsieh, and Krishnamurti, and will add to this the more recent results of Li (1982), Wang (1989), and Shen (1990).

15.2   Recent evidence for lexical diffusion

Wang (1969) suggested that exceptions to regular sound change might be caused by the overlapping operation of two rules in a bleeding relationship. From the standpoint of the Neogrammarian hypothesis, this was a new idea: that irregularities might be the result of two regular sound changes, rather than the competition of sound change and analogy. As Wang began to gather empirical evidence for this idea, he discovered data that had more serious consequences for the Neogrammarian position – findings of considerable scope that cast doubt on the whole idea of change by regular phonological rule.

In 1962, Peking University published the *Hanyu Fangyin Zihui*, the results of a massive research project of the 1950s, with phonetic transcriptions of 2,444 morphemes in 17 modern Chinese dialects. With data from the Middle Chinese Dictionary and Sino-Japanese sources, these materials formed the basis of the Dictionary on Computer, or DOC (see Streeter 1977). Wang, together with Hsieh, Cheng, Chen, and others, used this data set to trace the paths followed by Chinese sound changes. As Wang has pointed out, Chinese data are particularly useful for testing the Neogrammarian hypothesis because the morphological analogies that can interfere with the regularity of sound change in inflectional paradigms are practically nonexistent.

It quickly became evident that the exceptionless character of sound change received very little support from Chinese data. One of the most concise statements of the position that emerged is given by Wang and Cheng (1977). They analyze the Neogrammarian position, summarized in the Bloomfieldian dictum that "Phonemes change," into two components: sound change is *phonetically gradual*, proceeding by imperceptible increments, but *lexically abrupt*, affecting all relevant words simultaneously. They then point to the unsuitability of this model for a wide range of discrete phonetic changes: flip-flops, metatheses, epentheses, deletions, and changes in point of articulation. Given this limitation, plus the existence of many competing forms and exceptions and the artificiality of many explanations of dialect borrowing, they propose a different model:

We hold that words change their pronunciations by discrete, perceptible increments (i.e. phonetically abrupt), but severally at a time (i.e. lexically gradual) . . . (p. 150)

The strong position of Wang, Chen, Cheng, and Hsieh aligns them with the most radical of the Romance dialectologists, who were most skeptical of the Neogrammarian concept of sound laws.[5] For them, the process of change operates not upon sounds, but upon words. They call this conception *lexical diffusion*. They do not deny that sound change may be regular: in this respect, lexical diffusion may predict no less ultimate regularity than the Neogrammarian principle. However,

[t]he difference lies rather in the description (and ultimately, the explanation) of the change mechanism, i.e. how the change is actually implemented. (p. 151)

Tone splitting in Chaozhou

For Wang and Cheng, lexical diffusion is plainly more than a working principle: it is a substantive solution for the transition problem. They support their position with an impressive demonstration of lexical split in the reflexes of Middle Chinese tone III in the dialect of Chaozhou (Cheng and Wang 1977). No matter how narrowly the phonetic environments are analyzed, the split into modern tones 2b and 3b persists. Neither the Middle Chinese initial consonants or final vowels nor the modern initials or finals explain the massive splitting of word classes. Table 15.1 shows a typical distribution of Chaozhou tones afer modern initials. Cheng and Wang locate 12 pairs that were homonymous in Middle Chinese but are now split in this way.

The Chaozhou data provide a dramatic example of an even split without phonetic motivation – and with no analogical or grammatical motivation. In response, a number of Sino-Tibetan historical linguists took the Neogrammarian position: they pointed out that these data had no bearing on the regularity of sound change, since it was clear to them that there must have been extensive dialect borrowing in 13th-century Chaozhou.[6] My own reaction at the time was that this was an illegitimate use of the concept of dialect borrowing. Instead of introducing hard data on dialect mixture, the respondents argued that since sound change is known to be regular, there *must have been* dialect mixture. There seemed to be no difference between these reactions and the automatic response of certain Neogram-

---

[5] Thus Gauchat: "The phonetic *law* does not affect all items at the same time: some are destined to develop quickly, others remain behind, some offer strong resistance and succeed in turning back any effort at transformation" (cited in Dauzat 1922, my translation).
[6] This response was offered at the 1975 meeting of the LSA in San Francisco, where Chen and Hsieh first presented the Chaozhou data. Since then, it has been developed in Egerod 1976, 1982; Pulleyblank 1978; and Chan 1983. The initial counterresponse was that this criticism did not take into account the specific location of the split and the presumed borrowings. The splits are not randomly distributed throughout the lexicon, but are concentrated in certain etymological classes.

Table 15.1 Distribution of Middle Chinese tone III in modern Chaozhou by Middle Chinese initials (from Cheng and Wang 1977:94)

MIDDLE CHINESE INITIAL	CHAOZHOU TONE	
	2b	*3b*
b	6	7
v	1	3
d	11	14
dz	6	2
z	3	3
ɖ	3	4
dʐ	1	3
ʐ	3	5
dj	2	1
g	6	4
ɣ	14	15
TOTAL	56	61

marians to Gauchat's data on Charmey (see chapters 4, 16): they argued that the fluctuation of /l'/ and /y/ in the middle generation must have been the result of those speakers' borrowing half of their forms from their parents and half from their children. It also seemed to me unlikely that dialect borrowing would be specialized to reflexes of Middle Chinese tone III.

Final consonant shifts in Atayalic dialects

In 1982, Li published data on variation in the Atayalic dialects of Formosa, which showed the type of implicational scaling in word-final consonantal changes exemplified in table 15.2, for 10 speakers of the Skikun dialect. (Though Li presents a number of other sound changes, this velar/labial shift involves the largest number of words and the greatest number of informants.) Li concludes that there is evidence of a general drift in Atayalic dialects toward simplification of features of final segments, and that the changes are phonetically abrupt, and lexically gradual: "The Skikun speakers between ages 80 and 32 apply the rule -p > -k and -m > -ŋ to different lexical items and they differ in the number of items to which the rule applies, largely depending on the age and sex of each individual speaker" (1982:186).

The implicational scale of table 15.2 presents the 10 individual lects as vertical columns; each horizontal line shows a different linguistic environ-

Table 15.2 Lexical diffusion in velar/labial shift in Skikun (from Li 1982)

	S.T. f84	S.P. f80	Y.K. f71	B.M. m65	P.S. m61	Y.S. m54	M.W. m50	Y.N. f55	H.Y. m46	Y.K. m36	W.B. m32	
qciyap	-p	-p	-p	-p	-p	-p	-p	-p	-p	-p	-k	'opposite shore'
ʔiyup	-p	-p	-p	-p	-p	-p	-p	-p	-p	-p	-k	'goshawk'
qatap-	-p	-p	-p	-p	-p	-p	-p	-p	-p	-p	-k	'scissors'
tgtap	-p	-p	-p	-p	-p	-p	-p	-k	-p	-p	-k	'to fan'
ghap	-p	-p	-p	-p	-p	-p	-p	-p	-p/k	-p	-k	'seed'
qurip	-p	-p	-p	-p	-p	-p	-p	-p	-p/k	-p	-k	'ginger'
hmap	-p	-p	-p	-p	-p	-p	-p	-p	-k	-k	-k	'stab'
pshup	-p	-p	-p	-p	-p	-p	-p	-p	-k	-p	-k	'suck'
hmop	-p	-p	-p	-p	-p	-p	-p	-p	-k	-p	-k	'do magic'
talap	-p	-p	-p	-p	-p	-p	-p	-k	-p	-k	-k	'eaves'
tgiyup	-p	-p	-p	-p	-p	-p	-p	-k	-k	-p	-k	'sink'
miyup	-p	-p	-p	-p	-p	-p	-p	-k	-k	-k	-k	'enter'
qmalup	-p	-p	-p	-p	-p	-p	-p	-k	-k	-k	-k	'hunt'
mgop	-p	-p	-p	-p	-p	-p	-p	-k	-k	-k	-k	'share one cup'
qmuyup	-p	-p	-p	-p	-p	-p	-p	-k	-k	-p	-k	'fold'
kmiyap	-p	-p	-p	-p	-p	-p	-p	-k	-k	-k	-k	'catch'
mnep	-p	-p	-p	-p	-p	-k	-p	-k	-k	-k	-k	'to fish'
msuyap	-p	-p	-p	-p	-p/k	-k	-p	-k	-k	-k	-k	'yawn'
qom	-m	-m	-m	-m	-m	-m	-m	-m	-m	-ŋ	-ŋ	'anteater'
syam	-m	-m	-m/ŋ	-m	-m	-m	-m	-ŋ	-m	-ŋ	-ŋ	'pork'
qmtam	-m	-m	-m	-m	-m/ŋ	-m	-m/ŋ	-ŋ	-m	-ŋ	-ŋ	'swallow'
rom	-m	-m	-m	-m	-m	-m	-ŋ	-ŋ	-m	-ŋ	-ŋ	'needle'
qinam	-m	-m	-m	-m	-m	-m	-ŋ	-ŋ	-ŋ	-ŋ	-ŋ	'peach'
hmham	-m	-m	-ŋ	-m	-m/ŋ	-m	-ŋ	-m	-ŋ	-ŋ	-ŋ	'grope'
yuhum	-m	-m	-ŋ	-m	-m	-m	-ŋ	-ŋ	-m	-ŋ	-ŋ	'gall'
prahum	-m	-m	-m	-m	-m/ŋ	-ŋ	-ŋ	-ŋ	-ŋ	-ŋ	-ŋ	'lips'
tmalam	-m	-m	-m	-ŋ	-m/ŋ	-m	-ŋ	-ŋ	-ŋ	-ŋ	-ŋ	'taste'
mtlom	-m	-m	-m	-m	-m	-m	-ŋ	-ŋ	-ŋ	-ŋ	-ŋ	'burn'
lmom	-m	-m	-m	-m	-ŋ	-ŋ	-ŋ	-ŋ	-ŋ	-ŋ	-ŋ	'burn'
mktlium	-m	-m	-m	-m	-m	-ŋ	-ŋ	-ŋ	-ŋ	-ŋ	-ŋ	'run'
cmom	-m	-m	-m	-m	-ŋ	-ŋ	-ŋ	-ŋ	-ŋ	-ŋ	-ŋ	'wipe'
mnkum	-m	-m	-ŋ	-m	-m	-ŋ	-ŋ	-ŋ	-ŋ	-ŋ	-ŋ	'dark'

ment, in this case a particular word. The most conservative lect is that of the two oldest speakers S.T. and S. P. at left: their final consonants are the same as that of the full form of the word given in that column. The first part of the table shows the gradual replacement of the labial voiceless stop by a velar voiceless stop. The most conservative environment for final

/p/ is *qciyap*, where all speakers but the youngest keep the original labial; the most innovative is *msuyap*, where five speakers have velar /k/, and one varies between /p/ and /k/. The implicational scaling for age indicates that for the age dimension, the presence of a velar for a speaker of a given age implies that all younger speakers will have a velar, and the presence of a labial implies that all older speakers will have a labial. On the lexical dimension, it indicates that if a given word has a final labial, all words above it will have a labial; if it has a final velar, all words below it will have a velar. The table is not presented as a perfect implicational scale: there are "scaling errors." For example, the fourth item *tgtap* shows a scaling error for Y.N., who has final /k/, though the use of a final labial by the two younger speakers H.Y. and Y.K. would predict a /p/ for her as well. However, the overall regularity of the pattern is evident, and is submitted to support the conclusion that the significant linguistic environments for the change are individual words.

The second part of table 15.2 shows the corresponding shift for the final labial and velar nasals.

Vowel merger in Shanghai

In 1990, Shen presented similar tables documenting the progress of a vowel merger in Shanghai, collapsing the Middle Chinese distinction that is represented as /-ang/ vs. /-eng/ in Beijing, and as front /-ã/ vs. back /-ɑ̃/ in Shanghai. Shen obtained discrimination data from 376 Shanghai speakers, who were presented with a series of items, each consisting of three words that differed only in the vowel, and were asked to judge which if any of the three was different. There was extensive lexical variation: correlation of the merger with frequency of the word showed an r of .67. Furthermore, there was extensive homophone splitting: words that had the same vowel historically differed from each other about 20% of the time (Wang 1989:21–23).

Lexical diffusion in other language families

Evidence for lexical diffusion is of course not confined to Sino-Tibetan. The papers in Wang 1977 offer evidence from Swiss German, Classical Tibetan, Old Welsh, and Swedish, as well as discussions of acquisition in English and Chinese. Chen and Wang (1975) draw further arguments of lexical diffusion from Sherman's (1973) study of the historical development of English forestressing of nouns derived from verbs. Chapter 16 will consider work by Ogura (1987), which argues that the English Great Vowel Shift proceeded by lexical diffusion. Krishnamurti (1978) traces the development of Dravidian consonant clusters, using computational methods to analyze data presented by Burrow and Emeneau (1961); his results leave no doubt that these sound changes proceeded with the word, not the phoneme, as the basic unit.

15.3 Lexical diffusion in the speech community

With the exception of Shen's experiments in Shanghai, the evidence presented so far is based on changes long completed. This section will turn to evidence for lexical diffusion in studies of the spontaneous use of language within the speech community. The change in progress that we will examine is the tensing of short **a** words in the Middle Atlantic states, with special attention to Philadelphia. American dialects in general exhibit a fronting and raising of this class, and a number of chapters have dealt with the mechanism in one form or another.

The fronting and raising of short **a** continues a process that began in the 10th century. An earlier raising of long **ā** to **ɔ** (in *boat, stone,* etc.) had left a hole that was filled by lengthening of short **a** in open syllables. Fronting, raising, and participation in the Great Vowel Shift led to a merger of *name, gave,* etc., with several other classes in modern /ey/. The residual instances of short **a**, all in checked syllables, are now being affected in all American dialects of English. The most favored subset for raising are words ending in final front nasals: *hand, man, ham,* etc., which are raised almost everywhere. In the Northern Cities Shift, all short **a** words are tensed and raised. But in the Middle Atlantic states, the raising and tensing affect only some short **a** words, following a complex set of conditions that vary systematically from New York to Philadelphia to Baltimore. Chapters 3 and 4 dealt with this Middle Atlantic situation as part of the description of the Philadelphia vowel system, and chapter 11 treated the tense/lax opposition in Philadelphia as an example of a phonemic split.

The tensing of short **a**

There is a sizeable literature on the raising of short **a** in the Middle Atlantic states, beginning with a series of articles by Trager (1930, 1934, 1940), Cohen's (1970) analysis of New York City and surrounding New Jersey, and Ferguson's (1975) description of the Philadelphia system. Payne (1976, 1980) deals with the acquisition of the phonetic process of raising and the distributional pattern of which words are raised. Halle and Mohanan (1985) and Kiparsky (1989) relate these data to the phonological framework developed in their articles. Harris (1989) compares data from Belfast with the New York City and Philadelphia reports in relation to the theory of lexical phonology. Labov (1989a) is a detailed quantitative study of the tense/lax opposition in the speech of 100 Philadelphians. Before the end of part D, I will attempt to clarify a number of the unresolved questions raised in all of these treatments of short **a**.

In the Middle Atlantic dialects, a set of words with short low nonperipheral [æ] is opposed to another set with nuclei that are fronted to a peripheral position – generally mid to high, long, with a centering inglide (i.e., [e:ə]). As before, I will refer to this opposition as lax vs. tense. Figure 15.1 enlarges the view provided by figure 11.7; it shows for both New York City and Philadelphia the set of following consonants that yield tense vowels (when the next segment is [+consonant] or a Level 2 or word boundary): the outer line shows the New York system, and the inner line shows the consonants that condition tensing in Philadelphia, a proper subset of the New York system. The Philadelphia system is close to the minimal or core set that conditions the tensing of low vowels in English generally – front nasals and voiceless fricatives.[7]

In additon to the basic conditioning of the following consonant, there is an extensive set of special phonetic, grammatical, and lexical conditions for tensing to apply. It will be useful here to consider the relation of the major Philadelphia subconditions to the Neogrammarian hypotheses that sound change is lexically regular and mechanical in its operation.

1   *The tensing operation.* Short **a** is tensed before the set of consonants in figure 15.1 only when it is in a closed syllable. Thus *ham* and *hand* have tense vowels, but *hammer* has a lax vowel. This is a simple phonetic condition. But if the following syllable is a Level 2 inflectional suffix, the vowel remains tense, as in *hamming it up*. Again, *man* is tense, both as noun and verb, and *manner* is lax (since a vowel follows the consonant directly). But *manning* (as in *Who is manning the store?*) is tense, since the syllable is open only by virtue of the inflectional suffix *-ing*. This is clearly grammatical information, but no problem arises for the Neogrammarian principles, since this effect can plainly be attributed to analogy: tense /æh/ occurs in the participle *manning* by analogy with the simple verb *man*.

2   *The weak word condition.* To be tensed, the vowel in question cannot

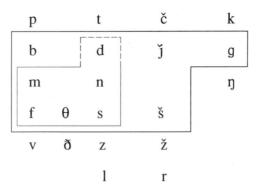

Figure 15.1.   Consonants following short **a** that condition tensing in Philadelphia (inner line) and New York City (outer line)

---

[7] As Ferguson first pointed out, this odd combination of features is also characteristic of the broad **a** class (though the nasal environment is even more limited). When we make the obvioius adjustment of front nasals to back nasals, it also applies to the tensing of short open *o*.

be in a "weak word," that is, one whose only vowel can be shwa. This condition is stated as though it were a phonetic condition, but weak words are of course a subset of "function words": auxiliaries, articles, etc. The classic contrast is tense *tin can* vs. lax *I can*. But any grammatical implications of this condition can also be handled by analogy. Auxiliaries such as *am* and articles like *an* have shwa in normally unstressed position, and shwa is a lax vowel; the marked stressed forms can be said to be lax by analogy with the unstressed forms.

3   *Derivational suffixes.* If a Level 1 derivational suffix follows the consonant after the vowel, there is considerable variation in the frequency of tensing. Thus we find widespread variation in *Lassie*, [laesi] or [le:əsi], and *plastic*, usually [plaestɪk] but possibly [ple:əstɪk]. The variability of the first may be said to reside in the variable identification of the isolated word *lass* as the first part of *Lassie* on the analogy of *Pat:Pattie::lass:Lassie*. But there is no free form *plast* that might support the same argument for *plastic*.

4   *Strong verbs.* Strong verbs ending in nasals remain lax, contrary to the general rule. Thus Philadelphians pronounce lax *ran, swam, began*, but tense *man, Dan, slam, understand*, etc. There is some variation in the *ran, swam, began* class; but the condition that excepts irregular verbs ending in nasals from the general rule is a strong one. In Philadelphia, the vernacular preterit of the verb *win* is always pronounced with a lax vowel, [wæn]. This kind of grammatical information certainly cannot be handled in the Neogrammarian framework. Nor can it be characterized as a unique exception, in the light of Toon's (1976) study of variability in the raising of West Germanic short **a** before nasals in Old English texts. In three sources – the Lindisfarnane Gospels, the Rushworth Gospels, and the Durham ritual – Toon found that the sound change is complete except for Class III strong verbs, which are lax as a group. Of the 106 tokens of these verbs in the Lindisfarnane Gospels, 106 were lax. The Philadelphia *ran, swam, began*, /wæn/ are the sole surviving members of this class in the environments of figure 15.1.

5   *The* mad, bad, glad *class.* All vowels followed by voiced stops are lax, except for those of *mad, bad,* and *glad*, which are always tense. The three words involved are all common affective adjectives, and so we might want to construct some kind of general rule to account for them. But *sad*, another common affective adjective, is lax along with all other short **a** words ending in /d/.[8] This is massively regular for the entire Philadelphia speech community – a clear case of lexical diffusion, arrested in mid-career at some point in the past.

---

[8] The stability of *sad* in Philadelphia will be demonstrated in table 15.5. It is not impossible that further progress of this sound change will make use of the obvious generalization. Some tendency to pronounce tense *sad* in word lists has been observed in Payne's work in the Philadelphia suburbs.

We must therefore concede that not all sound change in Philadelphia is Neogrammarian: one such process, at least in the past, did not share the Neogrammarian syndrome. To make further progress in understanding when regular sound change operates, and when sound change advances one word at a time, we will have to look more closely at short **a** in Philadelphis, to see what kind of rule is at work.

Unpredictable lexical distributions

Trager approached the problem of whether tense /æh/ and lax /æ/ constitute one phoneme or two in the framework of autonomous phonemics. Minimal pairs like *can* [N, V] vs. *can* [Aux], or lexical exceptions like New York City *avenue*, were not the only evidence. The fact that one could not predict whether *jazz* or *wagon* was tense or lax for any given speaker was the major factor that led Trager to entitle his 1940 article "One Phonemic Entity Becomes Two: The Case of 'short *a*'." Cohen (1970) found such extensive and unpredictable irregularity in the margins of the New York City and New Jersey rules – before voiced fricatives and velar stops, in polysyllables – that he concluded that no rule could be written. As noted above, the pronunciation of some groups of words is unpredictable in Philadelphia; for example, short **a** followed by an -stV- sequence (*master, plaster,* etc.) shows extensive individual variation that cannot easily be reduced to rule. In both New York City and Philadelphia, it is difficult to predict the pronunciation of "learned words" like *alas, wrath, Gath,* and *adz,* which are acquired late in life.

The present configuration of tense /æh/ and lax /æ/ in Philadelphia leads to the strong inference that lexical diffusion operated at some earlier state in the history of this redistribution. So far, the view of lexical diffusion is no more direct than the view obtained from the DOC studies. However, in dealing with other aspects of linguistic change, LCV found that the most profitable strategy is to track the mechanism involved by observing change in progress, rather than by weighing the residues of processes no longer operating. It was therefore welcome news to find that, in a subarea of the lexical distribution of short **a** in Philadelphia, lexical diffusion is still at work.

As noted in the previous section, one subcondition of tensing is that a consonantal segment or boundary must follow the first consonant after short **a**. Thus even when short **a** is followed by consonants /m/ and /n/, most favorable to tensing, we would find lax /æ/: *manner, camera, planet, damage, flannel.* I was more than a little surprised when, during an early exploration of the Philadelphia suburb of Radnor, I came across a group of 12-year-olds who read lists with *planet* tense, but the other words lax. This was not an isolated event. In every area of the city, LCV found the same tendency for speakers to break the pattern of the earlier distribution, pronouncing *planet* as tense. Word list data for 31 Philadelphians from

King of Prussia are shown in table 15.3. There is a trend to tense vowels throughout the __NV subclass, but *planet* leads the list with twice the frequency of any other word: two-thirds of the speakers read it with a tense vowel.

LCV also found lexical diffusion in the __LV subclass. In New York City, following /l/ is among the least likely environments for tensing. But Philadelphia postvocalic /l/ is most often realized as an unrounded mid back glide, and there is a general tendency for a nucleus followed by a lax glide to become tense. For adults as well as children, *pal* is homonymous with *Powell*: both words show a long tense nucleus followed by a back glide. Table 15.3 shows word list data from the same 31 King of Prussia subjects, comparing *personality, pal, algebra,* and *California.* Here *personality* and perhaps *pal* are good candidates for lexical diffusion; the data from spontaneous speech point in the same direction.[9]

Table 15.3 Tensing of short **a** in open syllables in King of
Prussia (from Payne 1976)

	N	% Tense
__NV		
planet	62	68
damage	31	35
manage	31	32
flannel	31	23
camera	31	19
family	31	19
__LV		
personality	30	20
pal	31	6
algebra	30	0
California	31	0

[9] The selection of *planet, pal,* and *personality* in the process of lexical diffusion is of course far from arbitrary. The effect of frequency is present, as in the earlier stages of the short **a** rule. The role of affect in *mad, bad,* and *glad* reappears in *pal* and *personality.* Phonetic conditioning can also be detected, not in the precise form of output rules like the fronting of /ow/, but in a rougher approximation: for example, *mad, bad,* and *glad* with grave initials, opposed to *sad* with a nongrave initial. The inclusion of the initial liquid cluster *gl* seems hard to explain, since such environments tend to lower F2 and F1 in the phonetic output (see *glass, traps,* and *black* in figure 6.10). Yet it is repeated in the selection of *planet* as a leading element in the change. More importantly, the following /ɪt/ syllable of *planet* contributes to the tensing of the first vowels, as opposed to the darker /l/ of *flannel* (first pointed out to me by C.-J.N. Bailey, p.c.). This echoes the umlaut rule of the Atlanta dialect described by Sledd (1966), which opposes *pillion* to *pillow.*

Table 15.4 looks more closely at the situation by adding the data from spontaneous speech, and by separating children (age 9–15) from parents (age 37–52). It appears that the pattern of lexical diffusion is not an artifact of word lists.[10] For both adults and children, in both styles, the leading position of *planet* is preserved. Children show an overwhelming tendency to tense *planet*; only two use a lax vowel consistently. Other words are moving as well, but *planet* is obviously the leader.

Lexical diffusion in the working-class neighborhoods

The vowel shifts studied by LCV are initiated and led by speakers in particular locations within the social structure (Labov 1980, 1990). But the lexical diffusion documented above for the middle-class suburb of King of Prussia is not limited to any one social group. Data from working-class neighborhoods in Kensington and South Philadelphia show the same pattern. These data illustrate the extraordinary stability of the core pattern: that is, words governed by subconditions 1 and 5. Labov (1989a) examined short **a** words in the spontaneous speech of 100 working-class speakers in the LCV Neighborhood Study, and found only one exception to the general pattern of tensing governed by the phonetic pattern of figure 15.1 and subcondition 1. It is even more remarkable to find such consistency in the highly specific lexical subcondition 5, as shown in table 15.5: in 259 spontaneous uses of *bad, mad, glad, sad,* and *dad,* one exception was found to the rule that vowels in the first three words are tense, the others are lax.

Table 15.6 shows that there is much less stability in the marginal distributions before intervocalic consonants that show lexical diffusion in King of Prussia. The __LV class provides the largest amount of data. One can observe a steady movement from 0% tensing among the oldest speakers,

Table 15.4   Tensing of short **a** by age and style in King of Prussia A/B/C = no. all tense / no. tense and lax / no. all lax (from Payne 1976)

	Adults, 37–52 years		Children, 9–15 years	
	Speech	Word list	Speech	Word list
planet	1/2/4	1/0/8	12/1/2	17/2/2
damage		0/0/9		10/0/11
manage		0/0/9		9/0/12
flannel	0/0/9	2/0/5		7/0/14

[10] In the King of Prussia interviews, Payne designed special techniques to concentrate occurrences of *planet* in spontaneous speech.

Table 15.5 Tensing and laxing of short **a** before /d/ in Philadelphia spontaneous speech

	Tense	*Lax*
bad	143	0
mad	73	0
glad	18	1
sad	0	14
dad	0	10

Table 15.6 Tensing and laxing of short **a** before /l/ in Philadelphia spontaneous speech ( ) = unclear cases

		AGE			
		8–19	*20–39*	*40–59*	*60+*
ALL __LV WORDS	Tense	7	6	(1)	0
	Lax	8	15(3)	7	10
INDIVIDUAL WORDS					
alley	Tense	5	(1)	(1)	0
	Lax	6	3	3	3
personality	Tense	2	(1)	0	0
	Lax	2	3	(1)	0
Italian	Tense	0	1	0	0
	Lax	4	3	4	2
Allegheny	Tense	0	0	0	0
	Lax	0	4	0	1

to a slight tendency toward tensing among speakers in their forties and fifties, to about 30% tensing among speakers in their twenties and thirties, to almost 50% tensing among preadolescents and adolescents. This increse does not occur evenly across all words. Table 15.6 also shows the record for the four most common words: *alley, personality, Italian,* and *Allegheny*. It is clear that tensing is concentrated in the first two. As in King of Prussia, the results show that *personality* is rapidly becoming a tense word. The same pattern can be observed in the __NV class, though the individual words are not as frequent.

Further progress of /æ/ tensing among young children

In 1990, Roberts began an investigation of the acquisition of sociolinguistic variables by young children, 3–4 years old, in the white community of South Philadelphia (1993), developing indications in the earlier work of Guy and Boyd (1990) and Labov (1990) that children acquire specific Philadelphia variables quite early in life. In this research, Roberts used a variety of techniques to obtain as much data from children at this age as is normally obtained from interviews of one to two hours with adults. The recording, which involved as many as 13 sessions with the same child, was done at a day-care center. To enrich the data on specific variables, Roberts used games and puppet plays to introduce names with phonological features of special interest in the development of the Philadelphia dialect. Included among these were short **a** words, particularly those that had shown indications of lexical diffusion in progress: words with short **a** before intervocalic laterals and nasals, and the class consisting of *mad, bad,* and *glad.* The results allow us to compare the state of the Philadelphia dialect in 1973, among adults and adolescents, with the developments among 3- and 4-year-olds in 1990. These children resembled the adults in their uniform use of the core pattern: for example, 30 tokens tense out of 31 for *mad* and 42 tense out of 42 for *bad,* as opposed to 42 lax out of 43 for *sad.*[11]

Roberts obtained considerable data on the pronunciation of three words with short **a** before intervocalic /l/ (*Sally, Allen,* and *alligator*), and five words with short **a** before intervocalic nasals (*planet, Janet, animals, camera,* and *hammer*). Table 15.7 shows the data for the 11 children from whom the most data were obtained. The first column shows all 11 children. The second uses the pronunciation of the word *giraffe* to distinguish between those children who had fully acquired the Philadelphia dialect and those who had not. The pattern for these 7 children is somewhat more consistent than for the 11 as a whole.

By this evidence, the tensing of short **a** before intervocalic /l/ has progressed considerably. The three words *Sally, Allen,* and *alligator* all show rates of tensing higher than 50%, though they do not give us enough evidence to show that the earlier pattern of lexical diffusion has continued.[12]

The results for short **a** before intervocalic nasals are more promising. Good data were obtained from the children on two of the words in table 15.3: *planet* and *camera.* In the King of Prussia study in 1973, *planet* showed twice as high a rate of tensing as other words, about 61% in word

---

[11] In is interesting to note that the one tense token of *sad* was given by a child with one black parent. In other respects as well, his speech pattern differed from that of most of the children.
[12] It was not possible to get good data on the words that had shown lexical diffusion among adults – *Italian, personality,* and *Allegheny* – since these words are not in the active vocabulary of 3-year-olds.

Table 15.7   Tensing of short **a** before intervocalic laterals and nasals by young Philadelphia children

	All children [N = 11]		Children with consistent /æh/ in giraffe [N = 7]	
	Tense	*Lax*	*Tense*	*Lax*
Sally	19	16	11	9
Allen	10	8	5	5
alligator	19	5	12	3
planet	87	5	57	1
Janet	14	14	8	6
animals	0	34	0	21
hammer	1	15	1	7
camera	0	41	0	24
giraffe	27	11	23	0

list data. In the spontaneous speech of adolescents, the rate was higher, about 80%. The South Philadelphia 3-year-olds of 1990 showed almost categorical tensing of *planet*. For all 11 children, the rate is 94.5%, and when we consider only those children who appear to have mastered the Philadelphia system, it reaches 98.3% – only one exception was recorded. On the other hand, words with a following /ər/ syllable, *hammer* and *camera*, are almost categorically lax. Instead of a general advance, there seems to be a polarization of tensing in this subset.

Might this distribution be the product of phonetic conditioning? The analysis of short /i/ in Southern English by Sledd (1966) shows that unstressed -/ɪt/ will condition brighter vowels in the preceding syllable, and the difference between *planet* and *camera* can be accounted for in this way. The absence of tensing in *animals* may be linked to the fact that polysyllabic words with initial short **a** have already appeared to favor laxing words with following voiceless fricatives like *aster* and *aspirin*. But it is very difficult to give a phonetic motivation for the contrast between *Janet* and *planet*. *Janet* was chosen to be phonetically comparable to *planet*; with the initial palatal /dʒ/, it should favor tensing even more than *planet*, with an initial obstruent-liquid cluster. Yet the difference between the tensing of the two words is large: *planet* shows almost 100% tensing, and *Janet* 50%. The most recent study of short **a** in Philadelphia therefore supports the earlier findings that assignment to the tense class is proceeded by a lexical redistribution of individual words.

15.4 Summary of the evidence so far

At this point no reasonable person would maintain what might be called
the Neogrammarian dogma: that sound change is always gradual, always
regular, affecting all words at the same time. The question now is whether
the Neogrammarian position retains any substantive value. Are *some* sound
changes phonetically regular and lexically abrupt? Chen and Wang
(1975:257) come close to saying no:

This lexically gradual view of sound changes is incompatible, in principle, with the
structuralist way of looking at sound change.

A later statement of Wang (1979) is more moderate: "The Neogrammarian conception of language change will probably continue to be part
of the truth." And in response to the first presentation of the approach
taken in these chapters (Labov 1981), a number of statements on behalf of
lexical diffusion began with an acknowledgment that both Neogrammarian
regularity and lexical diffusion exist. Yet over the past decade, it has
become evident that the lexical diffusionists do not accept the existence of
regular sound change in the sense that the Neogrammarians conceived it:
a phonetically motivated change of an articulatory target that affects every
word in which that target occurs. Wang and Lien (to appear) reinterpret
the Neogrammarian position as a description of the output of a change,
and not of the process of change itself. They return to the position of Chen
and Wang (1975) that lexical diffusion is "the basic mechanism in the
implementation of sound change." To the best of my knowledge, no parti-
san of lexical diffusion has presented evidence of regular sound change.[13]
In each case examined, the fundamental mechanism of change argued for
is that words migrate, one at a time, from one class to another (Barrack
1976; Toon 1976, 1978; Hooper 1976; Krishnamurti 1978; Milroy 1980;
Bauer 1982, 1986; Phillips 1980, 1984; Fagan 1985; Ogura 1987; Shen
1990; Wang 1977, 1989). This long list of publications would lead an
outside reader to the impression that the evidence is mounting inexorably
in favor of the principle of lexical diffusion. But there is an unfortunate
bias in what kinds of reports are submitted. Those who work within the
historical/comparative framework continue to assume regularity. Though
papers have been published that criticize certain claims for lexical diffusion,
it would not occur to a historical linguist to write a paper reporting that

---

[13] Wang and Lien refer to an unpublished study of the Wenxi variety of the Shanxi dialect
by H. Wang (1990), which does appear to recognize regular change as well as lexical diffusion.
She identifies "conditioned and diffusional sound change," which "involves a change in phonemic categories which are restricted by phonological conditions, but not by words and contexts."

his or her latest investigation showed regular sound change. Indeed, no one would publish such a report, for it does not bring anything new to light.

The next chapter will attempt to restore the balance by reviewing the data presented so far from the Neogrammarian perspective. It will then present some direct evidence to support the Neogrammarian view that it is sounds that change, and not words.

16

Expanding the Neogrammarian Viewpoint

16.1 The current status of the Neogrammarian position

Chapter 15 raised the question of whether we might indeed locate firm evidence of a Neogrammarian sound change: a phonetically motivated shift of an entire sound class, affecting all words in which that sound occurs at the same time. But before we proceed, we might well consider whether any reference to the Neogrammarian controversy is not out of date, since Hoenigswald 1978 may in fact have already resolved it. That paper brings to a precise statement a position that Hoenigswald has represented for a number of years: that the Neogrammarian hypothesis was not a substantive statement about sound change, but a working principle that defined sound change.

Hoenigswald points out that if we consider the *practice* of the Neogrammarians, rather than their ideological statements, it will be seen that they were motivating the choice between two competing regularities found in the course of comparative reconstruction. One was to be called *sound change*; the other *analogy* or *dialect borrowing*. He points out that the lexical variability of the split of IE voiced palatals into Old Persian **z** and **d** might well be taken as a case of "sporadic" sound change. However, he concludes that such a label is definitional, not substantive.

If this is only a case of labelling, in all sobriety, regularities of nonanalogical origin for which we cannot name or care to construct a reasonable historical background ... 'sporadic' means no more than 'somehow competing' and is noncommittal. ... It seems that sporadic sound change is either a contradiction in terms or merely a traditional and not particularly well chosen collective designation for other than main-channel material.

Thus sound change is defined as a certain kind of object. The argument may seem circular; but, as Hoenigswald suggests, it is a useful kind of circularity that may clarify our understanding of what we are doing in historical reconstruction.

This analysis may seem especially congenial in light of the evidence reviewed above for lexical diffusion as the primary mechanism of sound change. If this represents the underlying process, the Neogrammarian hypothesis can still be defended as a way of identifying the regular correspondences that result when all the words that have followed a change are finally gathered into a single class, and then as a way of using that regularity as a base for constructing language relations.

What then remains of the Neogrammarian controversy? Are we to put aside as misguided the long list of articles that have vigorously argued for or against the Neogrammarian principles? On the one side are Curtius, Leskien, Delbrück, Osthoff, Paul, Saussure, Bloomfield, Hockett; on the other, Schuchardt, Gilliéron, Jespersen, Sturtevant; and on all sides, commentators too numerous to mention. If Hoenigswald is right, the copious ink devoted to the Lautgesetzfrage has been spilt on a misunderstanding.

Perhaps; but it seems to me that a substantial question remains. In Bloomfield's (1933) formulation, we are talking about a theory of how sounds actually change.

[S]ound-change is merely a change in the speakers' manner of producing phonemes and accordingly affects a phoneme at every occurrence, regardless of the nature of any particular linguistic form in which the phoneme happens to occur. . . .[T]he whole assumption can be briefly put into the words: *phonemes change.* (pp. 353–4)

This formulation seems to me solid enough to deserve the title of a theory, rather than a mere working principle. The theoretical statement may not have determined real practice, or even reflected that practice, but it does give us the incentive to formulate observations and principles that can prove it to be right or wrong. One may argue that regular sound change and analogy are always present, even co-present; but, as Malkiel (1967) points out in his insightful review of the competing principle that "Each word has its own history," it makes quite a difference whether we have 90% of one type or 90% of the other.

In such a climate, the classic "sound laws" would not necessarily be abolished (in fact, their residue might be doubly important for genetic reconstruction), but they would, psychologically, lose a great deal of their immediate appeal, and certainly would no longer, without grave damage, dominate the scene of linguistic research. (p. 140)

Unfortunately, the Neogrammarian principle has often been promoted as though it were an ideological position rather than part of a scientific program. Chapter 15 referred to this ideological use of the Neogrammarian principle in reactions to the earliest example of research on sound change in progress – Goidanich's (1926) critique of Gauchat's (1905) description of sound change in progress in Charmey. Gauchat's report of variation did not fit the Neogrammarian conception of sound change; for example, in the lenition of /l'/, the oldest generation used [l'] and youngest used [j], but the middle generation used both. Goidanich argued that Gauchat could not have observed the true sound changes that lenited [l'] to a glide. He argued that since sound change was defined as a gradual shift of sound from one target to the other, the discrete fluctuations that Gauchat observed must have been the result of dialect mixture. And since Charmey had been selected as an isolated village where dialect mixture from outside sources was least likely, the dialect borrowing must have taken place *within* the community. The first and third generations evidently spoke different dialects, contrasting [l'] and [j]. Goidanich argued that the fluctuations of the middle generation must have been the result of members of that generation borrowing some of their forms from their parents, and some from their children!

This resistance to the findings of dialect geography echoes the earlier pessimism of Delbrück (1885), who thought it might be very difficult to assess "how great the uniformity will be within the sounds of a homogeneous language" (p. 117), and concluded that the exceptionless character of sound laws could only be derived deductively, never by induction.

From what an individual speaks or would speak at a definite moment in his life, if he allowed the whole mass of his vocabulary to pass through his vocal organs, we must subtract all that can be regarded as borrowed (in the broadest sense) and then all phonetic formations that depend on analogy. (p. 129)

The empirical task is defined as an impossible one. Following a parallel logic 70 years later, Hockett (1958:44) concluded that sound change was too slow to be observed, and phonological change was too fast to be observed (see Weinreich, Labov, and Herzog 1968).

It must be granted that this negative approach has successfully influenced the course of linguistic research. Dialectology has been effectively isolated from general linguistics, as any introductory text will show. Though Bloomfield himself engaged in the study of word history, his chapter on dialect geography appears to take a point of view quite distinct from that of his chapters on phonetic change (Malkiel 1967).[1] Scholars continue to search for universal principles by manipulating isolated examples – subtracting from the available data, rather than adding to them.

This was not the Neogrammarians' original intent. As the quotation in section 1.2 showed, Osthoff and Brugmann's enthusiasm for empirical research went far beyond their endorsement of Winteler 1876. There are remarkable parallels between the methodological issues that they con-

---

[1] But see Kiparsky 1989:371, fn. 1, which presents a different view of the matter, and chapter 17 of this volume.

fronted and those that we confront today, where we can profit from their emphasis on "the clear air of tangible reality" and their call "to renounce forever that . . . method of investigation according to which people observe language only on paper."

It seems to me that Osthoff and Brugmann were on the right track – and that the discouragement voiced by Delbrück, echoed by Hockett and many others, was premature. We can give new life to the Neogrammarians' ideas by opening up the field to the vast array of data provided by the study of sound change in progress. This is indeed the tenor of Kiparsky's assessment of the empirical content of the exceptionless hypothesis. In response to Hoenigswald, he argues that "any borrowing hypothesis must fit the known dialectological and sociolinguistic realities" (1989:371). And since the dialectology of dead languages (like the Old Persian case considered by Hoenigswald) is irrecoverable, it follows that "the Neogrammarians were right in insisting on evidence from living languages as the basis for the theory of change."

An empirical approach to regular sound change

The case for lexical diffusion has been presented by Wang, Cheng, and Chen within a framework closely aligned with that of Weinreich, Labov, and Herzog (1968): the empirical foundations for a theory of language change must include the capacity to deal with the "orderly heterogeneity" that is a fundamental characteristic of language. The evidence for lexical diffusion, as presented in chapter 15, is certainly an impressive example of such an orderly distribution of variables.

However, the critique of the Neogrammarian position presented by the proponents of lexical diffusion has tended to focus more on the slogans or ideological positions that have been published in the course of the controversy, than on the evidence that led the Neogrammarians to their position in the first place. But there have been extensive efforts by scholars to assemble this evidence and assess its impact on the issues. The most useful for our present purpose is the remarkable work of Fónagy (1956, 1967).

Fónagy presents data from over 60 studies of sound change in progress – concentrated in French, English, German, and Hungarian dialects – together with his own instrumental measurements of vowel lengthenings and shortenings in French and Hungarian; he also reviews a wider range of completed sound changes. He gives full weight to the critique of the Neogrammarian position that emerges from the evidence of dialectology. Much of his criticism of the Neogrammarians enlarges the position taken by Gauchat: it is directed at their portrait of sound change as a uniform, gradual process in a homogeneous community, where the old forms give way to the new without oscillation or variation. Fónagy also presents many studies that show lexical diffusion and grammatical conditioning of sound change. At the same time, he warns that the opposing slogan – that sound change proceeds from word to word – receives even less support from the available evidence. He points out that lexical conditioning is comparatively rare, and that sound change begins in the majority of cases with the entire relevant vocabulary (1956:218–20, 1967:109). In fact, he shows that the assumption of homogeneity can lead dialectologists to exaggerate the case for lexical conditioning; when a wider range of data from the speech community is taken into account, words that appeared to be exceptions may turn out to differ only in the frequency of the new variant (1956:219).

Typical of the cases presented by Fónagy is Remacle's 1944 study of the alternation of intervocalic /h/ with zero in the Ardenne Liègois of Regne-Bihain. A first study of an 11-year-old boy showed lexical variation. But as the interview proceeded, it became evident that stylistic variation affected all words. The /h/ was used most often in careful speech, and some words were used more often in casual style. Remacle's data thus foreshadowed the more systematic studies of style shifting in the speech community, beginning with Labov 1966 and Shuy, Wolfram, and Riley 1966. The deletion of /h/ may have been a well-established sociolinguistic variable rather than a new sound change in progress. There is also the possibility that Remacle was dealing with dialect mixture, in the alternation of a local form with a conservative, standard form. In general, then, we must be alert to the possibility that other reports of lexical diffusion may be the products of limited data or of dialect mixture of this type.

16.2   Reexamining the evidence on lexical diffusion

With these precautions in mind, let us return to the evidence on lexical diffusion presented in chapter 15, and examine it from the viewpoint of those Neogrammarians who were strongly oriented to empirical investigations of the issues. We will reopen the question of dialect mixture, and consider possible phonetic conditioning of what seemed to be lexical variation.

The Atayalic consonant shifts revisited

Table 15.2 presented Li's (1982) implicational scale of lexical items in an Atayalic dialect of Formosa that was undergoing the shift from a labial to a velar place of articulation, as an example of a change taking place by lexical diffusion.[2] Lexical diffusion does not rule out the possibility of phonetic conditioning; indeed, the selection of a word is frequently motivated

---

[2] The data of table 15.2 seem to have been derived from the elicitation of single words; there are no references to spontaneous speech, and many of the words are from specialized vocabulary. There is no indication, however, that formality of elicitation procedures interfered with the regularity of the data.

by its phonetic composition (Chen and Wang 1975). The essential point is that the phonetic conditioning does not entirely determine the successive selection of individual words: the irreducible fact of lexical identity is reflected in the data, since the fundamental mechanism of change is said to be the selection of words from one category to join another category.

Like many implicational scales, this one is more impressive at first glance than on repeated examination. In the top half of the table, which shows the shift from /p/ to /k/, half of the words show scaling errors. The usual way of presenting scaling errors is to calculate the percentage for all cells: this would be 9/180 or 5%. It can then be said that the table shows "95% scalability."[3] (Since only 6 of the 10 speakers show any variation, this degree of error for the change in progress is actually 9/108 or 8.3%.) This might lead one to believe that the selection of /p/ or /k/ for a given word is indeed determined by its lexical identity.

The number of scaling errors in the bottom half of the table, which shows the shift from /m/ to /ŋ/, is twice as great as for the top half: 14 out of 130, or 10.8%. On the whole, it appears that the vertical position of the various words is not fixed, and that many rearrangements would give equally regular results. Nevertheless, the rearrangements would be local: it is clear that there are words that strongly favor the change, and others that do not. The question is whether it is their lexical identity, or some other factor, that is responsible for their position. In chapter 15, we saw that phonetic factors are roughly correlated with the selection of short **a** words to be included in the Philadelphia tense category, but that an arbitrary lexical selection is also at play, which is the essential feature of lexical diffusion. Is that the case with the Atayalic data?

We must first of course grant that no categorical, exceptionless rule can be written for these data: they show just the kind of fluctuation that dogmatic Neogrammarians like Goidanich rejected. We will reexamine these data with the probabilistic tools of sociolinguistic method, and ask whether there are phonetic factors that assign the position of each word as narrowly as the data themselves permit, or whether there are radical lexical exceptions that cannot be accounted for phonetically.

Table 15.2 shows no obvious influence of the immediately preceding vowels that will account for the choice of velar or labial. Nor do the initial consonants of the final syllables show a tight correlation with the variable. But if we take one step back and examine the initial consonants of the words, it becomes evident that the use of velar or labial is strongly influenced by the place of articulation of those consonants, particularly the stops. Fricatives, liquids, and glides do not appear to influence the vari-

---

[3] See Rickford 1991 for a review of methods for assessing the statistical significance of implicational scales. The scalability criterion follows Guttman's original "Index of Reproducibility," but later critiques show that more rigorous measures are required.

ation, with the exception of the laryngeal /h/. The least change is found with initial uvular stop /q/, and the most change is found with initial labial /m/. Initial stops or clusters with intermediate places of articulation – velar or apical – show intermediate frequencies of final velars. In other words, table 15.2 shows a systematic form of dissimilation, where the place of articulation of the initials is differentiated as much as possible from the place of articulation of the final.

It is of course evident that final nasals shift to velar articulation much more rapidly than final oral stops. Table 16.1 therefore examines separately the percentage of velar finals for subcategories of preceding stops, summing across all 10 speakers of table 15.2. Many of the preceding stops occur in combinations, and each combination assumes a position in the scale proportionate to the combined effect of the individual items.

It is striking that the same ordering is found in the smaller group with final nasal consonants as in the larger group with oral consonants. This encourages us to believe that the entire process is governed by the same general phonetic factors. Since the data are given in binary form (presence or absence of the innovating velar feature), a multivariate analysis with the variable rule program will allow us to examine this possibility. Table 16.2 shows the results of a variable rule analysis of the Skikun labial-velar alterations. Sex and age are entered as separate factor groups. A third factor group registers whether the final consonant is oral or nasal, and a fourth registers the place of articulation of word-initial stops in table 16.1.

This analysis reveals a good fit of prediction to observation, with a chi-

Table 16.1 Percentage velar finals by initial place of articulation

		Oral final	N	Nasal final	N
Uvular, glottal	q-, qc-, ʔ	11.25	4	20.0	1
Velar+laryngeal	gh-	15.0	1		
Velar+apical	tgt-, tg-	20.0	2		
Labial+laryngeal	psh-	20.0	1		
Apical	t-	30.0	1		
Uvular+nasal	qm-, qmt-, qin-	35.0	2	36.7	2
No stop	r-, sy-, y-			41.6	3
Laryngeal+nasal	hm-, hmh-	30.0	2	55.0	1
Apical/velar+nasal	tm-, km-, mg-, mtl-, mktl-, mnk-	40.0	2	61.2	4
Labial, oral	pr-			65.0	1
Labial, nasal	m-, mn-, ms-, cm-, lm-	51.6	3	70.0	3
Total		28.6	18	52.9	15

Table 16.2 Variable rule analysis of Skikun labial-velar alternations by sex, age, final consonant, and initial consonant clusters; dependent variable: velar final

	% Velar	Varbrul weight
SEX		
Male	41	.90
Female	38	.32
AGE		
70–	12	.01
60–69	15	.21
50–59	42	.55
30–49	74	.97
FINAL CONSONANT		
Oral	24	.29
Nasal	56	.76
INITIAL CONSONANTS		
Uvular, glottal	5	.04
Labial+laryngeal	12	.22
Velar+apical	12	.24
Velar+laryngeal	19	.35
No stop	42	.35
Apical	25	.48
Uvular+nasal	41	.57
Laryngeal+nasal	38	.59
Apical/velar+nasal	56	.77
Labial, oral	75	.87
Labial, nasal	60	.89

square per cell of 1.08. The variable rule analysis considers data from only 8 of the 10 speakers, since the oldest and youngest speakers' pronunciations are invariant. In table 16.1, the cells that show both labial and velar forms were rated as .5 velar; in the variable rule analysis, they are grouped with the innovative velar cells, so that the dependent variable for table 16.2 represents any shift to a velar articulation.

Results for the social factors are sharp and clear. Though there are only two female speakers who are variable, the high value for male fits in with the fact that the two invariant conservative speakers and the most conservative variable speaker are female, and the invariant innovative speaker is male. The age grading is extremely steep. The conservative speakers are in their 80s, and differentiation of the 30s and 40s is even more evident when we take into account the invariant innovative speaker, who is 32.

Table 16.3   Comparison of the ordering of places of articulation in tables 16.1
                                    and 16.2

	Table 16.1 Percentages	Table 16.2 Multivariate analysis
1	Uvular, glottal	Uvular, glottal
2	Velar+laryngeal	Labial+laryngeal
3	Velar+apical	Velar+apical
4	Labial+laryngeal	Velar+laryngeal
5	Apical	No stop
6	Uvular+nasal	Apical
7	No stop	Uvular+nasal
8	Laryngeal+nasal	Laryngeal+nasal
9	Apical/velar+nasal	Apical/velar+nasal
10	Labial, oral	Labial, oral
11	Labial, nasal	Labial, nasal

Our major concern is with the phonetic environments. Though one
would not expect the orderings for raw percentages and multivariate analysis to be identical, the major effects are well preserved (see table 16.3). Of
the 11 environments listed, items 1, 3, and 8–11 are ordered in the same
way, but the others are rearranged to a certain extent. The important fact
is that the same set of rational environmental effects can be seen to be
operating on both the oral and nasal finals. Figure 16.1 graphs the variable

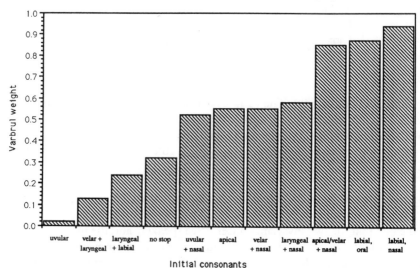

Figure 16.1.   Varbrul weights for initial consonant group in Skikun labial-velar
alternation

rule weights for the phonetic environments. At the two extremes are the most disfavoring and favoring environments in isolation. In the center are the neutral apicals. Velars fall toward the disfavoring side. All other combinations are positioned as the individual components would predict.

We can infer from figure 16.1 that the positive factors leading to verarization are nasality and labiality of the initial consonants; that apical and velar consonants have little effect, though velars are somewhat more conservative; and that laryngeal, glottal, and uvular consonants are very conservative. These inferences can be made more precise by a variable rule analysis that extracts all of the relevant features as separate factor groups from the sequence of preceding consonants: uvular, laryngeal, velar, apical, labial, nasal. Thus in *prahum*, the only factor group marked present is labial, since *p* is the only initial stop. For *mktlium*, the factors labial, nasal, velar, and apical are all marked present.

Figure 16.2 shows the results of a variable rule analysis that substitutes this set of six feature groups for the one environmental factor group of the preceding analysis. For each feature, the figure shown is the difference between the weight for the presence of that feature and the weight for its absence. The role of the six features is clear and unambiguous, confirming the general hypothesis of dissimilation in precise detail. The most disfavoring factor is the feature *uvular* (here a cover term for "uvular" and "glottal"), and the most favoring factor is the feature *labial*. *Velar* and *apical* are in the expected intermediate positions. The *laryngeal* feature has a dis-

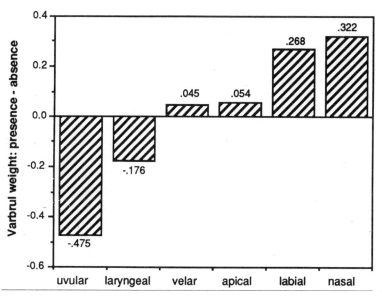

Figure 16.2. Effect of initial consonant features on velar realization of final consonants in Skikun

favoring effect, as we have seen: apparently its back articulation overbalances the fact that it is not a stop articulation.

We also note that *nasal* is the only feature here that is not a place of articulation, but a manner. It is obviously not a dissimilating feature, since it favors both oral and nasal final velars. The favoring effect of *nasal* as a feature of preceding consonants is consistent with its strongly favoring effect for the final consonant: .76 for *nasal* vs. .29 for *oral*, or a difference of .47 on the scale of figure 16.2.

The combination of figures 16.1 and 16.2 gives a clear view of the operation of the phonetic environment. It was already evident that the most powerful conservative feature is the uvular /q/ (and the glottal /ʔ/). It is now clear that the laryngeal /h/, though not a stop, is also strongly conservative, with about half the effect of /q/. In combination with the strongly positive labial feature, it leads to a very low value, though only one word is involved – *pshup*. Its combination with the positive nasal and labial factors in *hmap*, *hmop*, and *hmham* leads to a sizeable lowering of velarization. In addition to appearing strongly in the word *pshup*, the negative effect of the laryngeal /h/ shows up in combination with uvulars. If the major factor operating here is dissimilation, then the ambiguous character of /h/ – laryngeal fricative and oral voiceless vowel – is consistent with this weakly negative effect. A weaker influence is velarity, which gives quite low values in combination with other features in figure 16.2. Apicality is effectively neutral; combinations including this factor show little obvious effect that is not due to velarity.

This reexamination of the Atayalic data indicates that a change that was initially presented as a clear case of lexical diffusion is instead a likely example of Neogrammarian regularity. The Neogrammarian viewpoint must of course be modified to accept stochastic regularities in place of absolute rules. It is also possible that the limited data set conceals lexical irregularities of the type found in the development of Philadelphia short **a**. This case is therefore not presented as a demonstration of lexical regularity but instead is offered as a demonstration of the need to examine evidence for lexical diffusion more closely. Li's valuable presentation of the Atayalic data illustrates one of the dangers of the lexical view that the Neogrammarians anticipated. By accepting the word as the fundamental unit of change, the investigator is less likely to search for the deeper phonetic regularities that may underlie the process of change. This is of course not a necessary correlate of accepting lexical diffusion as an important mechanism of change: Chen and Wang (1975) show clearly how one may recognize both phonetic factors and lexical selection. But neglect of phonetic conditioning is a natural consequence of the view that the selection of individual words is the fundamental mechanism of change.

To sum up, the application of Neogrammarian techniques to the Atayalic consonant shift data shows that there is no clear evidence to support a mechanism of lexical diffusion, and until such evidence is advanced, we must accept the Atayalic case as an example of Neogrammarian regularity.

The Chaozhou tone split revisited

The Atayalic data do not provide the rich supply of homonyms that made Chinese dialects so useful in examining the regularity hypothesis. Pursuing our development of the Neogrammarian perspective, we must next reexamine the Chaozhou data of chapter 15.

It will be recalled that the immediate Neogrammarian response to these data was to claim that dialect mixture must have been responsible for the splitting. Wang and Lien (to appear) present a detailed reexamination of this question, based on Lien's (1987) recent research on Chaozhou. They find that the mixture of literary and colloquial dialects that Egerod, Pulleyblank, and others argued for in Chaozhou was in fact real, and actually more extensive than anyone had thought. It now appears that the irregular developments of Chaozhou tones are indeed the result of borrowings from literary Chinese. The literary stratum in Chaozhou, represented by the Northern Luoyang and Chang'an dialects, showed a merger of Middle Chinese tone III in words with voiced initials and the reflexes of MC tone II in words with voiced obstruent initials. Both groups surface as modern tone 2b. The colloquial stratum of Chaozhou is basically a southern Min dialect, with a Yue (Austro-asiatic) substratum. Here all words with MC tone III remain distinct from tone II, and tone III words with voiced initials appear with modern tone 3b. Reviewing Lien's work, Wang (1989) concludes that "it is clear now that this large influx of MC IIIv morphemes into 2b was the actuation mechanism for the tone change." Wang and Lien go further, and state that "as a result of the imposition of the literary system on the colloquial system, all the eight modern tone categories each contain both the literary stratum and the colloquial stratum." But the reason that the borrowing (or "diffusion" in their terms) appears to be phonetically selective is that the differences between the tone systems appear primarily as a result of the differences in the development of tone IIIv.

The intricate character of the dialect borrowing appears in an even more striking way in Lien's finding that many words cannot be assigned individually to a literary or colloquial stratum. He demonstrates that many modern Chaozhou words are hybrids, with all possible combinations of literary and colloquial reflexes in initials, finals, and tones. Table 16.4 illustrates some of these intimate combinations.

Here we see that the split of tones 2b/3b is not the only factor that leads to doublets; other original homonym pairs are split by segmental features. For example, *lou* 2b and *lou* 3b, both meaning 'dew', differ only in the colloquial versus the literary tone, but *nãũ* and *lau*, both meaning 'noisy', differ in the literary /n/ versus the colloquial /l/ as well as nasality.

Thus lexical diffusion is seen here as the mechanism of what Bloomfield

Table 16.4   Combinations of literary (L) and colloquial (C) patterns in
Chaozhou morphemes (from Wang 1989:12)

Initial	Final	Tone	Examples	
L	L	L	su 2b 'to feed'	nãũ 2b 'noisy'
C	C	C	ts'i 3b 'to feed'	
C	L	L		lau 2b 'noisy'
L	C	C	lou 3b 'dew'	
L	C	L	lou 2b 'dew'	
C	L	C	tsia 3b 'thank'	
C	C	L	nĩõ 2b 'quantity'	
L	L	C	sia 3b 'thank'	

called "intimate borrowing": something quite different from the split of
a homogeneous system that was originally projected for Chaozhou. The
exposition of Wang and Lien certainly enlarges our understanding of what
happened in Chaozhou. But it also seems to be a frank admission that the
critics of the 1972 argument of Cheng and Wang were right. How can the
Chaozhou case bear on the Neogrammarian hypothesis if it is admitted
that it is a case of dialect mixture after all?

Wang and Lien's analysis was not of course constructed with the intention of reinforcing the Neogrammarian perspective. They acknowledge that
Chaozhou is a case of borrowing, but go on to argue that there is no
"antinomy" between borrowing and sound change. They would resolve
this opposition by expanding the concept of "actuation" of Chen and
Wang (1975) to include the influence of language contact as well as physiological, acoustic, and conceptual factors. Actuation is described as an initial
"triggering" distinct from "implementation" – the actual process of the
change itself, which in their view is lexical diffusion. Thus there is no reason why the Chaozhou case could not have been simultaneously a case of
language contact and a case of lexical diffusion.

How is this position related to a criticism of the Neogrammarian concept
of regular sound change? Wang and Lien present their argument within a
view of a linguistic system "in which each and every component of a grammar is interrelated." While they reject Saussure's Neogrammarian position
on sound change, they endorse the Saussurian notion that *tout se tient* in
language structure and design. They acknowledge the existence of system-
internal phonetic changes, but argue that these cannot be isolated from
social factors (the influence of the literary language) and conceptual factors
(the influence of grammar and meaning).

Wang and Lien associate their position with the sociolinguistic recognition of the orderly heterogeneity of the speech community (Weinreich,

Labov, and Herzog 1968). Their view of the role of social factors in language change will enter into the discussion of the role of internal factors in language change in volume 2. But at this point, we must pursue further the implications of the association between lexical diffusion and the influence of the literary stratum in Chaozhou. Similar connections have appeared in other cases of lexical diffusion, and bear crucially upon the argument that lexical diffusion is the basic mechanism of sound change.

Social correction as dialect mixture

The example of Chaozhou suggests that historical records that are first interpreted as the result of internal sound changes may turn out to be the result of later and more conscious reactions to sound change. In sociolinguistic studies of the speech community, this opposition has been termed *change from below* and *change from above* (Labov 1966:chap. 9) In general, change from above involves lexical borrowing. Thus Haeri (1991) shows that the variable appearance of /q/ in Cairene Arabic is not a systematic sociolinguistic variable of the colloquial language, but rather a set of borrowings of individual words from Classical Arabic.

Words of course are not to be despised or neglected. One argument for lexical diffusion revolves around the social importance of words: that they are the basic carriers of social significance. It is certainly true that when people talk about sound change, it is usually in terms of particular words: the social correction of sound changes in New York City, Philadelphia, or Chicago is focused on individual words, not sounds. But these corrections occur only in the late stages of a change, when it is all but completed, and they are remarkably unsystematic and sporadic, with none of the predictable and regular behavior of the original sound changes.

The irregular character of lexical correction is not an argument for lexical diffusion, but rather a reason to doubt that words are the fundamental units of change. The detailed investigation of sound changes within the community that we have carried out show that the earlier stages of change are quite immune from such irregular lexical reactions; and even in a late stage, the unreflecting use of the vernacular preserves that regularity. Figure 16.3a shows the distribution of words in the two classes in the speech of Leon Alinsky, 30, from New York City. The change involved here – the raising of short **a** in certain closed syllables – is the New York City correlate of the Philadelphia change that we have studied so closely. In New York City, it appears to date back to at least the middle of the 19th century.[4] It currently affects words with short **a** before the consonants shown by the outer line in figure 15.1 (basically in closed syllables). As in

---

[4] Real-time data on this change in progress date back to the end of the 19th century. Babbitt (1896) described the raising of the words in the "broad *a*" class to mid front position, perhaps the same subset now characteristic of Philadelphia.

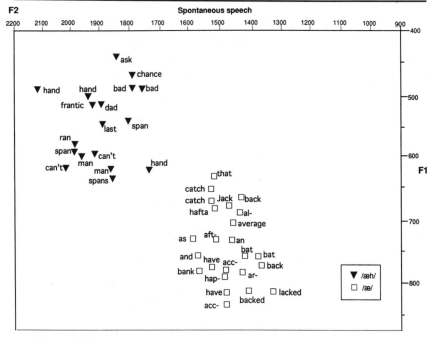

Figure 16.3. /æ/ and /æh/ classes for Leon Alinsky, 30, New York City
(a) Location of nuclei in spontaneous speech

Philadelphia, short **a** in these words becomes tense /æh/, rising from low to mid and eventually to high position. In figure 16.3a, the triangles, representing /æh/, are discretely separated from the squares that represent lax /æ/. Figure 16.3b is the pattern of short **a** words shown by Alinsky in reading a connected text; the two word classes are brought close together, but the distribution of spontaneous speech is preserved. Figure 16.3c shows the locations of the nuclei pronounced by the same speaker in reading word lists. A few words remain in the raised position: *pass, bad, bag,* and perhaps *dance.* The laxing of *half, ask, laugh,* and the other token of *pass* is just as inexplicable and unpredictable as the splitting of Chaozhou tone III.

Several cases of lexical diffusion cited in Wang 1977 involve such late stages in the correction of a socially stigmatized variable. Thus Janson (1977) gives clear evidence that the deletion of final /d/ in modern Stockholm Swedish is the crystallization of a 19th-century stereotype. And as we have seen, the mixtures found in Chaozhou itself actually were the result of such processes.

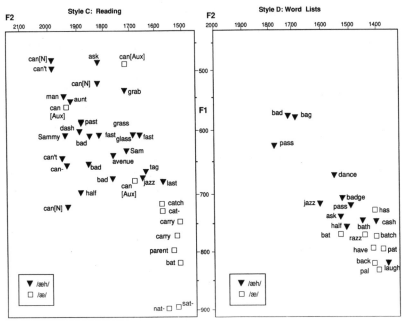

(b) Locations of nuclei when reading a connected text
(c) Locations of nuclei when reading word lists

16.3 The Neogrammarian regularity of change in progress

Chapters 3, 4, and 6 presented data from instrumental measurements of change in progress; the most detailed view of individual vowel systems was provided in chapter 6. These data were introduced to illustrate the principles of chain shifting, and did not focus on the lexical regularity of the changes. But it is now important to point out that these sound changes in progress show very different properties from those described for the cases of lexical diffusion. They exhibit all three central characteristics of a Neogrammarian sound change: lexical regularity, gradualness, and phonetic conditioning.

Lexical regularity

In general, the sound shifts of chapter 6 did not involve any changes in the membership of the historical word classes involved. The Northern Cities Shift has been studied in the greatest detail, not only as presented in LYS, but also in many more detailed analyses in connection with the CDC project that involve 30–50 tokens in each category. LYS and LCV did not find any changes or disturbances in the historical word classes /i/, /e/, /æ/,

/o/, /oh/, and /ʌ/: the make-up of these word classes characteristic of the oldest, most conservative speakers is identical with that of the youngest speakers. The same is generally true for our studies of the Southern Shift, in Philadelphia, Atlanta, Birmingham, Texas, and elsewhere. Others who have carried out detailed studies of changes in progress have reported the same situation (Feagin 1990; Laferrière 1977; Callary 1975; Eckert 1986, 1988, 1991; Di Paolo 1988). The fronting of /uw/ and /ow/, the fronting and raising of /aw/, the tensing and fronting of front short vowels, all appear to show Neogrammarian regularity.

Mergers tend to show a similar lexical regularity. Every word in the resultant /ohr/ class is affected by the raising process in New York City and Philadelphia. The raising of /ohr/ involves, not just the common *door, four, for, more, fork,* but every lexical item in this class that is uttered in spontaneous speech, no matter how common or uncommon, learned or vulgar: reading from the records of Leon Alinsky, I find *born, forth, fort, horns,* and *source.* None of these remain at the original cardinal [ɔ] or go off in another direction; instead, all move steadily upward toward [u:ə].

Herold's (1990) investigation of the merger of /o/ and /oh/ in Eastern Pennsylvania is the most detailed study of a merger carried out to date: she did not observe any evidence of lexical irregularity. The same is true for Di Paolo's and Bailey's studies of the ongoing merger of tense and lax high vowels before /l/, the merger of /i/ and /e/ before nasals, and the merger and near-merger of /er/ and /ʌr/ in Philadelphia, discussed in part C.

Gradualness

In general, these changes show no sign of discrete movement. It is difficult, of course, to prove the absence of discontinuities. To compare speakers across age levels, we must superpose one vowel system on another; and such superposition is hardly precise enough to establish continuity or discontinuity. The LCV study of Philadelphia developed an approach to the normalization problem (Hindle 1978) that permitted the joint analysis of several hundred vowel systems. It was demonstrated that the geometric mean normalization (Nearey 1977) was better than several others in selectively eliminating the effects of differences in vocal tract length, and no other differences. No obvious discontinuities appeared in the display of mean values for changes in progress that covered a large part of the possible phonetic range. Problems of incomplete normalization or overnormalization could easily mask a discontinuous distribution. But conversely, every effort made to find discontinuities, where they were most expected, has failed.[5]

---

[5] One of the most likely sites for such a discontinuity was in the tensing and raising of the nucleus of (aw), which was closely identified with [æ] for the oldest speakers in Philadelphia: LCV anticipated a discrete jump to an identification with the mid or lower high nucleus of

Phonetic conditioning

The changes in progress show detailed phonetic conditioning, with no indication of grammatical constraints.[6] The new and vigorous changes that we have located in various cities usually show long, elliptical distributions in the direction of the change, as opposed to the more globular distributions of stable vowels. Within these elliptical distributions, we find a fine subdivision of phonetic classes, as almost every feature that might favor or disfavor the shift comes into play. A number of the vowel charts of chapter 6 demonstrated this point in regard to the movements of /æh/ and /o/ in the Northern Cities Shift (figures 6.8, 6.9, 6.10, 6.11, 6.13, 6.14, 6.16), as well as the multivariate analysis of Frank Huber's system in table 6.1. A close view of the fine-grained phonetic control of the Northern Cities Shift is provided by figure 16.4, which displays a more detailed analysis of the raising of /æh/ in the vowel system of Bea White than was first presented in figure 6.10. Figure 16.4 examines the relative positions of 26 tokens of /æh/ and 8 tokens of /o/ with primary stress. (For ease of locating items, they are numbered in three successively less peripheral paths, from high to low.) The /æh/ tokens show the effect of eight intersecting effects of the phonetic environment.

Nasality A following nasal consonant has the strongest effect, as we have frequently seen, in maximizing peripherality and height, as seen by the leading positions of 1 *aunts*, 2 *dance*, and 3 *hand*. A preceding nasal consonant has a smaller effect in the same direction as shown by 5 *mass*.

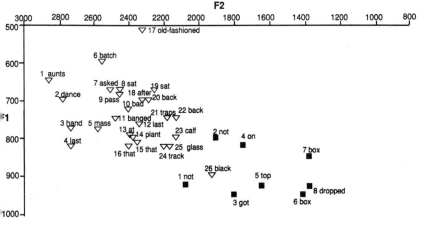

Figure 16.4.   Phonetic conditioning of /aeh/ for Bea White, 54, Buffalo [1970]

tense (æh), but found no evidence for this. The (aw) nucleus sometimes overlaps with (æh) but is usually lower, even when both vowels show parallel inglides.

[6] This statement has already been modified with respect to certain sound changes, such as the splitting of short **a** discussed in chapter 15.

Place of articulation   Following apicals and palatals show greater height than following labials and velars. Compare the position of 11 *banged* to the words with apical nasal consonants, 1–3. The two words with following palatals, 6 *batch* and 17 *old-fashioned*, are both located in high, nonperipheral position. On the other hand, words with following apicals are uniformly more peripheral and higher than words with following labials and velars – items 20–26, clustered at lower right.

Initial liquids   The effect of an initial /l/ is seen in the relatively low position of the two tokens of *last* (4,12). This is a small effect, however, compared to the influence of obstruent plus liquid clusters, seen in 14 *plant*, 21 *traps*, 24 *track*, 25 *glass*, and 26 *black*. While 21 and 24–26 show the combined effects of the preceding and following disfavoring environments, 14 *plant* shows how the disfavoring effect of an initial cluster can operate to reduce the effect of a favoring final nasal. Comparing 1 *aunts* with 14 *plant* shows that obstruent-liquid initial clusters have the most powerful effect upon the change in progress.

Polysyllables   The two words with following syllables, 17 *old-fashioned* and 18 *after*, are located on a nonperipheral path, showing the usual effect in reducing peripherality.

The regression analysis of Frank Huber's /æh/ data in table 6.1 (page 181) showed all of these effects except the effect for place of articulation. This regression analysis was given in terms of F1 and F2, before the present view of movement along the front diagonal had been presented. These two sets of dimensions are shown in figure 16.5, where F1 and F2 are contrasted with the more phonologically oriented dimensions of height, measured along the front diagonal, and peripherality – the distance from the front envelope, measured at right angles to height. Table 16.5 is a regression analysis of Bea White's /æh/ with height and peripherality as the dependent variables. Each line shows the estimated contribution of that environment to height or peripherality compared to a residual factor with

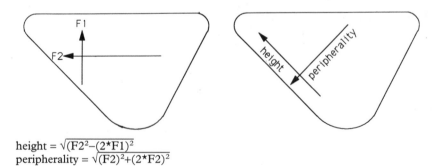

height = $\sqrt{(F2^2-(2\star F1)^2}$
peripherality = $\sqrt{(F2)^2+(2\star F2)^2}$

Figure 16.5.   Phonetic and phonological dimensions of vowel location and movement

Table 16.5 Effect of phonetic environment on height and
peripherality of /æh/ for Bea White, 54, Buffalo [1970]

	Height	*Peripherality*
Nasality		
Following nasal	433	300+
Preceding nasal	180	209
Place of articulation		
Following apical	279*	133+
Following palatal	545*	38
Following labial	49	47
(Following velar)	0	0
Initial liquids		
Initial /l/	94	194+
Obstruent+liquid	−454**	−80
Polysyllables		
Following syllable	28	−84

$+p < .10$ $*p < .05$ $**p < .01$

an effect of zero. In the case of nasality, the residual factor is a nonnasal
environment. For place of articulation, the residual factor is shown
explicitly as the least favorable environment of a following velar. Initial
liquids are of course compared with all other nonliquid initials, and two
following syllables with no following syllable.

With only 26 tokens, the effects are not significant or are only marginally
significant, but their repeated occurrence throughout the data makes it
plain that these are the influences that dictate the position of the individual
words in the phonological space. Most impressive is the amount of variance
explained by these factors; r^2 is .749 for height, and .729 for peripherality.

Figure 16.4 shows only 8 tokens of short **o** for Bea White, but even
with this small number, the phonetic conditioning is quite plain. The most
fronted word is *not*, with an initial nasal and a following apical. Both 1 *not*
and 2 *not* are fronter than the least favored word in the /æh/ set, 26 *black*.
The four words with apical finals are all fronter than the four words with
labial and velar finals, and the effect of an initial cluster in 8 *dropped* makes
it the least advanced token in this second stage of the Northern Cities Shift.

It might seem that this case approaches the endpoint where the Neogrammarian hypothesis merges with the view that every word has its own
history. If every phonetic feature of the environment affected phonetic
development, then homonyms would form the only word classes. This is
not the case, since many initial consonants have such slight effects on the

phonetic realization of a following vowel that they are lost in the random noise of subtle differences of stress or duration and of errors in measurement. But even if every word had its own history, this would not necessarily be lexical diffusion. Lexical diffusion involves the rejection of the idea that it is the phonetic composition of a word that solely determines its position in the process of change. If the word is to be taken as the fundamental unit of change, it is because some words undergo change for reasons that are not phonetic.[7]

Is there any evidence in figure 16.4 that individual words are being selected in the raising of Northern Cities /æh/? The chief anomaly in this diagram is the two widely separated articulations of *last* (4,14). Lexical diffusion would be shown instead by a cluster of pronunciations of the same word in a position not predicted by its phonetic composition. No such phenomenon appears in the Bea White data, which is based on an hour of spontaneous speech. A search of larger data bases is needed to pursue this possibility, given the firm evidence presented in chapter 15 of lexical diffusion in the splitting of Philadelphia short **a** into tense /æh/ and lax /æ/.

16.4 Do homonyms split?

We could hardly consider the illustration just given as proof that lexical diffusion is absent from the sound changes being examined. Lexical identity is certainly not a major factor. But it might still play a minor role – so that, over the course of a century, some words might gradually advance their position, or fall behind to be eventually filtered out and become members of another class. The LCV project searched for a precise way of testing this possibility.

The ideal test would be to measure a large number of words in the speech of one person, over a good stretch of time, and then carry out a regression analysis in which the identity of particular words would be entered into the equations – along with phonetic, prosodic, and social factors. This would require a fair number of items; otherwise, a nonsignificant result would be inevitable.

Interviews conducted in Philadelphia neighborhoods as part of the LCV project often involve two, three, or even four hours with a single speaker, and several series of recordings are made in most cases. But even then, the numbers of tokens of any one word are limited. If we were fortunate enough to find homonyms in spontaneous speech, we could hardly expect to find more than a few of each pair. The reading of word lists will give

---

[7] Lexical diffusion does not demand that the selection of words be entirely random: for example, frequency is often cited as an important factor. The crucial point is that no phonetic (or grammatical) explanation will fully account for the selection of a given word.

us all the lexical comparisons we need; but the absence of lexical diffusion in such lists would prove very little about the course of change in progress.[8] We could, of course, carry out the analysis on the entire set of normalized tokens for the 176 Philadelphia subjects whose speech has been analyzed; but we have no independent way of ensuring that any lack of significance in the effect of lexical items would not be caused by limitations of the normalization procedure.

The solution to this problem lies in a unique data set. In the exploratory stages of LCV, Arvilla Payne made a series of recordings of one speaker, Carol Meyers, 30 years old, over the course of an entire day: in a travel agency, dinner at home with her family, and a bridge game with close friends. Payne was then living at the Meyers's home, and knew all the people involved quite well, so that the effect of observation was reduced to a minimum.[9] Hindle (1980) then undertook a quantitative analysis of the effects of addressee, work situation, key, and many other independent variables on the formant positions of 3,600 vowels spoken by Carol Meyers.

To test the possibility of lexical diffusion in this system, Hindle and I located two word classes with large sets of homonyms and near-homonyms. These are free (uwF) and free (owF): the subsets of /uw/ and /ow/ words with no final consonants. One of the special features of the Philadelphia Pattern 3 chain shift (figure 3.6) is the sharp differentiation of checked and free allophones in the upgliding high and mid vowels. As we saw in chapters 3 and 4, the combined data from earlier observations in real time, the Philadelphia Neighborhood Studies, and the telephone survey show that (uwF) and (owF) are involved in change in progress.

Figure 16.6 shows the vowel system of Carol Meyers as analyzed by Hindle. Each vowel shows not one but three means, for each of the three major social settings: the travel agency, dinner at home, and the bridge game. Free (uwF) is well front of center – not as far front as /i/, but well ahead of checked (uwC). As always, (ow) runs behind (uw), and (owF) is ahead of (owC). The two free classes contain many words of high frequency; and since they do not differ in final consonants, we have a good chance of finding homonyms. In particular, we can expect a fair number of tokens of *two* and *too, know* and *no.*

Table 16.6 lists, for Carol Meyers, all words in these classes with 3 or

---

[8] One sort of bias in word lists is shown in figure 16.3c, typical of the late stages of a stigmatized change. Where there is less social affect, word lists can show the opposite effect: a concentration on an advanced target, eliminating much of the phonetic (and perhaps lexical) variation characteristic of spontaneous speech (LYS, figures 3–18; Yaeger 1975).
[9] The recordings of Carol Meyers were made with Nagra IVD and IVS tape recorders and Sennheiser 404 condenser microphones. The quality of these recordings is unparalleled for variety and spontaneity of social interaction, and for the fidelity of the signal from a physical point of view.

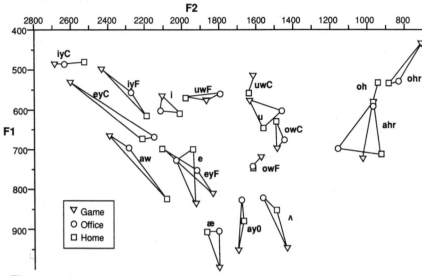

Figure 16.6.   Mean values for vowel nuclei of Carol Meyers, 48 [1972] in three
social contexts [from Hindle 1980, figure 4.4]

Table 16.6 Words with free /uw/ and /ow/
occurring more than twice in Carol Meyers corpus with mean F2 values

		N	Mean F2
(uwF)	two	40	1743
	too	14	1682
	do	19	1743
	to	5	1842
	through	3	1879
(owF)	know	50	1574
	go	38	1548
	no	32	1573
	oh	16	1587
	okay	27	1554
	so	15	1585
	goes	6	1591
	though	5	1701
	show	4	1461
	lower	3	1509

more tokens, and gives their mean F2 values.[10] In the case of (uwF), we are fortunate to have 40 tokens of *two* and 14 tokens of *too*. They differ by 61 Hz in F2, the crucial dimension. However, we do not know from the mean values alone whether this difference is significant, since the two sets of tokens may differ in duration, stress, pitch – or, most importantly, distribution by setting, since there is a 220 Hz difference between home and office means of (uwF). We also have the opportunity to examine *do*, which is almost identical to *two* in F1 and F2 measurements, and differs phonetically only by the voicing of the initial consonant.

In the (owF) class, we find 32 examples of *no* and 50 of *know*, with almost exactly the same F2 value. We must be particularly careful with the word *no* to exclude the possibility that prosodic factors play a role; the apparent identity of mean values might mask compensating differences between the two words. We also have *go*, which differs from *no* and *know* only by the /g/-/n/ contrast, with 38 tokens, about 27 Hz behind in the fronting process. This again is a small difference, compared to other factors.

A stepwise multiple regression analysis of these data allows us to distinguish the actual effect of phonetic environment from the effect of lexical identity. The data then permit a precise test of the hypothesis that the fundamental mechanism of the fronting of /uw/ and /ow/ is the differential advancement of individual words. There is ample evidence for powerful phonetic conditioning. Following liquids prevent fronting altogether, yielding differences of 500–1500 Hz between allophones before /l/ and not before /l/. Checked syllables are well behind free syllables, with distributions that overlap not at all or very little. Within the free (owF) and (uwF) classes, finer phonetic conditioning of the preceding consonants can be anticipated. The contrasts between *do/too* and *go/know* can be taken as representative of such finer phonetic differentiation. If the change is in fact proceeding word by word, we would expect that the differences between the two sets of homonyms would be at least as large as the smaller phonetic differences, and perhaps as great as the more powerful phonetic factors.

Table 16.7 shows the results of the stepwise regression analysis on F2 for Carol Meyers' (uwF) and (owF), including as independent variables the duration of the vowel, its fundamental frequency, stress, and position in the phrase group, and the identity of the lexical item. The words *two* and *do* are opposed to the residual class, *too*. The results show five coefficients, each about 100 Hz in magnitude, and each at about the .05 level of significance. The prosodic factors are in the direction we would expect for change in progress: the minimum constraint on articulation yields the

[10] The total number of tokens in the (uwF) category is 130; in (owF), 215. The three most common items analyzed for each class represent a sizeable percentage of this total, 77% and 56% respectively.

Table 16.7 Multiple regression analysis of homonyms in the Carol
Meyers data set

		Coefficient	*t*
(uwF)			
	PROSODIC FACTORS		
	Fundamental frequency	—	
	Duration [× 100 msec]	91	2.3*
	Secondary stress	−96	2.0*
	Phrase-final position	85	1.6
	SOCIAL SETTING		
	Office vs. game	−86	1.9*
	Home vs. game	116	1.8
	LEXICAL ITEM		
	two vs. *too*	—	
	do vs. *too*	103	2.5
(owF)			
	PROSODIC FACTORS		
	Fundamental frequency	—	
	Duration [× 100 msec]	—	
	Secondary stress	−72	2.3*
	Phrase-final position	−69	1.9
	SOCIAL SETTING		
	Office vs. game	47	1.5
	Home vs. game	−74	1.9
	LEXICAL ITEM		
	know vs. *no*	—	
	go vs. *no*	−165	4.4**

$*p < .05$ $**p < .01$

most advanced form. Thus longer duration favors higher F2, and secondary stress disfavors it. The social factors point in the same direction: the
home setting favors higher F2, and the office setting disfavors it. Finally,
we observe no difference at all between the two homonyms – and, contrary
to the unanalyzed means, a fairly strong advantage of 103 Hz for *do*
over *too*.

The findings for the (owF) class are somewhat different for the prosodic
factors. Neither pitch nor duration is significant. Secondary stress again
disfavors F2 as compared with primary stress. Most importantly, we
observe no difference between the homonyms *know* and *no*, but a very
large effect that predicts lower F2 values for *go* as compared with *no*.

The results of these two analyses are the same on the main point of
interest. The homonyms show parallel behavior, with no significant differences in expected formant positions. The largest significant differences

appear for words with different initial consonants, which may or may not represent phonetic conditioning. We cannot yet explain the *do* effect, since we have not identified any general influence of preceding voicing. But the higher F2 predicted for *no* as compared to *go* does fit in with all previous results that show *mad* with higher F2 than *bad* in Philadelphia and in the Northern Cities. Note the relatively higher F2 for *mass* and *not* in figure 16.4.

This is a test of only two homonym pairs; but it is a sensitive test, more closely connected to the mechanism of change than the analyses of completed changes in the DOC. We fail to find any evidence for lexical diffusion in these two changes in progress; all available data point to phonetically conditioned, gradual sound change in the spirit of the Neogrammarian proclamation.

16.5　Regularity within irregularity

Chapter 15 presented firm evidence of lexical diffusion in the splitting of short **a** in Philadelphia. This lexical split of short **a** into tense and lax members is not an isolated fact. The same word class is split in many other dialects of American English (New York City, Baltimore, and most Southern regions). Lexical irregularities are found in the relics of related earlier changes that split the broad **a** class and the short **o** class. The raising of the resulting /æh/ and /oh/ classes must be considered as a separate process, quite distinct from the formation of the classes themselves. Though we have seen that the fronting of /uw/ and /ow/ proceeds without evidence of lexical diffusion, this may not be the case with the raising of /æh/ and /oh/. If we have reason to think that lexical selection was involved in the formation of the classes, and speakers are therefore oriented toward words rather than sounds, it may be that lexical selection will continue in this further process.

The raising of the tense ingliding vowels /æh/ and /oh/ is not a minor adjustment. These word classes begin their career as low vowels, and in the course of several generations, become mid and then high vowels – in some cases, the highest vowels of the system. If words are individually raised to mid and high position, there is ample room to observe this lexical differentiation in the system of any one speaker. We can therefore take advantage of the special data set of Carol Meyers to examine this possibility.

The vowels studied by Hindle included all of the short **a** words pronounced by Carol Meyers: 149 words that he rated impressionistically as tense, and 247 that he rated as lax, before the formant positions were measured by LPC analysis. There is very little overlap between them: less than is normally found for neighboring phonemes like /i/ and /e/. Labov

(1989a) examines the distribution of the two sets and the overlapping area, and finds that it is populated by the most lax allophones of /æh/ and the most tense allophones of /æ/. Lax vowels after initial palatals, like the one in *jacket*, are among the highest; and among the tense vowels, the lowest positions are occupied by those in words with initial obstruent-liquid clusters and several following syllables, like *classical*. Here we will be concerned primarily with the distribution of the 149 tense vowels.

Table 16.8 is a multiple regression analysis of the Carol Meyers /æh/ data with height as defined in figure 16.5 as the dependent variable. The phonetic environment of /æh/ words is more limited than that for Bea White, where the entire short **a** word class is tensed, and we therefore can expect a more limited number of phonetic factors determining the degree of raising.

- The first two effects differentiate among the three major subclasses that are selected for tensing: short **a** before nasals, short **a** before voiceless fricatives, and the three words ending in /d/ (*mad, bad, glad*). Only two are shown here, since the class before voiceless fricatives acts as the residual group. When short **a** is followed by a nasal, the vowel is raised 158 units of height more than when it is followed by a voiceless fricative, and for *mad, bad, glad* 238 more.[11]
- A preceding nasal increases height by 99 units, but the effect is not significant.

Table 16.8 Effect of phonetic features on the height of (æh) in the speech of Carol Meyers

	Coefficient	t	p(2-tail)
Constant	2104		
Following nasal	158	3.57	0.000
Following /d/ (*mad, bad, glad*)	238	2.44	0.016
Preceding nasal	99	1.22	0.225
Preceding obstruent plus /l/	−210	−2.72	0.007
Two following syllables	−410	−2.75	0.007
Secondary stress	−95	−1.95	0.053

N = 149   Multiple r = .47   Squared multiple r = .22   F = 6.62

[11] The effect is more significant with nasals, since the sample contains many more words where short **a** precedes a nasal (77 of the 149) than words where it precedes /d/ (7 of the 149: 5 *mad*, 2 *glad*).

- A preceding obstruent plus /l/, as in *glad, plan, planted, Atlantic,* lowers the expected value for height by 210 units.
- Where two syllables follow the syllable with /æh/, height is decreased by 410 units. Though only three words are involved – *grandmother's, Bamberger's,* and *classical* – the effect is significant at the .01 level.
- When the syllable with /æh/ occurs in a position that dictates less than primary stress,[12] there is a small effect of decreasing height, significant at the .05 level.

The first two phonetic effects continue within the tense category the phonetic factors that were active in the original selection of words for that category. The other four are lower-level phonetic features that play no part in the original split, but determine relative height within the tense category. Three of them were also found in the analyses of Northern Cities Shift data in tables 6.1 and 16.5.

Table 16.9 shows the corresponding phonetic influences on the peripherality of the /æh/ nuclei.

- A strong effect is that of a following nasal consonant, a phonetic influence that is reproduced throughout the LYS data and the views of the Northern Cities Shift in this chapter. Thus following nasal consonants produce greater height and greater peripherality.
- A preceding nasal consonant, as in *man* and *Pan Am,* has a sizeable but somewhat smaller effect in increasing peripherality.
- Again, two following syllables have a powerful effect in centralizing the nucleus.
- A following consonant cluster, as in *last, stand, after,* etc., has a small but significant effect in centralizing the nucleus.

Table 16.9   Effect of phonetic features on the peripherality of (æh) in the speech of Carol Meyers

	Coefficient	t	p(2-tail)
Following nasal	145	4.84	0.000
Preceding nasal	125	2.19	0.030
Two following syllables	−300	−2.91	0.004
Two following consonants	−65	−2.18	0.031

N = 149   Multiple *r* = .52   Squared multiple *r* = .27   F = 13.14

[12] This category consists of syllables adjacent to those with primary stress, such as *Pan* in *Pan Am* and *Fran* in *San Francisco,* as well as auxiliaries like *can't.*

We are now ready to consider whether any lexical effects take part in determining the position of the /æh/ vowels in this large area of phonetic space. This set of 149 tense /æh/ words contains five items that occur more than five times:

half	7
pass	19
last	16
Pan Am[13]	8
can't	15

Table 16.10 shows the results of adding the five lexical identities to the analysis of height. No further significant results appear.

The addition of these five words does not materially change the results of table 16.8. The effect of a preceding nasal on height continues to be small and nonsignificant.[14] The effect of secondary stress is reduced, since *last* and *can't* normally occur with secondary stress, and some contribution of this factor is shifted to the words. Thus the close study of the /æh/ category does not yield any indication that lexical selection is active in the

Table 16.10   Effect of phonetic features and individual words on the height of (æh) in the speech of Carol Meyers

	Coefficient	t	p(2-tail)
Following nasal	182	2.87	0.005
Following /d/ (*mad, bad, glad*)	284	2.73	0.007
Preceding nasal	45	0.35	0.724
Preceding obstruent plus /l/	−176	−2.26	0.025
Two following syllables	−478	−2.57	0.011
Secondary stress	−111	−1.31	0.194
last	14	0.13	0.900
half	150	1.37	0.173
pass	137	1.71	0.090
Am	131	0.86	0.389
can't	155	1.51	0.134

N = 149   Multiple r = .467   Squared multiple r = .218   F = 6.62

---

[13] One-third of the recordings of Carol Meyers's speech took place at the travel agency where she worked – hence the numerous references to the airline *Pan Am* (*Pan American*).

[14] This phonetic effect does however have considerable value in explaining the special behavior of the syllable *Am*. If one does not take into account the fact that *Am* is always combined with *Pan* in *Pan Am*, and that is a single lexical item, then *Am* will appear to be lexically close to significance. But the proceding nasal is as much a part of the phonetic composition here as in *man*.

raising of this vowel. One could say that the five words we have been able to examine are accidents of the text; perhaps if five other words had been as frequent, we might have found lexical effects. But if lexical diffusion is said to be the fundamental mode in which change is implemented, then the examination of the Northern Cities Shift and the Philadelphia shift by the various methods used here should have produced at least one example of lexical selection.

Figure 16.7 gives a detailed view of the 149 tense vowels on an F1/F2 plot, with words at the extremes of the distribution labeled. It is immediately evident that the instances of /æh/ with following nasals are the highest and most peripheral, but they are also scattered to other extreme positions. The most peripheral vowels, at the extreme left, are heavily stressed words ending in nasals: *ham*, *Pan Am*, and *hands*. Among the most peripheral of the words ending in voiceless fricatives are *gas*, *half*, and *last*. It appears that initial /h/ yields peripheral vowels, without a consonantal transition to shift the value toward a more central position.

The most centralized /æh/ is in *grandmother's*. Though there are not enough /Kr-/ words to show a significant effect, they do exhibit a centralization factor parallel to the /Kl-/ words, and this, combined with the two following syllables, gives the extreme result.

The words ending in voiceless fricatives include *last* and *asked*. The effect of following consonant clusters is clear. What is not obvious is why *last* occurs both in the least peripheral positions, as its phonetic composition

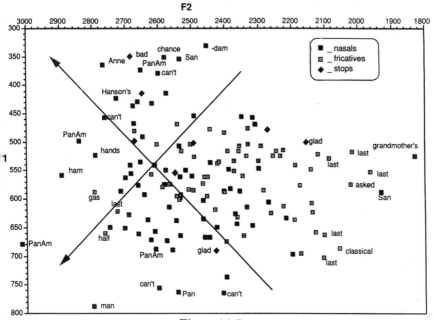

Figure 16.7.

woud lead us to expect, and in a very peripheral position. This would seem to be an error of measurement were it not that the same phenomenon was found in figure 16.4 for the speech of Bea White.

Among the highest vowels in the upper left corner are those found in some nonperipheral words that are members of multisyllabic combinations: *San (Francisco)*, *(Amster)dam*, *Hanson's*. This parallels effects observed throughout LYS, where words like *animal* are among the highest in the raising of /æh/, but less peripheral than others. *(Old)-fashioned* showed this behavior in figure 16.4.

Among the words ending in /d/, there is a clear contrast between *bad* and *glad*, where the initial obstruent-liquid cluster of *glad* leads to both low and nonperipheral position.

Thus the inspection of individual words in figure 16.7 reinforces the quantitative conclusions of the tables. There is no indication of any lexical selection in the raising of /æh/ in Carol Meyers's system. Words do not behave as though they were the fundamental units of the change. On the contrary, individual tokens of the same word vary considerably, sometimes ranging over the entire /æh/ space. To the extent that the position of words is determined within this space, it is determined phonetically.

16.6   The Neogrammarian conclusion

At the end of chapter 15, we had amassed considerable evidence for lexical diffusion in the process of change. This chapter has given voice to the perspective of the Neogrammarians, strengthening their position on dialect mixture and phonetic conditioning. We have added to the armory of tools available to Neogrammarian argument the quantitative techniques of linear predictive coding and multiple regression.

There can be little doubt that the originators of the Neogrammarian position would have welcomed modern advances in instrumental analysis of the phonetic continuum, which have implemented their trust in the importance of fine phonetic detail in establishing the mechanism of sound laws. They would not have been as likely to welcome the tools of statistical analysis and probabilistic reasoning, since they were committed to discrete solutions. Nevertheless, this extension of the Neogrammarians' argument seems to me wholly appropriate and completely in the spirit of their materialist orientation.[15]

---

[15] When proponents of lexical diffusion recognize the stochastic character of their data, their findings approximate the Neogrammarian position. Chapter 15 summarized the findings of Shen on the merger of the nasalized vowels /ã/ and /ɑ̃/ in Shanghai, based on self-reports of the merger by 350 or more high school students: each word of the vocabulary followed a characteristic logistic curve at different points in apparent time. Shen's most recent contribution to the discussion (1993) reports the analysis by the "bootstrap" method of these data

The use of these tools has considerably eroded the lexical diffusion position. There is no basis for contending that lexical diffusion is somehow more fundamental than regular, phonetically motivated sound change. On the contrary, if we were to decide the issue by counting cases, there appear to be far more substantially documented cases of Neogrammarian sound change than of lexical diffusion. The upshot of this discussion is not, however, a victory for the Neogrammarians. There are more than enough solid examples of sounds changing one word at a time to support the view that lexical diffusion is deeply rooted in the process of change. But where it is rooted, and where it flourishes, is more difficult to decide. We cannot resolve a paradox by saying that both parties are right. Though we have advanced evidence on both sides, the situation is no less chaotic than it was at the outset. If language changes in two different ways, the data must contain some hint that will tell us when it changes in one way, and when in the other.

One way of advancing toward a solution is to enlarge the field of data. So far we have been considering small numbers of speakers, and a few specific dialects. Chapter 17 will broaden the scope of the inquiry to examine the residues of sound change in the dialect geography of England, with evidence from 311 different speakers of the language. Dialect geography is the matrix in which the slogan "Every word has its own history" was formed. A systematic examination of these data should counter the Neogrammarian arguments advanced in this chapter, and strengthen the case for lexical diffusion.

and parallel data on the monophthongization of /Øy/ from Wenzhou. Whereas in the earlier report it appeared that lexical diffusion affected each word successively, he now finds that "the probability of change at a certain point in time only determines the changing chance of the words, but which words will get changed by an individual speaker is random." He concludes that "since every word has an equal chance of changing, no word should behave differently during the change, and change will be regular at the end." (Quotations are from the abstract to Shen 1993). The relationship between these perceptual judgments and speech production has not yet been determined, nor the degree of consistency of individual judgments over time. But it seems clear that in these mergers there is no lexical selection by the speech community comparable to the selection of *planet* by Philadelphians in the lexical split of the short **a** class.

17

Regular Sound Change in English Dialect Geography

17.1 The place of dialect geography in the Neogrammarian controversy

The last two chapters have provided evidence for and against the Neogrammarian principle that sound change proceeds by affecting whole classes of sounds – that is, phonemes. We are now ready to turn to the testimony of dialect geography on this issue.

The discussion so far would lead us to expect that any study of areal configurations could do no other than strengthen the case for lexical diffusion. Chapter 1 reviewed the initial enthusiasm of the Neogrammarians for the findings of dialect studies, their use of the regularities reported in Winteler's account of the Kerenzen dialect, and their subsequent disappointment when dialect studies reported fluctuations and irregularities quite different from what they had expected. For over a century, both supporters and opponents of the Neogrammarian position have accepted the idea that this evidence contradicts the testimony of historical and comparative linguistics and points toward a word-by-word evolution of sound change.

The slogan "Every word has its own history" ("Chaque mot a son histoire") is so deeply rooted in the tradition of dialect geography that it has been attributed to all the major figures in the field, particularly Gilliéron and Jaberg. The principle and the findings on which it is based have been uniformly used to dispute the Neogrammarian principle of the regularity of sound change. The Neogrammarians' first reaction to the dialectologists' findings was that the reported fluctuations were the result of hyperurbanisms and dialect mixture typical of complex communities, and it was in response to this interpretation that Gauchat returned to the Swiss village of Charmey, with the results reviewed in chapters 3 and 4. Gauchat argued that the Neogrammarian conception was essentially wrong, and that the individual word is the unit of change.

Phonetic laws do not affect all examples at the same time; some are destined to develop rapidly, others remain behind, while others show a strong resistance to the change and succeed in resisting any transformation whatsoever. (cited in Dauzat 1922:52; my translation)

What I have called the "Neogrammarian paradox" was therefore presented in its sharpest form by this opposition between historical linguistics and dialect geography. The most radical dialectologists argued that the Neogrammarians were the victims of an illusion, and the most rigid Neogrammarians were forced to reject the dialectologists' data as irrelevant. The picture that we have inherited from the earliest days of the controversy is that the procedures of historical and comparative grammar support, or even demand, the Neogrammarian position, while the facts of dialect geography are irrefutably against it.

This rigid opposition may have been generated by the search for a phonetic uniformity that is not found in any speech community. If the short **a** data of the last two chapters were reduced to the small number of forms usually reported in dialect atlases, we would undoubtedly find lexical variation in those environments that show regularity in spontaneous speech. From the citation forms of figure 16.3c, we would have deduced that *pass, bad, bag* are tense in New York City, while *half, ask, laugh* are lax.

The opposition of Neogrammarian and dialectological views was seen in a much more moderate light by Gilliéron and Dauzat. They were fully aware of the very regular developments across time of such sound changes as the palatalization of Latin /k/ before /a/, so that *cantare* corresponded to French *chant, campum* to *champ, calorem* to *chaleur, vacca* to *vache,* and so on. Dauzat cited the extraordinary success of Gaston Paris in tracing the regular diphthongization of Latin tonic free long **o**. As Gilliéron and Dauzat saw it, the irregularity of the dialect reflexes of these sound changes is the result, not of a process that is fundamentally irregular, but of the fact that the local dialects do not represent an uninterrupted inheritance of the Latin prototype. It is the long series of interactions between the dominant French language and the local dialects, and between city and villages, that has produced the irregular fluctuations of the dialect data (Dauzat 1922:52–3). Dauzat pointed out that while there are wide fluctuations in the geographical reflexes of individual words in the North, because of the more extensive influence of French on the northern dialects, one can find much more precise isoglosses in the Midi. Thus Gilliéron and Dauzat anticipated the position of Wang and Lien presented in chapter 16: that lexical irregularity was primarily the result of dialect contact, a position that considerably modifies the critique of the Neogrammarian position.

Along with others, I had the impression that Bloomfield never resolved the contradiction between his commitment to the Neogrammarian view and his passionate involvement with dialect geography (see Malkiel 1967). The general consensus was that dialect studies did not support the Neogrammarians, that "local dialects were no more consistent than the standard language in their relation to older speech-forms" (Bloomfield

1933:322). However, a closer examination shows that the two positions are not necessarily inconsistent.

[S]ound-change is merely a change in the speakers' manner of producing phonemes and accordingly affects a phoneme at every occurrence, regardless of the
nature of any particular linguistic form in which the phoneme happens to occur.
(1933:353)

Isoglosses for different forms rarely coincide along their whole extent. Almost every
feature of phonetics, lexicon, or grammar has its own area of prevalence – is
bounded by its own isogloss. The obvious conclusion has been well stated in the
form of a maxim: *Every word has its own history.* (1933:328)

In a closely reasoned argument, Kiparsky points out that "the prevalence
of language contact and diversity in no way disconfirms the [exceptionless
hypothesis], specifically not the *causal* claim which lies at the heart of it,
namely that exceptions do not develop internally to a system but only
through the interference between systems" (1989:370).

As noted in chapter 16, Kiparsky's position is not intended to echo
Hoenigswald's contention that the Neogrammarian principle was not an
empirical one. He argues that "any borrowing hypothesis must fit the
known dialectological and sociolinguistic realities" (1989:371). Yet it is
unlikely that we will ever have sufficient data on the social relations
between all dialects recorded in an atlas to submit the fluctuations in each
pair of neighboring communities to sociological scrutiny. It should be possible to use dialect atlases to confirm or disconfirm the Neogrammarian
position through a study of the spatial configurations of the linguistic
data themselves.

Bloomfield did not claim that individual words from the same word class
rarely coincide; he argued that they rarely coincide *along their entire length.*
To see how likely this is, let us consider an isogloss that intervenes between
25 communities on one side and 25 on the other. We need to calculate a
sociolinguistic equivalent of the lexicostatistic retention rate of 85% of the
basic vocabulary per millennium. Let us assume that the rate of disturbance of the words participating in the original sound change was no greater
than this.[1] Since most of the sound changes studied in a dialect atlas are
no older than half a millennium, we will posit the corresponding retention
rate of 92% per 500 years. The possibility of complete stability of dialect
histories for two words for 50 localities can be calculated as $.92^{100}$ or
.0239%. Thus given regular sound change disturbed by the usual rate of

---

[1] Much of the basic vocabulary of lexicostatistics is found in dialect atlases.

lexical replacement, in less than 1 out of 4000 cases would two words have the same history.[2]

What are the possible sources of the differentiation between two given words? We can group them into eight types.

1 Replacement of one word by a completely different word.
2 Lexical selection of one word by a sound change but not the other.
3 The effect of phonetic differences between words that have not been considered in the formulation of the sound change.
4 The effect of differential frequencies of the two words.
5 Accidental errors in transcription.
6 Inherent variation in speech production.
7 Borrowing of a more advanced or a more conservative form from neighboring dialects.
8 Borrowing of a more conservative form from the standard language.

These eight cases can be conceived as binary oppositions: either the given differentiation occurred or it did not. If we ask whether a particular change occurred in a given dialect, the answers yield four possibilities:

	1	2	3	4
Dialect A	Yes	Yes	No	No
Dialect B	Yes	No	Yes	No

Only cases 1, 2, 3 involve change. If the disturbances occurred independently, in one of these three dialects A and B would turn out to have the same form, and in two of them, different forms. Let us assume that the rate of differentiation is the same for all eight types: 100%–92%, or 8% per 500 years. Since only two-thirds of the replacements produce differences in the isoglosses, the number of identical results across the 50 villages must be somewhat larger than in the earlier calculation – not $.92^{100}$ but $.9467^{100}$, or .416% of the cases. The number of identical isoglosses is still quite small – less than 1%. This calculation shows that even the usual small rate of random disturbance in the vocabulary will cause 99% of the word pairs with the same relevant phonetic environment to follow different isoglosses for one community at least. One need not posit special sociological circumstances to produce such an effect.

Let us now consider the possibility that two words coincide in any *one* pair of communities on either side of an isogloss. If the sound change proceeded regularly, we would expect identical results in 100% of the

[2] In a certain number of cases, both words would be disturbed in the same way. The likelihood of this happening will differ according to the type of disturbance, as discussed below.

cases, less the number of times that a random disturbance had affected both words differently, or 94.67% of the time. If the sound change proceeded by lexical diffusion, we would expect identical results in 50% of the cases, less the same proportion of random disturbance, or 46.2%. For the 25 pairs of communities on either side of our hypothetical isogloss, the proportion of cases where the words were differentiated would be the same. Proponents of lexical diffusion would predict that only 12–13 pairs out of 25 would behave in the same way, while Neogrammarians would predict 23–24. This is a sizeable difference in the results expected for Neogrammarian change and lexical diffusion. We need not therefore turn aside from the evidence of dialect geography because it does not produce 100% uniformity of isoglosses. The data of dialect geography are an important source of evidence on the issue before us.

17.2   The lexical diffusionist approach to the Great Vowel Shift

Much of the recent evidence for lexical diffusion is derived from the computational analysis of data drawn from dialect geography. The original position of Wang, Chen, and Hsieh was based on the analysis of the 1958 survey of 17 Chinese dialects that formed the Dictionary on Computer (DOC) (Cheng and Wang 1972; Wang and Cheng 1977; Wang 1977). Wang and his students have also turned their attention to English dialect geography, and in 1987 Ogura published a detailed treatment of the geographic correlates of sound change, examining the progress of the Great Vowel Shift as it is reflected in the 311 localities of Orton and Dieth's *Survey of English Dialects* (SED). This fine-grained data set provides an opportunity to test the two competing views: whether it is sounds or words that change. The elements of the Great Vowel Shift comprise a variety of low-level sound changes – backing, fronting, raising, and lowering of the nuclei of the long vowels. The conclusions of chapter 16 would lead us to expect regular sound change in this case. But while Ogura accepts the idea that both regular sound change and lexical diffusion exist, she argues for lexical diffusion as the fundamental mechanism of all the sound changes considered here.

Ogura's appendices B and D tabulate all the phonetic forms for all the 311 communities for words that bear on the Great Vowel Shift. She refers to these tables in stating, "The data in Appendix B clearly show that the change of ME ī does not simultaneously occur but gradually extends its scope across the lexicon," and for ME ū, "it is clear that the change propagates itself across the lexicon." And at the end of chapter 1, she concludes, "We have claimed that the processes of the development of ME ī and ū have propagated themselves gradually from morpheme to morpheme" (1987:45).

These conclusions are presented as immediately obvious from an inspection of the data of appendices B and D. They are not based on quantitative analysis, though some quantitative methods are used to display the data. Appendix E condenses the data for each ME **ū** word by summing the number of times that each different phonetic form is reported in the SED. The type of data generated is illustrated in table 17.1, which gives the first five items in the series. Each horizontal line may be thought of as a sound spectrum for the given word. There are 45 different phonetic forms used for the 30 ME **ū** words that Ogura extracts from the SED materials. In addition, a frequency figure extracted from the American Heritage dictionary is given for each word.

The vowel shift index

At the top of each column in table 17.1 are numbers from 1 to 10 – categories assigned by Ogura to represent the relative degree of advancement of the Great Vowel Shift. The basis for these assignments is the scheme shown in figure 17.1, developed by Ogura to represent the successive stages of advancement of the vowel shift for ME **ū**.

The circled elements represent the stages that Ogura terms the "main routes," on the basis of their frequency in the data. Other sound changes branch off in different directions. I have superimposed on each phonetic category the numerical values that Ogura assigns to each phone in the SED data. The *index of vowel shift advancement* is calculated for each word by multiplying the number of occurrences of each phonetic form by the value of the category, and summing. The results are illustrated in table 17.2, with words classified by the voicing and place of articulation of the following consonant.

Table 17.2 provides an overview of the phonetic dimensions that might or might not influence the rate of the diphthongization of ME **ū**. Ogura uses it as a basis for general statements about phonetic conditioning ("words in which the **ū** precedes labials or velars are the laggers"). She also uses it to support the idea that phonetic conditioning does not determine the progress of the sound change, reasserting that individual words have very different values. It may be noted that the words ending in apicals are quite homogeneous in their various subgroups, with a relatively narrow range of index values from 2100 to 2120. The words ending in /r/ also form a uniform set, all with values below 2100. The eccentric values that would indicate lexical diffusion are to be found in the labial and velar columns. The single word *room* has a very low value; this could be the result of either lexical eccentricity or phonetic conditioning. Among the velars there is so much lexical variation that average values are meaningless. *Cow* shows a very high value; *eyebrow* is very low; and *bow* is much lower than any other velar word.

Table 17.1   Five ME **ū** words by phonetic environment and frequency (from Ogura 1987:app. E)

Word	Freq	1 u:	2 ʋu	3 ou	4 əu	4 o:	4 ɔu	5 ʌv	5 ʌu	6 ɒu	6 ɒ:	7 ɑ:	7 au	8 aə	8 a:	8 əu	9 æa
cow	46.95	29	10	1	31		1	6	2	2			46		10	52	1
eyebrow	1.18	41	5	4	35		1	11	9	3			50		3	43	
hour	159.7	19	4	1	28		1	5	10	2		10	78		4	45	
flower	52.2	15	6		28		2	7	9	4	1	9	85	1	3	44	
flour	21.08	11	6		28	1	1	6	8	4		13	84		5	40	

Word	9 ɛu	9 æa	9 ɛə	9 ɜ:	10 ɛ	10 œu	10 eu	10 ey	10 œy	10 ɛy	10 æi	10 ai	10 ɒi
cow	74	1	3	3	14	4	1		4	1	17	1	2
eyebrow	65		3		13	4	2	2	4		15		3
hour	64	1	2	2	8	4	1		4	1	6		2
flower	55	2	2	2	10	4	1	1	4	1	7		4
flour	52	1	2	2	11	4	1		4	1	7		4

Word	æ:	æa	ɛu	ɜ:	ɛ	ü:	y:	i:	a	ʊ	ʌ
cow	1	1	3					2			
eyebrow	1					1					
hour	2		1		1		1			16	
flower	3		1			1			2	14	
flour	4		1		1					20	1

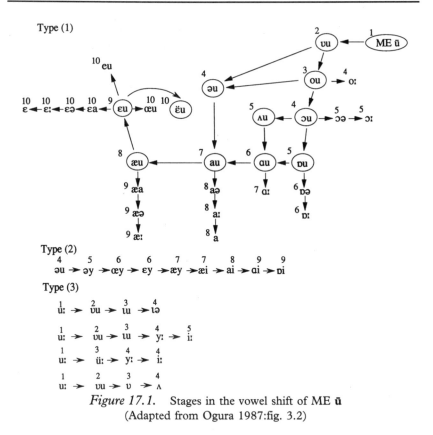

Figure 17.1. Stages in the vowel shift of ME **ū**
(Adapted from Ogura 1987:fig. 3.2)

17.3 Analysis of ME ū words

Let us now examine the data more closely, using mathematical tools that will allow us to decide whether or not there is evidence for lexical diffusion. The data exemplified in table 17.1 provide a distribution for each word across 45 phonetic categories. We can compare the distributions of any pair of words by a chi-square calculation that will show us the probability that differences in the distribution of phonetic categories are the result of chance fluctuations.[3] If each word had its own history, we would expect many of these pairs to differ significantly, without making reference to the geographic placement of the differences. Table 17.3 shows a number of such pairwise comparisons of ME **ū** words.

---

[3] The "expected value" (E) is here the mean of the occurrences of a given phonetic form for the pair of words. Chi-square is calculated by summing the squares of deviations from E divided by E. Since chi-square is not a reliable statistic when the expected value of any cell is less than 5, the values were taken only when E was greater than 4, and the N column in table 17.3 shows the number of such cases.

Table 17.2 Vowel shift advancement index of ME ū words by phonetic character of following segment (from Ogura 1987:tab. 3.2)

	Labial		Dental		Velar		Free	
Voiced			thousand	2107	bow	1623		
			trousers	2096	drought	1911		
					sow	2009		
Voiceless			house	2121	bough	2008	cow	2110
			mouse	2103	plough	1946	eyebrow	1941
			louse	2094				
			about	2091				
			out	2106				
			without	2129				
			snout	2112				
			south	2115				
			mouth	2098				
Nasal	room	711	down	2109				
			round	2098				
			crown	2088				
			ounce	2110				
			bounce	2091				
			drown	2108				
Liquid			hour	2069				
			flower	2069				
			flour	2071				
			owl	2110				

For the great majority of word pairs, the chi-square value shows no significant difference. A sampling of such nonsignificant results is shown on
the left. At the top of the column, with the lowest chi-square values, are
words that have the most similar phonetic environment, including
drown/crown, *house/louse*, *flour/hour*, *out/about*, and the homonymic pair
flour/flower. The chi-square values increase from top to bottom, and the
last five items show values over 10. Though this is still well below the .05
level of significance, it cannot be accidental that these are the items that
differ most in their phonetic environment. Some pairs contrast free with
checked environments (*cow* vs. *out*), whereas others contrast simple initials
with an initial cluster of obstruent plus liquid (*cow* vs. *eyebrow*); these clusters have been found to have considerable effect on changes in progress
(see chapters 3, 10, 16).

At the right are pairs that are significantly different. The first five items

Table 17.3 Pairwise chi-square evaluation of phonetic distribution of ME **ū** words

	χ^2	N		χ^2	N
Not significant					
down/crown	1.43	12	*p < .01*		
thousand/trousers	1.68	11	owl/out	24.18	11
house/louse	2.00	9			
cow/snout	2.12	10	*p < .001*		
down/round	2.37	12	flower/eyebrow	50.05	12
out/about	2.60	12	owl/hour	52.44	10
flower/hour	2.73	12	flour/thousand	62.80	13
ounce/crown	2.76	12	flower/about	71.05	13
crown/drown	2.85	11	drown/flower	73.80	13
flower/flour	2.87	12			
house/mouse	3.64	10	drought/cow	73.80	11
thousand/cloud	3.93	9	dought/without	76.76	11
cow/louse	4.00	10	drought/out	84.47	12
ounce/bounce	4.70	12			
out/without	6.50	13			
mouth/mouse	6.99	10	bow/bough	237.20	15
mouth/mouse	6.99	10	bow/drought	247.72	16
out/house	8.21	13	bow/out	269.62	14
sow/bough	9.00	10			
snout/without	9.02	11	room/plough	345.85	11
owl/bough	9.99	10	room/bough	398.45	13
south/mouth	11.94	10	room/out	403.81	12
cow/out	12.43	11			
thousand/bough	12.48	10			
cow/eyebrow	15.42	11			

N = number of phonetic values compared, where average occurrences > 4
Degrees of freedom = N − 2

also register the effects of phonetic conditioning, but of a more extreme kind than that shown by the nonsignificant pairs. These are the effects of following liquids, contrasting *owl* with *out*, *flower* with *eyebrow* and *about*, and *flour* with *thousand*. We also have different effects of the two liquids, differentiating *owl* and *hour*.

Next are three pairs that oppose *drought* to other words. *Drought* is a unique phonetic item, being the only word with an original ME velar in a checked syllable; the SED records show that this velar is retained as /f/ in many dialects.

The third set of pairs, with much higher chi-square values, show an extreme differentiation that goes beyond the previous examples. Phonetic conditioning cannot be invoked to account for the homonymic pair, *bow* and *bough*. Indeed, this would seem to be the kind of lexical diffusion that Ogura was looking for. Unfortunately, her interpretation of the ambiguous spelling *bow* was incorrect. The item is drawn from the SED question set VI-9 (Orton and Dieth 1962, Introduction).

5 Of a man whose legs are shaped like this [curving inward], you say he is . . .
   [expecting] **knock-kneed**.
6 Of a man whose legs are shaped like this [curving outward], you say he is . . .
   [expecting] **bow-legged**.

The target **bow** here is not the word meaning 'genuflect' with ME **ū**, from OE **bugen** 'to bend', but rather the word for the shape of a *bow*, the weapon, from ME **bowe** < OE **boga**, which followed a very different history and is a member of the /ow/ class in almost all dialects today.

The fourth set of pairs involved the word *room*, with even higher chi-square values. Ogura reports that 11 of the 311 points in the SED indicate the participation of *room* (from OE *rūm*) in the vowel shift; but my own reexamination of the original SED volumes locates only four such points, all in an isolated area in West Lancashire. In any case, since it is generally accepted that vowels before labials did not participate in the Great Vowel Shift, this is certainly an independent phenomenon.

Once we remove these last two sets, the chi-square evidence shows no significant differences that cannot be accounted for by the most obvious kind of phonetic conditioning. This application of chi-square is only a preliminary trial in approaching the problem. The pairs chosen are a judgment sample from a larger body of possible combinations of 30 words taken two at a time (435 pairs). Furthermore, the geographical differentiation of two words would be hidden in a chi-square comparison if two words randomly alternated the possible phonetic values at all localities.[4] The explorations to follow will address these questions. At this point we can observe that the failure to show any significant differences that are not connected with the phonetic environment of **ū** is not really consistent with the idea that each word has its own history.

Multiple regression analysis

The chi-square analysis of table 17.3 suggests the presence of phonetic conditioning in the reflexes of ME **ū** – in the influence of free vs. checked finals, following nasals, preceding liquid clusters, and so on. The chi-square measures simply indicate that certain pairs were more different than

---

[4] As pointed out by Wang (p.c.) in response to a draft of this chapter. This question is addressed at the end of this section.

others, without demonstrating what the effects were. If such phonetic effects held for all dialects, and if all the sound changes followed a single linear dimension of which the index of vowel shift advancement was a true measure, we could identify these effects through a single multivariate analysis. In the discussion to follow, these two assumptions will be called the *generality* and *linearity* conditions. Given the nature of the data, multiple regression would be the appropriate tool for such a multivariate analysis. First, the dependent variable – the index of vowel shift advancement – is a quantitative integral scale. Second, the phonetic environments that form the independent variables are partially but not completely independent of each other. For example, following nasals can occur with preceding liquid clusters (*drown*) but often do not (*down*). If the generality and linearity conditions hold, a multiple regression analysis would yield significant coefficients for the presence of a following nasal consonant, a preceding cluster, a free vowel and so on.

Table 17.4 shows results from a stepwise multiple regression analysis of the 30 ME ū words listed in Ogura's appendix E (the full data set from which table 17.1 is taken). The dependent variable is the index of vowel shift advancement, and the independent variables include all the phonetic features of the preceding and following segment that have been found to influence vowel shifts. Since we are testing for evidence that would support either of the two hypotheses – regular phonetically conditioned change or lexical diffusion – it is also useful to include an independent variable that would be sensitive to the presence of lexical diffusion. Such an indicator is frequency. Most of the studies that argue for lexical diffusion show a strong frequency effect, with the more frequent words favored in the change.

From the many environmental conditions tested, only a few effects emerge. Four negative coefficients, shown in bold type, indicate conditions that retard the advancement of ū words along the vowel shift path. The four are all significant, but sharply graded in the size of the effect. The

Table 17.4 Stepwise multiple regression analysis of reflexes of ME ū words. Dependent variable: Ogura's (1987) index of vowel shift advancement. Analysis of all ū words. N = 30, r^2 = .997

Variable	Coefficient	t	p(2-tail)
Following labial	**−1377**	−71.08	0.000
BOW	**−362**	−18.35	0.000
Following velar	**−149**	−9.87	0.000
Preceding liquid	**−33**	−3.75	0.002
Frequency	−0.008	−1.15	0.263

most powerful effect, −1377, is that of a following labial, which as we have seen is entirely the result of mistakenly including the word *room*. The second effect, −362, is the result of mistakenly including the word *bow*.

The third significant coefficient, −149, is the retarding effect of following velars. The velars that allowed the participation of the preceding vowel in the diphthongization are the ones that were eventually vocalized, as when *drought* is pronounced [draut]. The remaining velars inhibited the change categorically – there are no words with rhymes in /awk/ and /awg/ today. Ogura's coding of this class does not distinguish between vowels that have following velar or labial-dental consonants phonetically, and those that occur finally as the result of the total vocalization of the velar consonant. For example, the word *trough* is realized with a free vowel by 7 of the 14 Norfolk respondents, with a final /f/ by 2, with a final /θ/ by 1, and with either /f/ or a free vowel by 4. There are of course no /aw/ diphthongs before /f/ or /θ/, but all the free vowels are diphthongs ending in a back glide /w/. The value of −149 therefore registers the fact that in some dialects for some informants, the velar consonant is not vocalized. The lexical irregularity is not to be attributed to the vowel shift, but to the consonant vocalization.

Only one true phonetic condition emerges: the small effect of a preceding liquid, /l/ or /r/. This overall result might mean that in spite of the hints provided by the chi-square analysis, there is no sizeable influence of the phonetic environment on the vowel shift. This would then suggest the dominance of lexical diffusion, since most regular sound changes do show phonetic conditioning of some kind. On the other hand, the result may be due to the failure of either the generality or linearity condition. The generality condition is fairly well supported in most studies of phonetic influences on sound change, since it rests upon the general patterns of coarticulation and anticipatory assimilation.[5] However, the linearity condition seems much less likely to hold in this case.

Returning to figure 17.1, we see that the main path of the diphthongization of ū involves three different phonetic directions: first, the falling or opening of the nucleus from [u] to [a]; then a fronting from [a] to [æ]; and then a raising from [æ] to [e]. From a phonetic viewpoint, the route is curvilinear rather than linear. Different phonetic effects can be expected to apply to favor or disfavor the change at each stage. Furthermore, there are a number of side chains that involve entirely different types of sound changes: monophthongization, development of an inglide, shortening,

---

[5] In the diphthongization of ū as well as ī, we can expect that free vowels will show more open nuclei than checked vowels, and vowels before voiced finals more open nuclei than vowels before voiceless finals. Such relations are well preserved in modern Scottish dialects, reflecting the unfinished course of the original vowel shift, and in a number of centralizing processes that affect /ay/ in modern American dialects. There are limitations to the universality of such phonetic effects (LYS:chap. 3).

unrounding of the glide, and so on. In order to arrive at a single, straight-forward index of vowel shift advancement that would take all data into account, Ogura had to assign each of these side chains the same number as the next stage in the main series. Yet it is clear that very different types of phonetic conditioning will favor the advancement of sound change along these side chains. Linear correlations of the advancement index with particular phonetic conditions will therefore combine opposing conditioning effects in opposite directions, and average to zero.

Another aspect of this nonlinearity can be seen in the geographic distribution of the reflexes of ME **ū**, the proper domain of dialect geography. Figure 17.2 shows the values for all 311 points in England for the two words *house* and *mouse*. In the eastern half of England, there is a very regular progression of forms, starting with [u:] in the north, and proceeding to [ɷu], [aɷ], [æɷ], and [ɛɷ] in the southeast quadrant. This may be interpreted as the result of a steady expansion of the diphthongization process from an origin in the southeast toward the north. But in the western half of England, the situation is far more complex, with many local movements disturbing this regular progression, and many points of local origin. Some areas show the monophthongization of the diphthong, and others the shift of the glide from /w/ to /y/. The conservative effect of overlap with Welsh speakers can be seen in several of the subareas next to Wales. Thus there is a strong indication that the overall regression analysis of the data will be disturbed by a lack of linearity in the west.

Finally, the multiple regression analysis of table 17.4 shows that word frequency has no effect in favoring the change. This is another indication that the typical configuration of lexical diffusion is absent, although it does not rule out the possibility that lexical diffusion might be operating in the data to some extent.

Multidimensional scaling

In the light of this nonlinear configuration, and the limited results with regression analysis, it would seem advisable to follow an opposing mathematical approach. Instead of attempting to fit the histories of the 30 individual words into a preconceived format, we may apply a mode of analysis that maps the actual differences between the words as they are reflected in the distributions over the 45 phonetic forms. Factor analysis, which reduces the variation of the original data set to a smaller number of dimensions, is one useful approach to this task. However, it shares with multiple regression the assumption of linear relations among the elements involved, and often leads to a higher dimensionality than can easily be interpreted.[6]

---

[6] Factor analysis, in the form of principal component analysis, was applied to the data first, with interesting results; the first three components had useful phonetic interpretations. How-

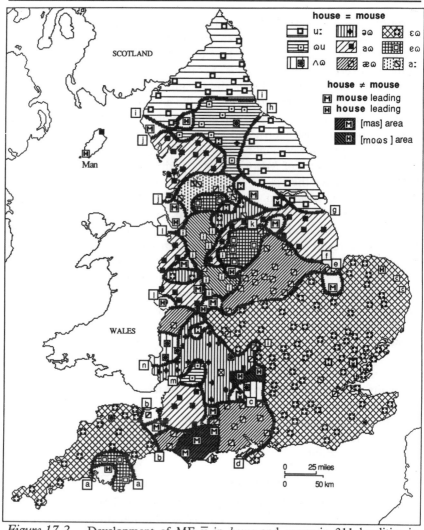

Figure 17.2. Development of ME **ū** in *house* and *mouse* in 311 localities in England

Multidimensional scaling (Shepard 1962; Kruskal 1964; Shepard, Romney, and Nerlove 1972) looks for any nonlinear relations between data points – similarity, association, correlation, interaction, etc. – that can be defined as a type of "proximity." The algorithm takes as input a matrix of partial correlations of all data, a more systematic organization of the information that we sampled in table 17.3 by the chi-square analysis of

ever, the results with multidimensional scaling described in this section were more precise and apparently are better fitted to the nonlinear character of the data.

pairs. The program then seeks by iterative means a set of distances in a small number of dimensions – usually two or three – that are monotonically related to the proximity data.

Figure 17.3 shows the two-dimensional display that is the result of entering the 30 ME **ū** words into a multidimensional scaling program.[7] The central set of 16 words without special phonetic conditioning is grouped in a tight cluster at the upper right. This is the central **ū** word class. All the other words scattered about the diagram contain allophones with particular phonetic conditioning.

1 The word *room* is at the far left, isolated from all others. As we have seen, it does not belong in this series.
2 The word *bow*, which also doesn't belong in the series, is isolated in low central position.
3 The word *drought* appears in low central position, even farther from the main distribution. As noted above, *drought* has a unique phonetic distribution that separates it from other words ending in velars.
4 Three words ending in /r/ are grouped closely together on the lower half of the vertical axis: *hour, flower, flour*.
5 The one word ending in a lateral, *owl*, occupies the same position as the /r/ words horizontally, but has the position of the main distribution vertically.

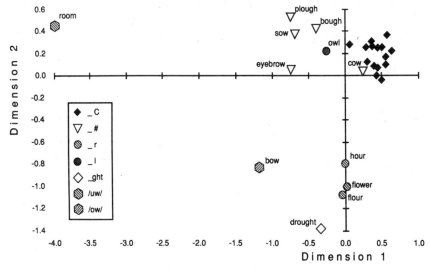

Figure 17.3.   Multidimensional scaling of all ME **ū** words

[7] The particular version of multidimensional scaling used here is that of the Systat program implemented on the Macintosh. Kruskal's (1964) stress formula was used with ordinary Euclidean distances.

6   Three words with free vowels originally ending in ME **g** are grouped
    together to the left of the vertical axis: *sow, plough, bough. Cow* and
    eyebrow, which have no etymological **g**, are grouped separately nearby.

It is not always easy to label the dimensions output by multidimensional
scaling, but figure 17.3 offers little difficulty. The horizontal Dimension 1
is related to participation in the vowel shift. The word *room,* which participates minimally, is at the extreme left. Next is *bow,* which does participate,
but as a member of another class – ME **ō**. The vertical Dimension 2 registers the influence of the following consonant, as we will see in more detail
in figure 17.4. Figure 17.3 also shows the degree to which underlying ME
g continues to determine the behavior of *bough, sow,* and *plough.*

Figure 17.4 is the result of an analysis in which the peripheral words
are dropped, and the main word class is submitted to multidimensional
scaling. The result is a fine-grained pattern of phonetic conditioning. At
the top are words ending in nasals – *thousand, bounce, crown, ounce, drown.*
The subset of words that begin with liquid clusters is concentrated at the
right. Next are the words ending with voiceless stops: *out, without, about.*
Below these, strung out along the horizontal axis, are words ending in
voiceless fricatives: *house* and *mouse* at the left, and *south* and *mouth* just
to the right of the vertical axis. Words with initial liquids are concentrated
to the right: this accounts for the separation of *louse* from *house* and *mouth.*

The phonetic interpretation of figures 17.3 and 17.4 is quite clear. Figure 17.3 isolates individual words that have distinctly different histories,
and in addition separates from the main body one phonetic subset – ME

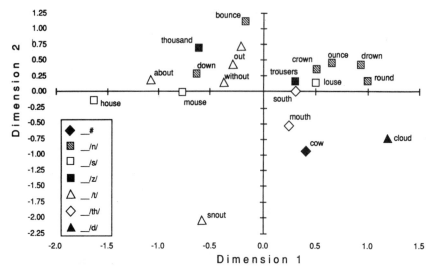

Figure 17.4.   Multidimensional scaling of core ME **ū words**

ū before liquids. Within the main subset, figure 17.4 displays a detailed phonetic conditioning.

These results have a significance that goes far beyond the case of ME ū. Although five generations of linguists have accepted the view that dialect geography establishes that "Each word has its own history," the evidence of figures 17.3 and 17.4 argues strongly in the other direction. Given the proper tools for quantitative analysis, the phonetic regularity of dialect patterns emerges in a form considerably stronger than the Neogrammarians themselves would have expected. No phonetic information is fed into the multidimensional scaling program: the fine-grained phonetic clustering of figure 17.4 is therefore a property of the data themselves.

There is one exception to this narrow phonetic specification: the word *snout*. It is different from the other words ending in /t/ in ways that cannot be accounted for phonetically, and must be considered the only example of a lexical variant.

Geographic evidence on ME *ū*

Figure 17.2 was first introduced to show the nonlinear character of the geographic distribution of ME ū. It is designed specifically to contrast the development of two words – *house* and *mouse* – in the SED. We can use this pair to explore the spatial distribution of the sound changes involved – the essential feature of dialect geography that has been missing to this point. Though the figure shows only a single pair, it will allow us to trace the process of geographic diffusion in detail. If the basic mechanism of sound change is Neogrammarian, the two words should show nearly identical spatial distributions; if the basic mechanism is lexical diffusion, we should observe independent shifts of *house* and *mouse*, especially visible in the boundary areas between the major dialect regions. For the great majority of the 311 communities, the same phonetic form is reported for these two words, indicated by one of the nine symbols shown at the top right of the diagram. The two words have different reflexes only in the 30 communities marked with an **M** or an **H** – less than 10% of the total. In general, *house* and *mouse* share the same history. But it is still possible that the change that produced this result involved a process of lexical diffusion, where words are selected randomly and advance individually. Evidence for such a process must be found on the boundaries between geographical areas, where most of the disagreement between *house* and *mouse* is located.

I originally chose *house* and *mouse* because Bloomfield gave considerable attention to these words in his discussion of the principles of dialect geography (1933:330ff.). Their differential behavior in the Netherlands appeared to be a classic case of lexical idiosyncrasy in spatial distributions:

The word *house* will occur much oftener than the word *mouse* in official speech and in conversation with persons who represent the cultural center; *mouse* is more confined to homely and familiar situations. Accordingly, we find that the word *house* in the upper-class and central form with [y:] spread into districts where the word *mouse* has persisted in the old-fashioned form with [u:]. (1933:330–1)

Like many explanations of lexical isoglosses, this is a post hoc account. But since it deals with general properties of the referents 'house' and 'mouse', it should apply generally to England as well as the Netherlands. Section 17.1 developed some quantitative arguments on how the data of dialect geography can be used to distinguish between regular sound change and lexical diffusion. Following this logic, we can use the data displayed in figure 17.2 to test two general propositions: that the sound change advances word by word, and that *house* will be more advanced than *mouse*.

Let us assume that at any given stage in the vowel shift, *house* and *mouse* do not advance together, but instead advance as individual lexical items with an equal possibility of being selected. Just as we saw earlier, there are four possible cases. If lexical diffusion were the basic mechanism, we should find the following distribution of the older form and the newer form in the communities that are undergoing this stage of the shift:

	1	2	3	4
house	newer	newer	older	older
mouse	newer	older	newer	older
	25%	25%	25%	25%

Let us neglect for the moment the effect of random differentiation of *house* and *mouse* due to the other causes of differentiation listed in section 17.1, and focus only on type 2: lexical selection of one word by a sound change but not the other. It follows that in the transitions between areas, change by lexical diffusion would produce 50% identical reports on the two words, and 50% differentiated. We can test this possibility by examining the isoglosses that surround the various regions of figure 17.2. If the transition between two points follows such a process, we would expect to find an **M** or an **H** between two regular points in one-half of the cases, corresponding to cells 2 and 3 above. Figure 17.5 displays an expanded view of the northernmost dialect area that illustrates the method used.

The northernmost area of England is the most conservative region, where the vowel shift has not affected ME **ū** at all. Just south of this area to the east, we find the first step in the vowel shift, the diphthongized high vowel [ɷu]. To the west, the next most southerly region has a more differentiated diphthong, [aɷ]. Each locality along this border in the [u:] region is matched with the nearest point just south of the isogloss, as indicated by the heavy dashed lines; there are seven such transitions.

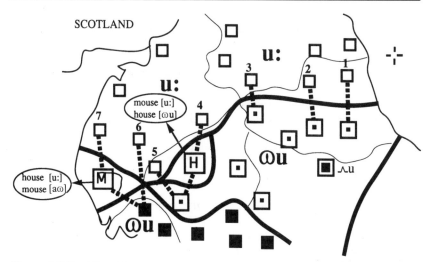

Figure 17.5.   Transitions across the southern boundary of the [u:] region in the North of England

- The localities labeled 1, 2, and 3 show a simultaneous transition from [u:] to [ɷu] in *mouse* and *house*.
- Locality 4 adjoins an intermediate locality marked **H**, where *house* is diphthongized and *mouse* is not. This is a lexical transition from the northern [u:] region to the diphthongized [ɷu] region, showing the kind of intermediate stage that the theory of lexical diffusion would predict.
- Locality 5 shows a simultaneous transition from [u:] in the north to [ɷu] to the south. It might also have been adjoined to the [aɷ] region, since it is the same distance from the black square to the southwest; but following the general procedure, Locality 6 is related to the [aɷ] region.
- Locality 6 shows a simultaneous transition from the [u:] region to the [ɷu] region.
- Locality 7 adjoins a second intermediate point marked **M**, where *mouse* is ahead of *house*. Again, the more advanced form is identical with that of the region to the south, as indicated by the continuation of the dashed line.

Localities 4 and 7 then show the type of lexical transitions that would support a theory of lexical diffusion; Localities 1, 2, 3, 5, 6 show simultaneous transitions consistent with a mechanism of regular sound change.

Table 17.5 lists the total number of transition points for all the isoglosses on figure 17.2. The isoglosses (indicated by the letters *a–n* on figure 17.2) are selected in a counterclockwise direction, beginning with Cornwall in the southwest. Each boundary and each of the differentiated localities

Table 17.5 Simultaneous and differentiated transitions for *house* and *mouse*

		house=mouse	house≠mouse	Lexical transitions
a.	Outer limits of [eɷ] in Cornwall	3	1	0
b.	Northeastern limit of [ɛɷ] in Cornwall	3	1	0
c.	Northwestern limit of [æɷ] in Dorset	4	5	1
d.	Western limit of [ɛɷ] in the Southeast	13	3	1
e.	Northern limit of [ɛɷ] in the Southeast	10	2	1
f.	Northern limit of [æɷ] in East Midlands	6	2	1
g.	Northern limit of [aɷ] in Lincolnshire/westward	7	1	0
h.	Eastern limit of [uː] in Yorkshire	4	3	0
i.	Southern limit of [uː] in the North	5	2	1
j.	Outer limit of [aɷ] in Westmorland	10	1	0
k.	Northern limit of [ɛɷ] in Central Midlands	2	1	0
l.	Outer limit of [aɷ] in Cheshire and Shropshire	6	3	1
m.	Southern/western limit of [əɷ] in Gloucestershire	5	0	0
n.	Outer limit of [ʌɷ] in Herefordshire	4	0	0
TOTAL: 107		82	25	6

marked **H** or **M** is selected once.[8] The first two columns show that there are 82 transitions where *house* and *mouse* shifted phonetic values simultaneously (as in 5 of the 7 transitions in figure 17.5) and 25 where the two words differed (as in the other 2 cases). This is 23% differentiated, half of the value predicted by a lexical diffusion model.

The 25 cases of differentiated transitions in the second column of table 17.5 do not all represent lexical transitions of type 2 listed in section 17.1.

[8] Two of the **H** localities were not used in this calculation, since they did not adjoin any major region.

Two other processes appear to be involved. The first is type 6, inherent variation in speech production. In Leeds, *house* is reportedly pronounced both as [a:] and as [aɷ], but *mouse* only as [aɷ]. From our knowledge of such variable situations elsewhere, we can assume with high probability that *mouse* would also show variation in a sizeable body of spontaneous speech. The second process is of type 3, conditioned sound changes due to phonetic differences between *house* and *mouse*. Most of these involve the labial onset of *mouse*. In the three points marked **M** in Dorset on the southern coast, the word *mouse* is shortened to [mas]: this has no relation to the vowel shift. The locality marked **M** on the west coast, just south of the Westmorland [aɷ] area, has [mạs] for *mouse* (with monophthongal [a]); there is no neighboring region with such a form. In the dark shaded south central area of Berkshire, there are two points marked **H**. Here the word *mouse* is realized as [moɷs], reflecting the rounded character of the initial: there are no neighboring areas with such phonetic forms. Since [oɷ] is a more conservative form in the history of the vowel shift, *house* is marked as leading, but this appears to be a case of phonetic conditioning of *mouse* rather than the lexical selection of *house*.

The third column of table 17.5 shows how many of the differentiated localities are actually *lexical* transitions, like points 4 and 7 in figure 17.5. Only 6 of the 25, or 5.6% of the total, can be identified as such by the methods illustrated in figure 17.5. This is far short of the 50% that the lexical diffusion theory would predict, and much closer to the effect that random perturbations would have on a regular process.

These results do not prove that lexical diffusion is not operating in the development of ME **ū**. It is always possible that words shift one at a time more rapidly and on a much smaller scale, so that they are rejoined within in each community shortly after that community is affected by the change. All that we can say is that no evidence for lexical diffusion has emerged in the data considered so far.

We can also ask whether this evidence supports the opposing model of regular sound change. One might argue that regular sound change would predict a 0% incidence of lexical transitions. However, there are many other sources of variation that make it unlikely that any community would show perfect regularity in production. As indicated in section 17.1, lexico-statistic calculations show that there will be roughly 8% differentiation of the vocabulary over 500 years. In these calculations, we are not considering lexical replacement, of course, but rather a series of small causes that can lead to phonetic differentiation of two words. These are not purely pho-netic effects, but the result of social interaction. The concept of "dialect mixture" has been used freely to account for such variation within the Neogrammarian perspective. On the dialectological side, Dauzat and Gil-liéron have made it plain that migration and intermarriage across dialect regions will ensure some representation of competing dialects in marginal areas. Thus the fact that 6 of 107 transitions are lexical transitions is not inconsistent with an underlying model of regular sound change, where the regular process is perturbed by a series of minor factors.

17.4 Analysis of ME ī words

We can now use the same tools to examine the front partner of the vowel shift, ME ī. Table 17.6 shows a sampling of 42 pairwise chi-square comparisons for ME ī, arranged in ascending order of chi-square. Forty-four out of 741 possible combinations of the 39 words are shown. Again, the majority of the comparisons show no significant difference in distribution: this is only a sampling of the number of pairwise comparisons that could be made. Pairs that are most similar phonetically show the lowest scores:

Table 17.6 Pairwise chi-square evaluation of phonetic distribution of ME ī words

	χ^2	N		χ^2	N
Not significant			*p < .05*		
ice/icicle	0.34	10	hive/wife	23.50	12
hive/ivy	1.58	10	eye/died	24.13	12
wife/knife	2.08	12			
mice/slice	3.00	11	*p < .01*		
white/writing	3.23	11	eye/dry	27.91	10
nine/mine	3.53	13	eye/sky	28.04	10
slice/lice	3.63	11			
died/flies	3.76	12	*p < .001*		
dry/sky	3.91	9	fire/ice	29.00	9
sight/lightning	3.94	12	thigh/might	30.55	12
spider/slide	4.37	13	right/night	33.43	13
fire/iron	4.45	9	iron/wife	42.83	10
might/writing	4.47	12	eye/light	43.77	12
hide/spider	5.16	13	might/wright	48.47	12
night/sight	5.70	11	died/slide	69.09	14
time/nine	6.42	13	might/light	74.03	13
died/light	7.47	11	died/hide	75.19	14
five/hive	8.58	11	sight/dike	76.81	12
stile/thigh	8.81	12	fight/white	97.82	11
beside/hide	8.90	13	fight/writing	99.54	11
dry/fire	14.58	8	might/fight	101.7	11
eye/flies	14.95	11	night/writing	102.9	13
might/sight	15.21	10	night/white	106.5	13
right/light	19.11	13	fight/night	131.8	13

ice/icicle, which combines phonetic with morphological similarity, is the very lowest. Next come phonetically similar pairs like *hive/ivy, wife/knife, mice/slice, white/writing, nine/mine, slice/lice*. Though the main function of the chi-square test is to distinguish significant from nonsignificant differences, we can also see an ordering within the nonsignificant group from lesser to greater phonetic similarity. Near the bottom of the left-hand column, we see *dry/fire*, where a free vowel is opposed to one before /r/. Greater phonetic contrast leads to significant differences in chi-square. However, we also see at the bottom of the left column a number of words that are near-minimal pairs, like *might/sight* and *right/light*.

Among pairs with significant differences, we find some that are phonetically distinctive, like *hive/wife*, opposed by final voicing, and at the .001 level, *fire/ice*, with even greater differentiation. But there are also a number of words with even higher chi-square values, with no clear phonetic differentiation: at the .01 level, the free pairs *eye/dry* and *eye/sky*, and at the .001 level, *died/hide, fight/white, fight/night*, etc. These involve two sets of words that were not members of the ī class in late Old English. If we refer to the main body of ME ī words as ī1, then these may be labeled ī2 and ī3.

The class labeled ī2 consists of ME short ĭ followed by a velar consonant and /t/ in *right, night, fight, sight, light, lightning*, and the compound form *-wright*. In the history of the best-known dialects, the velar was first realized as a voiceless palatal and then disappeared, with compensatory lengthening of the vowel. Two pronunciations, with and without the consonant, were competing in the London English of the 15th and 16th centuries (Jespersen 1949:284). This did not happen in all dialects. Americans are most familiar with the retention of the velar in Scots, as in the stereotypical phrase *braw bricht moonlicht nicht*. Unlike *drought*, ī2 shows no consonantal reflexes in any of the English dialects of the SED.

The class labeled ī3 consists of long ē followed by **g** in Old English in *lie, fly, die*, and long ɛ̄ in *eye*, etc. No consonantal reflexes survive in the dialects covered by the SED, but the raising did not occur in all dialects, as we will see. *Thigh*, which contained OE **eoh**, is related to this set.

Ogura (1987) lists several other words with different OE origins. *Fire, hive, mice, lice, hide, dry* all had the front rounded vowel **y** in late Old English, but there is no sign of this difference in any surviving dialect. The word *nine* contained /ig/ in late Old English, but chi-square and other tests show that it is identical in distribution to *mine*.

Multiple regression analysis

The multiple regression analysis of ME ī shows a pattern similar to that of ME ū. Table 17.7 displays the significant results from three separate runs. In the first analysis, shown in section (a) of the table, all 38 words are included, and the words with histories of membership in separate word classes are each assigned separate dummy variables. Frequency has no

Table 17.7 Stepwise multiple regression analysis of 38 ME ī words. Dependent variable: Ogura's (1987) index of vowel shift advancement.

Variable	Coefficient	t	p(2-tail)
a. *All words* [N = 38]			
Frequency	0.006	0.152	0.875
iç class (ī2)	−230.111	−3.689	0.001
ē class (ī3)	−189.384	−3.250	0.003
+grammatical	127.794	2.770	0.009
b. *Removing class ī2 and class ī3* [N = 27]			
Frequency	0.021	0.652	0.523
Following segment	83.060	1.987	0.062
Following liquid	−56.700	−1.874	0.078
c. *Removing all free and liquid-final words* [N = 21]			
Frequency	0.003	0.230	0.822
Following tense	−38.918	−3.296	0.006
Following nasal	77.090	2.372	0.034
Preceding nasal	−83.173	−3.325	0.005

effect at all, as in the case of ME ū. On the other hand, the two special classes have a strong effect in retarding the operation of the vowel shift on ī, with negative coefficients of −230 and −189. To the extent that the words in these classes were not a part of the main process, they would obviously fall behind the other words. Finally, grammatical forms – *beside* and *-wright* – have a small favoring effect.[9]

In analysis (b), the special word classes and grammatical items are removed, and with them, most of the sources of variation.[10] Frequency remains without effect, but two small phonetic effects emerge, just short of the .05 level of significance. Checked syllables have a small favoring effect, and following liquids a disfavoring effect.

When free vowels and liquid-final syllables are removed in the analyses of section (c), 21 words remain. Again, frequency has no effect. However, a small but significant disfavoring effect of a following tense (voiceless) consonant emerges, along with a favoring effect of a following nasal and a disfavoring effect of a preceding nasal. These small phonetic influences must be viewed with some skepticism in light of the absence of linearity

[9] The effect of membership in a grammatical class is probably due to reduced stress in ordinary discourse, though this would not necessarily show up in the elicitations of the dialect atlas fieldwork.

[10] A comparison of the ANOVA figures in runs (a) and (b) shows that only 5% of the original variance remains.

that we observed with ME **ū**. The procedure does suggest however that there are phonetic effects underlying the major sources of variation, the in-migrant word classes. On the whole, the situation resembles that of ME **ū**.

Multidimensional scaling

Let us now apply the technique of multidimensional scaling to the geo-graphic reflexes of ME **ī**. Figure 17.6 shows the results of a multidimen-sional scaling of the 38 ME **ī** words that Ogura (1987) extracted from the SED. All of these words have emerged in the standard language with /ay/. The lack of homogeneity that appeared in the chi-square and regression analyses is immediately obvious.

The main group of words, tightly clustered in the upper right, is re-presented with black diamonds. This is the **ī** class: the ME **ī** words that correspond directly to OE **ī**.

Scattered about the rest of the diagram are symbols that represent the migrants into the special classes **ī2** and **ī3**. Class **ī2**, depicted by triangles on figure 17.6, is the set of words with reflexes of OE long mid vowels before a final voiced velar. After a front vowel, the velar spelled **g** was shifted to palatal position and eventually vocalized to [j]; the preceding vowel was raised to high position in Late Old English or Middle English. *Eye* was usually spelled *eye, eiȝe,* or *eighe* in Middle English, reflecting OE **éa**, smoothed to ɛ: in late Old English. The spelling *ye, yen* is also found in Chaucer, showing the shift to a high vowel, but the *ey-* spelling is the one that survived in the standard language. In Middle English, *die* was variously spelled *dien, dyen, diȝen, deȝen, deyen,* akin to Icelandic *deyja*; the

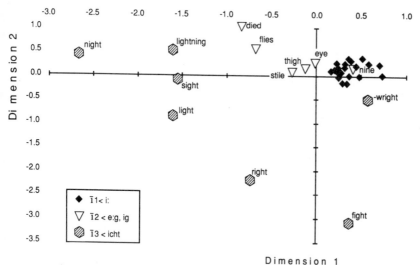

Figure 17.6.   Multidimensional scaling of all ME **ī** words

OE cognate stem was lost and later readapted from a Scandinavian source. The noun *fly* is from OE *fléoge*; the spelling *flyge* reflects an earlier raising. The word now spelled *thigh* is also from OE **éo**. It was spelled *thih* or *theiʒ* in Middle English, reflecting an earlier *théoh*. The words *stile* and *nine* had short high vowels that were lengthened with the disappearance of the velar, reflecting OE *stigon* and *nigon*.

On figure 17.6, five of these six **ī2** words show a distinct distribution outside the main body of ME **ī** words. *Died* and *flies* are well to the left, and *stile*, *thigh*, *and eye* form a tight cluster near the origin. Only *nine* is in the main distribution.[11] No phonetic conditioning accounts for the aberrant behavior of this subclass: here we see geographic evidence of lexical diffusion.

The words of the **ī2** class have a variety of different histories in Old English: *night*, *sight*, and *right* had short **i**, whereas *fight* had short **eo** and *light* a long **éo** that alternated with long **ī**. *Lightning* is derived from ME *lightenen* 'to lighten', with the same phonological history. In Middle English, all these words emerge with a short **i** and the spelling *-ight*, reflecting a pronunciation [ɪçt]. The velar realized as palatal [ç] apparently persisted as a consonantal articulation much later than the voiced velars. As noted above, parallel pronunciations with lengthened [i:] and short [iç] were found in the standard language as late as the 16th century (Jespersen 1949:284). Their differential history is reflected in the geographic dispersion as well. In figure 17.6, these words form an even more dramatic example of lexical diffusion than the first subset of migrants: they follow a widely dispersed pattern from upper left to lower right, with *-wright* off the main line of development.[12]

Figure 17.7 shows the fine-grained phonetic dispersion of the main distribution of the **ī1** class. Dimension 1 evidently reflects the effect of the voicing of the following segment. All the words with voiceless finals are to the right of the origin, and the others are to the left.

- Three words ending in /s/ are at the extreme right: *mice*, *lice*, and *slice*, while *icicle* and *ice* are close together a little higher up on Dimension 2.
- Two words ending in /f/ are just below and to the right of the origin: *wife* and *knife*.
- Three words with final nasals are to the left of the origin: *nine*, *mine*, and *time*, the last being differentiated in a way that may reflect its final labial.

---

[11] The disappearance of the palatal glide and compensatory lengthening seem to have happened earlier with *nine* than with *stile*. This seems to be the only major effect of frequency in the data reviewed here.
[12] The word *-wright* is the result of metathesis from OE *wyrht*, but the weakened stress on *-wright* is no doubt responsible for its distinct position.

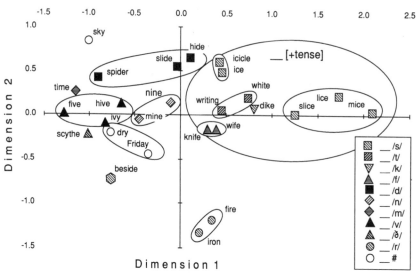

Figure 17.7.   Multidimensional scaling of core ME ī words

- Words ending in apical stops are closer to the vertical origin than words with other finals: *hide, slide,* and *Friday,* are closely aligned.
- Two words with initial *s-* clusters are at the upper left, *sky* and *spider.* This raises the possibility that the exceptional position of *snout* in figure 17.4 was not a lexical idiosyncrasy, but that its isolation was due to the absence of other words with *s-* clusters.
- Words with final voiced fricatives are at the extreme left; *five, ivy, hive, scythe.*
- *Slide* and *beside* are widely separated, but this is probably due to the grammatical status of the latter (see table 17.7a).

Dimension 2 reflects the effect of following and preceding liquid /r/, just as in figure 17.3. The strongest effect is that of following /r/: *fire* and *iron* are at low center, in the same relative position as *hour, flower,* and *flour* in figure 17.3. Preceding /r/, particularly in a consonant cluster, has a moderate effect in the same direction: *eyebrow* is below *sow* and *bough* in figure 17.3, just as *Friday* and *dry* are below *sky* in figure 17.7. Thus Dimension 2 appears to be roughly the same for **ū** and **ī**. The same cannot be said for Dimension 1, however. Though it clusters words by the place and manner of articulation of the following environment in both cases, the actual distributions are quite different.

Figures 17.3 and 17.7 show that there are no clear cases of lexical diffusion among the main distributions that reflect a continuous history from Old English to Middle English. Lexical diffusion is confined to those elements that have joined the ME **ī** class as the result of selective phonological processes that favor it: in this case, compensatory lengthening. The absence of lexical idiosyncrasies combined with strict phonetic conditioning leads to the conclusion that the mechanism involved in the Great Vowel Shift is regular sound change. The elements of the vowel shift proper – raising, lowering, fronting, and backing of vowel nuclei – display all the properties of a regular, Neogrammarian sound change.

Geographic dispersion of the migrant class ī3

Figure 17.8 shows the ī3 class in northern England, where the geographic source of its irregular behavior is evident. The three hatched areas show the regions in the north where *died*, *flies*, and *eye* have retained their membership in the ME ē and ɛ̄ classes along with *need*, *see*, and *freeze*, and are therefore realized as [iː] in modern dialects. Each one shows a different pattern. The *died* region covers the northern and western portions of northern England. The conservative behavior of *eye* is more limited: [iː] is found only in the southern half of this region. Finally, *flies* retains its original word class membership in the entire region, except for four points in the middle and one point in the southwest.

The scattered position of these words in figure 17.6 is entirely the result of this geographic irregularity, and has nothing to do with the operation of the vowel shift itself. In the midland and southern dialects, where this change of category membership is fully accomplished, all three words follow the history of their new class, long /iː/, with Neogrammarian regularity as it diphthongizes to /ay/ and /oy/.

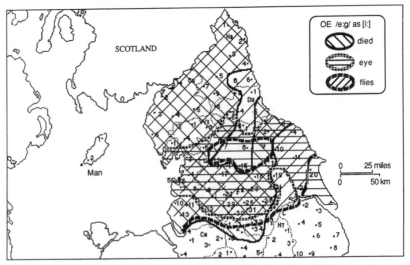

Figure 17.8.   Communities in northern England where Late OE ēg words retain membership in the ē class (= present = day [iː])

17.5   Conclusion

This chapter began with the normal expectation that the evidence of dialect geography would strengthen the case for lexical diffusion, but the opposite has proved to be the case. For over a century, linguists have assumed that the testimony of dialect geography was firmly aligned against the Neogrammarians, but instead we have found evidence for regular conditioned sound change with subtle and profound phonetic conditioning. We began with Ogura's argument that the diphthongization of ME ī and ū proceeded by lexical diffusion. But the quantitative methods used here give no support to this view. For the great majority of the data studied here, we can find no reason to posit a mechanism of lexical selection.

We can of course never rule out the possibility that lexical diffusion occurs in the major word classes in a manner more subtle than we can observe. If so, it must be confined to very short periods of time and space, and is far overshadowed by phonetic conditioning. There is no evidence here that lexical diffusion is the fundamental mechanism of sound change. Though some words may have their own history, each word does not have its own history. Once the data of dialect geography are examined with the appropriate mathematical tools, they are thoroughly consistent with the Neogrammarian view that sound change affects word classes and phonemes.

That is not to say that no evidence for lexical diffusion was found. In the case of ME ū, the most obvious candidates for lexical selection proved to be the result of errors of various types. But in the case of ME ī, two sets of words proved to be classical cases of lexical diffusion. Both were the result of earlier migrations into the OE ī class. In one case, long mid vowels were raised before voiced palatals to merge with ī, and in the other case, voiceless palatals were lost with compensatory lengthening of a preceding ĭ.

We are thus faced with another set of data that is parallel to the results of chapters 15–16. Lexical diffusion is not the basic mechanism of change, but once again it appears alongside regular change. With the rich data from dialect geography behind us, it may be possible to advance a general solution to the problem of predicting when and where lexical diffusion will actually be found.

18

A Proposed Resolution of the Regularity Question

No theory of language change can be considered adequate unless it includes a solution to the transition problem for sound change. Does sound change proceed one word at a time, or does it change phonemes as a whole? Our pursuit of this question has developed ample evidence that both regular sound change and lexical diffusion are active and productive processes. We have not yet advanced to the level of predicting when one type of transition occurs, and when the other. The task of this chapter is to advance a reasonable proposal for doing so.

Instead of reviewing all the evidence at once, we will begin by reviewing even more closely the development of short **a** in Philadelphia, where both lexical diffusion and regular sound change are intimately involved. Though we have observed lexical diffusion and regular sound change in the diphthongization of the ME high vowels, the SED materials do not allow us to make inferences about the situation within a single speech community. The program for this chapter is to juxtapose the two processes in Philadelphia and compare their properties on several different planes: physical, phonological, morphological, and social. For each process, we must then address the fundamental question of variation studies: what is it that is varying? To answer this question, we must determine by direct and indirect means the level or stratum of linguistic structure at which the variants are represented. The solution envisaged here is structural: to differentiate the areas of linguistic structure where regular sound change or lexical diffusion is most likely to be found.

There is a sizeable literature on the best way of representing the short **a** split in Philadelphia. Most of the arguments have been bound to a concept of *rule* or *process* that is specific to a grammatical theory. This is not an area of great stability, either in terminology or in proposed principles. It will of course be important to eventually relate our findings to current forms of phonological theory, but it would seem more prudent to begin with terms that are easily translatable into a variety of formal frameworks. We will therefore focus on the substantive nature of the variants concerned: the features or characteristics that differentiate the conservative from the innovative form. Both the quantity and quality of these features or characteristics will be important in determining the level of linguistic representation of the variation and its defining envelope. We will then consider how these differentiating elements are to be assembled into a rule or a lexical matrix.

18.1   Two contrasting short *a* developments in the Middle Atlantic states

At various points in this volume, we have had occasion to refer to the development of short **a** in the Middle Atlantic states. Two distinct aspects have been considered: the splitting of this category into tense and lax categories, and the raising of the tense category from a low to a high ingliding vowel.

- In chapter 3, tense /æh/ was distinguished from lax /æ/ as a part of the study of the Philadelphia vowel system, and the raising of the variable (æh) was traced in apparent time with age, sex, and social coefficients of regression equations.
- In chapter 4, the history of the split was traced in New York City and Philadelphia through reports in real time, and the raising of (æh) was assigned to the group of "nearly completed changes" in Philadelphia.
- In chapter 11, the separation of /æh/ and /æ/ was introduced in New York City and Philadelphia as an example of a lexical split, and a number of details of grammatical, phonological, and lexical conditions were provided.
- In chapter 15, it was shown that lexical diffusion had occurred in the past history of this split, and that new words were migrating into the /æh/ category before intervocalic nasals and before /l/.
- In chapter 16, the raising of (æh) was traced through regression analysis of instrumental measurements, demonstrating fine phonetic conditioning with no trace of lexical diffusion.

Since it has been shown that one of these closely associated processes is a prototypical case of lexical diffusion, and the other is an instance of regular sound change, we can compare their properties as a way of finding out when we can expect one of these types of change, and when the other.

The phonetic features involved

The earliest recorded stages of the split between /æh/ and /æ/ involve lengthening and a shift toward a more peripheral position (LYS:chap. 3); later developments involve raising, fronting, and the addition of an inglide:

$$[kæst] \rightarrow [kæ^<:st] \rightarrow [kɛ:st] \rightarrow [ke:əst] \rightarrow [ki^⊤:əst]$$

The phonetic opposition between the two forms of the original short **a** class eventually includes four features at least:

	Unchanged forms	*Changed forms*
Length	shorter	longer
Peripherality	less peripheral	more peripheral
Height	lower	higher
Inglide	absent	usually present

The acoustic trajectories followed by the changed form are considerably different from those followed by the unchanged form. As figure 18.1 illustrates, the unchanged form typically shows a simple, parabolic movement in which the consonantal transitions move down to a single F1 maximum. The changed trajectory is in a different area of F1/F2 space, shifted toward the high front area. It is also more complex, with three points of inflection instead of one. The initial transition typically moves down to an F1 maximum, then frontward to an F2 maximum, then upward and backward to an F1 minimum.

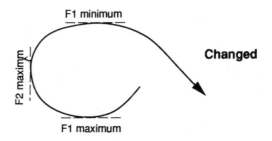

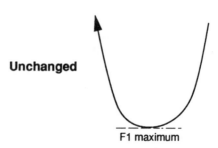

Figure 18.1.   Characteristic trajectories of unchanged (lax) and changed (tense) forms of short **a**

Measurements of the position of /æ/ are taken at the F1 maximum. The measurements of the nuclei of /æh/ are taken at the F2 maximum, since this best represents the phonetic impressions of relative height or advancement of the change. The F2 maximum is also a point of minimum energy, and in some of the more advanced tokens, the vowel becomes even more complex, and can be heard as two distinct nuclei.[1] The discontinuity between the two categories is therefore accentuated by two different strategies of measurement, which correspond to two different types of phonetic structure. The simple structure is similar to the trajectories of simple vowels like [ɛ] in *pet* and [ɑ] in *pot*; the complex structure is similar to the trajectories of *yeah* and *idea*, and it appears to be identified with one of these two vowels as it advances from mid to high position.

This frequently recurring combination of phonetic differences calls for a general term to distinguish the changed from the unchanged category. *Tense* and *lax* are the traditional and most appropriate terms, and I will continue to use them to distinguish /æh/ from /æ/, where the glide /h/ indicates that the tense vowel is ingliding. It should be clear that *tense* is a cover term for this combination of impressionistic and acoustic features. Though the advanced forms of /æh/ appear to require more muscular effort, *tense* cannot be used to refer to this property until we have electromyographic data to support this impression.

The raising of the variable (æh) is traced by following a series of small increments in fronting and raising of the tokens that we classify as tense by the criteria just given. Chapter 16 demonstrated that these small differences form a continuous range across phonetic space, and no indications of a discrete break within (æh) have been found (see figure 16.8).

The progress of the raising of (æh) can be traced by measurements of individual formant positions: F2 appears to be a more sensitive indicator than F1, both of phonetic conditioning (as chapter 16 showed) and of degree of advancement through the community (as chapter 3 showed). Chapter 16 showed that the most satisfactory way of tracking the change is through a combination of F2 and F1. This is the Cartesian distance along the front diagonal of acoustic space, which is heard impressionistically as the *height* of the vowel:

$$(\text{æh}) = \sqrt{(\text{F2})^2 - (2*\text{F1})^2}$$

We thus assign the variable (æh) to a phonological dimension, which is one step more complex than simple measurements of the central tendencies of

---

[1] Thus in CDC gating experiments, Chicago *that* is often heard as two words: *the act, the fact*, etc. (See chapter 6, p. 189).

formants, but much less complex than the combination of properties used to distinguish /æh/ from /æ/.

Parallels in phonological conditioning

The phonetic conditions that control the split of the short **a** category and the raising of the tense category are similar. Chapter 16 showed that the following properties of the phonetic environment increase the height or peripherality of (æh):

Favoring	*Disfavoring*
Following nasal consonant	Secondary stress
Following stop (/d/)	Two following syllables
Preceding nasal consonant	Obstruent/liquid initial cluster

Two of the three favoring elements also form part of the conditions for the split. It is clear that a following nasal consonant favors the selection of words for the /æh/ category more than a following stop, since almost all words were selected from the first category but only three from the second. A more subtle parallel is found in comparing the effect of nasals with that of voiceless fricatives (the residual category in the regression analysis). When word-initial short **a** occurs before a nasal, all words are selected: tense *aunt, answer, ancestors, anchovies, ambush, ambition, ambulance, anticipate, anti-*. But when it occurs before a voiceless fricative, only the more common, monosyllabic words are tensed: tense *ass* and *ask*; lax *ascot, aspirin, astronauts, aspect, athletic, after, African, Afghan*.

No effect of a preceding nasal consonant is observed in the selection process.

Of the disfavoring environments, the effect of secondary stress is parallel to the effect of auxiliary status: the grammatical functors *am, an, and, can* are not tensed. When these elements are stressed, they frequently have secondary stress. The word *can't* is usually tense; unlike the others, it is not a weak word, and cannot have shwa as its only vowel. However, 5 of the 139 instances of *can't* recorded from the 100 speakers of the Philadelphia Neighborhood Study were lax, while only 2 of the 145 instances of *aunt* were lax (Labov 1989a). This may also register the effect of secondary stress.

The effect of two following syllables was quite powerful in Carol Meyers's phonetic forms (table 16.4), though it involved only three items. This is a general phonological factor in the tensing of English vowels, which is reflected in oppositions like *sane/sanity, white/Whitsuntide*. In the selection of words for the /æh/ category, the effect of following syllables may be seen in the fact that words like *astronaut* are lax, but *ask* and *ass* are tense. However, this effect is confounded with frequency, and frequency appears to be the major factor in the Philadelphia Neighborhood Study. *Afghan,* which occurs only once, is lax, but *after,* with 152 tokens, is tense.

Finally, the selectional process exhibits no correlate of the disfavoring effect of initial liquid clusters. No words with initial obstruent-liquid clusters appeared as lexical exceptions parallel to *great, break,* and *drain* in the raising of $\overline{ea}$ discussed in chapters 10 and 13. Nevertheless, figure 16.8 showed that such words appear regularly among the least advanced of the tensed /æh/ words. In general, initial consonants have little effect upon the short **a** split: initial nasals do not have a powerful enough effect to tense words with disfavoring finals, and initial /KL/ clusters do not have a disfavoring effect strong enough to overcome the favoring effect of the following nasals, voiceless fricatives, and stops. It is actually quite surprising to note that *glad* is tensed, but not *sad.* The only initial effect registered at all in the selectional process is the fact that less common words with initial short **a** are lax before fricatives.

Contrasts in grammatical conditioning

Grammatical conditioning is quite extensive in the selectional process. The most important fact is that inflectional suffixes close the syllable: *planning* and *passes* are tense, indistinguishable in this respect from *plan* and *pass,* though *hammock* and *castle* are lax. This effect appears to include the comparative -*er* and superlative -*est* as well. While this may be ascribed to analogy in a Neogrammarian perspective, it is nonetheless a grammatical effect.[2] The irregular verbs *ran, swam, began* are regularly lax, as are all function words like *can, am, an.*[3]

On the other hand, no trace of grammatical conditioning can be found in the raising of (æh). A factor was introduced to identify grammatical words like *can't* and *after,* but no significant effects were found.

Contrasts in social conditioning

The study of 100 Philadelphians found no social differentiation regarding the split of short **a** in spontaneous speech. The oldest upper-class speaker, born in 1915, had essentially the same system as the oldest working-class speaker, born in 1892 (Labov 1989a:18). There are sizeable differences in

---

[2] Derivational suffixes also play some role in the tensing process, though the data here are sparse, even from the study of 100 speakers (Labov 1989a). One case of tense *classics* appeared, but two of the three instances of *classical* were lax, and though *photographed* was tense, *graphic* was lax. Diminutive suffixes provide clearer data. *Frannie, Danny,* and *Sammy* are regularly tense, but *Cassie* and *Cathy* are lax. Though the data involving derivational suffixes exhibit considerable variation, there is no doubt that they must be taken into account in an exact treatment of the tensing process.

[3] Though a phonological definition of "weak words" allows us to do away with using grammatical terminology in the case of *can, am, an,* no such resource is available for *ran, swam, began.*

the amount of correction that occurs in word lists – primarily a middle-class phenomenon – but none in the unreflecting production of ordinary conversation that displays the basic system of the vernacular. In speech, a small number of tense vowels are found where lax ones are expected, and lax where tense are expected, but these are distributed fairly evenly among all neighborhoods and all social classes.

In the new process of tensing before intervocalic nasals and before /l/, there is some suggestion of a social correlate. The latter effect appears to be confined to working-class neighborhoods, while the former is concentrated in middle-class neighborhoods and the suburbs.

The most general and striking fact is the complete absence of any social awareness of the distributional facts about short **a**. No one is ever stigmatized for saying [me:əd] but not [se:əd], or for saying [pe:əs] but not [ke:əš]. Nor does anyone ever characterize the Philadelphia dialect in terms of these distributions.[4]

On the other hand, the raising of (æh) shows a close correlation with age, social class, and sex. Figure 18.2 shows the mean height (distance

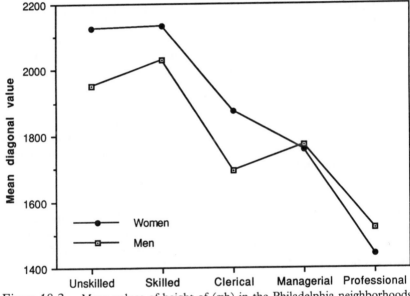

Figure 18.2.   Mean values of height of (æh) in the Philadelphia neighborhoods by sex and occupation. [Ht = $\sqrt{(F2)^2 - (2*F1)^2}$]

---

[4] One case illustrates the unconscious nature of the mechanism of dialect contact at this level. Murray A. was a New Yorker who moved to Philadelphia at the age of 12, went to high school there, and then returned to Queens. I asked him how Philadelphians pronounced various short **a** words: he knew that they used a lax vowel for *sad, cash,* and *bag,* but he had no idea how they pronounced *mad, bad,* or *man.* In other words, only the words that differed from his own New York City pattern had come to his attention; words that were the same had escaped his notice altogether.

along the front diagonal) for all (aeh) allophones combined according to occupation and sex – the sharply stratified pattern that is typical for a nearly completed change. This variable is the most highly stigmatized in the Philadelphia system. It is the most often mentioned in overt discussions of the Philadelphia dialect (the "harsh, nasal *a* in *bad* and *Camden*"), and as we have seen, it shows some degree of correction in word lists. The sharp slope of social stratification is steeper among women than among men. Women show higher values then men in the working classes, but the pattern is reversed for the middle classes. Figure 18.3 shows the more regular pattern that is the result of a multiple regression analysis. (Here the unskilled group is the residual class, where both men and women have a reference value of 0). Men show a slightly curvilinear pattern of correction, with the skilled working class showing positive coefficients, while women show a linear pattern, with each progressively higher social class showing more negative values.

Subjective evaluation tests show that these social distributions are correlated with a strong and consistent set of attitudes. Social stigmatization in Philadelphia is not readily evident in conscious discussion, but the matched guise technique used to elicit unconscious social evaluations shows the pattern clearly. The subjective reaction tests carried out in Philadelphia were based on a reading text, to be considered in more detail in volume 2. It concentrated five different phonological variables in separate sentences of a narrative, and a zero passage that contained none of them. In the experiment, four different female speakers alternated in a pattern

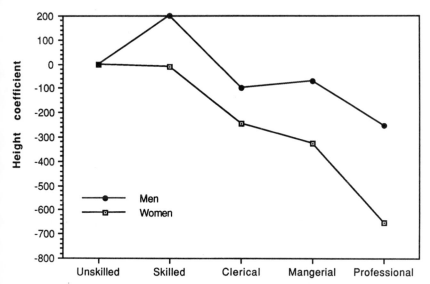

Figure 18.3.   Regression coefficients for height of (æh) in the Philadelphia neighborhoods by sex and occupation. [Ht = $\sqrt{(F2)^2-(2*F1)^2}$]

that exposed listeners to each variable for each speaker. Each speech sample was rated on a 7-point scale of job suitability, ranging from "television announcer" to "none at all." The social evaluation of each realization of the variable was registered by the difference in rating between the zero passage and that particular variable for the same speaker. Figure 18.4 is a two-formant plot of the positions of the nuclei for the (æh) words for the four speakers, who were drawn from four different social classes. The most advanced forms, with high front nuclei, were used by the upper working class speaker RD. More moderate forms of tense vowels were used by the lower working class speaker CS and the lower middle class speaker PH. The upper-class speaker CF read the (æh) passage with corrected forms of the variable, in the same low front position as lax /æ/.

Figure 18.5 shows the evaluation of (æh) in Philadelphia as registered by the differences between the ratings for the zero passage and the (æh) variable. The biggest single effect is the drop in the ratings of the upper working class speaker RD, who appears with the most advanced forms of (æh) in figure 18.4. Her mean rating in the zero passage is moderately high, 3.8, exceeded only by the upper-class speaker with 4.3. But the rating of her (æh) passage drop precipitously to 2.6. The more moderate pronunciations of (æh) by CS and PH did not produce such a strong reaction. The low front forms used by the upper-class speaker CF produced a clear increment over the zero passage, which was already quite high. The overall conclusion is that the phonetic form of the variable is highly evaluated,

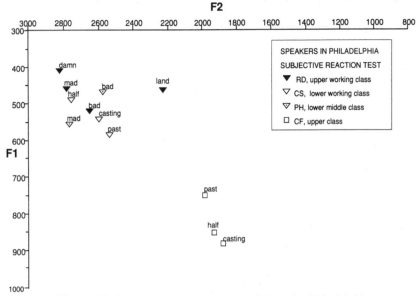

Figure 18.4.   Realizations of (æh) nuclei in the Philadelphia
subjective reaction test

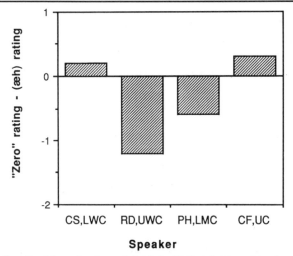

Figure 18.5.   Social evaluation of (æh) in Philadelphia subjective reaction test as shown by differential ratings of job suitability

and the sharp social stratification of figures 18.2 and 18.3 is reflected in a uniform social evaluation of Philadelphians by all members of the community.

It is important to note again that this regular pattern of social stratification and evaluation affects only the raising of (æh). It does not affect the distribution of the /æh/-/æ/ split in spontaneous speech. Though correction among middle-class speakers disturbs the pattern by merging tense forms with the lax category, it is largely confined to data from reading and word lists.

The problem of rule formulation

All of these contrasting features of the short **a** processes come into focus when we approach the problem of formulating them concisely as linguistic rules. The raising of (æh) is a paradigmatic case of a phonetic implementation rule. The nature of the splitting process is quite different, but whether it is a rule or a lexical distribution remains to be determined.

THE RAISING RULE FOR (æh)

As far as the phonetic conditioning of the raising of (æh) is concerned, we need only construct the equation that incorporates the figures already given, creating a phonetic implementation rule that would control the output of a speech synthesis program to replicate Philadelphia speech. We will begin with the values for internal conditioning derived for the Carol Meyers data in table 16.8. The first term of the equation in (1) – the constant – is specific to her nonnormalized vowel system, but the three favoring and three disfavoring environments should approximate the values of the speech community as a whole.

(1)   height(æh) = 2104 + 158 * [__+nas] + 238 * [__−cont]
          + 99 * [+nas__] − 210 * [−cons + voc__]
          − 410 * [__σσ] − 95 * [2 str]

These coefficients are based on a sampling of Carol Meyers's nonnormalized speech, with mean values for the coefficients that will vary from one sample to another. We can reduce the particularity of the results by adding information on the degree of internal variation within her system. Table 18.1 adds the standard errors to the coefficients originally given in table 16.8. These indicate that if we were to sample repeatedly the vowel output of Carol Meyers, 95% of the time the values for each factor would lie within twice the standard error of the coefficient given. Thus we can say that 19 times out of 20, the effect of a following nasal will be 158 ± 88, while the effect of two following syllables will be −409 ± 298.

This amount of fluctuation is also reflected in the significance figures, which tell us that there is less than one chance in 1000 that there is no positive effect of a following nasal; though 158 is the most probable mean for this coefficient, the distributions do not determine whether the actual value is 158, or 159, or 157. In the spirit of further data reduction, we must drop the nonsignificant preceding nasal constraint and write a rule using the qualitative formalism of the variable rule from chapter 7:

(2)   (æh) RAISING

$$\begin{bmatrix} +\text{tense} \\ +\text{ant} \end{bmatrix} \rightarrow \langle \text{z high} \rangle \Big/ \begin{bmatrix} C_0 \\ \langle -\text{voc} \rangle \end{bmatrix} \begin{bmatrix} \underline{\quad} \\ \langle 1 \text{ str} \rangle \end{bmatrix} \Big\langle \begin{matrix} -\text{cont} \\ +\text{nas} \end{matrix} \Big\rangle C_0 \ (\sigma)\langle \# \rangle$$

Table 18.1   Regression coefficients for height of (æh) with standard errors for Carol Meyers

	Coefficient	Standard error	t	p(2-tail)
Constant	2104	35	—	—
Following nasal	158	44	3.56	.000
Following stop	238	98	2.43	.016
Preceding nasal	99	81	1.21	.225
Preceding obstruent+/l/	−210	77	−2.71	.007
Two following syllables	−410	149	−2.75	.007
Secondary stress	−95	48	−1.95	.053

The symbolism of this rule may be read as follows. A front tense vowel is variably raised, in a manner favored by the following conditions: if the immediately preceding feature of a consonant is nonvocalic (i.e., it is not a liquid); if stress is primary; if the following consonant is not a continuant and is nasal; and if there is no more than one syllable before an inflectional boundary.[5] Some quantitative information is preserved here: the vertical arrangement of <–cont> and <+nas> shows that the most favoring factor is a following stop, as against a fricative, and that the rule is favored even more if that stop is nasal. We might also indicate relative strengths by ordering environments with Greek superscripts. But by appending table 18.1 to the rule, we provide information on relative strength in a more accurate and readable form.

There has been considerable discussion about whether external or social constraints should be incorporated into the rules that describe variation in the speech community. There are two major objections, both well founded: first, social factors do not form part of the hierarchical structure of closed sets that allow us to describe linguistic structure; second, rule symbolisms imply independence, and while internal constraints are characteristically independent, we normally expect interaction among social constraints. Nevertheless, there are reasons to believe that such conditions can and should be added to phonetic implementation rules like (2).

The number of social constraints that affect language in a significant way is not open-ended. All the factors that have been shown to be relevant can be grouped under six superordinates: sex, age, socioeconomic class, ethnicity, community size, and social network density. Though we cannot reduce these social data to the binary feature notation of rule (2), we can enter them into an elaboration of equation (1). To register the interactions among these social factors, we will eventually have to add several terms that indicate, for example, the special effect of sex in the lower middle class; but for the moment a relatively simple elaboration of the phonetic implementation rule will indicate the directions we can follow.

The pattern of figure 18.3 can be reduced to a single multiple regression analysis for all three allophones for both sexes in which occupation and age are treated as single quantitative variables.[6] Table 18.2 shows such an analysis of all allophones for both sexes. All factors are highly significant, well below the .01 level. The age coefficient, −2.73, is to be multiplied by the age of the subject: thus if we compare a 70-year-old speaker with a 20-year-old speaker, we will expect a difference of (−2.73 * 50 =) −136.5; a

---

[5] Though table 16.6 did not find a significant effect of a single following syllable, repeated studies show that this is a small disfavoring factor, and it would not be unreasonable to omit the optional single syllable in this rule, indicating that the rule is favored if it applies to a stem-final syllable.

[6] A certain amount of information will be lost. For *occupation*, the effect will be that of drawing a single regression line, and the curvilinear pattern for males will disappear.

Table 18.2   Regression coefficients for social constraints on the height of (æh)
in Philadelphia

	Coefficient	Standard error	t	p(2-tail)
Age	−2.73	0.87	−3.15	0.002
Sex (1 = female)	325	85	3.85	0.000
Occupation	−54	15	−3.58	0.001
Sex * occupation	−63	24	−2.68	0.009

N = 116   Constant = 2312 $r = .667$ $r^2 = .444$

moderately small difference compared with those for the new and vigorous
changes. If the speaker is female, the expected value of height will be 325
units higher – a much greater difference.[7] Occupation is a quantitative
variable ranging from 0 to 6. A professional speaker with a value of 6 on
this dimension, compared with a skilled working-class speaker with a value
of 3, will be expected to be (−54 * 3 =) −162 lower on this dimension. A
certain amount of information will be lost. For *occupation*, the effect will be
that of drawing a single regression line through all the points of figure 18.3.
   Finally, we have an interactive term: sex * occupation. This is computed
in a straightforward, mechanical fashion: if sex = 1 (female), then the value
of this interactive term will be −63 * occupation. This will increase the
difference between a female professional speaker and a female unskilled
working-class speaker by (4 * −63 =) −252. To this must be added the differences due to the simple term for occupation, or 4 * 54. Thus the difference between two such female speakers is (252 + 216 =) 478, while the
difference between two corresponding male speakers is only 216, since for
males, sex = 0. A comparison with the values displayed in figure 18.3 will
show that this is a good approximation of the more detailed view. One
could, of course, incorporate all the information in figure 18.3 into a rule
by returning to individual values for each occupational group, but the simplified form of table 18.2 seems to capture the main outlines of Philadelphia (æh). If we take the Carol Meyers data as a first approximation to
the internal constraints on the Philadelphia system, then the social information can be added as an elaboration of equation (1).

---

[7] It should be noted that these are normalized mean values, so that this difference is not due
to the differences in vocal tract length between men and women.

(3)   height(æh) = 2104 + 158 * [__+nas] + 238 * [__−cont]
          − 210 * [−cons + voc__] − 409 * [__σσ] − 94 *
          [2 str] −2.73 * age + 325 * female − 54 * occupation
          − 63 * sex * occupation

Whether equation (3) or rule (2) is the best way of representing the raising of (æh) seems to me a matter of focus and interest rather than theory. A raising rule can be written at various levels of precision or generality. Equation (3) would be a reasonable format for a phonetic implementation of the Philadelphia dialect. If one were to design a synthesis program to produce an approximation of that dialect, there would be no motivation for truncating the information to the linguistic formulation of (2). The program would require the social information of (3) in order to produce an appropriate output.

A RULE FOR THE TENSE/LAX SPLIT

There have been many efforts to write a rule that will generate or account for the distribution of /æ/ and /æh/ in the Middle Atlantic states. A formulation of the basic Philadelphia pattern given in chapter 15 would have to begin with something like the rule shown in (4).

$$(4) \quad \begin{bmatrix} +\text{low} \\ +\text{ant} \end{bmatrix} \rightarrow [+\text{tense}] \; / \; \left[\underline{\hspace{1cm}} \atop -\text{Weak} \right] \begin{bmatrix} +\text{ant} \\ +\text{nas} \\ \begin{bmatrix} +\text{cont} \\ +\text{tense} \end{bmatrix} \end{bmatrix} \left\{ \begin{matrix} \# \\ [+\text{cons}] \end{matrix} \right\}$$

Rule (4) states that a low front vowel is tense if it is followed by a front nasal or a front voiceless fricative in a syllable closed by two consonants or an inflectional boundary, and not in a "weak word" whose only vowel can be shwa. Before we consider irregular lexical items, (4) must be refined in several ways to take care of more subtle generalizations. Irregular verbs such as *ran*, *swam*, *began*, and *wan* (vernacular preterit of *win*) may be excluded by adding the notation [+Reg] to [−Weak].[8] We must also account for uncommon polysyllabic words, which always show a tense vowel if short **a** precedes a nasal, but otherwise are usually lax. If short **a** is followed by the cluser -*st*-, variation is also found. Thus:

---

[8] The data in Labov 1989a show that the laxing of irregular verbs is not as categorical as the conditions covered by rule (4). In spontaneous speech, 5 of 31 members of this class were tense. Furthermore, it may be simpler to give up this generalization and mark these four words as not undergoing the rule by a lexical feature.

$$
(5) \quad \begin{bmatrix} +\text{low} \\ +\text{ant} \end{bmatrix} \rightarrow [+\text{tense}] \;/\; (-\text{seg})^{\beta} \begin{bmatrix} - \\ -\text{Weak} \\ +\text{Reg} \end{bmatrix} \left\{ \begin{bmatrix} +\text{ant} \\ \alpha\text{nas} \\ \begin{bmatrix} \gamma\text{cont} \\ +\text{tense} \\ +\text{sib}^{\delta} \end{bmatrix} \end{bmatrix} \right\} \left(\begin{array}{c} \#^{\delta} \\ [+\text{cons}] \; C_0 V^{\beta} \end{array} \right)
$$

To take care of the polysyllabic constraint, it must be stipulated that if α is positive – there is a nasal consonant following short **a** – then the combination marked with β is possible: a preceding zero initial and a following syllable. Thus *ambush, ambassador* are tense, but *African* is lax unless specified otherwise.

Since (5) is designed to show only those environments where short **a** must be tense, the variable subcategory of *plastic, master*, etc., must be excluded. (5) specifies with δ that if the first consonant after **a** is a sibilant, then an inflectional or word boundary should follow.

So far, we have not taken care of facts that are intrinsically lexical. Some of these are obligatory subcategories; others are variable. In the dictionary, we would have to mark rule (5) as:

- applying categorically to the three words *mad, bad, glad.*
- not applying normally to *ran, swam, began, wan.*
- not applying to a number of learned words: *alas, wrath*, etc.
- not applying to a number of affective or onomatopoetic words: *bam! wham! mam*, etc.
- applying variably to words with derivational boundaries: *classical, Lassie, Annie*, etc.
- applying variably to polysyllabic words with initial /æh/ and following voiceless fricatives, but applying categorically to *after, afterwards*, etc.
- applying variably to a number of abbreviations: *gas, exam*, etc.
- applying variably to a number of specific words with short **a** followed by intervocalic /n/, headed by *planet.*
- applying variably to a number of specific words with short **a** followed by /l/, headed by *pal* and *personality.*

The question must now be raised whether such a complex rule can be justified, or whether the short **a** split is governed by a rule at all.

A SHORT **a** RULE VS. A SHORT **a** SPLIT

Since the short **a** situation was first described in the literature, many arguments have been presented on both sides of the question: Is this complex distribution the result of a rule of English phonology, or is it a lexical split into two phonemes? The majority opinion appears to be that it is a split. Trager (1930, 1934, 1940) ultimately came to this conclusion, as did Cohen (1970) and LYS. Ferguson's (1975) account of Philadelphia short **a** uses rules to describe the regular parts of the process, but makes no attempt to incorporate the many special conditions into a rule-like form. One can identify five objections to rule formulations such as (4) and (5).

1 Disjunctive curly brackets show that voiceless fricatives and nasals do not form a natural class, since there is no theoretically based label for them.

2 Disjunctive curly brackets also indicate that there is no theoretically adequate way to combine "stem-final and preconsonantal" into a single conjunctive description.

3 The notations [–Weak] and [+Reg] are ad hoc ways of incorporating what is in effect a derivational constraint – one that looks across derivations.

4 The Greek letter combinations of (5) are an ad hoc patchwork with no theoretical foundation.

5 Even if a formulation such as (5) is accepted, so many lexical specifications must be added that most of the words covered by (5) might just as well be listed lexically.

Halle and Mohanan (1985) write a rule for short **a** tensing, based on their acquaintance with Trager (1930), but the subset of facts on which their treatment rests is not large enough to bear on the current discussion. Kiparsky (1989) provides a much more complete treatment, which covers most of the facts in Labov 1989a, looks at a wider range of dialects, and takes into account the difference between the tense/lax split and a continuous raising rule for tensed (æh) like (2). Harris (1989) continues the analysis within Kiparsky's framework, adding data from the tensing of Belfast short **a**, and argues that if the structure-preserving condition is dropped from lexical phonology, the facts of all these dialects can be incorporated as lexical rules.

Kiparsky's versions of short **a** rules are presented informally, with lists of additional properties to be taken into account in the style of chapter 15, rather than being worked into a single statement by abbreviatory conventions in the style of (4) or (5). His solution to the short **a** problem in the framework of lexical phonology, locating the rule firmly in level 1, deals persuasively with many of the questions raised above.

Objection 2 is resolved because the syllables involved are all closed at level 1, before level 2 suffixes like *-ing* and *-er* are added.

Objection 3 is partially resolved because the level 1 ablaut rule "i → æ in the past tense of strong verbs" can be ordered after the tensing rule.[9]

Objection 5 is resolved because level 1 rules are quite compatible with dictionary entries. The complex conditions of objection 4 might also be resolved into dictionary entries.

In the framework of lexical phonology, the tense-lax distribution of short **a** words will therefore be treated by a feature-filling rule that will reduce the information content of lexical entries to a minimum. Kiparsky notes (p.c.) that for Philadelphia speech, "tensing is a feature-filling rule which assigns [+tense] to **a** in regular words in the tensing environment, and [−tense] by default elsewhere. The feature is then lexically specified only in exceptional words, such as *alas, wrath.*"

There remains objection 1: do voiceless fricatives and nasals form a natural class that can be reasonably referred to by a linguistic rule? Ferguson (1975) points out that this class has been associated with the lengthening of short **a** in English at least since the 17th century, and perhaps since as early as the 15th (Wyld 1936: 203–5). The southern British broad **a** class is derived from such early lengthenings. To this we add the observation that the same class, suitably adjusted for backness, operates in the American tensing of short **o**. The absence of a single category for this class may therefore be considered a defect in phonological theory rather than a defect in the short **a** rule.

Labov (1981) presents three bodies of evidence to show that the tense/lax division of short **a** words is a phonemic split into two distinct underlying forms, rather than a rule. One argument concerns the unpredictable distributions of the two classes, the issues we have just discussed. The second concerns experiments indicating that speakers from the Middle Atlantic states have a greater tendency to show categorical perception of an [æ] – [i:ə] continuum than speakers from the Northern Cities. In response, Harris (1989) argues that categorical perception may be as characteristic of a lexical rule as of a phonemic opposition. This is a difficult matter to decide, especially since we are dealing only with various degrees of categorical perception, with much individual variation. It is the third type of evidence that appears to be decisive for the issue raised here: the ways in which the Philadelphia short **a** distribution is learned by speakers of other dialects.

Differential acquisition of the Philadelphia short *a* pattern

Chapter 4 introduced Payne's (1976, 1980) study of the acquisition of the Philadelphia dialect by out-of-state families in order to show the relative

---

[9] Wedge is of course also included in the input of this ablaut rule. The difficulties of formulating an ablaut rule are well known, but there appears to be ample evidence for the rule-governed character of this process from generalizations by language learners.

stability of the parents' speech. As noted there, the Philadelphia suburb King of Prussia was selected for this study since it was composed of 50% Philadelphians and 50% families from out of state – mostly upper middle class parents from Ohio, Massachusetts, and New York. Payne studied 24 families on six blocks, recording parents, children, and peers in extended interviews, with both spontaneous speech and formal experiments. The 108 children interviewed included 34 children of out-of-state parents who were brought to Philadelphia at various ages and were exposed for varying lengths of time to the Philadelphia dialect.

The overall results of Payne's inquiry showed that children rapidly acquired the low-level sound changes first displayed in figure 3.6. The rate of acquisition of the five such Philadelphia variables is shown in table 18.3. Only a small percentage showed no pattern of acquisition, and these were heavily concentrated among children who had arrived after the age of 9.

The variable (æh) is not shown in table 18.3 because it is present in all the dialects concerned. These dialects differ only in the distribution of the tense forms – the issue that we will now consider.

There is no need to show a comparable table for the acquisition of the Philadelphia short **a** distribution. Of the 34 children born to out-of-state parents, only 1 acquired the core pattern. The contrast between the two kinds of variables is remarkable. All that is needed to acquire the Philadelphia vowel shifts is to be exposed to the dialect before the age of 8 or 9. To acquire the short **a** pattern, however, it is not enough to be born in the Philadelphia area; one must have parents born in Philadelphia. How can we explain this contrast? The only linguistic data that children must acquire from their parents, and cannot get elsewhere, are the first dictionary entries. It seems reasonable to conclude that the short **a** pattern is such a set of dictionary entries: that children in Philadelphia families acquire *mad* with an underlying tense vowel, and *sad* with an underlying lax vowel.

One might argue that this acquisition pattern might be produced by a rule of lexical phonology, which would be equally difficult to learn. Such

Table 18.3 Rate of acquisition of Philadelphia sound changes by out-of-state children in King of Prussia (from Payne 1976)

	(ay0)	*(aw)*	*(oy)*	*(uw)*	*(ow)*
Acquired	50%	40%	60%	52%	68%
Partially acquired	44	40	30	48	32
Not acquired	6	20	10	0	0
Number with parental pattern different from Philadelphia	34	20	20	25	25

a lexical rule would allow the native learner to make use of the generalizations that are inherent in the data, in addition to acquiring the irregular parts of the distribution word by word. If this is so, then all out-of-state children would have the same difficulty with a rule as with a completely lexical distribution: though they might learn the general features of the rule, they would not be able to master the long list of exceptions to those generalizations.

We can explore this issue by examining the degree of acquisition of the core pattern by out-of-state children from different dialect areas. Six of the out-of-state families came from Northern Cities areas. As we have seen, these parents have no split in the short **a** class: all short **a** words are tensed. Three of the out-of-state families came from New York City. The parents in these families have the distribution shown in figure 15.1, which is reproduced here as figure 18.6. In New York City, the basic pattern is that short **a** is tensed before all voiceless fricatives and voiced stops, but only before the anterior nasals. Given the fact that the New York City children have learned that system, they have two distinct tasks in learning the basic pattern of the Philadelphia dialect: (1) to learn that the restricting feature [+anterior] applies to all consonants, and so pronounce *cash, smash, ash* with lax vowels, and (2) to avoid tensing before voiced stops except for the three words *mad, bad, glad*.

Every linguist to whom I have posed the problem predicts – before seeing the data – that the first task is easier: it involves a simple generalization. The second task involves learning a set of lexical specifications that have no basis in the New York City dialect. In terms of rule-governed learning, it involves not only a new generalization ("Lax all words before voiced stops") but also an exception ("Reverse this rule for the three exceptional words").

Figure 18.7 shows the comparative degree of learning of the Philadelphia

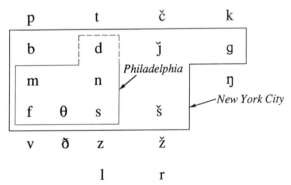

Figure 18.6.　Consonants following short **a** that condition tensing in Philadelphia (inner line) and New York City (outer line)

pattern by the two groups of families. For each of these diagrams, complete learning of the Philadelphia pattern would be represented by a diagonal line leading from 100% at the upper left, for those words that are tense in Philadelphia, to 0% on the lower right, for words that are lax in Philadelphia. The solid lines show the degree of tensing for *mad, bad, glad* on the left, and all other -/d/ words on the right. The dotted lines show the degree of tensing before front voiceless fricatives, on the left, and before /š/, on the right. The slopes of the lines show the degree of differentiation of the Philadelphia tense and lax categories – that is, the degree of learning.

For the Northern Cities families, there is no significant difference between the two lines. Though there is considerable difference among the families in the rate of tensing, in none of the six do we find a significant difference between the rates of learning before /d/ and before the voiceless fricatives. The New York City families, on the other hand, show a sharp difference in the rate of learning in a direction contrary to what the nature of the rules predicts. The rate of tensing before /š/ continues almost as high as the rate of tensing before the other voiceless fricatives. In contrast, the rate of tensing for the main body of -/d/ words falls to below 50%, while *mad, bad, glad* remain at 90%, the norm shared by New York City and Philadelphia.[10]

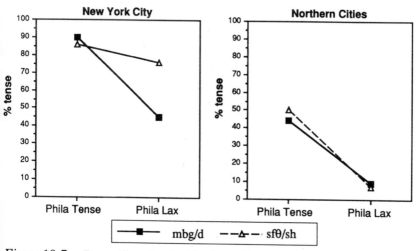

Figure 18.7. Rate of learning for Northern Cities and New York City families of Philadelphia short **a** pattern. Before /d/: tense *mad, bad, glad* vs. lax *sad, dad,* etc. Before voiceless, fricatives: tense *half, path, pass,* etc. vs. *cash, mash, ash,* etc.

---

[10] Payne shows that a certain amount of correction of short **a** is found in the spontaneous speech of the New York City parents, in a pattern consistent with the findings of Labov (1966), so that the 90% figure is close to the adult norm in interview style.

Figure 18.8 shows that this greater rate of learning is reflected in all three New York City families. The three families differ in the amount of learning of the Philadelphia pattern, with learning increasing from the Bakers to the Morgans to the Millers. In each case, the slope for the vowels before /d/ is greater than the slope for the vowels before voiceless fricatives. While the Northern Cities families give no support to the prediction that more learning would take place for the -/š/ category than the -/d/ category, the New York City families reverse our expectation that learning the lexical pattern before /d/ would be more difficult. How can we explain this result? It seems clear that the expectation rested on the assumption that the New York City and Northern Cities speakers approached the Philadelphia system as the same kind of learning problem. In the abstract, it seems that any language learner would be able to acquire a general rule – laxing all short **a** before any back consonant – more easily than one that laxed all short **a** before voiced stops with the exception of three common adjectives. Since children from Northern Cities families and New York City families perform differently, it seems more likely that the two groups approach the problem from a different point of view. We have seem ample evidence that the Northern Cities Shift is a regular sound change, affecting all short **a** words without any structural differentiation beyond the phonetic level. The children from Northern Cities families satisfy our expectation that the Philadelphia laxing before /š/ is easier to acquire than the *mad/bad/glad* pattern. It therefore seems reasonable that they are attempting to apply the simplest possible rules to the best of their ability.

New York City children, on the other hand, find it easier to learn the lexical distribution. It therefore seems likely that they approach the learning problem without using rules, one word at a time, and that this might be because their own system has two underlying forms, /æh/ and /æ/, unrelated by any rule. Let us see whether such an assumption would lead to the results of figures 18.7–18.8. Given the contrast between their own sys-

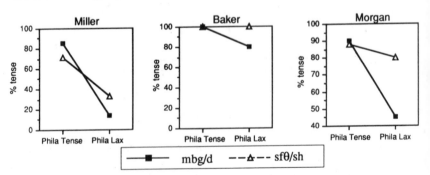

Figure 18.8. Rate of learning for 3 New York City families of the Philadelphia short **a** pattern, before /d/ and before voiceless fricatives

tem and the Philadelphia system (figure 18.6), the New York City children's task of learning not to tense short **a** before /š/ would then be equivalent to entering a [–tense] feature in the dictionary for *cash, dash, smash, hash, mash, trash, flash*, etc. This would involve adjusting the underlying forms of a very large number of words. But the same is even more true for learning the *mad/bad/glad* pattern word by word. This is not simply a matter of learning that *mad, bad*, and *glad* are lexically marked as [+tense]; it also means learning to mark as [–tense] a large number of words that are tense in the New York City system: *sad, fad, dad, Brad, plaid, shad, ad, cad*, etc. As figure 18.6 indicates, New Yorkers must learn to lax short **a** before /b/ and /g/. If learning occurs word by word, this generalization must increase, not decrease, the difficulty of learning the Philadelphia pattern of short **a** before voiced stops, with a dramatic rise in the number of dictionary entries to be changed: *cab, tab, stab, crab, drab, bag, hag, snag, brag*, etc. Therefore the relative success of the New York City children with the *mad, bad, glad* pattern does not support the view (first presented in Labov 1981) that they are relearning underlying forms one word at a time.

In response to an earlier draft of this chapter, Kiparsky (p.c.) points out that the data cited above *are* consistent with the view that the New York City (and Philadelphia) children are employing lexical rules in which general feature-filling operations are supplemented by lexical specifications for exceptional words. Such a lexical rule would give the New Yorkers a framework in which to anticipate lexical specification for [+tense] in the Philadelphia system. The immediate question is whether lexical rules would account for the crucial fact that New Yorkers do better in learning the *mad/bad/glad* pattern than the *mass/mash* pattern. Assuming that New Yorkers have a lexical rule, let us examine the rule changes necessary to pass from the basic New York City system to the basic Philadelphia system. The most economical representation of the New York City feature-filling rule is (6), which limits the nasal environment by bracketing it with [–anterior] to exclude tensing before /ŋ / and combines voiced stops and voiceless fricatives by an α notation.[11] This rule must of course be accompanied by a number of lexical specifications: *avenue* is marked as [+tense], *alas* as [–tense], while words with voiced fricatives such as *jazz, razz, wagon, imagine* are marked as variable in this respect.

---

[11] In the disjunctive convention being observed here, the first (upper) element in the bracket will select nasals and mark them as [+anterior], and nasals will not be governed by the second (lower) element, even though they contain the features [–continuant, –tense].

(6) NEW YORK CITY

$$\begin{bmatrix} +\text{low} \\ +\text{ant} \end{bmatrix} \rightarrow [+\text{tense}] \ / \ \underline{\hspace{1cm}} \ \left\{ \begin{matrix} \begin{bmatrix} +\text{nas} \\ +\text{ant} \end{bmatrix} \\ \begin{bmatrix} \alpha\text{cont} \\ \alpha\text{tense} \end{bmatrix} \end{matrix} \right\}$$

The adjustment of this basic system to the environments characteristic of Philadelphia requires two steps, which differ in their character according to the order in which they take place. If the New Yorker reacts first to the difference in words like *cash*, *dash*, etc., he or she will perceive the generalization that short **a** is lax before /š/. This is simple to state in terms of segments, but in terms of features, it requires the very complex rule (7).

(7) TRANSITIONAL FORM 1

$$\begin{bmatrix} +\text{low} \\ +\text{ant} \end{bmatrix} \rightarrow [+\text{tense}] \ / \ \underline{\hspace{1cm}} \ \left\{ \begin{matrix} \left\{ \left\{ \begin{bmatrix} +\text{ant} \\ +\text{nas} \\ +\text{cont} \\ +\text{tense} \end{bmatrix} \right\} \right\} \\ \begin{bmatrix} -\text{cont} \\ -\text{tense} \end{bmatrix} \end{matrix} \right\}$$

Rule (7) states that if the following consonant is either a nasal or a tense (voiceless) fricative, it must be [+anterior], but if it is a lax (voiced) stop, it need not be so combined. This leaves short **a** tense before /b, d, g/ but lax before /š/. If, on the other hand, the New Yorker first perceives that Philadelphia short **a** is lax before all voiced stops (except *mad*, *bad*, *glad*), rule (8) can be formed.

(8) TRANSITIONAL FORM 2

$$\begin{bmatrix} +\text{low} \\ +\text{ant} \end{bmatrix} \rightarrow [+\text{tense}] / \ \underline{\hspace{1cm}} \ \left\{ \begin{matrix} \begin{bmatrix} +\text{nas} \\ +\text{ant} \end{bmatrix} \\ \begin{bmatrix} +\text{cont} \\ +\text{tense} \end{bmatrix} \end{matrix} \right\}$$

This step merely involves changing the α features of (6) to +. Depending on one's attitude toward a notation, this is either a simplification or the abandonment of a generalization, but in any case it is a fairly simple and straightforward statement compared with (7). It only requires the capacity to add the dictionary notation that *mad*, *bad*, and *glad* are [+tense], which as we have seen is consistent with the character of the New York City rule. It is then a straightforward generalization for the New Yorker to pass to the Philadelphia system by generalizing the feature [+anterior] to all environments.

(9)   PHILADELPHIA

$$\begin{bmatrix} +\text{low} \\ +\text{ant} \end{bmatrix} \rightarrow [+\text{tense}] \ / \ \underline{\hspace{2em}} \ \begin{bmatrix} \begin{Bmatrix} +\text{ant} \\ +\text{nas} \\ \begin{bmatrix} +\text{cont} \\ +\text{tense} \end{bmatrix} \end{Bmatrix} \end{bmatrix}$$

This analysis is not intended to suggest that it is easy for New Yorkers to learn the Philadelphia system; on the contrary, we have seen that they have only partial success. It does show that a formulation of the problem in terms of rules reveals an asymmetry in the difficulty of the two aspects of the learning problem. A grasp of the fact that short **a** is lax before voiced stops will facilitate the recognition that it is lax before /š/. But laxing before /š/ is a peculiar and difficult condition to grasp if the situation before voiced stops is not recognized. This asymmetry accounts for the results of figures 18.7 and 18.8, that New Yorkers do relatively better in learning the *mad/bad/glad* pattern than laxing before /š/, and it reinforces the conclusion that the New York City children approach the problem with a system of lexical rules rather than a set of dictionary entries that are not associated with any generalization. It follows that other Middle Atlantic speech communities, including Philadelphia and Baltimore, also have lexical rules determining their short **a** distributions.

Kiparsky (p.c.) adds a further argument in favor of the existence of lexical rules in these short **a** systems: that the expansion of the rule documented in chapter 16 to new environments is consistently motivated by phonetic factors.

These environments are not arbitrary from a phonological point of view. There are no reported cases of tense **a** before voiceless stops, a natural class systematically excluded from the tensing environment. Also, there are no cases of lax **a** being extended into words which have regular tense **a**.[12] If we recognize that the distribution of tense and lax **a** in Philadelphia is governed by rule, then we can explain these facts. The phonological conditions under which tense spreads through the lexicon then appear as an extension of the rule's context. . . . On the other hand, if we assume that there is no rule behind the distribution of tense and lax **a**, we have no account for the orderly path that the lexical diffusion process takes.

The argument from a large-scale, evolutionary point of view reinforces strongly the evidence from the acquisition of the Philadelphia dialect, which is consistent with the position of Kiparsky and Harris that short **a**

---

[12] Labov 1989a reports 1.1% tensing before voiceless stops in the spontaneous speech of 100 subjects in the Philadelphia Neighborhood Study. But Kiparsky's general point is valid, in that these sporadic events do not show any consistent pattern and do not represent a general trend that would show an extension of the rule.

is governed by a lexical rule. We conclude that lexical diffusion of short **a** in Philadelphia takes place in the form of changes in the dictionary entries associated with such a rule. The process fits the framework for lexical diffusion set forth by Wang and Lien in chapter 16, where the phonetic motivation of the change precedes and limits its lexical implementation.[13] It is now clear that the view of lexical splits presented in chapter 11 must be modified. If the division of short **a** into tense and lax forms is governed by a lexical rule, the underlying forms are not changed, and there is no justification for writing /æ/ and /æh/. For short **a**, the process of "lexical splitting" is therefore a series of phonetic feature specifications within dictionary entries rather than changes in the headings that identify those entries. The abstract character of these changes is demonstrated by the fact that the dictionary entries so modified may refer to grammatical categories like "auxiliary" or "class III preterit strong verbs." Whether the other lexical splits presented in chapter 11 are also rule-governed remains to be seen. In the discussion to follow, I will use the term *lexical splitting* to refer to both changes in underlying forms and the development of contrast through the addition of features to lexical entries.

18.2 Where is lexical diffusion to be found?

The splitting of short **a** is clearly a classic case of lexical diffusion. By contrast, the vowel shifts of Philadelphia are classic cases of Neogrammarian sound change. The discussion has isolated a number of features that characterize these two polar types of change in progress, shown in table 18.4.

The characteristics shown for (æh) also hold for the other Philadelphia sound changes in progress: (aw), (ow), (uw), (ay0), (oy). These are either unconditioned shifts of the phonetic target of a phoneme, or rules with simple and exceptionless phonetic conditioning: (ow) and (uw) represent fronting except before liquids, (ay0) represents centralization before voiceless finals.

It remains to be seen whether the same opposition of properties appears for other cases of lexical diffusion or regular sound change, and whether

---

[13] It does not follow that this phonetic motivation is universally predictable. The selection of phonetic factors in individual dialects shows some dialect-specific traits. There is no trace in New York City of tensing before /l/ – this appears to be one of the least likely environments for tensing in that dialect. In Boston, tensing of short **a** before /t/ appears to be a favored environment in a dialect that originally showed tensing only before nasals. General explanations for such differentiation may eventually be found. For example, there may be a connection between the vocalization of /l/ in Philadelphia and the tensing of short **a** in this environment. Phonetic motivation must spring from the general characteristics of the speech apparatus. Nevertheless, we must be prepared to find dialect-specific aspects of phonetic conditioning within the range of data that we can presently account for.

Table 18.4 Opposing characteristics of two changes affecting short **a** in Philadelphia

		Raising of (æh)	*Tensing of /æ/*
1	Lexical diffusion found	no	yes
2	Discrete	no	yes
3	Phonetic differentiation	single feature	many features
4	Phonetic conditioning	precise	approximate
5	Grammatical conditioning	no	yes
6	Social affect	yes	no
7	Categorically perceived	no	yes
8	Learnable	easily	with great difficulty

the two sets of properties turn out to show a regular association. We will then be able to approach the larger question: Where in general can we expect to find lexical diffusion, and where can we expect Neogrammarian regularity? Since the cases examined so far involve vowel shifts in progress in English dialects, the logical first step is to examine the range of completed vowel changes in the history of English, at least insofar as the nature of residues or lexical irregularities is concerned. A complete review of the subject is beyond the scope of this chapter, but certain salient facts warrant our attention.

The differentiation of English vowel changes seems at first glance to be surprisingly clear-cut. Regular sound change appears in a wide range of vowel shifts that represent movements within subsystems of short upgliding diphthongs, or ingliding diphthongs: raising, lowering, fronting, backing, rounding, unrounding, nasalization. The Great Vowel Shift consisted of sound changes of this type, similar in their regular character to the vowel shifts studied by LYS in a range of English dialects, and by LCV in Philadelphia. Chapter 17 demonstrated that this was the basic mechanism in the diphthongization of the high vowels. But in addition, we located in the SED two examples of lexical diffusion, and it will be helpful to examine them first.

Chapter 17 showed that lexical diffusion is not characteristic of the diphthongization of ME ī, which was a perfectly regular constituent of the Great Vowel Shift; instead it accompanies the formation of ME ī out of Old English materials, a process that was uniform throughout the South and Midland but variable in the North. ME ī was formed from OE ī and ȳ, the latter unrounded in late Old English, along with the results of various lengthenings of short **i**. One of these lengthenings involved palatal **g** and **h**. Before final /t/ the voiceless palatal [ç] was deleted, with compensatory lengthening of short **i**. The data from the SED included *night, light, light-*

ning, sight, night, right, and *-wright.* (This process involves a much smaller set of words than the short **a** split.) No data are available that bear on characteristics 6–8 in table 18.4. Concerning characteristics 1–5, however, we can say that

1 Lexical diffusion was found.
2 It is a discrete process, involving the disappearance of a complete segment.
3 It involves at least two phonetic features and probably more, depending on the phonetic realizations of short **i** and long **ī** in late Old English.
4 There is some evidence of phonetic conditioning. Figure 17.7 shows that words with initial /r/ are at lower right, close to those with final /r/ in figure 17.7, and words with initial /l/ are at upper left.
5 No grammatical conditioning is evident.

In addition, OE short **i** was lengthened before final **g** and **h** as in *thigh, nine* (< OE *nigon*). These show some differentiation in figure 17.6, though *nine* is fully merged with the main cluster.

The second case of lexical diffusion from the Great Vowel Shift concerns the raising of long mid vowels before palatal **g**. The SED data include only three words (*eye, died,* and *flies*), but more were involved (*lie, sly,* etc.). It is not only in the SED materials that we find lexical irregularity. The common word *height* is derived by way of OE *hēhθu*. The current spelling indicates that this word was pronounced to rhyme with *eight*; as late as 1775, Walker considered [heit] to be the most general pronunciation. These words also show properties 1–5 in table 18.4.

Lexical diffusion in these lengthenings prompts us to examine other shortenings and lengthenings in the history of English.[14] We find a wide variety of lexically irregular cases. ME long **ē** was shortened in *head, dead, breath, sweat,* etc.,[15] while the great majority of words in this class stayed long and rose to [i]: *bead, read, mead,* etc. A second irregular shortening then produced *sick, silly, britches,* and other short /i/ reflexes. In the back, we find the result of two irregular shortenings (with rough phonetic conditioning) in *flood, blood, glove,* etc., and later *good, stood,* as opposed

---

[14] The available orthographic conventions usually lead to a differentiation between "long" and "short" vowels in the historical record. Though there are some cases (i.e., Hungarian high vowels) where the difference is purely one of length, such oppositions are unstable (Chen and Wang 1975); it is more common to find short and long subsets differentiated by a complex of many phonetic features that are best described with more abstract terms like *tense* and *lax*. The use of the /h/ symbol in /æh/ is appropriate for the tense long and ingliding vowels, but for a general discussion it is probably better replaced by /:/ – so long as the length sign is taken as an abstract representation of the class of long vowels, rather than phonetic length.
[15] See Jespersen 1949:242. This shortening shows great dialectal diversity; for example, *head* remained tense in Scots, and is [hi:d] in Glasgow.

to *food*, *mood*, *fool*, etc.[16] Wyld begins his discussion of shortenings and lengthenings in Early Modern English with the following troubled passage:

The whole question is beset by various difficulties. Lengthening and shortening of vowels has occurred at various periods during the history of English, sometimes under conditions which are clear and can be formulated without hesitation, since the results are found with regularity, and the apparent exceptions can be explained by a specific analogy, sometimes under conditions which are more or less obscure, since the lengthening or shortening is apparently intermittent, being present in some words, but absent in others in which the phonetic conditions seem to be identical. (1936:253)

In addition to the lengthening and shortening of mid and high vowels, an even more striking set of parallels to the historical lengthening of short **a** can be found in the modern lengthenings of English low vowels. Though I have described the change affecting short **a** as *tensing*, the lengthening of the nucleus is an essential phonetic component of tensing, and the change would certainly have been described as *lengthening* in the historical literature. The current lengthening and raising of short **a** is the fifth in a series of such processes in English.[17]

1   In Old English, ā underwent unconditioned and regular lengthening, raising, and backing to ɔ̄ in free and open syllables, with ɔ̄ later raising to [o:] and diphthongizing to [oʊ]; OE *tá*, *stán*, *bát* → Mod. E. /tow, stown, bowt/.

2   In Late Old English and Early Middle English, short **a** underwent lengthening in open syllables, with subsequent fronting, raising, and diphthongization; ME *name*, *grave* → Mod. E. /neym, greyv/.

3   In Modern Southern British English, short **a** in syllables closed by front

---

[16] This is one of the common examples explained by Neogrammarians as dialect borrowing (Bloomfield 1933), or used to illustrate lexical diffusion (Fónagy 1956; Wang 1977). But many oscillations have occurred since the process was new and vigorous, and there is little that can be recovered now of the original mechanism.

[17] These changes are alternately focused on open and closed syllables, in ways that have yet to be fully accounted for. The sound change involving short **a** in the Middle Atlantic states begins with the differentiation of a single category, the intact historical class of short **a** words. As with all other English short vowels, the distribution of this class is limited: there are no short vowels in word-final or free position. The short vowels do occur in both free and checked syllables (free *castle* vs. checked *Cass* and *cast*), and this is an important distinction in the development we are studying. The current lengthening, fronting, and raising of the short **a** category is primarily focused on vowels in closed syllables.

   The first of the five processes listed affected both closed and open syllables; the second only open syllables; the third only closed syllables. The fourth seems specific to closed syllables as described here, but there is a parallel alternation of free syllables with a somewhat different geographical distribution, so that words such as *pa*, *ma*, *ha ha* have alternate long open **o** forms *paw*, *maw*, *haw haw* merged with *caw*, *maw* 'stomach', *Hawthorne*, excepting less common or more recent formations like *spa* and *bra*.

voiceless fricatives and front nasals of French origin was lengthened to form the "broad **a**" class: *class, mass* ('church service'), *cast, pass, half, bath, aunt, dance,* etc., but not *mass* 'weight', *ant, fancy,* etc.

4   In American English, short open **o** was lengthened before voiceless fricatives and back nasals to join the long open **o** class, with subsequent raising, backing, and development of an inglide, so that (in Philadelphia) *lost, cloth, cough, strong, long* develop [ɔ:, Ω:, oə, ʊə] as opposed to *costume, Gothic, Goffman, ping pong* with [ɑ].

5   In American English, tensed short **a** is raised to mid and high position.

All these changes generally share the first five features of lexical diffusion listed in table 18.4.

1   Except for the first, they share the property of widespread lexical irregu-larities of the sort that Wyld reflected on. The amount of lexical irregu-larity in the broad **a** class was even greater in early stages than today. Jespersen (1949) notes that Holyband (1578) has broad **a** in *aunt, com-mand, demand,* etc., short **a** in *answer, branch, advance,* and both in *change.*

2   They are alternations between two discrete classes of vowels.

3   The phonetic differentiation involves various features besides length: usually fronting or backing, and/or raising or lowering. The broad **a** class in *after, glass, bath, aunt,* etc., is now realized as a long low central vowel, but it is generally considered that the lengthening took place in front position at "the time immediately following the change from /a:/ to a front vowel, while short **a** was still a back vowel" (Jespersen 1949:307; see also Wyld 1936:203–5). This means that the tensing of what is now broad **a** was originally accompanied by fronting and rais-ing, almost identical to the modern [æ] → [ɛ:].

4   The phonetic conditionings show rough patterns of striking similarity. The phonetic conditioning of broad **a** is almost identical to that of Philadelphia short **a**: voiceless fricatives and front nasals (see Ferguson 1975). Similar alternations are found in Hart's (1569) transcription of such words as *master* with both forms, echoing the Philadelphia situ-ation today. The same rough phonetic conditioning may be seen operating in the irregular lengthening of short open **o**. Every dialect and subdialect of American English shows a different distribution. Thus my own speech has tense *moth, wroth, cloth,* but lax *Goth*; tense *strong, long, song,* but lax *ping-pong, gong, thong*; tense *moral* and *coral,* but lax *sorrel* and *tomorrow.*[18]

5   Grammatical conditioning is common in these shortenings and length-

---

[18] The role of frequency is obvious in these cases. It is the back nasals that favor raising for the low back vowel, not the front nasals.

enings. Lengthening in open syllables in Early Middle English was directly conditioned by the grammatical paradigm: it did not affect past participles like *written* or *bitten*, even though they had only a single intervocalic consonant.[19] Further, it is commonly accepted that derivations from different elements of the inflectional paradigm produced many of the irregularities in the lengthening in open syllables. Jespersen (1949:308) argued persuasively that many modern lexical fluctuations are a continuation of the analogical irregularities in open syllable lengthening.

It is more difficult to examine properties (6–8) of Table 18.4 for these earlier changes. Though we have no experimental data on categorical perception, the social categorization associated with this variable is quite discrete. Furthermore, the well-known irregularity of the broad **a** class has consequences for its learnability: it serves as an ideal marker of a class dialect, since it can apparently be learned correctly only by children who have attended British public schools from an early age (Wyld 1936:3). One consequence of this development is that the broad **a** distribution did acquire the kind of social significance usually associated with lower-level changes like the opening of the nucleus of /ey/; in this respect, then, it is exceptional.

We can conclude that vowel lengthening and shortening in English are implemented by lexical diffusion, while raising, lowering, backing, and fronting proceed by regular sound change.

18.3   The concept of *abstractness* involved

Why should these shortenings and lengthenings be irregular? The explanation, I suggest, is that they are not sound changes in the literal sense. Rather, they are changes of membership in higher-order classes of long or short vowels. *Long/short*, like *tense/lax*, does not refer to any physical dimension – certainly not to duration alone – but instead refers to a set of features that may include length, height, fronting, the directions and contours of glides, and the temporal distribution of the overall energy of the vowel. The argument that led to our adopting *tense* and *lax* as cover terms applies to *long* and *short* as well. In these shortenings and lengthenings, the whole set of phonetic features change at once, at least in the cases that we have been able to examine in progress. A hierarchy of categories must be recognized, depending on the number of features involved in their

[19] I am grateful to Robert Stockwell for pointing out this grammatical conditioning of the original tensing process, which shows a much closer parallel to the modern complications than the variation explained by the choice of inflected or uninflected bases.

realization – a hierarchy of *abstractness*. Though *abstract* can be a vague term in everyday use, it takes on a precise meaning in linguistic analysis.

- A *concrete term* is a label for a physical trait or process, a unitary measure that is not a combination of other measurements. The central tendency of a particular formant, or bundle of reinforced harmonics, is such a concrete measurement, expressed in hertz.
- One step more abstract are the phonological dimensions of *height* and *peripherality*, Cartesian distances across the F1/F2 space, which are calculated from F2 and F1 measurements.
- The categories *diphthong* and *monophthong* are another step more abstract, since they involve measurement of changes in height and other dimensions over time.
- The cover terms *tense* and *lax* involve yet another level of abstraction, since they refer to contrasts of height, peripherality, duration, and diphthongization.
- At the highest level of abstraction in the English vowel system are the categories *long* and *short*, which are realized phonetically as tense and lax (realizations that may be reversed, as we have seen) and as various types of diphthongization, but which also involve distributional facts (i.e., checked vs. free).[20]

Though the terms may vary from one theoretical perspective to another, the concept of a hierarchy of abstraction is common to all linguistic analyses. A more abstract term occupies a higher node on a tree of hierarchical relations, defined by its relations to the terms that it dominates. The concept can be applied to the consonant system as readily as to the vowel system, to morphology and syntax as readily as to phonology.

The dimension of continuity and discreteness is intimately linked to the degree of abstractness. Concrete features like F1, F2, F0, and duration are by definition continuous, though any given system may show uneven distributions across those continua. Height is also continuous, since it is a function of F1 and F2. But the shift from tense to lax involves several qualitatively different features, which do not freely combine in all possible permutations. There are cooccurrence restrictions that make certain combinations less probable (e.g., short duration and diphthongization). Thus a shift from one abstract category to another usually involves the simultaneous and discrete shift of cooccurring features.

---

[20] A different type of abstraction leads in the direction of statistical generalization. Mean values of a group of vowels are obviously one step more abstract, and normalized mean values considerably more abstract. In this direction, further abstraction yields probability distributions around these means, with probabilistic weights that relate the values of differentiated groups within the community.

18.4   Changes within and across subsystems

The vowel system of English and other Germanic languages is not simply an aggregation of vowels, but is organized into subsystems, such that the contrast between subsystems is greater than the contrast within them. Chapter 9 presented evidence from various sources, including natural misunderstandings, for the existence of such subsystems. Within subsystems, changes are governed by the three general principles of chain shifting developed in chapters 5 and 6. Chapter 9 presented some principles that govern movements between the subsystems of short vowels, upgliding diphthongs, and ingliding diphthongs. The tensing of short low vowels is governed by the Lower Exit Principle, but whether a particular vowel moves to the front or the back is controlled by specific configurations of the phonetic and phonological structure (Moulton 1962). On both the front and back paths we have observed lexical diffusion in the earlier broad **a** class, the modern short **a** class, and the modern short **o** class. The brief observations made of other changes in the history of English suggest that, in general, we can look for lexical diffusion in shifts across subsystems, that is, changes of abstract features. Within vowel systems, we can expect regular Neogrammarian change.

Since short or lax nuclei fall by the general principles of vowel shifting, there is structural pressure on lax /æ/ to exit the system. The only available route is to the long and ingliding vowels (i.e., tensing); this is the structural matrix of the peripheralization and raising of (æh) that we have witnessed.

Within a subsystem, vowels can be opposed at a relatively abstract level, through combinations of the three lower-level dimensions of height, backing, and rounding. Milroy's (1980) study of lexical diffusion in Belfast shows such a result for a late stage of the sound changes involved, perhaps better characterized as the social alternation of a stable opposition of standard and local forms. One such set involves the splitting of words in the short **u** class: *butcher, hull,* etc. The phonetic alternants are opposed by height, fronting, and rounding: [ü] vs. [ʌ]. A second case concerns short **a** words, such as *carrot*, which show irregular alternation of extreme front and back forms, [æ] vs. [ɒ], differentiated by both fronting and rounding.

What about diphthongization and monophthongization? These processes seem to hold an intermediate position. The first case of irregularity discussed by Wang (1969) dealt with the monophthongization of Chinese /ay/. Yet the diphthongization of high vowels that apparently initiated the Great Vowel Shift was quite regular, like parallel movements in other Germanic and in Balto-Slavic languages (LYS:chap. 4). A detailed case of monophthongization studied by Malkiel (1976) involves the sporadic reversal of the general diphthongization of Gallo-Romance short mid vowels. Thus typically Latin *frons, fronte* 'forehead' became Old Spanish *fruente,*

La. *pressa* 'compressed' led to OS *priessa* 'hurry'. Malkiel's task is to explain the irregular process that led to Modern Sp. *frente, prisa,* and the contrast between French *siècle* and Sp. *siglo* 'century'. In his exhaustive discussion can be found all the features presented for the splitting of short **a**: rough phonetic conditioning, morphological influence, intersection from various directions, and finally, the ineradicable residue of lexical irregularity, "a residue of cases unsolved if not insoluble" (p. 768). At the same time, the parallel case of the perfectly regular monophthongization (*ie* → *e*) makes it clear that the addition or loss of glides seems to follow the Neogrammarian pattern as often as not, or more so.

A good source for further data on vowel change is the extensive study of sound change in progress by Copenhagen by Brink and Lund (1975). Their real-time data have greater depth and reliability than those of any other study I know. They include recordings of speakers born as early as 1810, and the sound changes are reported by means of an impressionistic transcription of considerable depth and precision. In a discussion of "sound laws," Brink (1977) reports a wide variety of exceptions to sound changes. Some of these irregularities are accounted for by the principles outlined above (e.g., orthographic influence on the late stages of change), and several shortenings affect only a few words and are conditioned by frequency. But exceptions are also reported for simple lowerings and raisings. In the lowering of the upper mid nucleus of a diphthong with a low back glide, analogy has operated to prevent the lowering of the common word *læger* 'doctors'. A raising of long [a:] does not affect Swedish and German loanwords. A lowering of [ø] before [n, m, f] (an environment strikingly similar to the tensing condition for Philadelphia short **a**) is characterized as "very slow and affecting the vocabulary less systematically" than many other sound changes.

On the whole, the findings of Brink and Lund indicate that analogy, frequency, and foreign status can influence the course of low-level output rules. At the same time, their overall findings support the principles presented above. Their most general observation on the consistency of sound change indicates not a word-by-word mechanism but a Neogrammarian regularity:

Once these exceptions have been established, we must then admit that the more recent laws observed in the oral data generally do show an extremely high degree of consistency; they actually operate rather mechanically. (Brink 1977:10)

The last short *a* question

Before we leave the study of vowel systems, it is necessary to face squarely the puzzle posed by the contrast between the Northern Cities short **a** system and that of the Middle Atlantic states. How can we explain the fact that short **a** underwent lexical splitting at a high level of abstraction in the Middle Atlantic states, but in the Northern Cities submitted as a whole to a regular, phonetically conditioned sound change?[21]

For a number of years, I felt that this was an insoluble puzzle, and that no linguistic factor could account for it. It seemed clear that the answer had to be a historical one, to be traced in the settlement patterns of the two areas and their earlier histories. The Northern Cities Shift is quite recent. Its rotation of the short vowels represents a new departure for English phonology, and we have no record of its earlier history. On the other hand, the history of short **a** has been traced by a great many writers, including Jespersen, Wyld, Trager, and Ferguson. Ferguson (1975) demonstrates that the history of short **a** is intimately entwined with the history of broad **a**. The lengthening of short **a** before voiceless fricatives and nasals goes back at least three hundred years (Jespersen 1949:304–10; Wyld 1936:203–5). It is generally agreed that this lengthening took place when short **a** was in front position, similar to the modern lengthening of /æ/, and that the backing to broad **a** followed it. Putting together the evidence advanced by Jespersen, Wyld, and Ferguson, it seems clear that the similarity between the conditioning of the Philadelphia short **a** split and that of broad **a** is not a parallel independent development. It is similar because it is the *same* sound change, transmitted to Philadelphia in the dialect of the early settlers.

Ferguson (1975) also argues, contrary to Trager (1940), that the Philadelphia distribution is close to that of the original short **a** lengthening, and that the New York City distribution was originally quite similar. This is particularly persuasive in light of the fact that Babbitt's (1896) early description of the New York City short **a** listed only words in the British broad **a** class as being raised to the level of *bared*. It seems probable, therefore, that the New York City short **a** pattern was similar to that of Philadelphia at an early date, and that words with short **a** before voiced stops were tensed later. The Philadelphia pattern was already generalized past the British model. Ferguson shows that the true core or nucleus of short **a** lengthening is found before final /s, f, θ/ and -*nt*, -*ns* clusters. The broad **a** class in England excludes words with final nasals like *man* and *ham*, includes only two instances of broad **a** before -*mp* (*sample*, *example*), and includes broad **a** before -*nd* only in the stem -*mand*. In all of these areas, the Philadelphia system is quite consistently generalized, though we did

---

[21] At the end of his own treatment of the short **a** development, Kiparsky (1989:404) rightly points out that in the account offered in Labov 1981, it remains "mysterious that *a*-tensing, which after all involves the same feature in all dialects, is subject to lexical diffusion in some dialects and not others."

note lax *wham, bam, mam,* which may be relics of the earlier pattern.[22] Conversely, we find some traces of continued development of short **a** tensing in England. Jones (1964) reports that some British speakers have a length contrast between short [jæm] 'crush' and long [ĭæ:m] 'fruit conserve'.

All this points to the conclusion that the Philadelphia short **a** system is a direct continuation of the 17th- and 18th-century lengthening of broad **a** in front position, free to generalize and expand on separation from British dialects. Though this simplifies the problem, it transfers the question of explaining lexical irregularity to the origins of the broad **a** split. Here the special theory of Jespersen has much to contribute. Jespersen (1949:308–12) argues that broad **a** lengthening is not a new Early Middle English process, but rather a continuation of the developments that followed open syllable lengthening in Early Middle English. In the light of Minkova's (1982) reanalysis of this phenomenon, the argument is particularly persuasive. She contends that the consistent core of this process is the word class with a single short vowel followed by a single consonant and a shwa, C V C ə, and argues that the loss of the shwa was accompanied by a lengthening of the prior syllable. This lengthening would therefore be homomorphic with the lengthening of short **a** in current dialects, where a short vowel in a closed syllable develops length with a centering inglide.

It is also interesting to note in Minkova's tables the extraordinary predominance of /a/ over /e/ and /o/ in this process. Of the 310 Old English words that were candidates for possible lengthening, 50% contained /a/, and of these, 20% were lengthened, as opposed to 8% for /e/ and 3% for /o/.

In later periods, the lengthened /a/ underwent fronting, and the phonetic distance between long and short pairs increased tremendously, leading to the present *sane/sanity* relation. This was accentuated by the fact that in the 17th century, short **a** in closed syllables was still a back or central [a]. The alternation between the short and the long form then exhibited many of the properties of lexical diffusion that we have been studying. Jespersen points to a number of fluctuations that are analogical retentions of the back position for the long vowel. For example, the French borrowing *passe* from *passer* had both closed and open reflexes, leading to *pass* and what was eventually respelled as *pace.* The broad **a** [pɑ:s] was an analogical reformation (or "compromise," in Jespersen's terms) from short [pas]. After the fronting of short **a** there were three forms: [pæs, pɑ:s, peis]. Another such triplet is [bæθ, bɑθ, beið]. Many of the doublets created at that time produced the contrast between standard "compromise" forms [fɑðə, rɑðə, vɑz] and "vulgar" forms [feiðə, reiðə, veiz]. To many such cases, one can

---

[22] Ferguson (1975) points out that Baltimore has lax /æ/ in *slam* and *ham.*

add the retention of the back vowel in affective words (*ah!, haha, mama*) and in more recent loans from Romance and other languages (*mustache, mirage, spa, adagio, lava, lama, drama*, etc.). We can thus observe in these developments the strong influence of the two major factors specifically said by the Neogrammarians to create irregular sound changes: analogy and dialect mixture. This irregular pattern then continued to expand along phonetically conditioned lines, in the word-by-word manner that led to so many lexically conditioned results in England and the Middle Atlantic states.

The Northern Cities tensing and raising of short **a** appears to be a recent and independent phenomenon in a dialect that did not inherit the lexically defined broad **a** distribution. The similarities between the phonetic conditions in the Northern Cities and Philadelphia that we saw in chapter 16 are due to the general character of the phonetic constraints, rather than historical transmission.

Kiparsky's (1989) illuminating treatment of the short **a** development is not inconsistent with this scenario. Without entering into the historical background, he posits that the broad **a** pattern in New England and Philadelphia is the same inherited rule. He argues that in New England, the broad **a** level 1 rule produced a back vowel, and all other short **a** words "are then subject to tensing postlexically by the same rule as in the 'Midwest'" (p. 403).[23] He further suggests that in Philadelphia, tensed broad **a** coincided with the tense vowel that was the output of the postlexical tensing rule. In Philadelphia, these two rules merged, yielding a lexical tensing rule.

To develop this view further, we will need some modification of the description of the New England short **a** pattern. It is one of the dialects with the "nasal pattern" governed by the simple rule (10), producing tensed and raised vowels in *man, manage, animal, hammer*, with other vowels remaining lax.

(10)   [+front, +ant] → [+tense]/ ____ [+nas]

LYS (fig. 27) shows the vowel system of a 70-year-old speaker from Cambridge, Massachusetts: there is a sharp differentiation between tense (æhN), coinciding in its nucleus with upper mid /ey/, and other /æ/ vow-

---

[23] Kiparsky's brief treatment of this "Midwest tensing rule" has a preliminary backing rule before /r/ and an informal schema for continuous raising of all other vowels with phonetic conditioning of the sort shown in figure 16.4. *Midwest* is an unfortunate term; its referent varies over much of the United States, but most of the area that it generally covers – in Ohio, Indiana, Illinois, Kansas, and Missouri – is not included in the Northern dialect region, and does not participate in the Northern Cities Shift. The preliminary backing rule may not be necessary, since /a/ is strongly fronted before /r/ in many of these areas, and occupies a position that is predictable from the phonetic conditioning of the continuum.

els.[24] This may be contrasted with the continuum shown by older speakers in the Northern Cities, as illustrated in figure 6.8 and elsewhere in this volume. Thus Eastern New England has two phonemes: the broad /ah/ category and the single /æ/ category, differentiated by a simple allophonic rule.

Kiparsky (p.c.) notes that the restriction of the older Boston dialect to tensing before nasals does not militate against the unified treatment of Philadelphia and New England, noting that the environments of the nasal dialect, added to the original broad **a** pattern, yield the Philadelphia pattern of figure 18.6. Whether the Philadelphia development is the product of direct contact with New England, the product of contact with some other nasal pattern, or a response to the general extension of tensing before nasals in American English can best be determined by further research on historical contacts and influences; but the unified approach to the further development of lexical rules seems an important direction to pursue.[25] An account of the further extension of the short **a** environments in New York City that depends on intersection with the Northern Cities Shift seems to me less plausible, considering that the latter is much more recent and has no lexical conditions.

The account derived from the theory of lexical phonology adds several dimensions to our understanding of the short **a** development. The concepts of postlexical rule and lexical rule encapsulate many of the properties that we have discussed, and link them to other properties and wider data bases. Within this theory a number of problems remain unsolved: whether the structure-preserving condition can be maintained (Harris 1989), whether strict cyclicity can be supported, and how many levels exist. Nevertheless, lexical phonology provides a framework that consistently illuminates our data, augmenting the insightful formulations of the Neogrammarians. The Philadelphia short **a** split is the continuation of a longstanding pattern of lengthening of English /a/, which proceeds by changes in lexical rules at a high level of abstraction. This change is characterized by dialect mixture and by analogical and other forms of grammatical conditioning, and it typically exhibits lexical diffusion. The Northern Cities tensing of short **a** appears to be an independent phenomenon: a postlexical

---

[24] In the lax class, vowels before /d/ and voiceless fricatives are somewhat higher than other lax vowels, and one vowel before /s/ is close to the /æhN/ category. In recent years, the Boston dialect has shown some tensing in other environments, especially before /t/ (Laferrière 1977), but the nasal pattern generally remains intact. See also Payne 1976 for the vowel system of out-of-state parents from New England, recorded during the King of Prussia study, who consistently showed the nasal pattern.

[25] Recent contacts between Philadelphia and New England are shown by the development in the 1930s of local terms for a submarine sandwich. In the Eastern New England area surrounding (but not including) Boston, *grinder* is the basic term. While the basic Philadelphia term is *hoagie, grinder* has been adopted regularly in Philadelphia for a submarine sandwich heated in the oven, sometimes called an *oven grinder* (Labov 1989c).

shift of height at a low level of abstraction. This change proceeds in a continuous manner, conditioned only by phonetic context, without any trace of lexical irregularity or grammatical conditioning.

18.5 Consonantal changes

We should briefly consider some of the more obvious issues regarding consonant changes, though less work has been done in this area than with vowels. In general, the importance of discreteness and graduality, emphasized by Wang, is thrown into relief. The most striking contradictions to the Neogrammarian notion of graduality appear in metathesis, haplology, and other discontinuous consonant shifts. The history of Dravidian initials traced by Krishnamurti (1978) involves such rearrangement of consonants groups, and it is only natural to expect lexical diffusion here. The same can be said for changes in place of articulation.

A detailed view of such diffusion can be obtained in Kinkade's (1972) study of the shift of velars to alveopalatals in the Salishan languages of the Pacific Northwest. At both geographic ends of this language family, alveopalatals are found among the plain and glottalized voiceless stops and the voiceless fricatives; but in a central region, a large group of languages show the conservative velars. Lower Cowlitz is exceptional in showing a split, "a case of sound-shift caught in transit" (p. 2): roughly one-third of all the morphemes are in the alveopalatal series. Kinkade accounts for 15 of the 124 cases by means of borrowing from Chinook Jargon, and for several dozen by phonetic processes. Like Malkiel (1976), he exhausts all possible sources of explanation, including dissimilation, before he concludes that this sound change is phonetically discrete but lexically gradual.

In a monograph on the labial-velar changes in English and Dutch, Bonebrake (1979) considers one of the most striking examples of discontinuous changes in place of articulation: the shifts of [x] to [f] and [f] to [x]. She necessarily begins with a well-known list of lexical irregularities such as regular *cough* vs. irregular *dough* or *slough*, and regular *daughter* vs. irregular *laughter*. The overall model that she presents for multiple conditioning of sound change is as complex as those of Malkiel or Kinkade – involving the possibility of perceptual continuity, morphological and semantic influence, and social differentiation.

Changes in place of articulation are necessarily more abstract than changes in manner. The placement of the tongue at various points along the midsagittal section is not a simple linear shift, but a rearrangement of the shape of the tongue by adjusting several different muscles. The acoustic consequences are in turn registered by a variety of signals: the frequency distribution and amplitudes of bursts, and the transitions of three formants. Manner of articulation involves a simpler set of dimensions, and changes in manner of articulation are most often phonetically gradual. They are also more likely to be lexically regular, as current studies of change in progress attest. The various phonetic shifts of palatals in South America show every sign of Neogrammarian regularity: the lenition of /č/ to a fricative in Panama City (Cedergren 1973) and the devoicing of /ž/ in Buenos Aires (Wolf and Jiménez 1979). The sizeable literature on the aspiration and deletion of /s/ shows no evidence of lexical conditioning in the many detailed quantitative investigations of Spanish (Ma and Herasimchuk 1968; Cedergren 1973; Poplack 1979; Terrell 1981; Hochberg 1986; Alba 1990) and of Portuguese (Oliveira 1983; Guy 1981). In English, detailed studies of the vocalization of liquids show no trace of lexical irregularity (Labov 1966; Ash 1982). A dramatic example of the lenition of postvocalic stops is found in Liverpool, where voiceless stops become affricates and fricatives – beginning with /k/, and now proceeding to /t/ and perhaps /p/ among younger children. My own explorations of this process show that it is both gradual and regular. Such a replay of Grimm's Law reminds us that it is no accident that the Neogrammarians' most brilliant successes were scored on the changes of manner that this law describes. There is every reason to think that this was a gradual process, a phonetic output rule: as paradigmatic an example of Neogrammarian change as we might look for.

One way to approach this brief survey in a more controlled way is to examine a group of sound changes that were assembled for a study with a different orientation. In his review of reported sound changes originally discussed in chapter 16, Fónagy (1956) organizes the 60 studies according to whether they show evidence of variation in individuals, the lexicon, prosodic or positional influence, and so on. His conclusions bear on the variety and complexity of factors that influence sound change, rather than the types of change that might favor one mode or the other. If we consider all the studies of modern dialects presented by Fónagy that include some evidence of change in progress,[26] the classification shown in table 18.5 yields some support to the principles outlined in this section. The one case of lexical diffusion reported for vowel changes within a subsystem is in Sommerfelt's (1930) account of the Welsh high unrounded vowel: the older variant is preserved in three archaic words: ('werewolf', 'warrior', and 'lamentation'). Otherwise, these distributions support the observation that regular sound changes are in the majority. Where lexical diffusion does

---

[26] I have not included, for example, Hermann's (1929) discussion of the alternation of /θ/ in Charmey, since comparison with Gauchat's data led Hermann to conclude that no change was involved. A number of observations of English data by Jespersen and Daniel Jones – concerning, for example, centralization of /i/ in *pretty* and *children* – seem to have no obvious connection with change in progress. However, there are a number of citations of British dialects with the same complex conditions of lengthening of short **a** that are found in the Middle Atlantic states.

Table 18.5   Lexical conditioning reported in sound changes
(data from Fónagy 1956)

	No lexical conditioning reported	Lexical conditioning reported
Vowel shifts		
Within subsystems	4	1
Diphthongization and monophthongization	3	1
Lengthening and shortening	0	7
Consonant shifts		
Change of manner	4	0
Change of place	5	2

occur, it is most often found in changes across subsystems – particularly lengthenings and shortenings in vowels,[27] and changes of place of articulation in consonants. One case of diphthongization and monophthongization showed lexical variation, but three were regular. Though these numbers are not large enough to be decisive, they have the advantage that they were collected with an independent perspective, and the fact that they follow the patterns we have found in the study of changes in progress is encouraging.

18.6   The resolution of the paradox

What progress has been made, then, in resolving the Neogrammarian controversy? – or, to the extent that we have come to recognize a substantive issue, in resolving the Neogrammarian paradox? Restated most simply, the paradox amounts to this: if Wang and his associates are right about lexical diffusion, and the Neogrammarians were more right than they knew about sound change, how can both be right?

One group has asserted that "Phonemes change," the other that "Words change." Neither formulation is very useful as it stands; they are abstract slogans that have lost their connection with what is actually happening. A close examination of change in progress has been more fruitful. We have located Neogrammarian regularity in low-level output rules, and lexical diffusion in the redistribution of an abstract word class into other abstract

---

[27] Fónagy documents lexical differences in his own meticulous studies of vowel length in French and Hungarian. But these may not bear directly on the issue, since the French data deal with a low-level phonetic continuum, and the Hungarian high vowels present the less common case of a phonemic difference based on phonetic length alone.

classes. I do not propose to resolve the original confrontation into a simple dichotomy – that here words change, there sounds change. I have exhibited two polar types, and have analyzed the clusters of properties that created these types. The whole array of sound changes will undoubtedly show many intermediate combinations of these properties of discreteness, abstractness, grammatical conditioning, and social conditioning.

Other dimensions should certainly be taken into account. On the basis of studying lexical diffusion in Breton, Dressler (1979) has suggested that diffusion is more likely when fortition is involved than lenition.[28] Henry Hoenigswald has brought to my attention a dimension that must be relevant to several of the cases examined here: the scope of the conditioning environment. Hoenigswald points out that when phonetic conditioning extends over two, three, or four segments, the probability that a grammatical boundary will be crossed increases dramatically – and with it, the probability of grammatical conditioning. Open-syllable lengthening is just such a case, since syllables are necessarily defined by segment sequences of some length. The modern tensing of short **a** considers a minimum of two, and up to four, following segments. By contrast, the fronting of /ow/ in Philadelphia has one simple exception – when a liquid is the next segment. Certainly there are other important properties to be considered. We will find some discontinuous shifts that are regular, like the shift of apical to uvular (r) throughout Western Europe. We will also no doubt find some lexical irregularities within subsystems, beyond those caused by correction at late stages of the change, as the materials of Brink and Lund indicate.

With these reservations, the following conceptions of the two types of change have gradually emerged:

Regular sound change is the result of a gradual transformation of a single phonetic feature of a phoneme in a continuous phonetic space. It is characteristic of the initial stages of a change that develops within a linguistic system, without lexical or grammatical conditioning or any degree of social awareness ("change from below").

Lexical diffusion is the result of the abrupt substitution of one phoneme for another in words that contain that phoneme. The older and newer forms of the word will usually differ by several phonetic features. This process is most characteristic of the late stages of an internal change that has been differentiated by lexical and grammatical conditioning, or has developed a high degree of social awareness or of borrowings from other systems ("change from above").

Given this range of properties, we would predict that the realms of regular

---

[28] It might be noted that the example analyzed in detail by Malkiel (1976), to which Dressler also refers, is a case of lenition rather than fortition.

sound change and lexical diffusion would display complementary distribution:

Regular sound change	*Lexical diffusion*
Vowel shifts in place of articulation	Shortening and lengthening of segments
Diphthongization of high vowels	Diphthongization of mid and low vowels
Consonant changes in manner of articulation	Consonant changes in place of articulation
Vocalization of liquids	Metathesis of liquids and stops
Deletion of glides and shwa	Deletion of obstruents

This resolution of the Neogrammarian controversy entails a shift of research strategies. It turns aside from the questions, Does every word have its own history?, Is it phonemes that change?, Are the Neogrammarians right or wrong?, toward a research program of a different sort. It begins with respect for the achievements of our predecessors; but that does not mean that it will rest content with the data they have gathered. We demonstrate an appreciation of their work, not by remanipulation of the original observations, but by undertaking a broader and deeper set of inquiries that will display the value and the limitations of their initial results. We can then ask, What is the full range of properties that determine the transition from one phonetic state to another? Following this path, we will eventually be able to predict with a high degree of probability the ways in which the phonological system reacts to the mysterious process of sound change. This is the problem of the final section of this volume, which is concerned with the relation between linguistic change and the system's ability to transmit information.

Part E

The Functional Character of Change

19

The Overestimation of Functionalism

The four chapters of part D were concerned with the resolution of the controversies and paradoxical findings that proceeded from the Neogrammarian position on the regularity of sound change. The results have provided remarkably strong support for their point of view. Once the Neogrammarian concept is modified by our present understanding of the hierarchy of abstractness of linguistic categories, the regularity of sound change appears as a substantive reality. In part E, our attention turns to another aspect of the disagreements that have followed from the original Neogrammarian statement: the relation of sound change to meaning.

The Neogrammarian position on this matter is quite simple: the course of sound change is not modified by the communicative needs of speakers and listeners. Grammatical systems do show adjustments that preserve meaningful relations, but these are the result of a separate process of analogical change. The problem of distinguishing analogical change from regular sound change has been argued continually since the Neogrammarians first articulated their position. But recent years have seen a revival of the view that sound change is directly affected by the need to preserve meaning, under the title of *functionalism* and the *functional hypothesis*. This general point of view applies to synchronic variation as well as to historical change. To assess functional arguments, we will have to deal with both types of variation. The most detailed developments have taken place with respect to synchronic, stable variation, and much of this chapter will focus on this area of investigation. It will first be helpful to look at the place of functional arguments in general and their relation to linguistic argumentation.

19.1 Functionalism and functionalists

Over the past half century a number of linguistic schools and tendencies have worked under the title of *functionalism*. They have oriented themselves toward the notions of "function," "communication," and "meaning," in a way that may be summed up as a default proposition:

(1)   The function of language is for the speaker (or writer) to communicate meaning to the listener (or reader).

The concept of "meaning" here is usually narrower than the concept used in information theory, but broader than that used in truth-definitional semantics. In general, discussions of functional effect refer to the need to represent *states of affairs* with propositions that will succeed in distinguishing what are true states from those that are not, along with their extensions into the interrogative, imperative, and other moods. In addition, such discussions have come to include various ways of calling attention to parts of the sentence, or withdrawing attention, as indicated by such terms as *focusing* and *defocusing*, *topicalization*, *foregrounding*, and *backgrounding*. But these discussions of functional effects usually do not include the function of representing the emotional state of the speaker, the social relations between speaker and addressee, or the facilitation of speech and communication by condensation, abbreviation, or mechanical means.

The range of linguists who devote their efforts to explaining language structure by the need to communicate is quite broad, and might include in diverse ways such major contributors as Martinet, Halliday, Kuno, Kiparsky, and Givón. The Parasession on Functionalism at the Chicago Linguistic Society's 1975 meeting gave full representation to functional views. The great majority of papers argued in favor of functional explanations, though at least two were skeptical.

One does not have to look far to find linguists who avoid "function" and functional explanations. Chomsky has shown a thoroughgoing skepticism in regard to functional explanations of language structure. In defending the autonomy of syntax, he concedes that the needs of communication may have influenced the structure of language as it evolved in human prehistory, but he argues that very little can be concluded from this observation (1975:56–60). Pursuing a biological analogy, he says:

There is no doubt that the physiologist, studying the heart, will pay attention to the fact that it pumps blood. But he will also study the structure of the heart, and the origin of this structure in the individual and the species, making no dogmatic assumptions about the possibility of "explaining" this structure in functional terms. (p. 57)[1]

Chomsky's negative view of functional explanations is certainly related to his position that the study of language use is quite distinct from the study of language structure, and possibly not very important to linguists; that

---

[1] This is certainly an extreme position, one not likely to evoke a sympathetic response from most physiologists, who have profited from their functional orientation since the time of Harvey.

syntax is autonomous and can be studied apart from semantics; and that the language faculty is an innate structure isolated from social interaction. Since those who investigate language in its social context do not usually hold any of these positions, one might expect that work in this area would fall into the functional camp. Yet over the past ten years, I and others who observe language in use have become increasingly doubtful of arguments for the controlling effect of meaning on language and language change. It is often asserted that speakers take the information state of their addressee into account as they speak, and that given a choice of two alternatives, they favor the one that will put across their meaning in the most efficient and effective way. But in what follows, we will see that quantitative studies of the use of language fail to confirm this assertion.

Functional arguments are not easily discouraged. *Communication* and *meaning* appear there as elements that are inherently good; a linguistic device is considered better if it communicates more information, and worse if it does not. I find myself inherently suspicious of anything that is inherently good.

What we might call naive or teleological functionalism has been tried in other fields and been found wanting. Merton points out that the structural-functionalism of sociology looks to the structural *consequences* of behaviors or institutions, not their motivations. In his discussion of functions and dysfunctions, he points out two types of confusion in his own field:

"the tendency to confine sociological observations to the *positive* contributions of a sociological item to the social or cultural system in which it is implicated; and the tendency to confuse the subjective category of *motive* with the objective category of *function.*" (1957:51)

This description might equally well be applied to linguists who have resonated to Jakobson's call for teleological thinking in linguistic analysis, under the program that the structure of language can only be understood as an implementation of speakers' intentions (Caton 1987). At the level of speech acts, one can appreciate the position of Searle and Grice that to understand the meaning of an utterance is to understand the intentions of the person who uttered it.[2] Yet I think we must be skeptical of all arguments that claim to explain linguistic changes through the speaker's desires or intentions to communicate a given message. There is no reason to think that our notions of what we intend or the intentions we attribute to others are very accurate, or that we have any way of knowing whether they are

---

[2] Searle 1970:43–4. Searle disagrees with Grice only in claiming that it is the illocutionary intention that must be grasped rather than the perlocutionary intention.

accurate.[3] Granted that the interpretation of utterances involves the attribution of intentions, attributing those intentions to others is not the same as saying that we have grasped their actual motivations. Even if we knew precisely what those motivations were, this would not mean that such motivations actively determined a speaker's choice of one linguistic variant or another. If functional theories of language change and variation are theories of intentions, they will be leading us down a very slippery path indeed.

Many functional arguments are aimed at the explication of invariant structures. In recent years, the same type of argument has been freely applied to the variable elements in language structure, and in particular to constraints on variable rules. In the functionalist milieu, these arguments seem almost self-evident. One might ask, if the communication of information does not determine the shape of linguistic variation and change, what does? Most linguists of the 19th century were clear on this point. Sound change, the major mechanism of linguistic change, was seen to operate in a mechanical fashion, without regard to meaning or the communicative needs of society. There is good reason to think that this is still the most common type of change. If this is so, we can expect that much synchronic variation is also unresponsive to the need to communicate information. In the discussion to follow, we will encounter ample evidence that morphological and syntactic variation is controlled by a tendency to preserve parallel structures in successive sentences. Other variants are the result of the arbitrary social evaluation of alternative ways of saying the same thing, the chance by-products of geographic contact. Some variation must be seen as historical residue, without any vestige of communicative function (Baugh 1983; Houston 1985). This is not to say that functional arguments are illusions. Rather, we will see that the need to preserve information is relatively weak, and can be overridden by a variety of other factors.

On the other hand, we find that, with certain losses, languages do adjust to preserve their capacity to transmit meaning. If speakers do not take meaning into account in their choice of linguistic variants, how does this adjustment come about? This is the major puzzle that chapter 20 is intended to resolve. I hope to show that we can come to a more balanced view of functional arguments by following the principle of accountability (paying attention to all the available data, rather than just those utterances that favor the ideas in view) and by using multivariate analysis that takes into account the operation of several influences that jointly determine the end result.

---

[3] See also Chomsky 1975:76. In addition to assessing functionalism negatively in general, as in the earlier quotation, Chomsky expresses a thoroughgoing skepticism of his own intuitions about his intentions in speaking, which as he sees it may not turn out to be directed toward the communication of information at all.

19.2   Functional explanations of sound change

A full consideration of functional arguments must certainly include the explanation of sound change. The chain shifting of vowels and consonants that we considered in part B has always been considered a major instance of functional behavior. Such coordinated changes have the effect of avoiding merger and the loss of the distinctions that are used to encode meaning (Martinet 1955; Haudricourt and Juilland 1949). It is well known that such arguments fail to deal in an accountable way with the fact that mergers are even more common than chain shifts, and that massive mergers do take place, with a concomitant increase in homonymy. Though it is often argued that the mergers that lose the least information are favored, part C gave many examples of unconditioned mergers that are hard to reconcile with this point of view.

Even where chain shifting does occur, it appears that functional arguments are often arbitrary. Chain shifts are only one kind of coordinated vowel change: the other is parallel movement, which is generally considered an example of rule generalization that leads (in terms of features) to simpler statements. Such simplifications can be said to facilitate the work of the speaker in producing language or the hearer in understanding it. This can be argued to be the function of the change, and such parallel shifts are sometimes given as instances of functional behavior. But the entire discussion will quickly become vacuous if we lump together explanations based on the facilitation of speech with those that are based on the preservation of meaning. Lenition processes that wear away forms, destroy inflectional contrasts, and confuse paradigms may be thought of as the result of a kind of functional facilitation, following a principle of least effort. In all that follows, "functional arguments" will be limited to those that are based on a tendency to preserve meaning in the course of linguistic variation and change.

In many cases, parallel or generalized sound changes turn out to alternate in an unpredictable manner with chain shifts. One of the clearest examples of parallelism is the fronting of (uw) and (ow) in Philadelphia (see figure 3.6 for the community means). The parallelism is never complete: it is normal for one vowel to lead, and the generalization appears in the gradual completion of the change in the slower member. In Philadelphia, as elsewhere, (uw) leads (ow).[4] Now, however, consider the London vowel system of Marie Colville, in figure 6.3. Here /uw/ has moved to the front and /ow/ has moved down to low back position, parallel with the

---

[4] Chapter 8 proposed that all such frontings of (ow) are forms of parallel movement rather than chain shifts, and that the fronting of mid vowels is not an inherent part of the general principles of vowel shifting.

lowering of /ey/ in front. There is no clear relation between the fronting of /uw/ and the lowering of /ow/. But there is a relation between the fronting of /aw/ and the lowering of /ow/: it is a chain shift, which eliminates the possibility of a merger of /aw/ and /ow/.

(2)   /ow/ → /aw/ →

In the central Texas vowel system of Jerry Thrasher in figure 6.4, the same chaining relationship of /ow/ and /aw/ can be observed. However, we cannot say that either one of these patterns – chain shift or parallel shift – is characteristic of Philadelphia, London, and Texas. Many London speakers do show a perfectly parallel arrangement of /uw/ and /ow/ – for example, the oldest London speaker reported by LYS, 83 years old (LYS:fig. 29). The same variations are found in Birmingham and Texas. In general, the height of (ow) is a sociolinguistic variable independent of fronting. The lower unrounded variants are characteristic of extreme working-class styles. Thus vernacular Cockney [ʌu] is parallel to the most advanced forms of (ey), [aɪ]. On the other hand, a very close fronted and rounded (ow) is associated with a clergyman's overrefined pronunciation, [øʊ]. As a result of this sociolinguistic variation, one can find idiosyncratic fluctuation within the community between a chain shift and a parallel shift analysis of the sound changes involved, with many indeterminate cases. This is an implausible consequence, and leads to the conclusion that if the difference between a functional and a nonfunctional structure is so malleable, there cannot be very much substance in it.

Even more basic to functional thinking about phonology is the belief that phonological oppositions are entirely determined by contrastive function: that speakers and listeners can hear only those differences in sound that signal distinctive differences in meaning. But chapters 12–14 have shown that this is not so: in near-mergers, speakers produce reliable and stable distinctions that neither they nor other listeners can use to distinguish one meaning from another. There is no doubt that phonemes do function to distinguish meaning; but the historical development of the system of phonemes is not narrowly controlled by that communicative function.

19.3   Constraints on morphological variation

Consonant cluster simplification in English

The first internal constraints on linguistic variation to be studied systematically concerned the simplification of final clusters in the African-American Vernacular English and then in many other dialects. The major focus has been on the deletion of final /t/ or /d/ in words such as *fist, hand, past, kept,* and *walked*. Two major factor groups emerged as general to almost all English speakers, as shown in figure 19.1.

One basic constraint on *-t,d* deletion is phonological: the effect of the following segment. A following consonant favors deletion more than a following vowel, as indicated by relations *a* and *b* in figure 19.1, and within this major division, greater sonority (and the possibility of resyllabification) favors deletion. One might argue, as Kiparsky has done (1971, 1982), that this kind of variation need not be entered into a grammar, since it can be predicted by universal considerations of markedness in syllable structure that facilitate articulation. The second constraint is independent of the first and more abstract in the sense defined in chapter 18: clusters formed by past tense inflections, as in *walked*, are less likely to be simplified than monomorphemic clusters, as in *fact* and *fist*, as indicated by relations *c* and *d* in figure 19.1.

A variable rule that records these and other facts about this process is given in (3).

(3)   t,d → <Ø> / <–str> <+cons> [+cons] <Ø> __ ## <–syl>

This may be read as follows: /t/ or /d/ is variably reduced after another consonant before a word boundary, and this happens more often in unstressed syllables than in stressed ones, more often when a third consonant precedes, as in *next*, more often when there is no grammatical boundary before the final consonant, and more often when a syllabic segment does not follow.

It is true enough that if all the stable constraints on variation were to be assigned to universal principles, there would be no need to represent variation in the grammars of particular languages. To this end, Kiparsky

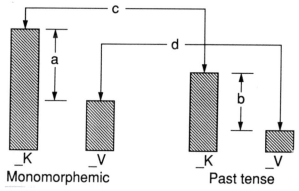

Figure 19.1. Two basic constraints on *-t,d* deletion in English

has consistently argued that the grammatical constraint on -*t,d* deletion be subsumed under a universal "functional" principle:[5]

[T]here is a tendency for semantically relevant information to be retained in surface structure . . . . It characteristically originates as a blocking of rules in environments in which their free application would wipe out morphological distinctions on the surface.[6] (1982:87)

Confidence in this universal lasted only until the next language was investigated. In Ma and Herasimchuk's (1968) study of Puerto Rican Spanish in Jersey City, it was found that final /s/ was deleted *less* often in monomorphemic words like *más* and *tres*, and *more* often when it was a grammatical inflection as in *padres*. Many other studies of Spanish and Portuguese, to be reviewed below, confirm this finding. But the limitations of a functional explanation also appeared in the study of English -*t,d*. The most extensive study of this variable is Guy 1980, an examination of -*t,d* deletion by 26 white Philadelphians and New Yorkers. In his extensive review of functional explanations of variation, Guy demonstrates that each individual mirrors the pattern of the group, and that the past tense constraint is acquired early in life by all speakers of the language. In a later application of these facts to functional explanations, he points to the data given in table 19.1. As usual, the most favoring factor is the monomorphemic status of the cluster. Regular past tense clusters are considerably

Table 19.1 Grammatical constraints on −*t,d* deletion for 19 Philadelphia speakers

Context	Varbrul weight	
Monomorphemic words (e.g., *west*)	1.00	⎫
Semiweak verbs (e.g., *kep+t, tol+d*)	.91	⎬ FUNCTIONAL
Regular past tense verbs (e.g., *walk#ed*)	.52	⎭
Regular participles (e.g., *have walk#ed*)	.49	COUNTERFUNCTIONAL

[5] The tendency to see the grammatical constraints on -*t,d* deletion as functional is a natural one. In Labov 1971 I proposed that whenever a single segment is variably deleted, it will be deleted less often if it is a separate morpheme. In the discussion to follow, it will be evident that this formulation is subject to the same criticism as Kiparsky's.

[6] The use of the word *tendency* in this formulation is problematic. Within the framework of the categorical view that limits rule types to obligatory or optional, it can only refer to the frequency of occurrence of rules that have the effect postulated. On the other hand, Kiparsky was responding to data from quantitative studies of consonant cluster simplification, so that we might interpret his constraint as a principle of universal grammar that applies to the distribution of tokens in spontaneous speech.

lower, at .52, as we would expect. The semiweak verbs are ambiguous in their grammatical status: some speakers appear to analyze the derivational *+t* suffix as a past tense signal, while others do not. The mean value of .91 is therefore intermediate, and the treatment of the semiweak verbs is not inconsistent with the functional explanation of the behavior of past tense forms.[7]

However, Guy (1991) points out that a functional explanation would predict that *-ed* in the present perfect *have walked* would be deleted much more often than *-ed* in the regular past tense, since the present perfect is marked primarily by the auxiliary *have*, and the /t/ or /d/ is redundant. This is not what we find, however. The treatment of this *-ed* suffix is not significantly different from that of the regular past tense *-ed*, and this is accordingly a counterfunctional effect.

It is reasonable to ask, if functional effects do not explain the *-t,d* grammatical pattern, what does? Guy has recently pursued this question within the structural framework of lexical phonology. The exponential hypothesis (Guy 1991) predicts that the actual numerical relations between monomorphemic, semiweak, and preterit forms will be in the ratios $x^3:x^2:x$ as a result of the fact that they have been affected by the *-t,d* deletion rule three times, twice, and once respectively: monomorphemic within the base morpheme; monomorphemic and semiweak forms after level 1 affixation and bracket erasure; and, after level 2 affixation and bracket erasure, all three types. Both preterit and past participle morphemes are level 2 affixes, and this treatment is thus perfectly consistent with the fact that the preterit and the past participle share the same values of *-t,d* retention. At this point, a number of issues remain to be resolved: what other languages show this effect (and why Ladakhi does not); whether the exponential relation fits the data better than other mathematical models; whether the stress constraint shows the effect of such iterative application, and so on. But the exponential hypothesis fits in with the general pattern found throughout this chapter: that variable morphological constraints are accounted for by mechanical and structural factors rather than functional tendencies to preserve information.

The perfect (s) of Ladakhi

An opportunity to test the generality of functional effects on the deletion of grammatical segments appeared in Koshal's sociolinguistic study of Ladakhi, a Sino-Tibetan language spoken in the Himalayan region of northwestern India. Ladakhi has final clusters ending in /s/ where the /s/ is variably deleted in a process that affects initial clusters as well. In final

---

[7] This intermediate value ultimately turned out to mask a wide range of individual values, correlated primarily with age, since the actual value assigned to the ambiguous class depends upon the developing grammatical analysis of the speaker (Guy and Boyd 1990).

position, the /s/ is sometimes a part of the stem, and sometimes the perfect marker. When the /s/ disappears, the perfect is then unmarked and opposed to many other tenses that are marked with suffixes. But the imperative is also unmarked, and it is not difficult to construct sentences that are ambiguous between imperative and perfect if the /s/ is missing. Thus the sentence *Khyo-rang-ngi pene khyer-s* is heard as 'You took the money' with a perfect indicative meaning. But when the perfect /s/ is deleted after the verb, it becomes *Khyo-rang-ngi pene khyer*, homonymous with the imperative 'Take the money'. An even more pernicious collapse of distinctions occurs when the /s/ is deleted before the participial suffix *-kan*. *Tang-s-kan* means 'something given'. But when the /s/ is deleted, one can no longer distinguish this participial construction from the result of adding *-kan* directly to the verbal root, where it functions as a noun-forming suffix. Thus *tang-kan* can mean either 'something given' with a deleted perfect /s/, or 'one who gives, a giver', with no /s/ understood.

The situation is quite parallel to English *-t,d* deletion, and offers an excellent opportunity to examine the generality of the functional hypothesis. Koshal's preliminary analysis, carried out at the Linguistics Laboratory of the University of Pennsylvania, made a distinction between lexical clusters and grammatical clusters. Men's and women's speech was analyzed separately, with the results shown in table 19.2. In neither case is there a significant difference between lexical and grammatical clusters. There appears to be no functional differentiation with respect to the deletion of Ladakhi /s/.

The deletion of plural /s/ in Spanish

The most intensively studied variable of this type is final /s/ in Spanish, which undergoes aspiration and deletion in a variety of European and Latin American dialects. Terrell (1981) summarizes a wide range of studies and shows that in the extreme case of the Dominican Republic, /s/ can no longer be considered a base form. The most careful exploration of func-

Table 19.2 Grammatical constraint on /s/ deletion in Ladakhi for men and women

| | VARBRUL WEIGHT FOR /s/ DELETION | |
	Lexical	Grammatical
Men	.50	.50
Women	.53	.47

tional effects on this process is found in the work of Poplack (1979, 1980, 1981). In her study of Puerto Rican Spanish in Philadelphia, Poplack considered many sources of information besides the plural inflection itself: morphological, syntactic, semantic, and cultural factors. The data to follow are drawn from Poplack 1980, to illustrate the relations between functional and counterfunctional effects, considering the deletion of both the variable (s) in the plural of noun phrases and the variable (n) in the third person plural of verbs.[8] To underline the application of the data to functional explanations, I will mark each data set as FUNCTIONAL or COUNTERFUNC-TIONAL.

To begin with, Poplack replicated the earlier finding of Ma and Heras-imchuk (1968) that the relationship between monomorphemic and grammatical forms reversed the English situation (see table 19.3). She then carried out an extensive variable rule analysis, simultaneously examining the effects of phonological, syntactic, morphological, and cultural factors on the realization of Spanish /s/. Each of the tables to follow is an extract from that single analysis, showing the constraints on deletion by the weights assigned to each possibility in a factor group.

The plural inflection /s/ can appear on several elements of the Spanish noun phrase. For example, there can be a determiner, a noun, and an adjective, as in (4).

(4)   la*s* cosa*s* bonita*s*

Poplack accordingly examined the effect of grammatical role in the noun

Table 19.3   Effect of grammatical status on deletion of /s/ and /n/ in Puerto Rican Spanish

Grammatical status	*% deletion*		
	(s)	*(n)*	
Inflectional	68	9	COUNTERFUNCTIONAL
Monomorphemic	54	1	

[8] Poplack studied the aspiration and deletion of the variable (s), and the nasalization, weakening, and deletion of (n). The tables to follow will present only the constraints on the deletion of these inflections. Aspiration and nasal weakening would not be subject to any functional constraint, since they leave some phonetic substance that can identify the inflection.

Table 19.4   Effect of grammatical category within the noun phrase on /s/ deletion

Grammatical category	Varbrul weight for /s/ deletion	
Determiner	.26	⎫
Noun	.57	⎬ FUNCTIONAL?
Adjective	.69	⎭

phrase in the factor group shown in table 19.4. For this factor group I have inserted FUNCTIONAL? with a question mark. To be sure, it is often argued that it is a functional effect for necessary information to be presented first, and not later, since it would then be redundant. Here the -*s* inflection is present most often with the determiner, in initial position, less often with the noun that follows, and still less often with the adjective that follows next. But this assumes that listeners process the information in each word of a phrase in the order in which they received it. This is a dubious assumption, and there is much psycholinguistic evidence against it. Furthermore, Guy points out that if we do accept this argument, we must then accept the idea that the English language is massively counterfunctional, for in English, the plural marker normally appears on the last element of the noun phrase:

(5)   the beautiful thing*s*

Poplack explored in more detail the effect of the position of the /s/ inflection in the linear order of the Spanish noun phrase, and her results have since been replicated by others. Consider first the case of the third element in three-element strings. As table 19.5 illustrates, there are four possible realizations of the inflections in the first two elements (where S represents the presence of /s/, and 0 its absence). These can be divided into two

Table 19.5   /s/ and 0 in three-element Spanish noun phrases

POSITION			
1	*2*	*3*	
S	S	—	las cosas bonita-
S	0	—	las cosa bonita-
0	S	—	la cosas bonita-
0	0	—	la cosa bonita-

relevant sets. In the first three cases, there is at least one preceding /s/, and so the plural information is preserved; in the fourth case, 00__, there is no such plural information, and the morphological plural information depends on an inflection in the third element alone. A functional theory must predict a lower probability of deletion in the 00__ case, but as table 19.6 shows, this is not what Poplack found. The same situation prevails with two-element strings.

In both cases, we see the tendency of a speaker to continue the pattern set at the beginning of the noun phrase: an /s/ tends to produce an /s/, and a zero tends to produce a zero. We may refer to this as *perseverance* or *concord*. Poplack relates this concordial tendency to a principle of least effort at the grammatical level, an extension of the principle of least effort at the phonetic level first articulated by Martinet (1961).

In the same factor group, there remains only one case to be examined in table 19.6: noun phrases that have a single member. If there is no supporting information in the noun phrase, there is the least tendency to delete the plural /s/, and we have what seems to be a clear functional effect. We will consider this case in more detail below.

Spanish sentences also show the plural by an /n/ inflection on the verb:

(6)   a.   La reina manda.   'The queen commands.'
       b.   Las reinas mandan.   'The queens command.'
(7)   a.   La reina es bonita.   'The queen is beautiful.'
       b.   Las reinas son bonitas.   'The queens are beautiful.'

The contrast between (6a) and (6b) shows the most common situation. Just as the /s/ is the sole indicator of the plural in the feminine noun phrase, so the /n/ is the sole indicator of the plural in the third person verb. But in (7a) and (7b), with the irregular verb *ser* 'to be', /n/ is not the only

Table 19.6   Effect of serial ordering in the noun phrase on deletion of plural /s/

	Varbrul weight for /s/ deletion	
Three-element string		
/s/ preceding [SS__, S0__, 0S__]	.44	COUNTERFUNCTIONAL
No /s/ preceding [00__]	.73	
Two-element string		
/s/ preceding [S__]	.44	COUNTERFUNCTIONAL
No /s/ preceding [0__]	.52	
Single noun phrase	.24	FUNCTIONAL

indicator of plurality in the verb. A functional theory would therefore predict a higher rate of deletion of the (n) in (6b) than in (7b). However, as table 19.7 shows, Poplack's analysis reveals the opposite.

This result parallels the pattern found in Brazilian Portuguese, termed the *principle of salience* by Lemle and Naro (1977). According to this principle, the more prominent the inflectional marking is, the more phonetic substance associated with it, the greater the tendency to retain the inflection (see also Guy 1981). The effect of salience has been demonstrated by a fine-grained correlation with phonetic substance. In Portuguese, as in Spanish, the results are the reverse of what a functional theory would predict.

Poplack also considered the position of the subject noun phrase with respect to the verb. A functional argument would predict that if the subject noun phrase occurs before the verb, and the noun carries plural marking, the /n/ of the verb is less likely to be needed; but if the subject noun phrase occurs after the verb, plural information on the verb is more likely to be needed. But table 19.7 also shows that these predictions are not borne out.

The great majority of Poplack's findings are therefore counterfunctional in nature, and call the generality of the functional hypothesis into question. But so far we have considered only inflectional information. Poplack explored many other sources of information that might support a plural interpretation:

(8) a. un grupo de plantas   'a group of plants'
     b. Hablan con muertos.   'They talk with the dead.'
     c. arroz con habichuelas   'rice with beans'
     d. Yo mis hijos les digo.   'I tell my kids.'

In (8a), the lexical item *grupo* lets us know that the speaker is referring to more than one plant, irrespective of the presence of the /s/. In (8b), syntactic structure tells us that 'dead' refers to more than one spirit: Spanish

Table 19.7 Constraints on the deletion of verbal /n/ in Puerto Rican Spanish

	Varbrul weight for /n/ deletion	
Regular verb	.78	COUNTERFUNCTIONAL
Irregular verb	.22	
NP after verb	.69	
NP before and after	.42	COUNTERFUNCTIONAL
NP before verb	.38	

never omits the article in the singular. In (8c), cultural knowledge defines the beans as more than one bean, whether or not the /s/ is realized. And in (8d), the listener's awareness of the speaker's family situation indicates that the speaker is referring to more than one child, even if the three /s/'s are deleted.

Poplack considered the effect of the presence of such morphological and syntactic information, along with pragmatic information, on the deletion of plural /s/ in two factor groups; her results are displayed in table 19.8.

These are relatively weak effects compared to the counterfunctional effects noted above. But the most powerful functional argument of all appeared when Poplack considered sentences containing no disambiguating information at all – neither morphological nor pragmatic nor cultural. Here plural /s/ and /n/ were never deleted. But as Guy (1981) points out, and Poplack (1981) emphasizes, this cannot be taken as evidence for a functional account. It is not possible for a listener to know that a speaker has signaled a plural inflection if the inflection does not appear and there is no other information telling the listener that it is a plural. Therefore, in a study like Poplack's, the coder doing the linguistic analysis will automatically classify such utterances as singular. Guy's study of parallel phenomena in Brazilian Portuguese shows that the analytical problem is not limited to the extreme case of no supporting information. The overestimation of functionalism is a more general process, a regular result of misclassifying sentences as singular instead of plural.

The loss of the plural in Portuguese

Guy's (1981) study of the deletion of /s/ in Brazilian Portuguese focused on a large body of data collected by MOBRAL, a research project concerned with increasing literacy among adults in Rio de Janeiro. In his exposition of the functional problem, Guy begins with 5,247 tokens of noun

Table 19.8 Comparative effects of morphological and nonmorphological information on the deletion of Puerto Rican Spanish plural /s/

	Varbrul weight for deletion of /s/	
Morphological disambiguating information		
Present	.57	FUNCTIONAL
Not present	.43	
Nonmorphological disambiguating information		
Present	.59	FUNCTIONAL
Not present	.41	

phrases consisting solely of a noun, where there is no opportunity for supporting inflections. As table 19.9 shows, the tendency to preserve the /s/ inflection in these cases is even greater than in Spanish: 95.4% /s/ and only 4.6% zero. With two-element noun phrases, the usual procedure is to focus on the possibility of deleting /s/ on the second element, and the effect of an inflection on the first element on such a deletion. Table 19.9 shows that there is a strong functional effect.

If we now turn our attention to the first element of these two-element noun phrases, we would expect to find the same percentage with zero inflections (hereafter, zeroes) as in one-element noun phrases, namely 4.6%. Nothing in a functional argument would predict otherwise, since this first element is not affected by any inflections before it, realized as zero or /s/.[9] Guy found 2,799 such two-element phrases in his data. One would accordingly expect 128 with zeroes, or 4.6%, but there were only 70, or 2.5%.

(9)   *Calculation of missing zeroes*

Total two-element NPs [= 2,729 + 70]	2,799
Zeroes expected from table 19.9 [= .046 * 2,799]	128
Zeroes found in table 19.9 [= 7 + 63]	70
Zeroes missing	58

What happened to the other 58 tokens? It stands to reason that they were tokens with a zero preceding a zero, since these are the type that are most likely to be classified as singulars instead of plurals. If we follow that logic

Table 19.9 Functional effects in plural marking of Brazilian Portuguese noun phrases

	0	/s/	Total	% deletion	
One-element noun phrases	241	5,201	5,247	4.6	
Second element of two-element noun phrase					
/s/ inflection preceding	2,046	683	2,729	75.0	} FUNCTIONAL
No /s/ preceding	7	63	70	10.0	

[9] Before we finish with the argument, however, we will consider the consequences of not making this assumption.

in replacing them, we obtain the revised figures shown in the top half of table 19.10.

The functional effect has shrunk considerably. Yet in all probability, it is still considerably overstated. Let us continue Guy's original argument by returning to the figure of 95.4% /s/ in single-element noun phrases. These instances of /s/ have no morphological support from other sites within the noun phrase, and their identification as plurals must depend on the various other sorts of information discussed above. It is inevitable that listeners would misinterpret a number of these plurals as singulars, just as they do with two-element noun phrases. Let us assume, as a first approximation, that the proportion of single-noun plurals misinterpreted as singulars is comparable to the proportion of two-element noun phrases misinterpreted as singulars. There we had to increase the number of zeroes by 82%. If we do the same for the single-element noun phrases, we obtain the revised figures shown in the bottom half of table 19.10. If 7.7% is a more correct estimate of the number of /s/'s deleted in single-noun plurals, then phrases intended as plurals will have no disambiguating support, and will consequently be heard as singulars. If that is so, the calculation of missing zeroes in (9) must also be revised:

(10) *Calculation of missing zeroes (revised)*
      Total two-element NPs   2,799
      Zeroes expected from table 19.10 [= .077 * 2,799]   215
      Zeroes found in table 19.9   70
      Zeroes missing   145

Next we must again revise the calculation for two-element noun phrases that was used to estimate the functional effect; the results appear in table 19.11.

At this point, the functional effect has disappeared. This particular mode of calculation is recursive, and would force the estimates for one- and two-

Table 19.10 Functional effects in plural marking of Brazilian Portuguese noun phrases: Revised estimate

	0	/s/	Total	% deletion	
Second element of two-element noun phrase					
/s/ inflection preceding	2,046	683	2,729	75.0	FUNCTIONAL
No /s/ preceding	63	65	128	49.2	
One-element noun phrases	438 [= 1.82 * 241]	5,201	5,639	7.77	

Table 19.11 Functional effects in plural marking of Brazilian Portuguese noun phrases: Second revision

	0	/s/	Total	% deletion
Second element of two-element noun phrase				
/s/ inflection preceding	2,046	683	2,729	75.0
No /s/ preceding	152	65	217	70.0

element noun phrases to readjust each other in an upwardly mounting spiral. In any case, it seems clear that the true percentage of deletion is higher than we would first estimate from the reported frequency of zeroes with single noun phrases, and the functional effect is accordingly smaller than the 75%–49% differential derived from the first calculation.

REEXAMINING THE ORIGINAL ASSUMPTION

These calculations were based on the assumption that the percentage of deletion for the first element of two-element noun phrases was the same as that for single noun phrases. Now let us consider the consequences if this assumption is not valid.

- If the rate of deletion for two-element noun phrases were actually *higher* than for single noun phrases, then the effect of these calculations would be increased: there would be more missing zeroes.
- If the rate of deletion for two-element noun phrases were actually *lower* than for single noun phrases, this in itself would be a counterfunctional argument. Since speakers have two opportunities rather than one to convey the plural information, a functional theory would predict more deletion when a second element follows than when one does not.

A functional theory therefore could not in principle adopt such an assumption.

We thus come to the conclusion, following Guy's elegant quantitative argument, that many of the functional effects reported in the literature are the result of loss of data in coding that leads to a systematic underestimation of the extent of deletion whenever a sentence contains less supporting information. The result is a systematic overestimation of functional arguments.

WHERE ARE THE MISSING ZEROES?

The critical reader must certainly have long since asked the question, "Where are the missing zeroes?" If there is so much misinterpretation of plurals as singulars in Brazilian Portuguese, why have these problems of communication not been reported? Would the frequency of misinterpretations be greater or lesser in actual conversation than in the linguistic coding? What would happen if the interview materials were meticulously reexamined for possible errors or ambiguities of number?

I do not have a complete answer to these questions, but some hints are available from the results of the CDC project in the United States.

Several chapters in this volume have drawn upon the CDC study of natural misunderstandings to make inferences about the effects of misunderstanding upon language change. The same study has demonstrated that the actual number of misunderstandings in everyday life is much greater than casual observations lead us to believe. If we ask someone to write down the misunderstandings that occur in the course of a day, we will receive a half dozen or so at the end of a week. If we don't succeed in getting people to write these events down, they will of course not remember the details. But it is surprising to find that people will not remember that any misunderstandings occurred at all.

The actual misunderstandings recorded are heavily concentrated among those that are quickly detected because they do not fit the pragmatics of the immediate situation. A smaller number are detected by accident. For 613 examples whose mode of detection was established, table 19.12 shows the percentages of the various modes.

The smallest categories are made up of errors that are detected only accidentally, or never. These are the most important, from several points of view: they represent a much larger number of errors that cause misunderstanding, but are never detected. How large the number is would be difficult to say, but it is not unlikely that it would be of the same order of magnitude as the missing zeroes in the Brazilian Portuguese situation. Here is an example of a naturally occurring misunderstanding of the last category. It took place at a dinner table in South Philadelphia, where I was a guest. The wife came out of the kitchen, saying, "All right, everybody to the table!"

Table 19.12 Modes of detection of naturally occurring misunderstandings

	%
Corrected by listener before the utterance was finished	13
Correction elicited by immediate inquiry of the listener	48
Inferred from later utterances in the conversation	27
Corrected from events that followed accidentally	10
Never corrected by hearer or listener [observed by a third person]	2

(11) WL [to wife]:   You run a tight ship.
      Husband: She makes us slaves.
      Wife [puzzled]:   Why would I want you to leave?
      Husband [irritated]: One day, we'll explain it all to R___ [her
                            name].

The misunderstanding here is the direct result of one of the new and vigorous changes in Philadelphia, the raising of checked (ey) from mid to high,
overlapping with /iy/. The vowel of *slave* is pronounced close to [i:]; the
initial /s/ of *slave* is neutralized by the preceding /s/ of *us*.

(12) She makes us slaves.   [šime⊥ksʌsli⊤:vz]
      She makes us leave.   [šime⊥ksʌsli:v]

The wife heard her husband's utterance as *She makes us leave*. She thus
heard from her husband a bad-tempered, even insulting utterance *makes
us leave*, instead of the intended joking remark, *She makes us slaves*. The
resulting irritation between husband and wife was not resolved.

   The frequency of this type of misunderstanding is difficult to estimate,
since in principle, the great majority of such events will escape observation.
It is interesting to note that in this case a plural inflection on *slaves* that
might have prevented the misunderstanding was not detected, even though
there is no variation in the use of the plural in this South Philadelphia
dialect. It stands to reason that a variable inflection would be associated
with many more cases of misinterpretation.

Subject-verb concord in Portuguese

Poplack's study of Puerto Rican Spanish in Philadelphia showed a powerful and consistent effect of concord, in that a preceding zero favored a
following zero, and a preceding /s/ favored a following /s/. The comparable
phenomenon in the Portuguese verbal system has been subjected to a penetrating study by Scherre and Naro (1991). Like Spanish, Portuguese
shows variation of plural marking in the verb phrase as well as the noun
phrase. Thus the utterance in (13) is possible, where all three parenthesized plural marks can be present or absent.

(13) A(s) pessoa(s)   não   pode(m)   chegar.
      people   [neg]   can   get there

Some verbs are marked with a simple nasal consonant (realized as nasality
of the vowel), while in other cases more phonetic substance is involved in
marking the plural. Scherre and Naro's study is not concerned with any
one form of plural marking, but with whether the plural is marked at all.

In this case, the strings did not consist of juxtaposed elements, but of successive finite verbs with the same plural subject. These were generally discontinuous: sometimes clauses were successive, but sometimes they were separated by a number of other clauses. The sequences that Scherre and Naro coded were defined as verbs with the same plural subject in continuous utterances of the same speaker, separated by no more than 10 other clauses.[10] Reviewing Poplack's findings, they raised the question whether a verb that was marked for plurality would be more likely to be followed by a verb unmarked for plurality, as the functionalist hypothesis would predict, or by a marked verb, as Poplack's noun phrase results would predict. The sample consisted of 64 speakers from Rio de Janeiro, stratified for sex, age, and education. From this data set, Scherre and Naro derived 4,073 tokens for subject-verb agreement. Table 19.13 shows the counterfunctional character of their basic findings. Scherre and Naro point out that isolated or first-of-a-series verbs show no effect at all: their frequency of marking is the same as the mean for the entire corpus. But when a plural-marked verb precedes, the probability of marking rises, and when an unmarked verb precedes, the probability of marking falls dramatically. These results then replicate the principle of concords shown by the Spanish noun phrase: marks beget marks, and zeroes beget zeroes.

This effect is remarkably robust. Since Portuguese is a pro-drop language, there are many verbs whose subjects are ambiguous. Scherre and Naro calculated the same figures with all ambiguous cases dropped, with the same result. They found identical patterns for sequences of predicate adjectives. Within the clause, they examined the relationship between the verbal plural marking, and whether the last element of the subject had an /s/ inflection or not. The results are shown in table 19.14. Again, similar results were found for predicate adjectives, in relation to the subject, and

Table 19.13 Marking of verbs at discourse level according to marking of preceding verb in Brazilian Portuguese

	N	% marked	Varbrul weight
Verb preceded by marked verb	1,671	84	.66
Verb preceded by unmarked verb	608	35	.18
Isolated or first of a series	1,794	73	.48
Total	4,073	72	

---

[10] The length of discourse over which this effect operates might seem surprising, but it is not atypical of other priming effects in syntax (Estival 1985). Chapter 20 will present data on the priming of passive constructions.

in relation to the mark on the preceding verb. Scherre and Naro's results leave no doubt that the dominant constraint on variation in the marking of Portuguese verbs is not a functional one. From the standpoint of the traditional functional argument, what we are seeing is not a tendency to preserve semantic information on the surface, but rather a tendency to use marks where they are least needed, and omit them where they are most needed. That is not to say that this parallelism of structure is without its contribution to the economy of the language. Rather, it joins the study of variation in inflections to the general study of concord in language, an area where it has long been recognized that functional arguments are very difficult to sustain.

Table 19.14   Marking of verbs at clausal level according to marking of preceding verb in Brazilian Portuguese

	N	% marked	Varbrul weight
/s/ present on last element	2,134	84	.56
0 present on last element	322	48	.18

19.4   Conclusion

The results of this chapter show an extraordinary consistency. Given phonological and morphological variation, the functional hypothesis predicts a tendency for speakers to choose one variant or the other in a fashion that will preserve information. Most of the results cited show the opposite: in the stream of speech, one variant or the other is chosen without regard to the maximization of information. On the contrary, the major effects that determine such choices are mechanical: phonetic conditioning and simple repetition of the preceding structure.

So far, the results favor the Neogrammarian view that language change is phonetically determined and mechanical. However, we have not yet looked at change: all of the cases considered here are examples of stable variation. When language changes, its information-carrying capacity is often threatened; but in the long run, most languages do preserve their means of conveying information, more or less, by one route or another. Though speakers may not behave wisely and thoughtfully as they choose one variant or the other, somehow the system does react. Chapter 20 will present some evidence of such reactions, and construct a model that suggests how they come about.

20

The Maintenance of Meaning

The developments of chapter 19 called into question the validity of most arguments for functional constraints on linguistic variation. Though most of the discussion considered stable variables, it would be hard to posit a functionally controlled process of change if there were no synchronic mechanism that allows functional constraints to emerge. Yet there is no doubt that in some way or other, linguistic systems respond to change in ways that maintain meaning – more or less.

A typical case is the radical reduction of final consonants in French. One of the results of this process was the elimination of the final /s/ that marked plural inflections in the noun phrase in the same way as the final /s/ in Portuguese and Spanish. French originally signaled the feminine plural of the article as *las* (vs. singular *la*), just as Spanish does. The /s/ is preserved in the underlying form of the article, since it is realized phonetically when the next word begins with a vowel. This does not of course satisfy the functional hypothesis, since liaison does not convey any plural information in the majority of cases, when the next word does not begin with a vowel. Through some process of systemic readjustment that is yet to be understood, the feminine plural is now consistently signaled by an opposition of vowel quality, opposing /le pɔm/ 'the apples' to /la pɔm/ 'the apple'. The readjustment is far from complete, since there are forms of the determiner that do not show such vowel change. This is illustrated in a sentence from one of de Gaulle's speeches:

(1) Je m'addresse aux peuples – *au pluriel.*
     'I address myself to the peoples – in the plural.'

The metaremark *au pluriel* was required since here the loss of final sibilants in the noun is not compensated for by vowel change in the determiner. The morphophonemic contraction of (2a) is not distinguished from the contraction of (2b) when a vowel does not follow.

(2)   a.   à   le   → au   b.   à   les   → aux
            /a   lə/   → /o/   /a   le/   → /o/
            'to   the [sg]'   'to   the [pl]'

Thus the processes that maintain meaning are effective on the whole but not compelling, so that some meaning is lost in the course of change.

Like the other Romance languages, French also formerly relied on final /s/ in the verbal system, most commonly to signal the difference between second and third person singular, as in (3).

(3)   a.   /va/ + /s/   b.   /va/ +   0
                 'go   2nd sg.'   'go   3rd sg.'

Here there was no vowel change in the paradigm that maintained the difference in meaning. Instead the burden of conveying information shifted to the pronoun, as French optional subjects became obligatory clitics.

(4)   a.   /tu/ + /va/   b.   /il/ +   /va/
                 '2nd sg. go'   '3rd sg. go'

These two examples show how long-range changes in the French phonological, morphological, and syntactic systems compensated for sound changes, in ways that suggest a causal link. This does not seem completely consistent with the results of chapter 19, which showed that speakers do not take meaning into account in choosing one variant or another. We can best approach this problem by examining some recent results of multivariate analysis that allow both functional and mechanical effects to emerge, and that measure their relative weights.

20.1   Some functional effects on the paradigmatic system of Spanish

The negative results on functional effects considered so far have been largely concentrated in the syntagmatic aspect of language. The studies of Spanish and Portuguese noun phrases, and concord with the verb phrase, have all envisaged a functional effect that operates in the stream of speech, where the speaker has the opportunity to adjust the choice of variants at one point to compensate for the presence or loss of information at other points: that is, structural differentiation. All the evidence accumulated so far indicates that this is not a strong influence on speakers' behavior. Rather, speakers are more influenced by the tendency toward structural parallelism.

The change in the vowel of the French plural determiner was a change in the paradigmatic system of morphological alternation. In long-range changes we do find evidence that the system has reacted to variable deletion in a way that tends to preserve information. Hochberg (1985) examines to orthogonal effects on the deletion of /s/ in a study of 10 Puerto

Rican speakers from Boston. One is the effect of the syntagmatic sequence of /s/ and zero that Poplack had measured. The other is a purely informational question: whether the form of the determiner itself conveys plural information, with or without an /s/. Thus (5a) is ambiguous, since no signals of plurality remain, but (5b) is not, since *much-* is itself a signal of plurality.

(5)   a.   la-0   planta-0   b.   mucha-0 planta-0
               'the-?   plant-?'   'many   plants'

The results shown in table 20.1 are from an interactive group of four factors, each a combination of two conditions: whether a zero or an /s/ precedes, and whether or not the determiner itself contains plural information. The results register two constraints: the counterfunctional and mechanical perseverance effect, which leads the speaker to follow a zero with a zero, and a functional information effect, which would lead the speaker to preserve an /s/ if it was needed to signal the plural.

The mechanical perseverance effect favors deletion wherever the determiner or quantifier (DET here is shorthand for both) has a zero inflection, and disfavors deletion wherever it has an /s/. Thus .68 is larger than .44, and .55 is larger than .33. Deletion is also favored when the determiner or quantifier is identifiable as a plural, even when the /s/ inflection is not present (.68 vs. .55); it is disfavored when the determiner or quantifier is not so identified (.44 vs. .33). The upper left cell then shows the confluence of both mechanical and functional effects, and consequently the highest probability of deletion; the lower right cell shows the case where both disfavor deletion, and consequently the lowest probability; and the mixed cases are intermediate. It is also clear that the mechanical perseverance

Table 20.1 Mechanical and functional constraints on deletion of Puerto Rican Spanish plural /s/

FUNCTIONAL CONSTRAINT		MECHANICAL CONSTRAINT	
		Favors deletion	*Disfavors deletion*
Determiner identifiable as plural	Favors deletion	DET + 0__ .68	DET + /s/__ .44
Determiner not identifiable as plural	Disfavors deletion	DET + 0__ .55	____ .33

effect outweighs the functional effect. In both cases where the mechanical effect is favorable, the probabilities are above .5; in both cases where it is not favorable, the probabilities are below .5.

The small paradigmatic adjustment that we are witnessing here is a tendency to preserve the /s/ more often with the feminine articles *las, unas* and to delete it more often with the quantifiers *muchas, todas*, etc. A rather different kind of paradigmatic adjustment was found in a small study by Flores, Myhill, and Tarallo (1983). They examined the difference between masculine and feminine determiners in a group of Puerto Rican speakers in Philadelphia. The structural situation would lead one to predict a functional difference:

(6)

	Singular	*Plural*
Masculine	el hombre	los hombres
Feminine	la mujer	las mujeres

In the masculine article, the presence or absence of /s/ is one of two marks of the singular/plural difference; in the feminine article, it is the only mark. As we see in table 20.2, the percentages of deletion show a small but significant difference. Thus it appears that the vowel difference in the masculine article will carry some of the plural information.

In her study of 10 Puerto Rican speakers in Boston, Hochberg (1986a,b) explored functional readjustments in the use of pronouns in relation to the -*s* of the second singular, in a pattern that resembles the long-range developments of French cited in (3)–(4). The following paradigm shows the use of final concordial inflections in the Spanish present tense for the root *estudia-* 'to study':

(7)

	Singular	*Plural*
1st	(yo) estudi*o*	(nosotros) estudi*amos*
2nd	(tu) estudia*s*	
3rd	(el, ella, usted) estudia	(ellos, ellas, ustedes) estudia*n*

In the present tense of *estudiar*, /s/ is the only segment that distinguishes

Table 20.2   Percentage deletion of Spanish /s/ in Philadelphia

	% deletion	*N*	
Masculine	19.7	269	FUNCTIONAL, $p < .05$
Feminine	12.5	191	

the second and third person singular, just as the *n* distinguishes the third plural. On the other hand, the /s/ of the first person plural is part of the salient inflection -*amos*, where it functions much like the monomorphemic /s/ in *más*. It should follow by the functional hypothesis that the tendency to delete the second singular /s/ would be the lowest. On this point, Hochberg's findings support the counterfunctional tendencies outlined in chapter 19: second person singular /s/ is dropped in 84% of the cases, as compared with an overall deletion rate of 53%.

However, Hochberg found that the system readjusts for this loss by the differential use of pronouns, which are variable in all Spanish dialects as indicated by the parentheses in (7). Figure 20.1 shows the percentage of pronoun use for the five subject pronoun types for three types of verbs. In type A, the loss of /s/ produces homonymy of first, second, and third persons singular (the conditional, the imperfect, and the present and imperfect subjunctive). In type B, only the second and third persons fall together (present, perfect, future indicative). In type C, the deletion of /s/ produces no loss of contrast in the verbal paradigm (preterit, present of *ser* 'to be').

Figure 20.1 shows a fine-grained adjustment of pronoun use to the frequent loss of /s/ in the second singular. First, *tu* is the most frequent pronoun across the board; the least frequent is *nosotros*, where the inflection is never in danger. The rate of /n/ deletion is much lower than that of /s/ deletion, and the use of third plural pronouns is accordingly quite low.

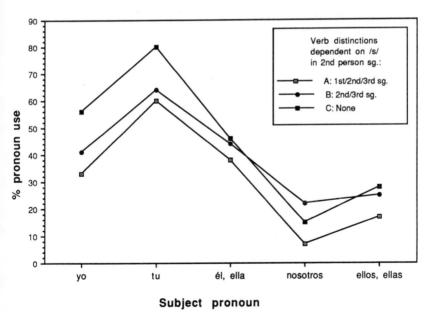

Figure 20.1. Percentage of pronoun use in Spanish by person and tense contrasts depending on /s/

Furthermore, the adjustment of pronoun use is fine-grained enough to match the amount of homonymy produced by the loss of /s/. The contrast between the two extreme types A and C is quite regular; there is some fluctuation with type B, especially where a low number of tokens is involved.

These results are quite different from those found in chapter 19. They are not based on the examination of individual uses of /s/ or *tu*, and they are not concerned with the relationship between a particular use of *tu* and a particular occurrence or nonoccurrence of second singular /s/. Instead, they register the overall paradigmatic shift in the frequency of elements that are systematically related. The fact that the second singular shows a rate of /s/ deletion much higher than the norm indicates again that the important contrast among first, second, and third singular is not preserved by a direct modification of the variable rule involved here, or by direct intervention in the process of linguistic change that produced this result, as Kiparsky's functional hypothesis would predict. Yet the system has readjusted by the differential use of pronouns.

20.2   Further exploration of functional effects in Puerto Rico and Madrid

Hochberg's analysis made good use of a small data base, a study of 10 Puerto Rican speakers in Boston. If the functional effects displayed were strong ones, we would expect them to be replicated in other studies, in proportion to the amount of deletion of verbal /s/. Furthermore, we should *not* find such pronominal distributions for Spanish dialects that have no /s/ deletion, like those of Madrid or Mexico City. Cameron (1992) explores these issues; it may be helpful at this stage to look briefly at the results that bear most directly on the question of functional compensation. Cameron draws 10 educated speakers from his larger sample of 62 from San Juan, Puerto Rico, to compare with 10 educated speakers from Madrid in the materials published in Esgueva and Cantarero 1981. Each group includes 5 men and 5 women.

A gross comparison of the Madrid and San Juan data shows a sizeable difference between the two cities in the use of pronouns in both singular and plural (see table 20.3). This table supports the functional argument advanced by Hochberg (1986a) that twice as high a percentage of pronouns is realized in Puerto Rico, where /s/ is aspirated and deleted, than in Spain, where it is not. This may be due to the same kind of systemic adjustment that was responsible for the overall rise of pronoun use in French. One way of seeing if this is true would be to compare various components of the functional effect in both speech communities. Cameron finds that switch reference – a change in the referent of the subject as

Table 20.3 Overall percentage of pronoun use in San Juan
and Madrid

	SAN JUAN		MADRID	
	+*Pro*	N	+*Pro*	N
Singular	50%	1,768	26%	1,509
Plural	19%	358	7%	549

compared to the last subject mentioned – is a strong determinant of pronoun use. This cannot be an immediate effect of the loss of /s/, since it appears prominently in Mexican Spanish (Silva-Corvalán 1982) as well as in Madrid. Table 20.4 shows a remarkable identity in the effect of switch reference and same reference on pronoun use for both San Juan and Madrid, despite the fact that the levels of pronoun use are quite different. The effect of switch reference appears to be the result of the factor that operates generally on the expression of pronouns in pro-drop languages: the pronoun provides contrastive information that reinforces switch reference.

We can make a finer comparison of the San Juan and Madrid systems by examining the correlation of pronoun use with the degrees of ambiguity of the verb that results from the deletion of second singular /s/. Figure 20.2 shows that the Varbrul weights for the two systems are again almost identical.[1] In the case of switch reference there is a significant correlation with verb class for both cities, with very similar values, while there is no

Table 20.4 Effect of switch reference on
pronoun use in San Juan and Madrid

	VARBRUL WEIGHTS FOR PRONOUN USE	
	San Juan	*Madrid*
Switch	.64	.65
Same	.34	.34

[1] In both Hochberg's and Cameron's analyses, the class of verbs that show no ambiguity with the loss of verbal /s/ is confined to the preterit, and does not include *ser* 'to be'. Cameron limited his analysis to the singular, where the situation is more straightforward than with the plural.

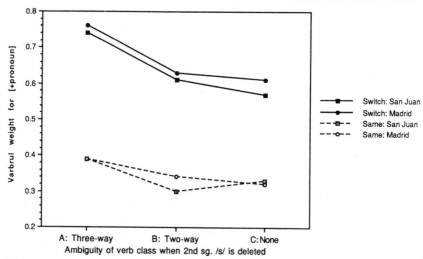

Figure 20.2.   Pronoun use in San Juan and Madrid by switch reference and potential ambiguity of verb (adapted from Cameron, 1992)

significant correlation for same reference, with the same low values for both cities. Thus whatever functional relations determine pronominal use in Spanish are not influenced by the variable deletion of verbal /s/, and there is no correlation between verbal morphology and pronominal use.

Cameron's detailed analyses of the distribution of pronoun use in San Juan do not show close correlations between the use of a given pronoun and the presence or absence of /s/. The greatest percentage of pronoun use is found with nonspecific *tu* (used for the generalized other, as in *uno*), where the least information is being conveyed on person and number. Cameron then studied the specific correlation between the presence or absence of second singular /s/ and the presence or absence of the pronoun *tu* in San Juan Spanish. Some significant evidence for functional compensation appeared at the .05 level, but it was distributed irregularly across social groups in a pattern that is difficult to explain. The existence of functional compensation in the stream of speech may exist, but if so, it is certainly the weakest of many effects operating upon the variable /s/ inflection and the pronoun. The comparison of San Juan and Madrid shows that whatever processes are operating to increase pronoun use in Latin American dialects, they cannot represent a response to speakers' perceived need to convey information, by providing pronouns in the particular utterances where verbal inflections are missing.

20.3   Arguments from syntax

The discussion so far has focused on the intersection of phonology and morphology, where the most detailed studies of the functional hypothesis have taken place. We may examine one case of parallel exploration in syntax, a study of constraints on the agentless passive carried out by Weiner and Labov (1983). This study concerns the choice between the passive (8a) and the generalized active (8b) in English.

(8)   a. The liquor closet was broken into.
      b. They broke into the liquor closet.

Figure 20.3 shows that the mechanical effects of priming and parallel structure were by far the most important.

- The passive was favored most strongly if the preceding instance of the variable was also a passive (.69 vs. .31).
- There was also a strong tendency to maintain parallel structure: that is, coreferential subjects are maintained in the same syntactic position (.62 vs. .38).

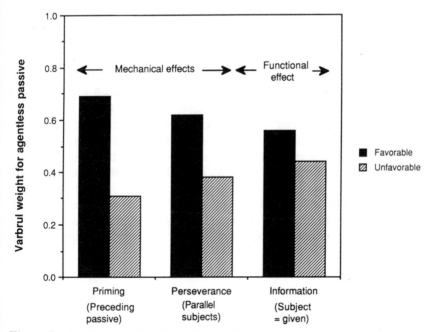

Figure 20.3.   Comparative effect of three factor groups on the choice of agentless passive vs. generalized active in English (from Weiner and Labov, 1983)

- The third effect is one that might be considered functional, though it does not involve the loss or retention of information. It involves the tendency for *given* information to be placed first, and *new* information to follow. There is a tendency to favor the passive if the subject of the passive is *given* information (.56 vs. .44), that is, if it occurs somewhere in the preceding four clauses.[2]

This approach to the agentless passive repeats the themes that were evoked in the morphological studies. It shows that informational considerations may well be present, but that mechanical factors are stronger. We must therefore return to the question posed at the beginning of chapter 19. If sound change is mechanical, if inflections are swept away, if distinctions are lost and people do not respond to the need for information as they speak, how is meaning maintained?

20.4 The acquisition of variable constraints

Before we can answer the question just posed, we must ask how children learn variable relations in the first place. A more complete treatment of this issue will be provided in volume 3, but a brief summary of the evidence will be helpful here.

There is every indication that these quantitative relations are acquired early in life. Labov et al. (1968) and Labov (1972) report that adolescents and preadolescents in Harlem show most of the variable constraints on the contraction and deletion of the copula that characterize the adult community, though some of the finer phonological constraints develop later. Guy and Boyd (1990) found that Philadelphia children 5 to 7 years old display the general quantitative constraints on -*t,d* deletion, both grammatical and phonological, and also the constraint specific to the Philadelphia community: the low probability of deletion before final pause. Again some of the more subtle constraints develop slowly – the treatment of the derivational suffix -*t* in *kept, lost, told*, etc. – but the major pattern is well established early in life.

Labov (1989b) analyzed the acquisition of variable constraints on (t,d) and (ing) by children 4 to 7 years old. Figure 20.4 shows the pattern of acquisition of grammatical constraints on (t,d) deletion by an upper middle

---

[2] The original study examines the second and third factor groups in greater detail, and shows that the parallel subject effect is proportional to the number of preceding clauses with this form, while the given/new effect does not show such fine gradations.

class family from King of Prussia. The vertical axis shows the Varbrul weights, and the horizontal axis shows five factors from the grammatical factor group. The two parents, Curt and Kay, are in lockstep with each other: the greatest degree of deletion is found with the *-n't* suffix, and the next highest with monomorphemic words. The lowest values are shown by the ambiguous derivational class of *kept, told, lost*, etc. The preterit and participle are not significantly different, both exhibiting the same low value in line with the data of Guy 1991 presented in chapter 19. Curt and Kay's son David shows values very close to his parents', with the outstanding exception of the derivational class. This is quite consistent with the fact that the probabilities learned are not attached to surface forms or even to morphological types, but to abstract elements like grammatical boundaries and categories. David does not have the same grammatical analysis of the derivational class as his parents and treats them like members of the mono-morphemic class. Thus the variable rule that David has acquired is similar to that of his parents, though his analysis of particular forms may vary.

Roberts (1993) undertook an extended examination of the variable patterns acquired by 14 South Philadelphia children from 3 to 6 years old, together with data from their parents. Using specially adapted methods for gathering data, Roberts obtained as many tokens from children as from adults. Her data confirm the pattern of figure 20.4, and show that children as young as 3 years old have acquired the constraints on variation that are specific to their family and the community. It is important to note that these are not general constraints that are the automatic products of physio-

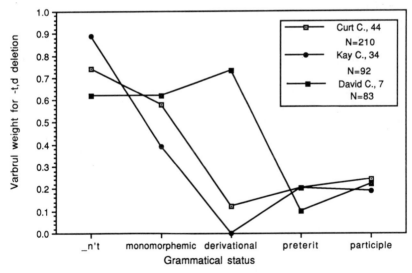

Figure 20.4. Acquisition of grammatical constraints on *-t,d* deletion by David C., 7, King of Prussia (from Labov 1989b)

logical or psychological principles. Children learn the community-specific aspects of their rule systems more quickly than some of the general ones. Figure 20.4 shows that children acquire very early the opposition of bimorphemic and monomorphemic clusters, which, as we saw in chapter 19, is quite specific to English. Guy (1980) shows that 3- or 4-year-old children growing up in Philadelphia display a form of -*t,d* deletion that shows a heavy disfavoring constraint of following pause, which is specific to that community as opposed to others like New York City.

In general, children learn the variable aspects of their local dialect in the same way that they learn the categorical rules. It is well known that neither overt correction nor direct instruction is an important factor in the learning of such categorical rules (Brown, Cazden, and Bellugi-Klima 1969). In the case of variable rules, it is hardly possible that such methods can operate. Variable rules are probabilistically controlled limits of variable behavior, which govern distributions over time, and no single utterance can be called acceptable or unacceptable, grammatical or ungrammatical, with respect to such a rule. What, then, is the mechanism of learning?

20.5   Probability matching

The learning of variable patterns of this kind is a familiar part of human behavior. Psychologists and ethologists refer to it as *probability matching:* a pattern first established in laboratory experiments, observed widely in animal behavior, and replicated in field experiments.[3] It is found in nonhuman animal species as well as in humans. Before we consider how it applies to human language learning, it may be helpful to look at its operation in other species.

Goldfish, rats, pigeons, and humans all show the capacity to replicate the observed frequencies of events in their behavioral responses. The classic laboratory experiment is running the T-maze. In the T-maze, the animal has only the basic choice of turning left or right. If food is placed on the left side 75% of the time, and on the right side 25% of the time, what pattern of behavior would one predict after 30, 50, or 100 trials? The optimal pattern, a rational one, might be to turn left 100% of the time. But in fact, most species of animals, including human beings, match the probability of food distribution very closely: they turn left 75% of the time and right 25% of the time.[4]

---

[3] In this discussion of probability matching, I am indebted to R. Gallistel for a perspective much broader than the linguistic situation.

[4] The rat actually displays this behavior less typically than other species. If incorrect choices are not rewarded, it will tend to maximize its reward for this behavior and turn always toward the higher rate of rewarding. Only if it is corrected at the end of each incorrect trial will the rat tend to match probabilities of choice with probabilities of reward. Human beings, on the other hand, will show more consistent probability matching (Gallistel 1990).

(9)

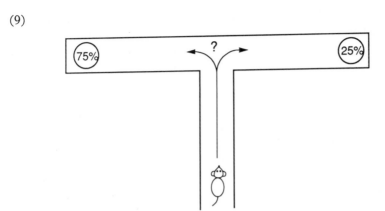

This form of binary choice can be matched in the laboratory with many different experimental paradigms: a pigeon may have the choice of pecking on one of two keys, or a fish may have the choice of swimming to one end of a tank or the other. The evidence for probability matching is not limited to the laboratory. Ethologists have shown that many species match the time spent in different foraging areas with the abundance of food in each area.[5] A number of experiments have demonstrated that this is not a simple case of matching the response to the frequency of the stimulus. Animals show the capacity to calculate rapidly the net reward for a given foraging area, and adjust the duration of their foraging to both the rate and the quantity of the food available.

Godin and Keenleyside (1984) examined the behavior of schools of cichlids in a tank with a feeding tube at each end. Fish larvae were fed at one end at a rate of 10 times each minute, and at the other end at rates of 10, 5, and 2 times each minute. Within 30 seconds of the start of each trial, the fish adjusted their numbers at each end of the tank in ways that were proportional to the rate of feeding. The average fish had not actually been rewarded before this behavior was established.

Harper (1982) reports an experiment with a flock of 33 mallard ducks at a lakeshore. Two experimenters stationed themselves 60 feet apart along the shore and threw out bread one morsel at a time at different rates, and the ducks rapidly distributed themselves accordingly. Figure 20.5a shows that when the rates of feeding were equal, the ducks were distributed in

[5] For example, Smith and Dawkins (1971) showed that the relative frequency with which individual Great Tits chose a given "patch" of food was roughly proportionate to the abundance of food in each patch.

successive trials close to the mean number of 16.5 for each experimenter. Figure 20.5b shows the results of a trial where one experimenter threw bread only half as fast as the other. Here the number of ducks near him dropped to a mean value of 11, and this adjustment was made within 60 seconds. These results indicate that the ducks have a mode of perception and calculation that allows them to represent rate of reward and size of reward as separate quantities, and multiply the two to arrive at the net rate of reward, which in turn is used to adjust the time spent foraging in any area. The adjustment of behavior must be the result of perception and calculation rather than reward, since in the 60 seconds that it takes to make the adjustment, only a minority of the ducks have actually obtained any food.

Probability matching seemed like blind, irrational behavior in the laboratory experiments, because they deal with individuals. At first glance, it seems contrary to the principle of evolutionary theory that the behavior of organisms would not optimize the amount of food that any individual would receive. But the foraging studies of ethologists, which deal with groups of animals, give us a different view of the matter. If we think of an individual animal, isolated in the wild, probability matching does seem

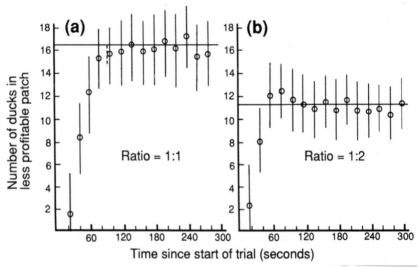

Figure 20.5. The mean numbers of ducks in front of experimenter 1 as a function of the time since the onset of throwing. The horizontal lines indicate the number to be expected if the 33 ducks apportion themselves in accord with the relative rate of throwing. Solid vertical bars are standard deviations. Dashed vertical line is representative of 95% confidence levels. (a) Experimenter 1 and 2 both throw once every 5 seconds. Circles are means of 29 trials. (b) Experimenter 1 throws every 10 seconds, Experimenter 2 every 5 seconds. Circles are means of 24 trials (from Gallistel 1990, adapted from Harper 1982)

counterproductive. Consider two garbage heaps, one with two morsels of food per square yard, and another with one morsel per square yard. One might think that a rational pigeon would go immediately to the first heap. But would it optimize its foraging by doing so? The amount of food to be gotten does not depend on the quantity in the heap alone, but also on the number of pigeons foraging on it. A lone pigeon who heads for the sparser garbage heap will soon get fat, until the other pigeons realize what is happening. This situation might lead to an unstable oscillation, where pigeons rush back and forth as the advantage of one situation or another becomes evident to them. But it can be demonstrated that there is a solution where no animal has the advantage of any other. On a large scale, this produces an evolutionary resolution that achieves a stable population dispersion: and that solution, as it turns out, is probability matching.

It is not difficult to relate human language learning to this more general pattern of behavior. There is ample evidence to indicate that human beings do probability matching in experimental situations, just as other animals do.[6] There is no need to consult the experimental literature, however. The actual evidence of language learning, as illustrated in figure 20.4, shows that children do match in their production the frequency of the variables in their environment. To put it another way, it is not a hypothesis that children do probability matching. It is simply a description of the observed facts.

20.6 Accounting for linguistic change

The child's ability to reproduce the frequencies of *-t,d* deletion or (ing) show how stable linguistic variation is transmitted across many generations. It is then easier to understand that much of synchronic variation is a residue of historical processes, rather than the immediate product of linguistic or physiological principles. In volume 2, we will see a number of examples of such long-term continuity. One of the major constraints on the variable (ing), for example, is differentiation by the grammatical function of the suffix. The apical form [ɪn] is favored by progressives and participles, and is progressively more disfavored by the nonverbal categories adjectives, gerunds, and nouns. It appears that this grammatical conditioning is the result of historical continuity of the original distinction between the participle suffix **-inde, -ende** and the verbal noun suffix **-ing**

---

[6] Gallistel (1990) reports a series of classroom demonstrations at Yale where students observed rats running a T-maze, and were asked to guess which arm of the maze would contain the reward before each trial. They were then shown that their own predictions were matched to the frequency with which the reward was distributed, more accurately than those of the rat, who, as noted above, will do probability matching with corrected but not uncorrected trials.

(Houston 1985). Though English speakers are not at all aware of this constraint, children acquire it very early in life (Labov 1989b).

As we come to understand better how such stability of variable relations is achieved, the problem of accounting for linguistic change becomes more difficult. Most of the cases discussed here and in chapter 19 have been stable linguistic variables: there is no evidence for ongoing change in Spanish or Portuguese (s) or (n). But the larger view of the history of the Romance languages, and the contrasting structure of modern dialects, requires us to reconstruct the changes that have led to the current situation. The comparison of modern Spanish dialects gives us a synchronic view of the result of such changes. Figure 20.6 is derived from Terrell's (1981) comparative study of the deletion of /s/ from 10 Latin American dialects of Spanish. There is a wide range in the rate of deletion across dialects. The differences are somewhat exaggerated because of the heterogeneous character of the data. The first four dialects in the figure represent educated, careful speech; the fifth, the educated fast speech of Miami; the sixth through ninth, four social class levels in Panama; and the tenth, lower-class speech from Santo Domingo. We can now supplement this diagram with more recent information from sociolinguistic studies that control for sex, social class, and education. In his study of the Spanish of Santiago in the Dominican Republic, Alba (1990) finds that the rate of deletion of plural /s/ varies from 77% for those with 0–6 years of schooling to only 28% for those with a university degree. His overall comparison of Caribbean dialects shows 46.5% deletion of /s/ in San Juan (from Lopez Morales 1978), 50% in Panama City (from Cedergren 1973), and 69% in Santiago (from his own data). On the whole, we must be impressed by the sweep of the

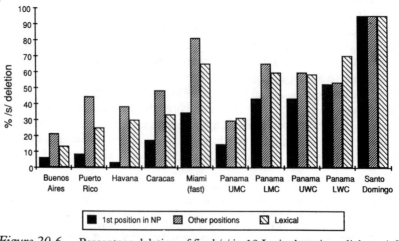

Figure 20.6. Percentage deletion of final /s/ in 10 Latin American dialects (after Terrell 1981)

variation. We do not know in what direction the change is heading – it may be moving toward the conservative norm of Buenos Aires, or toward the more radical deletion of the Dominican Republic. But in order to account for these data, we must argue that at some time in the past, many Spanish dialects underwent a massive weakening and deletion of final /s/, which affected grammatical suffixes as well as roots.

To understand the mechanism of this change, we need to find some behavior in everyday interaction that will lead to a gradual shift in the frequencies that are acquired by children. If speakers do not consciously or unconsciously adjust their sentences to maximize the transmission of meaning, then we need to find some other mechanism that accounts for the systemic adjustments that maintain informational content. The pages to follow will outline a mechanism that effects change and maintains meaning. It is not, however, a functional theory of the type that functional theorists have presupposed.

The mechanism involved has been illuminated by Kroch (1989a,b) in his studies of the development of periphrastic DO in Early Middle English, 1400–1700. Kroch has demonstrated that the four major sentence types – declarative, interrogative, negative declarative, and negative interrogative – follow distinct but parallel growth rates characterized by parallel logistic curves. It appears that at each stage in the history of the language, speakers learn a characteristic input level of periphrastic DO that controls their syntactic variation, determining the proportion of the DO-support variant (10b) in the subset of positive WH-questions.

(10) a. How lykyth you my boy of the kitchen?
      b. How do you like my boy of the kitchen?

The problem of learning to reproduce this proportion is not so very different for the child and the linguist. The first task is to define the envelope of variation: that is, to recognize all instances of WH-questions where DO-support might apply.[7]

A similar situation exists for acquiring the present-day constraints on -*t,d* deletion. Each observation of a word with final clusters simplified, and each observation of a word with intact clusters, contributes to the pool of cases that forms the basis for the calculation of frequency of -*t,d* deletion and the child's future use of the rule. But this includes only words that are identified as being subject to the rule – words with underlying final clusters. If children hear a pronunciation such as /hiy towl miy/, this will

---

[7] See Labov and Labov 1976 for a case where a child did not construct an envelope of variation that matched the adult form until a protracted learning period of $3\frac{1}{2}$ years had passed and some 25,000 questions were asked.

not contribute any data to the calculation of the frequency of *-t,d* deletion unless they identify /towl/ with an underlying /towld/, /towl#d/, or /towl+t/.

Each observation of a sentence with periphrastic DO, or a sentence without it, will then contribute to the pool of forms that determines the balance between the old and new variants. But if there is a tendency for one or the other type of form to be misunderstood more than the other, the misunderstood tokens may never form part of the pool of tokens that are used to establish the probabilities in question. In the case of periphrastic DO, there were several processes that led to occasional misunderstanding of older forms like (10a). If the progress of an earlier change, like the loss of case marking, leads to a greater tendency for the older form to be misunderstood, no matter how small the tendency, there will be a gradual shift, generation after generation, toward the newer form. If sentences with periphrastic DO are not subject to the same sources of misunderstanding, they will become a larger and larger part of the pool of tokens that establish these probabilities.

Such a mechanism is the reverse of the effect envisaged by functional theories in linguistics. Kroch's argument indicates that it is not the *desire* to be understood, but rather the *consequence* of misunderstanding that influences language change. This mechanism implies a mismatch between producer and interpreter: the type of built-in instability that we would expect to find behind long-term shifts in language behavior.

Misunderstanding in sound change

Let us now consider how such a mechanism of misunderstanding will affect the process of sound change that was the focus of much of this volume. For a stable linguistic system, this mechanism is inherently conservative. Consider a hypothetical distribution shown in figure 20.7. There are three low vowels in this figure: /æ/, /o/, and /oh/. A single aberrant token of /o/ is well within the /æ/ distribution. If it is contained in the word *drop*, it may well be identified as /o/, and contribute to the computed mean value of /o/. But the listener may also fail to comprehend the word and

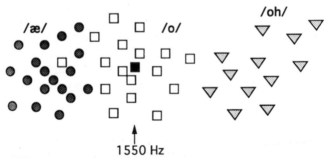

Figure 20.7.   A stable distribution of English low vowels

the sentence it contains. In that case, this token will not contribute to the mean value of /o/. If it is in the word *block*, there is a greater likelihood that the word will be identified as *black*,[8] and so be subtracted from the pool of tokens that determine the mean target of /o/. The end result is a computed mean for the second formant of F2 of 1550 Hz, shown as the black square.

If no sound change is involved, this mechanism of misunderstanding will have a conservative tendency, reinforcing the separation of /æ/ and /o/, and maintaining their margins of security. If a change is in progress, and /o/ is moving forward, the effect will be to retard the change.

For this mechanism to operate, it is not necessary that *every* outlying token of /o/ should be misidentified; this may occur in only a minority of the cases. But even if a small minority of cases are subtracted from the computation of the mean, the result will be to retard the direction of shift.

Now let us consider a distribution such as the one shown in figure 20.8. Here the vowel /æh/ has been fronted and raised, and is following an elliptical distribution that stretches toward the mid front peripheral region. The fronted token of /o/ will no longer be heard as within the range of the /æ/ distribution, and there is a much greater likelihood that it will be identified correctly as /o/. It will then contribute to the computation of the mean value of /o/, and accordingly, that mean will be shifted toward the front in comparison with the mean of figure 20.7: for these 17 tokens, the effect is to shift the mean of F2 from 1550 to 1571 Hz. In everyday life, speakers deal with a much larger number of tokens, and much smaller shifts would be expected. But no matter how small the effect, repeated misunderstandings will have the effect of facilitating the shift. The discussion of deviations

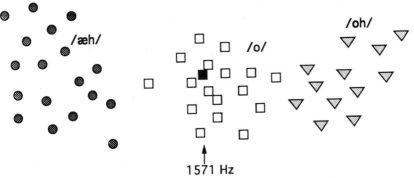

Figure 20.8. An unstable distribution of English low vowels

[8] These examples are in fact chosen from experiments on cross-dialectal comprehension to be discussed in volume 2. Even when the context strongly disfavors *black*, as in *Senior citizens living on one* —, up to 40% of listeners will continue to hear this token as *black*.

from the expected course of chain shifting at the end of chapter 8 showed a number of cases where the presence of a stable phoneme in the normal path sometimes led to merger, but more often led to avoidance – the leading element in the chain shift moved in an unexpected direction. Thus /ey/ shifted to the back in several cases rather than merging with an existent /ay/. In the Northern Cities Shift, an earlier pattern of the descent of /e/ to [æ] led to an overlap with advancing /o/, and a gradual shift of the movement of /e/ toward the back. These results would be explained by the mechanical effects operating in patterns such as those illustrated in figures 20.7 and 20.8, the result of probability matching by language learners.

20.7   The interpretation of zeroes

A different and more complex mechanism applies to the variable realization of segments in an inflectional paradigm such as the deletion of the Spanish plural /s/. (We might equally well consider the Spanish verbal /s/ or /n/, which would be just as relevant to our result). To match the probabilities of aspiration and deletion that are used in the surrounding community, language learners must do more than detect the phonetic signals. They must also define the envelope of variation, and interpret each signal as a potential member of the class in question. The analysis to follow projects the effect of probability matching on the deletion of an inflection /s/ for a hypothetical data set, which is not far removed from the real data sets discussed earlier. It will illustrate the calculations that language learners must make in order to interpret the zeroes produced by members of the speech community who surround them.

We begin by considering the references to plural objects made by a given speaker in the course of extended conversation. This will involve the speaker's producing a certain number of inflectable forms referring to those plural objects. Let us call that number **P**, and assign it the arbitrary value of 200. We will also assume a variable process of deletion of the infleciton /s/ that signals this plurality in the stream of speech, and set this rate of deletion **x** at 20%. We then proceed with the simple problem of analyzing the /s/ forms that are actually produced.

Stage 1. The interpretation of /s/ inflections

{1} **P**   **number of references to plural objects**   = 200
{2} **x**   **rate of deletion of plural /s/ in production**   = .20

The actual number of zeroes produced will be referred to as **P0**. This quantity is **P** * **x**, or 20% of 200, which is 40. The complement of this is the number of forms produced with /s/, or **Ps**; this quantity is 200 – 40 or 160.

{3}   **P0**   **number of zeroes produced** $= P * x$ $= 40$
{4}   **Ps**   **number of /s/ forms produced** $= P - P0$ $= 160$

The next step is to consider how the forms produced are interpreted by the language learner. The notation **PsP** follows a tripartite scheme, where the first letter indicates the target that the producer aimed at, the second its concrete realization, and the third the category communicated to the listener. Line {5} indicates the fact that all of these /s/'s are heard as plurals.

{5}   **PsP**   **number of /s/ forms heard as plurals** $= 160$

Stage 2. The interpretation of zeroes: The Privative Theory and The Minimal Calculation

The analysis of the zeroes produced is not quite as simple as the analysis of /s/'s. For this purpose, we will need to define a *supported* element of linguistic structure.

Definition: An element of linguistic structure is *supported* if it is accompanied in the stream of speech by other sources of the information that it carries.

This support may consist of morphological, lexical, syntactic, pragmatic, or cultural information, just as in the analyses of Poplack (1980, 1981). A structural element is *supported* in a particular sentence if it is accompanied by any of this information; otherwise, it is *unsupported*. The term *unsupported zero* then indicates the total absence of an inflection or any other mark of the plural. These are the crucial cases noted by Guy (1981) in the discussion of Rio de Janeiro Portuguese in chapter 19: 58 zeroes that had escaped the notice of the analyst. We will see in what follows that the language learner, equipped with the faculty of probability matching, will be faced with a comparable problem in dealing with unsupported zeroes.

Let us posit a rate of unsupported zeroes, **y**, of 5%. This is a reasonable estimate in light of the data we have just examined.

{6}   **y**   **rate of unsupported zeroes** $= .05$

It follows that the number of zeroes that are supported by disambiguating information is the number of zeroes produced, **P0**, multiplied by the complement of this rate, or **(1 − y)**, which yields 38. The notation **P0P** then symbolizes the unproblematic number of plurals produced as zeroes and recognized as plurals.

{7} **P0P** **number of zeroes in plural contexts** $= P0 * (1 - y)$ $= 38$

The analysis of the remaining unsupported zeroes depends on the interpretive theory held by the language learners. The first of these is the *Privative Theory* (represented in the following bracketed items by **P**).

Privative Theory: All unsupported zeroes are to be heard as singulars.

This theory is equivalent to the statement that /s/ versus zero is a privative opposition. This is certainly the case with the English plural, and it is characteristic of all inflectional systems with obligatory, or near-obligatory, rules. Romance systems with intact, invariant /s/ inflections are also privative systems, where the absence of an /s/ clearly signals the singular.

We next introduce the symbol **P0S**, signifying the number of plurals produced as zeroes and heard as singulars. This is calculated as the number of zeroes produced, **P0**, times the rate of unsupported zeroes, **y**, which is 40 times .05, or 2.

{8P} **P0S** **number of unsupported zeroes heard as singulars**
$$= P0 * y \quad = 2$$

Learners who accept this theory cannot include these two cases among the plural tokens they have heard, and the number of plurals that they can recognize remains at 38, the number of supported zeroes. The total number of plurals they have heard, **(P)**, is therefore not 200, but 198.

{9P} **(P) number of plurals perceived** $= P - P0S \quad = 198$

They must then base their calculations of the rate of deletion on the *perceived* plurals. Designating this perceived rate as **(x)**, we then show that it is calculated as the proportion of zeroes heard as plurals out of all tokens heard as plurals. This is 38/198, or .192.

{10P} **(x)** **perceived deletion rate by Privative Theory**
$$= P0P/(P) \quad = .192$$

This is a fairly simple and straightforward account of probability matching under the Privative Theory, but it leads to a somewhat surprising consequence. Instead of the long-term stability mentioned earlier in connection with (ing) and other variables, this result shows instability. Since the rate of deletion that the language learner perceives is lower than the 20% rate produced by the previous generation, it follows that each succeeding generation will show less deletion. This is therefore a conservative, damping out process, similar to the elimination of outlying vowels from the calculation of mean target frequencies. The result would be the gradual elimination of /s/ deletion. Yet we know that this does not happen. The situation in each of the dialects shown in figure 20.6 is remarkably stable, without any sign of change in apparent time or real time.

In the case of sound change, it is not hard to identify the sources that renew variation and create outlying forms, in spite of this conservative tendency: the principle of least effort, the difficulty of reaching the target in rapid speech, the occurrence of overarticulated forms, and the general inexactness of the articulatory apparatus. The aspiration of /s/, especially in preconsonantal position, is the formal norm of careful speech in many Latin American countries. Certainly the difficulty of controlling and hearing [h] at the ends of words contributes to a continued renewal and maintenance of a certain level of deletion. Furthermore, the aspiration and deletion of /s/ can take on a social value in itself, just as a fronted or raised vowel can be associated with a desired social identity and social values. These are matters reserved for volume 2. However, there is more to be said about the mechanism of probability matching before we conclude.

The Privative Theory is not the only theory that would produce the result just sketched. The categorical approach to the /s/ inflection need not be so strict. The language learner might take a simpler view: that given a certain amount of confusion, only the clear cases would be used to determine the frequency of deletion. This is equivalent to interpreting all unsupported zeroes as singulars. Thus the language learner may come to the conclusion that some /s/'s cannot be relied upon, without deviating from the conservative strategy that leads to the result {10P}. Let us call this atheoretical treatment the *Minimal Calculation*. At this stage, we cannot distinguish the results of the Minimal Calculation from those of the Privative Theory.

A more radical departure from the Privative Theory would take place when listeners come to the conclusion that they cannot in principle predict when speakers will decide to mark a plural with an /s/ and when they will not. This is an entirely different view of the matter, and it will demand an entirely different mode of calculation.

Stage 3. The interpretation of zeroes: The Facultative Theory

In a community with sizeable rates of /s/ deletion, it will be difficult for speakers and listeners to ignore the fact that the Privative Theory is false to the facts of language. Given the hypothetical data set just considered, listeners have observed that 38 plurals were produced without an /s/, and this observation clearly throws doubt on the Privative Theory. However, listeners have at their disposal an alternative theory: the *Facultative Theory* (represented in following display numbers by **F**).

Facultative Theory: For any given unsupported zero, there is no way of knowing whether it is to be interpreted as singular or plural.

The Facultative Theory holds that an /s/ signals plurality, but that a zero does not clearly signify plurality or singularity. This type of marking operates in many languages of the world. For speakers of Japanese, Korean, or Yucatec (Lucy 1987), for example, a noun phrase without a plural inflection is neither singular nor plural.

Let us pursue the consequences of the Facultative Theory for probability matching. Given a system where /s/ does mark the plural variably, it does not follow that there is no way of taking unsupported zeroes into account in calculating the rate of deletion. Even if language learners accept the fact that each unsupported zero is itself ambiguous, they still posit in their linguistic system an underlying /s/ and know (unconsciously) that a good number of them are the product of a deletion process. To evaluate these unsupported zeroes, they must find an algorithm to determine the proportion of zeroes that are derived from plurals. They can do this by using the proportion found in clear cases to decide the proportion of unclear cases. This might be done in the following way.

In the Facultative Theory, the number of unsupported plural zeroes is still 2, by the same calculation as in line {8P}. In the derivation of the Facultative Theory, the interpretation of unsupported plural zeroes will be indicated by **?** instead of **S**, since their interpretation is uncertain.

{8F} P0? **number of unsupported plural zeroes**
$$= P0 * y \quad = 2$$

Now language learners are faced with another group of relevant forms: the singulars. All singulars are produced as zeroes, of course, and a good proportion of these will be unsupported. The language learners must deal with the facts that (a) it is impossible to distinguish these from the unsupported zero plurals, and that (b) there are many more singulars than plurals.

The number of references to singular objects, **S**, will be posited as 400, twice the number of references to plural objects.[9] Let us assume for the moment that the proportion of these that are unsupported is the same as the proportion of unsupported plural references: the rate **y**, or 5%. This will yield 20 unsupported singulars, which will be designated as **S0?**.

{9F} S **number of references to singular objects** = 400
{10F} S0? **number of unsupported singulars**
$$S * y \quad = 20$$

---

[9] This is the proportion of singulars to plurals that I have found in a number of quantitative studies of spoken texts in University of Pennsylvania Linguistics Laboratory archives.

The total number of unsupported zeroes in the entire corpus, $T0?$, is then no longer 2, but rather 22, the sum of unsupported zeroes produced as plurals and those produced as singulars.

{11F} $T0?$ **total unsupported zeroes** $= P0? + S0?$ $= 22$

In order to divide up these uncertain cases into the likely proportion of singulars and plurals, the learner must have some perception of the proportion of plurals out of all inflectable nouns in the corpus. This perception must be based on the clear cases, that is, the supported cases. The number of singulars perceived by the language learner, (S), is the original 400 less the 20 unsupported, or 380 tokens. As far as the plural is concerned, we recall that 2 occurrences have disappeared, which leaves 198 clear cases as the perceived set (P).

{12F} (S) **number of perceived (supported) singulars**
                                $= S - S0?$ $= 380$
{13F} (P) **number of perceived (supported) plurals**
                                $= P - P0?$ $= 198$

The perceived proportion of plurals uttered follows simply from these totals.

{14F} (T) **total supported forms**
                                $= (P) + (S)$ $= 578$
{15F} (P/T) **perceived proportion of plurals** $= (P) / (T)$ $= .343$

The next stage of the calculation applies this proportion to the obscure cases, to assess which of these were likely to have been produced as plurals and which as singulars. We can then distribute the obscure cases into singulars and plurals, along with the clear cases, to arrive at the desired insight into the rate of deletion predicted by the Facultative Theory.

The number of unsupported forms estimated to be of plural origin will be indicated by $(P0 > P)$. This figure can be obtained by multiplying the number of obscure cases $T0?$ by the proportion derived in {15F}, that is, 22 times .343, or 8.

{16F} $(P0 > P)$ **number of unsupported forms inferred to**
              have been used for plurals $= (P) / (T) * T0?$ $= 8$

To arrive at an estimation of the total number of zero plurals, $P0P$, we must add to these unclear zero plurals to the clear zero plurals: the 38 original plus the 8 just derived, or 46. We can then do the same for the total number of plurals. The number of plurals perceived (P), which is

198, is increased by the 8 new zeroes to a sum of 206. We will indicate this corrected **(P)** as **(P′)**.

{17F} **(P0P)**   **inferred number of zero plurals**
$$= P0P + (P0 > P) \qquad = 46$$
{18F} **(P′)**   **inferred number of plurals uttered**
$$= (P) + (P0 > P) \qquad = 206$$

Finally, the desired rate of deletion predicted by the Facultative Theory is obtained by dividing the results of line {17F} by those of line {18F}, or 46 divided by 206, which yields a rate of .222.

{19F} **(x′)**   **inferred deletion rate, Facultative Theory**
$$= (P0P) / (P′) \qquad = .222$$

We have now arrived at a result opposite to that derived from the Privative Theory. The Facultative Theory estimates a rate 11% higher than the original, while the Privative Theory estimates a rate 0.8% lower. This is a striking result: the two theories each produce an unstable result, in that the learner is led to an estimate of the rate of deletion different from that actually used by speakers in the community. The two theories are unstable in opposing directions, with opposite mismatches of production and perception.

Figure 20.9 compares the effect of the Privative and Facultative Theories across the entire range of deletion rates: .05 to .95. Throughout, the error in estimation produced by the Facultative Theory is positive, indicating that the deletion rate will be advanced rapidly at the outset, and then more

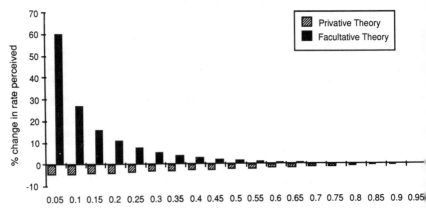

Figure 20.9.   Percentage changes in the perceived rate of /s/ plurals as compared to the original rate in speech production by the Privative Theory (privative opposition) and the Facultative Theory (facultative opposition)

slowly as the change goes to completion. On the other hand, the Privative Theory is conservative, and restrains the change at every stage of its development.

How likely are we to find these two theories in the speech community? Where and when will one or the other tend to dominate? The situation varies considerably from one end of figure 20.9 to the other. At the left, when the deletion rate is weak, the evidence for the Privative Theory is the strongest. It is unlikely that the Facultative Theory mismatch of 60% at the 5% deletion rate will ever apply, if there is only 5% deletion to support this theory. However, the preference for the Privative Theory will weaken rapidly if for one reason or another the deletion rate advances. At the right, with 95% deletion, the evidence for the Facultative Theory is overwhelming, but the rate of mismatch is quite small at this point, and as in most S-shaped curves, the process advances slowly toward completion.

Figure 20.9 predicts a catastrophic shift of the rate of deletion at some point in the process. At low levels of deletion, the Privative Theory acts in a conservative manner to restrain the process among speakers of the younger generation. But any increase in the rate can lead to the abrupt conversion of language learners to the Facultative Theory, and to the more rapid completion of the change.

Change and stability; stability and change

We must now confront the fact that reproducing the probabilities of /s/ deletion involves two unstable processes. If the language learner discards unsupported zeroes by the Minimal Calculation, or interprets them as singulars by the Privative Theory, the result will be a slight shrinkage of the perceived rate of deletion. If the language learner uses the unsupported zero plurals to calculate the rate of deletion by the Facultative Theory, these unsupported zero plurals will be inextricably confused with unsupported zero singulars, and the perceived rate of deletion will inflate.

How then can we account for the fact that the regional dialects of Spanish are highly differentiated but stable in their treatment of /s/? Is there a relationship between figures 20.6 and 20.7? The problem is not unrelated to the biological problem of the transformation of species. Despite the fact that we must recognize the long-term evolution of one species into another, the vast majority of surviving species are stable, and intermediate forms are relatively rare. One explanation of this situation is that transformations between species occur suddenly, under special conditions that disturb the normal stability (Gould 1980; Williamson 1981).

The current stability of Spanish (s) implies a balance of forces. Most previous discussions have attributed such stability to a balance between overt and covert prestige: on the one hand, the influence of the standard language, and on the other hand, the local values that maintain any non-standard features of colloquial speech. The other type of balance, presented here, is cognitive. On the one hand, there is the conservative effect of losing tokens from the calculations by the Privative Theory or the Minimal Calculation, which would lead to a gradually increasing consistency of underlying forms. On the other hand, there is the support given to the Facultative Theory by any recognition of the reality of inherent variation of /s/. In order to account for sudden transformations, we might look for either a sudden disturbance of the set of balanced sociolinguistic attitudes or a sudden shift toward one mode of cognitive representation or the other.

It seems most likely that the type of radical linguistic change that leads to the rapid reduction in inflectional systems must involve, in one way or another, a sudden increase in the mode of calculation shown here as the Facultative Theory. Such a change will not come about unless some outside force disturbs the system. That outside force usually involves intimate contact with speakers whose system is radically different, normally the result of large-scale migration into the speech community. Here we anticipate the central theme of volume 2, which will deal with the actuation problem of linguistic change by examining the interaction of language and society.

20.8   Probability matching and systemic readjustment

Let us now return to the central theme of this chapter: How is meaning maintained in the course of linguistic change? Chapter 19 showed through the perseverance or concord effect that speakers are not dominated by communicative needs in choosing a particular variant in the stream of speech. However, the history of languages and our own examples show that the system does react to preserve meaning in general. Number is conveyed by vowel changes rather than by inflection on the noun, as in the history of French, and person is identified by the pronoun rather than by inflection on the verb. The colloquial French negative is now expressed by the reinforcing adverbial, *pas* or *jamais*, and the English negative is transferred to a new site and attached to *do*. How do these systemic changes come about?

The preceding discussion demonstrates that probability matching, which is blind to communicative needs, will more or less automatically produce this result. The major part of the calculations outlined above involves the interpretation of zeroes by the inspection of the supporting environment. Whether support is found or not is the crucial variable in the calculation. The procedure inevitably directs the listener's attention to that range of objects that would qualify for the systemic readjustments that will ultimately preserve meaning.

When an element of the system is found to cooccur frequently with the signal being deleted, it is increasingly eligible to assume the distinctive feature representing the semantic feature in question. Thus at one point a variety of forms cooccurred with the preverbal negative *ne* in French: *point, jamais, miette, gout, pas, rien*, etc. Of these, *pas* has become accepted as the unmarked form of the negative. Throughout a long history of variable realization of *non* → *ne* → *n* → 0, the role of *pas* in identifying the negative sentences was forced into high relief by the process of probability matching.

The analysis advanced in section 20.7 applies to the insertion of these redundant elements as well as to the deletion of a segment. Let us consider *ne*. The language learner hears a certain proportion of *ne* realized as [n]; a certain proportion are also realized as zero. A small number of zeroes will occur in unsupported contexts, where it is impossible to know whether they were intended as positive or negative tokens. A certain proportion of these will be attributed to positive utterances, and so will be lost from the pool of negative utterances that the language learner uses in matching the probability of production of *ne*. But the very definition of "unsupported zero" means that none of these utterances that involve unsupported zeroes will contain *point* or *jamais* or *pas*. This means that the perceived proportion of negative utterances that contain *point* or *jamais* will increase, and the use of these redundant elements will increase with each successive generation.

At this point, we can return to the consequences of Cameron's study of functional relations between *tu* and the deletion of verbal /s/. This is the prototypical situation where a redundant element of the context is introduced with higher frequency as inflectional information is lost. A first view of functional compensation would expect this effect to appear just where that information is most important – with person-specific *tu*. However, the system appears to react in a more general way – by an overall rise in pronoun use, with an emphasis on nonspecific *tu*. The analysis given above indicates that listeners cannot distinguish between unsupported zeroes that are the products of an intended singular and those that proceed from an intended plural. Similarly, listeners cannot distinguish between unsupported zeroes that are the result of a specific second singular reference, a general reference, or a specific first or third person reference. The result will be a general loss in /s/, and a general rise in pronominal use not tied to any one context. The outcome in Modern French is that there is no tendency to realize one pronoun more than another; all are equally obligatory.

It goes without saying that the process of probability matching proceeds without conscious attention. Operating simply upon the needs of the learner to arrive at an estimate of the rate of deletion, it will automatically identify the most promising candidates to reinforce the system, and facilitate the transfer of the semantic load away from the elements that are undergoing phonetic weakening.

20.9   Overview of the functional question

The original impetus for the study of the functional hypothesis came from the work of Poplack, who examined most thoroughly possible influences on the deletion of information. With the help of variable rule models, she analyzed the contributions of morphological, syntactic, semantic, and cultural information and established a model for all future research. For a while, it seemed as if the close study of syntagmatic information in the stream of speech might be a dead end, since the results in chapter 19 were generally negative. Yet in light of the mechanism proposed here, it is all the more important that we turn our attention to the proportion of ambiguous and unambiguous signals. Like the naive listener of the Privative Theory, we first looked only at the plural, the marked case. But the distribution of information in the singular, the unmarked case, will be equally important if we are to follow through the logic of the Facultative Theory, which reflects the extraordinary sensitivity of human beings to frequency.

The general perspective advanced here will be most attractive to those who conceive of language as a social fact, rather than the result of individual choice. A good many theories of language put forward recently would explain language structure as the result of the intentions of the speaker to communicate meaning to the listener. There is a part of language behavior that is subject to conscious control, to deliberate choice, to purposeful and reflective behavior. But as far as I can see, it is not a major part of the language faculty, and it has relatively little influence on the long-range development of language structure. That is not to deny that we have intentions, goals, and aims in life. But what those intentions are, and what the motivations for our actions may be, is not as accessible as some formal and reflective linguists would like to believe.

It is no accident that the illustrations used to introduce probability matching were drawn from the behavior of other species. I have proposed here that abstract syntagmatic and paradigmatic relations, and the interpretation of zeroes, are controlled by faculties that are shared by animals that are both closely and distantly related to humans. Probability matching is a generalized learning device that transfers information from the environment to the organism. The most characteristic data on other species of animals are drawn from food-rewarded behavior in the laboratory and foraging in nature. But the observations on probability matching in humans are based on a calculation of abstract expectations that have no immediate reward. We should not be embarrassed if we find that systemic readjustments in the syntax and morphology of language are governed by the same cognitive faculty that governs the social behavior of mallard ducks.

The evolutionary and historical perspective that is presented here demands an understanding of human behavior in its social context, at least as thoroughgoing as our understanding of the social behavior of other species. We are products of evolving history, not only our own but that of the animal kingdom as a whole, and our efforts to understand language will be informed by an understanding of this continuity with other populations of socially oriented animals.

21

The Principles Reviewed

This volume has been devoted to a study of the general principles of linguistic change that determine the internal development of linguistic structures. The treatment is far from complete, and many topics and areas are not touched on at all. The central focus has been the systematic evolution of sound. Principles of morphological change have been considered only insofar as they are responses to the effects of sound change, and syntactic change has been involved in only the most marginal way. The selection of materials has been motivated by opportunities to study change in progress, following the general strategy of using the present to explain the past, and the past to explain the present. The most detailed and systematic views of changes in progress have been obtained from sound changes taking place in the Germanic and Romance branches of Indo-European, and in Sino-Tibetan. The focus on sound change is not accidental, since it is the motive force that is most responsible for the continued metamorphoses of languages throughout recorded and unrecorded history. Nor is it accidental that the various chapters of this volume have become successively involved with grammatical issues of increasing abstractness, since any sustained pressures upon the surface of a language will eventually reverberate throughout the structure as a whole.

The chapters of this volume have dealt with variation of considerable complexity, controlled by crosscutting influences that are even more complex. The purpose has not been to demonstrate that linguistic reality is complex, but on the contrary, to search for the simplest principles that underlie that complexity. In this respect, the study of change and variation does not differ from studies that pursue theoretical models on the basis of intuitions and examples. The simplification that we look for takes the form of general principles, of varying degrees of strength and certainty. Their generality is their value, and that generality springs from their relation to the properties of human physiology and psychology. In some modes of linguistic discussion, general findings are stated in terms of linguistic "universals" or a "universal grammar." The quotation marks that I have used here are intended to express a certain skepticism. I do not believe that we will succeed in finding human limitations or skills that are so isolated from all other factors that they will uniquely determine the outcome of linguistic evolution. The general principles that I will restate in this chapter interact with other principles, so that in the most unfavorable configuration, their effect may not be felt or may actually be reversed. Their force lies in the measurable way in which they assess the balance of forces that they dominate, and in which they influence the outcome of systems that they intersect.

These principles have been disengaged from the data by measurements and calculations, in such a form that it is possible to estimate the degree of error associated with them. But in a more qualitative vein, they have been tested by their ability to resolve paradoxes that have themselves endured the test of time.

The following discussion assembles the principles developed in chapters 5–20 to give an overall perspective on the findings of this volume. Some of the principles are restated in a more concise form than they took in the fuller treatment.

Part B: Chain shifting

The principles of chain shifting developed in part A all flow from the conception of phonological space that is organized by the feature of *peripherality*. Three general principles of chain shifting presented in chapter 5 were refined in chapter 8 to a single *Vowel Shift Principle*, which rests upon a view of vowel space that is defined by tongue position rather than acoustic parameters.

In chain shifts, peripheral vowels become more open and nonperipheral vowels become less open.

This principle rests upon the definition of peripherality given in chapter 6 (16): that peripheral vowels are closer to the periphery of the vowel space than nonperipheral vowels, a definition that holds for articulatory position as well as acoustic properties. In Germanic and Baltic languages, *tense* vowels are peripheral, and *lax* vowels are nonperipheral. In the phonological space of Romance languages, the front unrounded and back rounded vowels are peripheral; the front rounded or "mixed" vowels are nonperipheral.

Chapter 9 presented five principles governing chain shifts across subsystems, which also depend crucially upon this conception of peripheral and nonperipheral paths in phonological space. The general chain-shifting principle would lead to an accumulation of high vowels in the peripheral tense subsystem and of low vowels in the nonperipheral lax subsystem. The first three principles governing changes of subsystem locate three strategic crossover points that prevent this situation from arising. The *Lower Exit Principle* governs the tensing of low vowels as they reach the lower perimeter of phonological space.

In chain shifts, low nonperipheral vowels become peripheral.

The *Upper Exit Principle* registers two possibilities for tense monophthongs as they are raised to the least open position, developing into upgliding or ingliding diphthongs.

In chain shifts, the first of two high morae may change peripherality, and the second may become nonperipheral.

The *Mid Exit Principle* concerns the shift of monophthongs to ingliding diphthongs as they move from mid to high position.

In chain shifts, peripheral vowels rising from mid to high position develop inglides.

The other two principles concern the structural relations of subsystems. The *Redefinition Principle* recognizes that changes of fronting, backing, raising, and lowering within a subsystem can lead to its redefinition in relation to other subsystems.

Peripherality is defined relative to the vowel system as a whole.

Finally, changes of subsystems are influenced by the same *Unmarking Principle* that operates for individual changes.

In chain shifts, elements of the marked system are unmarked.

Part C: Mergers and splits

In the discussion of mergers, splits, and near-mergers, part C considered the converse of the chain-shifting configuration. Much of the discussion revolved about the validity of two principles that had been clearly set forth by earlier scholars. The basic position is articulated by *Garde's Principle*.

Mergers are irreversible by linguistic means.

The spatial correlate of Garde's Principle is *Herzog's Principle*, which makes predictions about areal distributions in dialect geography.

Mergers expand at the expense of distinctions.

The general discussion of mergers showed that there are several routes by which mergers can take place, but it is not yet possible to predict when a given language will show merger by approximation, lexical redistribution, or sudden expansion of two phonemes into the same phonological space.

　　The phenomenon of near-merger that was described and investigated in chapters 12–14 gave further confirmation to the basic principles of merger. No principle governing near-mergers was formulated, since the basic findings had to do with possibilities rather than general patterns. Though near-mergers have been located in many communities, they do not form a general or necessary part of phonological structure. The suspension of phonemic contrast is a possibility that has been recognized not only as one form of transition to a merger, but also as a relatively stable part of phonological structure. The existence of near-mergers forces us to abandon two principles that had traditionally been thought to govern linguistic behavior: that there is no such thing as a small difference in sound, and that the production and interpretation of linguistic forms are symmetrical.

Part D: The regularity of controversy

Part D was concerned with the Neogrammarian *Regularity Principle*, which may be restated as follows:

Sound change is a change in the phonetic realization of a phoneme, without regard to lexical identity.

Evidence was considered for an opposing principle of lexical diffusion, that sound change proceeds as a change in the phonetic form of individual words. The resolution proposed in part D, designed to predict when the regularity principle will apply and when change proceeds word by word, may be viewed as a reformulation of the lexical diffusion principle as the *Principle of Category Change*.

Changes that affect several features of a sound simultaneously proceed by altering the category membership of individual words.

Chapter 18 concluded that such changes in category membership may be registered as the addition or subtraction of a feature specification in a lexical rule, as well as alterations in underlying forms.

Part E: The functional character of change

Part E addressed the evidence for the second aspect of the Neogrammarian regularity principle, which we may call the *Mechanical Principle*:

The relative progress of sound change is determined by phonetic factors alone, without regard to the preservation of meaning.

Much of the discussion concerned synchronic variation; it was found that the choice of one linguistic variant or another is not determined by the need to preserve information, but is influenced by the tendency to maintain parallel structure and parallel articulation. The chapters in this part considered how this syntagmatic principle might affect the course of change, which is essentially paradigmatic, following the principle that functional effects are primarily the consequences of linguistic choices rather than the causes of them. It was suggested that the recognition of a privative opposition tends to work against the progressive deletion of inflections, but a shift to a facultative opposition can trigger a rapid increase in the rate of deletion. This can be summed up in a *Principle of Structural Compensation*.

When the rate of deletion of a meaningful feature of a language increases, the frequency of features that redundantly carry this meaning will increase.

The discussion of chapter 20 was limited to one type of language change: the gradual elimination of a meaningful inflection. However, the effects of probability matching on the rates of change would appear to be effective in a wide range of phenomena: the fluctuations of lexical items that result in the avoidance of homonymy, the tendency to increase transparency of derivation, and the regularization of paradigms. In all these cases, variation will be controlled by the language learner's need to estimate the pool of tokens that show one form and those that show another, and this estimation will in turn be limited by the rate of misunderstanding that occurs in sentences containing each form.

I have not considered here the possibility that speakers consciously recognize the advantages of one form over another and choose it to carry out their purposes. All sociolinguistic studies show that conscious choices in language are limited to surface forms and rarely reach the level where systematic linguistic change is operating. This will become much more evident in volume 2, which will consider the social factors that operate upon language, and which will present evidence for the radical differences between changes from above and changes from below.

On the whole, the findings of this volume show that the Neogrammarian characterization of language structure is essentially correct. That structure is a largely mechanical system, out of the reach of conscious recognition or adjustment by its users. There is no doubt that language is designed to carry propositional information, as the result of a radical reorganization of whatever communication systems operated for the nonhuman species from whom we have evolved. It therefore seems odd that we are not free to adjust this system to maximize its efficiency in conveying information of its kind. One possible explanation is that the efficiency of language depends upon its automatic character, and that a phonological or grammatical structure that was open for conscious inspection and manipulation would necessarily operate very slowly. Therefore our efforts to change language consciously must be confined to higher-level stylistic options: the selection of words, and the construction of phrases and sentences within a narrowly limited set of choices. The linguistic changes that have been discussed here operate well outside the range of conscious recognition and choice.

A second line of explanation will deal with social limits on the overall effectiveness of language as a means of conveying information. It is perfectly true that I can arrange with someone to meet me at a time and place quite distant from the time and place of speaking, and that no other animal can do this. Why, then, does the system so often fail, and we spend much of our time waiting for someone who never comes? Part of the answer lies in social pressures on the vernacular to reduce the amount of information conveyed, which will be explored in volume 2. A broader approach will carry us into the ways in which language structure fits into our social needs. Much of what we hear, we do not understand, and as the discussions of natural misunderstandings in this volume show, we systematically tend to underestimate how much. A full appreciation of this fact will return us to the question that opened chapter 1: How can we reconcile the fundamental fact that language continually changes with its basic function as a communicative device? Volume 2 will respond to that question and attempt to trace the forces that are responsible for the continual renewal of language change.

References

Abdel-Jawad, Hassan 1981. Phonological and social variation in Arabic in Amman. University of Pennsylvania dissertation.

Adams, J. 1799. *The Pronunciation of the English Language*. London.

Aicken, J. 1693. *The English Grammar*. London.

Alba, Orlando 1990. *Variación fonética y diversidad social en el español dominicano de Santiago*. Santiago: Pontificia Universidad Católica Madre y Maestra.

Allen, Harold B. 1964. The primary dialect areas of the Upper Midwest. In H. B. Allen (ed.), *Readings in Applied English Linguistics*, New York, 31–41.

Allen, Harold B. 1973. The use of Atlas informants of foreign parentage. *Festschrift Kurath*.

Arnaud, René 1980. Quelques observations quantitatives "en temps réel" sur un changement: L'accroissement d'emploi de la forme progressive dans la première moitié du XIX siècle. *Communications au XXe Congrès de la Société des Anglicistes de l'Enseignement supérieur*. Poitiers.

Ash, Sharon 1982. The vocalization of intervocalic /l/ in Philadelphia. *The SECOL Review* 6:162–75.

Ash, Sharon, and John Myhill 1986. Linguistic correlates of inter-ethnic contact. In D. Sankoff (ed.), *Diversity and Diachrony*, Amsterdam and Philadelphia: John Benjamins, 33–44.

Atlas Linguistique de France 1901–12. [ALF]. Paris: Champollion.

Babbitt, E. H. 1896. The English of the lower classes in New York City and vicinity. *Dialect Notes* 1:457–64.

Bach, Emmon, and Robert T. Harms 1972. How do languages get crazy rules? In R. Stockwell and R. Macaulay (eds.), *Linguistic Change and Generative Theory*, Bloomington: Indiana University Press.

Bailey, Charles-James N. 1973. *Variation and Linguistic Theory*. Washington, D.C.: Center for Applied Linguistics.

Bailey, Guy, Cynthia Bernstein, and Jan Tillery in press. The configuration of phonological change in Texas. To appear in *Language Variation and Change*.

Bailey, Guy, and Natalie Maynor 1985. The present tense of BE in Southern black folk speech. *American Speech* 60:195–213.

Bailey, Guy, and Natalie Maynor 1987. Decreolization? *Language in Society* 16:449–73.

Bailey, Guy, and Natalie Maynor 1989. The divergence controversy. *American Speech* 64:12–39.

Bailey, Guy, and Gary Ross 1992. The evolution of a vernacular. In M. Rissanen et al. (eds.), *History of Englishes: New Methods and Interpretations in Historical Linguistics*, Berlin: Mouton de Gruyter, 519–31.

Baker, P., and C. Corne 1982. *Isle de France Creole: Affinities and Origins*. Ann Arbor, Mich.: Karoma.

Barrack, C. M. 1976. Lexical diffusion and the High German consonant shift. *Lingua* 40:151–75.

Barry, Martin 1985. A palatographic study of connected speech processes. *Cambridge Papers in Phonetics and Experimental Linguistics* 4.

Barton, Michael 1830–32. *Something New, Comprising a New and Perfect Alphabet*. Boston and Harvard: Marsh, Capen and Lynn.

Bauer, Robert S. 1982. Lexical diffusion in Hong Kong Cantonese: "Five" leads the way. Paper given at the 8th Annual Meeting of the Berkeley Linguistics Society, Berkeley.

Bauer, Robert S. 1986. The microhistory of a sound change in progress in Hong Kong Cantonese. *Journal of Chinese Linguistics* 14:1–41.

Baugh, John 1979. Linguistic style-shifting in Black English. University of Pennsylvania dissertation.

Baugh, John 1983. *Black Street Speech: Its History, Structure and Survival*. Austin: University of Texas Press.

Bell, Allen 1984. Language style as audience design. *Language in Society* 13:145–204.

Bellot, J. 1580. *Le maistre d'escole anglois*. Theo Spira (ed.). Halle.

Benediktsson, Hreinn (ed.) 1970. *The Nordic Languages and Modern Linguistics*. Reykjavík: Societas Scientarium Islandica.

Bickerton, Derek 1984. The language bioprogram hypothesis. *The Behavioral and Brain Sciences* 7:173–221.

Bloomfield, Leonard 1926. A set of postulates for the science of language. *Language* 2:153–64.

Bloomfield, Leonard 1933. *Language*. New York: Henry Holt.

Bonebrake, Veronica 1979. Historical labial-velar changes in Germanic. *Umeå Studies in the Humanities*, 29. Umeå: Acta Universitatis Umensis.

Bradley, David 1969. Problems in Akha phonology: Synchronic and diachronic. Ms.

Bradley, David, and Maya Bradley 1979. Melbourne vowels. [*Working Papers in Linguistics*, 5]. University of Melbourne, Linguistics Section.

Brink, Lars 1977. On sound laws. Paper given at the Society for Nordic Philology, Copenhagen.

Brink, Lars, and Jørn Lund 1975. *Dansk Rigsmål I–II. Lydudviklingen siden 1840 med særligt henblink på sociolekterne i København*. Copenhagen: Gyldendal.

Brown, Roger, Courtney Cazden, and Ursula Bellugi-Klima 1969. The child's grammar from I to III. In J. P. Hill (ed.), *Minnesota Symposium on Child Psychology*, Vol. 2, Minneapolis: University of Minnesota Press, 28–73.

Brown, Vivian 1990. The social and linguistic history of a merger: /i/ and /e/ before nasals in Southern American English. Texas A&M University dissertation.

Brugmann, Karl 1897. *The Nature and Origin of the Noun Genders in the Indo-European Languages*. New York: Charles Scribner's Sons.

Brugmann, Karl 1922. *Kurze Vergleichende Grammatik der indogermanischen Sprachen*. Berlin: Walter de Gruyter.

Brunot, Ferdinand, and Charles Bruneau 1949. *Précis de grammaire historique de la langue française*. Berlin: Walter de Gruyter, 1922.

Bühler, Karl 1934. *Sprachtheorie*. Jena.

Bullokar, W. 1580. *Booke at Large for the Amendment of Orthographie for English Speech*. In M. Plessow (ed.), *Fabeldichtung in England*, Berlin: Palaestra, 1906.

Burrow, Thomas, and Murray B. Emeneau 1961. *Dravidian Etymological Dictionary*. Oxford: Clarendon Press.

Callary, R. E. 1975. Phonological change and the development of an urban dialect in Illinois. *Language in Society* 4:155–70.

Camenish, Werner 1962. *Beiträge zur altratoromanischen Lautlehre*. Zurich: Juris-Verlag.

Cameron, Richard 1992. Pronominal and null subject variation in Spanish: Constraints, dialects and functional compensation. University of Pennsylvania dissertation.

Caton, Steven C. 1987. Contributions of Roman Jakobson. *American Review of Anthropology* 16:223–60.

Cedergren, Henrietta 1973. The interplay of social and linguistic factors in Panama. Cornell University dissertation.

Cedergren, Henrietta 1984. Panama revisited: Sound change in real time. Paper given at NAVE, Philadelphia.

Cedergren, Henrietta 1987. The spread of language change: Verifying inferences of linguistic diffusion. In P. H. Lowenberg (ed.), *Language Spread and Language Policy: Issues, Implications and Case Studies*, Washington, D.C.: Georgetown University Press. [GURT '87].

Cedergren, Henrietta, and David Sankoff 1974. Variable rules: Performance as a statistical reflection of competence. *Language* 50:333–55.

Chadwick, Michael, and John Ventris 1958. *The Decipherment of Linear B*. Cambridge: Cambridge University Press.

Chan, Marjorie K. M. 1983. Lexical diffusion and two Chinese case studies re-analyzed. *Acta Orientalia* 44:117–52.

Chen, Matthew, and William S.-Y. Wang 1975. Sound change: Actuation and implementation. *Language* 51:255–81.

Cheng, Chin-chuan, and William S.-Y. Wang 1972. Tone change in Chaozhou Chinese: A study of lexical diffusion. In *Papers in Linguistics in Honor of Henry and Renee Kahane*, 99–113. [Reprinted 1977].

Chomsky, Noam 1964. The logical basis of linguistic theory. In H. Lunt (ed.),

Proceedings of the Ninth International Congress of Linguists, The Hague: Mouton, 914–78.

Chomsky, Noam 1975. *Reflections on Language*. New York: Pantheon Books.

Chomsky, Noam 1980. *Rules and Representations*. New York: Columbia University Press.

Chomsky, Noam, and Morris Halle 1968. *The Sound Pattern of English*. New York: Harper & Row.

Christy, Craig 1983. *Uniformitarianism in Linguistics*. Amsterdam and Philadelphia: John Benjamins.

Cohen, Paul 1970. The tensing and raising of short [a] in the metropolitan area of New York City. Columbia University Master's essay.

Coles, C. 1674. *The Compleat English Schoolmaster*. London. [Menston, England: Scolar Press facsimile, 1967].

Cooper, C. 1687. *The English Teacher*. B. Sundby (ed.). Lund, 1953.

Cooper, Franklin S., Pierre Delattre, A. M. Liberman, J. M. Borst, and Louis J. Gerstman 1952. Some experiments on the perception of synthetic speech sounds. *Journal of the Acoustical Society of America* 24:597–606.

Dauzat, A. 1922. *La géographie linguistique*. Paris.

De Camp, L. Sprague 1933. Transcription of "The North Wind" as spoken by a Philadelphian. *Le Maître Phonétique*.

Dees, Anthony 1971. *Etude sur l'évolution des démonstratifs en ancien et en moyen français*. Groningen: Wolters-Noordhoff Publishing.

Delamothe, G. 1592. *The French Alphabet*.

Delbrück, Berthold 1885. Die neueste Sprachforschung: Betrachtungen über George Curtius' Schrift "Zur Kritik der neuesten Sprachforschung." Leipzig: Breitkopf & Härtel.

Dinnsen, Daniel 1985. A re-examination of phonological neutralization. *Journal of Linguistics* 21:265–79.

Di Paolo, Marianna 1988. Pronunciation and categorization in sound change. In K. Ferrara et al. (eds.), *Linguistic Change and Contact: NWAV-XVI*, Austin: Department of Linguistics, University of Texas, 84–92.

Di Paolo, Marianna, and Alice Faber 1990. Phonation differences and the phonetic content of the tense-lax contrast in Utah English. *Language Variation and Change* 2:155–204.

Disner, Sandra 1978. Vowels in Germanic languages. UCLA dissertation. [*UCLA Working Papers in Phonetics*, 40].

Dobson, E. J. 1957. *English Pronunciation 1500–1700*. Vol. 2: *Phonology*. Oxford: Oxford University Press. [2nd ed. 1968].

Donegan, Patricia J. 1978. On the natural phonology of vowels. Ohio State University dissertation. [New York: Garland, 1985].

Dressler, Wolfgang 1979. Diachronic phonology. *Linguistics* (San Francisco).

Eckert, Penelope 1969. Grammatical constraints in phonological change: The unstressed vowels of southern France. Columbia University Master's essay.

Eckert, Penelope 1980. The structure of a long-term phonological process: The back vowel chain shift in Soulatan Gascon. In Labov 1980b, 179–217.

Eckert, Penelope 1986. The roles of high school social structure in phonological change. Paper given at the Chicago Linguistic Society, Chicago.

Eckert, Penelope 1988. Adolescent social structure and the spread of linguistic change. *Language in Society* 17:183–208.

Eckert, Penelope 1989. The whole woman: Sex and gender differences in variation. *Language Variation and Change* 1:245–68.

Eckert, Penelope 1991. Social polarization and the choice of linguistic variants. In P. Eckert (ed.), *New Ways of Analyzing Sound Change*, San Diego, Calif.: Academic Press, 213–32.

Egerod, Søren 1976. Tonal splits in Min. *Journal of Chinese Linguistics* 4:108–11.

Egerod, Søren 1982. How not to split tones: The Chaozhou case. *Fangyan* 3:169–73.

Ellis, A. J. 1874. *Early English Pronunciation.* Vol. 4. [New York: Greenwood Press reprint, 1968].

Endzelin, J. 1922. *Lettische Grammatik.* Riga: Lettischen Bildungsministerium.

Escure, Geneviève 1987. The acquisition of Putonghua (Mandarin) by speakers of the Wuhan dialect. In K. M. Denning et al. (eds.), *Variation in Language: NWAV-XV at Stanford*, Stanford, Calif.: Department of Linguistics, Stanford University, 121–36.

Esgueva, M., and M. Cantarero (eds) 1981. El habla de la ciudad de Madrid: Materiales para su estudio. Madrid: Consejo Superior de Investigaciones Cientificas, Instituto Miguel de Cervantes.

Estival, Dominique 1985. Syntactic priming of the passive in English. *Text* 5:7–21.

Fagan, D. S. 1985. Competing sound change via lexical diffusion in a Portuguese dialect. *Sezione Romanza* 27:263–92.

Fasold, Ralph 1969. A sociolinguistic study of the pronunciation of three vowels in Detroit speech. Georgetown University mimeograph.

Feagin, Crawford 1990. æ-raising in Southern States English? Paper given at NWAVE-XIX, Philadelphia.

Ferguson, Charles A. 1963. Assumptions about nasals: A sample study in phonological universals. In J. Greenberg (ed.), *Universals of Language*, Cambridge, Mass.: MIT Press, 53–60.

Ferguson, Charles A. 1975. "Short a" in Philadelphia English. In E. Smith (ed.), *Studies in Linguistics in Honor of George L. Trager*, The Hague: Mouton, 259–74.

Flanagan, J. 1955. A difference limen for vowel formant frequency. *Journal of the Acoustical Society of America* 27:613–17.

Flores, L., J. Myhill, and F. Tarallo 1983. Competing plural-morphemes in Puerto Rican Spanish. *Linguistics* 21:897–906.

Florio, John 1611. *Queen Anne's New World of Words, a Dictionarie of the Italian and English Tongues.* London: M. Bradwood.

Fónagy, Ivan 1956. Über den Verlauf des Lautwandels. *Acta Linguistica* (Budapest) 6:173–278.

Fónagy, Ivan 1967. *Variation und Lautwandel*. Monologentagung. Wien.

Fónagy, Ivan 1979. La métaphore en phonétique. Ottawa: Didier.

Fowler, Joy 1986. The social stratification of (r) in New York City department stores, 24 years after Labov. New York University ms.

Fries, Charles C., and Kenneth Pike 1949. Co-existent phonemic systems. *Language* 25:29–50.

Gallistel, Randolph 1990. *The Organization of Learning*. Cambridge, Mass.: MIT Press.

Garde, Paul 1961. Réflexions sur les différences phonétiques entre les langues slaves. *Word* 17:34–62.

Gauchat, Louis 1905. L'unité phonétique dans le patois d'une commune. In *Aus Romanischen Sprachen und Literaturen: Festschrift Heinrich Morf*, 175–232.

Gauchat, Louis, Jules Jeanjaquet, and Ernest Tappolet 1925. *Tableaux phonétiques des patois suisses romands*. Neuchâtel: Paul Attinger.

Gill, A. 1621. *Logonomia Anglica*. [J. Jiriczek (ed.), Strassburg, 1903].

Gilliéron, Jules 1918. *Pathologie et thérapeutique verbale*. Paris.

Godin, J. J., and M. H. A. Keenleyside 1984. Foraging on patchily distributed prey by a cichlid fish (Teleosti, Cichlidae): A test of the ideal free distribution theory. *Animal Behaviour* 32:120–31.

Goidanich, P. 1926. Saggio critico sullo studio de L. Gauchat. *Archivio Glottologico Italiano* 20:60–71.

Gould, Stephen J. 1980. *The Panda's Thumb: More Reflections in Natural History*. New York: W. W. Norton.

Gould, Stephen J., and N. Eldredge 1977. Punctuated equilibrium: The tempo and mode of evolution considered. *Paleobotany* 3:23–40.

Greenberg, Joseph 1969. Some methods of dynamic comparison in linguistics. In J. Puhvel (ed.), *Substance and Structure in Linguistics*, Berkeley: University of California Press, 147–204.

Grisch, Mena 1939. *Die Mundart von Surmeir (Ober- und Unterhalbstein)*. Paris: E. Droz.

Guy, Gregory 1980. Variation in the group and the individual: The case of final stop deletion. In Labov 1980b, 1–36.

Guy, Gregory 1981. Syntactic and phonetic variation in Carioca Portuguese. University of Pennsylvania dissertation.

Guy, Gregory 1991a. Functional constraints on linguistic variation. Ms.

Guy, Gregory 1991b. Explanation in variable phonology: An exponential model of morphological constraints. *Language Variation and Change* 3:1–22.

Guy, Gregory, and Sally Boyd 1990. The development of a morphological class. *Language Variation and Change* 2:1–18.

Habick, Timothy 1980. Sound change in Farmer City: A sociolinguistic study based on acoustic data. University of Illinois at Urbana-Champaign dissertation.

Hadlich, Roger 1965. *The Phonological History of Vegliote*.

Haeri, Niloofar 1991. Sociolinguistic variation in Cairene Arabic: Palatalization and the *qaf* in the speech of men and women. University of Pennsylvania dissertation.

Hahn, Reinhard F. 1991. *Spoken Uyghur*. Seattle: University of Washington Press.

Halle, Morris 1962. Phonology in generative grammar. *Word* 18:54–72.

Halle, Morris, and K. P. Mohanan 1985. Segmental Phonology of Modern English. *Linguistic Inquiry* 16:57–116.

Hammerberg, Robert 1970. Umlaut and vowel shift in Swedish. *Papers in Linguistics* 3:477–502.

Harnad, Stephen (ed.) 1987. *Categorical Perception: The Groundwork of Cognition*. Cambridge: Cambridge University Press.

Harper, D. G. C. 1982. Compatitive foraging in mallards: Ideal free ducks. *Animal Behaviour* 30:575–84.

Harris, John 1985. *Phonological Variation and Change: Studies in Hiberno-Irish*. Cambridge: Cambridge University Press.

Harris, John 1989. Towards a lexical analysis of sound change in progress. *Journal of Linguistics* 25:35–56.

Harris, Zellig 1951. *Methods in Structural Linguistics*. Chicago: University of Chicago Press.

Hart, J. 1551. *Works*. B. Danielson (ed.), 1955.

Hart, John 1569. *An orthographie, conteyning the due order and reason, howe to paint thimage of mannes voice*. London: Wm. Seres.

Hashimoto, K., and K. Sasaki 1982. On the relationship between the shape and position of the tongue for vowels. *Journal of Phonetics* 10:291–9.

Haudricourt, A. G., and A. G. Juilland 1949. *Essai pour une histoire structurale du phonétisme français*. Paris: C. Klincksieck.

Haugen, Einar 1970. The language history of Scandinavia: A profile of problems. In Benediktsson 1970, 41–79.

Hayes, Bruce 1992. On what to teach the undergraduates: Some changing orthodoxies in phonological theory. Paper given at Seoul International Conference on Linguistics 2. Seoul: The Linguistic Society of Korea, July, 1992.

Hedström, Gunnar 1932. *Sydsmåländska Folkmål*. Lund: Carl Blom.

Hermann, E. 1929. Lautveränderungen in der Individualsprache einer Mundart. *Nachrichten der Gesellsch. der Wissenschaften zu Göttingen. Phl.-his. Kll.*, 11, 195–214.

Herold, Ruth 1990. Mechanisms of merger: The implementation and distribution of the low back merger in Eastern Pennsylvania. University of Pennsylvania dissertation.

Herzog, Marvin I. 1965. *The Yiddish Language in Northern Poland*. Bloomington and The Hague [*IJAL* 31.2, part 2].

Hindle, Donald 1978. Approaches to vowel normalization in the study of natural speech. In D. Sankoff (ed.), *Linguistic Variation: Models and Methods*, New York: Academic Press, 161–72.

Hindle, Donald 1980. The social and structural conditioning of phonetic variation. University of Pennsylvania dissertation.

Hochberg, Judith 1985. Final /s/ deletion in Puerto Rican Spanish: Functional constraints and consequences. Ms.

Hochberg, Judith 1986. /s/ deletion and pronoun usage in Puerto Rican Spanish. In D. Sankoff (ed.), *Diachrony and Diversity*, New York: Academic Press, 199–210.

Hock, Hans Heinrich 1986. *Principles of Historical Linguistics*. Berlin: Mouton/de Gruyter.

Hockett, Charles F. 1950. Age-grading and linguistic continuity. *Language* 26:449–57.

Hockett, Charles F. 1958. *A Course in Modern Linguistics*. New York: Macmillan.

Hockett, Charles F. 1965. Sound change. *Language* 41:184–204.

Hoenigswald, Henry M. 1978. The Annus Mirabilis 1876 and posterity. *Transactions of the Philological Society*, 17–35.

Holmquist, Jonathan C. 1985. Social correlates of a linguistic variable: A study in a Spanish village. *Language in Society* 14:191–203.

Holmquist, Jonathan C. 1988. *Language Loyalty and Linguistic Variation: A Study in Spanish Cantabria*. Dordrecht: Foris Publications.

Holyband, Claudius 1578. *The French Littelton: A most easie, perfect and absolute way to learn the Frenche tongue*. London: Thos., Vautroullier.

Hong, Yunsook 1991. *A Sociolinguistic Study of Seoul Korean*. Seoul: Research Center for Peace and Unification of Korea.

Hooper, J. B. 1976. Word frequency in lexical diffusion and the source of morphophonological change. In W. M. Christie (ed.), *Current Progress in Historical Linguistics*, Amsterdam: North Holland, 95–105.

Houston, Ann 1985. Continuity and change in English morphology: The variable (ING). University of Pennsylvania dissertation.

Hubbell, Allan F. 1962. *The Pronunciation of English in New York City: Consonants and Vowels*. New York: King's Crown Press, Columbia University.

Hymes, Dell 1961. Functions of speech: An evolutionary approach. In F. C. Gruber (ed.), *Anthropology and Education*, Philadelphia: University of Pennsylvania Press.

Jackson, Michel T. T. 1988. Phonetic theory and cross-linguistic variation in vowel articulation. [*UCLA Working Papers in Phonetics, 71*].

Jakobson, Roman 1960. Concluding statement: Linguistics and poetics. In T. Sebeok (ed.), *Style in Language*, Cambridge, Mass.: MIT Press.

Janson, Tore 1977. Reversed lexical diffusion and lexical split: Loss of -d in Stockholm. In Wang 1977, 252–65.

Janson, Tore, and Richard Schulman 1983. Non-distinctive features and their use. *Journal of Linguistics* 19:321–36.

Jespersen, Otto 1949. *A Modern English Grammar on Historical Principles. Part I: Sounds and Spellings*. London: George Allen & Unwin.

Jones, Daniel 1964. *An Outline of English Phonetics*. 9th ed. Cambridge: Heffer.

Jones, J. 1701. *Practical Phonography*. London.

Joseph, Brian D., and Richard Janda 1988. The how and why of diachronic morphologization and demorphologization. In *Theoretical Morphology*, New York: Academic Press, 193–210.

Kaisse, Ellen 1992. Can [consonantal] spread? *Language* 68:313–32.

Katz, Elihu, and Paul Lazarsfeld 1955. *Personal Influence*. Glencoe, Ill.: Free Press.

Kenyon, John, and Thomas Knott 1953. *A Pronouncing Dictionary of American English*. Springfield, Mass.: G. C. Merriam.

King, Robert 1969. *Historical Linguistics and Generative Grammar*. New York: Holt, Rinehart and Winston.

King, Robert 1975. Integrating linguistic change. In K. H. Dahlstedt (ed.), *The Nordic Languages and Modern Linguistics*, Stockholm: Almqvist & Wiksell, 47–69.

Kinkade, Dale 1972. The alveopalatal shift in Cowlitz Salish. *IJAL* 39:224–31.

Kiparsky, Paul 1971. Historical linguistics. In W. Dingwall (ed.), *A Survey of Linguistic Science*, College Park: University of Maryland, 577–649.

Kiparsky, Paul 1982. *Explanation in Phonology*. Dordrecht: Foris.

Kiparsky, Paul 1989. Phonological change. In F. Newmeyer (ed.), *Linguistics: The Cambridge Survey*, Cambridge: Cambridge University Press, 363–415.

Kohlberg, Lawrence 1981. *Essays on Moral Development*. San Francisco: Harper & Row.

Kökeritz, Helge 1953. *Shakespeare's Pronunciation*. New Haven, Conn.: Yale University Press.

Koshal, Sanyukta 1982. Social and linguistic constraints on the deletion of Ladakhi perfect /s/. Ms.

Kotsinas, Ulla-Britt to appear. Sex differences in young people's language in Stockholm. To be published in B.-L. Gunnarsson and C. Liberg (eds.), *Rapport från ASLAs nordiska höstsymposium*, Uppsala, 9–11 Nov. 1991, ASLA:s skriftserie nr. 5. Uppsala: Uppsala Universitet.

Krishnamurti, Bh. 1978. Areal and lexical diffusion of sound change. *Language* 54:1–20.

Kroch, Anthony 1989a. Function and grammar in the history of English periphrastic "do". In R. Fasold and D. Schiffrin (eds.), *Language Variation and Change*, Orlando: Harcourt Brace Jovanovich, 133–72.

Kroch, Anthony 1989b. Reflexes of grammar in patterns of language change. *Language Variation and Change* 1:199–244.

Kruskal, Joseph B. 1964. Nonmetric multidimensional scaling: A numerical method. *Psychometrika* 29:115–29.

Kučera, Henry 1961. *The Phonology of Czech*. The Hague: Mouton.

Kuhn, Sherman, and Randolph Quirk 1953. Some recent interpretations of Old English digraph spellings. *Language* 29:143–53.

Kurath, Hans 1939. *Handbook of the Linguistic Geography of New England*. Providence, R.I.: American Council of Learned Societies.

Kurath, Hans 1949. *Word Geography of the Eastern United States*. Ann Arbor: University of Michigan Press.

Kurath, Hans, and Raven I. McDavid, Jr. 1961. *The Pronunciation of English in the Atlantic States*. Ann Arbor: University of Michigan Press.

Kurath, Hans, et al. 1941. *Linguistic Atlas of New England*. Providence, R.I.: American Council of Learned Societies.

Labov, William 1963. The social motivation of a sound change. *Word* 19:273–309.

Labov, William 1964. Stages in the acquisition of standard English. In R. Shuy (ed.), *Social Dialects and Language Learning*, Champaign, Ill.: National Council of Teachers of English.

Labov, William 1965. On the mechanism of linguistic change. In *Georgetown Monographs on Language and Linguistics* 18:91–114.

Labov, William 1966. *The Social Stratification of English in New York City*. Washington, D.C.: Center for Applied Linguistics.

Labov, William 1969. The logic of non-standard English. In J. Alatis (ed.), *Georgetown Monographs on Language and Linguistics* 22, 1–44.

Labov, William 1971. Methodology. In W. Dingwall (ed.), *A Survey of Linguistic Science*, College Park: University of Maryland, 412–97.

Labov, William 1972. Negative attraction and negative concord in English grammar. *Language* 48:773–818.

Labov, William 1973. The social setting of linguistic change. In T. A. Sebeok (ed.), *Current Trends in Linguistics 11: Diachronic, Areal and Typological Linguistics*, The Hague: Mouton. [Also published as chap. 9, *Language in the Inner City*].

Labov, William 1974. Language change as a form of communication. In A. Silverstein (ed.), *Human Communication*, Hillsdale, N.J.: Erlbaum, 221–56.

Labov, William 1975a. On the use of the present to explain the past. In L. Heilmann (ed.), *Proceedings of the 11th International Congress of Linguists*, Bologna: Il Mulino, 825–51.

Labov, William 1975b. *What Is a Linguistic Fact?* Lisse: Peter de Ridder Press. New York: Humanities Press.

Labov, William 1976. The relative influence of family and peers on the learning of language. In R. Simone et al. (eds.), *Aspetti Socioling. dell'Italia Contemporanea*, Rome: Bulzoni.

Labov, William 1980a. The social origins of sound change. In Labov 1980b, 251–66.

Labov, William (ed.) 1980b. *Locating Language in Time and Space*. New York: Academic Press.

Labov, William 1981. Resolving the Neogrammarian controversy. *Language* 57:267–309.

Labov, William 1984. Field methods of the Project on Linguistic Change and Variation. In J. Baugh and J. Sherzer (eds.), *Language in Use*, Englewood Cliffs, N.J.: Prentice-Hall.

Labov, William 1988. The judicial testing of linguistic theory. In D. Tannen (ed.), *Language in Context: Connecting Observation and Understanding*, Norwood, N.J.: Ablex, 159–82.

Labov, William 1989a. The exact description of the speech community: Short **a** in Philadelphia. In R. Fasold and D. Schiffrin (eds.), *Language Change and Variation*, Washington, D.C.: Georgetown University Press, 1–57.

Labov, William 1989b. The child as linguistic historian. *Language Variation and Change* 1:85–94.

Labov, William 1989c. The limitations of context. In *CLS*, part 2, Chicago: Chicago Linguistic Society, 171–200.

Labov, William 1990. The intersection of sex and social class in the course of linguistic change. *Language Variation and Change* 2:205–54.

Labov, William 1991. The three dialects of English. In P. Eckert (ed.), *New Ways of Analyzing Sound Change*, New York: Academic Press, 1–44.

Labov, William, and Sharon Ash to appear. The cognitive consequences of linguistic diversity. To appear in *Language Variation and Change*.

Labov, William, P. Cohen, C. Robins, and J. Lewis 1968. *A Study of the Nonstandard English of Negro and Puerto Rican Speakers in New York City*. Cooperative Research Report 3288. Vols. I and II. Philadelphia: U.S. Regional Survey.

Labov, William, and Wendell Harris 1986. De facto segregation of black and white vernaculars. In D. Sankoff (ed.), *Diversity and Diachrony*, Amsterdam and Philadelphia: John Benjamins, 1–24.

Labov, William, and Teresa Labov 1976. Learning the syntax of questions. In R. Campbell and P. Smith (eds.), *Recent Advances in the Psychology of Language*, New York: Plenum Press.

Labov, William, and B. Wald 1969. Some general principles of chain shifting. Paper given at the winter meeting of the LSA.

Labov, William, Malcah Yaeger, and Richard Steiner 1972. [LYS]. *A Quantitative Study of Sound Change in Progress*. Philadelphia: U.S. Regional Survey.

Ladefoged, Peter 1964. *A Phonetic Study of West African Languages*. [West African Language Monographs 1]. Cambridge: Cambridge University Press.

Laferrière, Martha 1977. Consideration of the vowel space in sound change: Boston /æ/. Paper given at the winter meeting of the LSA.

Laferrière, Martha 1979. Ethnicity in phonological variation and change. *Language* 55:603–17.

Lambert, Wallace 1967. A social psychology of bilingualism. In J. Macnamara (ed.), *Problems of Bilingualism. Journal of Social Issues* 23:91–109.

Laneham, Robert 1871. Letter. In Furnall (ed.), *Captain Cox, His Ballads and Books*. Ballad Society.

Lavandera, Beatriz 1978. Where does the sociolinguistic variable stop? *Language in Society* 7.2:1971–82.

Lee, Ki Moon 1961. *Kugŏsa Kaesol*. Seoul: Minjungsogwan. [Rev. 1983].

Lehiste, Ilse, and Gordon E. Peterson 1961. Transitions, glides, and diphthongs. *Journal of the Acoustical Society of America* 3:268–77.

Lehmann, Winfred P. (ed.) 1967. *A Reader in Nineteenth-Century Historical Indo-European Linguistics*. Bloomington: Indiana University Press.

Lehmann, Winfred P. (ed.) 1975. *Language and Linguistics in the People's Republic of China*. Austin: University of Texas Press.

Lehnert, M. 1936. *Die Grammatik des Englischen Sprachmeisters John Wallis* (1616–1703).

Lemle, Miriam, and Anthony Naro 1977. *Competencias básicas do portugues*. Rio de Janeiro: MOBRAL.

Lennig, Matthew 1978. Acoustic measurement of linguistic change: The modern Paris vowel system. University of Pennsylvania dissertation.

Li, Paul Jen-Kuei 1982. Linguistic variations of different age groups in the Atayalic dialects. *The Tsing Hua Journal of Chinese Studies*, new series, 14:167–91.

Liberman, Alvin, K. Harris, H. Hoffman, and B. Griffith 1957. The discrimination of speech sounds within and across phonemic boundaries. *Journal of Experimental Psychology* 54:358–68.

Liberman, Mark, and Janet Pierrehumbert 1984. Intonational invariance under changes in pitch range and length. In M. Aronoff and R. Oehrle (eds.), *Language Sound Structure: Studies Presented to Morris Halle by His Teacher and Students*, Cambridge, Mass.: MIT Press, 157–233.

Lien, Chinfa 1987. Coexistent tone systems in Chinese dialects. University of California at Berkeley dissertation.

Liljencrants, J., and B. Lindblom 1972. Numerical simulation of vowel quality systems: The role of perceptual contrast. *Language* 48:839–62.

Lindau, Monica 1978. Vowel features. *Language* 54:541–63.

López, Leticia 1983. A sociolinguistic analysis of /s/ variation in Honduran Spanish. University of Minnesota dissertation.

Lopez Morales, Humberto 1978. Dialectos verticales en San Juan: Indices de conciencia lingüística. *Boletin de la Academica Puertorriqueña de la Lengua Española* 6:5–23.

Lucy, John A. 1987. Grammatical categories and cognitive processes: An historical, theoretical, and empirical re-evaluation of the linguistic relativity hypothesis. University of Chicago dissertation.

Luick, Karl 1903. *Studien zur Englischen Lautgeschichte*. Vienna and Leipzig.

Luick, Karl 1921. *Historische Grammatik der englischen Sprache*. Leipzig: C. H. Tauchnitz.

Luthin, Herbert W. 1987. The story of California (ow): The coming-of-age of English in California. In K. M. Denning et al. (eds.), *Variation in Language: NWAV-XV at Stanford*, Stanford, Calif.: Department of Linguistics, Stanford University, 312–24.

Ma, Roxana, and Eleanor Herasimchuk 1968. The linguistic dimensions of a bilingual neighborhood. In J. Fishman, R. Ma, and R. Cooper (eds.), *Bilingualism in the Barrio*, Washington, D.C.: Office of Education.

MacDonald, Jeff 1984. The social stratification of (r) in New York City department stores revisited. Ms.

McKenzie, R. 1918. Notes sur l'histoire des diphthongues *ie* et *uo* dans les langues baltiques. *Bulletin de la Société de Linguistique* 66:156–74.

Malkiel, Yakov 1967. Every word has its own history. *Glossa* 1:137–49.

Malkiel, Yakov 1976. Multi-conditioned sound change in the impact of morphology on phonology. *Language* 52:757–79.

Marckwardt, Albert H. 1957. Principal and subsidiary dialect areas in the North-Central States. *PADS* 27:3–15.

Markey, Thomas L. 1973. Comparability, graduality and simplification in dialectology. *Orbis* 23.

Martinet, André 1952. Function, structure and sound change. *Word* 8:1–32.

Martinet, André 1955. *Economie des changements phonétiques*. Berne: Francke.

Martinet, André 1958. C'est jeuli le Mareuc. *Romance Philology* 11:345–55.

Martinet, André 1961. *Eléments de linguistique générale*. Paris: P. Colin.

Meillet, Antoine 1921. *Linguistique historique et linguistique générale*. Paris: La Société Linguistique de Paris.

Merton, Robert K. 1957. *Social Theory and Social Structure*. Glencoe, Ill.: Free Press.

Miège, G. 1688. *The English Grammar*. London. [Menston, England: Scolar Press facsimile, 1970].

Milroy, James 1980. Lexical alternation and the history of English: Evidence from an urban vernacular. In E. Traugott et al. (eds.), *Papers from the 4th International Conference on Historical Linguistics*, Amsterdam and Philadelphia: John Benjamins.

Milroy, James, and John Harris 1980. When is a merger not a merger? The MEAT/MATE problem in a present-day English vernacular. *English World-Wide* 1:199–210.

Minkova, Donka 1982. The environment for Middle English open syllable lengthening. *Folia Linguistica Historica* 3:29–58.

Mitchell, A. G., and A. Delbridge 1965. *The Pronunciation of English in Australia*. Sydney: Angus & Robertson.

Moulton, William G. 1962. Dialect geography and the concept of phonological space. *Word* 18:23–32.

Mulcaster, R. 1582. *The First Part of the Elementarie*. London. [Menston, England: Scolar Press facsimile, 1970].

Nares, R. 1784. *Elements of Orthoepy*. London.

Nearey, Terence 1977. Phonetic feature system for vowels. University of Connecticut dissertation.

Nolan, Francis in press. The descriptive role of segments: Evidence from assimilation. In D. R. Ladd (ed.), *Papers in Laboratory Phonology II*, Cambridge: Cambridge University Press.

Nöldeke, Theodor 1880. *Kurzgefasste Syrische Grammatik*. Leipzig: T. O. Weigel.

Nordberg, Bengt 1975. Contemporary social variation as a stage in a long-term phonological change. In K.-H. Dahlstedt (ed.), *The Nordic Languages and Modern Linguistics*. Stockholm: Almqvist & Wiksell, 587–608.

Nunberg, Geoffrey 1980. A falsely reported merger in eighteenth century English: A study in diachronic variation. In Labov 1980b, 221–50.

Ogura, Mieko 1987. *Historical English Phonology: A Lexical Perspective.* Tokyo: Kenkyusha.

Ogura, Mieko 1990. *Dynamic Dialectology.* Tokyo: Kenkyusha.

Oliveira, Marco de 1983. Phonological variation in Brazilian Portuguese. University of Pennsylvania dissertation.

Orton, Harold 1933. *The Phonology of a South Durham Dialect.* London: Kegan Paul, Trench, Trubner.

Orton, Harold, and Eugen Dieth 1962–67. *Survey of English Dialects.* [SED]. Leeds: E. J. Arnold & Son.

Orton, Harold, Stewart Sanderson, and John Widdowson 1977. *The Linguistic Atlas of England.* Atlantic Highlands, N.J.: Humanities Press.

Osthoff, Hermann, and Karl Brugmann 1878. *Morphologische Untersuchungen auf dem Gebiete der indogermanischen Sprachen,* I. Leipzig.

Patterson, H. W. 1860. A glossary of words in use in the counties of Antrim and Down. *English Dialect Society.* London: Trübner.

Payne, Arvilla 1976. The acquisition of the phonological system of a second dialect. University of Pennsylvania dissertation.

Payne, Arvilla 1980. Factors controlling the acquisition of the Philadelphia dialect by out-of-state children. In Labov 1980b, 143–78.

Pedersen, Holger 1962. *The Discovery of Language.* Bloomington: Indiana University Press.

Pederson, Lee A. 1965. *The pronunciation of English in metropolitan Chicago.* Publications of the American Dialect Society #44.

Perkell, J. 1971. Physiology of speech production: A preliminary study of two suggested revisions of the features specifying vowels. *Quarterly Progress Report* 102:123–39. Cambridge, Mass.: Research Laboratory of Electronics, MIT.

Peterson, Gordon E., and Harold L. Barney 1952. Control methods used in a study of the vowels. *Journal of the Acoustical Society of America* 24:175–84.

Phillips, B. S. 1980. Lexical diffusion and southern *tune, duke, news. American Speech* 56:72–8.

Phillips, B. S. 1984. Word frequency and the actuation of sound change. *Language* 60:320–42.

Pisoni, David 1971. *On the Nature of Categorical Perception of Speech Sounds.* Status Report on Speech Research SR-27. New Haven, Conn.: Haskins Laboratories.

Pope, M. K. 1934. *From Latin to Modern French with Especial Consideration of Anglo–Norman.* Manchester: University Press.

Poplack, Shana 1978. On dialect acquisition and communicative competence: The case of Puerto Rican bilinguals. *Language in Society* 7:89–104.

Poplack, Shana 1979. Function and process in a variable phonology. University of Pennsylvania dissertation.

Poplack, Shana 1980. The notion of the plural in Puerto Rican Spanish: Competing constraints on /s/ deletion. In Labov 1980b, 55–68.

Poplack, Shana 1981. Mortal phonemes as plural morphemes. In Sankoff and Cedergren 1981, 59–72.

Postal, Paul 1968. *Aspects of Phonological Theory*. New York: Harper & Row.

Price, O. 1665. *The Vocal Organ*. [Menston, England: Scolar Press facsimile, 1970].

Priebsch, R., and W. Collinson 1958. *The German Language*. London: Faber & Faber.

Prince, Ellen F. 1987. Sarah Gorby, Yiddish folksinger: A case study of dialect shift. Sociology of Jewish languages. *International Journal of the Sociology of Language* 67:83–116.

Prokosch, E. 1930. The Germanic vowel shift and the origin of mutation. In *Studies in Honor of Hermann Collitz*, Freeport, N.Y.: Books for Libraries Press, 70–82.

Pulleyblank, Edwin G. 1978. Abruptness and gradualness in phonological change. In M. A. Jazayery et al. (eds.), *Linguistics and Literary Studies in Honor of Archibald A. Hill*, The Hague: Mouton, 181–91.

Rauch, Irmengard 1967. *The Old High German Diphthongization*. The Hague: Mouton.

Read, Allen Walker 1963a. The first stage in the history of *O.K. American Speech* 38:5–27.

Read, Allen Walker 1963b. The second stage in the history of *O.K. American Speech* 38:83–102.

Read, Allen Walker 1964. Successive revisions in the explanation of *O.K. American Speech* 39:243–67.

Reed, Caroll E., and L. W. Seifert 1954. *A Linguistic Atlas of Pennsylvania German*. Marburg.

Remacle, Louis 1944. *Les variations de l' h secondaire en Ardenne liègeois: Le problème de l' h en liègeois*. Paris: Éditions Dion.

Rickford, John R. 1991. Variation theory: Implicational scaling and critical age limits in models of linguistic variation, acquisition and change. In T. Huebner and C. A. Ferguson (eds.), *Crosscurrents in Second Language Acquisition and Linguistic Theories*, Amsterdam and Philadelphia: John Benjamins, 225–45.

Roberts, Julia 1993. The acquisition of variable rules: *t,d* deletion and *-ing* production in preschool children. University of Pennsylvania dissertation.

Romaine, Suzanne 1981. On the problem of syntactic variation: A reply to Beatrice Lavandera and William Labov. [*Working Papers in Sociolinguistics*, 82]. Austin, Tex.: Southwest Educational Developmental Laboratory.

Rudd, S. 1755. *Prodromos*. London.

Samuels, M. L. 1965. *Linguistic Evolution with Special Reference to English*. Cambridge: Cambridge University Press, 1972.

Sankoff, David, and Henrietta J. Cedergren (eds.) 1981. *Variation Omnibus*. Edmonton, Alberta: Linguistic Research.

Sankoff, David, and William Labov 1979. On the uses of variable rules. *Language in Society* 8:189–222.

Sankoff, David, and Pascale Rousseau 1974. A method for assessing variable rule and implicational scale analyses of linguistic variation. In J. L. Mitchell (ed.), *Computers in the Humanities*, Edinburgh: Edinburgh University Press, 3–15.

Sankoff, David, and Gillian Sankoff 1973. Sample survey methods and computer-assisted analysis in the study of grammatical variation. In R. Darnell (ed.), *Canadian Languages in Their Social Context*, Edmonton, Alberta: Linguistic Research, 7–64.

Sankoff, David, and Pierrette Thibault 1981. Weak complementarity: Tense and aspect in Montreal French. In B. B. Johns and D. R. Strong (eds.), *Syntactic Change. Natural Language Studies* 25:205–16.

Sankoff, Gillian 1980. *The Social Life of Language*. Philadelphia: University of Pennsylvania Press.

Sankoff, Gillian, and Penelope Brown 1976. The origins of syntax in discourse: A case study of Tok Pisin relatives. *Language* 52:631–66. [Reprinted in Sankoff 1980, 211–55].

Santorini, Beatrice 1989. The generalization of the verb-second constraint in the history of Yiddish. University of Pennsylvania dissertation.

Saussure, Ferdinand de 1949. *Cours de linguistique générale*. 4th ed. Paris: Payot.

Scherre, Maria Marta Pereira, and Anthony J. Naro 1991. Marking in discourse: "Birds of a feather." *Language Variation and Change* 3:23–32.

Schmalstieg, William R. 1964. The phonemes of the Old Prussian Enchridion. *Word* 20:211–21.

Schmalstieg, William R. 1968. Primitive Baltic *ē. Word* 24:427–32.

Schuchardt, Hugo 1980. *The Ethnography of Variation: Selected Writings on Pidgins and Creoles*. Translated by Thomas Markey. Ann Arbor, Mich.: Karoma.

Searle, John 1970. *Speech Acts: An Essay in the Philosophy of Language*. Cambridge: Cambridge University Press.

Sedlak, Philip 1969. Typological considerations of vowel quality systems. [*Working Papers on Language Universals*, 1]. Stanford, Calif.: Stanford University.

Senn, Alfred 1966. *Handbuch der Litauischen Sprache*. Heidelberg: Carl Winter.

Shen, Zhongwei 1990. Lexical diffusion: A population perspective and a numerical model. *Journal of Chinese Linguistics* 18:159–200.

Shen, Zhongwei 1993. Stochastic diffusion and regularity of sound change. Paper given at NWAVE-XXII, Ottawa.

Shepard, Roger N. 1962. The analysis of proximities: Multidimensional scaling with an unknown distance function. *Psychometrika* 27:125–39, 219–46.

Shepard, Roger N., A. Kimball Romney, and Sara Beth Nerlove 1972. *Multidimensional Scaling: Theory and Applications in the Behavioral Sciences*. New York: Seminar Press.

Sherman, D. 1973. Noun-verb stress alternation: An example of the lexical diffusion of sound change in English. *Project on Linguistic Analysis, Reports, Second Series*, 17:46–81.

Shi, Ziqiang 1989. The grammaticalization of the particle *le* in Mandarin Chinese. *Language Variation and Change* 1:99–114.

Shuy, Roger, Walt Wolfram, and William K. Riley 1966. *A Study of Social Dialects in Detroit.* Final Report, Project 6-1347. Washington, D.C.: Office of Education.

Sievers, Eduard 1850. *Grundzüge der Phonetik: Zur Einführung in das Studium der Lautlehre der indogermanischen Sprachen.* Leipzig: Breitkopf und Hartel.

Silva-Corvalán, Carmen 1982. Subject expression and placement in Mexican-American Spanish. In J. Amastae and L. Elias-Olivares (eds.), *Subject Expression and Placement in Mexican-American Spanish,* Cambridge: Cambridge University Press, 93–120.

Singler, John 1987. Remarks in response to Derek Bickerton's "Creoles and universal grammar: The unmarked case?" *Journal of Pidgin and Creole Languages* 1:141–5.

Sivertsen, Eva 1960. *Cockney Phonology.* Oslo.

Sledd, James H. 1966. Breaking, umlaut, and the Southern drawl. *Language* 42:18–41.

Smith, J. N. M., and E. Dawkins 1971. The hunting behavior of individual great tits in relation to spatial variation in their food density. *Animal Behaviour* 19:695–706.

Smith, John Maynard (ed.) 1982. *Evolution Now: A Century after Darwin.* San Francisco: W. H. Freeman.

Soares, Marilia Facó, and Yonne Leite 1991. Vowel shift in the Tupi-Guarani language family: A typological approach. In Mary Ritchie Key (ed.), *Language Change in South American Indian Languages,* Philadelphia: University of Pennsylvania Press, 36–53.

Sommerfelt, Alf 1930. Sur la propagation de changements phonétiques. *Norsk Tids-skrift for Sprogvidenskap* 4:76–128.

Stampe, David 1972. On the natural history of diphthongs. In *CLS* 8, Chicago: Chicago Linguistic Society, 578–90.

Stevens, Kenneth N. 1972. The quantal nature of speech: Evidence from articulatory-acoustic data. In E. E. David and P. B. Denes (eds.), *Human Communication: A Unified View,* New York: McGraw-Hill, 51–66.

Stewart, J. M. 1967. Tongue root position in Akan vowel harmony. *Phonetica* 16:185–204.

Stockwell, Robert P. 1964a. On the utility of an overall pattern in historical English phonology. In H. Lunt (ed.), *Proceedings of the Ninth International Congress of Linguists,* The Hague: Mouton, 663–71.

Stockwell, Robert P. 1964b. Realism in historical English phonology. Paper given at the winter meeting of the LSA, Los Angeles.

Stockwell, Robert P. 1972. Problems in the interpretation of the Great Vowel Shift. In M. E. Smith (ed.), *Studies in Linguistics in Honor of George L. Trager,* The Hague: Mouton, 344–62.

Stockwell, Robert P. 1978. Perseverance in the English Vowel Shift. In J. Fisiak (ed.), *Recent Developments in Historical Phonology*, The Hague: Mouton, 337–48.

Stockwell, Robert P. 1985. Assessment of alternative explanations of the Middle English phenomenon of high vowel lowering when lengthened in the open syllable. In R. Eaton et al. (eds.), *Papers from the 4th International Conference on English Historical Linguistics*, Amsterdam and Philadelphia: John Benjamins, 303–18.

Stockwell, Robert P., and C. W. Barritt 1951. Some Old English graphemic-phonemic correspondences – *æ*, *ea*, and *a*. *Studies in Linguistics: Occasional Papers* 4. Washington, D.C.

Stockwell, Robert P., and C. W. Barritt 1955. The Old English short digraphs: Some considerations. *Language* 31:372–89.

Stockwell, Robert P., and C. W. Barritt 1961. Scribal practice: Some assumptions. *Language* 37:75–82.

Stockwell, Robert P., and R. Macaulay (eds.) 1967. *Linguistic Change and Generative Grammar*. Bloomington: Indiana University Press.

Stockwell, Robert P., and Donka Minkova 1990. The Early Modern English vowels, more o'Lass. *Diachronica* 7:199–214.

Streeter, Mary 1977. DOC, 1971: A Chinese dialect dictionary on computer. In Wang 1977, 101–19.

Sturtevant, Edgar H. 1940. *The Pronunciation of Greek and Latin*. Philadelphia: Linguistic Society of America.

Sturtevant, Edgar H. 1947. *An Introduction to Linguistic Science*. New Haven, Conn.: Yale University Press.

Sweet, Henry 1888. *A History of English Sounds*. Oxford: Clarendon Press.

Swenning, Julius 1909. *Utvecklingen av Samnordiskt Æi i Sydsvenska Mål*. Stockholm: P. A. Norstedt.

Terrell, Tracy 1975. Functional constraints on deletion of word final /s/ in Cuban Spanish. In *BLS* 1, Berkeley, Calif.: Berkeley Linguistics Society, 431–37.

Terrell, Tracy 1981. Diachronic reconstruction by dialect comparison of variable constraints: *s*-aspiration and deletion in Spanish. In Sankoff and Cedergren 1981, 115–24.

Texas Conference 1962. *First Texas Conference on Problems of Linguistic Analysis of English*. Austin: University of Texas.

Thibault, Pierrette, and Michelle Daveluy 1989. Quelques traces du passage du temps dans le parler des Montréalais, 1971–1984. *Language Variation and Change* 1:19–46.

Thibault, Pierrette, and Diane Vincent 1990. *Un corpus de français parlé*. Montreal: Recherches Sociolinguistiques.

Toon, Thomas E. 1976. The variationist analysis of Early Old English manuscript data. In W. M. Christie, Jr. (ed.), *Proceedings of the Second International Conference on Historical Linguistics*, Amsterdam: North Holland, 71–81.

Toon, Thomas E. 1978. Lexical diffusion in Old English. In *Papers from the Parasession on the Lexicon*, Chicago: Chicago Linguistic Society, 357–64.

Toon, Thomas E. 1983. *The Politics of Early Old English Sound Change*. New York: Academic Press.

Trager, George L. 1930. The pronunciation of "short A" in American Standard English. *American Speech* 5:396–400.

Trager, George L. 1934. What conditions limit variants of a phoneme? *American Speech* 9:313–15.

Trager, George L. 1940. One phonemic entity becomes two: The case of "short a." *American Speech* 17:30–41.

Trager, George L., and Henry Lee Smith, Jr. 1957. *An Outline of English Structure*. Washington, D.C.: American Council of Learned Societies.

Trudgill, Peter 1974a. *The Social Differentiation of English in Norwich*. Cambridge: Cambridge University Press.

Trudgill, Peter 1974b. Linguistic change and diffusion: Description and explanation in sociolinguistic dialect geography. *Language in Society* 3:215–46.

Trudgill, Peter 1986. *Dialects in Contact*. Oxford: Blackwell Publishers.

Trudgill, Peter 1988. Norwich revisited: Recent linguistic changes in an English urban dialect. *English World-Wide* 9:33–49.

Trudgill, Peter, and Nina Foxcroft 1978. On the sociolinguistics of vocalic mergers: Transfer and approximation in East Anglia. In P. Trudgill (ed.), *Sociolinguistic Patterns in British English*, London: Edwin Arnold, 69–79.

Tucker, R. Whitney 1944. Notes on the Philadelphia dialect. *American Speech* 19:39–42.

Tuite, Thomas 1726. *The Oxford Spelling Book*. London. [Menston, England: Scolar Press facsimile, 1967].

Voegelin, C. F., and Zellig S. Harris 1951. Methods for determining intelligibility among dialects of natural languages. *Proceedings of the American Philosophical Society* 95:322–9.

Walker, John 1791. *Pronouncing Dictionary*.

Wallace, Rex 1981. The variable deletion of final *s* in Latin. Ohio State University Master's thesis.

Wallace, Rex 1984. Variable deletion of -*s* in Latin: Its consequences for Romance. In P. Baldi (ed.), *Papers from the XIIth Linguistic Symposium on Romance Languages*, Amsterdam and Philadelphia: John Benjamins, 565–77.

Walsh, Thomas 1985. The historical origin of syllable-final aspirated /s/ in dialectal Spanish. *Journal of Hispanic Philology* 9:231–26.

Wang, William S.-Y. 1967. The measurement of functional load. *Phonetica* 16:36–54.

Wang, William S.-Y. 1969. Competing sound changes as a cause of residue. *Language* 45:9–25.

Wang, William S.-Y. (ed.) 1977. *The Lexicon in Phonological Change*. The Hague: Mouton.

Wang, William S.-Y. 1979. Language change: A lexical perspective. *Annual Review of Anthropology* 8:353–71.

Wang, William S.-Y. 1989. Theoretical issues in studying Chinese dialects. *Journal of the Chinese Language Teachers' Association* 25:1–34.

Wang, William S.-Y., and C.-C. Cheng 1977. Implementation of phonological change: The Shaungfeng Chinese case. In Wang 1977, 86–100.

Wang, William S.-Y., and Chinfa Lien to appear. Bidirectional diffusion in sound change. In C. Jones (ed.), *Historical Linguistics: Problems and Perspectives*, London: Longman.

Weinberg, Maria Fontanella de 1974. *Un aspecto sociolingüístico del español bonaerense: La -s en Bahía Blanca*. Bahia Blanca: Cuadernos de Linguisticca.

Weiner, E. Judith, and William Labov 1983. Constraints on the agentless passive. *Journal of Linguistics* 19:29–58.

Weinreich, Uriel 1968. *Languages in Contact: Findings and Problems*. The Hague: Mouton. [Originally published as Publications of the Linguistic Circle of New York, no. 1, 1953].

Weinreich, Uriel, William Labov, and Marvin Herzog 1968. Empirical foundations for a theory of language change. In W. Lehmann and Y. Malkiel (eds.), *Directions for Historical Linguistics*, Austin: University of Texas Press, 95–188.

Wetmore, Thomas 1959. *The Low-Central and Low-Back Vowels in the English of the Eastern United States*. Publications of the American Dialect Society 32. University: University of Alabama Press.

Whitney, William Dwight 1867. *Language and the Study of Language*. New York: Charles Scribner & Co.

Wilbur, Terence (ed.) 1977. *The Lautgesetz Controversy: A Documentation (1885–1886)*. Amsterdam and Philadelphia: John Benjamins.

Williamson, P. G. 1981. Paleontological documentation of speciation in Cenozoic molluscs from Turkana Basin. *Nature* 293:437–43.

Winteler, J. 1876. *Die Kerenzer Mundart*. Leipzig.

Wolf, Clara, and Elena Jiménez 1979. A sound change in progress: Devoicing of Buenos Aires /z/. Ms.

Wolfe, Patricia 1972. *Linguistic Change and the Great Vowel Shift in English*. Berkeley: University of California Press.

Wolfram, Walt, and Donna Christian 1976. *Sociolinguistic Variables in Appalachian Dialects*. Washington, D.C.: Center for Applied Linguistics.

Wood, S. 1982. X-ray and model studies of vowel articulation. Lund University dissertation. [Also, *Working Papers*, Lund University Department of Linguistics and Phonetics 23].

Wyld, Henry Cecil 1936. *A History of Modern Colloquial English*. London: Basil Blackwell.

Yaeger, Malcah 1975. Speaking style: Some phonetic realizations and their significance. [*Pennsylvania Working Papers* I, 1].

Zachrisson, R. 1913. *Pronunciation of English Vowels, 1400–1700*. Göteborg.

Index